CW00954164

Strategic Survey 2012
The Annual Review of World Affairs

published by

Routledge
Taylor & Francis Group

for

The International Institute for Strategic Studies

The International Institute for Strategic Studies
Arundel House I 13–15 Arundel Street I Temple Place I London I WC2R 3DX I UK

Strategic Survey 2012
The Annual Review of World Affairs

First published September 2012 by **Routledge**
4 Park Square, Milton Park, Abingdon, Oxon, OX14 4RN

for **The International Institute for Strategic Studies**
Arundel House, 13–15 Arundel Street, Temple Place, London, WC2R 3DX, UK

Simultaneously published in the USA and Canada by **Routledge**
270 Madison Ave., New York, NY 10016

Routledge is an imprint of Taylor & Francis, an Informa business

© 2012 The International Institute for Strategic Studies

DIRECTOR-GENERAL AND CHIEF EXECUTIVE Dr John Chipman
EDITOR Alexander Nicoll

ASSISTANT EDITOR Dr Jeffrey Mazo
MAP EDITORS Jessica Delaney, Sarah Johnstone
EDITORIAL Janis Lee, Jens Wardenaer, Carolyn West
DESIGN/PRODUCTION John Buck
ADDITIONAL MAP RESEARCH Henry Boyd
CARTOGRAPHY Martin J. Lubikowski

COVER IMAGES Getty Images
PRINTED BY Bell & Bain Ltd, Glasgow, UK

British Library Cataloguing in Publication Data
A catalogue record for this book is available from the British Library

Library of Congress Cataloguing in Publication Data

ISBN 978-1-85743-653-2
ISSN 0459-7230

Contents

Strategic Geography (after p. 170)

Index of Regional Maps

Events at a Glance

July 2011–June 2012

July 2011

3   **Thailand:** Pheu Thai Party wins general election, and Yingluck Shinawatra, sister of former Prime Minister Thaksin Shinawatra, who was ousted in a 2006 military coup, becomes prime minister.

9   **South Sudan:** The new country of South Sudan is formally created, gaining independence from Sudan, its northern neighbour with which it still has disputes over borders and oil revenues.

11   **Cyprus:** Confiscated Iranian munitions explode at a naval base, badly damaging the country's biggest power plant. Thirteen people including the navy chief are killed.

12   **Afghanistan:** Ahmed Wali Karzai, brother of President Hamid Karzai and a leading political figure in the southern province of Kandahar, is shot dead in his house by a bodyguard.

13   **India:** Three bombs kill 26 people in Mumbai.

17   **United Kingdom:** Britain's most senior police officer, Metropolitan (London) Police Chief Paul Stephenson, resigns amid allegations of links between senior officers and executives of News Corporation, the media group headed by Rupert Murdoch.

17   **Afghanistan:** Responsibility for security in Bamiyan province is handed from NATO to Afghan security forces, the first of a series of transfers intended to cover the whole country by 2014.

20   **Somalia:** UN declares famine in parts of southern Somalia, where there is acute malnutrition and high mortality.

21 **Greece:** European leaders agree a second financial bailout package for Greece, under which it will receive €109bn of new loans. In addition, private holders of €135bn of bonds are to be offered debt exchanges that will mean losses for them and a reduced debt burden for Greece. The deal, which follows months of negotiations among eurozone countries amid mounting concern in the markets, gives the €440bn European Financial Stability Facility (EFSF), the eurozone's bailout fund, greater flexibility to make loans, for example to countries that face temporary borrowing difficulties but have not received formal rescue packages. This would enable it to pre-empt problems of member countries, including by buying their bonds in the markets. Interest rates on rescue loans to Greece, Portugal and Ireland are reduced. The package requires approval by eurozone parliaments.

21 **United States:** Manned space flights by the US National Aeronautics and Space Administration (NASA) come to an end with the final landing of the Space Shuttle *Atlantis*.

22 **Norway:** Anders Breivik, a 32-year-old right-wing extremist, kills 77 people in terrorist attacks. He explodes a car bomb outside the prime minister's office in Oslo, killing eight people and destroying government buildings. He then travels to the island of Utoya, where a Labour Party youth camp is being held. Dressed in police uniform, he kills 69 people – mostly teenagers – in a gun rampage that ends with his arrest. In a manifesto, he describes his preparation for the attacks and his opposition to Muslim immigration. After conflicting medical reports on his sanity, he goes on trial for murder on 16 April 2012.

23 **China:** An accident involving two high-speed trains kills 40 people in Zhejiang province in eastern China. Three senior railway officials are dismissed. The crash is blamed on signalling flaws.

27 **Afghanistan:** Mayor of Kandahar, Ghulam Haider Hamidi, is killed by a suicide bomber carrying explosives in his turban.

29 **Turkey:** The armed forces chief, General Isik Kosaner, and all three service chiefs resign following a row with the government, which refused to promote officers who were being tried in criminal cases, including over a 2003 coup plot. Recep Tayyip Erdogan, prime minister, appoints new commanders and indicates plans for changes to extend civilian control over the military.

31 **Syria:** Tanks enter the city of Hama and step up attacks on demonstrators in other cities as stand-off between President Bashar al-Assad and anti-government protesters continues. More than 100 people are killed. In the following days, regional countries including Saudi Arabia and Turkey put pressure on Assad to cease attacks on protesters. On 14 August, Syrian warships shell the port city of Latakia and tanks also take part in an assault which kills 26 people.

August 2011

1 **United States:** Congress approves an increase to the US debt ceiling after acrimonious negotiations that had threatened to put the country in default. Parties agree on a $2.1 trillion package of spending cuts, to help reduce the fiscal deficit, but Tea Party Republicans block any tax increases. On 5 August, the credit-rating agency Standard & Poor's lowers the long-term credit rating of the United States from AAA to AA+, because of poor prospects for containing government spending and raising revenues. It says Congress's deal on spending cuts 'falls short of the amount that we believe is necessary to stabilise the ... debt burden'. It says America's governance and policymaking has become 'less stable, less effective and less predictable'.

6 **Afghanistan:** Taliban insurgents shoot down a US *Chinook* helicopter, killing 30 American special-forces troops and eight Afghans.

7 **Europe:** Mounting concern in financial markets about sovereign debt problems spreading across the eurozone prompts the European Central Bank to indicate that it could buy Italian and Spanish bonds to bolster confidence in the two countries' ability to borrow.

9 **United Kingdom:** 16,000 police are deployed in London to curb an outbreak of urban looting. As disturbances spread to other cities, three men are killed in Birmingham.

14 **Libya:** An offensive by rebel fighters takes them into the centre of Zawiya, 50km west of Tripoli. The advance continues in the following days.

15 **Iraq:** Bomb attacks in several cities, including Kut, kill more than 80 people.

18 **Israel:** Attacks on Israeli civilians and soldiers leave eight Israelis dead near the southern resort of Eilat, close to the Egyptian border. Ten attackers are killed by Israeli forces, who also kill five Egyptian soldiers in the chase, causing a diplomatic row. The incident brings violence in Gaza as Israel launches reprisal strikes.

18 **Syria:** US President Barack Obama calls on Assad to step down. The EU also does so.

19 **Afghanistan:** Taliban assault and briefly occupy offices of a British cultural centre in Kabul, resulting in the deaths of eight Afghan policemen and a New Zealand soldier, as well as all the attackers.

21 **Libya:** Rebel forces advance into Tripoli, signalling the end of the 42-year rule of Muammar Gadhafi. Their arrival triggers days of fighting against pockets of resistance from Gadhafi's forces, as well as scenes of jubilation in the capital and other cities. On 23 August, Gadhafi's compound is overrun. On 29 August, Gadhafi's wife and three of his children arrive in Algeria.

22 **Pakistan:** US drone strike kills Atiyah Abd al-Rahman, al-Qaeda second in command, a Libyan. On 15 September, a drone strike is reported to have killed al-Qaeda chief of operations in Pakistan, Abu Hafs al-Shahri, a Saudi.

25 **Mexico:** Armed men set fire to a casino in Monterrey, killing 52 people. Members of the Zetas drug cartel are arrested.

26 **Nigeria:** UN headquarters in Abuja, the capital, is attacked with a car bomb that kills 23 people. Boko Haram, an Islamist sect, claims responsibility.

26 **Japan:** Naoto Kan resigns after 15 months as prime minister after being criticised for his leadership after the 11 March earthquake. He is replaced by Finance Minister Yoshihiko Noda.

September 2011

7 **Germany:** Constitutional court rejects a legal challenge to the bailout package for Greece, but says the parliamentary budget committee must approve in advance any future German guarantee for eurozone loans. Chancellor Angela Merkel says 'the euro will not fail'.

7 **India:** Bomb at Delhi High Court kills 13 people.

10 **Egypt:** Israel's embassy in Cairo is stormed by protesters and the staff is rapidly evacuated to Israel.

13 **Afghanistan:** Insurgents launch multiple attacks in Kabul, firing rockets at the US embassy from a high-rise building and engaging in a shoot-out with Afghan forces until all 11 are dead, 19 hours after the attack began. Sixteen other people are killed. Admiral Mike Mullen, chairman of US Joint Chiefs of Staff, later says the attacks were carried out by the Haqqani network with the support of Pakistan.

15 **Denmark:** Centre-left bloc ousts incumbent centre-right coalition in general election. Helle Thorning-Schmidt becomes prime minister.

15 Five central banks (US Federal Reserve, European Central Bank, Bank of England, Bank of Japan and Swiss National Bank) take action to boost the ability of banks worldwide to obtain dollar funding, offering to provide three-month loans.

15 **United Kingdom:** Kweku Adoboli, a 31-year-old trader in the London operation of UBS, the Swiss bank, is arrested and charged with fraud. UBS estimates that fraudulent trades cost it $2.3bn. Oswald Grübel, UBS chief executive, later resigns.

20 **United States:** IMF says the global economy has slowed and has entered a 'dangerous new phase'. It criticises indecision on governments' policies and warns against excessive tightening of fiscal stances.

20 **Afghanistan:** Burhanuddin Rabbani, head of the council appointed to hold peace talks with the Taliban, is killed in his home in Kabul by a suicide bomber with a turban bomb.

21 **United States/China:** US announces plans to sell $5.9bn of arms to Taiwan, mainly upgrades to F-16 fighter aircraft. China strongly criticises the sale.

23 **Zambia:** Michael Sata becomes president after defeating the incumbent, Rupiah Banda, in general election.

23 **Yemen:** President Ali Abdullah Saleh returns after three months in Saudi Arabia, where he was treated for wounds suffered in an attack on his compound. His return follows an escalation in violence between protesters and government forces in Sana'a, the capital.

23 **Palestine:** President Mahmoud Abbas lodges an application for Palestine's statehood with the United Nations, asking whether the world will 'allow Israel to occupy us forever'.

24 **Russia:** Vladimir Putin and Dmitry Medvedev announce plans for a job swap in 2012, with Putin standing again as president and Medvedev to stand for the United Russia Party in parliament and become prime minister. Finance Minister Alexei Kudrin is sacked after voicing dissent.

25 **Saudi Arabia:** King Abdullah announces that women will be able to vote and stand in municipal elections from 2012, and to be members of the Majlis ash-Shura, the consultative assembly.

29 **Germany:** The Bundestag, by a large majority, backs expansion of powers of the European Financial Stability Facility, giving important support to Merkel's handling of the eurozone debt crisis.

30 **Bahrain:** Twenty doctors are jailed by a military court for between five and 15 years after treating protesters during unrest in March 2011. They later win a retrial in a civilian court.

30 **Yemen:** Anwar al-Awlaki, a US citizen accused of involvement in al-Qaeda attacks, is killed by a US drone strike in Yemen.

30 **Myanmar:** President Thein Sein suspends work on a Chinese-backed $3.6bn dam on the Irrawaddy River in Kachin state, saying the project was contrary to the will of the people.

October 2011

4 **Somalia:** Truck bomb kills more than 100 people at a government compound in Mogadishu, many of them students seeking scholarships to study in Turkey. Al-Shabaab claims responsibility.

5 **United States:** Steve Jobs, founder and chairman of Apple, the computer company, dies of cancer aged 56.

7 **Syria:** Mishaal al-Tammo, spokesman of an opposition Kurdish group, is killed by gunmen in his home. The death toll so far in the security forces' crackdown on protests is put at about 3,000.

9 **Egypt:** Troops attack a protest by Coptic Christians, leaving at least 25 people dead.

11 **Iran/United States:** The US says it has foiled an Iran-directed plot to assassinate the Saudi Arabian ambassador to Washington. One man is detained. Iran denies the allegation.

11 **Slovakia:** Coalition government of Prime Minister Iveta Radicova falls after failing to win parliamentary approval for the 21 July eurozone rescue package. Parliament later agrees to ratify the eurozone agreement.

11 **Myanmar:** Government frees about 200 political prisoners as part of an amnesty under which more than 6,000 prisoners are freed.

11 **Ukraine:** Yulia Tymoshenko, former prime minister, is jailed for seven years after being convicted of criminally exceeding her powers in a 2009 gas deal with Russia. The EU and Russia criticise the court decision.

14 **Uganda:** US President Obama notifies Congress he is sending 100 troops to Uganda to help combat the Lord's Resistance Army and seek to capture its leader, Joseph Kony.

14 **United Kingdom:** Defence Minister Liam Fox resigns following revelations over the role of an unofficial adviser.

18 **Israel/Palestine:** Israeli army soldier Gilad Shalit is released after five years in captivity in exchange for 1,027 Palestinian prisoners.

20 **Somalia:** African Union and Somali troops expel al-Shabaab fighters from Mogadishu, the capital.

20 **Spain:** ETA, the Basque separatist group, says it has ceased all military activities, 43 years after its first attack.

20 **Libya:** Muammar Gadhafi, former Libyan leader, and his son Mutassim are captured and killed as his home town of Sirte is overrun by forces of the new government. On 19 November, his son Saif al-Islam is captured in the south.

21 **Iraq:** US President Obama announces all 46,000 American troops in Iraq will withdraw by the end of the 2011, following the failure of negotiations with the Iraqi government on a new Status of Forces Agreement.

23 **Turkey:** Earthquake near the eastern city of Van kills 600 people.

23 **Tunisia:** First post-revolution election, for a constituent assembly to appoint a government and write a new constitution, results in victory for the Islamist An-Nahda Party, which wins 89 of 217 seats, with the centre-left Congress for the Republic winning 29 and the Popular Petition Party winning 26.

24 **South Africa:** Two government ministers are dismissed and the police chief is suspended over corruption allegations.

27 Leaders of the eurozone agree a revised package of measures to deal with the financial problems of Greece and to seek to augment the eurozone's resources for dealing with similar problems in other member countries. Private Greek bondholders are asked to take a 50% 'haircut' or write-down on their holdings. Some banks are to be asked to raise capital. The European Financial Stability Facility is to seek ways to 'leverage' its €440bn of committed resources in order to maximise the protection it can provide, by partially insuring debt or by raising money from outside countries such as China through a special financing vehicle. Leaders agree on a future series of summits and other measures to drive greater economic convergence.

31 **Palestine:** United Nations Educational, Scientific and Cultural Organisation (UNESCO) votes to admit Palestine as a member, with 107 nations in favour, 14 against and 52 abstentions.

November 2011

2 **Pakistan/India:** Pakistan's cabinet decides to grant most-favoured-nation trade status to India, a move that will reduce import barriers. India had granted it to Pakistan in 1996.

03 **Syria:** Government accepts Arab League peace plan under which it will withdraw the army from cities, free political prisoners and hold talks with the opposition. The ceasefire breaks down immediately and government forces continue to suppress protests, killing hundreds in the following days. Many of the deaths are in Homs.

4 **Colombia:** Alfonso Cano, FARC leader, is killed by the army in an intelligence-led operation.

8 **Iran:** International Atomic Energy Agency says Iran has worked on producing a nuclear weapon.

10 **Greece:** George Papandreou resigns as prime minister and is replaced by Lucas Papademos, former vice-president of the European Central Bank, at the head of an interim national unity government.

16 **Kuwait:** Protesters storm the National Assembly, demanding the resignation of Prime Minister Sheikh Nasser al-Mohammad al-Sabah. On 28 November he resigns, and on 6 December the emir dissolves parliament and calls elections.

16 **US/Australia:** Governments announce plans for up to 2,500 American troops to be based in northern Australia, beginning with 250 Marines in 2012.

16 **Italy:** Silvio Berlusconi resigns as prime minister and is replaced by Mario Monti, former EU commissioner, at the head of a government of 'technocrats', with no politicians in the cabinet.

19 **Egypt:** Protesters take over Cairo's Tahrir Square, scene of mass demonstrations earlier in the year, angry at military rule. In the following week, about 40 people are killed in clashes with police. Nevertheless, voting begins on 28 November in parliamentary elections spread over six weeks.

20 **Spain:** Centre-right Popular Party easily wins the general election, ousting the Socialist government. Mariano Rajoy becomes prime minister.

22 **Pakistan :** Husain Haqqani resigns as ambassador to the US over a memo that appeared to seek US help in asserting civilian control over the military. Haqqani denies involvement, and the origin and authenticity of the memo remain unclear.

23 **Bahrain:** Independent international commission appointed by King Hamad details abuses of protesters by security agencies in February and March, including beatings, electrocution and rape.

23 **Yemen:** Ali Abdullah Saleh signs an agreement in Riyadh to step down after elections to be held within three months.

26 **Pakistan:** US forces kill 24 Pakistani soldiers in an attack on a border post. Amid outrage in Pakistan, border crossings through which NATO sends supplies into Afghanistan are closed. Pakistan orders the US to close down drone activities from its Shamsi Air Base. A Pentagon investigation later finds errors by US forces in Afghanistan but also alleges the incident was triggered by Pakistani soldiers firing at them. Pakistan rejects the Pentagon's account.

27 **Syria:** Arab League members vote to suspend Syria's membership and impose sanctions over its violent crackdown on protests. On 28 November, an independent UN Human Rights Commission reports that security forces have committed crimes against humanity.

29 **Côte d'Ivoire:** Former President Laurent Gbagbo is flown to The Hague to face charges of crimes against humanity at the International Criminal Court.

29 **Iran:** Britain's embassy and residential compound in Tehran are stormed and ransacked by a mob. Britain, alleging regime consent in the attack, expels all Iranian diplomats and withdraws its staff from Iran.

December 2011

1 **Myanmar:** Hillary Clinton, making the first visit by a US secretary of state for more than 50 years, says the US will support lifting some restrictions on international aid, but will not yet remove economic sanctions. She holds talks with President Thein Sein and with Aung San Suu Kyi.

4 **Russia:** United Russia Party, led by Prime Minister Vladimir Putin, suffers a large fall in its majority in the Duma, winning 238 of 450 seats, down 77 from the 2007 elections. Its share of the vote, at 49.3%, is down 15 percentage points. Thousands demonstrate against Putin, claiming the elections were flawed. In

the largest demonstration in Moscow, on 24 December, tens of thousands of people take part, with one estimate at 80,000.

6 **Afghanistan:** Bomb at Shia shrine in Kabul kills about 70 people.

8 European Central Bank offers unlimited three-year credit to banks in order to boost liquidity and aid confidence in banks. On 21 December, it allots €489bn of three-year loans to banks, a record for an ECB refinancing operation.

9 Eurozone heads of government agree in Brussels on a 'fiscal compact' to strengthen economic policy coordination, backed by stronger rules on budget deficits. Losses being taken by private holders of Greek debt are deemed to be exceptional, not to be repeated for other debtors. However, British Prime Minister David Cameron blocks the new fiscal disciplinary procedures from being adopted into EU treaties.

11 **South Africa:** Durban climate-change conference agrees to extend the Kyoto Protocol on reducing emissions as a step to a new, more comprehensive agreement covering all countries.

12 **China:** Residents of Wukan, a small town in Guangdong province, eject police and Communist Party officials following the death in custody of a local representative, amid a dispute over land seizures. The protest continues until 21 December, when agreement is reached with provincial party officials. The leader of the rebellion is later named the local Communist Party secretary.

17 **Philippines:** Flash floods caused by a typhoon kill some 1,250 people in two southern cities.

17 **North Korea:** Kim Jong-il dies at the age of 70, reportedly of a heart attack, and is replaced as leader by his third son, Kim Jong-un.

18 **Iraq:** Last American troops leave Iraq, ending a presence which began with the invasion in March 2003.

19 **Syria:** Government signs an agreement with the Arab League intended to end the violence that has killed about 5,000 so far. On 22 December, an advance team of the Arab League monitoring mission arrives. The next day, explosions at offices of Syrian security services in Damascus kill 44 people. On 26 December, monitors begin to arrive and deploy to Syrian cities. But violence continues. On 28 January, the Arab League suspends its monitoring mission.

22 **Iraq:** More than a dozen bombs in Baghdad kill over 70 people, mostly in Shia districts.

25 **Nigeria:** Bombs planted by the Boko Haram sect kill about 40 people, with targets including three Christian churches.

January 2012

3 **Afghanistan:** Taliban reaches agreement with Qatar to establish an office there to facilitate international talks.

8 **Nigeria:** General strike is launched in protest at the removal of fuel subsidies, which caused petrol prices to more than double. The strike is suspended on 16 January after President Goodluck Jonathan partially reverses the price increase.

11 **Iran:** A nuclear scientist, reported to hold a senior position at the Natanz enrichment facility, is killed by a bomb attached by a motorcyclist to his car.

13 The AAA credit rating of France and Austria is cut to AA+ by Standard & Poor's, the US rating agency, which also downgrades seven other countries.

13 **Myanmar:** Government releases more than 600 political prisoners. US President Obama announces that diplomatic relations will be restored after 22 years.

20 **Nigeria:** About 200 people are killed in the northern city of Kano in multiple attacks by members of Boko Haram, the Islamist insurgent group.

20 **Afghanistan:** Four French soldiers are shot dead by an Afghan soldier, prompting President Nicolas Sarkozy to threaten to pull French troops out of Afghanistan ahead of schedule.

21 **Egypt:** Final results in parliamentary elections give Islamist parties a clear majority. Muslim Brotherhood wins 235 of the 498 seats, and the Salafist Al-Nour Party wins 125.

23 **South Sudan:** Production of oil is halted by the government of South Sudan in a dispute with Sudan over transit fees for the oil, which accounts for almost all government revenues but must be piped through Sudan for export.

23 **Iran:** EU foreign ministers agree to ban oil imports from Iran and to freeze assets of Iran's central bank.

23 **Kenya:** International Criminal Court rules that Uhuru Kenyatta, finance minister, and Francis Muthaura, cabinet secretary, will be indicted for crimes against humanity following post-election violence in 2007. Both resign.

February 2012

1 **Egypt:** More than 70 people are killed after one set of football supporters attacks the other at a match in Port Said. The incident prompts protests against the country's military rulers.

4 **Syria:** Russia and China veto a United Nations resolution, backed by the 13 other members of the Security Council and promoted by the Arab League, calling for President Assad to step down and to allow a transition to democracy. Just before the vote, Syrian forces launch an assault on the city of Homs, where hundreds are reported killed in the coming days. On 24 February,

former UN Secretary-General Kofi Annan is appointed special envoy of the UN and Arab League to Syria.

7 **Maldives:** President Mohamed Nasheed steps down and says he has been ousted in a police and military coup. He is replaced by Vice-President Mohammed Waheed Hassan.

8 **Palestine:** Rival factions Hamas and Fatah sign an agreement in Doha, Qatar to form a unity government under President Mahmoud Abbas.

13 **Israel:** Israeli diplomatic vehicles in New Delhi, India and Tbilisi, Georgia are targeted in attacks with magnetic explosive devices that appear to be the work of Iran. The next day, two Iranians are arrested after bombs detonate prematurely in Bangkok, Thailand.

14 **Honduras:** More than 350 people are killed in a prison fire.

21 **Afghanistan:** US apologises after copies of the Koran confiscated from detainees at Bagram Air Base are burned as rubbish. The burning prompts violent protests across Afghanistan. On 25 February, two US officers are killed by a policeman while working as advisers in the Interior Ministry.

22 **Yemen:** Voters elect the vice-president and sole candidate, Abdrabuh Mansur Hadi, to replace President Ali Abdullah Saleh.

29 European Central Bank provides a further €530bn of three-year loans to European banks to boost the liquidity of the banking system.

March 2012

1 **Serbia:** EU grants Serbia candidate status for membership, clearing the way for formal accession talks.

4 **Yemen:** Militants linked to al-Qaeda kill more than 100 Yemeni soldiers in a raid near the southern city of Zinjibar. In following weeks, a government offensive seeks to remove militants from territory they have taken in the south.

4 **Republic of the Congo:** More than 200 people are killed by explosions at a munitions depot in Brazzaville.

4 **Russia:** Vladimir Putin wins presidential election with 63.6% of the vote. Thousands protest against alleged voting fraud.

11 **Afghanistan:** American soldier kills 17 civilians, including nine children, after leaving his base in southern Afghanistan. Sergeant Robert Bales is arrested and flown back to the United States to face murder charges in a military court.

14 **Democratic Republic of the Congo:** International Criminal Court in The Hague issues its first verdict, convicting Thomas Lubanga of using child soldiers in the DRC civil war.

14 **China:** Bo Xilai, a rising Politburo member, is dismissed from his post as party secretary in Chongqing. Previously, the city's police chief, Wang Lijun, had taken refuge in a US consulate before being handed over to authorities. Subsequently, allegations emerge about the death of a British businessman, Neil Heywood, who was an associate of the Bo family and died in a hotel room in Chongqing. Wang had allegedly told US diplomats – and later Chinese authorities – that Heywood had been poisoned. On 10 April, Bo is formally dismissed from the Politburo and the Communist Party's Central Committee, and it is announced that his wife, Gu Kailai, has been arrested on suspicion of murdering Heywood. It is later alleged that Bo's wife had been seeking to move money out of China and that Heywood had sought a larger-than-usual commission for arranging this.

21 **Mali:** Renegade faction of the army, unhappy at the conduct of the fight against Tuareg rebels in north, overthrows President Amadou Toumani Touré. West African leaders condemn the coup, call for a return to democracy, and impose sanctions on Mali. On 1 April, Tuareg rebels take the city of Timbuktu. Following diplomatic efforts by ECOWAS leaders, both Touré and junta leader Captain Amadou Sanogo resign on 8 April. Power is formally passed to Dioncounda Traoré, speaker of the national assembly, who becomes interim president and is to hold elections. However, the junta led by Sanogo says it maintains a supervisory role.

22 **France:** Mohamed Merah, who had killed seven people in attacks inspired by radical Islamist views, is shot dead by police after a siege of his apartment in the southwestern city of Toulouse.

25 **Senegal:** Macky Sall, a former prime minister, wins presidential election, defeating the incumbent 86-year-old President Abdoulaye Wade, who had sought a third term although the constitution stipulated a maximum of two.

27 **Syria:** UN Special Envoy Kofi Annan says Syria has accepted a six-point plan for a UN-supervised ceasefire, a political process to address Syrian people's concerns, daily humanitarian access to conflict victims, and release of detainees. The government is to withdraw troops from heavily populated areas and UN monitors are to be sent. Violence continues and the UN estimates the death toll in the year-long uprising has reached 9,000. On 9 April, fighting spills across both the Turkish and the Lebanese borders. Government attacks on Syrian towns continue. On 12 April, a ceasefire begins. In the following days, breaches of the ceasefire by both sides are reported.

31 **Thailand:** Three bomb attacks in southern cities of Yala and Hat Yai kill 13 people.

April 2012

1 **Myanmar:** Aung San Suu Kyi is elected to parliament and her party, National League for Democracy, wins 43 of 45 seats in by-elections. On 6 April, the government strikes a peace deal with Karen rebels, one of a series of

agreements with ethnic groups long engaged in conflict. On 23 April, EU foreign ministers agree to suspend sanctions for a year while retaining a ban on arms sales.

7 **Pakistan:** Avalanche hits an army outpost near Siachen Glacier, site of a long-standing high-altitude military confrontation with India, trapping and killing 129 Pakistani soldiers and 11 civilians.

11 **Sudan/South Sudan:** Sudan halts talks with South Sudan on an oil-payments dispute and says it will mobilise its army. On 13 April, South Sudanese forces capture the disputed area of Heglig from Sudan and shut down its oil production. On 14 April, Sudanese aircraft bomb targets in the South, including the central oil-processing facility. Later, southern troops withdraw from Heglig.

13 **Guinea-Bissau:** Soldiers seize government buildings in a military coup ahead of a presidential election expected to be won by Carlos Gomes, following the death of Malam Bacai Sanha in January. ECOWAS and European Union impose sanctions on coup leaders. On 22 May, they hand power to a civilian transitional government under an agreement with ECOWAS, which deploys 600 troops to oversee the arrangement.

13 **North Korea:** Test of a long-range rocket fails when it breaks up shortly after launch.

15 **Afghanistan:** Taliban launches coordinated attacks on many targets in Kabul, including embassies and government buildings, but its fighters are repelled and killed.

16 **Argentina:** President Cristina Fernandez nationalises oil company YPF, which is majority-owned by Repsol of Spain. The move provokes widespread condemnation from European leaders.

16 **China:** Government allows renminbi to rise or fall by as much as 1% from the daily official rate against the dollar, doubling the permitted fluctuation band and marking a step towards a freely floating currency.

19 **India:** Successful test launch of long-range *Agni-V* nuclear-capable missile is carried out.

21 **Syria:** UN Security Council resolution formally establishes the UN Supervision Mission in Syria (UNSMIS), mandating up to 300 unarmed military observers to monitor the cessation of violence 'in all its forms by all parties'.

22 **China:** Chen Guangcheng, a blind human-rights activist, escapes house arrest in Shandong province and takes refuge in the US Embassy in Beijing. After high-level negotiations, on 19 May Chen leaves China to take up a scholarship at New York University.

23 **Netherlands:** Coalition government falls after far-right party refuses to support a new round of budget-cutting measures.

26 **Liberia:** Former Liberian President Charles Taylor is convicted by the UN Special Court for Sierra Leone of aiding and abetting war crimes during civil war in Sierra Leone. On 30 May, he is sentenced to 50 years in prison.

May 2012

1 **United Kingdom:** UK parliamentary committee, in a report on a telephone-hacking scandal, says Rupert Murdoch is not fit to run a major international company. Some MPs, however, dissent from this opinion. His company, News Corporation, acknowledges 'serious wrongdoing' by its now-defunct *News of the World* newspaper. On 15 May, Rebekah Brooks, former chief executive of the group's UK newspaper subsidiary, is charged with perverting the course of justice.

2 **Afghanistan:** US and Afghanistan sign a strategic partnership agreement under which US troops will support Afghan forces after the end-2014 deadline for withdrawal of NATO-led combat troops.

6 **Greece:** Parliamentary elections produce no clear result, with the previous leading parties, New Democracy and Pasok, suffering a sharp fall in vote share. The biggest gainer is the left-wing Syriza coalition, which wants to scrap the EU bailout austerity programme. Efforts to form a coalition swiftly fail and new elections are set for 17 June. The outcome increases speculation that Greece will quit the euro.

6 **France:** François Hollande, the Socialist candidate promising a growth policy instead of austerity, is elected president with 51.6% of the second-round vote, ousting Nicolas Sarkozy after one term.

8 **Israel:** Benjamin Netanyahu, prime minister, strikes a deal with centrist Kadima Party, headed by Shaul Mofaz, to form a national-unity government which is supported by 94 members of the 120-seat Knesset.

9 **Spain:** Bankia, Spain's third-largest bank, is partially nationalised with a capital injection of €4.5bn to strengthen it against exposure to losses on property lending, amid renewed market worries about the country's banking system and financial stability. Spanish and Italian borrowing costs rise as markets worry about the contagion effect of a possible Greek exit from the eurozone. Later, the Spanish government injects a further €19bn into Bankia.

10 **Syria:** Amid repeated violations of the ceasefire by both government and rebel forces, two bomb explosions kill 55 people in Damascus. The identity of the perpetrators is unclear.

20 **Serbia:** Tomislav Nikolic, a former extreme nationalist turned pro-European, wins presidential election, defeating Boris Tadic, president since 2004.

21 **Yemen:** Bomb attack kills 90 Yemeni soldiers at a parade in Sana'a.

25 **Syria:** More than 100 people, mainly women and children, are killed in Houla, near the city of Homs. The UN says most were 'summarily executed'. A pro-government militia is blamed. Kofi Annan, UN envoy, says the six-point plan is not being implemented. On 29 May, major Western countries expel senior Syrian diplomats. On 4 June, the rebel Free Syrian Army says it is no longer committed to a ceasefire, after some 80 government soldiers are killed in clashes. On 7 June, 78 people are reported killed near Hama and UN monitors are shot at as they try to reach the site.

25 **Afghanistan:** French President Hollande says all 2,000 combat troops will leave Afghanistan by end-2012, two years ahead of the NATO deadline, leaving some 1,500 non-combat troops.

25 **Egypt:** First-round results of presidential election produce a run-off between Muhammad Morsi of the Muslim Brotherhood and Ahmed Shafiq, last prime minister of ex-President Hosni Mubarak.

27 **Nepal:** Prime Minister Baburam Bhattarai dissolves the assembly, which has failed in four years to agree a new constitution, and calls new elections.

June 2012

2 **Egypt :** Former President Hosni Mubarak is sentenced to life imprisonment over the killing of protesters during the 2011 revolution. The former interior minister receives the same sentence, but the acquittal of four senior officials, as well as the acquittal of Mubarak and his two sons on corruption charges, provokes a furious response and demonstrations.

4 **Pakistan:** US drone strike kills Abu Yahya al-Libi, al-Qaeda second in command, a Libyan.

8 **Myanmar:** Violence breaks out in northwestern state of Rakhine between Muslims and Buddhists, following the murder of a Buddhist woman and the subsequent killing of 10 Muslim men. Tens of thousands of people flee their homes and a state of emergency is declared.

9 **Spain:** Government requests EU rescue package of up to €100bn to recapitalise its banks. Eurozone finance ministers agree to provide the funding, though details are yet to be worked out.

13 **Iraq:** Shia pilgrims are targeted in a wave of bombings which kill more than 80 people on the worst day of violence since the withdrawal of US forces.

14 **Egypt :** Military leadership dissolves recently elected parliament after the constitutional court rules results in one-third of seats were invalid. On 17 June, the final day of voting in the presidential election, it issues an interim constitution giving itself control of legislation until the election of a new parliament, as well as of the writing of a new constitution. It also limits the powers of the next president.

14 **Bahrain:** Civilian court reduces jail sentences on nine medical professionals convicted of roles in pro-democracy protests in 2011, and acquits nine others. The United States says it is 'deeply disappointed' at the court's failure to acquit all the accused.

16 **Syria:** UN Supervision Mission suspends patrols because of growing violence.

17 **Greece:** Centre-right New Democracy Party, which supports an EU bailout, wins re-run Greek parliamentary elections and forms a coalition with the socialist Pasok and Democratic Left parties. Antonis Samaras becomes prime minister. However, market concerns are not allayed.

19 **Pakistan:** Supreme Court disqualifies Prime Minister Yousuf Raza Gilani from office for contempt of court on the grounds that he did not pursue corruption charges against President Asif Ali Zardari. Raja Pervez Ashraf replaces him.

22 **Paraguay:** President Fernando Lugo is removed from office by a parliamentary vote after clashes over land evictions lead to the deaths of seven police and nine farmers. Vice-President Federico Franco replaces him. Mercosur and Unasur suspend Paraguay's membership, pending elections.

22 **Syria/Turkey:** A Turkish F-4 *Phantom* jet fighter on a reconnaissance mission is shot down by Syria over the Mediterranean, killing the two-man crew. Amid ensuing tension, President Assad later says he regrets the incident.

23 **Nigeria:** President Jonathan dismisses defence minister and national security adviser after attacks by Boko Haram on churches kill up to 150 people.

24 **Egypt:** Muhammad Morsi of the Muslim Brotherhood is announced as the winner of the presidential election with 52% of the vote, defeating Ahmed Shafiq.

25 **Cyprus:** Cyprus becomes the fifth eurozone member to seek an EU bailout.

28 **United States:** Supreme Court, in a 5–4 vote, rules that the Obama administration's health-care reforms were constitutional.

29 Eurozone leaders agree several steps that calm financial markets. A single banking supervisor will be created, run by the European Central Bank. The EU rescue funds can recapitalise banks directly, rather than debt-strapped governments. Spain's bank rescue is to be accomplished in this way. Irish banks are to receive better terms.

Chapter 1

Perspectives

After a short burst of bewildering change, the year to mid-2012 was one in which people whose interests were threatened tried to apply the brakes. Even as the Arab revolutions of 2011 were taking place, the extent to which youthful rebels would succeed in overturning the established order of their societies was questionable. In the aftermath, there was inevitable disillusionment: Egypt, for example, went through a remarkable series of elections, yet afterwards a military junta still wielded a great deal of power.

This is not to belittle what had been achieved by people power since Mohamed Bouazizi, a Tunisian street vendor, had set fire to himself in December 2010, epitomising the frustration felt by millions at their lack of opportunity in the face of venal bureaucracy and entrenched, corrupt dictatorships. The rapid removal of regimes in Tunisia and Egypt was followed by the more contested departures of Muammar Gadhafi in Libya and Ali Abdullah Saleh in Yemen, after tenures respectively of 42 and 34 years. Almost all the remaining Arab monarchies and regimes – in 2011 there were protests in 19 of the 22 countries of the Arab League – managed to deal with the popular forces that had been unleashed, some by enacting modest reforms. Notwithstanding the short civil war in Libya and continuing conflict in Yemen, these upheavals occurred with remarkably little bloodshed.

The exception was Syria, where security forces loyal to President Bashar al-Assad cracked down brutally on rebels in a conflict that was becoming more sectarian. At mid-2012, estimates of the total number of people killed on both sides ranged from 10,000 to 17,000. No end was in prospect – and violence escalated further in July with the assassinations of senior regime figures in a suicide bomb attack just as rebels conducted an offensive in the capital, Damascus. Efforts to mediate by the Arab League and the United Nations were unavailing, and there was no enthusiasm for foreign military intervention, especially as moves to put pressure on Assad were mostly blocked by Russia.

The revolutions of 2011 truly shook the world, and altered its perceptions. For decades, it had somehow been accepted that democracy was not appropriate for the Arab world. The George W. Bush administration, reacting to the September 2001 al-Qaeda terrorist attacks on the United States, had painted an image of a Middle East plagued by violent Islamism – and had used this as partial justification for the 2003 invasion of Iraq, a country in which al-Qaeda at the time had no significant foothold. But the Arab rebellions of 2011 reflected no such picture. Instead, they revealed that millions of young people wanted jobs and just societies, and were not at all persuaded by radical Islamism.

However, the removal of long-entrenched regimes lifted their expectations about what could be achieved. Egypt, Libya, Tunisia and Yemen were in the midst of difficult and fragile transitions. Events in Egypt, the most populous Arab country, were of particular significance. The military, having declined to save President Hosni Mubarak and having thus played an important role in making the revolution essentially peaceful, proved more ambivalent about shepherding in democracy. Islamists, who had been repressed by the former regime and had seemed irrelevant in the youth-led mass movement that ousted Mubarak, emerged to present themselves as a socially conservative force that appealed to voters who were concerned about instability. They won a series of elections. Even as presidential elections were under way, however, the army sought to reassert itself by dissolving parliament and issuing a draft constitution that gave it ultimate power. The new president, Muhammad Morsi of the Muslim Brotherhood, faced a delicate task in dealing with the generals. Yet here was a balance that seemed to leave out of account those who had brought about the revolution, but subsequently lacked the means to assert their interests. (See Arab Transitions, pp. 199–246.)

It was not only in the Arab world that old-established vested interests were reasserting themselves. In Russia, Vladimir Putin returned as president to re-emphasise the power of the state, relegating Dmitry Medvedev's hopes for a modernised economy to the second rank of priorities. In China, some of the intense but secret politics behind Beijing's version of state-led capitalism burst into the open with the scandal surrounding the politician

Bo Xilai, whose rise came to a sudden end. In India, entrenched bureau-cratic and commercial forces blocked the further opening of the economy, leaving in doubt the scope for continuing rapid growth. These were three of the 'emerging' economies that were expected to drive global growth in the decades to come, and to alter the balance of global power as they did so. But much was uncertain in these countries' future, and therefore also in prospects for the world.

This uncertainty was underlined by the meandering path taken by the longer-standing repositories of economic wealth and global influence: the United States and Europe. The former remained stuck in what has become an all-too-familiar unproductive political impasse. The most fundamental issue – how to steer a deficit-ridden economy, still suffering severely as a result of the 2008 financial crisis, to a position of more assured prosperity – remained utterly unresolved. The fury of radical 'Tea Party' Republicans seemed to dissipate as they were co-opted into the political realities of Washington; the non-radical establishment figure Mitt Romney emerged as the Republicans' presumptive nominee to face President Barack Obama in November 2012. But there was no hint of a bipartisan approach to economic and fiscal issues, and sheer political animosity – paying little regard to the merits of individual issues – seemed to be undermining the country.

In the realm of foreign policy, at least, the United States continued to move on to more sensible, firmer ground. It withdrew all troops from Iraq, remained on course for the exit from Afghanistan, played a limited role in the Libyan conflict and showed no inclination to become militarily involved in Syria's civil war. The interventionist, over-ambitious 'global war on terror' had been replaced by a more pragmatic approach, one that more accurately reflected America's true interests and played to its strengths. Iran's nuclear programme remained a primary concern, as did the security of the Middle East. But Washington engaged in a deliberate shift of strategic attention to the Pacific Ocean, where its formidable naval power had long reigned supreme. There, a rising China was altering the regional balance, but could not hope to match American military might – even if it wanted to – until some time in the distant future.

Europe remained stuck in its own impasse. It too faced the problem of how to generate economic growth when economies had become over-indebted. But the problem was compounded by the fact that 17 countries were tied together in an imperfect currency union that severely limited the scope for either individual or concerted action. The year to mid-2012 was characterised by bouts of fever in the financial markets, with borrowing costs for Spain and Italy, both large economies with the potential to carry the whole of Europe down with them, rising alarmingly. All the while, there were shrill forecasts that the eurozone, the group of countries using the euro as a common currency, would fall apart unless its leaders did – something! The question at the heart of this was whether the zone's member governments and electorates were still committed to being in the euro – essentially a political more than an economic choice. The evidence suggested that they did want to stay in the euro, since at each point at which action was demanded, voters and governments did just enough to prevent the derailment of the train. The euro kept puffing along. But economic growth was too slow to deal fundamentally with the problem of high debts, and so important questions remained to be resolved (see below).

Middle East in transition

While the Arab revolutions and the American withdrawal from Iraq drew much of the attention, the position of Iran remained an enduring issue of vital importance. Israel succeeded in creating the impression that a military strike on Iran's nuclear facilities was more than a remote possibility. Such an act, even if Western countries disavowed it, would almost certainly draw them into confrontation and even conflict with Iran. Amidst speculation about this potential short-term trigger for a global crisis, both Iran and the West upped the stakes in their long-term confrontation.

Tehran pressed ahead with its uranium-enrichment programme, for which there was no known civil purpose, since the fuel for its Russian-built nuclear power plant at Bushehr is supplied by Russia. In November 2011, the International Atomic Energy Agency, the UN's nuclear watchdog, revealed evidence (though of work done before 2004) of a comprehensive Iranian plan to develop all the technologies needed for an implosion-type nuclear weapon (see Iran, pp. 246–61). While there was no new indication over the past year that Tehran had decided to try to produce a weapon, it did dramatically increase the number of centrifuges that could enrich uranium to 20% purity – a level that covered 90% of the enrichment work needed to produce weapons-grade uranium. However, the programme continued to suffer from long-standing technical problems and in particular had difficulty in obtaining necessary materials because of international sanctions.

On the other side of the equation, sanctions were stepped up, and for the first time took a form that seemed to be having the kind of effect on the Iranian economy that could concentrate minds in Tehran. The United States and the European Union targeted Iran's oil exports and the payment and insurance transactions that were needed to keep them flowing. As an essay in this book spells out in detail (pp. 61–74), these measures could alter the cost–benefit equation for Iran's leaders. It appeared that the tightening of sanctions could have contributed to Iran's decision to attend a series of meetings with major powers in April–June 2012, though the talks made no significant progress. Separately, it appeared that sanctions imposed over the past two years had seriously inhibited Iran's development of the ballistic missiles that could deliver nuclear weapons.

Tehran's nuclear programme aroused much concern among states on the other side of the Persian Gulf. Over the year to mid-2012, regional competition intensified, with Iran accused of fomenting unrest in both Saudi Arabia and Bahrain, and of shipping arms to rebel groups in Yemen. When Iranian President Mahmoud Ahmadinejad visited an island claimed by both Iran and the United Arab Emirates, the Gulf Co-operation Council (GCC) issued a condemnation. Tehran also suffered regional setbacks, especially the rebellion against Assad in Syria and consequent disruption of links to allies in Lebanon. Hamas, the Islamist Palestinian faction, distanced itself from the Iran–Syria axis as it moved closer to the Muslim Brotherhood in Egypt.

This all formed part of a newly shifting regional landscape in the aftermath of the Arab uprisings. Saudi Arabia and other Gulf states had viewed with alarm the removal of the Mubarak regime in Egypt, and especially Washington's quick decision to drop the Egyptian dictator. Now, they saw in the election of the Muslim Brotherhood an unwelcome marriage of Islamism and democracy. This promised a difficult, even competitive relationship, in particular between Riyadh and Cairo. Gulf states were accused of interfering in post-revolutionary Tunisia, Egypt and Libya to provide resources to groups that might support their interests. But both sides had an eye to longer-term interests: when demonstrators sacked the Saudi Embassy in Cairo, senior Egyptian clerics and parliamentarians visited Riyadh to pay their respects to King Abdullah.

In contrast to their reaction to the Egyptian revolution, Gulf states saw in the Syrian rebellion a golden opportunity to weaken their regional rival Iran, and they tried to engineer international action against Assad and the arming of the rebels.

There was much to play for both in domestic political transitions (where new alliances were being made even as established interests were being protected) and in regional diplomatic relationships and extensions of influence. The longer-term question was how much the Arab upheavals would affect regional and religious divisions, and especially the position of Iran.

Israel's belligerence towards Iran appeared, for the time being, to have been countered by assurances given by Obama to Prime Minister Benjamin Netanyahu that the United States had 'Israel's back' and that Washington was not seeking to contain Iran but to prevent it from having a nuclear weapon. Obama urged Netanyahu to give tighter sanctions time to 'sink in'. In addition, former senior Israeli security officials publicly criticised the idea of attacking Iran, with a retired Mossad chief saying it was 'the stupidest thing I have ever heard'.

Europe: is muddling through sufficient?
In Europe, too, a great deal was at stake as the financial crisis afflicting the 17-member eurozone threatened continually to bring an economic disaster of a scale that could affect the continent – and the world – for decades. Repeated bouts of market instability, combined with political turmoil, suggested that Greece's stay in the common currency would soon come to an end, and that contagion could cause the same result for the much larger economies of Italy and Spain. The costs of eurozone exits or disintegration were deemed so high that even those who did not believe in a common currency – such as the Conservative-led government in the United Kingdom – wanted action taken to ensure that it did not fall apart. Markets and commentators alike yearned for governments to arrive at big solutions that would end uncertainties once and for all and begin to regenerate economic growth, which in turn would allow European countries to escape the burden of high sovereign debts. But the correct solution was a matter of intense debate, both in domestic politics and in inter-governmental crisis discussions. Germany – with, in effect, the fate of Europe at its disposal – resisted quick-fix steps which, it believed, would have only a short-term palliative effect.

In spite of the many forecasts of imminent financial Armageddon, at mid-2012 the euro was still intact. At each crisis point, governments and voters did just enough to contain negative market speculation. German Chancellor Angela Merkel insisted on a step-by-step approach that, she hoped, would in time convince markets of governments' collective will to retain the common currency and to build the fiscal and political structures needed to maintain it. She also believed that the budget-cutting 'austerity' policies which eurozone countries had introduced would, in the end, create sufficient business confidence in the health of economies to produce faster and more enduring economic growth. Many Europeans, however, disagreed with these German approaches, and governments and economists elsewhere viewed with considerable concern Europe's inability to resolve its internal issues and to remove uncertainties that were heavily overshadowing global economic prospects.

Viewed overall, the European economy was not in fact in especially terrible shape. The International Monetary Fund (IMF) forecast in July 2012 that the eurozone economy would contract in 2012 by 0.3%, and would grow by 0.7% in 2013. In other words, its trajectory was essentially flat – not sufficient to reduce joblessness, but not a severe recession either. By measures of public-sector debt, Europe was looking significantly healthier than America: the zone's collective budget deficit was forecast at 3.2% of GDP for 2012, compared with 8.2% for the United States. Total government debt would be 91.4% of GDP, compared with 106.7% for Washington. But these figures masked the particular problems of specific members: Greece, Ireland and Portugal, which had already arranged financial rescue packages; Spain, which was negotiating a eurozone bailout of its banks; and Italy, which had so far staved off the need for special assistance. Greece was in the grip of a steep and long recession, and unemployment was alarmingly high in several countries, notably Spain. The IMF noted that the most immediate risk to global growth was 'that delayed or insufficient policy action will further escalate the euro area crisis'.

The problem for the so-called 'periphery' countries was, in most cases, not that they had been especially profligate in public spending in the years leading up to the global financial crisis of 2008. However, they had benefited from plentiful finance via the banking system during the first decade of the euro's existence. During that period, markets had priced debt of all euro member countries at about the same level, on the basis that there was a common commitment to the single currency and a common central bank, the European Central Bank (ECB), which was assumed to stand behind them all (though it fact it was not set up to be the 'lender of last resort' like the US Federal Reserve or the Bank of England). The effect of the euro's introduction was therefore to set borrowing costs for some European countries lower than economic conditions might really warrant. With money easily available, they tended to channel it into consumption, unproductive investment (especially housing) and higher wages. The effect was to render economies less competitive and productive. For example, labour costs in several 'periphery' countries tended to rise significantly by comparison with those of Germany, which in turn benefited by being able to export large amounts of its goods to other eurozone members.

This merry-go-round stopped in two jolting stages. Firstly, the 2008 financial crisis caused a credit crunch that halted bank lending and caused a sharp recession, which in turn forced up governments' budget deficits. Secondly, Greece's revelation late in 2009 that it had grossly understated its budget deficit ended the period in which eurozone financing costs were essentially the same. Market differentiation between the creditworthiness of European governments was seen in widening spreads above yields on German government bonds. From then on, frenzied market speculation about the possible consequences repeatedly came to a head as Greece, Ireland and Portugal found themselves unable to meet their funding needs through the markets and had to be rescued.

The crisis of confidence became prolonged. At its heart was the poor state of Europe's banking system. Initially, banks suffered big losses because of exposure to US 'sub-prime' real-estate debt. Then their large holdings of European sovereign debt became the problem (and Spanish banks suffered from the end of a real-estate boom). To maintain their funding, governments relied on banks to buy their bonds. But banks in turn needed governments to rescue them if they made losses on bad loans (just as the US and British governments had injected capital into banks in 2008), and this would further increase sovereign debt. This created a dangerous mutual dependency: eurozone governments and private banks were compared to two drunks, each holding the other up.

At times during the year to mid-2012, market speculation became particularly intense. During summer 2011, it centred upon the terms of a second Greek rescue package and contagion to Italy and Spain. Later, the run-up to a December 2011 European summit came to be seen as a last chance to save the euro, with Olli Rehn, economic and monetary affairs commissioner, commenting beforehand that 'we are now entering the critical period of 10 days to complete and conclude the crisis response of the European Union'. Later still, elections in Greece that produced no clear result and had to be re-run created a frenzy of speculation about an imminent Greek exit (dubbed a 'Grexit') from the euro.

The responses of Europe's governments and authorities to these pressures were, in fact, substantial and multifaceted. But they fell far short of what some were calling for, and there remained considerable scepticism that enough had been done to stave off a variety of unpleasant possible outcomes such as continuing financial turmoil, a euro break-up, prolonged recession or depression, widespread social unrest and the end of the European Union.

What was done? Firstly, as each test of Greece's survival in the euro was reached, it was passed. A second rescue package was agreed, and Greece agreed to important measures to reform its economy and the tax system. The pain this would impose on Greeks caused the government that had negotiated the deal to be replaced by a technocrat, non-partisan prime minister, and later brought an election that underlined voters' anger. But a second election in June 2012 did produce a government, led by the conservative Antonis Samaras, that supported the bailout terms. Still, there would be further trials ahead. Secondly, the government of Italian Prime Minister Silvio Berlusconi, which had been reluctant to introduce economic reforms, was forced to stand down in favour of the respected non-partisan Mario Monti at the head of an entirely technocrat non-party government, which introduced labour and pension reforms. The question was for how long the consensus and political hiatus could hold. Thirdly, Spanish voters elected a government on the basis of plans for an austerity programme, which it proceeded to introduce even though the country was already under severe economic strain. Fourthly, eurozone governments agreed in December 2011 on a 'fiscal compact' which, while not really a step towards fiscal union, tightened monitoring and enforcement procedures for attaining common fiscal and debt targets. Fifthly, the ECB, faced with evidence of commitment to economic reforms and the euro's survival, offered to lend unlimited amounts of three-year money to banks. In two auctions, it lent about €1 trillion. This all but eliminated the risk of imminent bank bankruptcies and thus bought significant time for governments to produce more lasting solutions for weak banking systems, as well as to see some results from fiscal discipline and economic reforms. Sixthly, the zone's 'firewalls' – common funds to help countries in difficulties – were strengthened through modest changes. Finally, European leaders agreed in June 2012 to 'break the vicious circle between banks and sovereigns' – in other words, to separate the two drunks – by introducing common supervision of big banks and the ability to recapitalise them directly without adding to the sovereign country's debt burden.

None of these steps by itself held the key to solving the sovereign-debt crisis. But together, they showed a collective commitment of governments and voters. More radical solutions were rejected – and plenty had been proposed, such as much bigger action by the ECB, Keynesian stimulation of economies, heavy support from the IMF and other big economies, and so on. All such suggestions involved the conjuring-up of large amounts of money to help Europe through its wealth-threatening moment. Those who would be asked to produce such money were understandably not keen, seeing Europe as having the responsibility to deal with its own difficulty.

Germany also held out against many calls for it to produce even greater support than, as by far the largest contributor to bailouts, it was already providing. Events did, however, force it to show some flexibility, especially after François Hollande was elected as president of France on a pro-growth platform that enabled that country to band together with Italy and Spain in deliberations among European leaders. But Merkel would not countenance the mutualisation of debt through so-called 'eurobonds' issued by eurozone governments with mutual guarantees, seeing this as a solution that could only work after the zone's economies were truly bound together more closely both fiscally and politically. To her, it would remove all discipline on other countries to introduce reforms to make their economies more competitive. In parallel, she stuck to her belief that austerity programmes designed to reduce government debts were the only way back to health for countries that had over-spent, and that it was no solution for more creditworthy countries such as Germany to artificially stimulate their economies and undermine their own financial management. If Germany was carrying the whole of Europe on its shoulders, weakening Germany was, for Merkel, not the answer.

The problem, however, was that the mix of measures decided upon individually and collectively did almost nothing to generate the economic growth that would be needed, in the end, to resolve the sovereign-debt problem more fundamentally. They represented nothing more than 'muddling through' – an approach that bought time, but was perhaps insufficient. The danger was that further bouts of speculation could drive Spanish and Italian borrowing costs up to levels that were clearly unsustainable. At that point, more than muddling through would be required: real steps, including mutualisation of debt, would have to be taken towards fiscal and even political union. Otherwise, there could be disorderly exits from the euro. According to the OECD's November 2011 *Economic Outlook*, 'such turbulence in Europe, with the massive wealth destruction, bankruptcies and a collapse in confidence in European integration and cooperation, would most likely result in a deep depression in both the exiting and remaining euro area countries as well as in the world economy'.

An alternative scenario was that austerity programmes might become so unpopular that they could cause widespread unrest, and the election of populist, anti-European governments. Already by mid-2012 the radical leftist Syriza had emerged as the second-largest party in Greece, and anti-euro right-wing and left-wing parties were riding high in opinion polls ahead of a Dutch general election. If this trend continued, the existence of the EU itself, and its achievements over the past half-century, could come into question. Italian Prime Minister Monti, in his first speech to parliament in November 2011, said: 'We mustn't deceive ourselves that the European Union project can survive if monetary union fails. The end of the euro would unravel the single market, its rules, its institutions, and would take us back to where we were in the 1950s.'

Europe badly needed an injection of confidence that could spark bank lending and business investment to finance future growth. But it was not clear from there this would come. The vulnerability of the step-by-step approach was that it would need many years to succeed – and that, as elsewhere in the world, powerful vested interests stood in the way of reform.

Year of transition

It is perhaps a mark of changed times that this opening chapter of *Strategic Survey* has not, as it did four or eight years ago, dwelt on the US presidential election (though see extensive coverage on pp. 81–91). It may be a temporary phase, but much of the world now expects less of Washington and hangs on its actions to a much-reduced degree. This is not the fault of President Obama, nor of Hillary Clinton, his widely praised secretary of state who worked hard, for example, to deal with the Syrian crisis. After the tragedy of 9/11, the controversy of Iraq and the embarrassment of the WikiLeaks disclosures, Washington has been playing a more subtle and arguably more effective game. It was no mean feat for Obama to be seen, according to opinion polls, as a safer pair of hands in international security matters than the Republicans, even while managing the exit of combat troops from Afghanistan. Key moments for action could arrive regarding Iran, Syria and perhaps Pakistan. But America is drawing in its military horns, and cuts in defence spending are supported by a war-weary public across political lines – a rare area of agreement in a divided country. For Obama or Romney, the key areas at issue during the next presidential term seem likely to be domestic, with economic and fiscal matters paramount.

The good news in 2012 was of progress in two countries that have long been troubled. In Myanmar, a repressive military junta voluntarily moved – if only partially – towards democracy and liberalisation. It freed hundreds of political prisoners and moved to end conflicts with ethnic minorities. Western countries relaxed sanctions and re-opened relations. Aung San Suu Kyi was able to emerge from prolonged house arrest, be elected as an MP, travel abroad and receive the Nobel Peace Prize she was awarded in 1991 – an inspiring sight. (See Myanmar, pp. 378–83.) In Somalia, two decades without a proper government seemed to be coming to an end as clan-based factions hammered out a constitution and a plan for a transition to democracy. This was aided by foreign military intervention, which itself revealed Africa's slow but steady progress towards multinational military capabilities to deal with regional problems (see essay, pp. 47–61 and Somalia, pp. 282–7).

But there were also negative developments. West Africa (pp. 271–82) was an area of growing concern as the Islamist sect Boko Haram waged an increasingly violent campaign in Nigeria, while a spreading Tuareg rebellion caused a coup in Mali by soldiers unhappy that the revolt was not being properly countered (see *Strategic Geography*, pp. X–XI). In East Africa, important political moments were looming in Zimbabwe and Kenya, where the last elections had produced conflict.

The year to mid-2012 was, therefore, one dominated by transitions, with conflicting interests jockeying to secure their objectives. This was most obvious in the Arab world after the revolutionary wave of 2011, and in the surrounding region where the upheavals had upset traditional relationships and balances. But it was also occurring in a Europe struggling to work its own path to the future, in Russia after the re-election of Vladimir Putin, and in China where a leadership change was also under way. The United States remained in transition between an interventionist era and a new role, yet to take full shape.

Chapter 2
Strategic Policy Issues

Intelligence Agencies and the Cyber World

It took mankind until the turn of the last millennium to accumulate a corpus of data totalling five exabytes (10^{18} bytes). That amount of data is now being produced roughly every two days. And almost all of it is potentially – and instantaneously – available to a global community of Internet users, numbering in excess of two billion as of 2011 and expected to double by 2018. This tsunami of information, and the impact it has had in terms of public expectations of transparency, has presented a particular challenge for the world's intelligence services. They had been accustomed to operating in relative secrecy and with something close to a monopoly on certain kinds of information, but now face a world where far more material is in the public domain and the percentage of information that is truly secret is both smaller and ever better protected.

Even for the best-resourced and most technically proficient of the world's intelligence services, adapting to the new reality is a challenge, and will remain so for the foreseeable future. Over time it is likely that, although the fundamentals of intelligence work will remain unaltered, the phenomenon of 'Big Data' will significantly influence how intelligence is collected, stored, analysed and acted upon whilst simultaneously shaping the professional techniques or tradecraft associated with these activities. Indeed, this process is already well advanced.

Taming Big Data
The most immediate and publicly visible challenge facing intelligence and security organisations has been how to exploit Big Data for operational

purposes. This became urgent in the aftermath of the 9/11 attacks in 2001, when the extent of al-Qaeda's reach and operational capacity, much of it enabled by information and communications technologies (ICT), became evident. The challenge was particularly acute for the intelligence services of the United States and Western Europe, which were confronted with the task not just of looking for needles in haystacks but rather for needles in stacks of needles. Not only was Internet usage growing very rapidly, but this was accompanied by an explosion in the use of social media such as Facebook.

Jihadist groups were able to benefit from the IT skills of a generation of radicalised young muslims, often educated in the United Kingdom, to use the full spectrum of capabilities provided by the World Wide Web to enable covert communication. These included the use of encrypted Virtual Private Networks (VPNs), electronic 'dead letter boxes' (electronic mail-boxes in which draft messages can be accessed by those with the requisite password, so that messages never have to be sent and hence cannot be intercepted) and steganography (the concealment of data in seemingly innocuous formats such as pictures or maps). An example of the latter was furnished by a suspected jihadist arrested by the German authorities in April 2012. He was found to have concealed on his person a flash drive containing a pornographic film. German forensic experts uncovered within the film extensive al-Qaeda operational correspondence including confirmation of the role of the late Rashid Rauf in the abortive 2006 UK airline bombing plot.

Although faced with a daunting task, the Western intelligence community had some significant advantages which it was able to exploit over time. Foremost among these was the fact that the global system of undersea fibre-optic cables through which most Internet traffic passes was configured such that the bulk of the world's Internet communications physically transited the United States. At the turn of the millennium, this figure was in excess of 80%; and although alternative cabling routes have since been developed, it remains on the order of 60%. A jihadist message sent from Karachi to another location in Pakistan might well be wholly or partially routed via the United States and would hence become accessible to the US authorities (in modern ICT systems, individual messages are broken into data packets which are sent by whatever route is most readily available and reassembled at their destination).

In addition, counter-terrorism investigative activity is not just about analysing the content of specific messages, important though that is, but also about establishing connections between individuals who are trying to appear unconnected. Sophisticated relational analysis tools, some of which were developed for the Las Vegas gaming industry to defeat organised fraud, for example by gangs of card counters, were used. Such tools combine different forms of data, including records of travel and financial transactions – which collectively make up the 'electronic exhaust' which has become an inescapable feature of modern life – to identify linkages and patterns of movement that might not otherwise be apparent.

But for this to happen, these data sets have to be acquired by intelligence agencies. This need has given rise to widespread anxiety about the implications for individual privacy. Such concerns first manifested themselves in the furore that occurred in the United States when it became evident that the National Security Agency (NSA), the signals-intelligence body, had been authorised by President George W. Bush under the 2001 PATRIOT Act to access e-mail communications without the judicial warrants mandated by the 1978 Foreign Intelligence Surveillance Act (FISA). FISA, which was passed following the Church Commission investigation into illegal interception operations carried out at the behest of President Richard Nixon in the 1970s, had been designed to ensure that the government would not be able to intercept the communications of American citizens without judicial warrants. It also imposed limits on the circumstances in which the communications of foreign governments and organisations could be monitored within the United States (FISA did not seek to control such activities undertaken overseas).

However, as FISA pre-dated the Internet, it did not take into account the realities of the globalisation of electronic communications, which blurred the previously clear distinctions between foreign and domestic activities. Nor was FISA adequately configured to deal with the phenomenon of transnational terrorist groups comprised largely, if not exclusively, of non-US nationals, coverage of whose activities via intercept operations conducted on US soil FISA did not permit. In 2007, Congress passed the Protect America Act which sought to address some of the anomalies of FISA and to provide legal indemnity to Internet service providers (ISPs) that made data available to the US intelligence community.

Concern about the privacy implications of intelligence agencies accessing electronic correspondence was not confined to the United States. Pressure by Washington on the European Union (EU) to furnish substantial personal data on air travellers to the United States generated much controversy. So too did the discovery in 2006 that US intelligence agencies, as part of their Terrorist Finance Tracking Programme, had been accessing data about financial transactions stored in the Brussels databases of the Society for Worldwide Interbank Financial Telecommunication (SWIFT). (As with e-mails and other electronic intelligence, much of the value of this data was not in its content per se, but rather in terms of the ability it gave investigators to make connections between individuals and analyse patterns of behaviour.)

An interim agreement negotiated between Washington and Brussels, designed to address privacy concerns, has been the subject of as-yet-unresolved tensions between the European Commission and the European Parliament, with the latter rejecting the agreement. Similar friction has arisen in the United Kingdom, where the government announced in 2012 plans to require ISPs to retain the details of all electronic communications for a full year and to make this so-called metadata – not the actual content of e-mails or other communications – available to intelligence services on request. Reactions to these proposals have revealed low levels of public trust in government. On the one hand, the proposed system, which would be tightly regulated and subject to oversight mechanisms, is widely distrusted. On the other, Internet users are seemingly content to allow private-sector service providers not only to hold significant information about their personal lives but to accept that this data can be collated and made available to other companies for marketing purposes, with few controls.

Despite all the efforts made over the past decade to develop tools to filter and analyse large volumes of data, the ability of intelligence agencies to collect data far outstrips their capacity to analyse it. This is a serious problem: an abiding preoccupation of such services is that following a successful terrorist attack, information on their databases will come to light which, had it been registered and its significance appreciated at the time, might have played a role in preventing the attack.

The problem of data analysis is particularly acute in one area where modern communications have had a transformational effect, namely battlefield intelligence, surveillance and reconnaissance. In both Iraq and Afghanistan, the United States and its allies developed sophisticated methodologies for 'fusing' different kinds of intelligence, both human and technical, into packages that are used to conduct precision targeting of terrorist or insurgent groups either through missile attacks from unmanned aerial vehicles (UAVs) or night raids by special forces. The technical data comprises e-mail and mobile-phone intercepts as well as various forms of imagery, including data from satellites and video footage from loitering

UAVs. In conditions of high operational tempo such as exist in Afghanistan, these capabilities generate huge volumes of data which need to be analysed and packaged in something close to real time. At present, the capacity to do this is severely limited.

The continuing utility of such techniques for specialised counter-terrorism and counter-insurgency operations is self-evident, as is the scope to expand their use to deal with organised criminal groups such as narcotics traffickers and pirates. Such technologies could also have wider political and humanitarian purposes. For example, the mobilising and enabling role played by social media in the 2011 Arab uprisings, though its significance arguably was exaggerated, created awareness of the need to be able more effectively to analyse such media in real time in the hope of identifying patterns that might indicate a tipping point. Automated analysis of social media and other open-source data such as web searches and microblogs may in the future offer pre-emptive intelligence of social and political upheavals, economic crises or major outbreaks of disease. In terms of domestic security, some automated closed-circuit television (CCTV) systems can already pin-point anomalous behaviour, such as a group of people loitering in a location where this normally does not occur. Significant efforts are now being undertaken by the US Defense Advanced Research Projects Agency (DARPA) and Intelligence Advanced Research Projects Activity (IARPA) to promote the development of algorithm-based automated systems more capable of triaging large quantities of data from a variety of sources to produce actionable intelligence.

Such developments seem likely to have the effect of expanding responsibility for intelligence collection and analysis beyond what has traditionally been seen as the intelligence community and to alter the latter's relationships with customer departments. It is hard to imagine national intelligence agencies being able to meet more than a proportion of the demand from government departments and international organisations for intelligence to which these emerging capabilities are likely to give rise. Government departments could develop their own collection capabilities within their particular sector, or they could rely on a private intelligence community offering an increasing array of specialised services. Such a trend does not portend the demise of intelligence agencies as they currently exist. But it does point to wider operational collaboration with, for example, law-enforcement agencies – a trend now well established in the UK – and a greater readiness to leverage the capacity of private-sector contractors, a well-established process in the United States.

Authoritarian regimes: the other side of the coin

The intelligence communities of authoritarian states have been as preoccupied as their Western counterparts with monitoring the Internet and other forms of electronic media for evidence of threats – but with a focus on threats of a different kind. For governments such as those of China, Russia and Iran, the Internet is perceived as a Western-dominated system which, though providing significant benefits (including a substantially increased capability to conduct espionage against Western targets), serves as a vector for spreading subversive political ideas within their countries.

Approaches to this challenge have varied. Russia has not in the past sought to constrain Internet usage through content filtering or online censorship. But its security service, the FSB, and other government agencies such as the tax authorities, are able to monitor all Internet traffic under the SORM (an acronym meaning System for Operative Investigative Activity) programme, legislation for which was enacted in 1995, and to take action against people whose online activities they disapprove of. A bill passed by the Duma on 11 July 2012 made provision for Internet filtering on the basis of a judicial warrant, a measure ostensibly aimed at restricting access to pornography and other socially harmful content.

In China, techniques for controlling online activities by a 'Netizen' community that numbers in excess of 500 million have evolved into a sophisticated set of policies which have collectively been characterised as networked authoritarianism. As described by US researcher Rebecca MacKinnon, who coined the term, networked authoritarianism accepts that citizens will access and create online information well beyond what is normally deemed acceptable by authoritarian regimes. It allows such activity to take place within a controlled environment. One aspect of this control is engagement in online discussions by government stooges – the Fifty Cent Party, so-called because of the sum they are allegedly paid for each pro-government online intervention they make. Other aspects include an active filtering programme using sophisticated data-mining software, which prevents citizens from seeing content deemed to be objectionable; a requirement for all Internet users and microbloggers to register their real identities; and an onus on service providers to police the content displayed on their systems.

In spite of these constraints, the Chinese government is able to create the impression that citizens can debate and influence public policy. The Internet serves as a release valve for popular discontent and enables the government to take credit when it appears to take action in response to popular concerns. At the same time, the government can close down any online debate which looks like getting out of hand and punish those judged to be involved in anti-state activities.

The techniques developed by China's security and intelligence community to monitor and control dissent have proven to be a successful export model to other authoritarian states confronting ICT-enabled dissent. Conceptually, some of these techniques pre-date the Internet era and can be traced back to the approach adopted by the Chinese Ministry of State Security during the student demonstrations of 1989 which culminated in the 4 June Tiananmen Square massacre. At bottom, this approach amounts to allowing protesters and dissidents to have their heads whilst carefully observing their activities and connections so that arrests and prosecutions can take place at a time of the government's choosing. As Evgeny Morozov observes in his book *The Net Delusion*, ICT powerfully enables such investigative activity since online communications leave an indelible record of connectivity. This enables authoritarian regimes to detain and investigate not just individuals but entire networks. As Morozov notes, secret police forces love social media sites such as Facebook, as these do much of their investigative work for them.

Such was the case in Iran with the Green Movement, which protested against election results in 2009. Because levels of Internet penetration and use of social media were still relatively low, Iranian intelligence and security agencies found it easy to identify and close down the activities of those promoting dissent. Other governments confronted with similar challenges, such as Egypt's in 2011, resorted to the use of more blunt instruments such as shutting down the Internet for a brief period. Following a burst of urban rioting in August 2011, UK Prime Minister David Cameron briefly speculated on the possibility of closing down the social media sites perceived to have acted as an accelerant for anti-social behaviour. But in a world where societies are increasingly dependent on networked systems, such extreme activity is both counter-productive and, arguably, unnecessary. Intelligent and active monitoring by governments of social media, especially if this can be done using automated systems of the kind referred to earlier, is likely to prove a more effective response to situations of social disorder in whichever kind of society they occur.

The fact that opposition and dissident groups are heavily dependent on ICT has enabled the intelligence services of authoritarian states to extend their reach beyond their own borders to monitor, harass and intimidate individuals and groups located in states where they were formerly out of reach. The GhostNet investigation carried out in 2009 by Information Warfare Monitor, a Canadian not-for-profit Internet research group, revealed the scope of penetration – presumably by China though this could not be proved – of the networks of the Dalai Lama's Free Tibet Movement. This extended to penetrations of NGO and government networks in a large number of countries. The extent to which the Chinese government is able to intervene pre-emptively to constrain the activities of the Free Tibet Movement in neighbouring states such as Nepal testifies to the scope and effectiveness of its campaign. There are also indications that both Russia and Iran have resorted to ICT to put pressure on and curtail the activities of émigré and dissident groups located overseas.

Exploiting cyber capabilities
The widespread availability of cyber-exploitation techniques has had a significant empowering effect on intelligence services around the world. States which cannot afford to maintain traditional overseas collection networks of the kind operated by intelligence powers such as the US, the UK, France and Russia can easily muster the resources to develop cyber-collection capabilities, taking advantage of the low barriers to entry and the ubiquity of the techniques used to undertake such collection, many of which have been developed by criminal groups. China is widely seen as the country making the most ambitious and aggressive use of such techniques.

In the past, the ability of any intelligence service to collect information, particularly using human sources, depended on being able to identify and then obtain close access to potential sources of information, which could be hard to do in closed societies without coming to adverse attention. The Internet offers greatly expanded potential for targeting operations – identifying individuals with potential access to intelligence – and also multiple opportunities for making contact with them in seemingly innocuous and unthreatening ways. These provide insights into potential motivations that can be exploited, and ways of developing direct physical access. It is also possible that in some circumstances where physical contact is not an option, agents can be recruited and run wholly online – though this presents substantial challenges in respect of establishing bona fides and maintaining operational security. And from a practical perspective, the increasingly pervasive nature of ICT looks likely to reduce a long-standing problem faced by intelligence agencies of agents with good access but unable to report their intelligence in a timely manner.

The advent of the Internet means that intelligence can increasingly be collected by accessing the secure systems of target states and organisations, without the need to recruit human sources, though in the case of systems that are 'air-gapped' – not linked to the Internet – a secret agent may still be needed to facilitate access. The benefits of collecting intelligence by penetrating the networks of target organisations are self-evidently substantial. A successful covert penetration of a network provides access to enormous quantities of information which can be extracted instantaneously and, provided it is undetected, repeatedly. Most of the problems of validation associated with analysing and assessing traditional intelligence fall away; there can be no doubting the validity of material collected through cyber-exploitation operations. While it is not entirely unimaginable that some organisations might seek to create false databases or deliberately insert false or misleading data into their systems, the time and resources needed to do this are such that, in practice, it is unlikely to happen. And although it is not the case that, as is often asserted, attribution of a cyber attack is impossible, cyber-exploitation activities can be conducted at much lower levels of risk than is true of traditional collection techniques. Under the Law of Armed Conflict, espionage activities are not deemed to be the equivalent of an armed attack, and most if not all governments are likely to eschew the option of kinetic retaliation for such activities.

The most commonly used technique for penetration of a network is a so-called Trojan attack, in which a virus is introduced via an attachment to an e-mail. Opening the attachment introduces the virus into the network and activates it such that the system can be remotely instructed to download data without this being visible to the target system's operators. Such attacks have been greatly facilitated by the use of social networks such as Facebook and LinkedIn. A case in point is the successful attack in March 2011 carried out by a Chinese contractor apparently working for the 3rd Department of the General Staff of the People's Liberation Army against the RSA secure communications system used by US defence contractors. This operation, a sub-set of a much wider Chinese campaign collectively referred to as *Shady Rat*, targeting everything from secure US government and law-enforcement facilities to the International Olympic Committee, began with an analysis of participation in LinkedIn by employees of companies known to use the RSA system. The aim was to identify the most promising targets for so-called 'spear-phishing' attacks in which Trojans are sent to specific individuals in e-mail attachments, tailored to maximise the likelihood of their being opened. The attacks were just one phase in a much more complex and multi-faceted operation which involved acquiring a detailed understanding of the algorithms used in RSA, access to encrypted passwords and other operationally relevant detail amassed over an extended period.

Shady Rat is just one of many operations emanating from China designed to extract bulk data from the networks of the US government and private-sector corporations. The latter are targeted with the aim of gaining access both to intellectual property and the negotiating strategies of companies seen by China as competitors in sectors such as oil and gas exploration. This phenomenon has been described by General Keith Alexander, NSA director and head of US Cyber Command, as 'the greatest transfer of wealth the world has ever seen' and is thought to have led to the compromise of the corporate networks of every Fortune 500 company.

That such state-on-private-sector espionage, conducted on an industrial scale, represents a new and unprecedented phenomenon is not in doubt. What is less clear is how much damage such activities have in fact done, in terms of eroding the national advantage of the United States and other Western countries, which increasingly derives from their ability to leverage intellectual creativity. In some cases, the damage has been evident. The US wind-turbine manufacturer AMSC suffered an 80% decline in revenue in 2011 after its software had been stolen and its designs were allegedly pirated by the Chinese wind-turbine company Sinovel, previously AMSC's largest customer. Frequent problems of this nature for American companies would present a policy dilemma for the US government as it assesses the impact in the context of its overall relationship with China. The asymmetry of vulnerability between the United States and China made it hard for Washington to devise an effective and proportionate retaliatory strategy. After a period of equivocation, the US government finally raised the issue at the annual bilateral security and economic dialogue held in May 2012 in Beijing, accusing China of being responsible for large-scale and systematic theft of US intellectual property. It is not known how China, which has always denied any such activity, responded to these accusations.

Although China's cyber-exploitation operations have received intensive publicity, it is simply one player in what has become a constant and increasingly hard-fought triangular contest between the intelligence services of China, Russia and the United States.

There is no reliable way of determining the relative performance of these agencies since, by definition, successful cyber exploitations go undetected. It appears on balance that more exploitations emanating from China are discovered than from the United States or Russia. But there is an asymmetry of vulnerabilities insofar as there are many more things Russia and China want to steal from the United States than the United States wants to steal from them. At the same time, China in particular has significant vulnerabilities arising out of its extensive reliance on pirated Microsoft systems which do not benefit from regular security patches, with the result that criminal gangs often route their cyber activities via China to cover their tracks.

Many other states are active in this domain. The UK, Australia and Canada, all of which benefit from membership of the Five Eyes intelligence alliance with the United States, can safely be assumed to engage actively in cyber-espionage and cyber-exploitation operations. In 2011 the greatest number of cyber exploitations against China was found to emanate from Japan, the second largest number from the United States and the third largest from South Korea. Japan and South Korea are simply two of a growing number of developed economies with substantial cyber capabilities that are used for a wide range of activities including intelligence collection. And North Korea, a country where Internet penetration has been confined to a tiny elite, has developed impressive cyber-exploitation capabilities, apparently with assistance from China, which it has deployed against South Korea, Japan and possibly the United States.

Nor do intelligence services necessarily confine their cyber activities to pure espionage. They can also go on the offensive and sabotage other countries' systems. The Stuxnet attack on Iran's uranium-enrichment pro-gramme represents the first documented case in which physical damage was caused by cyber activities, though the extent and durability of the damage done remains unknown. From the outset it had been widely assumed that Stuxnet was a collaborative undertaking by United States and Israeli intel-ligence agencies with possible help from other Western partners sharing a common aspiration to degrade Iran's enrichment activities. In his June 2012 book *Confront and Conceal: Obama's Secret Wars and the Surprising Use of American Power*, US journalist David Sanger cites multiple sources indicating that Stuxnet was in fact developed by the NSA with help from Israel's Unit 8200. The fact that Sanger's claims have sparked a formal leak inquiry would seem to confirm their validity. The attack involved the introduction into the control system of Iran's P1 centrifuge cascade of a worm (a piece of self-perpetuating malware) designed to alter elements of the Siemens control systems. Centrifuges were made to spin at a faster-than-usual speed without this being apparent to those monitoring the system. After a brief period of spinning at the wrong speed, they were destroyed. It is unclear how Stuxnet was introduced into an air-gapped system, but it is likely that a secret agent was involved. What is clear is that Stuxnet was an intelligence-led attack which required detailed knowledge of how the Iranian P1 centrifuge cascade worked – it was even alleged that Israel had built a replica cascade in order to determine the precise effect that Stuxnet would have. There have also been suggestions that aspects of Microsoft technology shared with the US government for defensive purposes were deployed in this attack in ways Microsoft had not anticipated or approved. Awareness of the Stuxnet virus gave rise to much comment about the emergence of a cyber weapon capable of causing physical damage with the implication that such weapons could in future be widely and randomly deployed. But the reality is that such capabilities can only be deployed in an intelligence-based context and are likely to be used sparingly and for very specific purposes.

Networked systems in the West are also vulnerable to degradation and sabotage by foreign intelligence services. Targets could include elements of critical national infrastructure, banking systems, transport and any other services or amenities which depend on ICT. Attempts to damage them could come through logic bombs (malware which lurks in a network undetected until the originator decides to activate it) or 'zero-day attacks' which are designed to exploit network vulnerabilities which have not previously been identified by those monitoring the network. Western policymakers have expressed concerns that Chinese companies such as Huawei, which have made strenuous efforts to establish a commercial presence in Western countries and compete for contracts to sell communications technologies, could in the future be used as a vector for this kind of attack. Whether any state would be prepared to undertake such activities in a circumstance short of all-out war is debatable. Nor is it entirely clear how harmful such attacks would prove to be; for a logic bomb to be reliably effective at the point of activation it would need to have the capacity to adapt to a constant stream of software upgrades and security patches that are a characteristic of any networked system. But the existence of this threat is a reminder that in the cyber domain, all actors use broadly the same techniques; the only thing that distinguishes them is intent.

Dealing with such threats represents a constant challenge for the Western intelligence and security community and there are no easy answers. Asymmetries of vulnerability can make effective retaliation hard to achieve, and thinking about cyber deterrence is still in its infancy. Systems can be hardened to make them less attractive to attackers, but no defensive measures can offer complete assurance against penetration; with ICT-enabled systems configured as they are – and there is no foreseeable prospect of their being reconfigured differently – a determined attacker will eventually always get through. Most Western intelligence services have adopted a strategy based on active exploitation designed to find out as much as possible about the capabilities and intentions of potential adversaries – an approach which requires an integration of effort by signals and human intelligence agencies – to help identify effective security strategies. This requires intelligence communities to share intelligence with the private sector, which operates most of the systems likely to be attacked. This cultural adaptation has not come easily and it is clear that more work needs to be done to enable effective public-private collaboration.

Security threat to intelligence agencies

Just as 'electronic exhaust' makes terrorist groups vulnerable, the same is true of intelligence operatives engaged in covert operations. There are many ways in which their movements can be traced and monitored: travel bookings, credit-card use and banking history, mobile phones (now invariably equipped with GPS location), cars whose increasing dependence on computerised systems make them easy to monitor and even remotely control, CCTV and, potentially, more clandestine techniques such as nanotechnological sensors which can be concealed in items of clothing. Facial-recognition technologies, though still imperfect, are improving to the point where photographs can be used for active identification in ways not previously possible. Intelligence operatives – and their agents – are also vulnerable to detection via forensic techniques such as DNA – as American FBI agent Robert Hanssen found to his cost when he was exposed as a Russian spy in 2001 due to the discovery of his DNA on a document given to his KGB case officers and extracted covertly from KGB archives. Conversely, the absence of what now seems like a normal amount of 'electronic exhaust' – an absence of travel history, credit rating and so on —is inherently suspicious and any operative travelling with an identity lacking such underpinnings is inviting further scrutiny.

An example – albeit extreme – of the difficulties of mounting covert operations in an ICT-enabled era was the assassination of Hamas leader Mahmoud Abdul Rauf al-Mabhouh in the Al Bustan Rotana Hotel in Dubai on 19 January 2010. Mabhouh, who had been the primary conduit for providing Iranian and other weaponry to the al-Qassam Brigades, the military wing of Hamas in Gaza, was found in his hotel room suffocated after having been injected with a strong muscle relaxant. The Dubai authorities' investigation, relying on CCTV footage, revealed that the assassination team consisted of at least 18 people, some of whom had entered hotel washrooms which they then exited having altered their appearance. All were travelling on false identities using UK, Republic of Ireland, Australian, French or German passports in identities which had been stolen from individuals, some of whom were residents of Israel. The Dubai authorities unequivocally blamed the Israeli intelligence service Mossad. Although the Israeli government refused to comment, the Irish government expelled the Mossad representative from Dublin after investigating the use of Irish passports in the operation. Photographs of 11 of the assassination team were passed to Interpol for inclusion in their most-wanted list.

On one level, the operation could be deemed a success. Mabhouh was assassinated and Mossad, if indeed it was responsible, succeeded in exfiltrating the team from Dubai before the investigation began. But Mossad's activities were subjected to intensive publicity, and the impact on its wider operational capabilities will have been significant. Many of those involved are likely to have been involved in other operations, using either the same or other identities, possibly in conjunction with other operatives not involved in the Mabhouh case. Those agents could retrospectively be exposed as well. Determining the degree of operational contamination is likely to have been a time-consuming process, during which much planned operational activity will have been put on hold.

Among Western intelligence agencies, Mossad is unique in having authorisation to undertake assassinations. Therefore, the Mabhouh case was extreme, and perhaps unrepresentative. Most covert intelligence operations are designed to go undetected and to leave no traces that might give rise to investigation. But the ICT-enabled world offers less cover for covert activity than was previously the case. Another example was the identification by human-rights activists of covert CIA rendition flights through detailed analysis of flight plans and other records. The data were in the public domain but required significant expertise to make sense of – although the activists were unable to identify which flights were used for rendition rather than for purposes such as transfer of staff and equipment, and so exaggerated the scope of the rendition programme.

New tradecraft
The explosion of ICT technologies means that intelligence agencies face many new challenges as they try to carry out their activities undetected. It is by no means the first time that they have had to adapt to new technologies, starting with the advent of the telephone at the beginning of the twentieth century and the use of encrypted radio communications such as Enigma. That they will modify their tradecraft to cope with the realities of a networked world is not in doubt – though it may take time. But in any event,

they are unlikely to be rendered redundant. It may be possible to extrapolate important information from data available on the Internet, but the most important secrets are in the main unlikely to be found there. Moreover, intelligence work is not just about acquiring information not previously known, but equally about making sense of existing information and placing it in the correct context. Technical collection and analytical techniques will inevitably play an increasingly prominent role. But the most important secrets remain in the minds of people, and eliciting and interpreting these will continue to rely on techniques – more art than science – that have been in existence for many centuries.

African Defence: Building Cooperative Capacity

Africa has been home to some of the world's most complex wars and security problems. Increasingly, it is also the venue for ambitious initiatives designed to improve crisis management and the prevention and resolution of conflicts. Regional economic and security bodies have been important in generating new ideas, and at the continental level so too has the African Union (AU). Among the objectives have been the generation of new military and security capacities.

Key to these efforts is the goal of establishing African standby forces capable of tackling contingencies ranging from the simple provision of military advice to – at the other extreme – deployment of troops in situations to prevent or stop genocide. These forces were originally due to be operationally capable in 2010, but the date for full capability is now set for 2015. Though there is a need to be able to act anywhere in Africa, it is unclear whether the initiatives under way are shaped and resourced to meet this requirement. However, some national militaries, as well as the continent's security institutions and their international partners, have begun to demonstrate flexible and innovative approaches.

Desire for African solutions
The new initiatives have been spurred and shaped by security crises across the continent. The desire is to implement 'African solutions to African problems'. According to Jean Ping, then-chair of the AU Commission (AUC), speaking in 2010, 'with the transformation from the Organisation of African Unity into the African Union … African leaders expressed both their desire

and commitment to play a greater role in, and to take greater ownership of, peace and security on the African continent'. Ping said the Cold War era and its aftermath had shown that 'the international community could not always be relied upon to address threats to peace and security on the African continent'. Somalia and Rwanda had been painful lessons. 'Within this context, it became increasingly apparent that the AU would have to assume a greater responsibility for peace and security on the continent.'

In 2002, the AU established a Peace and Security Council (PSC) to 'strengthen [its] capacity for the prevention, management and resolution of conflicts'. The council was intended to 'anticipate and prevent disputes and conflicts, undertake peace-making and peace-building functions and authorise the mounting and deployment of peace support missions'. It is managed by the AU commissioner for peace and security; since 2008 this has been Ramtane Lamamra of Algeria who, assisted by a director, heads the Peace and Security Department. The overall framework for AU activities, the African Peace and Security Architecture (APSA), was designed to be a set of guiding principles for activities by the AU, UN partner agencies and non-governmental organisations, as well as regional economic communities such as ECOWAS (the Economic Community of West African States), and 'regional mechanisms for conflict prevention, management and resolution', such as the North African Regional Capability.

At the same time, a set of instruments was designed to enable the AU to analyse and manage conflicts through dialogue or intervention. The Union's Peace and Security Department is focused on generating capacities such as a continental early-warning system (comprising a situation centre, and analysis and monitoring personnel) and a military dimension in the form of an intervention capacity – the African Standby Forces (ASF). Other elements of the African Peace and Security Architecture include a Military Staff Committee, comprising the Addis Ababa-based defence attachés of the 15 PSC countries, the Common African Security and Defence Policy initiative, a 'panel of the wise', made up of eminent personalities and former officials to provide advice to the PSC, the Africa Peace Fund, and a Post-Conflict Reconstruction and Development Framework. While these instruments are still in gestation, they are central to understanding how African states, and their international partners, envisage effecting future conflict prevention and resolution.

The AU is increasingly being accepted as a central actor in African peace and security. This is apparent from the emphasis that some states have placed on giving an AU dimension to unilateral or regional security initiatives and military deployments. The AU has accepted these moves, such as the re-badging of Kenya's incursion into Somalia under the AU Mission in Somalia (AMISOM). In this way, the Kenyan force gains greater legitimacy, as well as access to the financial and logistics support available to those participating in activities sanctioned at the multilateral level, while the existing AMISOM force is further strengthened. The ECOWAS initiative in 2012 to deploy forces into Guinea Bissau and Mali, following military coups, also reflected the growing extroversion of regional economic communities.

Willingness to deploy forces as part of internationally mandated missions is becoming more apparent among certain African militaries. In April 2002, according to UN data, only four African countries (including North African states) had more than 500 military personnel deployed to UN operations; ten years later, 14 African nations met this criterion, with six deploying more than 2,000 troops. Meanwhile, five of the top ten overall contributors of military and police forces in April 2012 were from Africa: Egypt, Ethiopia, Ghana, Nigeria and Rwanda.

However, developing adequate capacity to support AU and AU/UN deployments, as well as to contribute to the ASF, hinges on more than just an ability to generate infantry battalions, engineer units or formed police units. It depends on whether they have the right capabilities in a much broader sense. It also depends on determining the roles that national armed forces are supposed to fulfil, and on the levels of ambition set for them – in other words, whether African nations see contributions to international forces as a core role for their armed and security forces. Indeed, the biggest challenge in realising APSA is not disagreement on the need to intervene in complex emergencies, but rather that African nations still lack the capacities to deal with many of the substantial challenges facing the continent.

New roles and capabilities

Some African security establishments are restructuring at a fast pace. They have realistic ambitions to become comparatively modern, responsive forces equipped to high standards. Examples include Uganda, where a 2012 estimate projects defence expenditure at around 12% of government spending and recent acquisitions have included advanced combat aircraft, and the new state of South Sudan, which is engaged in the creation of national armed forces. Others retain small forces that have changed little in size and capability since the 1960s. A number of countries are able to point to substantial experience in peacekeeping operations, strong professional training and military culture, as well as inventories and organisations that are being modernised. But few forces are capable of independently deploying and sustaining troops beyond their immediate regions.

Besides Uganda, which began its reform process in the early 2000s, another example is Ghana, which has a modernisation plan that extends to 2025. Its armed forces routinely participate in African peacekeeping missions, and it recently added to its tactical airlift capabilities.

African states have divergent priorities, and maintain armed forces to accomplish differing tasks. For many, territorial defence, support to the civilian population, internal security or police support remain central military duties. Deployments abroad in UN-mandated missions are a task for some armed forces, but ambitions to participate in such missions do not usually shape militaries' organisation and doctrine. Rather, armed forces and formed police units deployed abroad tend to be drawn from existing organisations. Force structures and procurement programmes are not necessarily geared towards producing capabilities that are ideal to be dispatched and sustained further afield (that is, small, well-trained and mobile forces with flexible airlift and support).

An examination of UN missions to sub-Saharan Africa in 2012, for example, shows that while African states deployed substantial infantry formations, combat support and combat service support units were deployed only by South Africa (engineers to MONUSCO in the Democratic Republic of the Congo), Ethiopia (logistics and transport assets in Darfur and engineer, medical and rotary-wing aviation assets in Abyei), and Nigeria (medics to Côte d'Ivoire). African forces have plenty of manpower, but often inadequate capabilities.

Defence and security reforms and force-development plans are primarily driven by domestic requirements. Scarce resources may be earmarked for territorial defence or static garrison deployments, and there can be bureaucratic inertia, as well as in-built military resistance to change. Meanwhile, some states that aspire to deploy forces abroad themselves suffer from domestic conflict and insurgency. This can lead them to develop capabilities, such as expertise in counter-insurgency, that could be useful on foreign operations. But it can also generate pressure to use armed forces internally or at least act in support of police forces, as has been seen in Nigeria, where the army was used to address the threat from the Boko Haram terrorist group.

Deployments such as these could be seen as potentially diluting the training and procurement requirements of armed forces, and taking them away from their core missions. But that is to assume that missions such as territorial defence are indeed the core tasks of a nation's armed forces. In recent unrest in Côte d'Ivoire, Guinea Bissau and Mali, militaries again played a role traditional for some African armed forces: that of actors in domestic politics, forces designed to bolster ruling elites or to preserve financial or other benefits. In these circumstances, or where the accountability of armed forces to government may be uncertain or relatively recent in origin, or where there are close ties between governments and armed forces, governments can channel scarce defence resources to units designed to support ruling regimes, such as presidential guards.

Such interests can affect the scope or implementation of defence reforms. For instance, according to a 2012 report by a group of 13 NGOs entitled *The Democratic Republic of Congo: Taking a Stand on Security Sector Reform*, the failure of reforms 'demonstrates the government has not wanted a professional and effective military, as it would constitute a threat to the entrenched political and financial interests of the Congolese elite'. While an armed forces law in 2011 gave 'legal foundation' to a blueprint for the Congolese military, the report said, 'the Presidential Guard and intelligence services have been systematically excluded from reform, and remain completely unaccountable'. It added that an ad hoc restructuring of military units in the eastern DRC in 2011 was 'intended to disrupt parallel chains of command'.

It is clear, therefore, that wide differences remain between African militaries in terms of their roles within their own societies. In many cases there is

---

ASF Regional Forces as of 30 June 2012:

North Africa Regional Capability (NARC – HQ: Tripoli, Libya): Algeria, Egypt, Libya, Tunisia, Western Sahara

East Africa Standby Force (EASF – HQ: Addis Ababa, Ethiopia): Burundi, Comoros, Djibouti, Ethiopia, Kenya, Rwanda, Seychelles, Somalia, Sudan, Uganda

Central African Multinational Force (Force Multinationale de l'Afrique Centrale (FOMAC – HQ: Libreville, Gabon)): Angola, Burundi, Cameroon, Central African Republic, Chad, Democratic Republic of the Congo, Equatorial Guinea, Gabon, São Tomé and Principe

Southern Africa Standby Force (SSF – HQ: Gaborone, Botswana): Angola, Botswana, Democratic Republic of the Congo, Lesotho, Madagascar, Malawi, Mozambique, Mauritius, Namibia, Seychelles, South Africa, Swaziland, Tanzania, Zambia, Zimbabwe

ECOWAS Standby Force (ESF – HQ: Abuja, Nigeria): Benin, Burkina Faso, Cape Verde, Côte d'Ivoire, Gambia, Ghana, Guinea, Guinea Bissau, Liberia, Mali, Niger, Nigeria, Senegal, Sierra Leone, Togo

little connection between defence ambitions and reform initiatives. Differing national-security priorities affect development of the capabilities required to act not only nationally, but also regionally and elsewhere. This means that, even if states want to deploy troops to support African initiatives, their armed forces might not be appropriately configured. For example, Ethiopia, a regular contributor to UN missions, does not have dedicated forces designed for overseas deployments, instead meeting the requirement from excess capacity. The same is true of other African troop-contributing countries, which very often deploy standard infantry or formed police units, rather than standing rapid-deployment contingents that have benefited from bespoke training and equipment. This is important, given that African regional economic communities – the building blocks of capability for AU initiatives – have as an objective the development of rapid-deployment forces before 2015.

Even some of the continent's larger armed forces have tended to retain local preoccupations and have deployed relatively few troops abroad. When armed forces do deploy on missions at distance, they generally do so with international assistance due to gaps in funding, transport, logistics support and planning. But this is not unique to deployments at distance: for example, Kenyan forces received foreign logistics support during their recent unilateral deployment into Somalia, and the re-badging of the operation under AMISOM then enabled access to UN and AU capacities and funding.

Gaps in equipment capability remain a major problem. Acquisition of basic capacities to deploy and sustain forces abroad, such as potable water supplies and secure communications sets, remains haphazard. This also means that troops often travel with equipment that is specific to them, which can hinder interoperability and access to common combat service support assets.

Airlift also remains a problem; this is not surprising given the cost of aircraft and maintenance. Limited regional airlift capacity is being improved by modest acquisitions such as Ghana and Cameroon's recent purchases of C-295 aircraft, as well as refit programmes such as the US-supported modernisation of Nigerian C-130 *Hercules* airlifters. But, in general, the lift capacity that does exist in national holdings is capable only of modest tactical troop movements. Moving larger numbers of personnel and equipment remains problematic and reliant on international assistance or contracted support.

South Africa is an exception, with capable platforms and highly trained staff. Though its focus has in recent years been on border surveillance and protection, the country's defence forces have recently been deployed on counter-piracy activities in the Mozambique Channel. A 2012 Defence Review consultation document explicitly noted that Pretoria 'envisages that, as a major power in Africa, it will play a leadership role in conflict prevention, peace support operations, peace-building, and reconstruction'. In terms of equipment holdings and ambitions, it is the only African state possessing what (on paper) come close to the capabilities of major Western armed forces. However, there are important caveats, principally concerning funding, platform availability and force readiness. The South African military, the document noted, was 'too poorly equipped and funded to execute the widening spectrum of tasks to the desired level'.

From a Western perspective, it might seem logical for states to collaborate on acquiring key capacities either too technically sophisticated or expensive for a single state to buy. But across Africa, collaboration on procurement remains elusive. There is no initiative at the multilateral, regional or continental level similar to the capability plans produced by the European Union or NATO. Where collaboration does take place, it is often dictated by circumstance, such as the development and employment in AMISOM of capacities to counter improvised explosive devices.

Closer alignment of security and defence policies could lead to better coordination on the structures, equipment and forces needed to deploy troops effectively or, as a start, agreement on what capabilities are required. It could also lead to enhanced transparency and confidence between states. But significant collaboration remains elusive.

AFRICOM, Europe and the UN

Foreign military support to African national and multinational defence bodies is nothing new. The EU and UN have long provided security assistance to African states and institutions, while many governments and armed forces have provided financial, technical and material assistance to African armed and security forces.

In recent years, international support to African defence institutions has tended to be viewed through the prism of counter-terrorism and counter-piracy imperatives. These concerns have driven the kinetic military engagements seen in recent years, including French hostage rescue missions in 2008 and the January 2012 rescue of two aid workers by US forces. They have also driven the increased use of US unmanned aerial systems, which are flown from the Seychelles, Ethiopia and reportedly Djibouti. These provide persistent surveillance in the Horn of Africa region, as well as targeted strike capacities in and off Somalia.

Washington maintains the broadest range of military and security assistance projects and programmes in Africa. The growth in its activities over the past ten years reflects Africa's rising strategic importance to the United States, notably Washington's desire since the 9/11 attacks to strengthen countries' ability to combat terrorism and transnational crime. According to the head of US Africa Command (AFRICOM), General Carter Ham, the main US preoccupation in Africa is the presence of violent extremist organisations 'that have very clearly articulated an intent to attack the United States, its allies, its citizens and its interests both within Africa and also more broadly, in Europe'.

AFRICOM was established in 2007 to help African countries build security capacity. The command still lacks an African home and is headquartered in Stuttgart, Germany, though it has forward-deployed forces at Camp Lemonnier, Djibouti, base for the US military's Combined Joint Task Force-Horn of Africa. US forces are actively engaged across Africa, both in counter-terrorism activities and also in support of AFRICOM's wider agenda, which emphasises conflict prevention, capacity building and African ownership.

One of AFRICOM's principal instruments is the US Navy's Africa Partnership Station (APS), which began in 2007 in West Africa and the Gulf of Guinea and now also covers East Africa and the western Indian Ocean. APS aims to build partner nations' maritime security capacities. Other US programmes include the Africa Contingency Operations Training and Assistance initiative, which offers training and equipment intended to help countries take part in multinational peace-support operations. The United States also funds international personnel to take part in US military training programmes. In addition, the Trans-Sahara Counter Terrorism Partnership is designed to enhance the capacities of Burkina Faso, Chad, Mali, Mauritania, Niger, Nigeria and Senegal to confront terrorist groups.

Among recent developments, the United States sent around 100 special-forces troops to help counter the Lord's Resistance Army, a militia led by Joseph Kony and implicated in conflict and human-rights abuses in the Central African Republic (CAR), the DRC, South Sudan and Uganda. This was significant not only because it led to more direct US military involvement in Africa but also because it indicated willingness to send troops for reasons not centrally connected to core US interests. Domestic lobbying in the United States might have been a motivating factor.

Other nations retain forces in Africa. France has a contingent in Côte d'Ivoire, which intervened during the civil war in 2004. It did so again in

2011, along with UN forces, at a critical stage in fighting between troops loyal to the incumbent President Laurent Gbagbo, who had been defeated in elections, and the successful candidate Alassane Ouattara. France maintains forces and equipment stocks in the CAR, Chad, Djibouti, Gabon and Senegal, and posts staff to training and planning roles in armed forces across Africa. It has a standing maritime patrol, *Operation Corymbe*, in the Gulf of Guinea. The United Kingdom has military missions with advisory roles in Kenya and Sierra Leone. British forces also train in Kenya. Meanwhile, French, British and other European armed forces, as well as the EU and UN, post experts to African institutions, including to the AU headquarters in Addis Ababa.

The UN, for decades a significant actor in African peace and security, remains active in mediation, peacekeeping and peace support. It first dispatched personnel in 1960 to the Congo (not counting the 1956 Emergency Force mission after the Suez crisis). Peacekeeping missions in Africa constitute the majority of UN operations and deployed personnel. The UN has become used to providing airlift and logistics support to the African forces (mainly infantry) taking part in UN peacekeeping missions on the continent. Importantly, the UN also provides funding to countries that contribute troops to its operations.

The 2008 Prodi Report, a joint AU–UN review of African peacekeeping operations, examined future UN support to AU capacity development. It noted that the AU was coping with the 'double challenge of building its institutions and responding to crises' but said problems in AU institutional capacity remained a significant constraint. It recommended improvements in training and logistics. In 2012, UN Secretary-General Ban Ki-moon said the UN had since strengthened its partnership with the AU. Institutional ties had developed following the 2008 deployment of the hybrid UN–AU mission to Darfur (UNAMID); this had previously been solely an AU operation. An AU–UN Joint Task Force on Peace and Security had been set up in 2010 for discussion of crises and longer-term strategic issues, and the two bodies were conducting joint assessment missions. The benefits of this closer association were being seen in the UN's role in the AMISOM mission to Somalia, to which its support office was providing planning and logistics support.

Deepening European involvement

In 2007, the EU entered into a strategic partnership with the AU, recognising the potential value of the AU's peace and security initiatives, as well as the importance to Europe of assisting security and stability on the continent. The EU has taken an active role. Its first stand-alone military mission was *Operation Artemis* in 2003, to improve security in the Bunia region of the eastern DRC. Since then four military missions and three civilian missions have been completed (civil/military support to AMIS II in Darfur is counted in both categories). Two military and two civilian missions were in progress at mid-2012, with a new civilian mission (with a military element) EUCAP *Nestor* due to be launched in summer 2012.

EUCAP *Nestor* was intended to build the capacity of regional states' maritime forces, including coastguard elements in Djibouti, Kenya, the Seychelles and Tanzania, as well as maritime police forces in Puntland, Somaliland and the Somali region of Galmudug. This mission complements other EU security- and capacity-building activities in the area prompted by the threat from piracy off the Horn of Africa. EUNAVFOR *Atalanta*, a naval mission launched in 2008, is intended to deter and prevent piracy off the coast of Somalia by protecting ships transiting the area, as well as vessels delivering supplies to Somalia for the World Food Programme. EUNAVFOR is assisting AMISOM to develop counter-piracy capacities such as detachments of personnel to protect ships delivering logistics support to AMISOM. On land, the EU Military Training Mission for Somalia is mainly based at Uganda's Bihanga training facility, helping to develop the command and control capabilities of Somali forces, as well as combat and training skills; the syllabus also covers international humanitarian law and the law of armed conflict.

Capacity building has always been a central objective of EU military involvement in Africa. The EU's African Peace Facility (APF) had channelled some €740 million in assistance by November 2010, and its scope had been broadened to cover conflict prevention and post-conflict stabilisation. The EU now organises an APSA Support Programme including support to the regional economic communities and regional mechanisms and, from 2012, a training centres support programme, backed by about €100 million from the APF.

Brussels has also supported development of ASFs intended for deployment to African hot spots. To assist in the generation of these, as well as helping the AU test the ASF concept, the EU developed a capacity-building programme, EURORECAMP, with a training and exercise cycle called *Amani Africa*. The EU activity is led by elements of the European External Action Service that support EU civil and military operations and planning.

Developing standby forces

The standby forces are the instrument with which the AU aims eventually to meet the demands of African security problems. They are the operational arm of the planned security architecture. Generated by the continent's regional economic communities and regional mechanisms, the five forces are each to be made up of around 6,500 military, police and civilian personnel.

The forces are intended to be flexible, mobile and capable of rapid deployment. This will be essential if they are to be able to carry out the six contingency-planning scenarios assigned to them:

- AU/regional military advice to a political mission, deployment within 30 days of mandate;
- AU/regional observer mission co-deployed with UN mission, within 30 days of mandate;
- standalone AU/regional observer mission, within 30 days of mandate;
- AU/regional peacekeeping force for preventive deployment missions and those mandated under Chapter VI of the UN Charter, within 30 days of mandate;
- AU peacekeeping force for complex multidimensional peacekeeping mission, within 30 days of mandate for military (90 days for other elements); and
- AU intervention within 14 days of mandate, for instance in genocide situations.

Implementation has been guided by a set of roadmaps. The first, from 2005 to 2008, was geared towards the establishment of infrastructures, including regional brigade headquarters, as well as development of doctrine, common operating procedures, and training and evaluation mechanisms. The second, from 2008 to 2010, established political and legal mandates; logistics, medical support, police and force protection and rapid-deployment concepts; and planning capacities. A multinational Command Post Exercise (CPX) – the culmination of the *Amani Africa* I cycle – was held in October 2010 to validate progress towards Roadmap II. A third roadmap began in 2011 and is scheduled to end in 2015; it introduces additional and broader threats to African security, such as the maritime dimension, into the ASF purview.

The original plan was for the ASF to be operationally capable by 2010. Documents now state 2010 as the target for initial operating capability, which some of the regional forces have already declared. Full operational capability for the whole force is now planned for 2015, while a continent-wide rapid-deployment capacity is due to be tested by December 2014.

The building blocks of the ASF, the various regional forces, carried out Field Training Exercises (FTX) during 2009 and 2010.

The Southern Africa Standby Force (SASF) FTX, *Exercise Golfinho*, held in South Africa in September 2009, involved 7,000 troops from 12 countries. Seeking to prove its operational competence, the Southern African Development Community decided not to draw on external support. Though some participants reported problems with logistics, organisation and communications, the SASF declared afterwards that it could deploy to any location in Africa, though this would depend on available strategic lift and logistics support. SASF is headquartered in Gaborone, Botswana.

ECOWAS initially aimed to establish a 6,500-strong task force by 2010, though just over 2,700 were confirmed as available in 2009. It is structured into two infantry battalions (western, led by Senegal, and eastern, led by Nigeria) and a composite logistics battalion. A headquarters was established in Abuja, Nigeria and training is carried out at centres in Ghana, Mali and Nigeria. An ECOWAS logistics depot was established in Freetown, Sierra Leone, with US support, while a second depot in Mali is to be oriented towards humanitarian crisis response. The ECOWAS Stand-by Force, supported by AFRICOM, executed *Exercise Cohesion Benin* in April 2010, with the objective of evaluating the eastern battalion's readiness. The western and logistics battalions were validated in 2007 and 2009 respectively.

The Economic Community of Central African States (ECCAS) conducted the *Kwanza 2010* exercise from May to June 2010 in Cabo Ledo, Angola. Themes included population security and medical provision, and deployed capacities included field hospitals and amphibious and airborne forces. ECCAS established a planning element, but decided not to set up a permanent force headquarters; it has yet to develop a rapid-deployment capability. However, the AU's decision to establish a Continental Logistics Base at Douala, Cameroon, close to the regional force's own base, may give impetus to the project.

The North African Regional Capability (NARC) was set up as a regional mechanism to enable North African countries to contribute to the ASF, with the executive secretariat to be located in Tripoli, Libya. A brigade headquarters was to be established in Cairo, and logistics depots in Algiers and Cairo. Though the upheavals in Arab countries have called into question the contribution of some northern states to future NARC activities, the AU completed an assessment of its capacity in 2012: headquarters staff in Libya occupy new buildings; EU funding support has been agreed, and training is scheduled to restart.

The Eastern African Standby Force (EASF) conducted its FTX, *Amani Carana*, in Djibouti in November 2009. Police and civilian specialists also participated, and the exercise relied on support from partner countries. A CPX was held in Khartoum in November 2011. The EASF was at first hampered by inadequate funding and regional tensions which limited contributions; logistics and planning were also problematic. However, it is now more active, with troops deployed to AMISOM in Somalia, though logistics, movement, sustainment and communications remain problematic.

An effective test?

Among the objectives of the first *Amani Africa* exercise cycle was to test the AU's ability to provide the core of a headquarters or operations centre that could be deployed to run a peace-support operation. In the event, however, the exercises only partially assessed the AU's capacity to organise such an operation, since most of the relevant posts were occupied by staff from outside the AU's Peace Support Operations Department. Furthermore, many personnel were unfamiliar with ASF guidance documentation, as well as UN best practice, and instead employed national procedures and standards.

Another objective, according to Jean Ping, the AU chair, was to 'practise the establishment of a mission headquarters for an ASF deployment, including the production of an integrated mission plan'. Analysts reported that linguistic differences caused problems in setting up a headquarters, even though English was to be used as a common language. Communication problems arose, partly because equipment was either unavailable or unfamiliar. Other issues included a lack of common operating procedures, so that national standards were often applied.

Low numbers of African ambassadors attended exercises, indicating that more could be done to encourage 'ownership' of the ASF concept. Added to this, there was a degree of uncertainty over the level of political agreement needed for deployment of standby force elements. Documentation issued afterwards asserted that unless there was political agreement on the use of assets comprising the ASF, the AU would be unable to carry out meaningful planning.

Amani Africa has led to developments in AU doctrine, policies and procedures. It was realised that a larger pool of dedicated AU staff was needed, that training in mission planning should be increased, and training for peace-support operations should be conducted in accordance with AU/UN standards. Among the main benefits of the ASF development process should be the emergence of common policy documentation and improved training standards. Progress on these remains limited. In addition, the CPX was dominated by military staff, though the goal had been a multidimensional deployment containing police and civilian elements. Indeed, problems persist in producing an active civilian component, due to a lack of understanding about potential functions and composition.

The lessons identified in the *Amani Africa* I cycle have been incorporated into the new APSA and ASF roadmaps and a second *Amani Africa* cycle is intended to help the AUC to learn relevant lessons. An ambitious planning, exercise and training schedule has been set by the AU for 2012 and beyond as part of the third roadmap, and *Amani Africa* II, a combined strategic-level CPX and an operational, tactical-level FTX, is due to take place in November 2014 prior to the ASF's planned full operational capability in 2015.

Ways forward

The increasing complexity of the standby-force concept may reflect the continent's security demands, but may delay its effective delivery. The AU has set the parameters within which the force will operate but does not have the authority over regional communities and mechanisms to impose a uniform process and structure. This has permitted regional actors to follow different paths in developing their standby forces. However, a pragmatic way for the AU to push forward its agenda may be to utilise the willingness of regional organisations to deploy troops. ECOWAS's initiatives in West Africa following the coups and unrest in Guinea Bissau and Mali are one example. Another is the deployment of EASF troops to Somalia, seen by the AU as the first operational deployment of a regional standby force.

More fundamentally, the original vision was that regional military forces could be deployed independently. But the addition of civilian and police components to form integrated missions reflects changing policy approaches, as well as debates over the nature of peacekeeping. It also means that AU and ASF planners face a challenge in broadening participation from ASF states beyond traditional contributors of military manpower.

Real-world lessons can be a guide for future capabilities. In rapidly evolving crises, the formal structures thus far envisaged might not always allow sufficient flexibility. Reactive ad hoc responses may be needed instead. One example is the AU-led Regional Cooperation Initiative against the Lord's Resistance Army, launched in March 2012 and due to field a 5,000-strong set of task forces drawn from CAR, the DRC, South Sudan and Uganda, with international support. This ad hoc development is important in that it consists of countries from different regional communities. Another example was the re-badging of Kenyan forces in Somalia under AMISOM, boosting their military capacity. The *Amani Africa* II cycle, including improved AU structures and staffing, and an effective and fully manned peace support operations department, should mark a further step forward. However, many African armed forces still lack the military assets that would allow them to dispatch and sustain forces abroad. In countries where there is capacity, maintaining it at the required readiness level is a material and financial challenge. Few states are yet willing to gear their defence planning, budgeting and training towards generating forces useful in sustained foreign missions. Gaps in capabilities tend to be filled by the UN or foreign countries. The need for external partners to support African defence ambitions, capabilities and missions is unlikely to diminish any time soon.

Economic Sanctions on Iran: A Case Study

A marked tightening of pressure on Iran began on 31 December 2011, when US President Barack Obama signed into law sanctions legislation passed by an overwhelming congressional majority. The European Union followed suit less than a month later with an agreement on new sanctions. These economic instruments are targeting a new area: Iran's hard-currency revenue from oil exports. This is being done in three ways. Firstly, an oil embargo by the European Union came into full effect on 1 July 2012. Secondly, sanctions are targeting Iran's financial system, particularly the central bank and its ability to receive payments for oil sales, as well as other exports. Thirdly, sanctions are challenging Iran's ability to transport exports (particularly crude oil and petrochemicals) to their destination markets by targeting not just oil companies but also European-based insurers of oil tankers. All these measures are aimed at diminishing Iranian access to its oil revenue in hard currency.

These developments stand in sharp contrast to the sanctions regime prior to 2012, which was generally targeted at Iran's nuclear and missile programmes and related activities rather than entire sectors of the economy. It seems likely that the cumulative effects of the new sets of sanctions, combined with poor domestic economic management, could undermine Iranians' confidence in the country's economic prospects and could contribute to economic dislocations in the country. It cannot yet be known whether these effects will compel Tehran to accept limits on its nuclear programme, as demanded by the United Nations Security Council and Iran's negotiating partners. However, at mid-2012 there was little doubt that the new measures were achieving their objective of putting substantive pressure on the Iranian economy. This helped to bring Iran to the negotiating table for a series of talks with major powers beginning in April.

If the new sanctions measures are successful in altering Iran's stance over its nuclear programme, they will be an interesting case study in the long-standing debate over the effectiveness of economic sanctions in achieving diplomatic objectives (see Brendan Taylor's *Sanctions As Grand Strategy* (IISS Adelphi 411) for an overview of the debate). In many cases, economic sanctions have not resulted in behavioural change on the part of targeted states. For example, long-running sanctions on Iraq, Cuba and North Korea all failed to induce desired shifts in their policies. Indeed, many have argued that economic sanctions have actually been counterproductive, serving to entrench hardline positions and to rally popular support for errant regimes. Sanctions on Iran since the revolution in 1979 had, until recently, been similarly ineffective, apart from impeding Tehran's acquisition of foreign parts for its missile and nuclear programmes. (Some recent polls, however, suggest the Iranian public is beginning to turn against the nuclear programme.) The latest measures are a renewed attempt on the part of the international community to change the cost–benefit calculus of the Iranian government and its clerical establishment. Two elements stand out over previous sanctions attempts: widespread international participation in sanctions measures, whether willingly or under US pressure, and the comprehensive targeting of key economic sectors such as oil and gas, banking and shipping. These elements raise the prospect that the new, ramped-up sanctions regime on Iran may yet prove to be a success. If so, this could change the nature of the debate over economic sanctions and their utility as instruments of geo-economic power.

Previous sanctions

Previous efforts to sanction Iran focused mainly on limiting the modernisation and technological development of its oil, gas and petrochemicals sector as well as the nuclear and missile programmes. Until 1995, these achieved little success because they contained significant loopholes. For example, while the 1987 US import ban on Iranian products prohibited US energy companies from importing Iranian crude oil into the US, it did not bar foreign subsidiaries of US firms from transacting with Iran – thereby permitting them to continue lifting Iranian oil and circumvent sanctions by establishing foreign subsidiaries and directing Iranian crude to non-US markets. As a result, by 1994, US firms had become the largest purchasers of Iranian crude in order to re-sell outside the US.

These loopholes were closed after 1995 by two presidential executive orders. Despite this, sanctions continued to founder, largely because they were imposed unilaterally (almost exclusively by the United States) and lacked international (especially European) support. In a post-Cold War world characterised by countries diversifying economic linkages and inte-grating themselves into the global economy, attempts at unilateral economic coercion through sanctions were less likely to be successful. The severance of links by one country created business opportunities for others. For example, when US energy companies were banned from energy investment in Iran by the March 1995 Executive Order 12957, they were quickly replaced by Japanese and other Asian companies. In 2009, after Total of France delayed investments in Iran's South Pars gas field on account of Iran's fractious rela-tions with Western states, it was replaced by China National Petroleum Corporation.

Before the Security Council adopted a series of sanctions resolutions begin-ning in 2007, there was little international support for sanctions on Iran. This was clearly seen in the diplomatic furore that greeted the US Iran Sanctions Act 1996, which sought to sanction foreign firms investing in Iran's energy sector. European governments in particular were vehemently opposed to this extraterritorial exercise of US jurisdiction over their companies. In effect, foreign energy companies were being forced to choose between participa-tion in the US market and continued involvement in Iran's energy sector. After European threats to raise the issue at the World Trade Organisation as an extraterritorial application of US national law and a transgression of international trade agreements, the Clinton administration sought to placate its allies by opting to waive sanctions on Total, which had energy invest-ments in Iran. Eventually, sanctions were only partially implemented as the United States adopted a practice of granting waivers to foreign companies despite their violation of the 1996 act's provisions. Thus, no determinations of violations were made between May 1998 and September 2010.

More effective US economic pressure on Iran was built incrementally between 2006 and 2010. During this period, the US Treasury persuaded 80 foreign banks to voluntarily discontinue their transactions with Iranian banks, and on 6 November 2008 the Treasury extended its restriction on so-called 'U-Turn' transactions – which prevented US banks from dealing with foreign banks handling transactions on behalf of Iranian banks – from solely applying to Bank Saderat (which was alleged to have handled transactions involving Hizbullah). The restriction now applied to all Iranian banks, except Bank Markazi, the central bank. However, these unilateral US measures still failed to achieve meaningful diplomatic pressure on Iran, which broke off negotiations over its nuclear activities in January 2010.

In response, on 9 June 2010, the UN Security Council adopted Resolution 1929, which imposed sanctions on activities that may assist Iran in its acquisition of uranium and of technology related to nuclear missiles, and in the development of its nuclear programme. Still, these UN measures were narrowly focused, and did not target the Iranian economy. The United States and European Union have now done precisely that.

EU oil embargo

On 23 January 2012, the European Union adopted measures imposing sanctions on European oil companies that import Iranian oil. Between January and June 2011, the EU imported over 450,000 barrels per day from Iran, approximately 5% of EU oil supplies and about 18% of Iranian exports.

France, the United Kingdom and Germany, which had been buying relatively little Iranian oil, envisaged the rapid imposition of a full oil embargo. But southern European states such as Greece and Italy, which respectively imported 30% and 13% of their annual crude requirement from Iran, argued for a longer phasing-in period to enable them to secure alternative supplies. Eventually, a five-month transition period was agreed, with the full embargo due to come into effect on 1 July 2012. An exemption was agreed for shipments being used to repay Iranian debts, a provision particularly important for Italy's ENI, which was owed $2bn by the Iranian government and was being repaid in crude.

Even though Greece's oil demand has fallen by around 20% since the onset of the financial crisis in 2008, it has been particularly hard hit by the EU embargo, especially in light of its poor credit rating. In some months of 2011, Iran supplied more than 50% of Greek oil imports, under generous 'open-credit' terms – a risky system whereby payments for shipments are deferred for 60–180 days, but where neither party has the security of a bank's letter of credit in the event of non-payment. Supplies from Iran ceased as of March 2012, when EU banks voluntarily declined to facilitate payments due to looming US financial sanctions (see below). Greece then had to resort to extraordinary measures to keep oil imports flowing. With most financial institutions refusing to extend it large amounts of credit without bank guarantees, Glencore and Vitol, the world's top two oil-trading houses, stepped in to act as suppliers of last resort, sourcing oil from Russia, Kazakhstan and Libya and extending open credit finance of around €300m to Hellenic, Greece's main refiner.

These difficulties notwithstanding, by April 2012, EU imports of Iranian crude has fallen from over 450,000 barrels per day in 2011 to around 350,000, and will drop to zero once the debt to Italy is paid off.

However, an embargo on European imports alone is not sufficient to pressure Iran. The Asia-Pacific region – particularly China, India, Japan and South Korea – has accounted for approximately 60% of Iranian oil exports. According to the US Energy Information Administration, between January and June 2011, of the 2.48m barrels per day exported by Iran, China accounted for 22% (543,000 b/d), Japan for 14% (341,000 b/d), India for 13% (328,000 b/d) and South Korea for 10% (244,000 b/d). It is these exports that US banking sanctions and EU insurance and reinsurance sanctions are targeting.

Banking sanctions
US sanctions on banks' non-petroleum-related transactions with the Iranian central bank came into effect on 29 February 2012, while similar sanctions for oil-related transactions commenced at the end of June. Rather than directly targeting companies or countries that import Iranian oil, these measures seek to sever access to the US financial system for foreign banks which handle payments for such transactions. This effectively forces banks to choose between doing business with the United States or with Iran, though Washington is granting waivers to countries that have shown a commitment to 'significantly reduce' their imports of Iranian oil.

As previous US measures under both the Bush and Obama administrations had already sanctioned more than 20 Iranian commercial banks because of their direct or indirect association with banned nuclear or missile programmes, the Iranian central bank had been clearing payments for most of the country's oil exports and was acting as a proxy for sanctioned Iranian banks, facilitating their transactions by obscuring their names from international payment messages. This made it more problematic for intermediary financial institutions to ascertain the true parties to a transaction and enabled circumvention of sanctions.

European banking sanctions implemented on 24 February 2012 by European Council Regulation No. 267/2012 and augmented on 16 March 2012 by European Council Decision 2012/152/CFSP, added to the pressure. In March 2012 SWIFT, the Society for Worldwide Interbank Financial Telecommunication, a Belgian firm that provides the secure private network used by almost all the world's banks to send payment messages to each other, expelled Iran's central bank and over 20 Iranian commercial banks from its services. This made it difficult for Iran to complete cross-border fund transfers through the international financial system. Such transfers are important to facilitate virtually all of Iran's international trade.

However, while barring Iranian access to the SWIFT system raises transaction costs for Iranian businesses, there are several ways to get around the measure even for the large transactions that characterise the oil trade (a supertanker full of crude can be worth more than $200m). For example, if counterparties to a trade have accounts in the same bank, then transfers between them would not need to utilise SWIFT. Other circumvention mechanisms involve setting up front companies, shipping gold bullion or carrying suitcases of money between trading partners. Iran has also established its own SWIFT equivalent.

In addition, Switzerland, an important hub for oil trading and a base for Iran's state trading firm Naftiran Intertrade, has exempted Iran's central bank from its asset freeze, although the degree to which Iran's oil exports are traded or financed through Switzerland is unclear. Additionally, while Swiss-based commodity traders such as Glencore stated that they had voluntarily ceased all oil trade with Iran, the use of shell companies and affiliates to disguise such lucrative trades would still be possible.

Iran and its trading partners adopted a variety of alternative methods to deal with the banking sanctions. Iran started accepting payment for its crude in Indian rupees, Chinese renminbi, Japanese yen and Korean won. China's two main purchasers of Iranian oil, Sinopec and Zhuhai Zhenrong, initially switched from settling payments in euros to using renminbi accounts in Beijing. However, as domestic Chinese banks ceased dealing with Iran due to US sanctions, they began routing the renminbi transfers through smaller Russian banks which do not have US operations. Tehran was using the proceeds to purchase Chinese goods and services.

India also explored the possibility of routing payments through alternative financial conduits, such as Russia's Gazprombank. It set up an account at the Indian state-owned UCO Bank, which does not have US operations, in the name of Iran's Bank Parsian, a privately owned Iranian bank free from sanctions against Iran's state-owned banks, to facilitate rupee payments to Iran. This covered up to 45% of the oil purchased by Indian oil refiners such as Mangalore Refinery and Petrochemicals, India's largest consumer of

Iranian crude, Essar Oil and Hindustan Petroleum. The total value of such purchases could be about $4bn per year. While such a move may be convenient for India, which previously settled trades in euros and dollars, Iran requested that part of Indian payments be made in Japanese yen, which had been appreciating even as the rupee's value had been falling.

In February 2012, Mahmoud Bahmani, governor of Iran's central bank, stated the country was willing to accept payment for oil in gold. Iran was also encouraging barter mechanisms. It offered to provide crude in return for wheat (an offer made to both Russia and Pakistan), soybean meal, grain (an offer made to India) and consumer products. It also asked China and India to pay for oil imports in kind, for example where companies from both countries undertake Iranian infrastructure projects in such areas as railways and power, which are not subject to sanctions. In March 2012, a delegation of Indian engineering companies visited Tehran and Tabriz to meet Iranian officials and business leaders and explore export opportunities in the service sector. If barter arrangements become a common payment mechanism for trade, this would still achieve the desired effect of international sanctions to starve Tehran of hard currency that it could use to purchase material for its nuclear programme.

Even though Tehran had not been completely shut off from international markets, by April 2012 banking sanctions had made it appreciably more difficult for it to receive payments for oil exports and were affecting the country's international trade. Most large banks around the world had US operations and were unwilling to risk these to maintain links with Iran.

However, the US was granting waivers to banks in countries that had shown a commitment to reducing Iranian oil imports. As of 12 June 2012, exemptions had been granted to Belgium, Czech Republic, France, Germany, Greece, Italy, Netherlands, Poland, Spain and the United Kingdom, and outside the EU to India, Japan, Malaysia, South Africa, South Korea, Sri Lanka, Turkey and Taiwan. On 29 June 2012, further exemptions were granted to China and Singapore. With all of Iran's major purchasers thus exempted, no penalties were imposed. Yet all had to reduce Iranian oil imports by 10–20%, and further cuts would be required when the first exemptions ran out in 180 days. So as not to spike prices, the strategy was not to cut off all Iranian oil exports at once but to do so gradually.

Even if covered by exemptions, many banks were no longer prepared to take the reputational risk of facilitating Iranian payments and were cutting links with Iran despite not being legally required to do so. Asian purchasers in particular struggled to pay for Iranian crude. For example, India's purchases encountered difficulties after the Reserve Bank of India dismantled a hard-currency payment mechanism utilising the Asian Clearing Union and German bank European–Iranian Trade Bank in response to UN sanctions adopted in June 2010. As a result of US and EU pressure, another transaction route, through Istanbul-based Turkiye Halk Bankasi (Halkbank), came under strain.

Payments for Iranian oil encountered problems. In February 2012, it emerged that the equivalent of $5bn-$6bn of South Korean payments to Iran were languishing in South Korean banks due to difficulties in repatriating funds to Tehran. Fearing that Iran would encounter payment difficulties as it was starved of hard currency, South Korea was considering imposing export quotas on Korean companies' sales to Iran, which consist mainly of steel, cars and electronics – Samsung Electronics and LG Electronics account for around 30% of Iran's mobile-phone market. In 2011, Iran ceased exporting crude to Pakistan after a state-owned refinery company failed to obtain financing for its purchases, as Pakistani banks refused to open letters of credit for Iran's National Iranian Oil Company. In May 2012, as a result of a court case unrelated to sanctions, the Bank of Tokyo-Mitsubishi UFJ, which accounted for almost all Iranian transactions handled by Japanese banks, and which facilitated most of Japan's payments for Iranian oil imports, froze dealings with Iranian banks after it was ordered to do so by the New York District Court.

Iran's trade was significantly affected in other ways. For example, Dubai experienced a decline in trade with Iran. It has been a major hub for transhipment of Iranian exports and imports, as traders sought to avoid international censure by routing goods through the Gulf port. But the sharp depreciation of the Iranian rial in 2012 drastically reduced Iranian demand for imported consumer goods. Although Dubai's direct re-exports to Iran grew by nearly 30% to 31 billion dirhams ($8.4bn) in 2011, figures indicated a slowdown in the last quarter of the year. In addition, Dubai appeared to have become a much less important conduit for the financing of Iranian oil sales since partly state-owned Noor Islamic Bank, which facilitated payments for as much as 60% of the roughly $70bn in annual Iranian oil sales, voluntarily ended business relations with Iranian banks at the end of 2011. This was a result of the US decision in November 2011, under the terms of the PATRIOT Act, to designate Iran as a territory of 'primary money laundering concern'.

EU shipping and insurance sanctions
The final and potentially most devastating element of the recent measures was aimed by the EU at European-based insurers and re-insurers of

oil tankers. From 1 July 2012, the regulations required the London-based International Group of Protection & Indemnity (P&I) Clubs, which reinsured around 95% of tankers around the world including those operated by Iran's Petrochemical Transportation Company, to cease issuing protection and indemnity for tankers carrying Iranian crude. P&I Clubs are collectively owned by ship-owners and provide insurance and reinsurance cover to companies and their insurers for third-party risks such as personal injury and pollution.

The measure was designed to prevent oil tankers from shipping oil from Iranian ports, since national P&I clubs in China, India, Japan, South Korea and elsewhere do not have the capacity to cover the risks of an oil tanker running aground or sinking – supertankers could require coverage of as much as $1bn, a risk few financial institutions can underwrite. The Japan Ship Owners' Mutual Protection & Indemnity Association and the China Shipowners Mutual Assurance Association, the largest ship insurers in their respective countries, both obtain reinsurance through the International Group of P&I Clubs in London, and would now be unable to do so for Iranian oil shipments. The EU sanctions also prevented ships from using Iranian fuel, and voided the insurance cover of ships carrying Iranian crude as of 1 July 2012. In February 2012, ship owners with more than 100 supertankers (including large shipping groups such as the Overseas Shipholding Group Inc., Frontline companies, Tankers International and Nova Tankers A/S) said they would stop loading cargo from Iran following the EU regulatory changes.

A similar EU ban on tankers carrying Iranian petrochemical products commenced on 1 May 2012, and immediately illustrated its potential effectiveness. Iranian petrochemical exports, which include methanol, caustic soda and xylene, fell by nearly 90% that month as compared to a year earlier, although this may be an overestimate as many Iranian ships may have had their transponders switched off to conceal their movements. Even Iran's Petrochemical Transportation Company was unable to obtain insurance from Iran's largest ship insurer, Kish P&I Club. It was believed that only China was able to purchase Iranian petrochemicals in May, with firms such as Sinochem and Nanjing Tankers able to secure insurance coverage from Chinese providers – and also to make significant profits on the cargoes as a result of virtual monopoly status.

The problem was not as severe for crude shipments as it was for shipments of petrochemicals, as Iran's main tanker operator, National Iranian Tanker Company (NITC), which lost its European maritime insurance cover in 2011, was able to obtain insurance coverage from Kish P&I Club. But it did not have sufficient capacity to transport all of Iran's crude sales. Additionally, new measures being considered by the US Congress would extend US banking sanctions to cover NITC (as well as National Iranian Oil), further inhibiting Iran's capacity to get its oil to export markets.

The UK considered asking other EU members to postpone the insurance sanctions by up to six months, to avoid a supply shock causing a spike in oil prices, and also to limit the impact on London, the centre for maritime insurance. Asian refiners warned that unless they received an EU waiver they would be forced to make drastic cuts to their crude imports or even cease their purchases of Iranian crude altogether. Japan and South Korea asked the EU to allow them access to European insurance after the embargo came into effect. Japan's legislature passed a bill allowing for as much as $7.6bn in sovereign guarantees for oil tankers transporting Iranian crude. China and India were also considering sovereign guarantees for oil tankers. However, it was likely that the two countries would require Iran to insure and deliver – effectively forcing Tehran to accept a massive discount on its crude – or would ship the crude themselves with scaled-back insurance coverage. As tanker owners became less willing to dock in Iran due to sanctions, three of NITC's supertankers started delivering crude to India's west-coast refineries.

International compliance and the Iranian response
China has relied on Iran for 11% of its oil, and has been Iran's largest single purchaser, accounting for 22% of Iranian crude exports. In the first four months of 2012, China imported 31% less from Iran than it did in the corresponding period of 2011. Although this was mainly due to a pricing dispute that was resolved in March, it gave the United States a justification for extending an exemption and to encourage continued reductions. It was reported that while Zhuhai Zhenrong and Chinaoil would keep up their levels of purchases, Sinopec's trading arm Unipec was set to purchase between 10% and 20% less Iranian crude under its 2012 annual contract.

India, which has accounted for 13% of Iranian sales, privately instructed its refineries to diversify away from Iranian crude and to curtail its purchases from Iran by at least 10%. It cut its purchase from Iran by a third in April 2012 as compared with March and, at around 243,000 barrels per day, its Iranian crude liftings in May 2012 were 10% lower than in April 2012, and about 38% lower than May last year. Essar Oil aimed to lift 15% less oil from Iran in 2012, while Mangalore Refinery and Petrochemicals nearly halved its Iranian imports in the January–May 2012 period. Meanwhile, Bharat Petroleum purchased no Iranian oil from February 2012 up to mid-year. India increased supplies from Saudi Arabia, Iraq and Latin America.

Japan, Iran's second-largest export market and which relied on Iran for 8.8% of its imports in 2011, imported between 15% and 22% less in the first half of 2012, increasing its supplies from Saudi Arabia, Qatar and the UAE. In February 2012, Japan's biggest refiner JX Nippon Oil & Energy announced it would match reductions by another Japanese oil importer, Cosmo Oil, by cutting its Iranian imports by 10,000 barrels per day to just under 30,000. South Korea, which has relied on Iran for 10% of its crude, bought 10% less from Iran in the first four months of 2012 than during the same period last year. Due to the EU insurance ban, South Korea cut off purchases entirely as of July.

Elsewhere, Turkey, which has accounted for 7% of Iran's oil exports, sharply cut its purchases in May and June 2012, having announced that it would reduce its purchases by 20% to avoid US banking sanctions. The short-fall would be made up by Saudi Arabian and Libyan imports. However, Iran still accounted for about 58% of Turkey's crude supplies between January and April 2012. South Africa, which has imported about 25% of its oil from Iran, its largest supplier, slashed its April 2012 imports of Iranian oil by 43% relative to March 2012, and nearly doubled supplies from Saudi Arabia. It increased its purchases from Nigeria. Sri Lanka, which has imported nearly all its oil from Iran, due in part to an interest-free credit facility, announced in May 2012 that it had reduced Iranian imports by 38%.

Iran sought to counter the reduction in demand for its crude in many ways. It offered large discounts, deferred payment plans and attractive credit terms. It was also stockpiling crude in supertankers anchored in the Gulf and at a newly constructed storage facility at Bahregan in southwest Bushehr province, which has the capacity to store a million barrels of oil. Tehran held talks with South Africa on storing excess fuel at Saldanha Bay, north of Cape Town. It also turned off transponders on its vessels, to foil Western intelligence monitoring. It was using flags of convenience and multiple shell companies – sometimes changing during a voyage – to disguise its tanker fleet and make it more difficult to track. Other methods included switching supplies between tankers using ship-to-ship transfers, blending Iranian crude with crude from other sources to disguise the origin (particularly using blenders operating floating storage off the coasts of Malaysia and Indonesia), as well as re-labelling. It could also use currencies such as Russian roubles or the Indonesian rupiah, or employ financial mechanisms such as swaps.

Effects on the Iranian economy

The net effect in the first half of 2012 of the EU oil embargo and cuts in purchases by other importers was a sharp reduction in the volume of Iranian oil exports. The International Energy Agency estimated that oil exports dropped to between 1.2 and 1.8 million barrels a day, compared with the first-half 2011 figure of 2.48m. Morgan Stanley, the investment bank, envisaged a further reduction of 150,000 barrels per day when the full EU embargo came into effect on 1 July 2012. As Iran began to run out of storage capacity for unsold oil, it was forced to reduce production, which could permanently damage oil fields. The IEA estimated that sanctions had reduced Iran's overall crude production by 250,000 barrels per day, or around 7% of its previous output, which had been 11% of the OPEC total.

According to US Department of Energy estimates, oil has accounted for 80% of Iranian export earnings, bringing in $73bn in 2010 and $72bn in 2011. But the London-based Centre for Global Energy Studies (CGES) estimated that the figure could fall by as much as 39% to $44bn in 2012 as a result of sanctions and a second-quarter fall in the oil price to around $100 per barrel from a peak of $128 per barrel in March 2012. Oil exports also accounted for over 50% of government revenue. The CGES estimated these had so far fallen by $12bn in the first six months of 2012, relative to what they might have been if sanctions had not been imposed. This would be equivalent to around 13% of the government's general budget, although this budget excludes expenditure on state-owned enterprises. According to the IMF, Iran needs an oil price of $117 per barrel to balance its budget. In May, parliament approved President Mahmoud Ahmadinejad's $462bn annual budget, which was lower in real terms than the 2011 budget. As sanctions continue to bite, the government could come under further pressure to reduce spending.

Sanctions contributed to the weakness of the Iranian currency, the rial. The rial–dollar exchange rate saw a high degree of volatility during the first half of 2012, in some cases fluctuating by 12% in a day. After the announcement of new US and EU sanctions, the rial depreciated by over 40% as citizens sought sanctuary in the dollar (see Figure 1). This made imports more expensive, adding to inflationary pressures. The large gap that emerged between the official and unofficial exchange rates introduced further inefficiencies and incentives for corruption. In response to the depreciation, in January 2012 the government permitted banks to set interest rates on deposits above the inflation rate (the maximum rate of interest was raised by six percentage points to 21%, just above the then official inflation level of 20.6%). Ahmadinejad had previously instituted below-inflation interest rates to enable poor Iranians access to cheap loans. While the measure did strengthen the rial and help combat inflation, higher rates will constrain economic growth. And the government found it impossible to keep ahead of the inflationary cycle. By June, the official rate hit 22.4%.

Heightened uncertainty over the economy's prospects would tend to restrain investment and infrastructure expenditure in sectors such as oil and gas. In addition, the decline of the rial would increase concerns about inflation, already under pressure because of the removal of subsidies and price controls. The outlook – to which sanctions have contributed – was for economic stagnation (the IMF's 2012 growth estimate for Iran was revised downwards from 3.44% in October 2011 to just 0.36% in April 2012) , with high unemployment and rising inflation, which was given in official figures at 22.4%, but in fact was likely to be much higher. Prices for food doubled or even tripled over the past year as Iran struggled to import rice, cooking oil, fruit and other staples. Public-transport prices and taxi fares rose. Official data from April 2012 showed that, relative to April 2011, prices for red meat, beans and dairy products rose by around 45%; rice, sugar and vegetable oil prices rose by around 30%, while the price of vegetables rose by 92%. As an indication of falling confidence, there was soaring Iranian demand for gold.

Meanwhile, unemployment was rising. A central bank report indicated that in 22.5% of Iranian families, all family members were unemployed. While official figures showed unemployment at 12.5% in urban areas and 29.1%, among young people, many believed the latter was closer to 50%, with graduates ten times more likely to be unemployed than those holding lesser qualifications.

In preparation for tighter sanctions from 1 July 2012, in May alone Iran ordered imports amounting to a large proportion of its annual wheat and sugar requirement. It settled the trades at a premium in local currencies rather than in hard currency. Iran's Government Trading Corporation, which purchases and distributes staple products such as sugar, bread and flour, increased its purchases to offset the reduced ability of private Iranian importers to overcome financial sanctions. In February, Iranian purchasers defaulted on $144m worth of Indian rice imports, prompting the president of the All India Rice Exporters Association to recommend to its members not to export to Iran on credit. European and Ukrainian suppliers also ceased booking shipments of grain to Iran. Earlier, Malaysian palm oil exporters halted shipments as sanctions complicated the ability of Iranian importers to obtain letters of credit and to pay for supplies through intermediaries in the UAE.

Conclusion

Until 2012, US-led sanctions on Iran raised the cost of business and impeded expansion of the nuclear and missile programmes but did not severely impact the Iranian economy as a whole. That changed with the three new sets of measures established by the United States and European Union since December 2011, which were phased in during the first half of 2012. Sanctions against Iran are now nearly universal and are having an increasingly severe impact on the Iranian economy. Not every country has joined the sanctions regime willingly. As an official position, most countries say they only support the UN sanctions that they are mandated to follow. Most countries that do business with the United States, however, have little recourse but to succumb to pressure from Washington. And EU sanctions on insurance and reinsurance and SWIFT communications apply whether one likes it or not.

Whether or not the sanctions will impact Iranian decision making remains to be seen. The new measures persuaded Iran in April to resume talks that had been in hiatus for 15 months and to drop preconditions for dialogue. As of mid-2012 three rounds of meetings at the political directors' level appeared to have reached a stalemate, as both sides made maximalist demands and said time was on their side. But there is no doubt about the pressure facing the Iranian economy. The question for the year ahead is whether this pressure will be biting enough to alter the government's position. There is some evidence that the Iranian public is beginning to calculate that the costs of defying the major powers are greater than the benefits of uranium enrichment. For the time being, however, other factors are more important to the government, including Supreme Leader Ayatollah Ali Khamenei's belief that the US strategy is to topple the regime and that making any concession will only encourage further pressure. In fact, the Western strategy is to persuade him that only by making concessions on the nuclear programme can he alleviate the economic pressure that poses the gravest threat to the regime. Should this turn out to be the case, the measures would have proved that sanctions can in fact be an effective tool of geo-economic power. Such an outcome is far from assured, but as this case study has shown, the current sanctions regime being brought to bear on Iran has a better chance of success than any previous attempt.

Chapter 3

The Americas

United States: Election Looms in Divided Nation

On 27 March 2012, CNN legal-affairs analyst Jeffrey Toobin attended the US Supreme Court's oral arguments on the challenges to President Barack Obama's health-care reforms, then walked outside and down the courthouse steps for a live broadcast. 'This was a train wreck for the Obama administration', Toobin declaimed, waving his arms for emphasis. 'This law looks like it's going to be struck down. I'm telling you, all of the predictions – including mine – that the justices would not have a problem with this law were wrong.'

Three months later, Chief Justice John Roberts led a 5–4 majority to strike down Toobin's new prediction. The court upheld the constitutionality of Obama's defining legislative accomplishment, including the 'mandate' – much maligned by conservative critics – that requires individuals to purchase health insurance. It did so even though Roberts found that the 'commerce clause' of the US constitution (which gives Congress the power to regulate interstate and international commerce) did not give the federal government authority to regulate 'inactivity' – that is to say, the inactivity of not purchasing health insurance. However, the federal government does have more or less unlimited authority to tax, and Roberts deemed the mandate penalty for not buying health insurance to be a tax by another name.

The mandate was important because among the crucial features of the Affordable Care Act (ACA) is the requirement that insurance companies offer health coverage to everyone at roughly similar rates (there are some

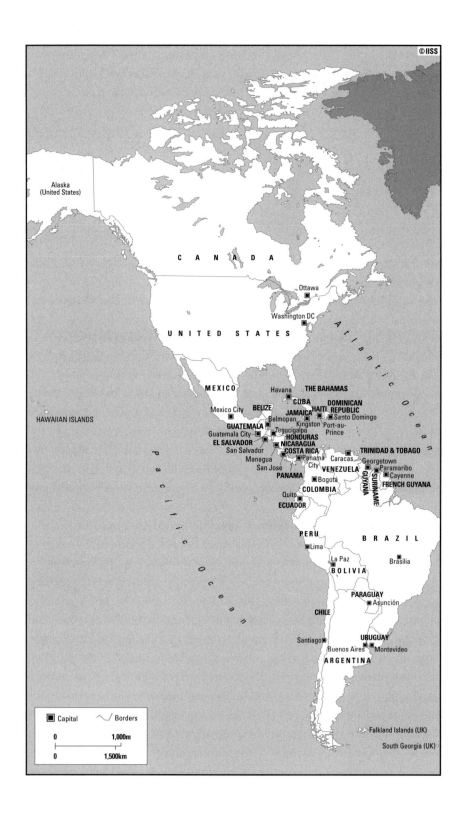

©IISS

Alaska
(United States)

C A N A D A

Ottawa

UNITED STATES

Washington DC

HAWAIIAN ISLANDS

MEXICO

Mexico City

Havana

THE BAHAMAS

BELIZE

CUBA

DOMINICAN
REPUBLIC

JAMAICA

HAITI

Belmopan

Kingston

Santo Domingo

GUATEMALA

Guatemala City

Tegucigalpa

Port-au-
Prince

EL SALVADOR

HONDURAS

San Salvador

NICARAGUA

COSTA RICA

TRINIDAD & TOBAGO

Managua

Panamá
City

Caracas

Georgetown

San José

PANAMA

VENEZUELA

Paramaribo

Cayenne

Bogotá

GUYANA

SURINAME

FRENCH GUYANA

COLOMBIA

Quito

ECUADOR

Atlantic Ocean

Pacific Ocean

PERU

B R A Z I L

Lima

La Paz

Brasília

BOLIVIA

PARAGUAY

Asunción

CHILE

Santiago

URUGUAY

Buenos Aires

Montevideo

ARGENTINA

Falkland Islands (UK)

South Georgia (UK)

■ Capital   ⌁ Borders

0   1,000m

0   1,500km

exceptions, such as age, where differential rates can be set). This requirement removes one of the great cruelties of the American system: the fact that many people with 'pre-existing conditions' could not find insurance at just about any price. Since 'pre-existing' applies to common chronic illnesses such as diabetes, the problem potentially affects a large number of Americans under the age of 65 (the elderly are provided for by a publicly funded system of government health insurance, Medicare, created in 1965). With the cruelty came huge economic inefficiencies: since most Americans are insured through their employers, losing one's job could be, in the most extreme circumstances, a death sentence for the employee or a family member. This situation did not enhance labour mobility or flexibility. The ACA ban on discrimination on the basis of pre-existing conditions was, unsurprisingly, a popular part of the reform. Republicans such as Mitt Romney, the presumptive Republican opponent for Obama in the November 2012 presidential election, said they were for it.

The problem, however, was that the ban on discrimination would probably not have worked without the mandate. It would have encouraged the young and healthy to game the system by waiting to buy insurance until they became sick. This would be akin to insuring a house after it burnt down: and if insurance companies were required to sell coverage under those conditions, they would most likely succumb to a 'death spiral' whereby they became financially unviable, charged astronomical rates, or both. (In this sense, the mandate is an inherently conservative instrument – and, indeed, it was first proposed by conservatives and in fact implemented by Romney as governor of Massachusetts in 2006 when he won approval of a very similar health care reform in that state.)

The ACA was a complicated piece of legislation with many moving parts. It turned insurance companies into something more like public utilities required to insure everyone. It provided subsidies to make coverage affordable for some of the 30 million people it would bring into the system for the first time, and it expanded Medicaid (government coverage for the indigent) to bring in the rest. And it introduced a long raft of measures to 'bend the curve' of rising American health costs downward.

A consensus had formed that the Supreme Court would strike down at least the mandate, if not the whole act, after conservative justices, including Roberts, asked harshly sceptical questions during oral arguments (Toobin's 'train wreck'). In the intervening months, some liberals started to argue that perhaps the overall reform could survive: other parts of the bill, including subsidies, might bring in enough healthy new subscribers to make the insurance system viable even without the mandate. But it was a risky proposition, and with such fierce Republican opposition to the whole package, it might have been easier after an adverse ruling for a new Republican president and congressional majority to dismantle it piece by piece.

It turned out that liberals had been somewhat carried away in their pessimism. Conservatives were correspondingly overconfident. In joining the more liberal justices to form a majority, Chief Justice Roberts looked clearly concerned about preserving the reputation and legitimacy of the court. A series of 5–4 decisions, including the 2000 *Bush v Gore* decision that stopped the Florida recount and put George W. Bush into the White House, were starting to make the Supreme Court look like a political animal riven by exactly the same left–right divisions as the rest of the country. Thus Roberts strained to find a solution that would reconcile his evident aversion to the law with a desire to avoid thrusting the Supreme Court into the battle between the American right and centre-left. Roberts apparently understood the perils of, and sought to avoid, a deepening rejection of the court's legitimacy on the left side of the political spectrum. He relied on the presumption that laws enacted by Congress and signed by the president should be considered constitutional unless the case against was overwhelming. And so, while rejecting the commerce-clause argument, he found another reason to uphold the law in Congress' designated authority to tax. It was still a 5–4 decision, but one that crossed the court's ideological dividing lines. 'The statute reads more naturally as a command to buy insurance than as a tax', Roberts wrote. But he added, in a key statement of restraint: 'we have a duty to construe a statute to save it, if fairly possible'. Since it was 'fairly possible' to view the mandate penalty, to be collected by the Internal Revenue Service, as a tax, that was what he did.

Contending visions of the American state

This effort at balance led to some fairly amazing praise. Charles Lane of the *Washington Post* wrote that 'the ruling is historic because it is a Compromise – a crisis-averting pact across lines of ideology, party and region, the likes of which we have not seen since pre-Civil War days'. Lane was referring to the 'Compromise of 1850 [that] reaffirmed the north–south line between slave states and free states'. This may sound like rhetorical over-reach, and less than reassuring, since a decade after the Compromise of 1850 the United States was riven by the great civil war that it was meant to avert. It is true enough, however, that Obama's health-care bill constituted one of the great pieces of social legislation of the past century, ranking with the landmark bills of Franklin Roosevelt's New Deal and Lyndon Johnson's Great Society. It fills what had been a gaping hole in the American welfare state, and removes the United States from the exceptional status of being the only rich democracy not to guarantee universal health care. Against this achievement stood an adamant American conservatism holding tight to the conviction that a private and largely unregulated health-care system was central to the vision of American exceptionalism. This exceptionalism was based on a largely economic – that is to say, free-market and property-based – definition of liberty.

How, then, was the court decision a compromise? The court did set limits on the federal government's ability to threaten to withhold Medicaid funding in order to coerce states into participating in an expansion of Medicaid that is another key element of the new law. And some conservative opponents took comfort from the rejection of the commerce clause as a basis for upholding the law. Time will tell if this was the beginning of a series of decisions that could undermine the constitutional basis of federal power as embodied in the New Deal welfare state. For the moment that seemed unlikely; health care really is *sui generis* insofar as the failure to do something – getting oneself insured – has a major deleterious effect on others. This is because, even though the uninsured could be deprived of basic and even life-saving treatment, it was not the case that they were left to die on the streets. There was already a law requiring hospital emergency rooms to treat emergency cases regardless of the ability to pay. This was *not* an American version of universal health care, however: it only applied to emergency care. Moreover, hospital emergency rooms would still present a bill, and indeed for many years health emergency had been the leading cause of personal bankruptcy. Still, the fact that they would treat you whether you could pay or not meant that the millions of wilfully uninsured constituted a vast army of free-riders on the health system, whose emergency treatment, however inadequate, was expensive for American tax-payers.

It was difficult to imagine many other areas where the federal government would find a necessity to 'regulate inactivity'. A military draft would be one possibility, but if conscription were reinstated it would not be conservatives leading the charge against it. The conservatives' case, argued seriously in the Supreme Court challenges, was that if government could force individuals to buy health insurance, there was no reason in principle that it could not force them to eat broccoli in the common interest of a healthy population. (This *reductio ad absurdum* was labelled the case of 'broccoli horrible' by Justice Ruth Bader Ginsburg.) A more practical example might be compulsory vaccination of children against infectious disease, something currently required by all 50 US states but not by federal law.

The Supreme Court ruling was handed down just over four months before the 2012 election. Obama immediately went on television to enumerate the concrete benefits of the legislation, something he had arguably done inadequately so far. Romney, his presumptive Republican challenger, stated: 'This is now a time for the American people to make a choice. You can choose whether to have a larger and larger government making intrusions into your life ... Or whether instead you want to return to a time where Americans have their own choice in health care.' There was no doubt that the two parties were presenting starkly opposed visions of the American state and its role in society. The conservatives' objection to universal health care appeared to be based on a definition of individual freedom that was fundamentally threatened by liberal governance of the kind that would establish health care as a right rather than a privilege – with commensurate taxation to fund that right. This conservative view required either a shrewd psychoanalysis or a fundamental misunderstanding of the liberal project. For example, George Will, an erudite and respected conservative columnist, has written repeatedly that liberals agitate for action against global warming and other environmental hazards because they are fundamentally determined to expand the role and control of government over the lives and liberties of individual Americans. Yet liberals would certainly not recognise this to be their motive. Rather, as liberal journalist Jonathan Chait has argued, liberals value government, and its control over people's lives, not as an end in itself, but as a necessary means to an end.

Making health care a right did, to be sure, entail a further redistribution of wealth via progressive taxation, and taxation is, at least in the abstract, an infringement on liberty. This infringement had become the other great cause of conservative anger, driving a 'Tea Party' movement that by 2012 had been more or less subsumed within the mainstream of the Republican Party. It was the Tea Party class of Republicans in Congress, elected in the conservative wave of 2010, which had brought the United States to the brink of default on its national debt in summer 2011 by refusing to authorise an increase in the federal debt ceiling unless there was a correspondingly huge and immediate cut in federal spending. Aside from plunging the economy back into recession, such cuts would have gutted federal programmes across the board. Since Obama and Congressional Democrats insisted, moreover, that at least some part of the plan to achieve fiscal balance had to include tax increases on the more wealthy, the disaster of default had been averted only through an eleventh-hour, jury-rigged deal. The Republican-controlled House of Representatives agreed at the last moment to raise the debt ceiling on the basis of setting up a bipartisan 'super committee' that would be tasked to reach a long-term budget agreement. If it failed, large automatic spending reductions would, under the agreement, be inflicted upon domestic and defence spending. The theory was that this would give left and right incentive to negotiate seriously. But the super committee indeed failed to reach an agreement, stymied by the same Republican refusal to consider tax increases.

The Republican parameters of this struggle were highlighted, if not set in stone, during the party's contest for the presidential nomination. During an 11 August 2011 candidates' debate at Iowa State University, Byron York of the *Washington Examiner* asked the candidates, 'Is there a ratio of cuts to taxes that you would accept? Three to one? Four to one? Or even ten to one?' The candidate to whom this was addressed, former Senator Rick Santorum of Pennsylvania, answered, 'No. The answer is no, because that's not the problem.' Fox News' Bret Baier then asked all the candidates: 'Say you had a deal, a real spending cuts deal, ten to one … spending cuts to tax increases … Who on this stage would walk away from that deal. Can you raise your hand if you feel so strongly about not raising taxes, you'd walk away on the ten-to-one deal?' All the candidates – Santorum, Herman Cain, Ron Paul, Michele Bachmann, Tim Pawlenty, Jon Huntsman, Newt Gingrich and Romney – raised their hands. It was a striking demonstration of the reality that, in American conservative discourse, budget deficits are not really discussed as the difference between revenue and spending. Rather, deficits are a stand-in for government spending, which – aside from military spending – is considered bad for the economy and threatening to liberty. An important question, if Romney were to become president, would be whether the absolute rejection of tax increases would continue.

Romney's turn

Republicans have a tradition of nominating as their presidential standard-bearer the candidate who appears to be next in line. In 1980 it was Ronald Reagan, who had come close to wresting the nomination from the incumbent Gerald Ford in 1976. George H.W. Bush (Reagan's vice president) got the nod in 1988, and Robert Dole, the Senate minority leader who had been Ford's running mate in 1976, won the contest to challenge Bill Clinton in 1996. As heir to a political dynasty, George W. Bush arguably fit the pattern in 2000. John McCain, Bush's chief challenger for the 2000 nomination, certainly fit the pattern in 2008.

By this admittedly loose standard, former Massachusetts Governor Mitt Romney, a leading candidate against McCain in 2008, appeared to be the presumptive choice for 2012. In most other respects, however, Romney was an implausible leader for a Republican Party that was moving ever farther to the political right. To begin with, Romney was a devout Mormon seeking the acclamation of a party whose most fervent base consisted of conservative Christians, many of whom derided Mormonism as a non-Christian cult. More important, perhaps, Romney had become governor of liberal-leaning Massachusetts by promising to pursue progressive policies on such matters as abortion and gay rights, promises on which he made good. In doing so he was following a family tradition; his father, George Romney, a former auto-company executive and governor of Michigan, was a leader alongside Nelson Rockefeller of the more liberal wing of the Republican Party, breaking with conservative orthodoxy during the 1960s to support civil-rights legislation and express scepticism about the war in Vietnam. Three decades later, the younger Romney's most disqualifying act was his key Massachusetts achievement: enactment of legislation providing near-universal health insurance to the state's citizens, by means of an individual mandate that became a model for the Obama-backed national health-care reform.

Romney's unfortunate reputation as a political chameleon had much to do with the necessity to sidestep the health-care achievement in front of a Republican electorate that had decided that such mandates constituted fundamental threats to American liberty. His somewhat contorted explanation – that American federalism rendered the mandate acceptable at the state level, but outrageous nationally – seemed unlikely to placate the white-hot anger of the Republican base. In any event, following the Supreme Court decision Romney repeated his vow that moving to repeal the Obama health-care legislation would be his first act as president.

It was the disadvantage of his former moderation – combined, perhaps, with a somewhat wooden political persona – that drove the cyclical dynamic of a Republican contest through seemingly endless candidate debates. Romney for many months was unable to break through a polling ceiling of roughly one-quarter of the national Republican vote. A succession of alternative candidates took the lead and then fell out of favour. Minnesota Governor Tim Pawlenty looked good on paper – a working-class background, a youthful and unassuming demeanour, and a record of political success as a Republican in an upper-Midwest bastion of traditional liberalism. He also coined a neologism – 'Obamney Care' – that was presumed to be extremely dangerous to the health-care reformer from Massachusetts.

Yet Pawlenty declined to repeat it to Romney's face when challenged to do so in a debate, a failure widely considered to reveal an inadequate instinct to go for the political jugular. Sarah Palin (the former Alaska governor and McCain's 2008 running mate) and Minnesota Congresswoman Michele Bachmann both appealed perhaps most viscerally to Tea Party conservatives. But Palin – who had come to enjoy a lucrative speaking circuit and a contract for regular appearances on Fox News, and who was almost certainly unelectable in a general election – ultimately decided against running. Bachmann did run but faded. Texas Governor Rick Perry offered suitably right-wing positions; he had broached the idea of Texas having to nullify federal laws it didn't like, and he threatened – presumably as a joke – rough physical treatment for Federal Reserve Chairman Ben Bernanke for the crime of conducting moderately expansive monetary policy against the recession, if Bernanke set foot in Perry's home state. Perry became instant front-runner in the polls when he announced his candidacy for the nomination (two days after the Iowa State University debate), and lost the status as soon as he opened his mouth in the next debate. His fumbles included a failure to remember the third of three federal departments that he had promised to abolish. Then came Herman Cain, a conservative black businessman who admitted he knew little about policy or the world beyond, but generated support with a variation on the idea of a flat tax – in his case, a 9% levy on income, business profits and retail sales. Although Cain too enjoyed some weeks of leading the polls, his candidacy was unviable for a number of reasons. The proximate cause of its demise was the emergence of several women who accused him of sexual harassment during his business career.

Then came Newt Gingrich. Gingrich's candidacy was also destined to implode – in fact, it imploded twice. But in between it revealed a great deal about the dynamics of modern American conservatism. In summer 2011, most of Gingrich's senior campaign staff resigned in exasperation at his failure to take the job of campaigning seriously enough – he had insisted on a break to take his wife on a Mediterranean cruise. Bereft of senior advisers, Gingrich gamely struggled on, visiting, it was reported, the local zoo, if there was one, at almost every campaign stop. The zoo visits were arguably endearing and certainly revealing. As much or more than Ronald Reagan, Gingrich was the founder of the contemporary strain of American conservatism. Or, to put it in the revolutionary terms that Gingrich keenly embraced, he was the Lenin to Reagan's Marx. He had engineered the 1994 election wave that installed a very conservative Republican majority in the House of Representatives, after 45 years of unbroken Democratic control. Gingrich proceeded to employ his signature combination of rough politics and rank demagoguery. Just before his 1994 victory, for example, Gingrich claimed that a North Carolina mother's horrific drowning of her two children embodied the sickness of society that could only be cured by voting Republican. A kind of giddy and ostentatious intellectualism sometimes seemed cartoonish, as in his 2012 campaign promise of a colony on the moon before 2020 with constitutional provisions for granting it American statehood. Volubility at other times got him into trouble: his campaign's first demise was associated at least partly with his reference to Medicare plans put forward by Republican star congressman Paul Ryan as 'right-wing' 'social engineering' – as unpalatable, he suggested, as the left-wing variety.

Yet, after the fall of Cain, the intellectualism and the demagoguery began to generate enthusiasm. At the start of 2012, the right-wing base still was not warming to Romney. Romney had apparently edged out Rick Santorum by a handful of votes in the Iowa caucuses on 3 January. He then won the New Hampshire primary a week later with a plurality of 25%, but failure to do so would have been catastrophic, since Romney was from next-door Massachusetts and owned a house in New Hampshire. At this point, Gingrich surged ahead in polls for the South Carolina primary scheduled for Saturday 21 January by exploiting his particular genius for tapping into the far-right id. At a candidates' debate the Monday before the primary, Gingrich repeatedly called Obama 'the food-stamp president'. The white southern audience gave him a standing ovation. He was replying to a question from Juan Williams, the black moderator, about whether he could understand the hurt of many black Americans at his use of such racially coded language. Gingrich, of whom there was no reason to suspect personal racism, replied by pretending that he had not repeatedly employed racialist dog whistles (language with a coded subtext that would be clear to the intended audience). 'First of all, Juan, the fact is that more people have been put on food stamps by Barack Obama than any president in history.' (Here he had to pause to soak in the crowd's approval.) 'I know among the politically correct you're not supposed to use facts that are uncomfortable.'

Three nights later, in another debate, Gingrich roused the audience on the subject of sex. ABC News was about to broadcast an interview with Gingrich's second ex-wife in which she claimed that he had proposed to deal with the problem of his affair with the woman who became his third (and current) wife through their agreement to an 'open marriage'. The claim was not new – it was contained in an *Esquire* article of many years ago. Asked about it as the first question of the debate, Gingrich impressively turned the question into an example of the media's determination to 'protect' Barack Obama. 'Every person in here has had someone close to them go through painful things. To take an ex-wife and make it two days before the primary, a significant question in a presidential campaign, is as close to despicable as anything I can imagine.' The audience loved this point – one that might be stated in the somewhat less heated argument that personal failings are not matters of public policy – though making that case arguably required forgetting that Gingrich had conducted his affair while leading an impeachment battle against President Clinton over Clinton's own affair. The Gingrich appeal had much to do with the conviction of many Republican voters that Obama was an intellectual lightweight, dependent on the use of teleprompters for the presentation of flowery but empty speeches. Gingrich, they believed, would demolish Obama in presidential debates.

In between these two performances by Gingrich, it was announced that a miscount of ballots in the effectively tied Iowa Caucuses meant that Santorum, rather than Romney, could now claim on the basis of a literal handful of votes to be the nominal winner of that contest. A few days later, Gingrich decisively won the South Carolina primary. So whereas just days before Romney looked poised to clinch an unprecedented triple victory of Iowa, New Hampshire and South Carolina, the contests were in fact divided three ways between Santorum, Romney and Gingrich.

Romney was able to dispatch Gingrich less than two weeks later in the Florida primary, mainly by pouring vast sums of money into a barrage of negative advertising. Then the final alternative, Santorum, rose to win in Minnesota, Missouri, Colorado, Mississippi, Alabama and Louisiana. Santorum, a devout and socially conservative Catholic, pushed the debate onto terrain that Romney would have preferred to avoid: religion and sex. The debate moved there also because of a separate battle that Obama found himself in with the hierarchy of the American Catholic Church over a provision in the health-care law requiring employers, including religious organisations, to include contraception coverage in their employees' health-insurance plans. The resulting brouhaha included one particularly unedifying episode in which Rush Limbaugh, a popular conservative talk-radio rabble-rouser, used the national radio waves to call a Georgetown University law student a 'slut' who should make videos of her bedroom activities available via the Internet to the general public, if she expected the public to subsidise those activities. (The student, whose law school is part of a Jesuit university, had enraged Limbaugh by testifying before a congressional panel in support of the contraception coverage.) The Limbaugh tirade led to a familiar piece of American public kabuki, wherein the remaining Republican candidates were all asked by journalists whether they would care to disassociate themselves from the remarks, and they all took pains not to ostentatiously alienate themselves from a highly influential right-wing figure. (Romney said simply 'it's not the language I would have used'.) In this raw climate, Santorum did himself and his party no favours by repeatedly returning to related subjects. He somehow found the presidential campaign an appropriate place to argue that sexual activity should be confined to within a marital relationship, and for the purpose of procreation. He also found occasion to observe that he was nauseated by the famous speech by America's only Catholic president, John F. Kennedy, in which he promised to respect a wall between religious obligation and state duties. Such reflections were arguably unfortunate for Santorum's political bid, since he otherwise presented a calm and modest blue-collar appeal that seemed, in some ways, more electorally promising than Romney's high net worth and background in private equity.

In the end, however, it was always hard to see Romney – a more plausible president with a much better campaign organisation and much more money – losing the nomination. In many ways Romney was lucky: although the Republican base did not warm to him and did not trust him, the candidates who emerged one by one to challenge his lead never looked like plausible winners against Obama.

Obama's predicament

This was ironic, since Obama looked (on paper at least) to be eminently beatable. The official jobless rate was stuck stubbornly above 8%, and economic growth was disappointingly slow. His most fervent supporters from 2008, including youth who had voted at higher-than-normal rates, were disillusioned, perhaps inevitably, by the compromising realities of a candidacy become presidency. And some less ideological voters who had backed him in 2008 no doubt noticed that his promise to transcend America's sharp partisan divide had failed.

Obama himself apparently drew the same conclusion. Whereas he had spent summer 2011 seeking bipartisan accord on a Grand Bargain to address the debt problem, the breakdown of negotiations persuaded him to campaign on a more populist and ideological basis. A speech on 6 December 2011 in Osawatomie, Kansas was crafted and staged as a conscious reprise of progressive Republican President Theodore Roosevelt's populist manifesto delivered in the same town 101 years earlier. Roosevelt had railed against the 'malefactors of great wealth'; Obama was not quite so acid, but did target what he portrayed as the injustice of vast concentrated wealth after decades during which the middle classes had failed to increase their incomes.

This approach made some political sense. The Obama campaign team was convinced that Romney's personal wealth, his alleged disconnect from the concerns of ordinary citizens, and business background as the head of the private equity firm Bain Capital, where he had made his fortune, could be usefully targeted to damage his image among undecided voters. They had a model for this in the Republican primaries, where the self-styled con-servatives in the race hammered Romney from the left – one might even say, the far left – for the allegedly predatory capitalism of that business career. And Romney's fortune had been the subject of unpleasant scrutiny as the candidate hummed and hawed about whether he would make public his tax returns which, due to favourable treatment of investment income, were pre-sumed to show a much lower effective rate of taxation than is paid by most middle-class Americans. (He eventually released his 2010 tax return and an estimate for 2011, and that was indeed what they showed.)

There were Democrats, to be sure, who questioned this line of attack. Newark Mayor Cory Booker, a charismatic and promising black politician, said (echoing Santorum) that attacks on private equity were 'nauseating'. This reaction made some sense for a New Jersey politician whose finan-cial backers were bound to include scores of hedge-fund managers. It also pointed to a danger area for Obama, who had received considerable Wall Street money for his initial presidential campaign, but who now found the taps drying up as an alienated financial industry turned towards the Republicans. Sure enough, initial campaign expenditure reports indicated that this might be the first presidential campaign in history in which the challenger raised more money than the incumbent. Early predictions that the president's campaign might raise and spend an astonishing one billion dollars were certainly looking premature. But the president's campaign managers in Chicago thought they saw evidence that attacks on Romney's Bain career were working to define Obama's opponent in negative terms in crucial upper Midwest battlegrounds such as Ohio (which Romney prob-ably had to take to win the election).

More generally, the Obama campaign against Romney eerily resembled the George W. Bush campaign for re-election against Democratic challenger John Kerry in 2004. Like Kerry, Romney was being attacked in the area of his supposed strength. For Kerry it was his background as a Vietnam war hero. For Romney it was his vaunted business competence. (Though it must be added that the Bain attacks, whether fair or unfair, did not involve the out-right lies that Bush-aligned groups had used to smear Kerry's war record.)

It was becoming clear that, to win re-election, Obama would, like Bush, have to grind out a narrow win by exploiting rather than overcoming the country's bitter divisions. Like Bush before 2004, Obama had a job-approval rating in polls just shy of 50%. There were demographic developments that appeared, for the long term, to favour the Democrats, leading some strate-gists to speak of an emerging Democratic majority. Socially, the country was clearly becoming more liberal; polls showed, for example, that in an aston-ishingly short span of years, a majority (albeit a thin one) of American voters had come to support gay marriage. Thus it seemed a reasonable, though by no means sure-fire, political bet for the president to come out in favour of homosexuals' right to marry, as he did in a spring 2012 television interview. This was of largely symbolic importance, since he left the actual resolution of the issue up to the courts and individual states, but Obama had already made the much more concrete contribution to gay rights of engineering the repeal of the military's 'don't ask, don't tell' ban on gays serving openly in the armed forces.

The most important demographic change involved ethnicity: year after year, the United States was becoming inexorably less white. The fastest growing minority population consisted of Hispanics, and this was the voting bloc for which the Republicans' steady march to the right looked most dam-aging. George W. Bush's political architect, Karl Rove, had considered the Hispanic population a natural target of Republican opportunity, since they were overwhelmingly Catholic, family oriented and – it was presumed – essentially conservative. Exit polling suggested that Bush, a former governor of Hispanic-rich Texas, had indeed won a relatively large 35% of Hispanic votes in 2000 and 41% in 2004. Since 2004, however, the Republican base had been gripped by a nativist fever. By 2010, this fever was reflected in both Republican political rhetoric and draconian laws in states such as Arizona intended to make life miserable for illegal immigrants and, it was hoped, encourage their 'self-deportation'. During the primaries Romney took care to stay to the right of his opponents on immigration issues: attacking Perry, for example, on his Texas policy of allowing the children of undocumented aliens who had grown up in Texas to attend state universities paying in-state fees rather than the significantly higher fees charged to non-residents.

Under these political circumstances, hopes for a bipartisan reform to nor-malise the status of millions of immigrants who were, by any reasonable reckoning, not going back, foundered. Even the more modest 'DREAM Act', offering a path to citizenship for young adults who had been brought to the United States as young children and therefore had not willingly violated immigration laws, had no chance of passage. With an undoubted eye on the political advantage, Obama decided to implement a mini-version of the DREAM Act by what constituted executive fiat. In June he announced that his administration would exercise broad discretion in a new policy to grant such young adults (under the age of 30) who had lived in the country for at least five years; had no criminal record; and were in school, had graduated from high school or were military veterans, a renewable two-year residence permit including the right to work.

Critics claimed he was stretching his authority and flouting laws duly passed by Congress and signed by previous presidents. Moral and policy considerations aside, the political advantage for Obama was not that these young adults could vote for him – they were still not citizens – but that the broader community of Hispanic citizens would be inspired and energised to come to the polls in greater numbers. In a closely divided country, turnout was going to be key, and indeed a number of Republican state legislatures, including Florida's, had passed 'voter ID' laws, ostensibly against the much-discussed, but practically non-existent, problem of voter fraud, but almost certainly intended to suppress turnout among heavily Democratic minorities. (These communities, disproportionately poor, contained more individuals who lacked photo identification such as driver's licences.)

The political disadvantage for Romney was that Obama's executive order made it, firstly, more difficult to move away from the hard-line immigration policies he had advocated during the primaries and, secondly, more difficult to confine himself to the single issue that he preferred to hammer every day: the dismal state of the economy. There had been a progression of positive monthly reports on job creation during the 2011–12 winter, raising hopes of a more robust recovery. As spring moved into summer, however, job creation slowed again: at less than 100,000 new jobs per month, it was not keeping up with population growth. Economists such as Paul Krugman spoke of an economy mired in depression: as in the 1930s, catastrophic financial collapse and economic recession were being followed by tepid growth and, potentially, new contraction, while the necessary antidote of government deficit spending was either inadequate or prematurely abandoned. Obama stated during a press conference in early June that 'the private sector is doing fine'; this political gaffe contained the truth that job losses were overwhelmingly in the public sector, where recession-strapped state governments had been forced to lay off teachers and public-safety workers, with damaging knock-on effects to the rest of the economy. Historical comparisons showed that total per-capita government spending (federal, state and local) was much lower under Obama than in previous economic downturns, for example in the early 1980s when the sharing of federal tax revenues with state governments helped the Reagan administration pull the country out of recession.

For all of this, with an annual growth rate just over 2% the United States was doing better than many of its European partners. The administration's bailout, early in its term, of a failing auto industry was showing results in increased car sales and economic upticks in Michigan and neighbouring Ohio, two electorally important states. The major stimulus package of Obama's first year in office, inadequate as it was, had been followed in 2011 by a 'mini-stimulus' whereby the president had leveraged the threat of an automatic increase in upper-income tax rates to gain Republican assent to a middle-income payroll tax holiday and extended unemployment benefits.

But the European comparison pointed to another election-year threat for the United States. The eurozone crisis had an important transatlantic dimension in that recession in Europe would limit the prospects for American recovery. The Obama administration tried without much success to convince German Chancellor Angela Merkel to act more decisively, and generously, against the debt crisis afflicting some eurozone members. This was, potentially, a rich field for transatlantic resentment. A common view among US analysts was that Europe's slow-motion catastrophe posed the single biggest threat to Obama's re-election. Meanwhile, the European crisis entered American politics in a highly ironic fashion. Through the past year of Republican presidential primaries, candidate after candidate had accused Obama of wanting to turn the United States into a version of 'socialist' Europe. But on the crucial question over economic stimulus versus fiscal austerity, the Republicans' thinking was very much in line with that of the Germans. Romney's economics adviser Glenn Hubbard made this explicit in a commentary published by the German financial paper *Handelsblatt*: 'The debate over fiscal policy in the eurozone is part of the global problem of excessive debt creation. While the US president advises the Europeans to lay on more debt-financed spending, he is presiding over an unparalleled peacetime deficit in the US.'

American pivot

There were bigger stakes, of course, than Obama's re-election. Europe's economic and political problems appeared to be the biggest pending threat to Western unity and coherence. After a decade of terrorism, war and economic crisis that had sapped American confidence, the Obama administration had made a decent start on redrawing a more sustainable, but still quite robust and assertive, world role for the United States. But this strategy depended crucially on having capable partners, and the strategic weight of the European partner was now in doubt. To the extent that Europe remained mired in financial crisis and economic stagnation, it would be more or less dead weight.

By early 2012, the Obama administration had both reaffirmed its deadline for withdrawal of combat troops from Afghanistan, and announced plans for substantial reductions in US infantry forces. In January, the Pentagon released new strategy guidance that set out the concept of a 'strategic pivot' – a rebalancing of US forces towards the Asia-Pacific – backed by plans for initially small military moves such as the deployment of US Marines to Northern Australia. A careful balancing of China's rise could, it was hoped, be accomplished without provoking a destructive arms race. Much of the 'pivot' was diplomatic; US officials argued that Washington's renewed attention to Asia-Pacific allies had already bolstered their confidence and restored a psychological balance vis-à-vis Beijing.

Meanwhile, the killing almost a year earlier of Osama bin Laden, along with continued targeted assassination via unmanned drones of the remaining al-Qaeda command structure, underscored that Obama's strategic retrenchment and earlier efforts at diplomatic conciliation in no way indicated a less robust defense of core US interests. 'There's a name', wrote the respected analyst Peter Beinart, 'for the strategy the Obama administration is increasingly pursuing from the Persian Gulf to the South China Sea: offshore balancing. It's the idea that America can best contain our adversaries not by confronting them on land, but by maintaining our naval and air power and strengthening those smaller nations that see us as a natural counterweight to their larger neighbors.'

This strategic doctrine seemed congenial to most Americans, insofar as in most surveys they gave Obama higher marks for foreign policy than they gave his presumptive Republican opponent. This was a virtually unprecedented advantage for a Democrat to enjoy. If Romney was going to score any political points against the incumbent's foreign policy, it would have to be in the Middle East with accusations that Obama was insufficiently devoted to Israel's welfare. Even this would be a difficult case to make. To be sure, the fraught personal relations between the president and Israeli Prime Minister Benjamin Netanyahu had not much improved. Netanyahu had handed the president what was arguably the biggest foreign-policy defeat of his presidency by refusing to halt Jewish settlements construction in occupied Palestinian territories. But the president swallowed this defeat, dutifully – and accurately – expressing the fundamental American support for Israeli security in a September 2011 speech to the UN General Assembly. At the UN, American diplomats promised to veto the Palestinians' bid for Security Council recognition of a unilaterally declared state, and they pressured Palestinian leaders not to sidestep this veto by seeking recognition in the General Assembly.

Washington's most acute difficulty with Israel came with renewed speculation in spring 2012 that the Israeli government was considering unilateral air strikes against Iranian nuclear facilities. The Obama administration pressed its Israeli counterparts not to do so, and asked for patience while increasingly onerous sanctions against Iran's defiance took effect. Those sanctions were, on their own terms, another undoubted success for the administration. By mid-summer 2012, countries in Europe and elsewhere had reduced imports of Iranian crude oil (see essay, pp. 61–74). For the regime in Tehran, the situation was starting to look grim: plummeting oil exports, a collapsing currency and banks that could not operate abroad. It was to this tightening of sanctions that administration officials attributed what they perceived as a renewed seriousness on the part of Iran about negotiating a solution. However, talks over the spring and early summer in Istanbul, Baghdad and Moscow arrived, once more, at a frustrating impasse. The administration's working theory was that Iran's economic conditions would become so dire that the regime would worry about its survival. However, the psychologically plausible alternative was that, seeing themselves practically at war, with regime survival at stake, Iran's leaders would view serious concessions to be a dangerous sign of weakness.

The Iran problem resonated in America's domestic politics. Romney, during a Republican debate, had declared flatly that the matter was simple: if Obama were re-elected, Iran would build a nuclear bomb; if Romney defeated him, Iran would be stopped. The clear implication was that Romney would be ready to use military force, but unanswered was the question of what a President Romney would do if US military action in fact only convinced the Iranians to leave the Non-Proliferation Treaty and to redouble their nuclear efforts. Was Romney prepared to follow air strikes with a military invasion?

In fact, Obama used a 4 March 2012 speech to the American Israel Public Affairs Committee's annual policy conference, to establish a clearer American red line: containment of an Iran armed with nuclear weapons was not an option. 'I made a commitment to the American people and said we would use all elements of American power to pressure Iran and prevent it from acquiring a nuclear weapon', he said. This was not as far as the Israeli government wanted to go in ruling out even a nuclear capability on Iran's part – that is, the capacity to manufacture nuclear fuel and thus be able to 'break out' suddenly for a weapons arsenal. But it certainly laid down a marker that might, in a second Obama or first Romney administration, lead to military conflict between America and Iran.

There were other possible roads to military conflict. Perhaps inevitably, the Arab uprisings of early 2011 had not led everywhere, a year later, to harmonious or peaceful results. The United States had engaged in a regime-changing war in Libya that resulted, from Washington's perspective, in successful results with minimal effort, since rebel forces and European allies had taken on the main burden of ground and air campaigns. Now, a comparable humanitarian emergency developed in Syria, where the regime used extreme violence against its people, pushing the country to the brink of civil war. In Libya the NATO effort had been helped by geography: Gadhafi's forces had battled the rebels mainly along a narrow coastal strip. In Syria, by contrast, the social and physical landscape seemed far less amenable to effective intervention from the air. Yet, although Washington had little appetite for direct intervention, administration officials were aware that atrocities might become so overwhelming as to create overwhelming pressure for another humanitarian intervention. Obama had already stated forcefully that solving the crisis would require the departure of Syrian President Bashar al-Assad from office. Although the president of the United States lacked the powers to make this happen, such statements tend to foreclose diplomatic solutions that might leave the current regime in power. In spite of Washington's reluctance to engage militarily, there were plausible scenarios in which this could happen. The recent history of such engagements – Iraq, Bosnia, Kosovo, Afghanistan, and most recently Libya – shows even tentative beginnings lead almost inexorably to regime change.

Future constraints

There were constraints that would apply to US foreign policy whoever won the election in November 2012. Likewise, domestic possibilities would be constrained by an overhang of government debt that would have to be serviced by an economy that looked to remain sluggish at best. This did not mean, however, that voters' decisions might not fundamentally affect America's future. On foreign policy, Romney was committed to a more confrontational posture towards those who did not fall in line with American policies and values. Russia was America's 'number one geo-political foe' and should be treated as such. There would be no more 'apologising' for American greatness. In other words, the Obama effort at conciliation would come to an end. In budgetary terms, Romney promised to set a floor under defence spending of 4% of GDP. Obama, by contrast, emphasised that 'over the past ten years, since 9/11, our defense budget grew at an extraordinary pace. Over the next ten years, the growth in the defense budget will slow, but the fact of the matter is this: it will still grow, because we have global responsibilities that demand our leadership.' The incumbent's bottom line, in other words, was to reconcile continued demands on America's military capabilities with the need for a 'peace divi-dend' such as helped return the US budget to balance and then surplus during Bill Clinton's presidency.

The capacity for a robust foreign policy would depend, under either president, on the ability to form a political consensus on the domestic pur-poses of the American state. Romney had backed the Paul Ryan budget plan, an iconic document for conservatives, which proposed to ultimately reduce the federal government's share of GDP to less than 15%, a level not seen since the Truman administration. Since defence spending was to be at least 4%, this would require the wholesale termination of many other federal responsibilities – a project that did not seem realistic. A re-elected Obama, on the other hand, would face a sullen and still obstructionist Republican opposition. His first-term ambitions – for effective strategies against global warming, to take one example – did not look that much more feasible in a second term.

Either man would enter office in a time of crisis. The parties' failure to agree on the basic structure of revenue and spending had created a time bomb set to go off on 31 December, eight weeks after the presidential elec-tion. On that date, the tax cuts enacted during George W. Bush's first term would automatically expire, payroll taxes would increase by 2%, and ben-efits for 3m unemployed would come to an end. At the same time, budget sequesters, the mandated consequence of the super committee's failure to reach agreement, would chop an additional $500bn from the Pentagon over ten years and an equal amount from discretionary domestic spending – with a strongly negative effect on economic growth. If the November election does not produce a catharsis that forces a minimal bipartisan consensus, there will be a renewed recession from which the American political system will find it hard to recover.

Latin America's Shifting Regional Landscape

Latin America has reached a critical juncture. Democratic advances have been matched by economic progress, with poverty and inequality declining, albeit from very high levels, in a number of countries in the region. Moreover, Latin America is making a name for itself in international decision-making bodies such as the G20. Brazil, in particular, has become an important actor on the international stage, while many of its neighbours are fostering closer economic and political ties with China and other Asia-Pacific nations. Yet drug-related violence has continued to spread across the region, and social protest threatens to undermine progress in several South American countries. Still, the dominant feature of the year to mid-2012 was the consolidation of a slow shift in political dynamics across the Western Hemisphere. Old power balances have been upset, both by the rise of new regional players and the decline of established hemispheric bodies.

Although the United States continued to play an important role in the hemisphere, Latin American nations asserted themselves in new ways, supported by growing political and economic clout. The shift in hemispheric relations was notable at the first meeting of the Community of Latin America and Caribbean States (CELAC) in December 2011. Despite being convened in Venezuela, the meeting was not dominated by Venezuelan President Hugo Chávez, but instead served to unite disparate actors from across the region. Twenty years ago it would have been unimaginable that 33 Latin American and Caribbean nations would establish a body that pointedly excluded the United States and Canada. But as many Latin American nations had come to view the United States as less relevant to their needs, the growing political distance between the United States and its Latin American 'backyard' was unsurprising.

The emergence of CELAC was mirrored by the declining influence and relevance of the Organisation of American States (OAS). While the OAS has always had its critics in the region, it suffered several setbacks in the year to mid-2012, particularly in responses to decisions by its human-rights bodies. In September 2011, Venezuela's Supreme Court overruled a decision by the Inter-American Court of Human Rights, which had declared that the disqualification of presidential candidate Leopoldo Lopez violated his political rights. Later, in April 2012, Chávez announced plans for Venezuela to leave the Inter-American Commission on Human Rights, claiming that it was too heavily influenced by the United States. Yet there was little evidence to support the president's reasoning, given that the commission had weighed in on several human-rights issues in the United States in the past year, including the treatment of journalists covering the Occupy Wall Street protests in 2011. Ecuador's courts also challenged statements by the commission, in particular its special rapporteur for freedom of expression. In March 2012, the courts proceeded with a defamation case against three executives and a columnist from national newspaper *El Universo*, going against recommendations by the human-rights body. The paper had published a column critical of President Rafael Correa.

The diminished role of the OAS was symptomatic of broader geopolitical changes both within the region and in Latin America's relations with the rest of the world. In November 2011, shortly before the CELAC meeting, new International Monetary Fund (IMF) President Christine Lagarde made her first visit to the region. It had not been so long ago that Latin American economies were being rescued by international financial institutions, including the IMF. A visit to the region would have been cause for concern, if not panic, by local finance ministers. Instead, Lagarde's tour of Peru, Mexico and Brazil highlighted just how far things had come in a few short decades. The IMF praised the region's macroeconomic stability and discipline, and sought assistance for an ailing Europe.

Hemispheric relations took another turn at the sixth Summit of the Americas, held in Cartagena, Colombia in April 2012. While the official themes were negotiated months in advance, the usual discussions about poverty, inequality, infrastructure and economic integration were overshadowed by three issues that had long divided the Western Hemisphere: drugs, Cuba and the Falkland Islands/Malvinas. While no formal agreement emerged from the meeting, Latin American heads of state agreed that this should be the last summit without Cuba. They argued that isolating the island had not led to democratic reform and that incorporating Cuba into regional forums such as the OAS would be a better mechanism for promoting a democratic transition. Canada and the United States did not, however, share this view. They were likewise separated from Latin Americans on the Falklands Islands/Malvinas issue and did not support Argentina's calls for negotiations with the United Kingdom over sovereignty. The debate on drug policy was the single issue that split countries within the region, with Colombia, Mexico, Costa Rica and Guatemala calling for renewed discussions on the legalisation or decriminalisation of several drugs, including cocaine. Despite these divisions, the fact that drug policy was discussed publicly represented a step forward in the debate. While there was little expectation that any of these issues would be resolved in the short term, the discussions were indicative of the changing nature of hemispheric relations. They highlighted both the growing confidence of Latin American states and the willingness of the United States to engage in discussions with Latin Americans on a more equal footing.

For Colombian President Juan Manuel Santos, the summit represented an opportunity to establish the country's position as a regional political and diplomatic leader. A spat over Cuba gave Santos a chance to illustrate a reorientation of Colombia's foreign policy, distancing him from his predecessor Alvaro Uribe. Santos played an important role in defusing a potentially volatile situation after ALBA (Bolivarian Alliance for the Americas) countries demanded that Cuba be invited to the summit. Cuba's attendance might well have resulted in a US boycott, particularly given that President Barack Obama was facing re-election in November 2012 and did not want to

China: Latin America's banker

In addition to steadily growing trade and investment – China has become the number-one trading partner of Brazil, Peru and Chile, and was in the top five trading partners for at least 16 countries in Latin America in 2011 – Chinese loans constitute another important link to the region. According to a 2012 report by the Inter-American Dialogue, a Washington think tank, Chinese loans to Latin America totalled over $75bn since 2005. China's commitments in 2010, at $37bn, exceed those of the World Bank, Inter-American Development Bank (IDB) and the US Import–Export Bank combined. Yet the terms on Chinese loans differed significantly from those of international financial institutions and Western banks, rarely coming with policy conditions. Such requirements have been controversial in Latin America since the 'structural adjustment plans' of the 1980s and 1990s. Yet the terms on Chinese loans are otherwise less favourable, and often require equipment purchases or oil-sales agreements.

China's loans are also directed towards different purposes. Energy, mining, infrastructure, transportation and housing comprise 87% of Chinese loans, compared to 29% of Inter-American Development Bank and 34% of World Bank loans. Chinese banks also loan to different countries, with Venezuela, Argentina, Brazil and Ecuador accounting for 91% of loan recipients since 2005. Oil sale agreements account for approximately $46bn – or 60% – of loans to the region. These loans generally have requirements set in terms of barrels of oil per day, for which China pays market price.

Despite these concerns, China has become the lender of last resort for several Latin American countries that have difficulty accessing global capital markets. Although the loans are more costly than those from international institutions or Western banks, in some cases they represent the only credit available. One positive development was the March 2012 announcement that the IDB and China's Export-Import Bank will establish a $1bn fund, which will make equity investments in areas highlighted for economic growth, including infrastructure and commodities-based natural resources. However, several concerns have been raised over the region's increasing reliance on Chinese financing. The loans tend to have lower environmental, and health and safety standards than other financers, which may become a problem in the future.

draw unnecessary criticism from the influential Cuban-American community. For Santos it was also an opportunity to demonstrate that Colombia had become an important leader in the region, willing to deviate from US policy where necessary, and committed to good diplomatic relations with its neighbours. Both Ecuadorian President Rafael Correa and Nicaraguan President Daniel Ortega skipped the meeting in a display of solidarity with Cuba. Chávez also missed the summit, going instead to Cuba for further cancer treatment, fuelling speculation on the state of the Venezuelan president's health.

The summit was also an important gauge of US relations with the region. Although Obama remained well-liked across Latin America, the region had been consistently overshadowed by US foreign-policy priorities in the Middle East and elsewhere. To be sure, the United States and Latin America continued to enjoy an important economic relationship. Around 40% of Latin America's exports still went to the United States and the region received 40% of US foreign investment. The United States also remained a valuable source of technology for Latin American countries. And despite tensions surrounding the issues of drugs, immigration and Cuba, there were several opportunities for the US to cooperate with the region, particularly on global issues of climate change, nuclear non-proliferation, energy security, and democratic governance. Both Latin America's success and the United States' domestic woes contributed to the distancing between the region and its northern neighbour. However, Latin Americans looked to have potential new opportunities to deal with the United States in other contexts, including extra-regional groupings such as the Trans-Pacific Partnership (TPP). The TPP sought to establish a trade bloc to facilitate investment, innovation and economic growth across the Asia-Pacific, and was a critical element in the US strategy for engagement with the Pacific.

Mexico: return to the PRI

As Mexico's drug war raged on, the country prepared for July 2012 presidential elections. The elections saw the return of the Institutional Revolutionary Party (PRI), which had governed virtually uninterrupted for seven decades until 2000. Mexico's new president, 45-year-old Enrique Peña Nieto, former governor of the state of Mexico, consistently enjoyed double-digit leads in national polls. Analysts agreed it was Peña Nieto's election to lose, but many Mexicans had not forgotten the PRI's past, in particular the widespread corruption, bribery and electoral fraud that characterised its long authoritarian rule, once described by Peruvian Nobel Laureate Mario Vargas Llosa as the 'perfect dictatorship'. The new president, due to assume office in December, faced several challenges.

In addition to tackling drug-related violence, Peña Nieto needed to revive the economy, which was particularly hard hit by the 2008 financial crisis, given its deep connections to the United States. The US receives 80%

Latin America in the Pacific Century

The twenty-first century's 'pivot' toward the Pacific is not limited to the United States. While China has become an important actor in Latin America, the region's countries are also reaching out to their far-Pacific neighbours; and beyond China to Japan, Korea and Southeast Asian nations. With renewed interest in the broadly defined Pacific region both in the United States and elsewhere, this represents an opportunity to better engage with Asia, boosting economic and political ties both bilaterally and within extra-regional groupings.

Although Mexico, Chile and Peru are long-standing members of APEC, the new Trans-Pacific Partnership (TPP) negotiations have revived interest in the relationship, and offered new economic opportunities for Latin America abroad. Colombia has made Asia-Pacific engagement a priority in its trade agenda, although the moratorium restricting new membership to APEC, and by association the TPP, has kept it on the fringes of negotiations. That said, Colombia is part of the Pacific Alliance (Colombia, Peru, Chile, Mexico) and has been invited to take part in several committees surrounding APEC. These Pacific rim countries agreed to formally launch their bloc in 2012 in Chile. Panama currently participates as an observer but there is a real possibility that other Central American countries could become involved in Pacific negotiations should the TPP present genuine opportunities for extra-regional political and economic cooperation.

Latin America has also expanded bilateral trade links in Asia. China has free-trade agreements with Chile, Peru and Costa Rica. South Korea has agreements with Peru and Chile, and is in negotiations with Colombia. Peru continues to lead the region; its trade with the Philippines, Thailand and South Korea (all APEC members) doubled during 2011. The government signed a free-trade agreement with Japan in May 2011 – it went into effect in March 2012 – and was engaged in negotiations with Thailand. Chile has also been important, signing a free-trade agreement with Vietnam at the APEC meeting in November 2011, and was to begin negotiations with Thailand in 2012. While Peru and Chile have embraced Asian trade, Mexico has continued to see the region as a competitor for the US market, which receives approximately 80% of the country's exports.

Emerging opportunities for Pacific nations in Latin America could precipitate a divide between a Pacific and Atlantic bloc, reducing a sense of regionalism that has been vital to hemispheric cooperation. The Pacific Alliance, for example, could function as a facilitator of intra-regional trade within the Pacific bloc as well as creating opportunities to participate in extra-regional, Asia-Pacific negotiations and alliances. These alliances also give some comfort to those who fear Brazil as the single, dominant power in the region. In the short term, however, regional integration is unlikely to suffer, particularly as the so-called Atlantic bloc includes commodity exporters Venezuela, Brazil and Argentina, which will continue to trade with China with or without access to a Pacific trade bloc.

of Mexican exports and more than $20 billion in remittances is sent every year from across the border. Although Mexico did not look likely to post growth rates as buoyant as some of its neighbours, GDP was expected to grow between 3.5 and 4% in 2012. In addition to economic recovery, the election campaign focused on employment, foreign investment and resource exploitation. Mexico's declining oil production stemmed in part from dwindling resources in major oil fields but also inefficient management of state-owned Pemex. While all parties opposed privatisation during the campaign, the more business-oriented PRI and PAN (National Action Party) argued for greater private competition, as well as increasing exploration and the development of alternative energy sources.

On crime, candidates promoted police and judicial reform, as well as longer prison sentences, and greater support for victims of violent crime. However, polls indicated that security was no longer the most important concern for many Mexicans. A poll conducted in February 2012 found that 33% of Mexicans cited security at their number-one concern, down from 48% in May 2011. The candidates' decisions to focus on economic policy rather than security may also have been a response to the perceived policy failures of President Felipe Calderón. Many voters were disappointed with Calderón's efforts to reduce violence, combat corruption and increase employment opportunities. Still, he looked likely to end his term with approval ratings in the high 50s. (Mexican presidents each serve a single six-year term).

Meanwhile, Mexico's drug wars continued to claim thousands of lives. In 2011 alone more than 12,000 drug-related homicides were reported, continuing a rising trend that saw at least 50,000 people killed and 5,000 missing since Calderón declared the drug war in December 2006. Mexico's position had long made it an important transit route for contraband, including drugs and arms. The increasingly wealthy and powerful Mexican cartels had consolidated their routes through turf wars and shaky alliances with rivals. While there were several big players involved – the Sinaloa Cartel, the Beltrán Leyva Cartel, Los Zetas, La Familia, Gulf Cartel and Juárez Cartel (and to a lesser extent the Tijuana Cartel) – some security experts argued that the drug trade had become dominated by two groups: Los Zetas, which controlled much of eastern Mexico, and the Sinaloa Cartel, which controlled much of the west.

A seemingly endless stream of murders continued to dominate the front pages in Mexico. In Monterrey in August 2011, a casino fire killed 52 people. Reports implicated the mayor's brother in the incident, which was believed to be the work of Los Zetas. The attack was reportedly provoked by the casino owner's refusal to pay a weekly extortion fee of approximately

$11,000. In September, 35 bodies were left on a busy road during rush hour in Veracruz. Gunmen who dumped the bodies were suspected members of a new, smaller group called 'New Generation', linked to Sinaloa Cartel leader Joaquín 'Chapo' Guzman. The attack was reportedly part of an ongoing attempt to wrest control of Veracruz (Mexico's largest and oldest port) from Los Zetas. In March 2012, 12 police in the state of Guerrero were ambushed and killed while searching for the bodies of ten recent murder victims. The incident came days after one of the bloodiest weeks in the drug wars, during which 421 people were killed.

Although the majority of victims were linked to turf wars, drug trafficking groups continued to target activists and journalists across Mexico. In December 2011, peace activist Trinidad de la Cruz was murdered in the central state of Michoacán, and two journalists were killed in Mexico City.

The Drugs Debate

Drug policy has landed firmly on the regional agenda. Four sitting presidents in Latin America have joined the voices of ex-presidents Ernesto Zedillo (Mexico), Fernando Henrique Cardoso (Brazil) and César Gaviria (Colombia), among many influential figures, in calling for a serious discussion of drug legalisation in the Americas. The latest to support the debate is Costa Rican President Laura Chinchilla, who joins Mexican President Felipe Calderón, Colombian President Juan Manuel Santos, and Guatemalan President Otto Peréz Molina. Interestingly, Calderón, Santos and Molina hail from the centre-right, which has traditionally tended to oppose drug-policy reform, although the debate has had little traction on either side of the political spectrum in Latin America until recently. Molina raised the issue at a March 2012 meeting of Central American leaders after sending his vice-president, Roxana Baldetti, on a regional tour to promote the government's position. In a sign of how much things have changed, the United States agreed to have a discussion on the issue at the Summit of the Americas in April 2012.

While drug policy is not a new debate in the Americas, these latest efforts are historically significant. Firstly, former and current leaders in Latin America have come together to form a critical mass to support renewed debate on drug policy and more progressive policy responses to drug-related violence. Secondly, the willingness of the United States to discuss drug policy in a public space such as the summit is an important step forward. Although the United States has explicitly stated that it has no intention of altering its drug policy, it has created the space for a multifaceted policy discussion. The debate is far more complex than simply over legalisation or decriminalisation, encompassing a broad set of alternatives and mechanisms that differ between producer, transit and consumption countries. There are already some experiences in the region that can inform the discussion, including the decriminalisation of marijuana for personal consumption in Argentina, Brazil, Colombia, Ecuador, Mexico and Uruguay.

For more on this topic see Nigel Inkster and Virginia Comolli, *Drugs, Insecurity and Failed States: The Problems of Prohibition*, Adelphi 428 (Abingdon: Routledge for the IISS, 2012).

In April, three more journalists were murdered in Veracruz. While Veracruz remained the most dangerous state for journalists, the murders in Mexico City were particularly significant as the Federal District had not previously been a locus of drug violence.

There were reports of the emergence of smaller groups involved in drug trafficking and other illicit activities. This fragmentation resulted in an explosion of extortion across the country, as newer groups sought sources of revenue. While bribery had long been part of daily life, experts estimated that extortion attempts had come to affect up to 60% of businesses countrywide. Schoolteachers, food-stall owners and even priests reported extortion attempts. While the authorities said 24,000 complaints had been received since December 2006, experts put the real figure much higher, with the Citizen's Institute for the Study of Insecurity estimating that two-thirds of cases had gone unreported. With most cases involving threats against a person or their family, such incidents added to the fear and insecurity felt by ordinary Mexicans otherwise removed from the drug war.

The Mexican government made some gains in the fight against the cartels. In February 2012 the reputed enforcer for the Sinaloa Cartel, José Antonio Torres Marrufo, was arrested. The cartel, effectively a coalition of drug 'capos', was headed by Joaquín 'Chapo' Guzman. In early 2012 rumours surfaced that the Mexican government was close to capturing El Chapo. Other important arrests included that of Saúl Solis Solis, allegedly an important player in the Knights Templar gang and implicated in a 2007 attack that killed five soldiers. In June 2012, authorities announced they had arrested José de Jesus 'El Chango' Mendez, leader of La Familia, a cartel based in Michoacán.

The Mexican government also targeted money laundering in an effort to cripple the drug traffickers' finances. The government estimated that up to $50 billion is laundered every year, an amount equivalent to approximately 3% of Mexico's legitimate economy and more than it spends on social programmes or receives from oil exports. In 2011, the government passed the Federal Law for the Prevention and Identification of Operations with Illicit Resources and Terrorism Financing, which raised minimum sentences and fines for money-laundering activities. Similar legislation had been effective in reducing laundering in Colombia and Italy. Further legislation under consideration in the Chamber of Deputies would require reporting of large, suspicious transactions. These 'know your customer' laws had previously applied only to banks but would now require investigation of real-estate agencies, car dealerships, bookmakers, art galleries, notaries and, potentially, religious institutions. The laws would also require disclosure of large cash purchases of vehicles, artworks and real estate. The government brought in US experts to train tax inspectors, and selected former Washington-based diplomat José Alberto Balbuena to lead the anti-money-laundering process in the Ministry of Finance.

In spite of these efforts, US–Mexico relations had a turbulent year. As details of the *Operation Fast and Furious* weapons scandal emerged, tensions rose between US and Mexican authorities. The gun surveillance programme, originally established in 2009 by the US Department of Justice and implemented by the Bureau for Alcohol, Tobacco, Firearms and Explosives, hoped to identify drug-trafficking organisations by tracking guns destined for Mexico. The 'gunwalking' scheme allowed into Mexico hundreds of assault rifles and other weapons that were then implicated in 150 murders of Mexican nationals, including the state prosecutor of Chihuahua, Mario González, as well as two US agents. Calderón criticised US actions, particularly in allowing the operation to continue even after the weapons began to turn up at grisly crime scenes south of the border. The US congressional investigation into the failed operation heightened tensions with Mexico, particularly as Mexican Attorney General Marisela Morales claimed that the Mexican authorities were not consulted about the operation, contradicting a statement by US Attorney General Eric Holder that the US government had cooperated with the Mexicans on the initiative.

The United States and Mexico also remained at odds over US immigration policy. In April 2012, a report by the Pew Hispanic Center reported that net migration from Mexico had reached zero, and possibly gone into reverse. At the same time, the US Supreme Court was determining the constitutionality of strict immigration laws in the state of Arizona. Calderón had criticised the Arizona laws for criminalising immigration and discriminating against Mexicans regardless of their immigration status. The drop in immigration also pointed to improvements in Mexico's economy. Sluggish recovery from the financial crisis in the United States, by contrast, saw a drop in the agricultural and construction jobs often filled by migrants. Nevertheless, Mexicans still comprised approximately 30% of foreign-born residents in the United States, and it was estimated around 50% were unauthorised.

Central America: a broader security challenge

For Central America's 'northern triangle' – Honduras, Guatemala and El Salvador – 2011 confirmed the sub-region's status as the most violent place in the Americas. Homicide rates reached 82 per 100,000 in Honduras, 41 in

Guatemala, and 66 in El Salvador. (The United States, by comparison, had a homicide rate of 5.2 per 100,000.) Despite the small size of these three countries, there were an estimated 17,000 homicides in 2011 alone, many of them attributable to drug trafficking and organised crime. The countries lacked the financial resources and capable state institutions to deal with either problem effectively. Also worrying was that drug-related violence was spreading to previously 'safe' areas such as Costa Rica and Panama, where homicides have increased in the past five years by 63% and 140% respectively.

Guatemala's presidential elections came at a critical moment as the country suffered from escalating violence and increasingly influential criminal organisations. It was unsurprising in this context that former general Otto Pérez Molina won the second round of presidential elections in November 2011. Many observers feared his promise to return to hard-line, 'iron fist' policies that had been criticised for having no discernible effect on levels of violence. Yet the new president drew praise from across the political spectrum, in particular for his three policy 'pacts' he announced after taking office – the fiscal pact, pact for peace security and justice, and zero hunger pact – each of which was aimed at advancing the social agenda. The fiscal pact raised taxes on the upper middle classes and the wealthy, and sought to both lower national debt and raise much-needed resources for security and development.

Honduras continued to struggle to address violence with its fragile political institutions and weak economy. In June 2011, the government announced a security tax that would generate up to $80m per year over the next five years. However, in September legislators reversed some elements of the law under pressure from the private sector. The Honduran Congress' decision in November 2011 to use the army to fight drug-trafficking organisations was also of concern. Critics noted that similar efforts in Mexico resulted in more deaths from drug-related violence. They argued that soldiers were ineffective in restoring public order and controlling crime. Moreover, in the Mexican case, allegations of human-rights abuses at the hands of the military sky-rocketed after they were brought into the drug war. While military intervention might be controversial, the police force was beset by problems of its own. It had gained a reputation for corruption, with entire units reportedly working with known affiliates of criminal organisations. These problems were difficult to eradicate as many of the most corrupt officials were supervisors and commissioners. Those who targeted these problems also put themselves at risk: Gustavo Alfredo Landaverde, former deputy drug tsar and a source for the US-based newspaper *Miami Herald*, was murdered in December 2011.

Honduras tragically made international headlines when over 350 inmates were killed in a prison fire in February 2012. Reports that many prisoners were left trapped in their cells and others shot as they tried to flee underscored the severe structural challenges facing the country's public institutions. In a further testament to the inefficient and ineffective justice system in Honduras, over half of those who died were on pre-trial detention, many having spent up to three years in prison while awaiting court dates. Overcrowding and inhospitable conditions have been a common problem across Latin America's prisons but the worst affected countries are those that have responded to rising violence by imposing tougher sentences. The fact that many of these security problems, particularly gang violence, follow criminals into the prisons has been another contributing factor. Loose security has also meant that weapons are freely available in prisons.

In March 2011, Obama's visit to El Salvador highlighted the country's success. In spite of security challenges, Salvadoran leaders had recently transferred power to the political party of the former guerrilla group Farabundo Martí National Liberation Front (FMLN), an important step in the consolidation of democracy two decades after the end of the civil war. A year later, however, the government of FMLN President Mauricio Funes was under pressure. In January 2012, opposition and civil society groups criticised Funes's decision to appoint former military officials to civilian political roles, including former General Francisco Salinas Rivera as head of police and retired General David Munguía Payés as minister for justice and public security. Critics claimed that the appointments were unconstitutional and undermined the spirit of the 1992 Peace Accords. At mid-2012, a case brought by civil-society groups was being considered by the Supreme Court. Payés's predecessor, Manuel Melgar, left suddenly in November 2011, sparking suspicion that the United States had influenced his resignation, or even made it a condition of assistance through the 'Partnership for Growth' initiative. Melgar had been implicated in a 1985 attack during the civil war that killed four US marines. The appointments could have been signs of a policy shift towards more repressive measures in tackling violence and insecurity in El Salvador.

Despite concerns about democratic governance in the executive branch, the results of El Salvador's legislative elections in March 2012 were a positive indicator of the country's democratic systems. The right-wing opposition Nationalist Republican Alliance (ARENA) capitalised on an anti-crime platform to win 33 seats in the 84-seat National Assembly; FMLN won 31 seats. The GANA Party (which had been formed by 12 deputies who defected from ARENA in 2009) won 11 seats in its first election, making it the real success story and a legitimate third force in Salvadoran politics. As a result, the FMLN needed to build consensus with ARENA or minority parties in order to pass legislative reforms.

Possibly the most unexpected event in the region in the year to mid-2012 was a truce negotiated between MS-18 and Mara Salvatrucha, the two most important transnational gangs in Central America. The rival gangs had been responsible for much of the violence in El Salvador in the last two decades and the truce offered an historic opportunity for the government to reduce insecurity. When El Salvador's left-leaning online newspaper *El Faro* first reported the government's role in negotiating a truce on 11 March 2012, Funes denied any involvement. Gang leaders then stated that Monsignor Fabio Colindres, head chaplain of the El Salvador armed forces and police, had facilitated the process. Colindres did not deny his role but insisted that he was not negotiating on behalf of the government but in his capacity as a representative of the Catholic Church. Former congressman Raul Mijango was also involved in the negotiations. Although Funes denied any quid pro quo for the truce, 30 Mara prisoners were transferred from maximum-security to low-security prisons, raising suspicion among Funes's critics. In May 2012, the Maras made a second show of good faith, announcing that the truce would extend to schools, which they declared formal 'peace zones'.

In the short term, a drop in the average daily homicide rate from 14 to 5 was a positive outcome; on 14 April El Salvador recorded its first day without homicides in nearly three years. However, it was too soon to tell whether the truce would last. There were concerns that the government might have made other, as yet unknown concessions to the gangs to secure the truce, and that gangs might be emboldened to seek further concessions. The government, while recognising the early results, remained cautious about the truce's long-term success. The agreement did not preclude extortion, which continued unabated after the truce was announced.

Nicaragua, while largely spared the crippling violence that beset its northern neighbours, did not escape a series of governance problems in 2011. Daniel Ortega won the November 2011 election easily, with 62% of the vote, although not without allegations of irregularities and voter fraud. His candidacy was disputed as he violated a constitutional ban on re-election, which was later overruled by the country's Supreme Court. Ortega's increasingly authoritarian actions were not limited to electoral politics. By mid-2012 he had virtual control over all three branches of government, while new laws also gave him the power to censor the media. He had a supermajority in the legislature and also controlled the Supreme Court. However, his continued popularity was unsurprising. His macroeconomic policies had maintained stability amidst the global financial crisis, and both foreign and domestic investment had increased. Venezuelan aid, meanwhile, allowed Ortega to finance social programmes that benefited the poor and tackled rural poverty by granting land titles to thousands of farmers and poor urban families.

As drug-related violence spread across Central America, leaders recognised the need for a regional response, primarily through the Central American Integration System (SICA). At a SICA meeting in June 2011, the World Bank and Inter-American Development Bank pledged $1.5bn over the next five years for regional security programmes, though it was unclear how much of this figure represented unfinished loans and projects. The other significant outcome of the meeting was a list of 22 projects covering four areas – law enforcement, crime prevention, rehabilitation and prisons, and institutional strengthening – that would shape the region's response to organised crime and violence in the coming years. Despite pledges of $300m from the United States, and other international support, the funding to tackle violence in Mexico and Central America was less than the $8bn that had been spent to improve security in Colombia over the last decade. However, experts questioned whether SICA had the capacity to carry out a regional security agenda, and whether Central American states were capable of absorbing such an amount of international funding and of carrying out the agreed projects.

Peru: in Lula's footsteps?

On 5 June 2011, Peruvians elected a new president, former Lieutenant-Colonel Ollanta Humala, on a platform of moderate reform that promised strong economic growth with 'social inclusion'. His social policy agenda sought a more equitable distribution of the country's wealth that was closely modelled on Brazil's experience. Indeed, several of former Brazilian President Luiz Inácio Lula da Silva's advisers served on Humala's campaign. Yet given Peru's significantly smaller economy and population, social conflicts and political instability, there were real questions about whether Peru could achieve economic growth while improving the lives of its poorest citizens. Humala's first step towards social policy reform was the establishment of a new Ministry of Development and Social Inclusion, headed by respected Peruvian economist Carolina Trivelli. This was a small but important move which, if successful, would distinguish the president from his predecessors and advance his social-policy objectives.

The Humala administration pursued a strategy of 'mining-based social development', aiming to redistribute natural resource wealth. In 2011, Peru passed legislation the government believed would raise mining revenues from around $650m to $1bn annually. The new law established a sliding scale to calculate royalties as a proportion of net profits or operating income, depending on whether the company had a tax stability agreement with the Peruvian government. Many of the larger companies – including BHP Billiton, Xstrata and Barrick Gold, which did have stability agreements – were to be subject to a special mining levy of up to 13.12% of operating income. Both royalties were in addition to a 30% corporate income tax. The revenue would be distributed to local and regional authorities, with funds earmarked for social programmes and education.

However, mining was also at the root of 100 disputes across the country that threatened to undermine the president's development goals. While many such conflicts were inherited from previous administrations, the underlying distrust among government, the private sector and civil society remained a significant hurdle to building support for mining projects. A standoff over the $4.8bn Conga copper and gold mine was one example. It halted mining activities in Cajamarca from late 2011 and forced the government to commission an environmental-impact assessment by international experts. The report recommended that the government undertake 'substantial improvements' to several technical aspects of the mine, potentially raising costs for majority owner Newmont Mining Corporation. Local organisations sought recourse in the Inter-American Commission on Human Rights, arguing that the mine would empty several alpine lakes, causing immense environmental damage and depleting water sources. The country's Constitutional Tribunal also considered a decision by the president of Cajamarca province, in which the mine was located, to declare the project 'unviable'. The court ruled against the departmental authorities, stating that it was beyond their powers to halt mining projects.

The Conga dispute coincided with disquiet over the government's efforts to eliminate illegal mining. Clashes between police and protesters in the southeastern Amazon region of Madre de Dios in March left three dead and more than three dozen injured. In Madre de Dios alone there were an estimated 50,000 illegal miners producing approximately 18 tonnes of gold per year. For one of the poorest regions in Peru, this $800m per year business was particularly lucrative. The Humala administration was attempting to incorporate illegal miners into the formal economy to ensure that mining was regulated and in compliance with environmental and safety standards, as well as to tax profits. According to Peru's national tax agency, illegal mining in Madre de Dios represented an estimated $186m in lost taxes every year.

The government was able to reach agreement with the illegal miners in Madre de Dios by granting temporary entitlements as part of a long-term effort to formalise mining activities in the region. If the agreement were to prove successful, it would set an important precedent for dealing with other illegal mining operations. However, Humala's decision not to side with protesters over the Conga mine caused some of his previously ardent supporters to lose faith in his leadership. It remained to be seen whether a new 'prior consultation' law, based on the International Labour Organisation's Convention 169 on Indigenous and Tribal Peoples, would help defuse the tensions.

In addition to social unrest, Peruvian authorities had to contend with the country's location at the centre of the region's drug trade. In 2011, the US Drug Enforcement Administration announced that Peru had overtaken Colombia to become the world's largest cocaine producer. Humala responded with a far tougher line on coca, including measures to step up the coca-eradication programme. His four-year plan aimed to remove 14,000ha in 2012, increasing over the next four years to 30,000 in 2016. The plan took a three-pronged approach, incorporating alternative development, interdiction and punishment, as well as prevention of drug use and rehabilitation of drug users. The strategy was a turnaround for Humala, who spoke against eradication during his election campaign. His replacement of progressive Ricardo Soberon by Carmen Masias as head of the national drug agency sent a further signal that Humala had no immediate plans to reform Peruvian drug policy.

February 2012 saw the end of an important chapter in Peru's history with the capture of Florindo Flores, alias 'Comrade Artemio', the last remaining leader of the Shining Path movement that terrorised the country in the 1980s and early 1990s. In December 2011, Flores admitted that Shining Path had been defeated. While the group was a shadow of its former self, the capture of the last member of the central committee was symbolic. As the group was based in remote jungle areas of the country where cocaine was produced, it was also an important step in tackling the country's drug trade. Shortly after Comrade Artemio was captured, his replacement, Walter Díaz Vega, was also taken. But Shining Path remained active, though on a smaller scale, with an estimated 300–500 members. In early April, they kidnapped 40 oil workers and demanded $10m for their release, prompting Humala to declare a state of emergency. Although the hostages were later released unharmed, the group declared that its military objectives had been achieved after six Peruvian soldiers were killed and a US helicopter shot down. The Peruvian government negotiated the workers' release without paying a ransom.

Humala struggled with his cabinet. His first prime minister, Salomón Lerner, resigned in December, citing the Conga mining dispute as the catalyst although experts suggested his difficulty in uniting a disparate cabinet undermined executive decision-making. This followed corruption allegations against Humala's second vice-president, Omar Chehade, who then stepped aside in November. Humala replaced the prime minister with former Lieutenant-Colonel and Interior Minister Oscar Valdés, taking advantage of the opportunity to switch 11 of the 19 ministers in his cabinet. The new cabinet marked a significant move towards the centre, with leftists replaced by technocrats. These decisions also reflected trends in other policy areas, indicating that far from pursuing a radical agenda, Humala was more closely following the approach of his predecessor Alan García, and veering minimally from the economic status quo.

Despite some setbacks, the president continued to enjoy the support of the Peruvian people, although by April his approval rating had declined to around 56%. Still, this was high by Peruvian standards; his predecessor Alan García (2006–11) frequently had approval rates below 30%, while Alejandro Toledo (2001–06) dropped to single digits. Humala successfully allayed the fears of the private sector and centre-right voters by pursuing an agenda of economic continuity with moderate change. Some supporters questioned whether, in seeking to placate the majority, he would fall short of implementing some of the most-needed reforms, particularly rooting out corruption in some of Peru's institutions. For Humala to be remembered as a truly transformative president he would need to make greater progress on social reforms and translate these into quantitative reductions in poverty and inequality.

One thing was certain: Humala's cabinet shake-up, new drug policy and approach to the mining sector indicated that he was going to be a far more pro-business, pro-investment president than many on the left had hoped. But it remained to be seen whether he could translate economic gains into social progress.

Colombia: prospects for peace?

At mid-2012, Colombia's President Juan Manuel Santos appeared poised to end his second year on a high. He had enacted several key reforms, maintained economic growth at around 6%, weakened the Revolutionary Armed

Forces of Colombia (FARC), improved relations with neighbouring Ecuador and Venezuela, and established the nation as a regional diplomatic leader. And yet, by May 2012, Santos's popularity had dropped to 64% from 76% in mid-2011. The drop could be attributed to several factors, including his handling of widespread floods, mudslides and destruction of property caused by heavy rains in 2011. Close to 300 people died, while tens of thousands were left homeless, and there were estimates the damage bill could reach $5bn. Security challenges, and the perception that insecurity was rising, as well as persistent unemployment and a lack of progress on social policy, further contributed to the president's declining popularity.

Colombia's trade ministry made significant advances. After years of delays and negotiations over labour and human rights, the US Congress finally ratified the bilateral free-trade agreement with Colombia in October 2011. Meanwhile, Colombia signed a free-trade agreement with Canada in August, and progressed in negotiations with Turkey, Panama and South Korea. In addition to bilateral trade agreements, Colombia continued to channel much effort into gaining entry to the Asia-Pacific Economic Cooperation (APEC) grouping and the Trans-Pacific Partnership. While APEC remained closed by a moratorium on new membership, Colombia was represented on several APEC committees, including the Investment Group and the Sub-committee on Customs Procedures.

While much of the country had benefited from a reduction in insecurity under former President Alvaro Uribe, there was a perception that violence was once again on the rise. This was reflected in the resignation of Defense Minister Rodrigo Rivera in August 2011 at a time when increased attacks by FARC on infrastructure sparked concern over foreign investment in Colombia's growing oil industry. He was quickly replaced by Juan Carlos Pinzón, although the bombing of oil pipelines, extortion and kidnapping of oil workers continued unabated. Between January and February 2012, national oil company Ecopetrol reported 13 separate attacks on Colombia's main pipeline. In other parts of the country there were reports that FARC was extorting $10 per barrel of oil. Although Santos put these attacks down to the 'desperation' of a weakened FARC, they may instead have been a herald of new tactics and targets pursued by the guerrilla group. In May 2012, a bomb in Bogotá killed two and injured dozens, including former Interior Minister Fernando Londoño. For many Bogotanos, this brought back memories of the city's violent past.

The changing nature of violence challenged the outdated assumptions and strategies of the Colombian government. 2011–12 saw new tactics emerging not only from FARC but also among increasingly violent and agile *bandas criminales* (criminal groups, or BACRIM) – paramilitary gangs that now control much of the country's drug trafficking operations. Colombia's other leftist guerrilla group, the National Liberation Army (ELN), also posed a renewed threat, amid reports it had rebuilt its ranks to around 2,500 members. In contrast to historically violent clashes between guerrilla groups and the paramilitaries, FARC and the ELN developed a non-combative relationship with the BACRIM. Some analysts compared the relations to those between 'mafia' groups in Europe, in which territory and interests are negotiated, and violence is unnecessary unless there is a departure from the agreed terms. The BACRIM were not politically motivated and were explicitly concerned with control of the drug trade, illicit gold mining and kidnapping. The motivation behind a more business-oriented relationship may stem from the fact that guerrilla groups control some 70% of coca cultivation. The BACRIM, with an estimated 6,000 members, demonstrated their capabilities with a shut-down of businesses, trade and public transport by the one of the most powerful groups, Los Urabeños, in January 2012 that affected six departments in the north and east of the country.

The rise of the BACRIM could be seen as an unintended consequence of the Uribe government's success. As successive Colombian administrations eliminated large-scale cartels, they were replaced by 'micro-trafficking', in which the trade was spread across numerous smaller groups. These groups were also involved in Colombia's domestic drug consumption, including cocaine, which had become a growing concern particularly in secondary cities such as Ibagué, Baranquilla and Barancabermeja. The demobilisation of over 32,000 paramilitaries in 2008 also contributed to the rise in new illegal armed groups as they sought to fill the vacuum left by the older forces. Some paramilitaries re-joined these groups after demobilising.

Colombian drug trafficking continued to affect other countries, with Mexican and Central American organisations helping to transport cocaine through Venezuela and up to Honduras. Operations carried out in Venezuela resulted in the capture of several leading FARC and paramilitary figures, including a key paramilitary leader, Héctor Germán Buitrago, alias 'Martin Llanos', arrested in February 2012. He was said to be the leader of a paramilitary group that refused to demobilise. Buitrago's father had been arrested in Colombia in 2010, while the Venezuelans had arrested his brother. It was believed that Martin Llanos played an important role in violence in the Llanos Orientales region of Colombia, with, according to Santos, potentially thousands of victims.

Santos's greatest achievement in 2011 was the weakening of FARC, particularly through the intelligence operation that resulted in the death of leader Alfonso Cano in November. Then, on 2 April 2012, FARC released its final ten uniformed hostages, many of whom had been held for over a decade. The release was coordinated with the assistance of the Red Cross, the Brazilian government, and several local peace activists, including the former senator and negotiator, Piedad Córdoba. FARC stated that it would no longer engage in kidnapping for ransom. While these were all important steps forward for Colombia, and many observers looked for a move towards peace negotiations, Santos made clear that FARC's gestures were insufficient.

One important obstacle to negotiations was the large number of civilian hostages still in FARC's hands. According to local non-government organisation Fundación País Libre, the figure could be as high as 400. While the real figure is likely to be lower – some hostages will have died in captivity, and there are reports that others have been re-kidnapped by other groups to demand a higher ransom – there are still hundreds of hostages unaccounted for. The Colombian public has little sympathy for FARC, with tens of thousands of Colombians protesting in December 2011 after the guerrillas killed four hostages during a rescue attempt by the Colombian military. Public sympathy was further eroded by the attack on the former interior minister in May.

While Santos made no secret of his desire for peace, and stated that he was prepared to speak with FARC directly, he also made clear that FARC must end all violent acts and release all hostages. The bombing in Bogotá tarnished these early hopes for peace. There remained the possibility that back-channel communications could allow for preliminary discussions before these conditions were met. However, Santos looked likely to take a more cautious route, mindful of failed negotiations in the past. It appeared unlikely that Santos would make any concessions to FARC in his first term as president, and it was questionable whether FARC was ready to make any concessions toward the government. However, peace negotiations had the potential to be a powerful basis for a 2014 re-election campaign. As a second-term president, Santos might also expect to have more room to make concessions that would allow peace talks to take place.

Venezuela: *Chavismo* without Chávez?

In mid-2011, much of the analysis of Venezuela focused on the October 2012 presidential elections, with experts predicting that they represented the best chance for the opposition to regain power in the 13 years since Hugo Chávez had become president. All this changed when Chávez announced in June 2011 that he was undergoing cancer treatment in Cuba. Speculation quickly turned to questions about whether Chávez would even be able to run in the elections and, if not, whether his United Socialist Party of Venezuela (PSUV) would survive without him. More importantly, could *Chavismo* survive without Chávez? There were questions as to how his illness would affect his election chances and whether it would lead to greater instability in his own party, as occurred in the immediate aftermath of the surgery in 2011.

Venezuela had become economically weak and politically polarised. Public institutions were fragile and Chávez consistently undermined democratic principles in his efforts to maintain power. The Inter-American Commission on Human Rights expressed concern with the situation in Venezuela, recommending in a report released in April 2012 that the government 'refrain from taking reprisals or using the punitive power of the State to intimidate or sanction individuals based on their political opinions'. These concerns extended to the country's lack of judicial independence and restrictions on freedom of expression. Chávez had fined or closed media outlets, including weekly magazines and television stations, and used the judicial system to punish his critics. Several opposition political figures and non-governmental organisations remained under criminal investigation for criticism of the government or receiving foreign aid, which could have amounted to treason under 2010 Supreme Court rulings.

The opposition, meanwhile, capitalised on the turmoil within the ruling party to rebuild its strength and prepare for primary elections in February 2012. Henrique Capriles, the 39-year-old governor of Miranda state, easily won the primary elections to become the candidate to oppose Chávez in October. Capriles's victory owed much to his strong record as governor, president of the Chamber of Deputies, and mayor of Baruta (a municipality of Caracas), as well as his ability to learn from the opposition's mistakes. Throughout his campaign, Capriles appealed to voters rather than seeking directly to confront Chávez. Capriles represented a new model of opposition for Venezuela and a departure from the traditional leaders of the past. He ran a moderate campaign, acknowledging the important progress made under Chávez in social policy. Critically, Capriles vowed not only to maintain Chávez' 'missions' – social programmes that benefit the poorest Venezuelans – but to expand them. It remained important for the opposition Unified Democratic Platform (MUD) to present a unified front in the lead up to the elections if they were to build on the 3m votes cast in the primaries.

This high figure was particularly promising given the history of government retaliation against opposition supporters.

However, the Venezuelan opposition faced a series of obstacles, not least of which was Chávez' well-funded political machine. Chávez controlled the majority of media outlets in the country and had access to enormous resources to fund the social initiatives that benefited his staunchest supporters. His long-standing popularity and the emotional connection many Venezuelans felt with the president would also be difficult to overcome in the few months before they were scheduled to go to the polls. Compassion for Chávez during his battle with cancer also looked likely to boost his chances. Many Venezuelans still saw Capriles as representing the traditional, elitist vote, which many also tied to a pro-US stance. These factors contributed to Chávez's 17-point lead in opinion polls, which he maintained in spite of his health and absence from the campaign.

Instead, both parties looked to compete for the estimated 30% of voters who were unaligned. The so-called 'ni ni' (neither nor) supported neither Chávez nor the opposition, and were distrustful of politicians. Polls indicated that economic factors were less important determinants for these voters but that they were instead defined by an interest in moving away from populist politics, and were not convinced that Chávez or the opposition were able to respond to Venezuela's problems. Capriles's moderate programme would need to respond to the concerns of these independents if he was to succeed against the incumbent Chávez.

Yet the real question for Venezuelan observers was what would happen to the country without Chávez. The president had resisted grooming a successor, although Venezuelan media outlets speculated that Foreign Affairs Minister Nicolas Maduro, Vice President Elías Jaua, head of the National Assembly Diosdado Cabello, or even Chávez's brother, Adán, could be in line for the leadership. Chávez appointed an eight-member 'council of state', the role of which remained murky but could include appointing his successor. That Chávez acknowledged his own mortality was significant, but he was unlikely to give up power anytime soon. And it appeared unlikely that any of the potential candidates could win an election in the event of Chávez's death. Instead, the uncertainty and jockeying served to increase tension within the PSUV. Internationally, the loss of Chávez would be a huge blow to Cuba, which remained heavily dependent on Venezuelan aid. There were estimates the country received up to $5bn annually, helping to offset the US embargo.

Although markets responded positively to boosts in support for the opposition, an election win would not necessarily mean a return to political stability, a well-functioning public and private sector, or a revival of the country's economy. The last 13 years had seen a fractured opposition struggle to put together a campaign that stood any chance of challenging Chávez and, even if the various actors were able to put on a united front for the 2012 elections, they could splinter again after a victory. There was also much work to be done to repair public institutions and to rebuild relations with the private sector. The state-owned oil company Petróleos de Venezuela (PDVSA) exemplified the opposition's challenges. Continued mismanagement saw its output reduced to the point where many wondered whether it could honour its contracts as well as continue to run Petrocaribe, its subsidised fuel-loans scheme in the Caribbean and Central America. There were also fears that the country's armed forces could intervene in an attempt to manage a difficult transition. The appointment of General Henry Rangel Silva as defence minister in January 2012 raised concerns among the opposition. He had said in 2010 that the military would not accept an opposition victory. Regardless of the outcome of the presidential election, political instability and uncertainty looked likely to remain the norm, at least in the short term.

Chávez's often antagonistic relationship with the United States was tested further in January 2012 when the Venezuelan president hosted Iranian President Mahmoud Ahmadinejad. Ahmadinejad's sixth trip to the region took him to the left-leaning countries Ecuador, Cuba, Nicaragua and Venezuela. The United States, and the Republican Party in particular, had been concerned for some time about Latin America's links with Iran, yet the trip received relatively little attention in Washington. Venezuela was Iran's closest ally in the hemisphere but as its influence in the region had declined its utility to Iran was more limited.

Argentina: Fernández's growing unpredictability

President Cristina Fernández de Kirchner won a landslide re-election in October 2011, securing 54% of the vote, 34 points ahead of her nearest challenger, Hermes Binner. Argentina had enjoyed strong economic growth and an expansion of social policies assisting the lower and middle-classes, which boosted the president's popularity. A weak opposition at the national level also helped. Yet despite the president's popularity at home, Argentina's troubles were far from over. Persistently high inflation, capital flight and declining international sympathy for unpaid debts isolated Argentina from the rest of the continent. The president's erratic policy decisions, such as the nationalisation of oil company YPF (Yacimientos Petrolíferos Fiscales), looked set to deepen that divide.

In February 2012, Argentina was formally scolded by the IMF for inaccurate reporting of the consumer price index for Greater Buenos Aires and GDP figures. While the government claimed inflation was hovering around 9.5%, private economists contended that the real figure was over 20%, making it the second highest in the region after Venezuela. Private firms calculating inflation figures different from the government's were slapped with large fines, forced to make public apologies, and even found themselves the subject of criminal investigations. The efforts of opposition congressmen to raise the issue in public took some of the pressure off private financial consultants, but the government was unlikely to adjust its figures in the short term.

There were several internal and external implications of the underestimation of inflation figures. Internally, it caused tension between the government and unionists, who sought wage increases in line with real inflation rather than the official single-digit figures. International creditors who accepted bonds as part of a debt-restructuring deal in the wake of Argentina's collapse in 2001 found their bonds were now worth a mere 30% of their original value plus interest. Capital flight was also a problem, with an estimated $200bn held abroad. Fernández attempted to crack down on the problem, passing new laws in December 2011 that increased border security to stop the transport of large quantities of US dollars to Uruguay and elsewhere.

International creditors were not just unhappy about inaccurate data but were losing their patience with Argentina's inability to repay loans as its economy recovered – the country posted 9% GDP growth in 2011. Obama was under pressure from Congress and the Treasury Department to be tough on Argentina, which led to a decision to vote against new loans from the World Bank and Inter-American Development Bank. The United States called on Argentina to first fulfil its debt obligations and resolve disputes with international bond holders. Argentina failed to agree on rescheduling repayment of a $9bn debt to the Paris Club of official creditors. Reaching such agreements was a condition for Argentina to regain access to international credit markets.

The IMF rebuke was followed in April by criticism at the World Trade Organisation from the United States, EU, Japan and ten other countries over trade restrictions. On 1 February, Fernández announced a new approval system that critics argued amounted to a near-blanket import restriction. Argentina also put pressure on importers to balance trade; there were reports that BMW, the German carmaker, was matching car imports with rice exports, while other carmakers were exporting olive oil, soy meal and wine.

Spain was infuriated by Fernández's decision in April 2012 to nationalise YPF, the country's leading energy company, in which the Spanish company Repsol held a 57% stake. Repsol was unlikely to receive anything near the $10.5bn it sought in compensation. As European and Latin American leaders expressed extreme concern, Argentina risked damage to trade as well as a decline in foreign direct investment. Spain limited imports of Argentinian biofuels, valued at $1bn per year. Argentina's move also put an end to any plans by Chinese state-owned Sinopec to purchase Repsol's holding. The government tried to tempt investors back with opportunities in shale gas, of which Argentina reportedly had the world's third largest reserves after the United States and China.

Argentina also sought to assert itself internationally over its claims to sovereignty over the Falkland Islands, which it calls the Malvinas. The issue returned to Argentina's national agenda in anticipation of the 30th anniversary of its invasion of the islands in April 1982. Argentine troops were expelled by a British military task force, and the United Kingdom has since stepped up investment in the islands, as well as increasing the military garrison. The sparsely-populated islands are inhabited by about 2,500 islanders, with a military presence of about 1,200 soldiers as well as naval and air assets.

Tensions resurfaced in 2011, boosted by interest in potential oil reserves in South Atlantic waters, which were being explored by British companies. In February 2012, two British cruise ships were prevented from docking in Ushuaia, a popular entry to Patagonia on Argentina's southern tip. There were reports that Argentine firms were being urged to boycott British goods. In support of Argentina, Peru denied port access to a British frigate on a scheduled visit in March. Mercosur, UNASUR and CELAC released statements supporting the rights of Argentina, and expressing disappointment over the UK's refusal to enter into negotiations. Fernández repeatedly sought UN support for negotiations, but Britain stated it would not discuss the issue without the support of the island's residents, who appeared solidly to back continued UK sovereignty.

International tussles were unable to distract Argentinians from troubles at home. A train crash in February during rush hour in Buenos Aires, which killed 51 people and injured over 700, underscored the decay of infrastructure. The opposition used the accident to attack government policies and the widening gap between rich and poor. While trains originating in the wealthy suburbs are modern and air-conditioned, those carrying residents from poorer regions are little more than shells. Transportation Minister Juan Pablo Schiavi pointed to similar accidents in Europe and the United States in an effort to downplay the government's failures.

Together, these factors underscored the challenges facing Argentina's president. Fernández had traditionally benefited as much from populist support as from a weak opposition. Support for the president, however, began to wane, even within her Peronist alliance. Corruption allegations against Vice-President Amado Boudou increased the pressure. The president had taken a risk in selecting the inexperienced businessman-turned-politician. Yet investigations in April 2012 into Boudou's alleged influence peddling dented the president's already declining popularity, with her approval rating dropping to a low of 42%. There was a fear that these factors might encourage Fernández's supporters to seek to consolidate power while they still could. Some called for constitutional reforms to implement a parliamentary system that would remove limits on presidential re-election.

In a region marked by a political shift to the centre, Argentina's recent policy agenda went against the trend. While the going might have looked good for Fernández in the short term, her populist and increasingly erratic policy decisions risked isolating the country from its regional allies.

Chile's year of protests

Long considered one of Latin America's success stories, Chile had enjoyed consistent economic growth (averaging 4.8% per year since 2004), was democratic, competitive and open, enjoyed low levels of violence, and had a strong middle class. And yet, in 2011, the country was wracked by a series of protests calling for education and political reforms. In part, the discontent reflected persistently high levels of inequality. As a result, President Sebastián Piñera had a particularly bad year. His approval ratings reached a nadir of 22%, a steep drop from the 63% he enjoyed after the dramatic rescue of 33 miners in October 2010.

Starting in May 2011, student protests captured international attention. Although students were not the only protesters – educators, unions and centre-left political parties were also involved – some 80,000 students led the demonstrations with calls for education reforms. Student leaders claimed that the current system entrenched inequality. Education was undoubtedly expensive and skewed towards the wealthy. A university degree cost approximately $3,400 a year, while the average annual salary was about $8,500. Some private universities charged up to $10,000 per year. Secondary education was also affected, with almost half of Chile's students in subsidised private education in which the costs were split between households and the state. Parents paid on average $400 per child per year, out of a monthly minimum wage of $363. Close to 40% of secondary and higher education spending was covered by households, the highest figure in the OECD. Across OECD countries, an average 69% of higher education funding comes from public sources. In Chile it is a mere 15%, leaving students and families to take out private loans to cover the remainder and keeping higher education out of the reach of many.

In spite of the sometimes violent nature of the protests, they enjoyed broad popular sympathy. A Centre for the Study of Contemporary Reality (CERC) poll conducted in September 2011 showed 89% supported the students' demands for free education and an end to public funding for private education, while 72% felt the protesters were winning. The same survey highlighted education's growing political importance, with 73% of respondents citing the issue as Chile's main concern; the figure had been a mere 24% earlier in the year. Chilean Education Minister Felipe Bulnes met student leaders in October 2011 but talks broke down after several hours. The teachers' union responded by calling an unofficial referendum on free education, in which 90% of the over 1.2 million voters expressed their support. Although the Piñera administration presented a new education budget, which increased funding by $350m in 2012, the final $11.6bn figure was less than student protesters requested.

The protests, while damaging to Piñera, were only one facet of the political problems facing Chile, and led to a broader discussion on much-needed reforms. While Piñera's coalition was performing poorly, so was the opposition Concertación, with approval ratings falling to historic lows of 14%. The protests reflected a deeper dissatisfaction with the political establishment. The discontent could be characterised as a generational shift: after 20 years of the Concertación government, voters were dissatisfied with Chile's progress. The change to a centre-right government under Piñera in 2010 created the space for those on centre-left to express such concerns. Moreover, new, younger voters were free from the country's political heritage – the dictatorship of Augusto Pinochet from 1973 to 1990 – and sought a democratic system in which the government listened to citizens' concerns and responded to their needs.

Piñera promised voters he would enact reforms in 2011. He met four of his presidential predecessors to discuss how to restructure the political system. In the existing de facto two-party system each constituency is represented by two MPs, making it virtually impossible for third parties to win congressional seats. The system was devised after the fall of Pinochet to limit the power of the right, but has long since lost relevance in a changing political climate. Piñera was, however, likely to meet resistance from his own party in attempting to dismantle the binomial system, and said he would not move forward without consensus from both coalitions. Instead, the government successfully passed smaller-scale, but still significant, reforms that made voter registration automatic and ended compulsory voting, eliminating a fine for failing to vote that had acted as a disincentive to register.

The student demonstrations sparked broader social protest movements. Local communities in the isolated Patagonian region of Aysén argued that the cost of living was up to 40% higher than in other regions of Chile. Limited infrastructure meant that the region was only accessible by air or sea, and flights to the capital Santiago, 1,700km to the north, were routed via Argentina, involving rigorous border checks. After 40 days of protests, the government agreed to talks with local residents who demanded a subsidy for high gasoline prices and a duty free area for food. Piñera asked them to be patient, and agreed to build new hospitals in Chile Chico and Cochrane. In October 2011 he announced a land route would be constructed to the region, but would not be completed until 2017.

A miners' movement in the northern Antafogasta region also took advantage of the move for social change, with the Calama Civic Assembly and Copper Workers Federation calling for a greater share of profits to remain within mining regions. While copper was one of the main drivers of Chile's economic success, local citizens saw little of the resource wealth, and demanded the implementation of a Northern Development Fund, which would reserve 5% of copper-mining profits for local administration.

As in many of its South American neighbours, Chile's desire for energy sustainability caused tension between the government and civil-society groups. In April 2012, the Supreme Court approved the construction of hydroelectric projects in the Patagonia region that could generate up to 20% of the country's electricity by 2020. Project HydroAysén, managed by Italian company Endesa and Chilean firm Colbun, planned to build five dams on two rivers, flooding approximately 6,000 hectares. Piñera supported the $7bn project, arguing that it was critical to meeting Chile's energy needs, which were projected to triple by 2030. Local communities and conservation groups claimed that the project failed to consider the environmental impact on wildlife and national parks, and threatened the local way of life in one of the most isolated areas of Chile. There were also implications for the region's tourist industry, built on the natural beauty of Patagonia.

sonroleitle#

Brazil: maintaining the country's rise

Latin America's unquestioned economic leader Brazil's steady economic growth was bolstered by a growing domestic market and commodity exports to China and elsewhere. The $2.6 trillion economy overtook the United Kingdom to become the sixth largest in the world. Although Brazil's economy had slowed since posting dramatic growth in excess of 7% in 2010, it was still predicted to expand about 3.3% in 2012.

When President Dilma Rousseff took over from Luis Ignacio Lula da Silva, it was unclear how she would make her mark on a presidency so clearly identified with her predecessor. Rousseff chose to shake up Brazilian politics by campaigning against corruption, making an example of her cabinet ministers. Although she successfully ousted several high-level officials, there were concerns that the president did not go far enough in leading an anti-corruption campaign with broader reach.

Since she took office in January 2011, six ministers had resigned, as well as Rousseff's chief of staff Antonio Palocci and the head of the Brazilian Football Confederation. Others remained under investigation. Palocci, who ran a political consulting firm while serving the president, resigned in June 2011 amid revelations that his personal fortune had grown 20-fold over the previous four years. In July, Transport Minister Alfredo Nascimiento stepped down four days after two of his chief aides quit in light of an article in Brazilian magazine *Veja* alleging that staff were taking kickbacks on transport and infrastructure contracts. In August it was Agriculture Minister Wagner Rossi's turn to resign, while denying allegations that he accepted bribes and free air travel from agriculture companies. In September 2011, Tourism Minister Pedro Novais resigned after prominent newspaper *Folha de São Paulo* reported misuse of funds in the tourism ministry. Some 30 ministry officials were arrested in August. The 81-year-old had previously been accused of using public money to fund a late-night party in a hotel in 2010.

In October 2011, Sports Minister Orlando Silva stepped down amid allegations he arranged payments from a fund established to promote sport for poor children. He was also responsible for preparations ahead of the 2014 football World Cup tournament and 2016 Olympic Games. In December, Labour Minister Carlos Lupi resigned after *Veja* magazine alleged that he and some of his aides demanded kickbacks from non-profit organisations in return for funding. *Folha de São Paulo* also reported that the minister was being investigated for allegedly receiving a salary from both the state of Rio de Janeiro and the Federal Congress, while only serving in the former capacity. In February 2012, Cities Minister Mario Negromonte became the sixth minister to step down after reports that his executive secretary met with a businessman interested in bidding for a public-works programme in Cuiaba, which would be awarded by the ministry. That same month, Development, Industry and Foreign Trade Minister Fernando Pimentel was questioned by the ethics committee after *O Globo* newspaper reported that his consultancy services had brought in $1.2m in less than a year (as of mid-2012 the investigation was pending).

Finally, in March 2012, the head of the Brazil Football Confederation (CBF), Ricardo Teixeira, resigned. Although he cited health problems, corruption allegations had for months surrounded the CBF leader, who was also the head of 2014 World Cup organising committee. Rousseff also dismissed the defence minister, Nelson Jobim, in August 2011, after he made disparaging remarks about his fellow ministers. He was reportedly angry that the president overruled him on a multi-billion-dollar contract to buy fighter jets.

Despite making gains in the domestic political realm, Rousseff came under fire internationally for increasingly protectionist trade policies. Foreign investors and exporters argued that the 'buy Brazil' policy, which awarded a 25% margin of preference to local goods in government procurement, violated WTO principles. However, as industry was suffering from the strength of the Brazilian real and an increase in cheap – mostly Chinese – imports, Rousseff was under pressure to protect local producers. The policy also included a 30-percentage-point tax increase on cars with less than 65% local content, taking the tax on some imported models to a punitive 55% on top of import tariffs. The president's 'Brasil Maior' (Bigger Brazil) policy was also criticised for its attempts to offset the rising value of the Brazilian currency by offering 20% tax cuts to domestic manufacturers of clothing, shoes, furniture and software. Rousseff maintained these policies were essential to keep Brazil afloat in what she described as a 'monetary tsunami'. The Brazilian government argued that loose monetary policy in Europe and the United States had flooded emerging markets, causing local currencies to appreciate. Instead, the president called on developed countries to boost recovery from the financial crisis through government investment in job creation rather than expanding the money supply. These policies had an adverse effect on US–Brazil relations, and it was unsurprising that economics and trade policy dominated the Brazilian president's first trip to the United States in April 2012.

Brazil's success was undermined by the continuing challenge of urban insecurity. In Rio de Janeiro, local government kept up a 'pacification programme' designed to reduce drug trafficking and drug-related violence in the city's *favelas* by first sending in military forces and later establishing a regular police presence in the community. In November 2011, Rio drug kingpin Antônio Bonfim Lopes ('Nem') was captured ahead of the pacification of the notorious Rocinha and Vidigal *favelas*. The police also arrested two of his accomplices, including his right-hand man. However, in March 2012, a Rio community leader who was prepared to testify against Nem was shot in broad daylight – casting doubt on hopes that pacification could reduce violent crime. Some experts argued that a spike in violence could be a result of the disruption of established power dynamics, and that a police presence might eventually calm this down. In Rocinha, authorities had few options other than increasing the police forces in the *favela,* as its location made it critical to maintaining a secure loop around the areas in which most activities were to take place during the World Cup and Olympic Games.

As Brazil sought to boost its international economic clout, Rousseff focused on building the country's human capital. In December 2011, she announced the 'science without borders' programme, which aimed to fund over 100,000 scholarships for undergraduate and PhD students by 2015. The students would spend a year abroad studying in areas such as engineering and biotechnology. Approximately a quarter of the cost would be covered by the private sector, the remainder by the Brazilian government. The programme would boost Brazil's credentials in areas considered critical to economic success, with the government recognising that many of Brazil's universities and programmes were mediocre. Students would spend their year at universities in the United States, Europe, South Korea, Canada and Australia.

Brazil continued to assert itself as a global power, seeking to translate its economic weight into political clout. At the February G20 meeting in Mexico, Finance Minister Guido Mantega said emerging countries such as Brazil would be willing to provide more funds to the IMF in order to assist the eurozone, in exchange for increased decision-making power within the organisation. But nowhere was Brazil's ambition more evident than in its active pursuit of a permanent seat on the UN Security Council. Some analysts suggested that Brazil's campaign has been hampered by the fact that it has no nuclear capability, comes from a region of lower strategic importance, and that it simply does not wield the political influence to merit a seat at the table. The counter-argument was that Brazil's relative stability and lack of nuclear ambitions should work in its favour, particularly when compared to other contenders such as India. The US has supported India's campaign for a permanent seat, but not Brazil's.

Shifting balances

Nowhere is the changing power balance in the Western Hemisphere more evident than in Washington's willingness to publicly debate drug policy with Latin American leaders. This highly controversial issue would have received little traction a decade ago. Several of South America's top economic performers have recognised this shift as part of a broader international trend. While China looked as though it would soon become the region's largest trading partner, Peru, Colombia and Chile in particular have sought new alliances with several Asia-Pacific nations, diversifying their interests outside the region.

Yet Latin America continued to struggle with internal problems that threatened to undermine this success. Drug-trafficking has come to affect almost every country in the region, either as producer, transporter or consumer. Central America and Mexico have experienced the worst of the drug wars, making them some of the most violent places in the world. South American nations, while relatively free of drug-related violence, have seen a rise in social protest that has detracted from economic gains. In part, democratic consolidation has been responsible for the empowerment of the region's citizens. Environmental groups, local communities, and students have been seeking greater input into democratic decision-making, as well as a more equitable distribution of the region's wealth. Despite advances in reducing poverty and inequality in Latin America, it remained the most unequal region in the world, and inequality continued to undermine the region's potential.

One important, and successful, response has been the renewed focus on social policy goals, including social inclusion. Latin America's economic success has been uneven, and the rise in social protest in the last year highlighted an undercurrent of discontent among Latin Americans. Although social programmes such as conditional cash transfers have contributed to declining inequality in several Latin American countries, social policy could continue to play a critical role in ensuring that more citizens of Latin America benefit from the region's wealth. The events of the year to mid-2012 also underscored the importance of fostering relations between the government, private sector and civil society, both on social issues such as education, as well as infrastructure and energy projects. Overall, Latin America's outlook remained positive, but a greater focus on social inclusion and better dialogue between governments and citizens would go some way towards addressing the region's challenges in the next year.

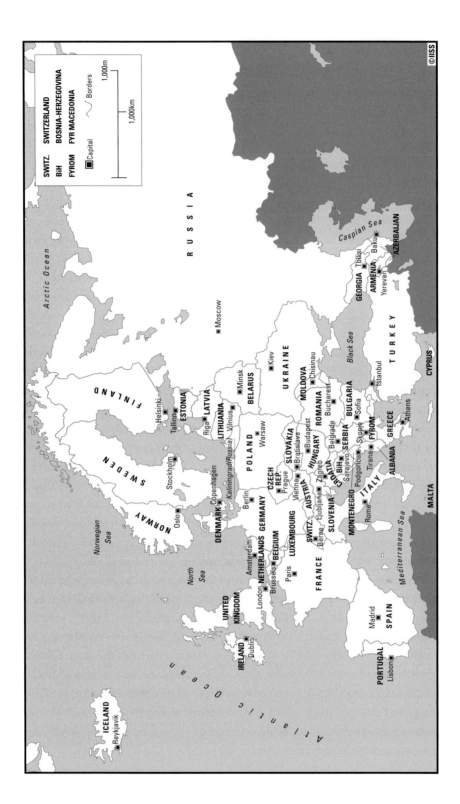

Chapter 4

Europe

Events in Europe in the year to mid-2012 were dominated by economic and financial problems that threatened to break apart the euro, the common currency used by 17 European nations; the potential disintegration of the currency was generally agreed to spell disaster on a global scale. The risk of a partial or total breakup grew during the year as governments failed to achieve consensus on big, bold solutions and continued to muddle through. The effect of the financial crisis was evident across Europe not only in poor or negative economic growth rates but in the fact that, by mid-2012, ten of the 17 eurozone countries had changed their governments. (See Perspectives, pp. 26–31 and *Strategic Geography*, pp. XVI–XVII.)

The highest-profile political casualty was Nicolas Sarkozy, ousted as president of France after one term by the Socialist François Hollande, though it was not simply the state of the economy that accounted for voters' choices, but a range of political and personality factors. The eurozone crisis underlined the strong leadership position of Germany and of Chancellor Angela Merkel, who nevertheless tried to reduce expectations of what Germany could do for Europe and stressed the responsibility of other governments to improve their finances. Merkel was not deaf to calls for compromise from more 'pro-growth' leaders, but stuck to her insistence that long-term solutions, rather than quick fixes, were needed to cure Europe's malaise. The danger of this approach was that events might sweep governments towards an outcome that they did not want.

The most dramatic departure was that of Silvio Berlusconi in Italy, replaced by the non-political technocrat Mario Monti. Political chaos in

Greece was testimony to the deep effects of the country's financial travails. Across Europe, the key to everything was the restoration of confidence among businesses and investors, so that economic activity could improve fiscal positions, lower debts, boost jobs, and eliminate the atmosphere of chronic crisis. But confidence was proving elusive.

France: Election of a 'Normal' President

A cloud of paradox descended over France between summer 2011 and summer 2012. While the media, the political class and public intellectuals obsessed relentlessly about the forthcoming presidential election, the public showed an unprecedented lack of interest. While commentators raised the putative stakes to ever higher levels, the voters yawned and declared themselves bored. In an opinion poll published by Le Monde on 7 March, two-thirds of the electorate declared that the campaign was 'not interesting', while only 6% found it 'very interesting'. The technical details surrounding both the crisis of the eurozone and the parlous state of French public finances, while offering fine outlets for grandiose opinion columns, were hardly the mainstay of the back-and-forth in the Café du Commerce. Pollsters in early spring predicted record levels of abstention in both the presidential first round (22 April) and the run-off (6 May). Most observers agreed that the election was at least as much about the visceral personal hatred Nicolas Sarkozy had aroused among large swathes of the population as it was about genuine policy issues. The widespread loathing of the outgoing president was matched by an equally widespread lack of enthusiasm for his Socialist challenger, about whom most people (even among the elites) knew virtually nothing. Of those who voted for François Hollande, with his slogan of 'Change is Now', in the second round, 55% did so to oust Sarkozy, against 45% who expressed genuine enthusiasm for Hollande's policies.

In any case, Hollande's election appeared to be a foregone conclusion. Never in the history of the Fifth Republic had either the left or the right succeeded in winning four straight presidential elections (which the right would have done had Sarkozy prevailed). All over Europe – in Spain, Hungary, Ireland, Greece and Italy – leaders from both right and left were being held responsible for the economic malaise sweeping the continent, and turfed out (see Strategic Geography, pp. XVI–XVII). Not a single poll throughout the year preceding the first round of voting on 22 April 2012 had forecast a Sarkozy win. The election was Hollande's to lose, which explains in large part his low-key and excessively vague campaign with no dramatic policy initiatives and no grand narrative – in short, a 'normal' campaign for the man who declared he wished to be a 'normal' president. Hollande's calm and understated demeanour made Sarkozy seem even more agitated and impulsive – precisely the style voters had come to abhor. Indeed, the only issue seemed to be the scale of Hollande's victory. In November 2011, one month after his triumph in the Socialist Party primaries, Hollande was credited with a potential score of 60% in the second round of the presidentials. This would have been unprecedented. Except for 2002, when Jacques Chirac beat the 'renegade' National Front candidate Jean-Marie Le Pen with 82% of the vote, the strongest showing for any candidate in the second round had been the 54% for the re-elected François Mitterrand in 1988, running against Chirac. Yet the polls continued, against all reason, to predict a landslide for Hollande – some even crediting him with 58% as late as mid-April. In 2012, there were more polls than ever before and they all told the same story.

In the event, French voters proved more canny (or more predictable) than the pollsters had suggested. Hollande's 51.63% share of the vote in the second round was lower than that of any winner since 1974. But it was far more in line with the reality of contemporary French politics than the polls had been. The outcome could have relatively easily been extrapolated from the results of the first round, when the five left-wing candidates collectively won 43.75% of the vote, with Hollande himself notching up 28.63%. This is socio-political reality in twenty-first-century France. For three decades, the French Socialist Party has witnessed the steady erosion of its working-class base.

In 2012 the three overtly right-of-centre candidates garnered 46.87% in the first round (Sarkozy took 27.18%). The balance was held by the only centrist candidate, François Bayrou, with 9.13% of the vote. Since Bayrou indicated after the first round that he would personally vote for Hollande in the second (as, indeed, did former President Jacques Chirac – his final act of revenge against Sarkozy), and since Marine Le Pen, leader of the National Front, announced she was not supporting Sarkozy, the arithmetic was relatively straightforward. In the event, only 45% of Bayrou's first-round supporters followed his lead in the second, with 35% supporting Sarkozy and 20% abstaining – hardly a rousing vote of confidence from the centre for the new president. Similarly, despite Le Pen's refusal to back Sarkozy (which might have turned out to be a poisoned chalice), over 50% of her first-round supporters voted for the outgoing president while only 20% voted for

Hollande (many National Front voters are former communists who swung from one extreme to the other) and 30% abstained. But the approximately 1.5 million voters Hollande was able to attract from Bayrou and an equivalent number from Le Pen gave him the comfortable margin he needed to win. He was thus indebted to huge numbers of voters from across the entire political spectrum.

Beyond the raw numbers, political analysts detected a less noble dynamic at work. Sarkozy, it was widely asserted, suffered from his status as an outsider. Unlike nearly all other French leaders, he had not risen through elite channels, such as the schools of Sciences Po and the École Nationale d'Administration (ENA). He lacked the high culture expected of a French president and was ill at ease discussing art, literature or film. Within weeks of his election, he was engaged in a messy divorce with his second wife and shortly afterwards threw himself into a very public affair with heiress, model and pop-singer Carla Bruni. He then committed the cultural blunder of dating her at Disneyland Paris, before eventually marrying her and fathering a child. He preferred Coca Cola to burgundy wines, he smoked fat cigars, he enjoyed consorting with the rich and the flashy. He was the son of an immigrant. He was overtly pro-American. In short, he made many French people squirm. French presidents are expected to act like monarchs – with refinement, distinction and decorum. Sarkozy manifestly did not fit the bill. Hollande, on the other hand, epitomised all of the unstated virtues of the ruling class: a long lineage from the middle class, along with old money; attendance at all of the best schools, Sciences Po, ENA and Hautes Études Commerciales; a man who could hold his own with Parisian intellectuals; a politician deeply rooted in a rural department, Corrèze, who could also converse knowledgeably about the French football league. Some analysts suggested that the 2012 election was an instance of class war. If that was the case, the outcome was entirely appropriate: power was stripped from the interloper and returned to the social stratum from which it had been pur-loined. Sarkozy announced that he was leaving politics.

The economy, stupid...

The major events of French public life during the year preceding the election were connected with the European and French financial crises. Sarkozy had been fortunate in June 2011 to be able to replace the disgraced Dominique Strauss-Kahn with Christine Lagarde as managing director of the International Monetary Fund (IMF), but this appointment did little to stem the economic tide. In August, the IMF warned that France's economy, with debt at 85% of GDP, a budget deficit of almost 8% of GDP, and a trade deficit of €70bn, was spiralling out of control and making unattainable the government's deficit target of 3% by 2013. By some benchmarks, France's economy was in worse shape than those of Spain and Italy. High unemployment, especially for the young and over-55s, high labour costs and weak external competitiveness all aggravated the structural problem. The budget had not been balanced since 1974; all French leaders had preferred to borrow to finance government expenditure, knowing full well that this was unsustainable in the long run without a serious return to growth. Sarkozy's embrace of the German-inspired 'golden rule', whereby the requirement to balance the budget every three years should be written into the constitution, was supported by Lagarde and the IMF, but was seen as an electoral trap by the Socialists. By late summer, Sarkozy and his new finance minister, François Baroin, were already focusing all their efforts on retaining the country's AAA credit rating. Growth forecasts for 2012 were revised downwards from 2.25% to 1.75% and new austerity measures worth €12bn, mainly taxes affecting big business, were introduced. In October, government growth forecasts were again reduced, to 1%, falling further in January to 0.5% when additional austerity measures were introduced. None of this was enough to satisfy the rating agencies. On Friday 13 January, Standard & Poor's downgraded France from AAA to AA+ (the same rating as the United States). No matter how hard the government tried to downplay the symbolic significance of this event, it was electoral manna for Hollande.

Yet the structural problems of the French economy dictated that the differences between Sarkozy's and Hollande's electoral platforms were limited. Both men were committed to controlling public finances, to stimulating growth and to improving competitiveness. Hollande made no secret of his intention to create a new tax bracket of 45% for incomes over €150,000 and controversially proposed to tax incomes over €1m at 75%. His campaign assault against 'finance', which had, he claimed, 'taken control of the economy, society and even our lives', and his attacks on the irresponsibility of the banking sector were geared to maximising support on the left. Some of his proposals appeared difficult to implement: the separation of speculative activities from legitimate investment within the banking sector; placing a limit on bank fees; banning toxic derivatives; and increasing the corporate income tax on banks. Both he and Sarkozy proposed the introduction of a tax on financial transactions (Tobin tax). Measures to help small and medium-sized companies improve their competitiveness and stimulate growth were also promoted by both candidates. Their biggest differences came in the areas of pensions, jobs and labour costs, with Hollande determined to restore the right to retirement at 60 for those having worked over 40 years (one of Sarkozy's most successful reforms had been raising the retirement age to 62); and Sarkozy targeting France's exceptionally high labour costs. During the one televised debate between the two men, on 2 May, the overwhelming majority of the exchanges dealt with the nitty-gritty of these policies, the bemused viewers trying their best to stay abreast of the cut and thrust of statistics and counter-statistics. Most commentators agreed that Hollande won the debate, less by the deployment of more convincing statistics than by his imposing presidential demeanour and his obvious ability to (more than) hold his own with the man who had predicted he would make mincemeat of him during the one-on-one confrontation. At the end of the day, the precise economic arguments made little difference. France's economy was manifestly in terrible shape, Sarkozy had been in charge of it for five years and the electorate was looking for change. In a sense, given these realities, Sarkozy's second-round score of 48.37% was not unimpressive. But it was the first time in the history of the Fifth Republic that an incumbent president failed to come first in the first round of voting.

Hollande lost no time appointing his government, on 15 May, under Prime Minister Jean-Marc Ayrault, a stalwart of the Socialist Party, mayor of Nantes and, since 1997, the president of the socialist group in the National Assembly. He was considered an extremely safe pair of hands in managing complex socio-political tensions. His government, comprising 18 full ministers and 16 junior ministers, with 50% men and 50% women, was a sophisticated balancing act among the many different factions within the Socialist Party, and included two Left Radicals and two Greens. Apart from the foreign and defence ministers (see below), three appointments stood out. Pierre Moscovici, at Finance, was expected to be a rock of orthodoxy for his long-time friend Hollande. The two men taught a joint course in political economy at Sciences Po in the 1980s and Moscovici was Hollande's campaign director for the 2012 election. At the Ministry of the Interior, Manuel Valls, a former aide to two prime ministers (Michel Rocard and Lionel Jospin), emerged as a leading specialist in issues of security. Arnaud Montebourg, a gadfly on the party's left wing, was put in charge of Industrial Renewal, where he would be constrained to channel his boundless energy into constructive projects.

From Merkozy to Merlande?

One key difference between the presidential contenders was their respective relations with German Chancellor Angela Merkel. Although Sarkozy and

Merkel were very different personalities, with, at least initially, quite different approaches to economics, and although the chemistry between them was
unstable, the French president progressively aligned France's eurozone economic and financial preferences with those of Germany. The media dubbed
this development 'Merkozy', shorthand for the alleged seamlessness of
views between the two leaders. But there was little doubt who was calling
the shots. For Merkel, Germany's participation in the eurozone was only
thinkable under the terms of German 'ordoliberalism', the principles which
had dominated in the early decades of the Federal Republic: a limited role for
the state, wages properly controlled by consensus between employers and
unions, strict budgetary policy and absolute independence for the central
bank whose sole focus should be on monetary policy and control of inflation. It was hard to imagine an economic worldview more removed from
traditional French statist preferences. By stepping in line with Berlin during
the negotiation of the austerity-inducing EU fiscal compact of December
2011, Sarkozy made himself complicit in what opponents castigated as a
German straitjacket for Europe which would prevent the very growth that
was required, according to a growing number of economists, to allow deeply
indebted countries to survive. And yet so strong was the German influence
over the European debate on this issue that it seemed almost pointless to
challenge it. On 15 April, one week before the first round of the election,
Sarkozy made a rather feeble attempt to suggest that if he were re-elected
he would demand a revision of the statutes of the European Central Bank
to balance austerity with growth. It was too little too late, and too blatantly
driven by electoral politics. Merkel responded instantly by saying that
Sarkozy knew what Berlin's position was and she could assure him it had
not changed. It proved the last sputtering of a tortuous relationship.

Hollande was considered by many to be unrealistic – or even reckless
– when he announced in December that, if elected, he would seek to renegotiate the terms of the fiscal compact. One consequence was that Merkel openly
supported Sarkozy's re-election bid and refused to meet Hollande. But the
Socialist candidate remained unfazed. He sensed that the political climate
was changing across Europe and that the austerity recipe being served up
by Germany would prove counterproductive. His timing could not have
been better. Three days before the second round of the presidential elections, the president of the European Central Bank, Mario Draghi, elaborating
on hints he had been giving out for some weeks, asked European leaders 'to
place economic growth at the centre of the battle against the financial crisis'.
He called for a binding 'Growth Pact' to counteract the austerity effects of

the fiscal compact. Two days later, on 5 May, European Commissioner for Economic and Monetary Affairs Olli Rehn demanded increased government spending on infrastructure projects, and promised a loosening of the EU's draconian budget rules for countries such as Spain. He too insisted that growth was the key to survival for the European economies. And the very day of Hollande's victory, parliamentary elections in Greece resulted in the decisive defeat of the pro-austerity parties.

Hollande had his first encounter with the German chancellor in Berlin on 15 May, the day after he took office. They had a 'full and frank exchange', in which both sides stuck closely to their guns – while agreeing that they would attempt to narrow their differences before the European Council meeting at the end of June. Merkel could not afford to be seen making early concessions to Hollande in advance of the French parliamentary elections, even though – or perhaps because – she had suffered a major political reversal in losing North Rhine–Westphalia to the Social Democratic Party (SPD) on 13 May. On the other hand, when Hollande met Barack Obama in the White House on 18 May, there was an instant recognition that the two men were of one mind on how best to end the economic crisis. Obama had spent his first term painstakingly putting into practice many of the growth-oriented policies on which Hollande had campaigned.

The Franco-German axis had been a fundamental and permanent instrument for driving forward European integration and there was no structural reason why leaders from different political families could not work well together. In the past, many of Europe's greatest achievements had come from an alliance between a French conservative and a German socialist (Valéry Giscard d'Estaing/Helmut Schmidt; Chirac/Gerhard Schröder) or vice versa (Mitterrand/Helmut Kohl). On the other hand, several newly elected French presidents, including Chirac and Sarkozy, had made early efforts to break out of this constraint and forge alliances with other European leaders. But before long they were forced to accept that the Paris–Berlin axis was vital. Without Franco-German agreement, there can be no majority in the European Council. The two countries represent approximately 50% of the European economy and no major financial steps forward are possible if they disagree. This is not to say, as some critics have asserted, that Paris and Berlin exercise a kind of condominium in European affairs. The starting positions of French and German leaders have rarely been in sync and only after intense bilateral negotiations have they appeared to converge. As Hollande embarked on his presidential career, this remained as true as ever. In France, there was a growing sense of resentment that successive French presidents had allowed Germany to dictate austerity measures. The truth is that those same presidents simply paid lip-service to German norms and continued to spend and borrow as usual. In Germany, there was an equally strong illusion that, because austerity and belt-tightening had worked at home, they could be applied in a one-size-fits-all manner to all European countries in trouble. Both of these myths needed re-examining. The discussions between Merkel and Hollande in the run-up to the June summit could not afford myth or illusion. Hollande, like some of his predecessors, insisted that he did not want the Franco-German axis to dominate. He stressed that it was urgent to bring all EU member states into the conversation. But the reality of the past 50 years of European integration suggested that he was going to have to learn to establish a very special relationship with Merkel. Journalists quickly began dubbing the phenomenon 'Merlande', 'Frangela' and even 'Homer'.

Legislative elections and the National Front

Hollande's next political challenge was to ensure that the legislative elections of 10 and 17 June provided him with a majority in the National Assembly. The narrowness of his presidential victory made speculation about the outcome of the parliamentary elections hazardous. Several 'known unknowns' further complicated the electoral procedure. What would be the level of abstention? What would be the attitude towards the Socialists of the radical left parties grouped under the 'Left Front'? Would the National Front succeed, as threatened by Marine Le Pen, in 'destroying' the mainstream conservative Union pour un Mouvement Populaire (UMP), of which Sarkozy had been the political soul? In the event, a strange dynamic, which has consolidated itself in the French electoral cycle, kicked in once again. Unlike most Western parliamentary electoral systems, where the government is chosen as a result of the outcome of parliamentary elections, the French Fifth Republic has in effect enshrined a practice in which the parliament is elected as a follow-on to the election of the president and the appointment of his government. This is the result of the constitutional reform introduced in 2000 whereby the presidential term was reduced from seven to five years, with the parliamentary elections following several weeks after the presidential vote. The aim was to avoid 'cohabitation' between a president from one political family and a prime minister from another, which had tended to happen when the presidential cycle was seven years and the parliamentary cycle five years. Thus President Mitterrand had had to 'cohabit' with Chirac as prime minister between 1986 and 1988, and again with Édouard Balladur from 1993 to

1995, the conservative prime ministers having won the legislative elections in 1986 and 1993. The 2000 reform aimed to allow a newly elected president to capitalise on his victory by ensuring that the outcome of parliamentary elections would give him a working majority. The result is not guaranteed, but has now become a self-fulfilling prophecy, with potentially negative consequences for the legitimacy of parliamentary democracy. Voters feel constrained to step in line and avoid cohabitation. A massive and unprecedented 44% showed their displeasure in 2012 by abstaining.

Hollande benefited handsomely from this loading of the electoral dice. On 10 June, the Socialists won 302 seats in the 577-seat assembly, while the right-wing parties grouped under the UMP secured 206. The Socialists alone thus had more than an absolute majority in the Assembly and, together with their radical and Green governing allies, a total of 333 seats. The 'Left Front', headed by former presidential candidate Jean-Luc Mélenchon, and including the former Communist Party, secured only ten seats; Mélenchon himself failed in his attempt to challenge Marine Le Pen in her Pas-de-Calais constituency. The Socialists succeeded in pulling off a historically unprecedented clean sweep, since they controlled the Elysée, the Senate, the National Assembly, 21 of the 22 Regional Councils of metropolitan France (with Alsace the only exception), and the vast majority of the departments. They did not, however, command three-fifths of the seats in the 'Congress' (the joint meeting, at Versailles, of the Senate and the National Assembly), the majority required to authorise constitutional change. This could be significant in light of possible eventual changes in the eurozone. If Hollande failed to get a vote through the Congress, he would be loath to subject the proposal to a referendum, given French voters' propensity to vote down European constitutional initiatives.

On the right, the UMP suffered a severe defeat; the number of its deputies fell from 314 to 188. The combined right (excluding the National Front) secured 229 seats. One potential fly in the ointment was Marine Le Pen. Her performance in the presidential race had been impressive. Opinion polls throughout 2011 suggested that it was not impossible that Le Pen, like her father in 2002, could just squeak into the second round, especially if the right-wing vote was split between too many candidates. That did not happen. Le Pen came in third in the presidential election with 18% of the vote (when her father made it to the second round in 2002 he took 16.86%, but had managed barely 10% in 2007). She was widely credited with having scored highest of all the candidates (around 26%) among 18–24-year-olds, but she did poorly among university students while her appeal was exceptionally strong among the growing ranks of less educated, less well-trained and unemployed young people. She also made serious inroads, for the first time in the party's history, into rural areas of eastern France and Corsica.

A parliamentary candidate must win at least 12.5% of the votes in the first round of legislative elections to advance to the second round. This threshold means that it is not uncommon for three or even four candidates to stand in the second round. Since the National Front vote comes largely from constituencies with right-wing majorities, there have often been two right-wing candidates with more than 12.5% in the first round standing against a single left-wing candidate in the second. In these circumstances, there has often been an arrangement between the two right-wing candidates whereby the one with the lower score in the first round stands down so that the left-wing candidate will not prevail. (In the second round, the winner only requires a plurality of the vote.) In June 2012, the National Front was in a strong position to negotiate such reciprocal deals with the UMP. Of the 353 parliamentary constituencies in which Le Pen scored more than 12.5% in the first round of the presidential elections of 22 April, she placed first in 23 and second in another 93. The National Front was thus theoretically in a position to influence the outcome in as many as 100 constituencies. Officially, the UMP insisted that there would be no deals. In reality, two tendencies emerged. The first was that the UMP did not hesitate to communicate a hard-right discourse, in an effort to attract National Front voters. The second was that it refused to engage in 'republican front' arrangements with other parties in order to isolate the National Front. The result was that the latter, by maintaining its own candidates in several dozen right-leaning constituencies, quite often ensured victory for the socialist candidate. At the same time, it succeeded in getting only three of its own deputies elected, including Jean-Marie Le Pen's 22-year-old granddaughter (and Marine's niece), Marion Maréchal-Le Pen. Marine Le Pen lost her own bid for a seat by 100 votes out of an electorate of 56,000 in her Northern constituency.

The problem for the UMP was that, under Marine Le Pen, the National Front emerged as a party with genuine cross-sectoral appeal. It was not confined to embittered crypto-fascists or narrow-minded racists, but appealed to all parts of society and had become a party that ordinary French men and women were not ashamed to belong to or vote for. A poll conducted in January 2012 indicated that 31% of French voters 'agree[d] with the ideas' of the National Front (versus 22% in January 2011 and 11% in 1999). And, while in 1999 70% of voters declared themselves 'utterly opposed' to the National Front (hence the tidal wave of support for Chirac against Jean-

Marie Le Pen in the 2002 second round), that figure had been whittled down under Marine's leadership to only 35%. Even practising Catholics professed growing support for the party which, in the hands of Jean-Marie, was essentially taboo for Christians. The National Front had become a fixture in French politics, with which the mainstream parties would have to come to terms.

There was a dramatic moment in mid-March 2012 during the presidential election campaign when Mohamed Merah, a 24-year-old self-proclaimed Islamist jihadist born in Toulouse of Algerian parents, committed a series of murders in that town against French soldiers and Jewish schoolchildren and their teacher. Seven people were shot dead at point-blank range. Merah's name figured on lists held by both US and French counter-terrorism authorities, because of trips he had taken to Syria, Afghanistan and Pakistan. He was eventually surrounded and, after a 30-hour stand-off, shot dead by an elite police unit, RAID. This event allowed Sarkozy to appear as the tough chief executive who took charge of the police operation, while Hollande was obliged merely to look on, as campaigning was suspended for several days. Le Pen attempted to make political capital out of the drama by highlighting the numbers of immigrants (mainly Muslim) in France (approaching 10% in 2012) and banging the drum on crime. Pollsters predicted the Toulouse shootings would be enough to turn the race around. They were wrong. But the event did draw attention in dramatic form to growing concerns in France, fuelled by the upheavals in the Arab world, about immigration policy. Le Pen's proposal to re-establish full control of all France's borders found resonance with large numbers of voters. Sarkozy tried to capitalise on these concerns by proposing that if the Schengen borders were not secured by December 2012, he would leave the Schengen system altogether and re-establish full French border controls. Hollande promised an annual parliamentary debate on numbers of immigrants. The problem was not going to go away.

The results of the legislative elections confirmed the domination of the electoral process by the two main governing parties. Any party which stood clearly apart from the mainstream – the Left Front, the centre under François Bayrou, and the National Front, was decimated. Although such parties represented one-third of the electorate, they wound up with only 15 deputies in the 577-member National Assembly. This is potentially unhealthy for French democracy. But each of the two governing parties is split down the middle on European policy. Indeed, the difference between federalists and 'sovereignists' (large numbers of whom exist in both main parties) is politically more significant than the distinction between left and right. Hitherto, all French presidents have tended, through judiciously modulated discourse, to avoid taking unequivocal sides on this issue. Given the seriousness of the stakes in the eurozone crisis, it looked as if Hollande would find it difficult to avoid grasping the constitutional nettle. The choices were becoming narrower: to embrace some degree of federalism or to risk allowing the European project to unravel. Whichever course he took, there would likely be protests in the streets and a potential recalibration of French politics.

Foreign and security policy
Foreign and security policy played a very minor role in the presidential election campaign. Of the '60 Promises for France' Hollande included in his electoral platform, only the last four related to overseas policy: the creation of a World Environment Organisation (intended to appeal to the Green vote, this had been proposed by Sarkozy in his 2007 campaign, but never acted upon); priority to relations with the countries of the Southern Mediterranean (an indirect reminder of Sarkozy's blunders during the early months of the Arab uprisings); the withdrawal of French troops from Afghanistan by the end of 2012 (an unambiguous vote winner); and the maintenance of a robust defence capacity based on the nuclear deterrent and a strong defence-industrial base (a standard incantation for any credible presidential candidate). Those who felt inspired (or were called upon by their editors) to speculate on what a Hollande foreign policy would look like invariably began their analyses by recognising that there was extremely little to go on.

Sarkozy's record on foreign and security policy was somewhat patchy. After a number of early successes, his ability to influence world events became bogged down in part because of his deliberate practice of centralising all decisions in the Elysée and of marginalising the Quai d'Orsay, in part because the problems themselves became more and more intractable. The Libyan campaign in mid-2011 allowed him to claw back some semblance of honour from the wreckage of his Tunisian and Egyptian mistakes, and the sale of *Rafale* fighter jets to India – the first overseas market for this expensive and politically controversial aircraft – was an important breakthrough. Sarkozy's decision to bring France back into NATO's integrated command structures was almost universally seen as a reflection of his Atlanticism, as opposed to the traditional French diplomatic preference for what is called Gaullo-Mitterrandism. The debate around these two (equally overstated) concepts was as furious as it was sterile. According to Gaullo-Mitterrandism, France had a special role to play, outside of the Western family of nations, with respect to the global South or the rising powers. This approach was alleged to be in stark contrast with the Atlanticist (or, since the end of the Cold War, the 'Occidentalist') notion that France's overseas activities should be tightly coordinated with those of its Western allies. This was a game French foreign-policy intellectuals enjoyed playing. But it hardly corresponded to anything tangible or sustainable. One could easily find elements of both approaches in the actions of all French presidents of the Fifth Republic, including Charles de Gaulle himself.

Speculation as to which of these two ostensibly incompatible camps Hollande would associate himself with was hardly dampened by his major speech on defence policy on 11 March 2012. Predictably, there were plenty of elements of both Gaullo-Mitterrandism and Atlanticism in this set-piece oration, which contained no surprises and no departures from the estab-lished canon. Apart from dispatching a number of subtle poisoned arrows in Sarkozy's direction (Hollande intended to 'restore' France's rank in the world and make its distinctive voice heard 'once again'), the speech was exceedingly vague on all substantive issues. The Socialist candidate perceived three main threats – terrorism; natural disasters (such as the Fukushima nuclear accident in Japan); and arms races in general and WMD proliferation in particular. He enunciated five commitments. The first was to offer a strategic vision for France's defence efforts (a vision which, reading between the lines, would navigate astutely between the EU Common Security and Defence Policy (CSDP) and NATO). The second was to deliver a credible and achievable level of military capacity based on a rationalised defence industry. The third was to establish a new balance in decision-making between the presidency, the prime minister and the parliament – an old chestnut which different presidents have played out in different ways over the decades without ever changing the basic fact that defence policy remains the clear prerogative of the Elysée. This idea was intended as a reminder that Sarkozy had short-circuited the other agencies. The fourth commitment was to a better deal for the armed forces, their families and other associated personnel – a promise presidential candidate Ségolène Royal had made in 2007, and on which Sarkozy had in part delivered. Hollande's final promise was to tighten the links between the defence sector and the nation – again, an issue to which all would-be executives have systematically paid lip service. He ended on a distinctly Gaullist note, as any major speech on the subject must: 'France is a great and beautiful nation. It is not just any nation. In the global concert it has always managed to voice original, independ-ent, generous and supportive contributions.' The speech extended hands to various constituencies without offending anybody and without offering any hostages to fortune.

When the victorious Hollande appointed as foreign minister his most bitter rival within the Socialist Party, former Prime Minister Laurent Fabius, overtly placing his faith in the one individual within the party who carried gravitas and commanded respect within the international community, he highlighted his own lack of experience in foreign and security policy. Fabius's support for the 'No' campaign during the referendum on the EU Constitutional Treaty in 2005 had been forgiven as the decision of a politician eager to appeal to the Socialist rank and file in the run-up to the presidential primaries of 2006. Fabius could be relied upon to adopt a purely pragmatic approach to international affairs and, during his first major interview after taking office, when pressed repeatedly to pronounce himself either a Gaullo-Mitterrandist or an Atlanticist, rejected these categories as meaningless. The only objective, he insisted, was to ensure that France wielded influence in international affairs. The appointment as minister of defence of Hollande's long-standing friend Jean-Yves Le Drian was a clear statement that there would be seamless continuity with the past. Le Drian, formerly the ranking Socialist on the Defence Commission of the National Assembly, a former minister under Mitterrand, president of the Regional Council of Brittany, and Hollande's adviser on defence issues during the electoral campaign, had twice been asked by Sarkozy to accept the defence ministry, but had twice refused. He had been discreetly dispatched by Hollande to both Washington and NATO headquarters in Brussels in March 2012 to reassure France's allies that there would be no rocking of any boats if the Socialist candidate won.

Hollande's performance at the NATO Summit in Chicago, less than a week after assuming office, delivered on these assurances. His electoral promise to bring back French combat troops from Afghanistan by the end of 2012 was quietly endorsed by his NATO partners, all of whom were also seeking the exit door. French forces in Kapisa province, whose task was to secure the Kapisa Valley route from the military base at Bagram to major combat areas further south without passing through Kabul, were to be replaced by Afghan forces. If the operation succeeded, it would redound to Hollande's credit. If it failed, it would be his first major mistake. The semantic distinction between combat troops and non-combat troops was a fudge. Some 1,200 French troops were to remain in Afghanistan in 2013 to help train the Afghan Army, but if they were to be required by the United States for combat duty, they would be ready and able. Some 400 French troops were to remain alongside their allies until the final withdrawal date of December 2014. But Hollande, who had criticised the NATO project for a missile-defence shield, chose not to raise this issue in Chicago. He was torn between industrial interests (France's major defence companies dearly want a share of the contracts) and politico-military interests (the missile shield would be US-dominated and would call into question France's sacrosanct commitment to nuclear deterrence).

More generally, Hollande looked likely to keep an open mind about the long-term development of NATO. During his 11 March speech on defence, he allowed himself the luxury of formulating questions about the present and future purpose of the Alliance. It was widely believed that Hollande would likely prioritise the re-launch of the EU Common Security and Defence Policy (CSDP), which had been in limbo since the 2009 Lisbon Treaty and which suffered a severe blow to its credibility when the Libyan campaign had to fall back on NATO. But, as Hollande made clear in his 60 Commitments, the major problem for the CSDP was the generation of capacity, which would require pooling and sharing at the EU level. This would involve sensitive sovereignty issues. Nor was it clear whether Hollande would be as enthusiastic as his predecessor for cooperation with the United Kingdom, whose prime minister blatantly snubbed him during the electoral campaign. Much looked to depend on UK preferences in times of austerity. Le Drian announced that, given France's parlous finances, the French defence budget would have to be cut – but in the same proportion, no more and no less, as other programmes. Perhaps the most likely course, already under discussion within the defence community, and to which Le Drian paid allusive lip-service, was an increasing level of cooperation and even integration between the CSDP and a new NATO which, in the post-Afghanistan period, would return explicitly to Europe and its hinterland to allow the United States to engage its tilt to Asia by offering Europeans leadership responsibilities in their own back yard. A new Defence White Paper was to be published by the end of 2012. Work on this document began immediately in June with the appointment of a special commission in which the role of Jean-Claude Mallet, who presided under Sarkozy over the drafting of the previous 2008 White Paper, was to be significant. Mallet was appointed special adviser to Le Drian. Seamlessness between the two White Papers appeared to be inevitable. A new military programme law was also to be submitted to parliament in summer 2013.

The Hollande administration was fully committed to working within the multilateral and institutional frameworks of the emerging multipolar world, with special emphasis on the UN, the G20 and, of course, the EU. The president and his foreign minister insisted on crafting a new relationship with Africa, based far less on the traditional dimensions of *Françafrique* (clientelism, military intervention and conditional aid) and far more on working with the African Union and the primary stakeholders to help develop the continent's own immense resources. That was easier said than done. Hollande personally had far fewer links with major African leaders than any of his predecessors and his latest book devoted only one page to African issues. His first real test was likely to be France's commitment to a new EU mission in the Sahel. France's historic role in this area, which has been destabilised by the fall of Libyan strongman Muammar Gadhafi, suggested that Hollande would be forced to take action, even perhaps against his own better judgement. Hollande had spoken of his determination to do more to promote Palestinian statehood (without, of course, offending Israel), but had failed to be specific, other than to maintain Sarkozy's preference for multilateral international recognition rather than unilateral French recognition. In May 2012, he indicated that, if a UN mandate authorised military action against the Bashar al-Assad regime in Syria, he would be prepared to engage French forces. He called in March 2012 for Assad to be transferred to the International Criminal Court. On Iran, Fabius indicated that the Chirac and Sarkozy policy will not be changed: strictly enforced sanctions, coupled with constant dialogue. An Iranian bomb, Hollande reiterated, was 'unacceptable'. Military action against Iran, however, was viewed with clear disfavour in Paris. It was believed that the new president (unlike Sarkozy) was open-minded about Turkey's membership of the EU, and would engage in more constructive relations with Prime Minister Recep Tayyip Erdogan, whom Sarkozy could not abide – and vice versa. Rumour had it that Hollande's price for re-engaging with Turkey would be Ankara's recognition of the Armenian genocide. This did not seem like a sensible way of proceeding. The new president would also seek, like all his predecessors, but with no greater guarantees of success, to develop strategic partnerships with Russia and China, as well as with the other emerging powers.

Relations with Barack Obama got off to a very good start during Hollande's visit to Washington, Camp David and Chicago in May. Despite the fact that the US president had appeared to favour the devil he knew, the two men proved to be on the same wavelength on the key economic issues of the day – and there was more than policy in common between the centrist American liberal and the centrist French socialist. Franco-American relations stood at a post-war high between Sarkozy and Obama and, although Hollande was by no means the instinctive Atlanticist that Sarkozy appeared to be, there was no reason to believe that he would attempt to row back from that level of harmony. Hollande insisted that he wished to entertain constructive relations with all international partners – by implication (and occasionally explicitly) distancing himself from the notion of special relationships. But with the United States, as with Germany, he looked likely to be squeezed into a situation in which he would have to pay special attention to bilateralism. It was not at all clear how he would relate to a (French-speaking) Mitt Romney, whose primary campaign castigated the type of European social values that Hollande epitomised as the polar opposite of good American values.

France has always perceived itself as an important player on the international stage. New presidents do not step into a vacuum. Their policy options are largely dictated by the structure of the international system they inherit. Their personality can play a part, but only within limits. De Gaulle, Mitterrand and, in a different way, Sarkozy, all tried to maximise their personal influence over the course of events. Hollande said that that, too, was his intention, but at the same time he insisted he wished to be a 'normal' president. How he would reconcile the two remained to be seen.

Germany: To Lead or Not to Lead

With the eurozone locked into a seemingly never-ending cycle of inadequate economic crisis management, which failed to address both slow economic growth and persistent sovereign-debt problems, policymakers and commentators focused on Germany as holding the key to a more stable future for Europe. Not only did it have the largest and strongest economy, but it was by far the biggest contributor to rescue packages for troubled debtor countries and to the 'firewalls' established to deal with future problems. In addition, its long-standing and dogmatic anti-inflationary stance lay behind the philosophy of the European Central Bank.

However, external demands for a German approach decisively geared towards generating faster economic growth clashed with the determined preference of Chancellor Angela Merkel's government for a course of action that focused on addressing budget deficits and reducing debt. Meanwhile, although the German economy performed better than most others in Europe, the outlook deteriorated. In the field of defence, plans to make the German Bundeswehr into a smaller yet more capable force moved to the implementation stage.

Saving Europe?

Merkel was criticised from two angles for her international economic policy. Germany, having weathered the economic crisis better than other economies in the eurozone, was seen as uncompromising and as dictating tough choices to other governments. In addition, analysts and leaders in Europe and the United States questioned Berlin's diagnosis of the eurozone's problem. They doubted whether the level of government debt was really at the root of the crisis, especially given that several of the countries in difficulties had not been fiscally irresponsible in the years leading up to the crisis. However, Merkel clearly believed that fiscal policy was at the heart of the matter – hence her successful advocacy of the 'fiscal compact' agreed by eurozone leaders in December 2011. She also understood that economic growth was needed for the eurozone to escape from the debt burden. However, she believed this must come not as a result of short-term stimulus but from structural reforms of economies. Up to mid-2012, Merkel, well aware of German popular support for her approach on this issue, continued to insist that taking on more debt was not acceptable as a measure to stimulate growth. She argued in the German parliament that 'debt reduction and strengthening growth and employment are the two pillars of the strategy … Growth through structural reforms, that makes sense, that is important, that is necessary … Growth on the nod would lead us back to the beginning of the crisis, which is why we will not do it this way.'

European leaders were unsure whether the Merkel government shared their sense of urgency. Polish Foreign Minister Radek Sikorski told an audience in Berlin that he was no longer worried about a dominant Germany, but a Germany that failed to act decisively. He said: 'I am deeply convinced that the biggest shareholder in a company – even if he, like Germany, does not hold a majority of the shares – has to shoulder the biggest responsibility for the welfare and rescue of the company.'

Among experts in Germany, debate raged about whether the government should change course and take on more risk for the greater good of the eurozone. Hans-Werner Sinn, a leading economist, argued that Germany was heavily exposed already and could not take on a greater burden. He calculated that should Greece, Ireland, Italy and Spain default on their debt yet the euro still survive, Germany stood to lose about $900bn. The cost to Germany of a collapse of the euro was put by Sinn at $1.35 trillion. He argued that for Germany to agree to assume greater liability for eurozone debts would be both illegal and economically unwise. Other commentators, such as Wolfgang Münchau, a leading financial writer, rejected the argument that Germany would be overwhelmed by the magnitude of the task as being beside the point, and questioned whether Germany could achieve its dual goals of limiting its own exposure to risk and preventing the eurozone from breaking apart.

Merkel, for her part, warned ahead of the June 2012 G20 Summit in Mexico that other countries must not over-estimate Germany's ability to solve the crisis. 'Germany's strength is not infinite ... Consequently, our special responsibility as the leading economy in Europe means we must be able to realistically size up our powers, so we can use them for Germany and Europe with full force.' She continued to dismiss calls for new forms of shared debt, such as so-called eurobonds (under which eurozone members would guarantee each other's debt), as 'simple' and 'counterproductive'. Merkel seemed set to pursue a long-term strategy which sought to marry immediate cuts in budget deficits with deeper fiscal and political integration among the countries of the eurozone. In her view, only if eurozone countries were moving closer together in terms of economic policies, fiscal stances and political structures could Germany justify pouring further significant resources into the eurozone's survival. She said: 'I know it is arduous, that it is painful, that it is a drawn-out task ... It is a Herculean task, but it is unavoidable.'

Earlier volumes of *Strategic Survey: The Annual Review of World Affairs* have reflected on how domestic determinants severely limited Germany's ability to satisfy the external demands put on it by partners in the realm of security and defence policy (see *Strategic Survey 2008*, pp. 149–54). Only when cherished norms of the German post-war security policy consensus were no longer compatible with each other, because the security environment had changed, did leaders adapt policy. While the stakes and the issues are different, the past 12 months suggest a similar pattern could unfold in the economic and financial sphere. The German electorate and politicians continued to equate high inflation with political instability, citing the Weimar Republic (1919–33) as the prime example. For this reason, Germans could not countenance calls for Germany to stimulate its economy for the greater good of Europe; that, to them, presented unacceptable risks of igniting German inflation. Voters pointed to productivity gains achieved in Germany over the past decade at the expense of limiting wage increases and of welfare reforms, and asked why they should give these up. They contrasted them with what they saw as profligate spending and excessive state-funded benefits in the countries that they were being asked to support.

But Germans did want the euro to survive. They believed that closer cooperation among eurozone economies was the appropriate recipe. The price could be a gradual adaptation of policy towards a more accommodative approach – but it would take strong political leadership to make this happen.

Domestic economic and political uncertainties

Despite its enduring strength, there were increasing worries about the state of the domestic economy. It grew by 3% in 2011, but slowed significantly towards the end of the year – in fact, negative growth of 0.2% was recorded for the fourth quarter. For 2012, the outlook advanced by independent economic institutes suggested annual growth might be as low as 0.4–0.8%. Economists did not, however, expect a repeat of the 2008 recession, because low unemployment and higher incomes were expected to boost domestic consumption, a traditional weak spot in the German economy. While investments by the private sector were likely to remain constrained, exports proved resilient. Unemployment fell below 5.5% by May 2012 according to the harmonised rate of the OECD, which showed 11% unemployment in the eurozone overall. Unemployment among people under 25 was at 5.4%, the lowest level since unification and the lowest in the eurozone.

The party-political scene remained in flux with a lot of movement outside the two big established parties, the Christian Democratic Union/Christian Social Union (CDU/CSU) and Social Democratic Party (SPD). The junior partner in Merkel's coalition, the Free Democratic Party (FDP), continued to be hit hardest, losing many seats in state-level elections and hovering between 3% and 5% in federal-level opinion polls in April and May 2012. The SPD failed significantly to close the gap to Merkel's CDU/CSU, with the big parties polling at 26–29% and 34–36% respectively. The most important development in the political landscape over the year to mid-2012, however, was the growth of the Pirate Party, which, building on success in local and regional elections, was supported by 9–12% of the electorate on the federal level in spring 2012. Advancing an agenda of transparency and Internet freedom, with party meetings streamed live and an online platform on which members could insert policy proposals in real time, the Pirates seemed to appeal to a segment of the electorate that had grown tired of the established parties. However, the party's allure was fragile, as it remained unclear whether a comprehensive political platform would emerge.

The Bundestag extended the mandates for the NATO-led KFOR mission and the EU-led counter-piracy mission *Atalanta* for one year in May 2012. Even though the 'over-the-horizon' reserve force, at the time involving a large German contingent, had to be deployed to Kosovo to deal with tensions on the ground, the KFOR deployment remained uncontroversial. Changes to *Atalanta*'s mandate, agreed among EU member states, did however generate heated debate. From March 2012 the EU force had been authorised to engage and destroy pirate infrastructure up to 2km onshore, and thus on Somali soil. While this shift did not foresee deployment of forces on the ground, except in emergency situations such as search and rescue, it triggered resistance from SPD parliamentarians who had previously supported the mission. The Greens also mostly abstained for similar reasons. Concerns focused on civilian casualties that might result from operating onshore. Gernot Erler, SPD deputy leader in the Bundestag, argued that 'there are some options that you are better off not having'. Green MP Kerstin Müller said the government had turned 'a reasonable mission into an adventurous mission'. While the *Atalanta* mandate was passed with the government's majority, the debate served as a reminder that domestic support for overseas deployments was still fragile in Germany.

In this context, the unfolding agenda of pooling and sharing military capability among NATO and EU members, for example in the framework of NATO's smart-defence initiative formally launched at the Alliance's Chicago summit of May 2012, created pressure to rethink parliamentary arrangements for the deployment of German forces overseas. Defence Minister Thomas de Maizière suggested NATO had to have guaranteed access to multinational command and control facilities, logistics and reconnaissance assets, and that these might have to be exempted from a case-by-case vote of approval in parliament. Opposition parliamentarians reacted strongly. Erler maintained that the Bundestag 'has to have the last word when German soldiers are sent abroad on combat missions'. Jürgen Trittin, parliamentary leader of the Greens, said such plans were not constitutional. Roderich Kiesewetter and Andreas Schockenhoff, respectively CDU/CSU spokesman for disarmament and arms control and CDU/CSU deputy leader, published a policy paper arguing Europe could only hope to improve its capacities in the security realm through closer cooperation, which had to include the willingness to constrain sovereignty in relation to the use of the armed forces abroad. They suggested that a reform of the German legal framework should give the government the right to deploy troops, and parliament the right to call them back if no parliamentary majority emerged. Currently, the government needs parliamentary approval in advance in most cases. Similar ideas had been voiced occasionally before, but never generated wider political support. In the context of pressure on defence budgets across Europe and a reorientation of US policy towards the Pacific, which would leave Europe with greater responsibility for its own neighbourhood, a window of opportunity seemed to have opened for fresh thinking.

Armed forces restructure

In 2011, Germany suspended universal conscription and initiated a fundamental restructuring of its armed forces which would see the Bundeswehr shrink and professionalise, with reduced financial resources. Though the changes were controversial, they swiftly faded from the public glare after the announcements were made, and the focus shifted to implementation.

Defence-spending cuts had been modest compared to other European NATO members, but were likely to accelerate between 2014 and 2016. This was because, although the government had decided in 2010 to cut spending significantly in the following years, the reforms decided upon later would actually cost money upfront, for example because of the cost of reducing the number of civilian employees. The government was funding these costs on top of the previously allocated defence budget, but was expected to accelerate reductions from 2014.

A central element of the restructuring was the move to a smaller, all-volunteer force consisting of 170,000 contracted and professional personnel and up to 12,500 short-term volunteers and 2,500 active reservists. The total of 185,000 compares to a strength of approximately 220,000, including 188,000 contracted and professional soldiers, as of May 2011. The number of civilian staff was set to decline from 75,000 to 55,000. In capability terms, a guiding principle was to prioritise breadth over depth. Germany would try to maintain as broad a spectrum of capabilities as possible while accepting a diminished capacity to sustain simultaneous and long-term operations. This decision was driven on the one hand by the assumption that the security environment would continue to be characterised by high levels of uncertainty, underpinning the need for flexible and adaptable forces; and on the other by the belief that a country of Germany's size and economic weight would have to be able to provide a broad spectrum of capability to exert political influence, including in NATO.

A more capable and restructured Bundeswehr, possibly enabled by more flexible handling of parliamentary control of executive decision-making regarding overseas deployments, would make Germany a more credible partner in NATO and the EU – a core interest of the government. Germany's emergence, through the eurozone crisis, as the dominant actor in Europe led to rising expectations and critical debate about its leadership role. But the government faced the need to continue to balance external and domestic demands.

United Kingdom: Search for Growth

The second year of coalition government was a challenging one for Prime Minister David Cameron and his deputy Nick Clegg. Having forged a surprisingly ambitious programme of reform following the unclear election outcome of May 2010, they ran into predictable difficulties in implementing it, causing squabbles and compromises. Yet the coalition held together, with few signs that it would not last the agreed five-year term.

The biggest problem for the Conservative-led government was the refusal of the economy to grow, in spite of low interest rates and business-friendly measures. It was officially forecast to expand by only 0.8% in 2012, the same pace as in 2011, and provisional figures in the first half of 2012 indicated that the economy had slipped back into a 'double-dip' recession. Its sluggishness laid the government open to criticism for sticking to its plan to shrink the public sector in order to reduce the country's high budget deficit. The coalition's determination to do this, and to reduce the national debt, impressed the financial markets, in which British government bonds were far more in demand than those of European countries with lower budget deficits. For example, the UK budget deficit in 2011 was 8.3% of GDP, below the peak of 11.6% reached in 2009 but well above Italy's 3.9%. Yet the interest-rate yield on UK ten-year government bonds was below 2% at mid-2012 and on Italy's about 6%. (As prices of bonds rise, their yields fall.) The difference lay in the markets' confidence – or lack of it – that planned deficit reductions could be achieved in the face of political and economic difficulties.

In theory, such confidence and the resulting prospect of continued low interest rates – combined with injections of money into the economy by the Bank of England in rounds of 'quantitative easing' – should foster UK economic activity and investment and provide the foundation for solid growth in future years. But the economy remained frustratingly anaemic. The shock of the 2008 financial crisis, in which several British banks were rescued by the government, continued to have an effect, with banks being urged to boost credit but seemingly unable to do so. Damaged confidence among businesses, homeowners and consumers was the most likely reason for a slide back into recession. Private-sector jobs created in 2011, at 226,000, did not match the 270,000 eliminated in the public sector in the same year.

Another important factor was the crisis in the eurozone: although the United Kingdom is not one of the 17 European countries that have the euro as a common currency, a significant proportion of its exports go to those countries. The mood in Britain was severely affected by fears of a eurozone collapse. The government, however, remained very reluctant to relax its stern fiscal stance and to take more creative steps to boost growth. With parliament now intended to have fixed five-year terms, the coalition still had time for the economy to recover and so offset the negative electoral impact.

Tactical politics

The impression was of a country in uneasy stasis, not moving backwards but unable to move forward. This was accentuated by the realities of coalition government, a phenomenon with which the country was unfamiliar, having not had one since the 1930s. Even with three years to go, both the Conservatives and the Liberal Democrats needed to look forward to the day when they were not bound together in government.

Although the coalition gave the Liberal Democrats, who came third in the 2010 election, positions of power that they could not otherwise have hoped for, with Clegg as deputy prime minister and four other ministers in cabinet, the experience was uncomfortable for them. Their role so far was to temper to some degree – but not to stop – reforms that they would otherwise have opposed, including higher university tuition fees and large-scale changes to the National Health Service. With wealthy bankers still being blamed for the financial crisis and its consequences, the Liberal Democrats had to watch as the government reduced the top rate of income tax. Above all, they shared the political backlash from public-sector cuts, unemployment and low growth. Meanwhile, items on the Liberal Democrats' own agenda, such as reform of the upper House of Lords, were not given high priority. As a result, it seemed inevitable that many core supporters would become disillusioned, and that the party was at risk of a major setback at the next election.

For the Conservatives, coalition was no doubt a tiresome drag on their freedom to manoeuvre. But they had to pay attention to its sometimes awkward requirements, since Cameron certainly did not wish to face the verdict of voters until the economy showed more vigour. He needed to keep the coalition in existence, and therefore he had to avoid humiliating his partners. In fact, this constraint might sometimes be useful for Cameron, who has shown himself on occasion to be a hasty leader. The most obvious example of this came in a late-night European Union summit at which he blocked agreement on the 'fiscal compact' treaty, only to see other members press on with it regardless. His clumsy move embarrassed the pro-European Clegg, and appeared afterwards to have been a dramatic but meaningless gesture.

Cameron seemed assured as he pressed ahead with the government's major projects, such as cutting the budget deficit and removing combat troops from Afghanistan. His most significant international move so far was to champion, jointly with French President Nicolas Sarkozy, the campaign that toppled Muammar Gadhafi in Libya – an impulsive but successful venture. But in the to-and-fro of tactical politics, Cameron was proving less adept, and was even being described as gaffe prone. Reforms of the National Health Service were mishandled to an extraordinary degree. The lowering of the top rate of income tax, while perhaps justified on budgetary grounds (a previous increase did not seem to have generated additional revenue), appeared crass politically.

Court drama

In the absence of major developments, a soap opera of a very British kind was being played out, month after month, in Court 73 at the Royal Courts of Justice on the Strand, London. This was the Leveson Inquiry, set up by the government to examine the role of the press and the police following a scandal. The formal outcome will be that Brian Leveson, a senior judge, will recommend a new, as yet unknown form of media regulation in the UK. But the main significance was that it seemed to spell the end of the prominent position that Rupert Murdoch and his companies had held in British life. The issues raised were likely to have ramifications in other countries where Murdoch's News Corporation had large interests – such as the United States – and perhaps for the media business more broadly.

The scandal was sparked by the hacking of telephones by the *News of the World*, a Sunday tabloid in the Murdoch stable, to obtain news stories. The affair had been pursued doggedly by the *Guardian* newspaper and some members of parliament for six years, after the royal household deduced that a story about a knee injury to Prince William, second in line to the throne, could only have been obtained in this illicit manner. Later, it emerged that the *News of the World* had routinely hacked the phones of thousands of people: celebrities, sports personalities, politicians and relatives of such figures. However, the scandal only really broke upon the nation with extraordinary force in July 2011 when it was reported that the same newspaper had in 2002 hacked the telephone of 13-year-old Milly Dowler, who was missing and was later found murdered. It was alleged that messages on her phone had been deleted, leading her family to think that she might still be alive, though evidence for this particular assertion was later found to be lacking. A wave of opprobrium swamped the Murdochs and their companies.

Murdoch's response was to close the *News of the World* down and apologise abjectly. However, his close association with prime ministers including Margaret Thatcher, Tony Blair and Gordon Brown was lavishly detailed in the press. Since Murdoch controlled four newspapers including the best-selling tabloid daily the *Sun*, political leaders had found him important to cultivate, and not just through fireside chats in the prime minister's Downing Street office but through extensive social and family contact. Cameron perhaps came on the scene too late for such a close association with the Murdochs themselves, but was a good friend of Rebekah Brooks, who had been editor of the *News of the World* and the *Sun* and had become chief executive of the News Corporation UK subsidiary which owned the newspapers. As the scandal raged, she resigned. Andy Coulson, who had succeeded Brooks as editor of the *News of the World*, had gone on to become Cameron's spokesman. He had resigned earlier in 2011.

Murdoch and his son James were interrogated by a parliamentary inquiry, where James's denial that he knew the hacking was the work of more than one 'rogue reporter' was met with scepticism. Previously seen as a likely successor to his father, he later resigned from all executive positions he held in the UK. The parliamentary committee deemed Rupert Murdoch not fit to run a major international company, but failed to reach a unanimous decision and thus undermined its own strongly critical report. Brooks was one of many people arrested in a police investigation, and in May 2012 she was charged with perverting the course of justice. The scandal also rebounded on the police, which had not pursued the hacking investigation even though they had the evidence to do so – and even more damaging, it was alleged that journalists used to pay policemen for information. Paul Stephenson, the (London) Metropolitan Police chief, resigned.

Hence the Leveson Inquiry. From November 2011 onwards, celebrities, victims of press intrusion, government ministers, newspaper editors and experts of all kinds were invited to have their say to the judge. If anything, the process seemed to be inflating the importance of newspaper editors, rather than putting them in their place. The inquiry was the place to be seen. Murdoch and Brooks were among those quizzed, and used the opportunity to reveal e-mails that embarrassed the government – perhaps because another effect of the scandal was that Murdoch had to drop his intended biggest move yet into UK broadcasting, the takeover of satellite broadcaster BSkyB. Politicians including Cameron, Blair and Brown trooped down to the High Court to be questioned. Meanwhile, Murdoch began the break-up of News Corporation by splitting off its newspapers from the main group.

Mood changer?

While the scandal claimed plenty of victims, Cameron himself at least appeared to be emerging fairly unscathed. His government could meanwhile claim a number of successes: the messy finances of the Ministry of Defence, which had found itself with at least £38bn of unfunded commitments to acquire equipment, were sorted out. NATO was on track to end its combat presence in Afghanistan in 2014. Real progress was being made in education reforms. But amidst economic stagnation, the national mood could best be described as sullen. The number of economists and politicians who questioned whether the government's dogged pursuit of lower public spending was the correct path, and sought more Keynesian, pro-growth measures, seemed to be growing.

The poor mood meant that much was invested in the London Olympic Games, which were to take place in July and August 2012. The hope was that these would not only boost the economy, but would create a more positive atmosphere.

Developments in European Defence

The economic and financial travails of European countries overshadowed security and defence discussions in the year to mid-2012. Defence spending is being cut in most European NATO member states: between 2008 and 2010 it fell by an average of 7.4% in real terms with a further 2.8% reduction from 2010 to 2011. Meanwhile, the United States was rebalancing its own defence commitments towards the Asia-Pacific region, raising the prospect of greater responsibilities for Europe, at the very least in its own periphery. Yet NATO's campaign in Libya in 2011 had again revealed the dependence of European forces on US enablers such as air-to-air refuelling and intelligence assets. Hence, attempts to promote a climate of closer defence cooperation to safeguard capability in times of austerity remained at the top of the agenda for both NATO and the EU under the rubrics of, respectively, 'smart defence' and 'pooling and sharing'. NATO tried to build momentum for closer cooperation at its summit meeting in Chicago in May 2012. The EU, however, seemed to suffer from a lack of high-level commitment to push forward its Common Security and Defence Policy (CSDP).

NATO leaders, meeting in Chicago, focused on the implementation of an agenda largely defined by the adoption in 2010 of the Alliance's new

Strategic Concept. A key theme was the development of capabilities over the longer term as NATO disengaged from Afghanistan, from which combat troops were due to be withdrawn by the end of 2014. Nevertheless, the summit emphasised that the Alliance would remain engaged in Afghanistan after 2014, and would seek to set up a UN-mandated training, advisory and assistance mission.

Progress was made on NATO's institutional reform process. Defence ministers agreed to cut one Joint Force Command, three component commands (one for each service) and two combined air operations centres. This would reduce the number of posts in NATO's command structure from 13,000 to about 8,800 by 2015. In addition, NATO's planned move into a new headquarters in Brussels in 2016 would bring a streamlining of its international staff, and a sprawling network of agencies was being reorganised in 2012 into just three, for procurement, support, and communication and information.

A further important move was the determination that counter-terrorism was not primarily a military task and that NATO's added value in this area was limited. Hence, the Alliance saw itself as playing a supporting role to other organisations, such as the EU and the UN, and pledged to avoid duplication. NATO did, however, continue to see a strong continuing role for itself in deterrence. Leaders, publishing findings of a posture review, said that 'NATO is committed to maintaining an appropriate mix of nuclear, conventional and missile defence capabilities for deterrence and defence'. While the overall role of nuclear weapons was to remain unchanged, the review indicated that NATO might be willing to reduce its reliance on non-strategic nuclear weapons in Europe in the context of negotiations with Russia, which had a far greater stockpile. It was thus likely that sub-strategic weapons, which are of little military value, would eventually become a bargaining chip in future disarmament talks. Missile defence, it was argued, could complement the role of nuclear weapons in deterrence, but could not substitute for them.

Smart defence
The summit determined that conventional forces should continue to become more flexible, inter-operable, sustainable and deployable, goals that NATO had pursued for the last decade. The latest push towards this was the 'smart-defence' initiative launched by Secretary-General Anders Fogh Rasmussen, former Danish prime minister. He told the European Parliament: 'Today's economic difficulties may tempt European nations to become introverted.

But the need for a confident, compelling, outward-looking Europe has never been greater. This is why European nations must continue to invest in critical military capabilities – smartly and sufficiently.' NATO leaders committed to create, by 2020, 'modern, tightly connected forces equipped, trained, exercised and commanded so that they can operate together and with partners in any environment.' This would be done through prioritisation, cooperation and specialisation – the building blocks of 'smart defence'.

Rasmussen's initiative was designed to cope with the triple challenge of austerity, continuing operational needs and a security environment characterised by deep uncertainty. Prioritisation implied that member states were encouraged to align their armed forces more closely with NATO's capability goals. Cooperation was an attempt to induce the pooling of military capability among Allies in order to generate economies of scale and improve inter-operability. Specialisation was by far the most difficult of the three elements, as it directly impacted on member-state sovereignty. It would entail member governments choosing to use scarce defence funds to invest in areas of excellence while giving up capability in other areas – a process that would be coordinated through NATO to shepherd a set of Alliance capabilities that was coherent and mutually supportive. The ambitious goal of smart defence was to change the way NATO members design, operate, maintain and discard military capabilities. It was not primarily about saving money, but rather about creating better value. Leaders adopted 20 smart-defence projects including pooling of maritime patrol aircraft and improving the availability of precision weapons. Each would be taken forward by a volunteering lead nation. Some were essentially symbolic, intended to build mutual confidence. A central element of the narrative behind smart defence was the promotion of transatlantic solidarity and common security in times of austerity. In the short term, electorates across the Alliance would want NATO to do its share to address the economic crisis by becoming more efficient. In the long run, smart defence could be a tool to reorganise the way in which the Alliance generated common security.

In the EU, ambitions very similar to smart defence continued to be pursued under the heading of 'pooling and sharing', launched in 2010. The rationale was clearly expressed at a Foreign Affairs Council meeting in March 2012: 'European cooperation on pooling and sharing military capabilities represents a common response to European capability shortfalls, aiming at enhancing operational effectiveness in a context of financial austerity and a changing security environment.' In November 2011, the European Defence Agency board endorsed 11 projects, selected from a much longer list, to be taken forward. They included helicopter training and networking of maritime surveillance. A satellite-communication procurement cell would explore the significant savings potential of pooling demand. Italy would lead a project aimed at generating a pooled deployable medical capability by 2014. As in NATO, the projects illustrated the potential to generate value in terms of efficiency, effectiveness, and mutual trust and transparency.

The EU's limited operational ambitions

Though these initiatives made progress, it was less clear what ambitions leading European countries had for operational capabilities, especially through the EU's Common Security and Defence Policy. Previously, the three biggest defence players, France, Germany and the United Kingdom, had launched initiatives within the EU, but by 2011 it had become apparent that their interest had lessened. France had become disillusioned with lack of progress on improved capabilities following its EU presidency in 2008. The UK clearly indicated that it would not play an active role following the 2010 election which brought a coalition government under the leadership of the Conservative party. Germany was struggling with its economic leadership role in Europe and invited doubts about its reliability in defence matters when it abstained in the 2011 UN Security Council vote authorising military action against the Gadhafi regime in Libya.

Perhaps as a consequence, the scope of the CSDP was gradually limited to civilian missions at the softer end of the security spectrum. Its military ambitions were now obscure. Though the US 'pivot' to Asia seemed likely to increase demand for EU missions in its periphery, it looked as if the CSDP would be unable to deliver.

To be sure, there was still a lot of operational activity in the CSDP framework – at mid-2012, the EU was running 12 operations and planned to launch two more during the calendar year. But their strategic effect was limited. For example, mandates for an EU monitoring mission in Georgia, a police and security-sector assistance mission in the Democratic Republic of the Congo, a police mission in Afghanistan, and the counter-piracy operation *Atalanta* were extended. The *Atalanta* mandate now allowed forces to engage pirate infrastructure up to 2km onshore in Somalia. In Bosnia, the EU terminated its police mission on 30 June 2012 but continued to conduct its military mission, *Althea*, albeit at reduced force levels and with an increasing focus on capacity building and training. *Althea* had some 1,200 troops in theatre and could be reinforced through an over-the-horizon force.

A symbol of the CSDP's lack of direction was EUFOR Libya, an operation that the EU offered in 2011 to the UN but stood down after it was clear that the request for activation would never come. On 24 March 2011, the European Council approved a crisis-management concept under which the EU offered a military operation to support humanitarian actors in Libya. The decision to launch was made dependent on a request by the UN Office for the Coordination of Humanitarian Assistance and it was suggested that the operation would not interfere with the neutrality and impartiality of humanitarian activities. On 1 April 2011, the Council formally made this offer to the UN with two specific objectives in mind: to contribute to the safe movement, and if necessary evacuation, of displaced persons, and to support humanitarian agencies in their activities. It was envisioned that operations would last up to four months. An operational headquarters was set up in Rome and a force commander was appointed. Contingency plans were developed covering different options including protection of humanitarian staff, securing and running a seaport and airport, a naval escort for humanitarian aid, and evacuation operations. It was likely that some of the contingencies discussed would have required a force of over 3,000 soldiers. Over the coming months, however, it became clear that neither the UN, nor local actors in Libya, were interested in taking the EU up on its offer. EUFOR Libya was an operation that nobody had asked for and nobody wanted. Ana Gomes, a member of the European Parliament and rapporteur on Libya, suggested it was an 'April Fool's joke'.

The EU nonetheless drew up plans for new CSDP missions. A concept was approved for a regional maritime capacity-building mission in the Horn of Africa and Western Indian Ocean, to be coordinated with *Atalanta* and an EU training mission for Somali security forces in Uganda, already under way. It was expected that the operation, EUCAP NESTOR, would be launched in July 2012 with an initial mandate of two years, and would be a civilian mission augmented with military expertise for a total of 175 staff. Key objectives would be to improve the capacity of regional governments to control their territorial waters with a view to fighting piracy. In the context of planning for this, the EU activated its Operations Centre in March 2012, for the first time since the centre was created in 2003 to coordinate the activities of the three EU operations in the area. Meanwhile, a second new operation was to be launched in the Sahel, a civilian assistance mission to help local police forces to improve inter-operability and strengthen capacity to counter terrorist activities and organised crime. Deployment, with a focus on Niger, was expected in the second half of

2012. The two missions seemed to strengthen the tendency for the CSDP to develop primarily as a civilian crisis-management tool employed in Africa – important, but not sufficient for the EU to become a security actor with global reach.

The Balkans: Roads to Europe

With the eurozone in financial turmoil and neighbouring Greece in political and economic chaos, the countries of the western Balkans remained a comparative oasis of calm in the year to mid-2012. They continued to progress towards integration into the rest of Europe, pursuing a path that began after the Kosovo War of 1999. (See *Strategic Geography*, p. XVIII.)

Albania and Croatia have joined NATO, and all countries in the region except Serbia aspire to do so. All have worked towards joining the European Union, and Croatia is due to enter in 2013. Montenegro and Kosovo, though not members of the eurozone, use the euro, and Bosnia's currency is pegged to it. All except Kosovo have gained visa-free access for their citizens to the Schengen zone. However, the travails of Greece – which has played an important role in shepherding the rehabilitation of the Balkans – and nerves over the Italian economy caused trepidation in the region because of its economic exposure. Historically, the economies of southeast Europe have prospered only when richer European economies were doing well, and have suffered in European downturns.

On the political front, the key event of the year to mid-2012 was the election in Serbia, which saw incumbent president Boris Tadic lose power to a former extreme nationalist, Tomislav Nikolic. In Croatia, a left-leaning coalition took power and in Bosnia the formation of a government almost 15 months after elections in October 2010 was a significant event. Macedonia scored a victory in its two-decade-old struggle with Greece when the International Court of Justice (ICJ) upheld a Macedonian claim that Greece had violated a 1995 agreement between them. Kosovo's leader Hashim Thaci emerged from international isolation caused by accusations in a 2010 Council of Europe report that he was a mafia boss. Throughout the year there were flare-ups of violence in Serb-inhabited northern Kosovo. There were protests in Montenegro against the government, but these had dwindled considerably by mid-year. In Albania the saga of political conflict, which had in effect paralysed governance since 2009, continued for another year.

Economic spillover

The effects of the Greek crisis were felt across the region, though not as dramatically as many feared. In 2011 average GDP growth across the entire Balkans (including Romania and Bulgaria) was a modest 1.9%, but all economies were expected to contract in 2012. A significant proportion of the region's exports are to Greece, Greek banks hold an approximate 20% market share, and Greek investment has been an important factor in the region.

An example of the effects of the eurozone crisis was US Steel's exit in January 2012 from the factory at Smederevo, Serbia, purchased in a privatisation in 2003. A collapse in demand forced the decision to sell the plant, which employs 5,400 people. Albania was especially vulnerable to the crisis, suffering a sharp fall in remittances from Albanians who had been working in Greece. Another effect was a sharp rise in the number of illegal migrants smuggled from Greece via Macedonia to Serbia and on to Hungary, which is part of the Schengen zone. In the past large numbers of migrants from Afghanistan and Bangladesh, as well as Kurds and Africans, could find work in Greece or acquire false papers which could get them to Italy. Over the past year there were few jobs in Greece, coupled with the rise of xenophobic, nationalist parties. Balkan smugglers turned to channelling migrants northwards; one indicator was the fact that more than 3,000 people sought asylum in Serbia in 2011, compared with 51 in 2008. The true number of those moving northwards was unknown – asylum seekers do not stay, but the application gives time for rest and medical attention.

Kosovo's status and Serbia's EU candidacy

The diplomatic struggle between Kosovo and Serbia continued. By June 2012 Kosovo claimed that 91 countries had recognised its independence, though the figure was disputed by Serbia, which maintained that Kosovo was still a Serbian province. Kosovo's international standing improved after the battering it took in 2010 following elections marred by fraud and publication of the Council of Europe report. The report alleged that Thaci had been involved in drug smuggling, murder and organ trafficking. In August 2011, Clint Williamson, a former US ambassador-at-large for war-crimes issues, was appointed to investigate the allegations, which were denied by the government. By June 2012 Williamson had not reported back, but Thaci had meanwhile met US Secretary of State Hillary Clinton, who praised him for helping promote democracy, stability and the rule of law.

In March 2011, at the insistence of the EU, Kosovo and Serbia began a dialogue in Brussels on so-called technical issues. Both sides had an incentive to participate in the talks: Serbia's government wanted to gain candidate status for EU membership while Kosovo wanted to make progress towards visa liberalisation for countries within the Schengen zone. A breakthrough came in July with a deal struck on vehicle license plates, the use of identity cards for travelling and the recognition of university diplomas. However, Kosovo, which was not able to export any goods to or via Serbia, then imposed a ban on Serbian imports and sent special police units to seize the two border checkpoints between Serbia and Serbian-controlled northern Kosovo. The Kosovo police reached one checkpoint but not the second. For the next year there were periodic clashes between NATO troops and local Serbs.

In the clashes, two German soldiers were shot and wounded in November as they tried to remove roadblocks put up by Serbs. German Chancellor Angela Merkel blocked agreement on the granting of EU candidate status. Later, however, intense lobbying and a desire to help Tadic in forthcoming elections led to Serbia being awarded candidate status in March 2012. The EU also opened the way for Kosovo to begin negotiating over visas, and a green light was given for work to begin on a feasibility study, one of the first steps on the road to EU membership for Kosovo.

EU candidacy did not, however, result in Tadic's re-election. In May, having called early elections, he was defeated after eight years as president by Tomislav Nikolic of the Serbian Progressive Party (SNS), formed in 2008 when Nikolic led his followers out of the extreme nationalist Serbian Radical Party. Though he had forsworn extremism and favoured EU membership, most regional leaders boycotted his inauguration after he denied that the massacre of 8,000 Bosnian Muslim men and boys by Bosnian Serb forces at Srebrenica in 1995 constituted an act of genocide. He alienated Croatia by declaring that Vukovar, the eastern Croatian town levelled by the Yugoslav Army and Serbian forces in 1991–92, was a Serbian town and that Croats should not return there.

Croatia's general election in December 2011 resulted in the Croatian Democratic Union (HDZ) being swept from power and replaced by the parties of the *Kukuriku* or 'cock-a-doodle-doo' coalition led by the Social Democratic Party. Two days later the country received the final stamp of approval for EU accession from the European Council, and in January more than two-thirds of those voting in a referendum agreed that they wanted their country to join the EU, which it is due to do on 1 July 2013.

Turkey: Fragile Dreams

At mid-2012 Turkey appeared to be on the brink of another of the periods of uncertainty that have characterised so much of its recent history. There was a palpable sense that an era was coming to a close, but it was unclear what would come next.

Nearly a decade after it first took office in November 2002, the Justice and Development Party (AKP) under its charismatic leader Prime Minister Recep Tayyip Erdogan still dominated the political landscape, with seemingly little prospect of opposition parties being able to loosen its grip on power. Yet Erdogan had announced that he would not stand again for prime minister, arguing that a new constitution was needed to replace the parliamentary system with one in which political power was concentrated in the office of the presidency. After this was done, the 58-year-old Erdogan planned to stand for president for two five-year terms.

Despite concerns about what critics alleged were his increasingly autocratic and authoritarian tendencies, there was no doubting Erdogan's continued popularity. Opinion polls showed his approval ratings consistently over 55%, more than twice the figure for any other politician. But two emergency operations to treat an intestinal growth, in November 2011 and February 2012, reinforced rumours about the prime minister's health. No obvious successor was waiting to take over. There was a general consensus that the AKP would break into different factions if Erdogan were forced to step down.

There was considerable uncertainty about Turkey's role in its region. In his victory speech after the AKP won a third successive term in the June 2011 general election, Erdogan made clear that his ambitions now extended well beyond the country's borders. He confidently predicted that the newly emerging political actors in the Arab world would look to Ankara for leadership, enabling Turkey to establish itself as the pre-eminent power in the Middle East. Twelve months later, those dreams had begun to fade. Instead of becoming a leader, Turkey appeared increasingly marginalised in the region, lacking the ability to shape events even along its own southern border with Syria and Iraq.

An ambition too far?

During its first years in office, the AKP had sought to balance a closer engagement with the Muslim countries of the Middle East with maintaining good relations with Turkey's traditional allies in the EU and the United

States. However, as it grew in confidence, the government began not only to identify more with other Muslim countries in the region but to try to assume a leadership role. The process accelerated after Ahmet Davutoglu, who had previously been Erdogan's foreign-policy adviser, was appointed foreign minister in 2009. In addition to appealing directly to the Muslim masses, particularly through the use of harsh anti-Israeli rhetoric, the government sought to forge closer political, economic and personal ties with the long-entrenched authoritarian regimes in the region.

Like many other countries, Turkey was caught unprepared when – starting in Tunisia in December 2010 – the region's ruling elites came under pressure from a wave of pro-democracy demonstrations. Initially, with the exception of Egypt, where its relations with the government of President Hosni Mubarak had always been strained, the AKP prevaricated, uncertain whether to jettison the relationships it had gone to such trouble to cultivate. But, by summer 2011, Erdogan had become one of the most outspoken supporters of the protesters, even citing his government in Turkey as a model to which they could aspire. Privately, officials confidently predicted that a new generation of democratic regimes in the Middle East would look to Turkey not only for inspiration but also for leadership.

Such hopes were raised still higher in September 2011, when Erdogan paid a five-day visit to Egypt, Tunisia and Libya, where he was received by cheering crowds brandishing his photograph and waving Turkish flags. Caught up in the enthusiasm, Erdogan gave a series of speeches, delivered in a hectoring tone reminiscent of his domestic election campaign, and repeatedly encouraged listeners to emulate his achievements in Turkey.

Although the flags and photographs had been supplied by Turkish businesses active in the countries Erdogan visited, much of the fervour appeared genuine. Many in the Arab world had long admired Erdogan's willingness to confront Israel while their own leaders remained silent. None had forgotten how, in 2010, Turkish NGOs had organised a flotilla of ships to carry aid to the Palestinians and break the Israeli naval blockade of Gaza. On 31 May 2010, Israeli commandos had stormed the flotilla while it was in international waters, killing nine ethnic Turks. In September 2011, after the *New York Times* published a leaked UN report which stopped short of holding Israel entirely responsible for the incident, Erdogan expelled the Israeli ambassador and downgraded bilateral diplomatic ties between the two countries to second-secretary level. The next time that Turkish NGOs attempted to break the Gaza blockade, he said, he would ensure that they were escorted by Turkish warships.

But neither Erdogan nor his advisers appeared to realise that admiration of Turkey's stand against Israel did not imply a widespread desire to accede to Turkish leadership. Nor did they understand that, however much Arabs might resent the West, few shared the Ottoman nostalgia that underpinned Turkish dreams of regional pre-eminence. Indeed, many resented being lectured on how to run their countries. During a visit to Cairo, Erdogan infuriated religious conservatives – including the Muslim Brotherhood, with which the AKP had long had good relations – when he bluntly informed the Egyptian people that they should adopt the Turkish model of secularism, which rigorously excludes any reference to sharia from the country's laws. To many, this was tantamount to instructing them to defy the word of God. In a poll conducted by the US-based Pew Research Center in March–April 2012, when asked whether Saudi Arabia or Turkey served as a better model for their country, 61% of Egyptians named Saudi Arabia and 17% Turkey, with the remaining 22% saying neither was an appropriate model.

The uprising in Syria provided an even starker reminder of the limits of Turkish influence. When protesters first took to the streets in February 2011, Turkey publicly expressed its support for Syrian President Bashar al-Assad while privately encouraging him to defuse the tensions by implementing democratic reforms. When he ignored this advice and opted instead to suppress protests by force, Ankara gradually turned against him. As the death toll rose, Syrians began to flee to Turkey. By June 2011, there were more than 10,000 Syrian refugees in temporary camps in Turkey's southeastern province of Hatay. Although the inflow slowed through the summer months, violence inside Syria showed no sign of abating and Turkey's fury and frustration continued to grow. On 22 November 2011, Erdogan called on Assad to step down. Yet Turkey hesitated to take measures to try to force him from power.

A disparate coalition of Syrian opposition groups was able to organise and hold meetings in Turkey. The Turkish authorities also allowed elements of the armed resistance to Assad, the Free Syrian Army (FSA), to operate out of refugee camps in Hatay and some wounded FSA fighters were treated in Turkish hospitals. But the government avoided providing the FSA with substantial quantities of arms. It was also reluctant to intervene in Syria unilaterally. In February 2012, Turkish officials privately briefed journalists that the government had drawn up military plans for the establishment of a humanitarian aid corridor in Syria. When the news broke, the government hastily issued a statement describing the plans as being merely a contingency measure, insisting that Turkey would only act in cooperation with the rest of the international community. It was aware that, unless it had the backing of the Arab League, the presence of Turkish troops on the ground in a former Ottoman province could be interpreted not as a humanitarian gesture but as imperial recidivism.

Later, an upsurge in violence in Syria led to another increase in the inflow of refugees. By June 2012, refugee camps in Turkey housed over 28,000 Syrians. Publicly, Turkish officials expressed support for the peace plan agreed by Assad and former UN Secretary-General Kofi Annan. Privately, they were sceptical about its chances of success and argued that the only solution was for Assad to be removed from power.

Iran tensions

The turmoil in Syria dealt another blow to Turkey's deteriorating relations with Iran. In 2009 and 2010, the government had aligned itself with Iran in resisting US-led international pressure on Tehran over its nuclear programme. But this was tactical rather than strategic, offering Turkey an opportunity to demonstrate its growing power by defying the West. Within the region, Turkey and Iran remained rivals, not allies. Underlying tensions surfaced when Turkey supported the crackdown by Bahrain's ruling Sunni elite on protests by the country's Shia majority.

For Turkey, even more galling than Assad ignoring its advice was his decision to ally himself more closely with Tehran. As a result, anger in Ankara at the brutality of Assad's domestic crackdown was mixed with pique at his preference for Iran – particularly as many in the AKP regarded Syria as part of Turkey's natural sphere of influence. A key point was reached in September 2011 when Turkey announced that it would deploy an early-warning radar in Kurecik in eastern Anatolia as part of NATO's proposed missile shield. Although officials denied that the radar was primarily aimed at Iran, Tehran was under no illusions. Iranian officials issued a string of furious denunciations, with some threatening to target the radar if the United States or Israel launched air-strikes against nuclear sites in Iran. Turkey remained unmoved, and in January it was announced that the radar was operational.

Friction between Turkey and Iran increased still further as a result of events in Iraq, where the two had long been rivals for influence. Although he was not as subservient to Tehran's wishes as his domestic opponents maintained, Nuri al-Maliki, the Shia prime minister of Iraq, had always had close ties with Iran and a troubled relationship with Turkey. In the run-up to the December 2011 withdrawal of the last US troops from the country, Maliki began to pursue increasingly sectarian policies. An arrest warrant was issued for Iraq's Sunni vice-president, Tariq al-Hashemi, on charges of running death squads which had targeted members of the country's Shia majority. Turkey had regarded Hashemi as one of its allies in Baghdad and angrily denounced the arrest warrant. When he fled to the semi-autonomous – and predominantly Sunni – Kurdish north of Iraq, Ankara made it known that it would be prepared to offer Hashemi political asylum in Turkey, for which it was accused by Maliki of interfering in internal Iraqi affairs.

After the US-led invasion and occupation of Iraq in 2003, Turkey had refused to deal with the Kurdistan Regional Government (KRG), which administers the north of the country, for fear that it would be encouraged to push for full independence – something that Ankara feared could inspire its own restive Kurdish minority. In spite of these fears, it had gradually begun to engage with the KRG, mainly to seek its cooperation in countering the militant Kurdistan Workers' Party (PKK), whose main bases and training camps are located in the inaccessible Qandil Mountains of northern Iraq. In addition, economic ties have grown in recent years, with cross-border trade flourishing. The confrontation over Hashemi strengthened the relationship further. When KRG President Masoud Barzani paid a two day visit to Turkey in April 2012, he was treated virtually as a head of state.

Yet for Turkey, improved relations with the KRG were little recompense for what now appeared to be a belt of Shia-dominated Iranian influence along its southern borders. It remained defiant. In April 2012 Hashemi travelled to Turkey for medical treatment. Following a request by Iraq, Interpol issued an international Red Notice for his arrest. Turkish Deputy Prime Minister Bekir Bozdag announced that Ankara had no intention of implementing the Red Notice and that Hashemi would be free to return to northern Iraq as soon as his treatment had finished.

The West: converging interests, continuing tensions

After several years in which Turkey's policies towards the Middle East had often been at variance with those of the European Union and the United States, Ankara's estrangement from Iran and Syria brought it closer to them on two key regional issues. Yet this in itself posed a challenge for the government, which had used its willingness to oppose the West to bolster claims to regional pre-eminence and remained wary of being perceived as a lackey of outside powers. Nor were Turkey's policies in complete alignment with those of its Western allies.

On Syria, Erdogan repeatedly called for a more aggressive, interventionist approach than that favoured by either the West or Sunni Arab countries such as Saudi Arabia and Qatar. Privately, Turkish officials repeatedly expressed impatience at the international community's reluctance to be more decisive in trying to force Assad from power or to dispatch a multinational force to secure a humanitarian aid corridor. In contrast, Ankara remained adamantly opposed to any military strike against Iran's uranium-enrichment programme. But, unlike in June 2010, when it had attempted to block additional UN sanctions against Iran, it was no longer willing to confront the international community on Tehran's behalf. Instead, Ankara simply called for the stand-off over Iran's nuclear ambitions to be resolved through negotiation rather than force.

Although Ankara had agreed to the deployment of the NATO radar and continued to contribute troops to the NATO-led International Security Assistance Force (ISAF) in Afghanistan, Turkey's relations with fellow Alliance members remained strained. Its refusal to recognise the government of Cyprus continued to block sharing of information between NATO and the EU.

By mid-2012, hopes were fading that this stand-off could be resolved through the reunification of Cyprus, which has been divided on ethnic lines since the Turkish invasion of 1974. UN-brokered negotiations under way since 2008 appeared to be on the point of collapse. On 13 June 2011, the UN Security Council issued a statement expressing its concern at the lack of progress in negotiations and urged the two sides to intensify their efforts. Over the next 12 months, leaders of the Greek Cypriot and Turkish Cypriot communities held regular meetings, usually once a week. They attended two summits in New York hosted by UN Secretary-General Ban Ki-moon. But no substantive progress was made on any of the main points of contention, such as the right of return for refugees who had lost their homes in 1974, power-sharing in a reunified state or the status of Turkish settlers in the Turkish Cypriot-administered north of the island. With the discussions deadlocked, the Turkish Cypriots declared they would suspend negotiations when Cyprus took over the rotating six-month presidency of the EU on 1 July 2012. They made clear that they saw no reason to resume talks once the EU presidency was over.

Turkey also warned that it would suspend relations with the EU for the duration of the Cypriot presidency, a move which appeared likely to deal a final blow to Ankara's EU accession negotiations. In practice, by mid-2012, the process was already moribund. Two years had passed since the EU opened a chapter in Turkey's accession process in June 2010, the longest period any candidate has ever gone without opening a chapter. Not only was there strong public opposition to Turkish accession in member states such as France and Germany, but the government appeared to have lost interest in membership, apparently confident that it could establish Turkey as a power in its own right rather than as a member of a bloc of countries.

Kurdish stand-off

In the general election of 12 June 2011, the AKP had won 49.8% of the vote and 327 seats in Turkey's 550-member unicameral parliament. Erdogan interpreted the result as a personal triumph, an endorsement of his leadership and a validation of his policies. In June 2009, the government had embarked on a bold, if poorly planned and implemented, engagement with Kurdish nationalists in an attempt to negotiate an end to the 25-year-old PKK insurgency. Alarmed by nationalist protests, the AKP had abandoned the public dialogue in October 2009. But government representatives had continued to hold secret negotiations with the PKK, in what became known as the 'Oslo Process' after a recording of a meeting in the city was posted on a PKK website in September 2011. However, by the time the recording became public, the AKP had also halted the Oslo Process, apparently not out of fear of a nationalist backlash but a sense that, after its convincing election victory, it no longer needed to compromise.

While the Oslo Process was continuing, the government had ordered the military to scale back offensive operations against the PKK in the mountains of southeast Turkey. However, from June 2011, a more aggressive approach was adopted, with more search and destroy missions and air raids against PKK camps and bases in northern Iraq. Erdogan issued a series of belligerent public statements, ruling out negotiations and vowing to eradicate the PKK unless it surrendered and laid down its arms. Although the full circumstances remained unclear, it appeared that it was Erdogan's refusal even to contemplate negotiations that prompted elements within the PKK to post the recording of the Oslo meeting on the Internet.

It was not only the AKP that was emboldened by the election. A pro-Kurdish informal coalition of independent candidates, led by the Peace and Democracy Party (BDP), many of whose members are sympathetic to the PKK, won 35 seats, up from 20 in the previous parliament. Buoyed by this, the Democratic Society Congress (DTK), a BDP-dominated coalition of Kurdish nationalist organisations, proclaimed what they described as 'democratic autonomy' for southeast Turkey. They called on Ankara to grant a large measure of self-government to the region and to allow Kurdish to be used as a language of instruction in local schools. In response, the government backed a judicial crackdown on Kurdish nationalist activists. Over the next 12 months, over 8,500 people were taken into custody and more than 4,000 formally arrested and imprisoned on charges of belonging to a PKK umbrella organisation, the Union of Communities in Kurdistan (KCK). Some were probably PKK members and sympathisers. But many, including a number of prominent academics and journalists, were as well known for their opposition to the violence of the PKK as for their support for Kurdish rights.

Although violence declined with the onset of winter, clashes between the PKK and the Turkish security forces began to escalate again in the spring. By mid-2012, both the fighting and the broader Kurdish issue appeared deadlocked, with little prospect of an imminent return to negotiations, much less a solution.

There was also an acceleration in the arrests of serving and retired military personnel on charges either of belonging to a clandestine Turkish ultranationalist organisation, which prosecutors claimed was called Ergenekon, or of plotting a coup in 2003. The rise in arrests ran parallel to growing concerns that some evidence in the cases had been fabricated. However, two independent forensic reports showing that the 2003 'coup plan' had been written using Microsoft Office 2007, which did not appear until 2006, appeared merely to spur prosecutors on. In January 2012, General Ilker Basbug, chief of the General Staff from 2008 to 2010, became the highest-ranking officer to be arrested and charged with membership of the 'Ergenekon terrorist organisation'. By June 2012, a total of 68 serving generals and admirals were in prison, nearly one in five of the 362 serving generals and admirals in the Turkish armed forces.

Gathering uncertainties

Although Erdogan promised to make a new constitution his government's first priority, in practice he had little incentive to introduce a presidential system before August 2014, when President Abdullah Gul is due to step down. Privately, the prime minister made clear he intended to serve as president for two five-year terms, which would ensure that he was still president in 2023, the 100th anniversary of the foundation of the modern Turkish Republic.

These plans, however, were thrown into doubt on 25 November 2011, when he was taken to hospital in Istanbul for an emergency operation to remove a growth in his intestines. After a 48-hour news blackout, it was announced that he had undergone a minor surgical procedure, had made a full recovery and would return to work within a week. In fact, it was 15 December before he was back in his office in Ankara. On 10 February 2012, Erdogan underwent another operation to remove more tissue from his intestines. While officials denied publicly that Erdogan had cancer, privately they acknowledged that the growth had been malignant. On each occasion that he was incapacitated, government business almost came to a halt – indicating that even without a presidential system, political power had already become concentrated in his hands.

These events reinforced concerns about the sustainability of the political stability and economic boom that had characterised the AKP's term in office. Although there was no expectation of an economic crisis, by mid-2012 annual inflation stood at over 8% and the IMF was forecasting that economic growth would slow to around 2.3%, compared with a previous annual average of 4.9% under the AKP.

The most pressing concern was political. There was no convincing heir apparent able to unite the AKP and take over from Erdogan if his health deteriorated to the point where he was unable to remain in office. Neither did any of the opposition parties appear to represent a credible alternative. As a result, if Erdogan were to step down, the likelihood would be a power vacuum as various factions in the AKP put forward candidates for leadership, perhaps even leading to the break-up of the party. The alternative, if Erdogan's health allows him to remain in office, seemed to be an even greater concentration of power in his hands, particularly if he succeeded in introducing a presidential system.

Neither scenario boded well for Turkey's ambitions of regional pre-eminence, which many Turks now regarded as preferable to disappearing hopes of EU membership. Among the new political forces emerging from the Arab uprisings, there was no sign of any desire to live under Turkey's shadow or leadership. Ironically, although Erdogan promoted Turkey as a democratic model, in practice it appeared to be becoming more authoritarian.

Strategic Geography 2012

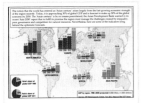

II
The birth of an Asian century?

IV
The US pivot to the Asia-Pacific

VI
The United States' drone wars

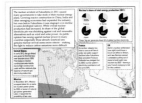

VIII
The nuclear industry after Fukushima

X
Mali's growing insecurity

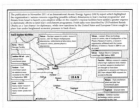

XII
Renewed efforts to limit Iran's nuclear programme

XIV
Civil war in Syria

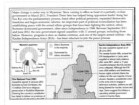

XV
Myanmar's obdurate ethnic conflicts

XVI
Changes of government in the eurozone

XVIII
The Balkans still look to Europe

XIX
Global scientific innovation: new players emerge

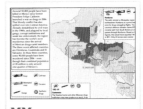

XX
Central America's drugs strife

The birth of an Asian century?

The notion that the world has entered an 'Asian century' arises largely from the fast-growing economic strength of the region recently. Today, it is approaching 30% of global GDP and is forecast to make up 50% of the global economy by 2050. The 'Asian century' is by no means preordained; the Asian Development Bank warned in its recent 'Asia 2050' report that to fulfil its promise the region must manage the challenges created by inequality, poor governance and competition for natural resources. Nevertheless, here are some of the indicators lying behind the optimistic forecasts.

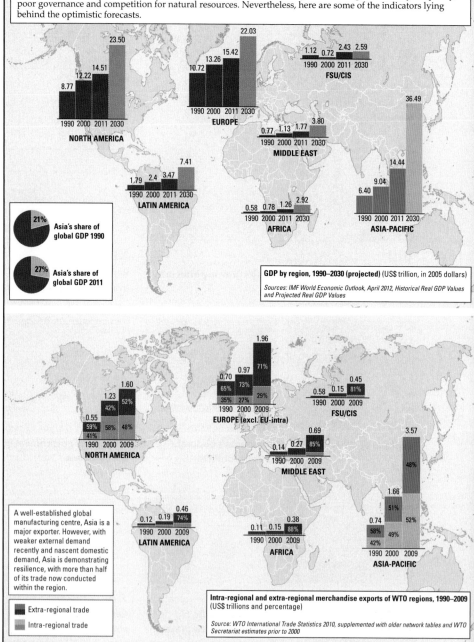

North America — 1990: 8.77, 2000: 12.22, 2011: 14.51, 2030: 23.50

Europe — 1990: 10.72, 2000: 13.26, 2011: 15.42, 2030: 22.03

FSU/CIS — 1990: 1.12, 2000: 0.72, 2011: 2.43, 2030: 2.59

Middle East — 1990: 0.77, 2000: 1.13, 2011: 1.77, 2030: 3.80

Latin America — 1990: 1.79, 2000: 2.4, 2011: 3.47, 2030: 7.41

Africa — 1990: 0.58, 2000: 0.78, 2011: 1.26, 2030: 2.92

Asia-Pacific — 1990: 6.40, 2000: 9.04, 2011: 14.44, 2030: 36.49

21% Asia's share of global GDP 1990

27% Asia's share of global GDP 2011

GDP by region, 1990–2030 (projected) (US$ trillion, in 2005 dollars)

Sources: IMF World Economic Outlook, April 2012, Historical Real GDP Values and Projected Real GDP Values

North America — 1990: 0.55 (59%/41%), 2000: 1.23 (42%/58%), 2009: 1.60 (52%/48%)

Europe (excl. EU-intra) — 1990: 0.70 (65%/35%), 2000: 0.97 (73%/27%), 2009: 1.96 (71%/29%)

FSU/CIS — 1990: 0.58, 2000: 0.15, 2009: 0.45 (81%)

Middle East — 1990: 0.14, 2000: 0.27 (85%), 2009: 0.69

Latin America — 1990: 0.12, 2000: 0.19, 2009: 0.46 (74%)

Africa — 1990: 0.11, 2000: 0.15, 2009: 0.38 (88%)

Asia-Pacific — 1990: 0.74 (58%/42%), 2000: 1.66 (51%/49%), 2009: 3.57 (48%/52%)

A well-established global manufacturing centre, Asia is a major exporter. However, with weaker external demand recently and nascent domestic demand, Asia is demonstrating resilience, with more than half of its trade now conducted within the region.

Extra-regional trade

Intra-regional trade

Intra-regional and extra-regional merchandise exports of WTO regions, 1990–2009 (US$ trillions and percentage)

Source: WTO International Trade Statistics 2010, supplemented with older network tables and WTO Secretariat estimates prior to 2000

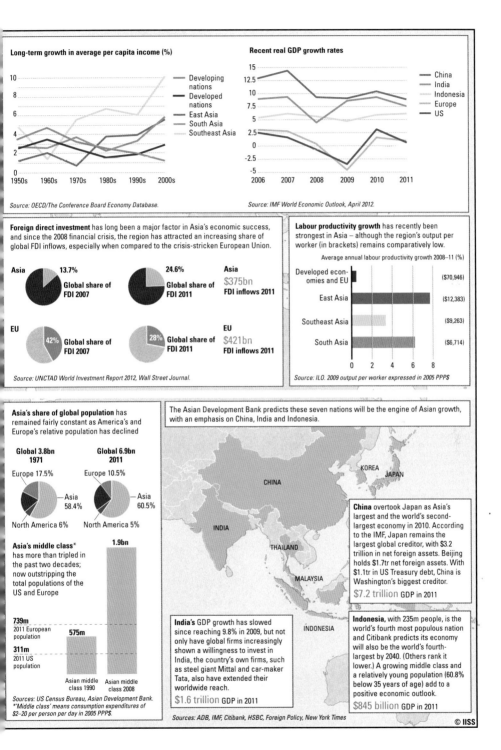

Long-term growth in average per capita income (%)

- Developing nations
- Developed nations
- East Asia
- South Asia
- Southeast Asia

Source: OECD/The Conference Board Economy Database.

Recent real GDP growth rates

- China
- India
- Indonesia
- Europe
- US

Source: IMF World Economic Outlook, April 2012.

Foreign direct investment has long been a major factor in Asia's economic success, and since the 2008 financial crisis, the region has attracted an increasing share of global FDI inflows, especially when compared to the crisis-stricken European Union.

Asia — 13.7% Global share of FDI 2007

Asia — 24.6% Global share of FDI 2011

Asia $375bn FDI inflows 2011

EU — 42% Global share of FDI 2007

EU — 28% Global share of FDI 2011

EU $421bn FDI inflows 2011

Source: UNCTAD World Investment Report 2012, Wall Street Journal.

Labour productivity growth has recently been strongest in Asia – although the region's output per worker (in brackets) remains comparatively low.

Average annual labour productivity growth 2008–11 (%)

- Developed economies and EU ($70,946)
- East Asia ($12,383)
- Southeast Asia ($9,263)
- South Asia ($6,714)

Source: ILO. 2009 output per worker expressed in 2005 PPP$

Asia's share of global population has remained fairly constant as America's and Europe's relative population has declined

Global 3.8bn 1971
- Europe 17.5%
- Asia 58.4%
- North America 6%

Global 6.9bn 2011
- Europe 10.5%
- Asia 60.5%
- North America 5%

Asia's middle class* has more than tripled in the past two decades; now outstripping the total populations of the US and Europe

- 739m 2011 European population
- 311m 2011 US population
- Asian middle class 1990: 575m
- Asian middle class 2008: 1.9bn

Sources: US Census Bureau, Asian Development Bank.
*"Middle class" means consumption expenditures of $2–20 per person per day in 2005 PPP$.

The Asian Development Bank predicts these seven nations will be the engine of Asian growth, with an emphasis on China, India and Indonesia.

KOREA, JAPAN, CHINA, INDIA, THAILAND, MALAYSIA, INDONESIA

China overtook Japan as Asia's largest and the world's second-largest economy in 2010. According to the IMF, Japan remains the largest global creditor, with $3.2 trillion in net foreign assets. Beijing holds $1.7tr net foreign assets. With $1.1tr in US Treasury debt, China is Washington's biggest creditor.
$7.2 trillion GDP in 2011

India's GDP growth has slowed since reaching 9.8% in 2009, but not only have global firms increasingly shown a willingness to invest in India, the country's own firms, such as steel giant Mittal and car-maker Tata, also have extended their worldwide reach.
$1.6 trillion GDP in 2011

Indonesia, with 235m people, is the world's fourth most populous nation and Citibank predicts its economy will also be the world's fourth-largest by 2040. (Others rank it lower.) A growing middle class and a relatively young population (60.8% below 35 years of age) add to a positive economic outlook.
$845 billion GDP in 2011

Sources: ADB, IMF, Citibank, HSBC, Foreign Policy, New York Times

© IISS

The US pivot to the Asia-Pacific

Announcing his government's future defence strategy in January 2012, United States President Barack Obama explained that after ten years of combat in Iraq and Afghanistan, the US military would shift its focus towards the Asia-Pacific. Motivated by the need to respond to the growing sophistication of China's military inventory and to reassure its allies in the region, Washington is consolidating and redeploying its forces. While there is currently a 50/50 split in naval forces deployed in the Pacific and the Atlantic, by 2020 the split will be 60/40.

US Forces Korea
Comprising 20,000 Army and 8,000 Air Force personnel, as well as a further 500 including Navy and Marines, US Forces Korea are charged with defending the Republic of Korea 'against external aggression' and maintaining stability in Northeast Asia. The size of the force has been reduced from 35,000 in 2002, and a number of US bases have been consolidated and relocated under 2002 and 2004 bilateral agreements, with the aim that South Korean forces should increasingly take the lead in operations.

Cam Ranh Bay
A key deep-water port, Cam Ranh Bay served as a US naval base during the Vietnam War and was later taken over by the Soviets before being handed back to Vietnam in 2002. Hanoi announced in late 2010 that it would be opening repair facilities for foreign navies. US Secretary of Defense Leon Panetta visited in June 2012, seeking greater access to the port for the US Navy, while USNS *Richard E. Byrd* was undergoing repairs there.

Littoral combat ships
Building on a 2005 Strategic Framework Agreement that seeks to promote bilateral defence cooperation, Singapore has agreed in principle that up to four US littoral combat ships can dock there on a rotational basis. Crews will live on board and the first ship is set to arrive by mid-2013. A naval repair facility at Changi already provides logistics and maintenance support for ships in the US Navy's 5th and 7th fleets.

Subic Bay, Clark Air Force Base and Joint Special Operations Task Force-Philippines
Two private companies, Huntington Ingall Industries and Hanjin Heavy Industries and Construction Philippines, Inc., signed an agreement in April 2012 to operate out of Subic Bay to repair and maintain US Navy vessels in the western Pacific. Hanjin already operates civilian facilities there, which are being expanded. Subic was a major logistics base for the US navy from 1945 until 1992. Clark US Air Force Base at nearby Angeles City was closed in 1991, but Manila announced in early June 2012 that US forces could once again rotate through Subic and Clark. Joint Special Operations Task Force-Philippines was set up in 2002 with its headquarters in Zamboanga City, Mindanao. Its main focus is to support counter-terrorism operations, provide aid and train air-force personnel in the southern Philippines.

RUSSIA

NORTH KOREA

CHINA

SOUTH KOREA

JAPAN

Okinawa

Commonwealth of Northern Mariana Islands

PHILIPPINES

THAILAND

VIETNAM

Luzon

Subic Bay

Tinian

Cam Ranh Bay

Guam

Mindanao

Zamboanga City

Singapore

Darwin

Indian Ocean

AUSTRALIA

Sources: Australian Department of Defence; Associated Press; Bloomberg; IISS; Singapore Ministry of Defence; Time; US Department of Defense

Marines redeployed from Okinawa
In April 2012 it was announced by Washington and Tokyo that nearly 9,000 US Marines would be shipped off the Japanese island of Okinawa to Guam, Hawaii and the US mainland, and Australia. A further 10,000 Marines will remain, along with 4,000 army/navy and 7,700 air force personnel. The US military presence in Japan dates back to WWII, when defeated Tokyo signed an agreement for the Americans to keep bases on its soil provided the US acted as its security force. This 'keystone of the Pacific' was an important US base during the Korean and Vietnam wars.

US–Japan training range
The US–Japan Okinawa redeployment agreement included funds to develop a joint training range. The location is set to be confirmed by the end of 2012, but Tinian, one of the three principal islands of the Northern Marianas archipelago, is the most likely option. The islands are a commonwealth territory of the US and two-thirds of Tinian is currently leased by the US Department of Defense.

Joint Region Marianas–Andersen Air Force Base and Naval Base Guam
A key hub for US Pacific Command's operations, the US territory of Guam plays host to two military bases, manned by over 4,100 active service members. As part of the redeployment of Marines from Okinawa, 4,700 are to be sent to Guam. Established in 1944, Andersen Air Force Base is described by the US Air Force as 'an important forward-based logistics support center for contingency forces deploying throughout the southwest Pacific and Indian oceans'. A new expeditionary air wing was added in 2003, which has seen deployments of B-2, B-52, F-15, F-16 and F-22, as well as RQ-4 *Global Hawk* unmanned aerial vehicles. In 2001 it was announced that three *Los Angeles*-class nuclear-powered fast attack submarines would be forward deployed to Naval Base Guam. The first arrived in 2002 and the last in 2007. A new support facility was built there in 2010.

Hawaii

Pacific Ocean

US Pacific Command and Pacific Fleet
Based at Camp H.M. Smith, US Pacific Command (PACOM) covers the 36 nations of the Asia-Pacific region. Its aims are to 'strengthen and advance alliances and partnerships', 'mature the US–China military-to-military relationship', 'develop the US–India strategic partnership', prepare for any contingency on the Korean Peninsula and 'counter transnational threats'. The US Pacific Fleet currently consists of approximately 180 ships, nearly 2,000 aircraft and 140,000 naval and civilian personnel. Its operations stretch between the west coast of the US and the Indian Ocean. Around 2,700 of the Marines being redeployed from Okinawa will be sent here.

Marine Air Ground Task Force
US Marines are to deploy to Darwin on a six-monthly basis to undertake bilateral training with the Australian Defence Force. The first rotation began in April 2012 and consisted of an infantry company of 200 Marines, but they did not bring any heavy equipment, vehicles or aircraft with them. Future rotations will include up to 2,500 personnel and will feature command, ground, aviation and logistics elements, supported by major equipment such as artillery pieces, light armoured vehicles and aircraft, as well as ground personnel. They will not have their own bases, but instead share Australian Defence Force facilities.

Washington's regional defence-treaty obligations

The US has historic defence treaties with five regional allies (shaded in orange), each forged in an attempt to stem the tide of communism in East Asia. These represent a 'hub-and-spokes' system, with the US as the central provider of defence agreements to a variety of separate allies. However, in recent years there has been a gradual development of a 'spoke-to-spoke' system, as the various states assume greater defence responsibilities and cooperate directly with each other.

Australia	1951 ANZUS Treaty
Japan	1951 Security Treaty; 1954 Mutual Defense Assistance Agreement; 1960 Treaty of Mutual Cooperation and Security
The Philippines	1951 Mutual Defense Treaty
South Korea	1951 Mutual Defense Treaty
Thailand	Based on the multilateral 1954 Manila Pact of the now-defunct Southeast Asia Treaty Organisation and the 1962 Thanat-Rusk communiqué, which reaffirmed the Manila Pact.

Previous agreements

Taiwan	A 1954 treaty on mutual defence was repudiated in 1980 after the US shifted its diplomatic recognition to China and adopted a policy of strategic ambiguity towards Taiwan.
New Zealand	The 1951 ANZUS Treaty has lapsed where it concerns New Zealand owing to Wellington's refusal since the mid-1980s to allow nuclear-powered or -armed ships to visit the country. However, a new bilateral cooperation agreement on maritime security, counter-terrorism and counter-piracy measures, as well as humanitarian assistance, was signed in June 2012.

The United States' drone wars

Unmanned aerial vehicles (UAVs) have become the Obama administration's – controversial – counter-terrorism weapon of choice. 'Drones', as they are commonly called, began as reconnaissance vehicles. Now militants are being killed by remotely controlled, armed UAVs belonging to the US Air Force and CIA from the battlefields of Afghanistan to Pakistan, Yemen and Somalia. Some 30 other countries possess UAVs, but the size and deadly nature of the US drone programme has put it in the spotlight. Increasing civilian deaths have particularly created resentment in Pakistan, where the CIA has operated UAVs for years. President Barack Obama's counter-terrorism adviser, John Brennan, has defended drone strikes as 'legal, ethical and wise', but the asymmetric nature of 'robotic' warfare, where the risks to the attacker are greatly reduced, has raised questions, as has the killing of high-profile militants accused but not convicted of crimes.

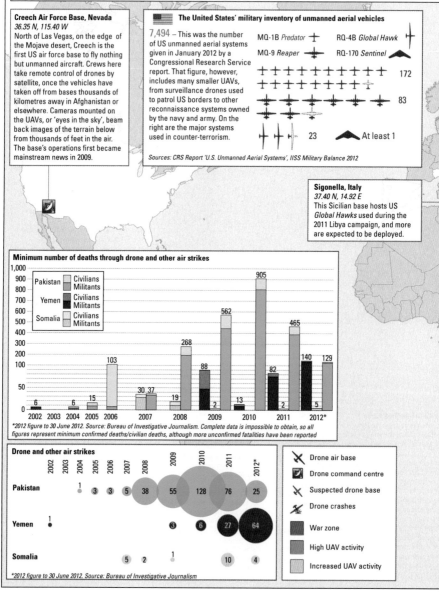

Creech Air Force Base, Nevada
36.35 N, 115.40 W
North of Las Vegas, on the edge of the Mojave desert, Creech is the first US air force base to fly nothing but unmanned aircraft. Crews here take remote control of drones by satellite, once the vehicles have taken off from bases thousands of kilometres away in Afghanistan or elsewhere. Cameras mounted on the UAVs, or 'eyes in the sky', beam back images of the terrain below from thousands of feet in the air. The base's operations first became mainstream news in 2009.

The United States' military inventory of unmanned aerial vehicles

7,494 – This was the number of US unmanned aerial systems given in January 2012 by a Congressional Research Service report. That figure, however, includes many smaller UAVs, from surveillance drones used to patrol US borders to other reconnaissance systems owned by the navy and army. On the right are the major systems used in counter-terrorism.

MQ-1B *Predator* | RQ-4B *Global Hawk*
MQ-9 *Reaper* | RQ-170 *Sentinel*

172
83
23
At least 1

Sources: CRS Report 'U.S. Unmanned Aerial Systems', IISS Military Balance 2012

Sigonella, Italy
37.40 N, 14.92 E
This Sicilian base hosts US *Global Hawks* used during the 2011 Libya campaign, and more are expected to be deployed.

Minimum number of deaths through drone and other air strikes

Pakistan: Civilians / Militants
Yemen: Civilians / Militants
Somalia: Civilians / Militants

2002: 6
2003: 6
2004: 15
2005: —
2006: 103
2007: 30, 37
2008: 268, 19
2009: 88, 562, 2
2010: 905, 82, 13
2011: 465, 140, 2
2012*: 129, 5

2012 figure to 30 June 2012. Source: Bureau of Investigative Journalism. Complete data is impossible to obtain, so all figures represent minimum confirmed deaths/civilian deaths, although more unconfirmed fatalities have been reported

Drone and other air strikes

	2002	2003	2004	2005	2006	2007	2008	2009	2010	2011	2012*
Pakistan	1		3	3	5	38	55	128	76	25	
Yemen	1							3	6	27	64
Somalia					5	2	1		10	4	

Drone air base
Drone command centre
Suspected drone base
Drone crashes
War zone
High UAV activity
Increased UAV activity

2012 figure to 30 June 2012. Source: Bureau of Investigative Journalism

ncirlik, Turkey
37 N, 35.42 E
Before its forces left Iraq at the end of 2011, the US transferred four unarmed *Predators* here. Turkish Foreign Minister Ahmet Davutoglu said the US would operate these in Iraq-related surveillance of the outlawed Kurdistan Workers' Party (PKK). Turkey has also been looking to buy armed US *Reapers*.

Al-Anad, Yemen
13.18 N, 44.76 E
At Al-Anad, the US military works with Yemeni forces against al-Qaeda in the Arabian Peninsula (AQAP). US drones provide surveillance data to Yemeni forces, and launch air strikes. This close cooperation was revealed in a January 2010 diplomatic cable published by WikiLeaks.

Al-Udeid, Qatar
25.12 N, 51.32 E
In a billion-dollar facility in a converted medical warehouse, the Combined Air and Space Operations Center (CAOC) oversees UAV operations throughout the Middle East, Iraq and Afghanistan. Lawyers are on 24-hour call to authorise US military drone strikes. Some drones are also based here.

Al-Dhafra, UAE
24.25 N, 54.55 E
The 380th Air Expeditionary Wing, based at Al-Dhafra since 2002, has around five *Global Hawks*. These are reportedly used for reconnaissance along Iran's borders with Afghanistan and Iraq and along the Persian Gulf; they are also thought to have a node to aid communications between F-22 and F-15 fighters.

Afghanistan
Jalalabad (1) *34.40 N, 70.50 E*
Kandahar (2) *31.50 N, 65.85 E*
Khost (3) *33.33 N, 69.95 E*
Shindand (4) *33.39 N, 62.26 E*
Both the CIA and US military host *Predators* and *Reapers* at Jalalabad; Khost is a CIA base. Largest airstrip Kandahar hosts the *Sentinel* advanced spy drone (the 'beast of Kandahar') used, reportedly, to monitor the Abbottabad compound where al-Qaeda leader Osama bin Laden was killed. A Shindand *Sentinel* crashed in Iran in late 2011.

Shamsi, Pakistan
27.51 N, 65.10 E
Controversy over civilian deaths had already led Islamabad to demand that the US halt CIA drone strikes on its soil. Then the US mistakenly killed Pakistani troops in November 2011 and the CIA was asked to leave its long-term base at Shamsi. The agency is thought to retain access to Shahbaz-Jacobabad and other Pakistani air bases.

Guam
13.58 N, 144.93 E
The first US *Global Hawk* in the Pacific arrived in late 2010 at Andersen Air Base, which is now a major UAV operations centre.

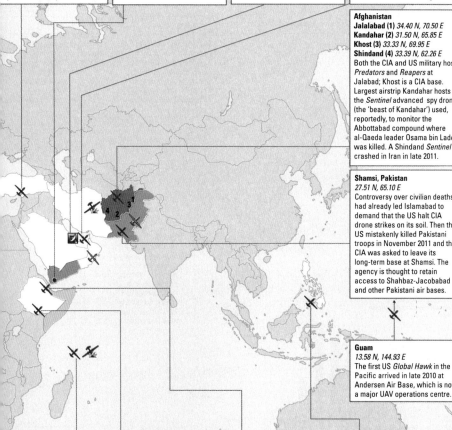

Mahe, Seychelles
4.67 S, 55.51 E
Unmanned drones arrived here in 2009 to track pirates in the Indian Ocean. After a brief withdrawal, US operations resumed in late 2011, with conflicting reports as to whether the *Reaper* drones now being used were armed. Flights were suspended again in April 2012 after two crashes in four months.

Arba Minch, Ethiopia
6.04 N, 37.59 E
In October 2011 the US military said it had established drone operations from this remote base in southern Ethiopia, using *Reapers* to spy on al-Shabaab Islamists in neighbouring Somalia. Ethiopia had shut the air base to the US military in 2007, after news of deadly US aircraft strikes on Somalia emerged.

Camp Lemonnier, Djibouti
11.54 N, 43.15 E
The launchpad for Yemen drone strikes against a leading *USS Cole* attack plotter (in 2002) and, possibly, radical cleric Anwar al-Awlaki (in 2011), this also has Somalia in range. As home to Combined Joint Task Force – Horn of Africa, the US defence secretary calls it 'central' to the ongoing fight against terrorism.

Zamboanga, Philippines
6.92 N, 122.06 E
After February 2012 reports that American drones had provided intelligence for Filipino strikes killing Abu Sayyaf and Jemaah Islamiah terrorists on the island of Jolo, President Benigno Aquino said reconnaissance UAV use was acceptable, but that no US drone strikes would be tolerated on Philippine territory.

urces: Bureau of Investigative Journalism, Foreign Policy, IISS Military Balance, Google Maps, Aviation Week, CBS, Hurriyet, Long War Journal, New York Times, PBS, ters, Rolling Stone, Stars and Stripes, USA Today, US Navy, US Air Force, Washington Post, Wired Danger Room.

The nuclear industry after Fukushima

The nuclear accident at Fukushima in 2011 caused many governments to take stock of their nuclear energy plans. Growing reactor construction in China, India and other emerging economies had expanded the industry, but even before Fukushima it was stagnant or in decline in some developed nations. While overall nuclear production had increased, its share of the global electricity pie was shrinking against coal and renewable alternatives such as wind and solar power. As public opinion has swung against nuclear power in many countries (especially those already sceptical) any genuine nuclear revival seems more remote – making the fight to reduce carbon emissions more difficult.

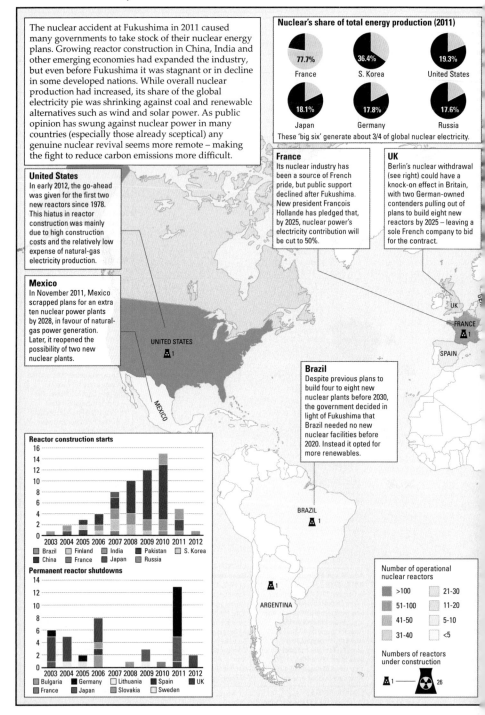

Nuclear's share of total energy production (2011)

77.7% France

36.4% S. Korea

19.3% United States

18.1% Japan

17.8% Germany

17.6% Russia

These 'big six' generate about 3/4 of global nuclear electricity.

United States
In early 2012, the go-ahead was given for the first two new reactors since 1978. This hiatus in reactor construction was mainly due to high construction costs and the relatively low expense of natural-gas electricity production.

Mexico
In November 2011, Mexico scrapped plans for an extra ten nuclear power plants by 2028, in favour of natural-gas power generation. Later, it reopened the possibility of two new nuclear plants.

France
Its nuclear industry has been a source of French pride, but public support declined after Fukushima. New president Francois Hollande has pledged that, by 2025, nuclear power's electricity contribution will be cut to 50%.

UK
Berlin's nuclear withdrawal (see right) could have a knock-on effect in Britain, with two German-owned contenders pulling out of plans to build eight new reactors by 2025 – leaving a sole French company to bid for the contract.

Brazil
Despite previous plans to build four to eight new nuclear plants before 2030, the government decided in light of Fukushima that Brazil needed no new nuclear facilities before 2020. Instead it opted for more renewables.

UNITED STATES
MEXICO
UK
FRANCE
SPAIN
BRAZIL
ARGENTINA

Reactor construction starts
16
14
12
10
8
6
4
2
0
2003 2004 2005 2006 2007 2008 2009 2010 2011 2012

Brazil | Finland | India | Pakistan | S. Korea
China | France | Japan | Russia

Permanent reactor shutdowns
14
12
10
8
6
4
2
0
2003 2004 2005 2006 2007 2008 2009 2010 2011 2012

Bulgaria | Germany | Lithuania | Spain | UK
France | Japan | Slovakia | Sweden

Number of operational nuclear reactors
>100 | 21-30
51-100 | 11-20
41-50 | 5-10
31-40 | <5

Numbers of reactors under construction

1 ———— 26

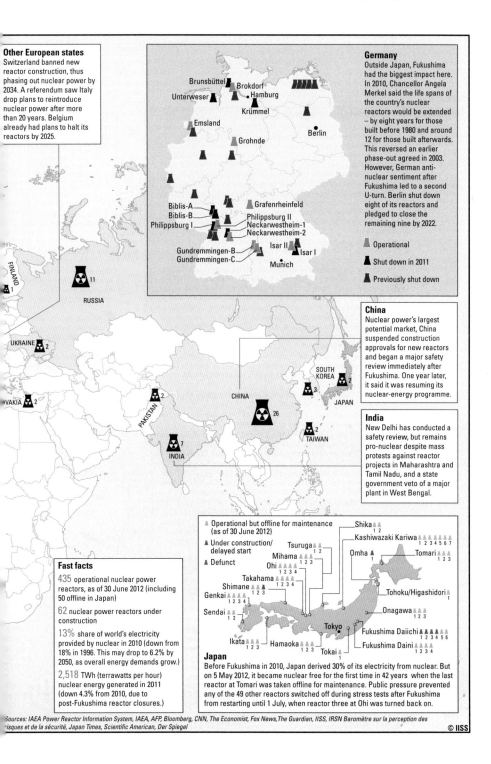

Other European states
Switzerland banned new reactor construction, thus phasing out nuclear power by 2034. A referendum saw Italy drop plans to reintroduce nuclear power after more than 20 years. Belgium already had plans to halt its reactors by 2025.

Germany
Outside Japan, Fukushima had the biggest impact here. In 2010, Chancellor Angela Merkel said the life spans of the country's nuclear reactors would be extended – by eight years for those built before 1980 and around 12 for those built afterwards. This reversed an earlier phase-out agreed in 2003. However, German anti-nuclear sentiment after Fukushima led to a second U-turn. Berlin shut down eight of its reactors and pledged to close the remaining nine by 2022.

Operational
Shut down in 2011
Previously shut down

China
Nuclear power's largest potential market, China suspended construction approvals for new reactors and began a major safety review immediately after Fukushima. One year later, it said it was resuming its nuclear-energy programme.

India
New Delhi has conducted a safety review, but remains pro-nuclear despite mass protests against reactor projects in Maharashtra and Tamil Nadu, and a state government veto of a major plant in West Bengal.

Fast facts
435 operational nuclear power reactors, as of 30 June 2012 (including 50 offline in Japan)

62 nuclear power reactors under construction

13% share of world's electricity provided by nuclear in 2010 (down from 18% in 1996. This may drop to 6.2% by 2050, as overall energy demands grow.)

2,518 TWh (terrawatts per hour) nuclear energy generated in 2011 (down 4.3% from 2010, due to post-Fukushima reactor closures.)

Japan
Before Fukushima in 2010, Japan derived 30% of its electricity from nuclear. But on 5 May 2012, it became nuclear free for the first time in 42 years when the last reactor at Tomari was taken offline for maintenance. Public pressure prevented any of the 49 other reactors switched off during stress tests after Fukushima from restarting until 1 July, when reactor three at Ohi was turned back on.

Sources: IAEA Power Reactor Information System, IAEA, AFP, Bloomberg, CNN, The Economist, Fox News, The Guardian, IISS, IRSN Baromètre sur la perception des risques et de la sécurité, Japan Times, Scientific American, Der Spiegel

© IISS

Mali's growing insecurity

The security situation in Mali has deteriorated significantly this year after an uprising by various Tuareg rebel factions in the north led members of the Malian army to launch a coup in protest at President Amadou Toumani Touré's poor handling of the crisis. Though Tuareg nomads across the Sahel have been opposing local governments since the 1960s, an influx of well-armed former officers of Muammar Gadhafi's armed forces into Mali after the collapse of the Libyan regime in 2011 has given the rebels a decisive advantage over Mali's poorly

Timeline of the coup and rebel gains in the north

Late January 2012	The Mouvement National pour la Libération de l'Azawad (MNLA), whose aim is the creation of an independent state of Azawad in northern Mali, conducts a series of assaults across the country, including on Ménaka in southcentral Mali, Tessalit and nearby Aguelhok in the north and Léré in the centre. The raid on an Aguelhok military base leaves 82 soldiers and civilians dead. The disparate nature of the attacks makes an effective military response very difficult.
February	As government and MNLA forces fight for the control of key towns, popular frustration at the actions of the MNLA and the government's inability to tackle them leads to violence against Tuaregs living in the south. The MNLA attempts to distance itself from al-Qaeda in the Islamic Maghreb (AQIM), stating that the group's aim is the creation of a 'secular republic of Azawad' in northern Mali.
21/22 March	Angry at their government's handling of the Tuareg uprising, Malian soldiers stage a coup against President Amadou Toumani Touré, a month before presidential elections are set to take place. Led by Captain Amadou Haya Sanogo, the coup leaders introduce themselves as the Comité National pour le Redressement de la Démocratie et la Restauration de l'État (CNRDR), and pledge to 'return power to a democratically elected president as soon as national unity and territorial integrity are restored' in the north of the country.
Late March	A high-level delegation representing the Economic Community of West African States (ECOWAS) urges the CNRDR to stand down or face the consequences, which could include the use of force. The African Union suspends Mali's membership; aid payments from the World Bank, African Development Bank and United States are suspended.
Late March/ early April	Divisions within the Tuareg rebel movement emerge. Ansar al-Din, a faction of Islamist Tuaregs that had worked in concert with the MNLA, begins to assert its authority and calls for the imposition of sharia law across Mali. It is thought to have close links with AQIM.
30 March– 1 April	Tuareg rebels gain control of Timbuktu, Gao and Kidal. The MNLA is forced out of Timbuktu by Ansar al-Din on 4 April.
2 April	ECOWAS imposes economic sanctions on Mali, halting trade and freezing bank accounts until 'constitutional order' is re-established.
6 April	MNLA declares independence for Azawad. Military coup leader Sanogo hands over power to National Assembly Speaker Dioncounda Traoré. He is sworn in on 12 April and will serve as interim head of state for 40 days. ECOWAS lifts its sanctions.
26 April	ECOWAS approves in principle the deployment of a 3,000-strong intervention force, despite the objections of Sanogo. The force could be used to maintain stability in Bamako and reclaim territory from Tuareg rebels in the north.
30 April–1 May	An uprising in Bamako by members of Touré's former presidential guard, the Malian army's 33rd battalion, is quashed by troops loyal to Sanogo.
14 May	ECOWAS threatens to reimpose its sanctions, accusing Sanogo of continued interference in Malian politics. He had called for the nomination of a new interim president as Traoré's 40-day term came to an end, while ECOWAS wanted Traoré to stay on for a year.
20 May	In a deal brokered by ECOWAS, Sanogo gives his backing for Traoré to stay on as president until an election can be held; in return Sanogo is granted the status of a former head of state with its accompanying salary, mansion, security detail and other privileges.
21 May	A planned convention by civilian supporters of the coup results in the storming of the presidential palace; Traoré is beaten unconscious and later flown to France for treatment.
26 May	After weeks of negotiations, the MNLA and Ansar al-Din announce the creation of the 'Islamic Republic of Azawad' and agree to what is ultimately a short-lived merger – it falls apart after disagreements over whether sharia law should be imposed across the Azawad region.
15 June	The African Union and ECOWAS member states fail in their effort to convince the UN Security Council to sanction the deployment of the ECOWAS intervention force into Mali.
28 June	Underlining the divisions between the various Tuareg rebel factions, Ansar al-Din rebels take control of Gao from the MNLA.
1 July	Ansar al-Din attack UNESCO-listed mausoleums and tombs of Sufi saints in Timbuktu – the worship of saints runs counter to their Salafist beliefs.

Incidence of armed conflict, as reported by the United Nations Office for the Coordination of Humanitarian Affairs (UNOCHA)

Internally displaced population, UNOCHA June 2012
167,250

Refugee population, UNOCHA June 2012
61,650

Area inhabited by Tuaregs

'Stressed' food security situation, as judged by the United States Agency for International Development, May 2012

Major seizures of illicit weapons and smuggling routes, 2008–2011

Approximate line of division between army and rebel-held territory

Direction of Tuareg offensive

Army reinforcements sent to the front

52 Infantry battalions

trained and under-equipped military. Mali's neighbours are watching the situation closely: they fear that Ansar al-Din, a faction of Tuareg Islamists thought to have close ties with al-Qaeda in the Islamic Maghreb, could use Mali's insecurity to spread Islamic extremism further across the Sahel. Meanwhile, much of the country is in the grip of a food crisis and many Malians are fleeing their homes.

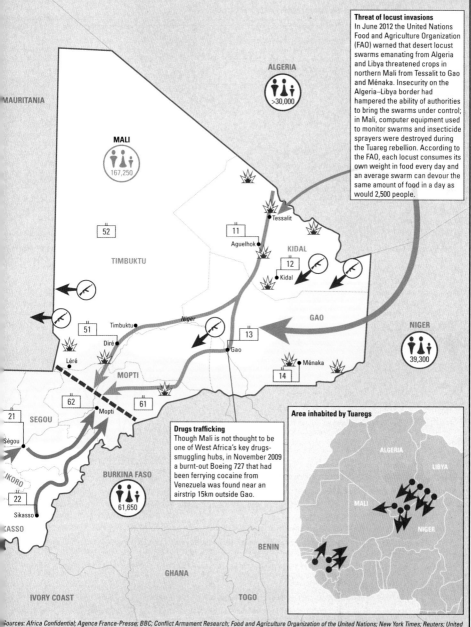

Threat of locust invasions
In June 2012 the United Nations Food and Agriculture Organization (FAO) warned that desert locust swarms emanating from Algeria and Libya threatened crops in northern Mali from Tessalit to Gao and Ménaka. Insecurity on the Algeria–Libya border had hampered the ability of authorities to bring the swarms under control; in Mali, computer equipment used to monitor swarms and insecticide sprayers were destroyed during the Tuareg rebellion. According to the FAO, each locust consumes its own weight in food every day and an average swarm can devour the same amount of food in a day as would 2,500 people.

Drugs trafficking
Though Mali is not thought to be one of West Africa's key drugs-smuggling hubs, in November 2009 a burnt-out Boeing 727 that had been ferrying cocaine from Venezuela was found near an airstrip 15km outside Gao.

Area inhabited by Tuaregs

Sources: Africa Confidential; Agence France-Presse; BBC; Conflict Armament Research; Food and Agriculture Organization of the United Nations; New York Times; Reuters; United ns Food and Agriculture Organization; United Nations Office for the Coordination of Humanitarian Affairs; United States Agency for International Development; www.allafrica.com.

Renewed efforts to limit Iran's nuclear programme

The publication in November 2011 of an International Atomic Energy Agency (IAEA) report which highlighted the organisation's 'serious concerns regarding possible military dimensions to Iran's nuclear programme' and threats from Israel to launch a pre-emptive strike on the country's nuclear facilities have added a greater urgency to diplomatic efforts to limit Iran's enrichment programme. Fresh talks were described by US President Barack Obama as a 'last chance' for diplomacy, while new sanctions by the United States and European Union sought to place Iran under heightened economic pressure to back down.

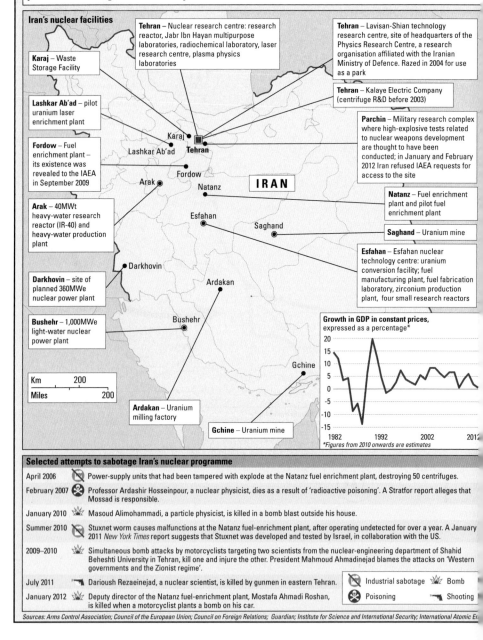

Iran's nuclear facilities

Karaj – Waste Storage Facility

Lashkar Ab'ad – pilot uranium laser enrichment plant

Fordow – Fuel enrichment plant – its existence was revealed to the IAEA in September 2009

Arak – 40MWt heavy-water research reactor (IR-40) and heavy-water production plant

Darkhovin – site of planned 360MWe nuclear power plant

Bushehr – 1,000MWe light-water nuclear power plant

Tehran – Nuclear research centre: research reactor, Jabr Ibn Hayan multipurpose laboratories, radiochemical laboratory, laser research centre, plasma physics laboratories

Tehran – Lavisan-Shian technology research centre, site of headquarters of the Physics Research Centre, a research organisation affiliated with the Iranian Ministry of Defence. Razed in 2004 for use as a park

Tehran – Kalaye Electric Company (centrifuge R&D before 2003)

Parchin – Military research complex where high-explosive tests related to nuclear weapons development are thought to have been conducted; in January and February 2012 Iran refused IAEA requests for access to the site

Natanz – Fuel enrichment plant and pilot fuel enrichment plant

Saghand – Uranium mine

Esfahan – Esfahan nuclear technology centre: uranium conversion facility; fuel manufacturing plant, fuel fabrication laboratory, zirconium production plant, four small research reactors

Ardakan – Uranium milling factory

Gchine – Uranium mine

Km 200
Miles 200

Growth in GDP in constant prices, expressed as a percentage*

20
15
10
5
0
-5
-10
-15

1982   1992   2002   2012

*Figures from 2010 onwards are estimates

Selected attempts to sabotage Iran's nuclear programme

April 2006	Industrial sabotage	Power-supply units that had been tampered with explode at the Natanz fuel enrichment plant, destroying 50 centrifuges.
February 2007	Poisoning	Professor Ardashir Hosseinpour, a nuclear physicist, dies as a result of 'radioactive poisoning'. A Stratfor report alleges that Mossad is responsible.
January 2010	Bomb	Masoud Alimohammadi, a particle physicist, is killed in a bomb blast outside his house.
Summer 2010	Industrial sabotage	Stuxnet worm causes malfunctions at the Natanz fuel-enrichment plant, after operating undetected for over a year. A January 2011 *New York Times* report suggests that Stuxnet was developed and tested by Israel, in collaboration with the US.
2009–2010	Bomb	Simultaneous bomb attacks by motorcyclists targeting two scientists from the nuclear-engineering department of Shahid Beheshti University in Tehran, kill one and injure the other. President Mahmoud Ahmadinejad blames the attacks on 'Western governments and the Zionist regime'.
July 2011	Shooting	Darioush Rezaeinejad, a nuclear scientist, is killed by gunmen in eastern Tehran.
January 2012	Bomb	Deputy director of the Natanz fuel-enrichment plant, Mostafa Ahmadi Roshan, is killed when a motorcyclist plants a bomb on his car.

Industrial sabotage   Bomb
Poisoning   Shooting

Sources: Arms Control Association; Council of the European Union; Council on Foreign Relations; Guardian; Institute for Science and International Security; International Atomic En

Diplomatic timeline

▢ = United Nations sanctions

July 2006	United Nations Security Council Resolution 1696 mandates that Iran halt uranium-enrichment and -reprocessing activities, including R&D.
December 2006	UNSCR 1737 imposes first sanctions on Iran's nuclear programme, freezing the foreign-held assets of 22 Iranian individuals and entities, and restricting IAEA technical cooperation with Iran.
March 2007	UNSCR 1747 mandates further sanctions, adding a further 28 Iranian individuals and entities subject to asset freeze, and banning Iranian arms exports, while restricting arms imports.
March 2008	UNSCR 1803 restricts the activities of Iranian banks, and reiterates that diplomatic talks remain a possibility provided Iran halts its uranium-enrichment activities.
September 2008	Reaffirming previous sanctions, UNSCR 1835 calls on Iran to comply 'fully and without delay'.
October 2009	US, France and Russia put forward a nuclear-fuel-exchange plan, under which Russia and France would provide replacement fuel for the Tehran Research Reactor (TRR) after Iran exported 1,200kg (75%) of its stockpile of low-enriched uranium (LEU). The plan is rejected by Iran a month later.
May 2010	Brazil and Turkey broker 'Tehran Joint Agreement' whereby Iran agrees to send 1,200kg of LEU to Turkey in return for 120kg of fuel for the TRR within one year. The agreement is rejected by the US and allies, who press for further sanctions.
June 2010	UNSCR 1929 expands the existing arms embargo, tightens restrictions on financial and shipping enterprises, and calls for 'cargo inspections to detect and stop Iran's acquisition of illicit materials'.
July 2010	The EU agrees to new sanctions to complement UNSCR 1929 which target Iran's foreign trade, banking and energy sectors.
January 2011	Talks between the E3+3 (Britain, France, Germany, China, Russia and the US) and Iran collapse.
November 2011	IAEA quarterly report on the Iranian nuclear programme, outlining its 'serious concerns regarding possible military dimensions to Iran's nuclear programme'. The US, UK and Canada blacklist the entire Iranian banking sector.
December 2011	Washington tightens its sanctions regime by threatening to cut off access to the US banking system to any foreign institution that purchases oil through the Central Bank of Iran, where Iranian oil revenues are channelled.
January 2012	The EU imposes new sanctions banning the purchase of Iranian crude oil and petroleum products by its members, with effect from 1 July 2012.
April–June 2012	During three rounds of talks with Iran, the E3+3 seek pledges from Iran that it will stop 20% uranium enrichment, shut the Fordow plant and ship out its stockpile of 20% enriched uranium. In return, Iran seeks an acknowledgement of its right to enrich and the lifting of sanctions.

Iranian and Western military assets in the Strait of Hormuz

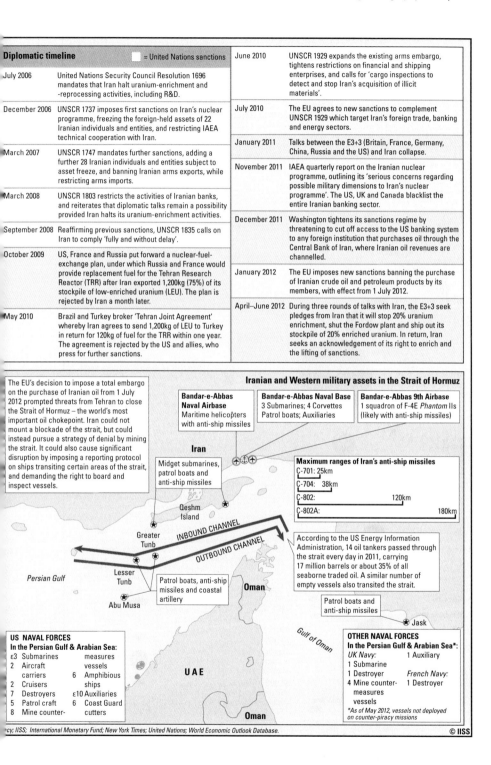

The EU's decision to impose a total embargo on the purchase of Iranian oil from 1 July 2012 prompted threats from Tehran to close the Strait of Hormuz – the world's most important oil chokepoint. Iran could not mount a blockade of the strait, but could instead pursue a strategy of denial by mining the strait. It could also cause significant disruption by imposing a reporting protocol on ships transiting certain areas of the strait, and demanding the right to board and inspect vessels.

Bandar-e-Abbas Naval Airbase
Maritime helicopters with anti-ship missiles

Bandar-e-Abbas Naval Base
3 Submarines; 4 Corvettes
Patrol boats; Auxiliaries

Bandar-e-Abbas 9th Airbase
1 squadron of F-4E *Phantom* IIs
(likely with anti-ship missiles)

Iran

Midget submarines, patrol boats and anti-ship missiles

Qeshm Island

Maximum ranges of Iran's anti-ship missiles
C-701: 25km
C-704: 38km
C-802: 120km
C-802A: 180km

Greater Tunb

INBOUND CHANNEL

OUTBOUND CHANNEL

Persian Gulf

Lesser Tunb

Patrol boats, anti-ship missiles and coastal artillery

Abu Musa

Oman

According to the US Energy Information Administration, 14 oil tankers passed through the strait every day in 2011, carrying 17 million barrels or about 35% of all seaborne traded oil. A similar number of empty vessels also transited the strait.

Patrol boats and anti-ship missiles

✦ Jask

Gulf of Oman

UAE

Oman

US NAVAL FORCES
In the Persian Gulf & Arabian Sea:
ε3	Submarines		measures vessels
2	Aircraft carriers	6	Amphibious ships
2	Cruisers	ε10	Auxiliaries
7	Destroyers	6	Coast Guard cutters
5	Patrol craft		
8	Mine counter-		

OTHER NAVAL FORCES
In the Persian Gulf & Arabian Sea*:
UK Navy:	1 Auxiliary
1 Submarine	
1 Destroyer	*French Navy:*
4 Mine counter- measures vessels	1 Destroyer

*As of May 2012, vessels not deployed on counter-piracy missions

Civil war in Syria

What started in March 2011 as peaceful protests for reform eventually degenerated into civil war in Syria. The shooting and torture of protesters led government opponents to take up arms and soldiers to defect to the rebel Free Syrian Army. By mid-2012 up to 17,000 had been killed, while tens of thousands had fled to Turkey, Lebanon and Jordan. Syria was increasingly split between a Sunni-Muslim-dominated opposition and supporters of President Bashar al-Assad's Alawite (Shia) regime. Despite a 'peace' plan struck by UN and Arab League special envoy Kofi Annan and the arrival of UN monitors, bloodshed continued. Suicide attacks raised suspicions that Al-Qaeda had begun operating in Syria, while a series of civilian massacres was widely (but not universally) blamed on 'shabiha' militia loyal to the regime.

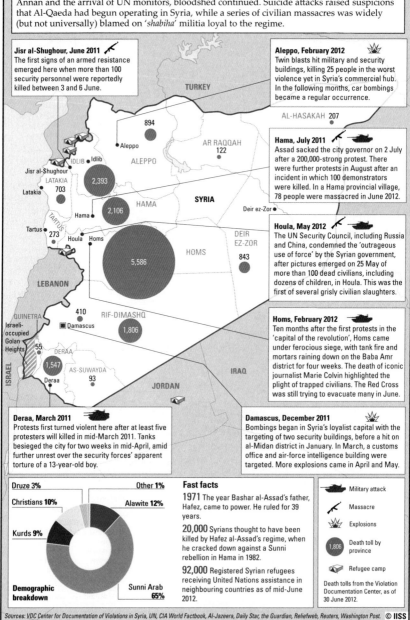

Jisr al-Shughour, June 2011
The first signs of an armed resistance emerged here when more than 100 security personnel were reportedly killed between 3 and 6 June.

Aleppo, February 2012
Twin blasts hit military and security buildings, killing 25 people in the worst violence yet in Syria's commercial hub. In the following months, car bombings became a regular occurrence.

Hama, July 2011
Assad sacked the city governor on 2 July after a 200,000-strong protest. There were further protests in August after an incident in which 100 demonstrators were killed. In a Hama provincial village, 78 people were massacred in June 2012.

Houla, May 2012
The UN Security Council, including Russia and China, condemned the 'outrageous use of force' by the Syrian government, after pictures emerged on 25 May of more than 100 dead civilians, including dozens of children, in Houla. This was the first of several grisly civilian slaughters.

Homs, February 2012
Ten months after the first protests in the 'capital of the revolution', Homs came under ferocious siege, with tank fire and mortars raining down on the Baba Amr district for four weeks. The death of iconic journalist Marie Colvin highlighted the plight of trapped civilians. The Red Cross was still trying to evacuate many in June.

Deraa, March 2011
Protests first turned violent here after at least five protesters will killed in mid-March 2011. Tanks besieged the city for two weeks in mid-April, amid further unrest over the security forces' apparent torture of a 13-year-old boy.

Damascus, December 2011
Bombings began in Syria's loyalist capital with the targeting of two security buildings, before a hit on al-Midan district in January. In March, a customs office and air-force intelligence building were targeted. More explosions came in April and May.

Druze 3%
Christians 10%
Kurds 9%
Other 1%
Alawite 12%
Sunni Arab 65%

Demographic breakdown

Fast facts

1971 The year Bashar al-Assad's father, Hafez, came to power. He ruled for 39 years.

20,000 Syrians thought to have been killed by Hafez al-Assad's regime, when he cracked down against a Sunni rebellion in Hama in 1982.

92,000 Registered Syrian refugees receiving United Nations assistance in neighbouring countries as of mid-June 2012.

Military attack

Massacre

Explosions

1,806 Death toll by province

Refugee camp

Death tolls from the Violation Documentation Center, as of 30 June 2012.

Sources: VDC Center for Documentation of Violations in Syria, UN, CIA World Factbook, Al-Jazeera, Daily Star, the Guardian, Reliefweb, Reuters, Washington Post. © IISS

Myanmar's obdurate ethnic conflicts

Major change is under way in Myanmar. Since coming to office as head of a partially civilian government in March 2011, President Thein Sein has helped bring opposition leader Aung San Suu Kyi into the parliamentary process, freed other political prisoners, expanded democratic freedoms and begun economic reforms. An important part of political reconciliation has been establishing peace with the armed ethnic groups that have been fighting the central, ethnic Burmese-dominated government, often since independence in 1948. Between September 2011 and June 2012, the new government signed ceasefires with 11 armed groups, including those below. However, progress is slow as clashes continue, and one of the largest armed militias – the Kachin Independence Army (KIA) – has been reluctant to join the peace process.

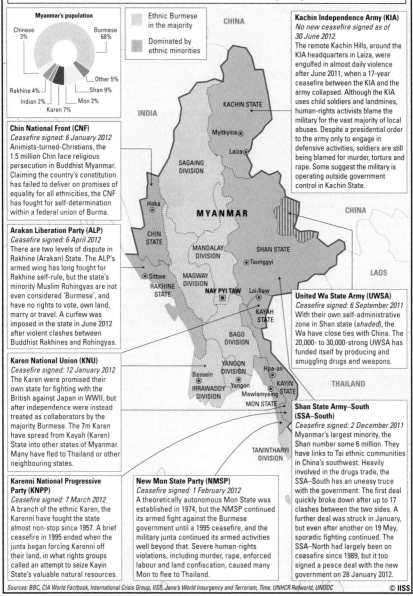

Myanmar's population

Chinese 3%
Burmese 68%
Other 5%
Rakhine 4%
Shan 9%
Indian 2%
Mon 2%
Karen 7%

Ethnic Burmese in the majority

Dominated by ethnic minorities

Kachin Independence Army (KIA)
No new ceasefire signed as of 30 June 2012
The remote Kachin Hills, around the KIA headquarters in Laiza, were engulfed in almost daily violence after June 2011, when a 17-year ceasefire between the KIA and the army collapsed. Although the KIA uses child soldiers and landmines, human-rights activists blame the military for the vast majority of local abuses. Despite a presidential order to the army only to engage in defensive activities, soldiers are still being blamed for murder, torture and rape. Some suggest the military is operating outside government control in Kachin State.

Chin National Front (CNF)
Ceasefire signed: 6 January 2012
Animists-turned-Christians, the 1.5 million Chin face religious persecution in Buddhist Myanmar. Claiming the country's constitution has failed to deliver on promises of equality for all ethnicities, the CNF has fought for self-determination within a federal union of Burma.

Arakan Liberation Party (ALP)
Ceasefire signed: 6 April 2012
There are two levels of dispute in Rakhine (Arakan) State. The ALP's armed wing has long fought for Rakhine self-rule, but the state's minority Muslim Rohingyas are not even considered 'Burmese', and have no rights to vote, own land, marry or travel. A curfew was imposed in the state in June 2012 after violent clashes between Buddhist Rakhines and Rohingyas.

Karen National Union (KNU)
Ceasefire signed: 12 January 2012
The Karen were promised their own state for fighting with the British against Japan in WWII, but after independence were instead treated as collaborators by the majority Burmese. The 7m Karen have spread from Kayah (Karen) State into other states of Myanmar. Many have fled to Thailand or other neighbouring states.

United Wa State Army (UWSA)
Ceasefire signed: 6 September 2011
With their own self-administrative zone in Shan state (*shaded*), the Wa have close ties with China. The 20,000- to 30,000-strong UWSA has funded itself by producing and smuggling drugs and weapons.

Shan State Army–South (SSA–South)
Ceasefire signed: 2 December 2011
Myanmar's largest minority, the Shan number some 6 million. They have links to Tai ethnic communities in China's southwest. Heavily involved in the drugs trade, the SSA–South has an uneasy truce with the government. The first deal quickly broke down after up to 17 clashes between the two sides. A further deal was struck in January, but even after another on 19 May, sporadic fighting continued. The SSA–North had largely been on ceasefire since 1989, but it too signed a peace deal with the new government on 28 January 2012.

Karenni National Progressive Party (KNPP)
Ceasefire signed: 7 March 2012
A branch of the ethnic Karen, the Karenni have fought the state almost non-stop since 1957. A brief ceasefire in 1995 ended when the junta began forcing Karenni off their land, in what rights groups called an attempt to seize Kayin State's valuable natural resources.

New Mon State Party (NMSP)
Ceasefire signed: 1 February 2012
A theoretically autonomous Mon State was established in 1974, but the NMSP continued its armed fight against the Burmese government until a 1995 ceasefire, and the military junta continued its armed activities well beyond that. Severe human-rights violations, including murder, rape, enforced labour and land confiscation, caused many Mon to flee to Thailand.

Map labels: CHINA, INDIA, KACHIN STATE, Myitkyina, Laiza, SAGAING DIVISION, Haka, MYANMAR, CHINA, CHIN STATE, MANDALAY DIVISION, SHAN STATE, Taunggyi, LAOS, Sittwe, MAGWAY DIVISION, RAKHINE STATE, NAY PYI TAW, Loi-kaw, KAYAH STATE, BAGO DIVISION, YANGON DIVISION, Hpa-an, Bassein, Yangon, KAYIN STATE, IRRAWADDY DIVISION, Mawlamyaing, MON STATE, THAILAND, TANINTHARYI DIVISION

Sources: BBC, CIA World Factbook, International Crisis Group, IISS, Jane's World Insurgency and Terrorism, Time, UNHCR Refworld, UNODC   © IISS

Changes of government in the eurozone

The eurozone crisis has claimed the heads of at least ten countries' leaders since the spring of 2011. Frustrated at the apparent economic mismanagement of their governments and the impact of austerity measures on living standards, Europe's electorate has been voting for change.

1952 — Date of accession to the EU

€ 1999 — Year of entry into Eurozone

▼BBB+ — Standard & Poor's credit rating as at January 2012 with indication of rise or fall

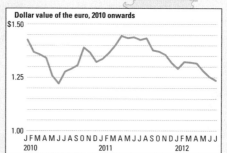

Dollar value of the euro, 2010 onwards

$1.50

1.25

1.00

J F M A M J J A S O N D J F M A M J J A S O N D J F M A M J J
2010   2011   2012

FINLAND
Finland's political scene was rocked in April 2011 when the far-right True Finns party, which ran on a ticket of euro-scepticism and opposition to euro bailouts, won 19% of the vote in parliamentary elections (up from 4.05% in 2007). The centre-right National Coalition Party leader Jyrki Katainen took office as prime minister in June, but only after forming a six-party coalition encompassing both far-left and right-wing parties that excludes the True Finns.

Standard & Poor's ratings ladder

AAA	AA	A	BBB	BB	B	CCC	CC	C	D

Investment grade   Junk   Default

NETHERLANDS
Prime Minister Mark Rutte of the People's Party for Freedom and Democracy resigned in April 2012 after failing to establish a parliamentary consensus in favour of budget cuts intended to avoid plunging the Dutch economy into crisis. Parliament passed a €14bn debt-reduction bill just five days later; Rutte agreed to lead a caretaker government until new elections in September.

IRELAND
Centre-right Fine Gael Party candidate Enda Kenny took office as Taoiseach in March 2011 after a snap election, ousting the centrist Fianna Fail Party. Kenny pledged to renegotiate the 'penal' 5.8% interest rate on the country's €85bn bailout. The economy returned to growth in 2011.

FRANCE
François Hollande defeated Nicolas Sarkozy in a May 2012 presidential run-off to become France's first socialist president in 17 years. He pledged to promote economic growth, countering Angela Merkel's commitment to austerity as the solution to the eurozone's economic woes.

PORTUGAL
Jose Socrates of the Socialist Party resigned as prime minister in March 2011 after the opposition rejected what would have been Portugal's fourth austerity package. Portugal received a €78bn bailout from the EU and IMF in May. Pedro Passos Coelho took over as prime minister in June, leading a centre-right coalition of the Social Democratic and Popular parties.

SPAIN
The People's Party, led by Mariano Rajoy, won a widely expected victory over the ruling Spanish Socialist Workers' Party in November 2011 parliamentary elections. The election was dominated by Spain's economic troubles; the unemployment rate reached 24.4% in March 2012.

ITALY
Mario Monti took over from Silvio Berlusconi as prime minister in November 2011 at the head of a technocrat government which introduced economic reform measures.

1973 € 1999
IRELAND
BBB+

1952 € 1999
NETHERLANDS
AAA

1952 € 1999
BELGIUM
AA

1952 € 1999
GERMANY
AAA

1952 € 1999
LUXEMBOURG
AAA

1952 € 1999
FRANCE
▼AA+

1995 € 1999
AUSTRIA
AA+

1986 € 1999
PORTUGAL
▼BB+

1952 € 1999
SPAIN
▼A

1952 € 1999
ITALY
▼BBB+

Sources: BBC; Bloomberg; Daily Telegraph; European Central Bank; Financial Times; Guardian; IFES Election Guide; New York Times; this is FINLAND; ThomsonReuters via The Financ

Key milestones in the eurozone crisis

November 2009	Newly elected Greek Prime Minister George Papandreou announces that the country's published budget deficit has jumped from 3.7% in early 2009 to 12.7%.
May 2010	The EU and IMF agree on a €110bn bailout for Greece; in return Athens submits to austerity measures. EU finance ministers set up the European Financial Stability Facility, a rescue mechanism worth €750bn for countries in financial distress.
November 2010	Ireland receives a €85bn bailout from the EU and IMF.
May 2011	EU finance ministers and the IMF approve a €78bn bailout package for Portugal.
July 2011	EU leaders agree on a second support package for Greece worth €109bn, to which private bondholders contribute a further €37bn.
October 2011	Private debt holders agree to a 'haircut' of 50% off the value of their bonds.
December 2011	The ECB offers to lend unlimited amounts of three-year money to eurozone banks to improve their liquidity.
June 2012	Spain requests a €100bn bailout for its banks. Cyprus also requests a bailout.

Interest rates on ten-year government bonds, expressed as a percentage

Interest rates of over 7% are considered unsustainable and put an economy at high risk of defaulting on its debts

France, Germany, Greece, Ireland, Italy, Portugal, Spain

SLOVAKIA
Iveta Radicova's government fell in October 2011 following a dispute among members of the four-party coalition led by her Slovak Democratic and Christian Union-Democratic Party as to whether to support an increased eurozone bailout fund. The Smer Party, led by former PM Robert Fico, won a March 2012 vote decisively and pledged to defend the eurozone while reducing the national budget deficit.

SLOVENIA
Borut Pahor lost a September 2011 confidence vote after his referendum on raising the retirement age was rejected. Although Ljubljana's centre-left mayor, Zoran Jankovic, won a December election, legislators later rejected his candidacy and awarded the post of prime minister to the runner-up, Janez Jansa, leader of a five-party centre-right coalition.

GREECE
The New Democracy party won a June 2012 parliamentary re-vote, promising to push through austerity measures to secure Greece's EU/IMF bailouts. The June election was seen as a referendum on the future of the euro: though no party had pledged to withdraw, the scrapping of the terms of the bailouts would have led the EU/IMF to withdraw their loan offers and risked a Greek exit from the euro.

FINLAND AAA — ESTONIA AA- — SLOVAKIA A — SLOVENIA A+ — GREECE CC — MALTA A- — CYPRUS BB+

© IISS

The Balkans still look to Europe

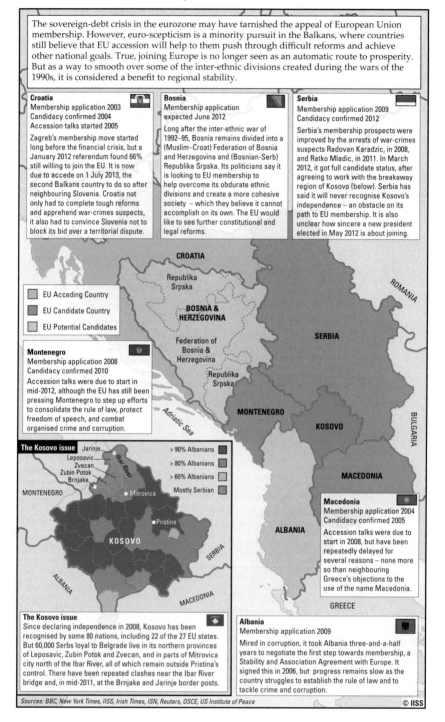

The sovereign-debt crisis in the eurozone may have tarnished the appeal of European Union membership. However, euro-scepticism is a minority pursuit in the Balkans, where countries still believe that EU accession will help to them push through difficult reforms and achieve other national goals. True, joining Europe is no longer seen as an automatic route to prosperity. But as a way to smooth over some of the inter-ethnic divisions created during the wars of the 1990s, it is considered a benefit to regional stability.

Croatia
Membership application 2003
Candidacy confirmed 2004
Accession talks started 2005

Zagreb's membership move started long before the financial crisis, but a January 2012 referendum found 66% still willing to join the EU. It is now due to accede on 1 July 2013, the second Balkans country to do so after neighbouring Slovenia. Croatia not only had to complete tough reforms and apprehend war-crimes suspects, it also had to convince Slovenia not to block its bid over a territorial dispute.

Bosnia
Membership application expected June 2012

Long after the inter-ethnic war of 1992–95, Bosnia remains divided into a (Muslim–Croat) Federation of Bosnia and Herzegovina and (Bosnian-Serb) Republika Srpska. Its politicians say it is looking to EU membership to help overcome its obdurate ethnic divisions and create a more cohesive society – which they believe it cannot accomplish on its own. The EU would like to see further constitutional and legal reforms.

Serbia
Membership application 2009
Candidacy confirmed 2012

Serbia's membership prospects were improved by the arrests of war-crimes suspects Radovan Karadzic, in 2008, and Ratko Mladic, in 2011. In March 2012, it got full candidate status, after agreeing to work with the breakaway region of Kosovo (below). Serbia has said it will never recognise Kosovo's independence – an obstacle on its path to EU membership. It is also unclear how sincere a new president elected in May 2012 is about joining.

EU Acceding Country
EU Candidate Country
EU Potential Candidates

CROATIA

Republika Srpska

BOSNIA & HERZEGOVINA

ROMANIA

Montenegro
Membership application 2008
Candidacy confirmed 2010

Accession talks were due to start in mid-2012, although the EU has still been pressing Montenegro to step up efforts to consolidate the rule of law, protect freedom of speech, and combat organised crime and corruption.

Federation of Bosnia & Herzegovina

Republika Srpska

SERBIA

Adriatic Sea

MONTENEGRO

KOSOVO

BULGARIA

The Kosovo issue
Jarinje
Leposavic
Zvecan
Zubin Potok
Brnjake

Ibar River

MONTENEGRO

Mitrovica

Pristina

KOSOVO

SERBIA

ALBANIA

MACEDONIA

> 90% Albanians
> 80% Albanians
> 60% Albanians
Mostly Serbian

MACEDONIA

Macedonia
Membership application 2004
Candidacy confirmed 2005

Accession talks were due to start in 2008, but have been repeatedly delayed for several reasons – none more so than neighbouring Greece's objections to the use of the name Macedonia.

ALBANIA

GREECE

The Kosovo issue
Since declaring independence in 2008, Kosovo has been recognised by some 80 nations, including 22 of the 27 EU states. But 60,000 Serbs loyal to Belgrade live in its northern provinces of Leposavic, Zubin Potok and Zvecan, and in parts of Mitrovica city north of the Ibar River, all of which remain outside Pristina's control. There have been repeated clashes near the Ibar River bridge and, in mid-2011, at the Brnjake and Jarinje border posts.

Albania
Membership application 2009

Mired in corruption, it took Albania three-and-a-half years to negotiate the first step towards membership, a Stability and Association Agreement with Europe. It signed this in 2006, but progress remains slow as the country struggles to establish the rule of law and to tackle crime and corruption.

Sources: BBC, New York Times, IISS, Irish Times, ISN, Reuters, OSCE, US Institute of Peace

© IISS

Global scientific innovation: new players emerge

There has been a gradual shift in the global balance of scientific innovation in recent years. Emerging economies including Brazil, Russia, India and China – known as the 'BRICs' – are now catching up with the traditional leaders in scientific research – the United States, Japan and Western Europe – in publishing larger numbers of scientific papers, being cited by other researchers more frequently and filing more patent applications. The number of patent applications filed by China, for example, ballooned between 1995 and 2008 compared with the 1980s. The global spread of Nobel Prizes awarded for scientific endeavour, however, does not yet reflect this new reality.

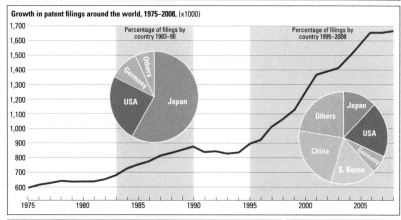

Growth in patent filings around the world, 1975–2008, (x1000)

Percentage of filings by country 1983–90

Percentage of filings by country 1995–2008

Number of Nobel Prizes won for scientific endeavour by country

United States: 261

United Kingdom: 80

Germany: 22

Russia: 11   Japan: 10

France: 29   India: 1   China: 1

Fast facts

2nd – China's ranking for journal citations; the United States still leads the world in journal citations, the United Kingdom ranks third.

32% of global expenditure on R&D took place in Asia in 2007, up from 27% in 2002; China's R&D spend grew by 3.9% in the same period.

13,238 scientific publications produced by Iran in 2008, up from 736 in 1996.

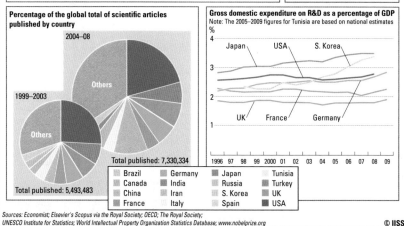

Percentage of the global total of scientific articles published by country

2004–08

Others

1999–2003

Others

Total published: 7,330,334

Total published: 5,493,483

Brazil	Germany	Japan	Tunisia
Canada	India	Russia	Turkey
China	Iran	S. Korea	UK
France	Italy	Spain	USA

Gross domestic expenditure on R&D as a percentage of GDP
Note: The 2005–2009 figures for Tunisia are based on national estimates
%

Japan   USA   S. Korea

UK   France   Germany

1996 97 98 99 2000 01 02 03 04 05 06 07 08 09

Sources: Economist; Elsevier's Scopus via the Royal Society; OECD; The Royal Society; UNESCO Institute for Statistics; World Intellectual Property Organization Statistics Database; www.nobelprize.org

© IISS

Central America's drugs strife

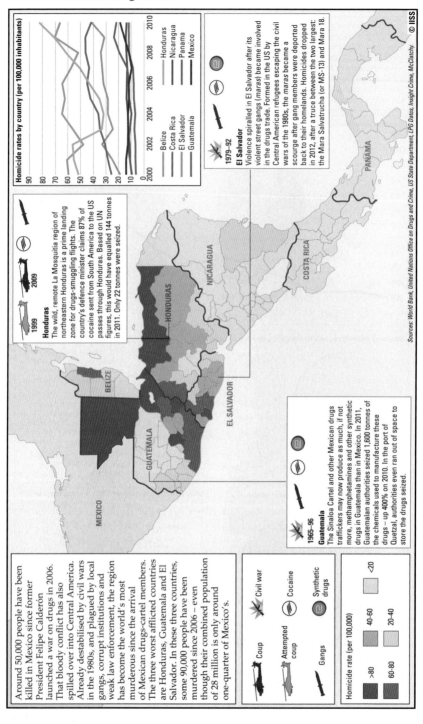

Homicide rates by country (per 100,000 inhabitants)

Belize
Costa Rica
El Salvador
Guatemala
Honduras
Nicaragua
Panama
Mexico

Honduras
The wild, remote La Mosquitia region of northeastern Honduras is a prime landing zone for drugs-smuggling flights. The country's defence minister claims 87% of cocaine sent from South America to the US passes through Honduras. Based on UN figures, this would have equalled 144 tonnes in 2011. Only 22 tonnes were seized.

El Salvador
Violence spiralled in El Salvador after its violent street gangs (maras) became involved in the drugs trade. Formed in the US by Central American refugees escaping the civil wars of the 1980s, the maras became a scourge after gang members were deported back to their homelands. Homicides dropped in 2012, after a truce between the two largest: the Mara Salvatrucha (or MS-13) and Mara 18.

Guatemala
The Sinaloa Cartel and other Mexican drugs traffickers may now produce as much, if not more, methamphetamines and other synthetic drugs in Guatemala than in Mexico. In 2011, Guatemalan authorities seized 1,600 tonnes of the chemicals used to manufacture these drugs – up 400% on 2010. In the port of Quetzal, authorities even ran out of space to store the drugs seized.

Around 50,000 people have been killed in Mexico since former President Felipe Calderón launched a war on drugs in 2006. That bloody conflict has also spilled over into Central America. Already destabilised by civil wars in the 1980s, and plagued by local gangs, corrupt institutions and weak law enforcement, the region has become the world's most murderous since the arrival of Mexican drugs-cartel members. The three worst afflicted countries are Honduras, Guatemala and El Salvador. In these three countries, some 90,000 people have been murdered since 2006 – even though their combined population of 28 million is only around one-quarter of Mexico's.

Coup
Attempted coup
Gangs
Civil war
Cocaine
Synthetic drugs

Homicide rate (per 100,000)
>80
60-80
40-60
20-40
<20

Sources: World Bank, United Nations Office on Drugs and Crime, US State Department, LPG Datos, Insight Crime, McClatchy.

© IISS

Chapter 5

Russia and Eurasia

Russia: Putin Returns

Many of the questions surrounding Russia's future for the next six years were resolved between autumn 2011 and spring 2012. Vladimir Putin, the two-term president who had observed the constitutional niceties in 2008 by becoming prime minister, announced in September 2011 that he would run again for president. This ended the younger, more liberally inclined incumbent Dmitry Medvedev's hopes of a second term during which his supporters had hoped he would move out of Putin's shadow. Putin duly won the March 2012 presidential election in the first round of voting, with 64% – a comfortable winning margin, although markedly lower than his performance in the 2000 and 2004 ballots.

He appointed Medvedev prime minister and, while promising certain reforms and a measure of modernisation, indicated that there would be little change in the direction of state policy. Putin indicated that the state-run companies against which Medvedev had taken aim would not be sold off or broken up. State spending on wages, pensions and benefits would continue to rise. So too would the defence budget. In the foreign-policy sphere, Putin promised that Russia would pursue reintegration with former Soviet states. The country would be open to cooperation with the West, but would vigorously oppose the construction of a missile shield in Europe. Seemingly, Putin's return promised continuity across the board.

However, other developments over the year to mid-2012 increased uncertainty about Russia's prospects beyond the six-year term that Putin began in

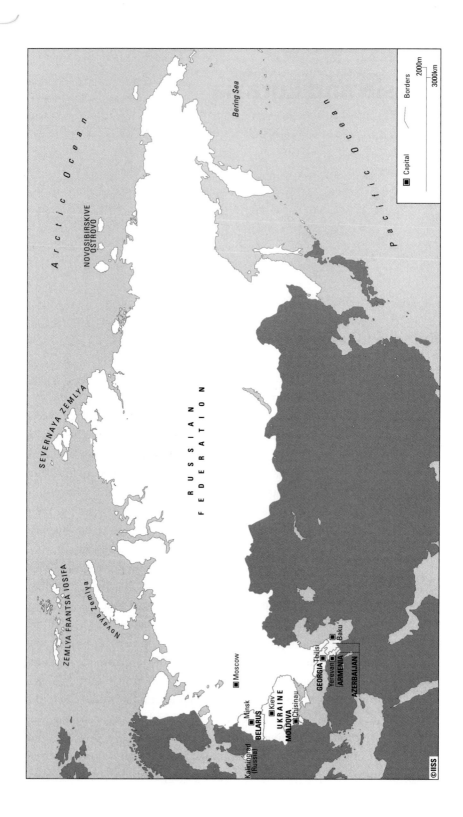

Arctic Ocean

Bering Sea

Pacific Ocean

NOVOSIBIRSKIVE
OSTROVO

SEVERNAYA ZEMLYA

ZEMLYA FRANTSA IOSIFA

Novaya Zemlya

R U S S I A N
F E D E R A T I O N

Moscow

Minsk
BELARUS
Kiev
UKRAINE
MOLDOVA
Chisinau
GEORGIA
Tbilisi
Yerevan
ARMENIA
Baku
AZERBAIJAN

Kaliningrad
(Russia)

2000m
3000km
Borders
■ Capital

©IISS

May 2012. The governing system established by Putin rested on a number of pillars, including broad support across society, control of the information space in which television predominates, a booming economy underpinned by rising oil output and rising oil prices, and strong budgetary surpluses that provided protection against external shocks. All these pillars showed signs of erosion in 2011–12.

Putin remained Russia's most popular politician, but sections of society – in particular the growing urban middle class and young people – turned against him in the wake of the fraudulent December 2011 election for the federal parliament. The rise of the Internet and social networking in Russia severely challenged the government's informal monopoly on information via television, which had been central to high approval ratings and vote shares recorded over the last decade. The economy returned to growth after the contraction of 2009, and oil output edged up in 2011, but few forecast-ers believed that GDP growth rates seen prior to 2008 could be restored or that oil output could rise much above the 10.25m barrels per day posted in 2011 – indeed, maintaining such a level was not expected to be easy. It was thus questionable what the main driver of GDP growth would be. Data for 2011–12 underlined that consumption was now the main engine of growth, but this was partly a result of increased state spending that put pressure on the federal budget. Even though tax revenues were swelled by high oil prices in 2011 and the first half of 2012, Russia was unable to return to the healthy budget surpluses it had run throughout Putin's first two presiden-tial terms. Indeed, current plans anticipated that the budget would remain in deficit up to 2015 and fiscal policy was counting to a much greater extent than before on the price of oil staying close to $100 per barrel. Many Russian commentators feared that Putin's stability would turn within a few years to political and economic stagnation.

Rise of the protest movement

Putin and Medvedev had agreed that only one of them would run in the 2012 presidential election. Speculation over which of them would appear on the ballot paper came to an abrupt halt in September, when at a con-gress of the United Russia Party Medvedev and Putin announced that the latter would return to the Kremlin while the former would become prime minister. Both men insisted that the arrangement had been long planned, but it was difficult to square this assertion with Medvedev's campaigning initiatives over the previous months. Indeed this claim, which implied that the population had been duped during Medvedev's presidency, did much to fire the protest movement in the following months. Putin also passed to Medvedev the leadership of United Russia, on the basis that as president Putin should stand above politics whereas the prime minister could benefit from the support of the largest party in the federal Duma. However, Medvedev and United Russia looked an odd match from the outset, not least because Medvedev had argued for the party's power to be diluted and in favour of a reformist programme that sat ill with United Russia's conservative mainstream.

United Russia, moreover, was a party in decline when Putin handed it to Medvedev. It had been embarrassed by numerous reports of corruption within its ranks, and the lawyer-turned-blogger Alexei Navalny's description of it as the 'party of thieves and swindlers' had lodged in the public's consciousness. United Russia had enjoyed a 60% approval rating at the time of the previous parliamentary election, but its rating was down to 40% by the time voters went to the polls in December 2011. The announcement of the Putin–Medvedev switch, moreover, stoked disenchantment in some parts of society with the closed nature of Russian politics and so fanned an anti-Kremlin vote. Opposition groups called on the electorate to back whichever candidate they felt was best able to defeat United Russia in their constituency, rather than not voting or spoiling their ballot paper. The leading beneficiary of this tactic was the Communist Party, which claimed nearly 20% of the vote. Another left-of-centre party, A Just Russia, surged past Vladimir Zhirinovsky's Liberal Democratic Party to claim third place with over 13% of the vote. On the official tally, United Russia took a little less than 50% of the vote in the December election and as a result it was reduced to a bare majority in the chamber.

Nationally, the results were in line with expectations and pre-election polls. The results in Moscow were not, and in the days and weeks following the election many videos emerged on the Internet that showed ballot fraud in favour of United Russia. Officially, United Russia took 46% of the vote in Moscow but some exit polls put its actual showing as low as 28%. On 5 December, about 10,000 people demonstrated in central Moscow. This was a large protest by the standards of Russia's marginal opposition and the authorities responded in a heavy-handed way, arresting over 1,000 people and dispensing short prison sentences. The popular reaction was extraordinary: on 10 December an estimated 60–70,000 people rallied at Bolotnaya Square in central Moscow to demand a re-run of the election. The dramatic growth in the size of the protests shocked the authorities, who thereafter adopted a less confrontational attitude, perhaps out of a concern to avoid further increases in the size of protests. It was also possible that a crackdown was not an option because there were insufficient numbers of riot police and internal troops close to Moscow that could be relied upon to suppress the demonstrations.

Putin was caught unprepared by the eruption of protests and he struggled to respond appropriately. He avoided commenting on some occasions, and on others he turned his crude wit on the protesting Muscovite middle class, likening them to chattering monkeys, suggesting that their white ribbons (a badge of protest) looked like condoms, and accusing them of being in the pay of foreign governments. This demonstrated paranoia, part genuine and part feigned, over the intentions and actions of Western states in Russia, the former Soviet Union and the Arab world. Yet it also betrayed Putin's struggle to understand how a population that was largely passive during years of chaos and economic decline (the 1990s), and appreciative of the economic growth and political stability during his two presidential terms (2000–08), could be demanding political change at a time when the Russian economy had returned to growth and the government had announced a new round of increases in wages and pensions. A segment of the population was breaking its social contract with the national leader. Notably, Putin's preference to ignore or demean the protesters was not shared by all his ministers and advisers. Two of the most prominent, his long-serving Finance Minister Alexei Kudrin and his chief ideologist Vladislav Surkov, recognised that a rise in protest sentiment was an inevitable consequence of rising incomes and the emergence of a sizeable middle class. Both men argued that the protesters deserved to be taken seriously; Surkov even called them 'the best part of society'.

Changes in Russian society were not the only structural factor behind the increasing salience of Russia's opposition: changes in the information sphere mattered just as much. Russia's media landscape is more diverse than it is often given credit for: newspapers and local radio stations are often a platform for investigative reporting and views that are openly critical of the authorities. However, by far the most influential parts of the media have been the national television stations. Surveys in the last decade showed that television was easily the most important source of news for most Russians; a distant second place was often occupied by conversation among families, ahead of newspapers, radio or the Internet. The national television channels were firmly under Kremlin control during Putin's first two terms – he understood their importance and so gained control of them years before targeting the oil and gas sectors. This near-monopoly in the information space helped explain Putin's consistently high approval ratings and the very low level of recognition for opposition figures. However, the 2011–12 electoral season marked a transition, with the rise of a largely unregulated Internet creating a widely available alternative to television as a source of information. According to data from the International Telecoms Union, Russia had just under 60m Internet users, amounting to some 43% of the population. The opportunities afforded to the political opposition by the Internet, as a means of organising and disseminating information, posed a profound challenge to the system that Putin had inherited and remade.

Opposition countered

Anti-government protests largely maintained their momentum between December and March, and activists hoped to repeat their success in denying the authorities more than 50% of the vote in the March presidential election, and so force Putin into a demeaning run-off. Among Putin's circle, there was a debate about whether it would be more legitimate to win narrowly in the first round, or to proceed to a run-off (most likely against Gennady Zyuganov, the Communist leader and habitual loser of presidential elections) and win by a wider margin.

Faced with this electoral challenge, the authorities were active on several fronts. Medvedev sought to placate the opposition by initiating legal changes to lower the thresholds for participation in elections and winning seats, and to reintroduce the direct election of regional governors, a practice Putin had scrapped in the wake of the 2004 Beslan hostage crisis. Some state officials encouraged their employees to join counter-demonstrations in cities where the opposition was rallying. The electoral authority denied Grigory Yavlinsky, the leader of the liberal party Yabloko, registration as a candidate. This barred several tens of thousands of Yabloko observers from electoral commissions countrywide and so gave greater scope for electoral fraud.

Putin played safe by refusing to join presidential debates, which could have cast him as on a par with the other candidates as well as exposing him to potentially awkward questions about some of the controversies of his first two terms. Instead, he focused on a vigorous programme of campaigning while still serving as prime minister. State television regularly showed him solving practical problems across the country, including the relocation of several thousand villagers in the Urals whose homes had suffered from mining-related subsidence. His manifesto was designed to appeal to ordinary Russians, by promising higher state salaries and benefits, anti-corruption initiatives and affordable housing. These measures, plus Putin's enduring popularity among the non-metropolitan working class and uneasiness in provincial Russia about where anti-Putin protests in Moscow and other large cities might lead, were sufficient to give Putin a clear victory in the first round. He claimed 63% of the vote, on turnout of 65%. The opposition again alleged (and presented some evidence for) widespread fraud, but the result was in line with many opinion polls taken in the months leading up to the election. Balloting in Moscow was marked by fewer violations than in December, and it was noteworthy that Moscow was the only territory where Putin got less than 50% of the vote. The republics of the North Caucasus once again reported implausibly high levels of turnout and support for Putin. In Chechnya, for example, Putin took 99.8% of the vote on 99.7% turnout.

Putin's inauguration on 7 May was accompanied by a fresh effort on the part of the authorities to snuff out the protest movement. The day before, police used violence to break up a protest rally of some 20,000 people and arrested 400. Rather than continuing on a path of confrontation, protesters thereafter shifted to organising spontaneous gatherings and marches around Moscow's streets. Ahead of an officially sanctioned demonstration five weeks later, police raided the homes of opposition leaders and their parents, and brought a number of them into police stations for questioning. At the same time, legislation was rushed through parliament to increase the maximum fine for violence at such demonstrations from 1,000 roubles to 300,000. As an estimated 40,000 people attended the rally, it seemed this did little to deter Muscovites from attending and may in fact have galvanised the opposition. Further legislation to limit the opposition's room for manoeuvre was prepared in June and July, in the form of two laws. The first obliged all non-governmental organisations engaging in political activity and in receipt of foreign funding to register with the authorities as 'foreign agents' and to report twice a year on their activities. The second established a single register of banned websites and obliged Internet service providers to block content that the authorities deemed extremist.

The protests that began in December 2011 marked a sea change in Russia's political system, as rising awareness and dissatisfaction on the part or the urban middle class put them at odds with the rest of the population. An affluent, educated segment of society resident in Russia's largest cities and employed in the private sector was flatly opposed to Putin's return to power and his system of government. They wished for a more active political role and a more accountable government, neither of which Putin seemed minded to offer them. Another opposition grouping comprised radical ethno-nationalists who rejected Putin's policy of pumping vast sums of money into the febrile and corrupt North Caucasus. They had the potential to appeal to a wider section of society than the liberal opposition and posed a greater threat to peace in Russia. Whereas Putin's nationalism celebrated Russia as a unique multi-ethnic civilisation, the ethno-nationalists sought to divide Russia on ethnic lines. Nationally, however, there was no mass politicisation. Apathy remained the dominant mood, together with support for Putin as the face of authority. Polls taken after May gave him an approval rating of around 70%.

And what of Medvedev, Putin's former protégé and the president for the previous four years? In the wake of Putin's inauguration as president, the word 'tandem' disappeared from the vocabulary; it was widely accepted that Medvedev would be a less powerful prime minister than Putin had been during the period 2008–12. His task was primarily to implement the decisions taken by Putin. The latter moved a number of his most trusted ministers out of the government and into the presidential administration as advisers, creating a parallel government structure. Complex decisions tended to cut across departmental lines, and in the post-May 2012 political landscape it fell to presidential advisers to coordinate positions and make recommendations to the president. Thus Medvedev took over a cabinet that had less authority than before. Furthermore, he clashed with some of the longer-serving ministers, which led some commentators to question whether Medvedev could command sufficient respect among cabinet veterans to be an effective prime minister.

State capitalism bolstered

During his term as prime minister, Putin had pushed Russia towards a more redistributive economic model, using the proceeds of the country's resource-export windfall to finance large increases in pensions and public-sector wages. In the period 2009–11, public spending averaged 22% of GDP, compared with 16% in 2004–06. In US dollar terms, social spending quadrupled between 2004 and 2010. The rise of middle-class protests confirmed the political expediency of higher state spending to Putin, for whom public-sector workers, welfare recipients and the provincial working class were more important constituencies than ever before. However, the state was left far more exposed to the price of oil. In 2008, an oil price of $60 per barrel was sufficient to balance the federal budget; by 2012 the break-even figure had risen to almost $120 per barrel.

These changes in fiscal policy had several implications. Firstly, the federal government accumulated a fiscal cushion against future shocks much more slowly than it had done in the years prior to the 2008–09 global economic downturn. This curtailed its ability to run a counter-cyclical stimulus in the event of another setback to the Russian economy – if, for example, disintegration of the euro were to trigger a deep recession in the eurozone, the largest market for Russian exports.

Secondly, it increased the budget's reliance on the oil and gas sectors to deliver the tax revenue needed to pay for the promised rearmament programme, investment in new transport infrastructure and future rounds of increases in wages and benefits. This exposure went beyond simply the oil price, which Russia cannot control; it also made budget fulfilment reliant on sustaining current levels of oil and gas output. In 2012, taxes paid by gas producers were raised fourfold over the next three years. Yet the increased tax burden on the gas sector, and the maintenance of a heavy tax burden on the oil sector, posed a threat to future hydrocarbons production at a time the main producing fields were mature and largely depleted. Thus the government found itself caught between the short-term need to maximise tax revenue from oil and gas, and the medium-term imperative to preserve output through a tax policy that encouraged fresh investment.

Thirdly, the government planned a return to debt issuance, after a decade of near abstinence. It was notable that most of the debt would be rouble-denominated, which posed less repayment risk for the state, and that it was not expected to result in a marked rise in Russia's sovereign debt ratio which, at roughly 10% of GDP, was very low compared with OECD states.

Alexei Kudrin, Putin's highly regarded finance minister, who resigned rather than serve in a Medvedev-led government, had been warning for over a year that fiscal policy was on a loosening trajectory. The drift away from fiscal conservatism had been apparent from 2008 onwards and was exacerbated during the presidential campaign, particularly in circumstances where the authorities were eager to stem the momentum of an emboldened opposition. However, by mid-2012 there was speculation that the government was preparing to put back the start of a planned six-year $600bn rearmament programme by three years and to set aside some $10bn in 2012–13 in case a new economic crisis took hold.

The other major policy in the economic sphere concerned privatisation and the modernisation of the Russian economy. Many technocrats had hoped that Medvedev would win a second term because he had promised to increase competition and reduce the role of the state and its powerful corporations. Putin, by contrast, had repeatedly signalled his preference for a conservative policy course. He did not reject the notion of modernisation outright – indeed, he had done more than Medvedev to encourage Russia's resource producers to move up the value chain – but he was not inclined to follow the Medvedev call for replacing the country's resource-based economy with a fundamentally different model. His election manifesto stressed the importance of state-led development through the establishment and promotion of gigantic state corporations, some of which dominated an entire sector of the economy.

Shortly after taking office, Putin issued decrees that directed Medvedev's government to fulfil his campaign pledges, including the creation of millions of high-tech jobs, markedly higher capital investment and a place for Russia by 2018 in the top 20 places of the World Bank's *Doing Business* index. The stress placed on the index marked a departure for the Russian authorities, who had paid little attention to it, in contrast to states such as Georgia and Kazakhstan that actively and successfully sought to improve their position. Russia was ranked 120 out of 183 states in the 2012 index, while Georgia was 16, Kazakhstan 47 and Armenia 55. The former Soviet Baltic states all appeared in the top 30. Putin's top-20 ambition could only be realised through a complete overhaul of Russia's regulatory environment, to which vested bureaucratic interests would be a formidable obstacle.

Putin's conservative inclinations swiftly made an impression on the new government's privatisation programme. Plans to sell stakes in oil-pipeline monopoly Transneft, power grids FSK and MRSK Holding, power generator RusHydro and leading oil company Rosneft were shelved. The president also indicated that state holding company Rosneftegaz, which holds the government's shares in Rosneft and Gazprom and is headed by Putin ally Igor Sechin, might increase its portfolio of assets. Putin told investors that he did not wish to develop state capitalism still further, but was against private-sector monopolies replacing state-run ones. His pronouncements and appointments left the impression that sensitive industries such as oil, gas, energy and some types of manufacturing would be subject to further state-led consolidation, while other parts of the economy could see more privatisation.

By approving three major deals between Rosneft and foreign companies, Putin demonstrated that strong state involvement in the energy sector would still create opportunities for investors. The first deal, with ExxonMobil, created a partnership to drill in a part of the Kara Sea with estimated reserves of 36bn barrels of oil. It also gave Rosneft a 30% stake in tight oil, shale and deepwater projects in North America, and provided for the transfer of unconventional know-how and technology for use in Western Siberia. The second and third deals, with Italy's ENI and Norway's Statoil respectively, also provided for joint exploration offshore in return for Rosneft's entry into projects run by its partner companies globally. By offering foreign companies access to Russia's huge offshore reserves, and the ability to book a pro rata share of them, Rosneft was able to attract the know-how and financing for offshore exploration that it lacked, while expanding the state champion's global footprint and acquiring the technology needed to wring further production out of the West Siberian fields that are the mainstay of Russia's oil industry. The last of these benefits is probably vital if Russia is to sustain oil output at 10m barrels per day over the next decade, and so keep the state budget in good order.

Developing an eastern dimension

After he won the presidential election but before taking office, Putin outlined his priorities for the next six years: alongside economic growth and reversing Russia's population decline, he stressed the importance of developing Eastern Siberia and the Russian Far East. The Far East accounts for one-third of Russia's territory but just 4% of its population. The eastern territories have lagged behind European Russia economically, suffering from depopulation and poor physical links with the rest of the country – despite Russia's vast gas production and exports, sizeable parts of the Far East are not connected to the pipeline network. The sense of separation between these territories and the rest of Russia is reflected in surveys that show large numbers of people there think of themselves as Siberian first and Russian second. These factors exacerbate Russian fears over a potential loss of resource-rich land to neighbouring China: hence Putin's focus on tying these territories more closely to the rest of Russia, encouraging their rapid development and reversing the trend of depopulation. To these security imperatives must be added an opportunity: just as the conquered territory of St Petersburg became Russia's window on the West in the eighteenth century, when Europe was the world's economic and military powerhouse, so Eastern Siberia and the Far East have the potential to serve as Russia's interface with Asia in the twenty-first century, as global economic and military power tilts from West to East.

Allowance was made in the federal budget for greater infrastructure spending in the eastern territories, alongside measures to encourage families to resettle. The authorities established a state corporation to develop the Russian Far East and, after the presidential election, created a federal ministry for the same purpose. Yet the scale of the development challenge necessitated attracting foreign capital to help develop the region's oil, gas and mineral reserves, to establish steel and aluminium plants and to make better use of timber resources. Here, China loomed large. In October 2011 the two countries established a $2bn bilateral fund that aimed to invest 70% of its resources in Russia and 30% in China. China Investment Corporation already had stakes in Polyus Gold and Vneshtorgbank (VTB), two companies that Putin viewed as strategically important. Chinese companies also provided the finance to build the first stage of the East Siberia Pacific Ocean (ESPO) pipeline, through which Rosneft delivers 300,000 barrels per day of oil to China. Developing Eastern Siberia's gas reserves will depend partly on the conclusion of a long-prepared agreement for Russia to sell 68bn cubic metres of gas per year to China, to be delivered from two directions – from West Siberia to western China, and from fields in Eastern Siberia and Sakhalin Island to northeastern China and the Pacific seaboard. Progress was reportedly made in talks, but no conclusion was reached. The main sticking point was price: Gazprom was used to getting two to three times the price for its gas in Europe than China pays Turkmenistan for gas supply.

The difficulty for Russia in engaging with China over Eastern Siberia is to strike a balance between tapping China's economic power – to 'catch the Chinese wind' in our sails, as Putin put it – and avoiding a soft takeover of Russian territory by Chinese capital and workers. Officially, China accounts for barely 1% of foreign investment in Eastern Siberia and the Far East. However, reports in the Russian press indicate that unrecorded investment is considerably higher and is often accompanied by illicit Chinese labour. Russia faces a related dilemma with regard to Central Asia, where it has joined with China in an effort to organise regional security structures and limit the Central Asians' interaction with Western states. Alongside this common interest, however, the two are commercial rivals in the region. China has arguably supplanted Russia as the region's leading trade and investment partner and has, for instance, much greater presence than Russia in the oil and gas sectors of Turkmenistan and Uzbekistan.

This duality was also apparent in politico-military relations between Russia and China. Russia had cut back on arms supplies to China in recent years, partly out of a concern to protect its own manufacturing base but also a reluctance to share advanced military technologies with a potential adversary. Senior Russian military officials noted that China's military had undertaken large-scale land warfare exercises in recent years, which seemed unlikely to be directed against the United States but were consistent with planning for war against a large neighbour. Yet Putin consistently rejected any suggestion of a Chinese threat and in May 2012 naval vessels from Russia's Northern and Pacific Fleets conducted exercises with their Chinese counterparts in the Yellow Sea. This involved not only drills for humanitarian assistance and disaster relief, but also war-fighting elements such as the protection of strategic lines of communication and anti-submarine warfare. The two states remained in lockstep at the UN Security Council and shared a preference to defend the international order and legal system as it existed in the second half of the twentieth century, with a stress on respect for state sovereignty and the principle of non-intervention. The rise of China and India was fully consistent with Russian desires for a multipolar world in which the United States no longer played a hegemonic role.

Syrian interests

Throughout the year to mid-2012, Russia played the leading role in restraining Western and Arab states from applying pressure on Syria over the repression of its domestic opposition, and on Iran over its nuclear programme. Initially, Russia not only blocked efforts to sanction Syria at the UN Security Council, it refused even to issue mild criticism of Damascus. From September 2011, as violence in Syria increased, it began to criticise the Syrian authorities but steadfastly refused to countenance any resolution that could be construed as making demands of the Syrian government or blaming it exclusively for violence in the country. Moscow suspected Western states and the Arab League of harbouring ulterior motives. In January 2012 Nikolai Patrushev, secretary of Russia's Security Council, said Western and Arab states were using the crisis to engineer a change of regime in Syria, not because of Assad's treatment of the opposition, but because of his alliance with Iran. Russia insisted that opposition forces were also to blame for the violence and pressed for this to be reflected in UN Security Council resolutions. It twice vetoed resolutions that sought to threaten or compel the Bashar al-Assad regime and backed former UN Secretary-General Kofi Annan's plan for a ceasefire and a Syrian-led political process. Throughout the first half of 2012, as Syria moved ever closer to civil war, Russia resisted efforts to make the departure of President Assad a precondition for the end of hostilities and the start of a political process. In late 2011 and again in 2012, Russia despatched naval vessels to the Syrian coast as a signal of support for the Assad regime and continued to supply arms, though it hotly contested US Secretary of State Hillary Clinton's assertion in June 2012 that these supplies included equipment used to attack the Syrian opposition. Although Russia remained one of the two closest supporters of the Syrian government, it also kept an open line of communication with the Syrian opposition and welcomed an opposition delegation to Moscow.

Russia's stance on Syria was informed by a range of interests. Firstly, Moscow was determined to ensure that the UN Security Council remained the prime body for dealing with international security crises and was equally determined to ensure there would be no Security Council blessing, explicit or implicit, for external military intervention in Syria. The systematic destruction of the Libyan armed forces and the lynching of Muammar Gadhafi in October 2011 underscored for Putin the importance of not allowing through the UN Security Council any resolution that opened the door for Western military action in a crisis-torn state such as Syria. Secondly, Moscow was eager to forestall the toppling of a government by a popular uprising, and saw parallels in Syria to the upheavals witnessed in the previous nine years in Georgia, Ukraine and Kyrgyzstan, as well as in Tunisia and Egypt. The unstated fear in the Kremlin was that the revolutionary wave in the Arab world might eventually lap at the shores of the former Soviet Union, or even Russia itself.

Thirdly, Russia was wary of the regional fallout that could accompany the collapse of the Assad regime, including the outbreak of Sunni–Shia violence, attacks on religious minorities and the dispersal of Syria's stockpile of weapons of mass destruction. It was also concerned that Iran would react to the loss of its principal regional client by seeking to assert more influence in Iraq, stepping up its nuclear programme or fomenting Shia discontent in the Sunni Arab monarchies. Commentators who pondered why Russia was courting so much unpopularity in the Middle East by backing the Assad regime failed to recognise how much Russia was obliged to take into account Iranian preferences because of close commercial and diplomatic ties between Moscow and Tehran, as well as Iran's potential to cause instability along Russia's southern periphery.

The fourth factor was that Syria under Assad and his father had been an ally of Moscow for several decades and one of the few Middle Eastern customers for Russia's arms and power-engineering industries. The naval supply base at Tartus was Russia's only naval facility beyond the territory of the former Soviet Union, creating a bridgehead should Russia one day have the wherewithal to re-establish itself as a naval power in the eastern Mediterranean. If the Syrian regime survived, moreover, there would be fresh opportunities for Russian companies, including the state-run oil and gas giants.

Finally, Russia had citizens on the ground in Syria, in the form of military personnel working at Tartus and supporting Russian-made military equipment in service with the Syrian armed forces. In addition, some 30,000 Russians were married to Syrian nationals and lived in Syria. If the country were to descend into full-scale civil war, or if the Sunni opposition were to win power, Russian policymakers worried that they could face a refugee crisis. The scale of this could potentially be magnified by pressure from Syria's Circassian community to return to their ancestral homelands in the Russian North Caucasus, where their kin still lived. Already by spring 2012, a trickle of Syrian Circassian families had resettled in the republic of Kabardino-Balkaria.

Moscow's preferred outcome was to have Assad remain in power and stability restored. Russian decision-makers supported the notion of peace talks, but their insistence on there being a Syrian-led process without any preconditions such as Assad's departure appeared designed to ensure that Assad or another member of the Alawite elite remained in control. Though some observers accused Russia of having the ability to persuade Assad to stand down but failing to do so, this probably exaggerated Russian influence. However, by acting as Assad's sole supporter on the Security Council while also engaging with some parts of the Syrian opposition, Russia kept open the possibility that it could negotiate a transition if Assad concluded that his position was untenable.

Moscow also opposed efforts by Washington and Brussels to increase sanctions on Iran. It denounced a report by the International Atomic Energy Agency (IAEA) in November 2011 that concluded that the only plausible purpose of certain Iranian research activities was to develop nuclear weapons. The Foreign Ministry suggested the IAEA was seeking to wreck Russian mediation efforts, and even went so far as to draw comparisons with the dossiers on Iraq's supposed nuclear programme in the run-up to the 2003 invasion.

Faced with calls in the UN Security Council for a fifth round of sanctions on Iran, Russian diplomats argued that the previous four rounds had failed and so a fifth would be counterproductive. Russia suggested instead offering Iran a road map for lifting the sanctions progressively, as a reward for transparency measures to assure the IAEA of the Iranian programme's peaceful intentions. This was consistent with Russia's desire to improve relations with Iran, which had been strained by Moscow's previous support for sanctions and the decision in 2010 to cancel a contract for the sale to Iran of the S-300 air-defence system. After many delays, Russian specialists completed their work to start the reactor at the Russian-designed Bushehr nuclear power plant and in September 2011 the plant was connected to the

Iranian grid. Iran is arguably the most likely future customer in the Middle East for Russia's state-owned and export-oriented nuclear power industry.

Eurasian integration

Putin's early announcements as president indicated that reintegration in the former Soviet Union would be a priority of his third term. Russia had already established a customs union with Belarus and Kazakhstan, and in January 2012 the three countries established a Common Economic Space and a Eurasian Commission, inspired by the European Commission, with the aim of creating a Eurasian Union by 2015. The intended purpose of the supranational authority was to coordinate economic and currency policy.

Putin suggested that Russia would unite the former Soviet states to form a bridge between the EU and the Asia-Pacific. The next two states in line to join were Kyrgyzstan and Tajikistan, both of which depended on access to Russian products and labour markets and so could ill afford to remain outside. Armenia was also mentioned as a potential member, although its inclusion would be complicated by the fact that it does not share a border with any of the existing members. The membership offer included lifting of migration quotas, privileged prices for Russian oil and gas, and access to Russian state procurement. By grouping together, Putin argued that members would have more bargaining power in trade talks with the EU.

Over the previous two decades, Russia had created plenty of intergovernmental bodies to facilitate reintegration, but with little success. The latest proposals, however, seemed to have more potential, by focusing on trade and leveraging access to Russia's large and developing markets. In tandem, efforts were put in train to introduce the rouble as a currency of settlement between members of the customs union and other former Soviet states.

Ukraine was a principal focus for Russian policymakers in the context of the Eurasian Union. (See next section, pp. 189–92.) Viktor Yanukovych's election as president in February 2010, and his agreement to grant Russia a long lease on Crimean naval facilities used by the Russian Black Sea Fleet, raised Putin's hopes for integration. Yanukovych thereafter jealously guarded his and Ukraine's sovereign prerogatives, but in 2011 sought a new deal to lower the price of the large volumes of Russian gas that Ukraine imported. Gazprom showed little interest in negotiating a price reduction for Ukraine, which during 2011 became a more valuable export market for the Russian company than Germany; it insisted there could be no revision unless Ukraine agreed to follow Belarus in selling a stake in its gas-pipeline network to Russia. Yanukovych rejected this proposal. Russia advanced an alternative proposal: that Ukraine could obtain a lower price if it joined the customs union. Again, Yanukovych refused, preferring to focus on a free-trade agreement with the EU. Russia's response was to await a Ukrainian change of heart, on the basis that Yanukovych would ultimately have to reach a deal to cut the gas price. Russian strategic patience was apparent in decisions in March 2012 to allow the well-connected Gazprombank to advance Ukrainian gas utility Naftogaz a $2bn credit line, and in June 2012 for Gazprom to advance Naftogaz $2bn on gas-transit fees.

Sun sets on the reset

US President Barack Obama and other Western leaders made a point of praising Medvedev's performance in bilateral and G8 meetings, in the hope that this would bolster Medvedev's chances of running instead of Putin in the March 2012 presidential election. In the second half of 2011, both the United States and the European Union reached final agreement with Russia on the terms of Moscow's entry to the World Trade Organisation, bringing to a close the longest accession process in the organisation's history. Western involvement was central to avoiding a veto by Georgia.

However, by autumn 2011 tensions between Russia and the West were rising. One of the main reasons was the American plan for anti-ballistic-missile facilities in Europe. NATO states rejected Moscow's proposal for organising missile defence in Europe on a sectoral basis, which would have made Russia an integral part of the system. Medvedev underscored that Russia's concerns centred on the fourth phase of the approach favoured by Obama. By 2020, the system was supposed to have the capability to counter ICBMs, which Moscow feared could blunt its own deterrent. It also feared that this was, in fact, the real motive behind missile defence. Putin's subsequent comments left little doubt that his country's relations with NATO would be conditioned primarily by whether Russian objections to missile defence were taken into account. One issue that could be affected by the stand-off was Obama's desire to pursue fresh nuclear-arms talks with Russia, including on tactical nuclear weapons and warheads held in reserve.

A second source of tension was a US decision to put on a visa blacklist a number of Russian government officials suspected of involvement in the detention and death in a Moscow prison of Sergei Magnitsky, a Russian lawyer who worked for a Western-owned investment fund and sought to bring to justice officials from the Interior Ministry who submitted a fraudulent claim for a $230m tax rebate. Magnitsky was denied medical treatment during 11 months in prison and, according to the Kremlin's human-rights council, was probably beaten to death. In response, the Russian government produced its own visa blacklist of US officials and pressured Magnitsky's Russian supporters.

Russia and the United States clashed repeatedly over Syria and to an increasing extent over trade relations. Russia was on course to join the WTO in mid-2012. For US business to obtain the full benefits of this, it was necessary for the US Congress to grant Russia permanent normal trade relations (PNTR) by repealing the 1974 Jackson–Vanik Amendment that withheld PNTR because of Soviet restrictions on Jewish emigration. Although Russia had not put any bars on emigration since the end of the Soviet Union, Jackson–Vanik still applied to Russia. From March 2012 onwards, hearings in the US Senate and House revealed a struggle between those favouring the repeal of Jackson–Vanik to improve the prospects for US business, and others eager to maintain pressure on Russia because of its support for Syria and Iran, as well as its perceived shortcomings on human rights, free trade and protection of intellectual property. By late June it was clear that PNTR would be granted, but there was considerable support in Congress for a new bill, perhaps tagged to the repeal of Jackson–Vanik, to deny visas and freeze US assets of Russian officials suspected of involvement in the Magnitsky case.

Putin's grip

The protests that followed the December 2011 parliamentary election marked a watershed for Russia's political system, confirming that the country had reached a level of socio-economic development at which it was no longer possible for a single leader to unite the entire country. However, the disparate opposition failed to create a body or executive able to conduct negotiations with the authorities; though even if it had, Putin might have refused to engage with it. Moreover, Putin retained the support of a majority of the population and kept control over the state apparatus. Although liberal commentators predicted that Putin would only stay in power for another two or three years, few could paint a credible scenario as to how he would be ejected from power. Just as the opposition which crystallised in 2011 and 2012 gave every appearance of being a permanent fixture, there were few signs that Putin's core support across the country or within the bureaucracy was eroding. The evident divisions in society did not seem to threaten his ability to remain in power.

The changes made in government following Putin's re-election were designed to ensure that every important decision would rest with him as national leader. The course that he set was more conservative than that proposed by Medvedev, but arguably more grounded in reality because it sought to leverage Russia's resource riches rather than to build a new, high-tech economy largely from scratch. The new governing structure seemed to suggest that Medvedev would have scope to encourage the development of technology and finance, but that Putin's closest allies would retain a grip on the commanding heights of the economy – oil, gas, power and metals included. While Putin had adopted a redistributive economic model, fiscal policy still had a safety cushion in the form of the reserve fund. This meant that the budget policy laid out for 2013–15 could probably survive a fall in the oil price to $70 per barrel, although economists feared that at that price Russia's economy would fall into recession.

In its dealings with the outside world, Putin signalled that Russia would remain open to cooperation with governments and companies, but would strictly defend its red lines. International oil companies accepted those terms with enthusiasm. Western states hoping for Russian cooperation on Syria were left frustrated, and the United States was put on notice that Russia would not simply acquiesce to plans for missile-defence facilities in Europe. Putin's return to the Kremlin dampened hopes for improved US–Russian relations. His promise of a less accommodating stance towards the West was made more credible by his emphasis on reintegration in the former Soviet space, and signs of a deepening partnership with China.

Ukraine: Difficult Path

Ukraine saw hoped-for closer ties to the European Union recede when former Prime Minister Yulia Tymoshenko, one of the leaders of 2004's Orange Revolution, was jailed in October 2011, after a trial widely criticised as politically motivated. A free Tymoshenko posed the biggest political challenge to President Viktor Yanukovych. Her imprisonment, on the other hand, created a major foreign-policy problem for Kyiv, by stalling an important EU cooperation agreement. With additional controversy over Tymoshenko's treatment in prison, and several foreign politicians' refusal to visit Ukraine during the Euro 2012 football championship in June, the country frequently attracted publicity for the wrong reasons.

Early in his presidency, Yanukovych had adopted a more pro-European stance than expected. A month after taking office in February 2010, he chose

Brussels for his first overseas visit, and negotiations started in September 2008 soon continued on an Association Agreement between the EU and Ukraine. However Yanukovych, who ran a pro-Russian electoral campaign in 2010 and was backed by Moscow in 2004's fraudulent presidential elections, was not really making a large shift. In a return to Ukraine's traditional balancing act between Russia and the West, he flew straight from Brussels to Moscow on that first official trip abroad.

Designed to replace a 1998 Partnership and Cooperation Agreement, the Association Agreement with the EU foresees a free-trade zone and will deepen Ukraine's political association with the continent. European Commission President José Manuel Barroso announced in August 2011 that the EU would support existing Ukrainian reforms by signing the agreement in December, but this positive mood was short-lived. Yanukovych insisted he had no influence in the Tymoshenko court case, but European politicians expressed grave misgivings in October about the former premier's seven-year sentence for 'abuse of office' in signing a gas deal with Moscow in January 2009.

Tymoshenko was a controversial figure, having amassed great wealth through gas trades in the early 1990s, but the deal in question had restored gas supplies to Europe that winter and her conviction elicited little but sympathy. The EU refused to sign the Association Agreement when negotiations were concluded in December, and after initialing it in March 2012 so as to remind Ukraine what it would be relinquishing, Brussels put the process on ice in May.

In the meantime, further charges were brought against Tymoshenko, and more opposition politicians were sent to jail, including former Interior Minister Yuriy Lutsenko who was jailed for four years in February for paying his driver 'illegal' bonuses. There was further outcry in April, after Tymoshenko reported being beaten in prison. Despite having to cancel a summit in Crimea in May when heads of states refused to attend because of Tymoshenko, and despite the threatened Euro 2012 boycott, Kyiv showed little sign of yielding.

Ukrainian politics are highly unpredictable. To be sure, in parliamentary elections due in October 2012, Yanukovych's Party of Regions (PoR) had little real risk of losing control of the Verkhovna Rada (parliament). However, Yanukovych's appointment of loyalists to key security positions demonstrated insecurity within the administration about its position.

Although Tymoshenko's Fatherland party and the Front of Changes Party, led by former parliamentary speaker Arseniy Yatseniuk, formed a coalition in April, voting arrangements made it difficult for this opposition coalition to win more than half of the 450 Rada seats. The opposition was almost certain to win the 225 seats elected by proportional representation from party lists, but would be at a disadvantage in simple majority districts, where PoR could afford lavish campaigns or persuade individual candidates to join it. Champion boxer Vitaliy Klitschko, who was leading the Strike Party, had not yet joined the 'united opposition', believing his grouping would perform better outside it.

'Is there life (for us) after the Euros?' billboards around Kyiv asked during June 2012's football championship. Following the Association Agreement rebuff by Europe, Yanukovych made more positive noises about accepting Russia's invitation to join a customs union with it, Kazakhstan and Belarus. However, his pronouncements lacked conviction. When in 2010 he had extended the Russian lease on the Ukrainian Black Sea port of Sevastopol and abandoned Ukrainian plans to join NATO, Yanukovych was motivated by a desire to repair relations with Russia damaged under his pro-Western predecessor Viktor Yushchenko. He was also hoping Moscow would agree to changes in the 2009 Tymoshenko gas deal.

Russia did respond with a small gas discount, but rising oil prices largely eroded the savings, and even with the discount, Ukraine was paying nearly as much as Germany for Russian gas. During the first half of 2012, for example, it was paying $416 per 1,000 cubic metre, compared to the $164 paid by Belarus.

To cut costs, Kyiv unilaterally cut the large volume of gas it was required to take from Russia under the contract. The Kremlin – which expressed 'puzzlement' over Tymoshenko's imprisonment – hinted it might reduce the gas price further were Ukraine to join its customs union or relinquish control of its gas-pipeline network. Russian gas giant Gazprom was less tolerant, issuing a threat to Ukraine in June that it would be sued if it did not take the full contracted amount of gas for 2012.

Yanukovych's power base is a coterie of businessmen and family from his own Donbass region, the heart of Ukraine's premier coal-mining and steel-producing industries. Although they would welcome lower gas prices because of their company activities, these people wanted neither to work within the post-Soviet economies of Russia's customs union, nor to face increased regulatory scrutiny from Europe. For them, the Ukraine's traditional 'multi-vector' foreign policy has been ideal for keeping the country in a grey zone between Russia and Europe.

The problem for Yanukovych was that the Ukrainian economy faced continuing difficulties from the 2008 financial crisis. Kyiv would need

Western backing to unblock $15bn in IMF loans, or it would need assistance from Russia. Even with a $2.6bn currency-swap deal with China in late June, it may be difficult for Ukraine to remain in this grey zone, where it was increasingly alienated from, instead of connected to, both of its neighbours.

South Caucasus: Limited Progress

The countries of the South Caucasus – Armenia, Azerbaijan and Georgia – witnessed an uptick in political opposition, prompted in part by protests in the Arab world. In Armenia and Georgia, opposition movements showed signs of consolidation and became an integral part of mainstream politics. Azerbaijan, however, shifted further into authoritarianism.

As Georgia prepared for parliamentary elections in October 2012 and Armenia for a presidential vote in February 2013, opposition groups in all three countries remained vulnerable. While the European Union had been active in promoting democracy in the region, Brussels and European capitals were preoccupied by the eurozone debt crisis, though there was still a commitment to nudge the region towards deeper reforms. An important signal came in August 2011 when Ambassador Philippe Lefort was appointed as EU Special Representative for the South Caucasus and the crisis in Georgia. The EU also said it would push ahead with negotiations on free-trade agreements with Georgia and Armenia. With Azerbaijan, by contrast, there was little progress in talks on an Association Agreement, the first formal step towards a free-trade deal. Nor was there much progress towards resolving the region's chronic conflicts, and Iran's difficult foreign relations cast a shadow over the South Caucasus.

Democratic evolution

The Arab uprisings had only limited resonance in the South Caucasus. Nevertheless, political opposition made inroads to varying degrees in each country. In Azerbaijan and Armenia there were marked signs of social discontent against polarised distribution of wealth. In Georgia, there was vocal dissatisfaction with monopolisation of power by President Mikheil Saakashvili, and about continuing economic woes.

The Armenian National Congress (ANC), the main opposition bloc uniting 18 parties and movements, held its first big rallies in mid-2011. Led by the first Armenian president, Levon Ter-Petrosyan, it started a 'Step-by-Step Revolution': a roadmap for change that would begin with the release of political prisoners and end with a peaceful change of government though early elections. It marked its first victory when the last remaining 15 political prisoners were released, but failed in a bid to bring forward to 2011 parliamentary elections planned for May 2012. Still, the elections saw an unprecedented, vibrant political debate both on the streets and on television. The ruling coalition of President Serzh Sargsyan's Republican Party and wealthy businessman Gagik Tsarukian's Prosperous Armenia Party split ahead of the May vote, revealing fissures within the ruling elite.

However, the ruling Republican Party won a parliamentary majority in elections that drew a mixed response from international monitors. Modest results for the opposition did not bode well for its performance in the presidential election in 2013. The Armenian opposition was relatively strong compared to others in the region, but perhaps not yet in a position to pose a serious challenge to the government. Many parties in opposition were linked to previous political leaders, which perhaps did not help to stir voters out of political apathy.

One potentially significant development in Georgia was the emergence of a political movement led by a wealthy businessman, Bidzina Ivanishvili. In April 2012 he launched Georgian Dream – Democratic Georgia Party, coordinating a coalition with three other opposition parties led by Irakli Alasania (Free Democrats), David Usupashvili (Republican Party of Georgia), and Kakha Kartava (National Forum). A sizeable demonstration, organised by the Georgian Dream coalition, took place in Tbilisi on 27 May 2012 around Freedom Square, and passed off peacefully. Previously, mass rallies in Tbilisi had petered out in mid-2011 after riot police and protesters clashed, leaving two dead. At the time, the authorities were quick to dismiss the protests as an 'anti-Saakashvili plot' orchestrated by Moscow.

Ivanishvili was at the centre of controversy. A French passport holder, he was stripped of his Georgian nationality, which barred him from heading his party. However, in May 2012 the parliament made constitutional changes allowing EU citizens meeting five-year residency criteria to take part in the October elections. But it was still unclear what part Ivanishvili would play, as he argued that his Georgian citizenship must be restored.

The stakes were high in the parliamentary elections scheduled for October 2012. This was because earlier constitutional amendments were set to bolster the powers of the prime minister at the expense of the presidential office at the end of Saakashvili's second and final term in late 2013. The opposition feared the president would use the device of a constitutional fix to hold on to power under a different guise.

In Baku, the reaction of the Azerbaijani authorities to anti-government protests underscored the deepening authoritarian and assertive streak of the country's leadership, headed by President Ilham Aliyev. The authorities sought to suppress public protests through disproportionate force and mass arrests – and had largely put a lid on these by mid-2011. The opposition, already weakened and without a locus in parliament following the November 2010 elections, suffered a new setback with the arrests of some of its key leaders, including Arif Hajili, chief of staff of the opposition Musavat Party, and Mohammed Mejidli, from the Popular Front Party. Despite this heavy-handed treatment, small-scale protests continued. In March 2012, rioters in the northeastern town of Quba set local governor Rauf Habibov's house alight in protest against pervasive corruption in the town. The central government was quick to remove Habibov and portray the incident as an isolated case. But it seemed possible that protests driven by social grievances could be replicated and even spark a larger show of discontent against the widening wealth gap in the energy-rich country.

Conflicts: wars of words
Little progress was made towards resolving the protracted conflicts of the South Caucasus. Several rounds of talks were held in the Geneva framework established to resolve territorial disputes following the 2008 war in Georgia, co-chaired by the EU, the UN and the OSCE. In summer 2011 the 16th round had a difficult start when Tbilisi threatened to pull out, accusing Russia of sponsoring terrorism on Georgian territory. Earlier the Georgian authorities arrested three people accused of plotting bomb attacks and having links with Russian military intelligence officers based in Abkhazia and South Ossetia. Moscow robustly rejected the charges.

Though the Geneva process continued, it made little progress. The main stumbling block was the insistence of the breakaway entities of Abkhazia and South Ossetia that Georgia should pledge not to use force while seeking resolution of the two conflicts. Georgia maintained that it had already done so in the ceasefire agreement and, based on the premise that both entities were occupied territories, demanded that Russia should make the same pledge. Russia adhered to its position that it was not a party to the conflict but merely a security guarantor. Abkhazia and South Ossetia warned that Georgia's decision to view them as occupied territories rather than self-governing entities could derail the talks. Despite the lack of progress, the talks remained a key channel of communication between Tbilisi, its break-away entities and Moscow.

Abkhazia and South Ossetia held de facto presidential elections in 2011 and 2012 respectively, both dismissed by Georgia as illegal. Following the death of Abkhazia's de facto president Sergei Bagapsh in May 2011, his deputy Alexander Ankvab won the August elections. A subsequent assassination attempt on Ankvab in February 2012, the sixth since 2005, underlined the rivalries beneath an apparently calm surface. The attacks were thought to stem from criminal elements pursuing a vendetta against Ankvab. In South Ossetia, elections in November 2011 gave a surprise victory to opposition candidate Alla Dzhioyeva, who defeated the Kremlin-backed Emergency Situations Minister Anatoly Bibilov. The subsequent decision by the Constitutional Court in Tskhinvali to invalidate the result plunged the territory into crisis, triggering political intervention from Moscow. Leonid Tibilov, former de facto deputy prime minister, won the rescheduled election in spring 2012, securing the support of Dzhioyeva, a factor that helped calm unrest.

In spite of the tensions arising out of the territorial disputes, there was a glimmer of hope for normalisation of relations between Russia and Georgia. After difficult negotiations Georgia agreed to a deal which allowed Russia to finalise its 18-year long pursuit of World Trade Organisation (WTO) membership. The parties agreed that a third-party commercial entity would monitor goods passing through Abkhaz–Russian and South Ossetian–Russian customs, and share that information with Tbilisi. However, implementation of the format proved problematic.

The agreement proved to be the only bright spot in otherwise troubled bilateral relations. Following the leadership switch in Moscow, Russia was even more firm in its view that the Georgian leader was *persona non grata* and should not have the privilege of diplomatic ties with Moscow. Russia still viewed a potential accession to NATO by Georgia as a red line. Nevertheless, Tbilisi planned to double its military contingent in NATO's Afghan mission in late 2012, becoming the largest non-NATO contributor. While Georgia's ambition was acknowledged at the Alliance's Chicago summit in May 2012, it was made clear that dialogue would be centred, for now, on strengthening ties and not on accession.

In the Nagorno-Karabakh conflict, hopes had been raised – not least by the OSCE Minsk Group co-chairs France, Russia and the United States – in the run-up to June 2011 talks between the Armenian and Azerbaijani presidents in Kazan, Russia, mediated by Russian President Dmitry Medvedev. The Minsk process had already evolved a set of Basic Principles, a delicate balance between the principles of non-use of force, territorial integrity and rights to self-determination. The United States and the European Union were hoping that if the parties agreed to endorse the Basic Principles, this would also help resuscitate Armenian–Turkish protocols from 2010 that by early 2011 had already run into the ground. The Kazan talks, however, produced no breakthrough and ended sourly.

With no progress being made, Aliyev said all options, including military, were on the table for Azerbaijan to bring the breakaway entity under its control. The Armenian and Azerbaijani presidents met, again at Medvedev's initiative, in the Russian city of Sochi in January 2012, and Azerbaijan was urged not to seek a military solution.

Meanwhile, the Line of Contact around Nagorno-Karabakh continued to be tense over the year to mid-2012 with dozens of deaths on both sides as a result of sniper incidents and other ceasefire violations. In September 2011 Armenian forces shot down an Azerbaijani unmanned aerial vehicle (UAV) over Nagorno-Karabakh. Azerbaijan said it was boosting its capabilities with 60 *Orbiter* and *Aerostar* UAVs to be imported from Israel and a further new fleet to be built by a joint Azerbaijani–Israeli joint venture. Azerbaijan also agreed a $1.6bn arms-supply deal with Israel, though the precise make-up of the agreement was not known. The war of words, and in particular military rhetoric from Baku, continued unabated. A clash on the Armenia–Azerbaijan border in June 2012 left eight soldiers (three Armenians and five Azerbaijanis) dead.

Azerbaijan's arms imports from Israel served further to aggravate relations between Baku and Tehran. Between August 2011 and March 2012 the Azerbaijani authorities arrested and charged at least 24 people who reportedly had links with Iran. They were accused of an attempted coup to install a theocratic regime, and of plotting acts of terrorism in Azerbaijan. Tehran, denying Baku's claims, accused the latter of plotting with Israel against the Islamic Republic. Some of those charged and convicted, including seven members of Azerbaijan's Islamic Party, dismissed their imprisonment as political persecution in response to party leader Movsum Samedov's interview in the *Washington Post* in 2010. Samedov had accused the Aliyev family of corruption and criticised the government's ban on wearing headscarves at schools.

The confrontation between Iran and Israel risked spilling over into the region. In February 2012 Israeli Embassy staff in Georgia (as well as in India and Thailand) were targeted in attacks. An explosive device in Tbilisi was detected and defused.

Azerbaijani Defence Minister Safar Abiyev attempted to calm Iranian concerns over the arms deal during a visit to Tehran in March 2012. He said that the military hardware was intended to be used to 'bring back occupied territories' – a reference to Nagorno-Karabakh. But Tehran remained deeply suspicious. A report in *Foreign Policy* magazine quoted an unnamed US intelligence officer as saying that Azerbaijan might grant Israel use of an air strip for a potential attack against Iran. Although Baku denied this, Iran was reluctant to trust its northern neighbour.

Russia, meanwhile, was stepping up its presence in the South Caucasus and the wider region in the light of emerging tensions. In September 2012 it was due to hold the *Kavkaz-2012* military exercise to test the interoperability of Russian troops stationed in the North Caucasus and, as envisaged, those in Armenia, as well as in Abkhazia and South Ossetia. Saakashvili accused Moscow of deliberately staging the exercise less than a month before Georgia's parliamentary elections, so as to intimidate voters. He depicted it as a preparation for a 'new Russian war against Georgia' – claims dismissed by Russian Deputy Foreign Minister Grigory Karasin.

In fact, the risk of another conflict between Georgia and Russia seemed low. Moscow largely had what it wanted through the status quo in South Ossetia and Abkhazia, as it looked for a secure atmosphere in which to hold the 2014 Winter Olympics in Sochi, just over the border from Abkhazia. However, there were concerns in the region that any emergency in Iran could prompt Moscow to boost troop levels at its military base at Gyumri in northern Armenia. Partly for this reason, the West was likely to continue to view the region as having strategic importance: in June 2012, US Secretary of State Hillary Clinton visited all three countries.

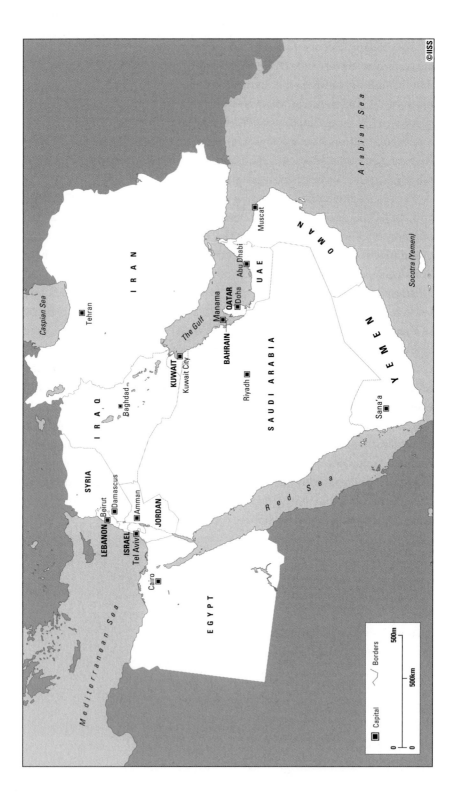

©IISS

Arabian Sea

Socotra (Yemen)

Muscat

O M A N

Abu Dhabi

U A E

Doha

QATAR

Manama

BAHRAIN

The Gulf

Kuwait City

KUWAIT

Riyadh

S A U D I   A R A B I A

Sana'a

Y E M E N

Tehran

Caspian Sea

I R A N

Baghdad

I R A Q

SYRIA

Damascus

Beirut

LEBANON

Amman

JORDAN

Tel Aviv

ISRAEL

Cairo

E G Y P T

Red Sea

Mediterranean Sea

■ Capital

⌄ Borders

500m

0   500km

0

Chapter 6

Middle East/Gulf

Difficult Transitions Follow Arab Uprisings

By the middle of 2012, the optimism and exaltation of the first few months of the Arab uprisings had unsurprisingly given way to a more sombre mood as the daunting realities of political transition became clear. While the grievances that led to popular revolts were in many cases shared across nations, the subsequent trajectories followed by each country proved increasingly distinct and singular.

Unwelcome truths emerged for those who had been caught up in revolutionary fervour. Change at the top did not, in fact, entail rapid or comprehensive transformation of the system, its instruments of control and the political culture. Bureaucrats and elites, unwilling to lose power, stymied calls for change. Those who had led the uprisings – revolutionary youth and secular factions – found themselves in a position of weakness. Revolutions emboldened formerly cautious but better organised groups, notably Islamists, to emerge on the political scene. After intense but brief moments of communion and solidarity, the new politics proved divisive and volatile, exposing long-suppressed emotions, fears and rivalries. Minority groups feared that rule by the majority would reverse their rights. Revolutionary successes also came at a steep social and economic price that stumbling transition processes only compounded. Meanwhile, large segments of populations longed for the stability provided by the old regimes.

The troubled transitions of Egypt and Libya and the mounting death toll in Syria inevitably eroded the romance and hopes initially attached to the uprisings. The tone of media coverage and social-media commentary darkened significantly as Arabs realised that change and progress would be costlier and less certain than initially thought – and also that powerful constituencies still favoured the status quo. Examples included the strong showing of former Prime Minister Ahmed Shafiq in the Egyptian presidential election, as well as the determination of the Egyptian ruling military council to protect its power and privileges.

In countries where the demand for reform was opposed or defeated, the prospect of protracted political and military confrontation loomed large. Syria sank deeper into a civil war with sectarian undertones, with the Bashar al-Assad regime determined to crush a multifaceted uprising. Yemen benefited from a respite after a negotiated settlement eased out its dictator but did not address the profound problems plaguing the country. Protesters in Bahrain found themselves weakened by intense government repression and regional support for the ruling family, leading to the rise of radical opposition voices.

Crucially, Egypt's transition proved volatile and uncertain. By mid-2012, the country finally had a president but still no constitution, and the military had ordered parliament dissolved. The revolution's achievements were far from being consolidated. Each of the three main actors – the ruling military council, the Islamists and the secular revolutionaries – repeatedly changed their posture and behaviour to maximise political gains. Revolutionary energy faded as the Muslim Brotherhood and the army emerged as the main actors and were seemingly amenable to power sharing. In Libya, the fall of the Gadhafi regime opened up politics but left a security vacuum that was filled by a multitude of armed groups which challenged the authority of transitional bodies. In Tunisia, however, a better-designed transitional process seemed on the verge of delivering the country's first democratic constitution, even as political polarisation grew.

Elsewhere, in countries that had experienced limited tremors like Morocco or Jordan, where timid political reforms were introduced, or had placated demands early on through increased state spending and patronage, like the Gulf states and Algeria, there was a sense that the moment of acute danger had passed. Still, political turbulence in Jordan and Kuwait, demonstrations in Oman, a crackdown on Islamists and activists in the United Arab Emirates (UAE), and discontent in Saudi Arabia in the form of Islamist, Shia and youth protests, all suggested that the popular challenge could again resurface.

Sectarianism and political Islam

Sectarian affiliation played a role wherever sects co-existed (prominently in Syria and Bahrain), but sectarianism did not become the dominant characteristic of the uprisings. However, in a tense regional environment, it came to play a role in how states and peoples perceived another country's uprising. Many Sunnis largely encouraged the Syrian revolution against President Assad, an Alawite, but vilified the Bahraini uprising for alleged pro-Iranian sympathies and Shia ambitions. Likewise, many Shias and minorities stood by Assad but supported the Bahraini revolutionaries. The potency of sectarianism came also from its association with the tense regional competition between the Gulf states and Iran.

Political Islam proved its vigour and appeal. The election of Muhammad Morsi as president of Egypt in June 2012 illustrated best the rise of the Muslim Brotherhood, which also did very well in the legislative elections. Its Tunisian branch, An-Nahda, came first at the polls in October 2011, winning the most seats in the constituent assembly and forming the government. In Libya, too, Islamist movements, especially the Justice and Construction Party and the Nation Party, were expected to do well in national elections despite an election law designed to constrain their power.

Well-organised and patient, Islamist factions showed caution in confronting the state, and opportunism when openings appeared. But their electoral victories put them in charge of societies that were under great social, economic and political stress; their governing skills, commitment to revolutionary and reformist ideals, and ability to engage and reassure non-Islamist segments of their populations would be tested decisively. The Muslim Brotherhood was also under pressure from its right flank: the strong showing and assertiveness of the Salafist movement suggested fragmentation and competition among Islamists.

Conversely, the aftermath of the revolutions exposed the weakness and lack of political and organisational savvy of non-Islamist political forces. Despite a relatively good showing in the first round of the Egyptian presidential election, they suffered from a lack of resources and organisation, political disputes, wavering commitment and an inability to appeal to the poor and the lower middle class. They faced the prospect of irrelevance should the Brotherhood and the military reach an arrangement. In Tunisia, non-Islamist forces carried a significant portion of the vote but could not translate this into political leverage, divided as they were over whether and how to engage the victorious An-Nahda. In Libya, too, Islamist sentiments seemed strong. In his first speech after the death of Muammar Gadhafi, the head of the National Transitional Council, Mustafa Abdul Jalil, spoke of enforcing sharia law and removing restrictions on polygamy. Later, his secular prime minister came under intense Islamist criticism and resigned.

Ironically, Islamist electoral victories elsewhere were used to galvanise support for the Assad regime in Syria, which presented itself as the ultimate rampart against Islamic radicalism sweeping the Arab world.

Impact on regional order

The Islamist upsurge looked likely to affect the region's geopolitics. Israel already appeared worried that it would re-energise Hamas in Palestine and would lead Egypt to adopt a more confrontational approach with regard to the peace accord between the two countries. Hizbullah, Lebanon's Shia movement, was torn between the satisfaction of seeing an Islamist movement dominate the Arab world's largest state and the prospect of sectarian-based rivalry with the Muslim Brotherhood. Gulf states saw a direct challenge from a group that married Muslim ideals to republican values, but also showed concern at losing Egypt as a reliable if docile partner. This promised a fraught, even competitive relationship at the heart of the Arab world.

Accusations that the Gulf states had sought to manipulate or hijack the revolutions were rife. Tunisian, Egyptian and Libyan political leaders, civilian activists and the media accused Qatar, Saudi Arabia and the UAE of providing funding, religious cover, media coverage and even weaponry to factions upholding their interests and in ways that would limit revolutionary aftershocks. At the same time, the importance of preserving economic ties and not alienating the strategically powerful Gulf states often served to allay tensions. After Egyptian demonstrators sacked the Saudi Embassy in Cairo, senior Egyptian clerics and parliamentarians travelled to Riyadh to pay their respects to the Saudi monarch, and the Egyptian military council seemed to be a reliable ally.

In Bahrain and Yemen, Gulf states were similarly accused of blocking change. Gulf and especially Saudi leverage was essential to engineer the negotiated departure of Ali Abdullah Saleh from Yemen and his replacement by the vice president. But this manoeuvring was perceived by Yemeni protesters as a way to preserve the corrupt structures of the state and to prevent more fundamental change. In Bahrain, Gulf states provided strong support for the ruling family against a perceived Shia threat. The Saudi–Bahrain proposal for a Gulf union was accordingly interpreted as a way to further constrain Bahraini politics and prevent the resurgence of the opposition.

The uprising in Syria served to crystallise political divisions in the Arab world. Eager to reverse the perceived loss of Iraq, counter Iran's influence in the Levant and weaken a regime often at odds with their interests, the Gulf states embraced the rebellion. They provided cover to Arab and UN diplomatic initiatives to put pressure on Assad, and provided money and weapons to the various rebel forces. Conversely, the prospect of losing Syria mobilised support from Assad's partners, notably Iran and Hizbullah. However, the Palestinian group Hamas – the Palestinian branch of the Sunni Muslim Brotherhood and once a staunch ally of Assad – gradually distanced itself from this alliance.

As the violence in Syria grew and acquired a sectarian dimension, the fear of regional contagion increased. In particular, the Syrian crisis accentuated Lebanon's own political and sectarian tensions. In the northern city of Tripoli, clashes between Sunni and Alawite fighters led to dozens of deaths. The fragile Lebanese cabinet, dominated by parties close to Syria but headed by a Sunni prime minister, sought to dissociate itself from the Syrian crisis and minimise its repercussions. Even so, North Lebanon provided refuge for Syrian refugees, activists and rebels, who channelled assistance and weaponry into Syria. Pro-Syrian factions, which dominate Lebanon's security forces, sought to constrain the activities of dissidents and Lebanese sympathisers in Beirut. Jordan, too, was exposed to the crisis, compounding its own problems. As refugees and defectors fled there, Jordan's frailty became more apparent. While the Jordanian king was the first Arab leader to urge Assad to resign, the government seemed unwilling to adopt a tougher line for fear of Syrian retaliation.

The region lived in fear of an inter-state war prompted by a miscalculation or a deliberate move by the Syrian regime. Heated rhetoric between Damascus and Ankara, Syrian incursions into Lebanon and questions about the posture of Hizbullah regarding the possible loss of its logistics route and strategic depth all held the potential for military escalation.

Unsurprisingly, the turmoil on its borders worried Israel. After decades of relative stability on the Golan Heights, civil war in Syria and the prospect of a new, unknown regime raised delicate strategic questions for the Israeli leadership, which was already facing significant changes in its relationship with Egypt, difficult choices regarding a nuclear-capable Iran, and an entrenched and strong Hizbullah in Lebanon.

Egypt: rollercoaster politics

After the dramatic resignation of President Hosni Mubarak in February 2011, Egypt careened from one political crisis to another, with new and old actors jockeying for influence over the transition to democracy and, ultimately, for power. Islamists gained political prominence and institutional power thanks to electoral victories. The military, however, retained ultimate political power. The country remained formally ruled by a 20-member panel of senior military figures known as the Supreme Council of the Armed Forces (SCAF). Headed by Field Marshal Mohammed Hussein Tantawi, who had been Mubarak's minister of defence, SCAF successfully resisted popular calls for a faster transfer of power to civilian authorities and passed legal and constitutional measures to entrench the armed forces' own power, raising fears of prolonged military rule.

On the surface, some of the most immediate demands of the revolutionary movement were placated. In June, a civilian court sentenced Mubarak and his interior minister, Habib al-Adly, to life in prison after finding them complicit in the deaths of protesters during the uprising of January and February 2011. But Mubarak was cleared of other charges, including bribery, and his two sons and six former interior ministers and police chiefs were cleared of most charges linked to the uprising. The sentences frustrated many Egyptians seeking justice for those killed during the revolution, prompting renewed demonstrations in Cairo's Tahrir Square and demands for the cleansing of the judiciary, which remained dominated by judges appointed by Mubarak and was supportive of SCAF. Egypt's top prosecutor announced that the verdict would be appealed.

The military's bid for power

The verdict in Mubarak's trial added to growing anger over perceived manipulation of the country's transition by SCAF to enhance its powers and preserve its privileges. After it took over from Mubarak, the military focused on preserving its rights and standing. The central feature of this effort was the creation of constitutional provisions that prevented or limited civilian oversight of and interference in matters the military deemed vital. But its expansive definition of such matters suggested a desire for autonomy. It won strong support among many segments of society eager for a return to order, including business elites, the judiciary and many ordinary citizens.

In November, the SCAF-appointed government introduced a proposal known as the Selmi document, which would have allowed the army to veto any military-related legislation. It said SCAF should form the panel that would write the new constitution, with only 20 members drawn from parliament. It also gave the military council veto power over the draft constitution, and enshrined the army as the protector of 'constitutional legitimacy' – a term ambiguous enough to allow military intervention in policymaking.

The proposal was met with outrage. Massive protests followed, with particular anger directed against Tantawi. On 20 November, fierce fighting broke out between protesters and security forces, leaving at least 40 dead. The cabinet of Prime Minister Essam Sharaf resigned. Tantawi, accused of delaying the transfer of power to civilian rule, promised to hold presidential elections by the following June; former Prime Minister Kamal Ganzouri was appointed to head a new cabinet. The Selmi proposal was eventually shelved.

Even then, the military council continued to shape the transition with a heavy hand. It resorted to military tribunals for civilians and refused to allow investigations into the use of deadly violence by soldiers against Coptic Christian protesters in October and November. It even obtained from the Justice Ministry a decree granting military personnel the right, normally reserved to the police, to arrest civilians, but the supreme administrative court later annulled the decree.

While ostensibly committed to Egypt's transition to democracy, the military proved reluctant to hand power to civilians. Even after parliament convened following elections in November and December, SCAF kept the prime minister and cabinet it had appointed and asserted the authority to overrule both the government and the assembly. Only after parliamentary sessions were suspended in April in protest did the ruling generals concede to a limited cabinet reshuffle.

The army's attempt to shape the future institutional order focused on the constitutional process. In a constitutional declaration issued in June 2012, SCAF gave itself the power to appoint a Constituent Assembly to draft the next constitution. After the Supreme Court deemed unconstitutional the electoral law under which parliamentary elections had taken place and thus dissolved the new Assembly, SCAF also seized the power to dissolve parliament and assume its responsibilities until a new body was elected. The issue became a focus of contention between the military and political forces, including the Muslim Brotherhood.

The military's deadly crackdowns on peaceful protesters and its referral of some 12,000 civilians to military courts deepened rifts with the revolutionaries. An activist campaign called Kazeboon ('Liars') sought to highlight SCAF's dishonesty and brutality by showing video evidence of beatings and killings of protesters by the army; organisers put up film projectors in public places to bypass SCAF-controlled state media. The campaign aimed to restore the credibility of Tahrir Square activists in the eyes of many Egyptians, who had come to see them as disruptive.

Islamists' electoral success

Elections for parliament's lower house, known as the People's Assembly, were held in November and December, with high turnout reported in three rounds of a complex voting system. The Muslim Brotherhood's political party, the Freedom and Justice Party (FJP), swept the elections, winning 47% of the vote and thereby dominating parliament. Second came the ultra-conservative Salafist Nour Party, which made a surprisingly strong showing with 25% of vote. A smattering of secular liberal and leftist parties won about 16%. Elected representatives met for the first time on 23 January, and SCAF officially transferred legislative authority to them. Saad al-Katani, a member of the Muslim Brotherhood, became the speaker of parliament. Elections for the upper house (the Shura Council) followed, with a lower turnout but similar results.

Parliament was tasked with appointing a 100-member panel to write Egypt's new constitution, including provisions for the distribution of powers, the rights of minority groups, the role of the military and the position of Islam. According to the timetable set by SCAF, this was to be completed and put to a referendum before presidential elections in June. The panel formed by the Islamist-dominated assembly was composed predominantly of Islamist figures; only a handful of seats were given to youth groups, women and Copts. This led to an outcry from groups calling for an inclusive constitution and a civil state. Many liberal and leftist members withdrew in protest, while Copts boycotted the panel; even Al-Azhar University, the centre of Islamic learning, withdrew its representative, citing the rejection of its draft constitutional principles. On 10 April, an Egyptian court suspended the constitutional assembly in response to numerous lawsuits alleging that it was unrepresentative and questioning the legality of the selection process. The assembly was later invalidated, but this episode, seen as an Islamist power grab, soured relations between the various political groups. The army seized on this tension to impose a new constitutional mechanism less dominated by Islamists.

This dispute also set the stage for Egypt's first-ever open presidential election, which stirred excitement and passion among citizens and was heavily contested between new and old political forces. It was portrayed as a race for the soul of the revolution against the remnants of the old order. With the exception of leading figure Mohamed ElBaradei, who withdrew from the race to protest at continued military rule and the lack of a constitution, all major political forces joined the contest. The Muslim Brotherhood had initially pledged not to field a presidential candidate, in a show of good faith that it was not seeking political hegemony. It even expelled popular party member Abd al-Moneim Aboul Fotouh after he joined the race, exposing the Brotherhood's internal divisions. However, the Brotherhood reversed its decision on 31 March, announcing the nomination of its chief strategist Khairat al-Shater.

Weeks before the election, ten of the 23 candidates were disqualified by Egypt's election commission. These included Omar Suleiman, Mubarak's former spy chief and rumoured to be the military's candidate, for not mustering enough signatures in support of his candidacy; the Muslim Brotherhood's al-Shater, for his criminal record during the Mubarak era; Hazem Salih Abu Ismail, a Salafist leader whose mother was found to hold American citizenship; and former Prime Minister Ahmed Shafiq, in line with a new rule banning Mubarak-era officials. All four appealed, but only Shafiq's candidacy was reinstated. There was a perception that the judiciary and the military were seeking to remove polarising figures so as to have a better chance at achieving consensus. After protesting the disqualification of Shater, the Brotherhood put forward a backup candidate, Muhammad Morsi, the relatively uncharismatic president of the FJP.

The first round in May saw Morsi come first with 25% of the vote, closely followed by Shafiq, by then the favourite of the military. Two candidates vocally supportive of the revolution, the Nasserite Hamdeen Sabbahi and the neo-Islamist Aboul Fotouh, placed third and fourth. That result seemed to validate the view that Islamists and secular authoritarians would vie for Egypt's future. It also created intense debate among revolutionaries: many argued that Morsi would be a lesser evil and that Shafiq represented a return to the old order; others, especially liberals and Copts, preferred Shafiq because of his secular outlook; still others, considering that the new president would either be a pawn of the military or constrained by it, advocated a boycott or blank ballots.

Following a tightly contested second round, much tension between the two camps and rumours of an impending military coup, Morsi was declared Egypt's first civilian president with 51.7% of the vote. As election results were announced on 24 June, thousands flooded to Tahrir Square to celebrate. Yet, in the absence of a constitution and a legislative branch, the extent of executive powers held by Morsi remained unclear.

The electoral success of Islamist parties owed much to their long history of welfare work, tight organisation, influence in professional organisations and legitimacy derived from identity-based campaigning. However, the FJP and the Nour Party, although both ostensibly Islamist, showed no particular inclination to collaborate in government. Ideological differences and political rivalries seemed to preclude any sustained alliance, as illustrated by the decision of the Nour Party to endorse Aboul Fotouh in the presidential election. However, the clear political dominance of Islamists made the role of religion in public life one of the most prominent and contentious issues in post-Mubarak Egypt.

The Muslim Brotherhood's decision to field a presidential candidate further complicated its already volatile relationship with a military historically antagonistic toward organised Islamic movements. Fearing that the Brotherhood would advance an Islamist agenda and would contest the military's privileges thanks to its newfound electoral legitimacy, the military looked for ways to weaken it, including using state media and instruments of the state such as the judiciary. However, the two factions appeared conscious of each other's respective power and sought to avoid direct conflict. The reluctance of the Brotherhood to enter into a direct challenge with the military – in contrast to revolutionary youths who were more eager to demonstrate and clash with security forces – led many to suspect an arrangement between the two aimed at marginalising other actors.

Both the Brotherhood and the military seemed to have lost standing: SCAF's increasingly obvious determination to hold on to power alienated many while the Brotherhood's broken political promises eroded its image. Still, with institutional competition now contained between these two forces, the presidential election and its aftermath reinforced the dichotomy between military-enforced order and Islamist-led change.

Breakdown of order

Following the tumult of the revolution, order continued to suffer. On 1 February 2012, deadly clashes broke out after a football match in the city of Port Said between rival supporters, leaving 74 dead. There were widespread accusations that security forces in Port Said had been complicit or incompetent, allowing people to come into the stadium with knives and other weapons, and failing to intervene when violence broke out. Some interpreted the police actions as revenge for the revolution, since football supporters had played an important role in street battles with the police. However, the military blamed foreign conspirators, raising the spectre of instability and chaos and highlighting the need for a strong army presence. Opposition leaders worried that the military would deliberately sow unrest to justify the maintenance of emergency laws. Eventually, 75 people were charged with murder or negligence in the Port Said killings, including nine police officers and the city's security chief. Parliament started proceedings to charge the interior minister with negligence, and pledged to examine several draft laws to reform the security sector.

This did not end suspicion that the military was insidiously attacking protesters. In early May, protesters camping outside the Ministry of Defence in Cairo were attacked by unidentified assailants, who threw petrol bombs and fired live ammunition and tear gas at them. At least 20 people were killed while police and soldiers standing nearby failed to intervene. The incident generated further anger towards the military, which was accused of complicity in the incident.

Coptic Christians, many of whom considered that the Mubarak regime had provided them security against Islamism, felt increasingly vulnerable as Salafists and the Muslim Brotherhood asserted themselves. Salafist MPs walked out of parliament when a minute of silence was held in memory of Pope Shenouda III, the long-time patriarch of the Coptic community, who died on 17 March after a long illness. The sense that the community was under attack had already been heightened when soldiers attacked Coptic demonstrators protesting against an attack on a church by Salafists in October, killing 25. SCAF later blamed Christians for triggering the violence.

Foreign-policy dilemmas

Among the controversial issues arising out of Egypt's new politics was its relationship with the United States. Egypt's political class was united in promising new rules in dealing with Washington, which was seen as having been complicit in Mubarak's rule, and as treacherous and unreliable. Revolutionaries hoped to scrutinise US military assistance while the army and remnants of the Mubarak regime focused on the role of US-funded NGOs in the unfolding of the revolution.

For its part, the United States recognised that the new situation in Egypt required a policy adjustment. US diplomats and visiting officials intensified their contacts with the FJP. American officials, while noting a convergence on economic matters, were nevertheless keen to obtain assurances that Egypt would maintain its strategic orientation, especially with regard to peace with Israel and relations with Iran.

US–Egyptian relations, however, were affected when, in a clear attempt to discredit pro-democracy groups, the offices of ten NGOs were unexpectedly raided by Egyptian security in December. The government justified the action by alleging that these NGOs had received foreign funds without government approval or that they had failed to register properly. Egyptian security also accused workers of carrying out political activities unrelated to their work. Forty-three people, including many foreigners, were charged; 15 were jailed or banned from leaving the country. State media inflamed the dispute by alleging that the NGOs were planning the break-up of Egypt. The issue significantly increased tensions between the United States and Egypt. US diplomatic pressure to solve the problem led to suggestions that the quarrel could jeopardise US military assistance. Ultimately, an arrangement to free foreign NGO workers was made, though its terms were not revealed. This development created much domestic controversy, with Egyptians outraged at what they saw as American and political interference in the judicial process.

Egypt's relations with Israel, governed by the 1979 peace treaty, suffered. Anti-Israeli sentiments were evident in demonstrations. Security in the Sinai deteriorated, prompting the deployment of Egyptian soldiers. After the accidental killing of Egyptian troops by an Israeli patrol in the Sinai in September, thousands of protesters attacked the Israeli Embassy in Cairo, stormed the offices and forced the staff to evacuate. The army declared a state of alert and reinstated martial law. There were more than a dozen attacks on pipelines carrying gas to Israel through the Sinai Peninsula. In April, the Egyptian General Petroleum Corporation abruptly announced that it was cancelling deliveries to Israel under the pretext of a financial dispute.

The Muslim Brotherhood leadership, however, promoted a more accommodating stance towards Israel, perhaps to cultivate better relations with Western nations. In his presidential acceptance speech, Morsi stated that all existing treaties would be respected. But an April visit by the grand mufti of Egypt to Jerusalem, which broke an unwritten rule not to visit any areas under Israeli occupation, was publicly condemned by senior Muslim Brotherhood and FJP figures for granting legitimacy to the Israeli occupation and offending Muslim sentiment.

A new Egypt?

Despite optimistic expectations, Mubarak's departure did not smoothly usher in peace and democracy: the transition was rocky, and a sense of chaos pervaded public life. Security suffered: an increase in both serious and petty crimes was reported, and the police remained ineffective and absent. Although abuses by security forces were a key driver of the protest movement, security-sector reform was still lagging. Instability hurt the Egyptian economy by scaring tourists and investors.

Political activity and freedom of expression expanded greatly. Public political debate was vigorous and abundant. But society was becoming increasingly polarised, with divisions emerging between ideological factions, particularly Islamists and secularists.

Libya: fragile authority

The international community became militarily involved in Libya in 2011, through a NATO intervention that proved decisive in helping Libyan rebels to oust Colonel Muammar Gadhafi from power. With a United Nations mandate to enforce a no-fly zone and to take 'all necessary measures' to protect civilians, NATO had moved immediately into more direct action, undertaking a bombing campaign on government targets, particularly around Tripoli. These effectively disabled the regime's military capabilities, which had been far superior to those of the largely disorganised rebels and would otherwise have easily overwhelmed them – as in fact was indicated by the first months of fighting. Air strikes by a multinational coalition, led mainly by France, Britain and the United States, began in March, and the mission came to an official end when the UN Security Council voted to end NATO's mandate from 31 October 2011.

Throughout the summer, there were repeated rebel offensives, backed by NATO helicopter and missile strikes. These were met by fierce counterattacks from regime forces. The Nafusa Mountains became an important rebel stronghold in the mostly Gadhafi-controlled western part of the country, while cities such as Misrata and Zliten, each less than 200km from the capital, saw intense fighting. On 29 July 2011, the rebels' military leader (formerly Gadhafi's interior minister), General Abdel Fattah Younes, was shot dead, a likely victim of distrust among rebels and tribal infighting. By then, the rebel movement seemed fractured and locked in a stalemate.

However, the rebels suddenly made significant progress in August, rapidly moving on Tripoli. Anti-Gadhafi protests and street fighting erupted in the capital, and on 22 August, the central landmark Green Square was overrun by rebels and renamed Martyrs Square. On 23 August, Gadhafi's compound was seized; he went into hiding while most of his family fled to Algeria. On 20 October he was found on the outskirts of his hometown Sirte, and beaten, shot and killed by a mob. Three days later, the National Transitional Council (NTC), which had been recognised in July by the international community as the legitimate government of Libya, declared the country officially liberated.

At mid-2012, the unelected NTC was still in control. Its chairman, Mustafa Abdul Jalil (formerly Gadhafi's justice minister), was the effective head of state, while former Gadhafi critic Abdel Rahim el-Keeb, who had spent many years abroad, was prime minister. El-Keeb headed a 24-member cabinet comprising figures from across the country. Its diverse composition was an effort to appease and co-opt tribal and regional factions and balance rival power interests.

The provisional government set a timetable and mechanisms for Libya's democratic transition. Elections were scheduled for June 2012 – they were later postponed to July – to form a 200-member national assembly tasked with drafting a new constitution. According to laws drafted with popular input and announced in February, 80 seats would be reserved for political parties, which were still nascent, having been banned under Gadhafi. Concerns ran high that allowing only independents to run would lead to an assembly (and a political process) dominated by wealthy and powerful tribal figures. An earlier proposal to have a 10% quota for women was scrapped. All those associated with the Gadhafi regime, as well as NTC officials, were banned from running for office. In March, details of the 13 constituencies comprising the national electoral map were announced.

Although most of the key figures of the Gadhafi regime were killed, integrated into the transition process or had fled, there were some high-profile exceptions. Saif al-Islam, Gadhafi's second son and heir apparent, was captured and arrested while trying to flee the country on 19 November. Although also wanted by the International Criminal Court (ICC) for crimes against humanity, at mid-2012 he was still being held in Libya pending trial. The NTC put considerable diplomatic pressure on Mauritania to extradite Abdallah Senoussi, Gadhafi's former spy chief, who was also wanted by the ICC and by France. The NTC also demanded that Niger hand over Saadi Gadhafi, the ex-leader's third son who was under house arrest there. Trials of hundreds of detained loyalists lagged behind schedule. However, dealing with the past continued to be important for the transition: the NTC appealed to Libyans to give evidence against former regime officials.

Libya's biggest challenge was to rein in the militias: awash with guns after raiding weapons depots, and empowered since the ouster of Gadhafi, they were a serious threat to central authority and to stability. A Human Rights Watch report estimated that there were over 250 armed groups in the city of Misrata alone, while other sources counted as many as 200,000 militia members throughout the country. The militias were often competing for space and control: inter-militia clashes killed 147 people in the southern city of Sabha in March. Across the country, armed militia men roamed streets and occupied government facilities. Militias were accused of serious human-rights violations, including extra-legal detention and torture of suspected

Gadhafi loyalists. These included black Africans, perceived as Gadhafi's hired mercenaries, even though Libya has its own indigenous black population. Innocent civilians were often beaten and detained for ransom.

Though it acknowledged these problems, the interim government proved mostly powerless. When local fighters attacked the NTC base in the former loyalist stronghold of Bani Walid on 23 January 2012, the NTC was forced to recognise the council they created as the new authority of the town. Popular demand for reining in militias increased, with regular demonstrations demanding their breakup and disarmament. On 20 April 2012, the government finally took control of Tripoli's international airport, after months of negotiations with the militia that had been running it since Gadhafi's ouster.

The NTC sought to persuade militiamen to join a new national army and police force, but with very limited success. Amid a widespread perception that the central government was weak, the militias could exert far more power and influence as independent entities. Some tribal factions and militias would prefer a weak government, following the experience of the strong rule of Gadhafi. Moreover, the electoral law stated that members of the military could not vote, providing a disincentive for militia members to join security institutions.

The role of religion in public and political life was another significant issue in post-Gadhafi Libya. In October, Abdul Jalil and other NTC officials announced that sharia would be the principal source of legislation, thus making the new Libya an Islamic state. However, in April, ahead of the elections, the NTC issued an unexpected and controversial law that banned parties based on religion, in order to preserve 'national unity'. The move was denounced by Islamist groups, particularly Libya's newly formed Muslim Brotherhood, which was expected to make a strong showing.

Fears also rose about the country breaking apart. In March, inter-tribal clashes broke out in the southern city of Sabha, killing 50, when the tribal leader threatened to demand independence for his allegedly oppressed people – a move that indicated the politicisation of tribal identities. In other cities, notably Misrata, local and municipal elections were held independently, as people resorted to their own local governance structures, further fragmenting central authority. Prominent figures in the eastern part of the country toyed with autonomy for Cyrenaica (one of the three semi-autonomous administrative regions of pre-Gadhafi Libya). A decision to base regional representation in the national assembly on population size, giving 102 seats to western cities and only 98 to the east and south combined, raised the spectre of marginalisation, angering many and sowing disenchantment with the transition. Greater support for regional autonomy would be divisive, particularly since most of Libya's oil reserves were in the east. However, proponents of regional autonomy appeared to lack clear goals. Protests in Benghazi, the eastern capital, revealed a lack of consensus.

These trends highlighted a deeper malaise: the struggle for the legitimacy of central authority, or at least of the unelected, shadowy NTC – and by extension, its questionable ability to shepherd a democratic transition. Assertions of strength by NTC leaders, such as a vow by Abdul Jalil to use force if needed to keep the country together, could not disguise the NTC's fundamental inability to exert nationwide control. Moreover, the NTC came under fire from fast-developing Libyan media and civil society for its lack of political and financial transparency. Its inclusion of Gadhafi-era officials bred discontent. Although spirits remained high in Tripoli, the interim government's failure to formulate, let alone promote, a unified or inclusive national vision was proving deeply problematic.

Tunisia: managing expectations

Just as Tunisia was the unlikely harbinger of a wave of democratic transitions in the Arab world, it proved to be the pioneer in the trend that followed: the attainment of political power by Islamists through democratic elections. The moderate Islamist An-Nahda party swept parliamentary elections held in October: competing with more than 100 other parties, it won 41% of the vote, amounting to 90 of 217 seats. More unusually, it formed a coalition government with two non-Islamist allies, pledging to work together with the secularist Congress for the Republic (CPR) and the leftist Democratic Forum for Labour and Liberties (known as Ettakatol). A 41-member coalition cabinet was formed in December, headed by Prime Minister Hamadi Jebali of An-Nahda, with CPR's Moncef Marzouki, formerly a human-rights activist, as president, and Ettakatol's Mustapha Ben Jaafar as speaker of the Constituent Assembly.

An-Nahda had been banned under the rule of ousted President Zine el-Abedine Ben Ali, and thousands of its activists were jailed; however, its philosophy had continued to evolve, and networks were maintained in exile. The party emphasised its commitment to secularism and pluralism, referring to the AKP in Turkey as an inspirational model. It was widely recognised as the early front-runner because of perceived honesty and credibility, particularly in light of its long-standing opposition to and suffering under the previous regime. However, political opposition to An-Nahda ran high in the run-up to elections, with fears that Islamism would creep into Tunisian society and politics, and would shape the constitution that the new assembly was due to write. However, with 90% voter turnout in free and fair elections, An-Nahda could safely claim a genuine popular mandate. Grassroots campaigning, excellent countrywide organisation and a moderate discourse won over voters, while secular parties that ran on an anti-Nahda platform performed badly. A shadowy, populist movement known as Arrida Ach-Chaabia came fourth, doing well in the deprived rural areas. The Salafist Nour party was not allowed to run in the elections.

As a committee drafted the new constitution, there were fears that Salafists, increasingly vociferous in their demands for conservative Islamist reforms, would influence the process. They were resorting to attacks on alcohol users and on theatres and actors. However, An-Nahda unequivocally distanced itself from such tendencies, declaring that the new constitution would not cite sharia as a source of legislation. Instead, the party emphasised the need for consensus and inclusion, saying that the constitution would merely repeat the existing reference to Islam as the religion of the state. An-Nahda was sticking to its promise to maintain Tunisia's secular nature, including by reaching out to the country's Jewish community. Further debates, including over whether to ban alcohol, and more complex questions over women's rights, were likely to emerge.

After coming to power, An-Nahda attempted to tackle head on the country's considerable economic challenges. Hampered by decades of dictatorship and associated corruption and mismanagement, the Tunisian economy, particularly the important tourism sector, was badly hit by the turmoil of 2011. Even after Ben Ali's departure, near-daily protests by those airing long-repressed grievances crippled the interim government. In an effort to spur investment, An-Nahda announced a series of economic reforms as well as an anti-corruption campaign. The United States pledged $100m to Tunisia to help it pay its debts, having already provided $190m in assistance to aid economic recovery.

Significant improvements, however, were slow in coming. The economy contracted by 1.8% in 2011, and unemployment rose to 19%. Public-works schemes expanded by the interim government were ineffective, and may only have engendered further corruption. Food inflation also rose. There was increasing recognition that structural reforms were needed. The country was paralysed by near-constant industrial strikes (directed by powerful labour unions) and protests over poor living standards, prompting the president and the prime minister to appeal for a six-month truce to break the cycle of unrest and economic stagnation. Strikes became less frequent and the finance minister, left-wing economist Hocine Dimassi, pledged infrastructure development, the creation of industrial zones and attention to marginalised regions. But there was little evident progress. The socio-political disaffection and frustration that had provoked fruit vendor Mohamed Bouazizi to set himself alight in December 2010, sparking a revolution, had not dissipated: in fact, there was a five-fold increase in self-immolations across Tunisia, including four in a single week in January 2012.

There were some positive steps. Most significant was the dissolution, even before the elections, of the state security apparatus, which had been the mainstay of state repression. In a widely lauded move, the head of the riot police was demoted by the new interior minister. Ben Ali and his wife were sentenced *in absentia* to 35 years in jail by a court in Tunis; some former ministers were also charged. With a flowering of civil-society groups and vigorous public debates and discussions, including in the media, Tunisian society was making a decisive and peaceful break with the past.

However, a ban on demonstrations was instituted in April 2012 after weeks of protests by those demanding and opposing the implementation of sharia. The government, emphasising the need for public order, forcibly dispersed a demonstration by thousands of unemployed graduates. Two days later, some 2,000 members of the labour movement and civil-society groups took to the streets in central Tunis, and attempted to march down Habib Bourguiba Avenue, the main site of the protests that overthrew Ben Ali. Riot police used tear gas and batons to disperse protesters, and charged them down with trucks and motorbikes. After 15 civilians and eight police-men were injured, Marzouki denounced 'unacceptable violence' from both sides. Although the numbers of demonstrators were not large, the incidents reflected growing frustration with the pace of change, as well as anger at An-Nahda's handling of the transition. The government repeatedly called for patience, highlighting the difficulties of rebuilding institutions and authori-ties tainted by decades of dictatorship. However, its biggest challenge was to meet very high popular economic and political expectations. It also had to manage socio-religious pressures in a society revelling in democracy and newfound freedoms. The coming months would be critical for Tunisia's transition, as the government attempted to strike a balance between main-taining stability and progress, and keeping popular support.

Algeria: political reforms spark disputes

Although Algeria nominally had a multiparty system from 1989, its politics were largely dominated by the military and by the National Liberation Front

(FLN), which faced repeated allegations of electoral fraud and boycotts by opposition parties. However, in response to the discontent that swept across the Arab world and hit Algeria sporadically in 2011, the regime reformed political laws. Nearly half the country's 44 political parties were legalised, creating a more open political environment. In addition, sweeping media reforms were passed in September, freeing radio and television from state control.

A sense of excitement and optimism preceded the parliamentary elections of May 2012. However, the elections, with a turnout of 42% and in which the country's governing FLN and its allies secured over 60% of seats, were tarnished by allegations of fraud from opposition candidates. An EU observer mission endorsed the election process, despite what were described as technical shortcomings. At the inaugural session of parliament, 49 legislators from the main Islamist coalition, Green Algeria Alliance, and MPs from two smaller parties held up signs that read 'no to voter fraud' and refused to attend. An opposition alliance of 14 small political parties led by Islamist party the Front for Justice and Democracy announced that it would boycott parliament in protest at the 'shameful fraud'. The alliance held 28 of the 462 seats. The largest Islamist party, the Movement of Society for Peace, led by Abdalla Djaballah, said it would not participate in the new government. The arguments were likely to delay debates on proposed constitutional amendments.

Demands for political reform did figure in the relatively contained mass demonstrations in 2011, and succeeded in having the 19-year-old state of emergency lifted. But popular demands centred on economic issues, in light of widespread poverty and unemployment, particularly among young people. Given that Algeria is the world's twelfth-largest exporter of oil and the fourth largest of natural gas, the poor economic situation indicated corruption and bad governance. The government has used energy revenues to raise wages and to increase subsidies, helping to placate protesters. However, most Algerians have seen little benefit from energy wealth, with living standards, public services and unemployment all worsening. Among other challenges were rising food prices and poor housing. Discontent was evident in almost daily protests, strikes and riots, particularly in January 2012.

With the memory of Algeria's long and bloody civil war still vivid, the competition between political factions, the role of the military and the uncertain position of Islamist groups made for a volatile mix, compounded by questions about the sincerity of the FLN's political reform agenda. However, there were also powerful factors supporting stability: despite decaying institutions, the state remained rich and omnipresent; the Islamists, after decades of violent repression, were weak and had to share the political space with other, less polarising political forces. It was unclear whether worsening problems would translate into sustained unrest. The capacity of the political process to be inclusive would be important.

Morocco: protests blunted

The legitimacy enjoyed by King Mohammed VI did not prevent the tide of Arab discontent from reaching Morocco, with nationwide protests breaking out in February 2011. Anger centred on perceptions of cronyism, corruption and deteriorating economic conditions, and translated into growing calls for political reform. The king announced constitutional reforms in June, and these were endorsed in a July referendum, with a disputed 72% turnout but 98% approval of the new document. The changes stipulated that the prime minister must come from the largest party in parliament whereas previously, the king could choose whomever he wished. The prime minister was also granted greater powers, including the authority to appoint and fire ministers, as well as to dissolve parliament. Parliament and the judiciary were strengthened, though as supreme leader of the armed forces and 'commander of the faithful', the king retained key decision-making powers.

Elections were held in November, a year earlier than scheduled. In the newly expanded lower house of parliament, 31 parties competed for 395 seats, with 60 seats reserved for women and 30 for young people. A turnout of around 45% was reported. The moderate Islamist Justice and Development Party (PJD) won 107 seats, and its leader Abdelilah Benkirane became prime minister. A centrist coalition government was formed, with the PJD allying with the royalist National Rally for Independents and the Independence Party (Istiqlal). Cabinet posts were divided between these three groups. However, allies of the king were given charge of the key ministries of finance and the interior.

The youth-led February 20 movement, which spearheaded the initial protests, lost energy and support in a society that appeared to want to avoid the instability seen elsewhere, even at the cost of a slower pace of political change. However, February 20 activists, including the rapper known as El Haqed ('the enraged one') whose critical songs became a rallying cry for the movement, argued that reforms were timid and continued to press for a full constitutional monarchy. Although protest rallies were held almost weekly, they did not manage to sustain momentum, especially after the withdrawal of Al Adl Wal Ihsan (Justice and Spirituality), Morocco's best-organised Islamist group. Although banned from politics, Al Adl has a strong social presence and influence; it organised and led a 40,000-strong pro-Palestinian rally in March 2012. The protest community remained divided mainly into youth and Islamist groupings. Although calls for greater political representation had undoubtedly increased, popular discontent centred on poverty, corruption and unemployment, issues that fundamentally frustrated, drove, and unified Moroccans. Benkirane emphasised the fight against corruption as a high priority, pitting the government against an entrenched nepotistic system of which the king was seen as a main beneficiary.

Economic pressures included a particularly high rate of youth unemployment. Although the government tried to placate protesters by increasing social spending, the economic crisis in Europe threatened to have a serious impact as Morocco's economy is heavily dependent on European markets and tourists, as well as on remittances. Soaring prices and unemployment provoked demonstrations and violent clashes with security forces in the northern city of Taza. In the capital, Rabat, protests outside the parliament building by unemployed graduates became a regular occurrence, and escalated briefly into an occupation of the education ministry. In January 2012, there were five self-immolations in one week.

Moroccan civil society was mobilised in March when a 16-year-old girl, who was forced to marry her rapist and then suffered abuse by him, killed herself. This provoked a national outcry and demands to overturn laws that allowed rapists to escape punishment by marrying their victims. Although the protests were not overtly political in nature, they did highlight the growing ability of Moroccan society to mobilise. The king's limited but genuine accommodation of popular demands appeared to have broken the momentum of protests, but this could be reversed if economic conditions continued to worsen.

Syria: civil war

The Syrian uprising, which began as a popular protest movement for greater civil and political rights, evolved into a civil war as the regime adopted repressive tactics and opposition groups resorted to self-defence and violence.

The regime of President Bashar al-Assad deployed all its instruments of repression to crush both mass peaceful demonstrations and, at a later stage, armed resistance. It sought to deepen sectarian fears and resentment in an attempt to ensure loyalty to key sectarian and social groups. While introducing cosmetic political reforms, Assad also pushed a narrative that blamed foreign-backed terrorist and jihadist groups for the uprising. Nevertheless, the rebellion spread across the country, with violence and unrest reaching every major city, including the capital Damascus and Aleppo, the largest city. By mid-2012, it was estimated that up to 17,000 Syrians had died, and at least 230,000 had fled their homes. In March 2012, the UN Human Rights Council's Commission of Inquiry on Syria reported that most of those killed and injured were victims of full-scale military attacks on entire towns and villages, while earlier victims had been mainly anti-regime protesters shot during demonstrations. This, among other factors, pointed to the transformation of the uprising into a civil war with sectarian undertones. (See *Strategic Geography*, p. XIV.)

Opposition to Assad

Even as rebel factions and exile groups suffered severe political and military setbacks, opposition to the Assad regime strengthened and radicalised. By mid-2012, it had yet to organise and unify sufficiently to pose an immediate threat to the Assad regime. It struggled to define strategies to weaken support for Assad among minorities, undermine the cohesion of his regime and security forces and rally effective international support. Fragmentation of the opposition was caused by political rivalries, disconnection between on-the-ground rebels and foreign-based opposition leaders, and differences about the wisdom and methods of militarising the uprising and courting foreign support.

Although there was international outrage at Assad's crimes, this did not translate into international action beyond the dispatch of monitors to observe a ceasefire agreement that was repeatedly breached. Western governments were held back by the high perceived strategic costs of intervention, by war fatigue, and by uncertainty about what precise actions they might take given Syria's difficult geographical and sectarian terrain, and the unclear nature of opposition groups. In particular, they were restrained from UN-backed military action by Russian and Chinese opposition.

The Syrian National Council (SNC), formed in summer 2011, gradually became the public face of opposition to the Assad regime, though in fact it was simply the most prominent of many groups. Headed by a secular intellectual, Burhan Ghalioun, it focused on persuading the international community to provide material and political support to the rebels. The SNC obtained recognition as the main opposition front from the Friends of Syria contact group and, as such, attended meetings in Tunis, Istanbul and Paris at which options for helping the Syrian opposition were discussed. Within the SNC, there were different opinions on the type of assistance needed, with some advocating direct foreign intervention and others arguing for external funding and arming of the rebellion. Several opposition figures, including SNC members, opposed militarisation of the uprising for fear it would deepen political and sectarian rifts and give the regime the upper hand. The SNC's inability to deliver decisive international action, despite attempts by Western and Arab states to muster a consensus on UN-supported action, eroded its standing among Syrian rebels and activists. Its fractiousness, combined with anxieties about the growing influence of the Muslim Brotherhood, greatly hampered its effectiveness and credibility. Disillusionment with the SNC prompted secular and neo-Islamist members to break away and form splinter opposition groups. Other respected opposition members preferred to remain apart from it.

On the ground, local coordination committees, a decentralised network of activists, emerged as the backbone of popular mobilisation. By February 2012, 14 local committees in cities across the country had formed into an umbrella organisation that documented abuses of protesters for the international media. In August 2011, they declared their opposition to the militarisation of the uprising in any way, emphasising indigenous civil disobedience instead. However, mass arrests in still quiescent Damascus seemed to affect the activist community.

As the brutality of Assad's crackdown intensified, armed resistance to his regime grew, especially after the regime's assault on Hama and border towns during the summer. The armed resistance grew to include a wide variety of groups with different motivations. The Free Syrian Army (FSA), formed in July 2011, emerged as the leading rebel force. Made up mostly of defectors from Assad's military and armed with weapons stolen from the regime's depots or bought from arms smugglers, the FSA claimed to have 40,000 fighters, mostly in the north and the cities of Homs, Hama and Rastan. Several generals joined the defectors' ranks. In March 2012, Human Rights Watch criticised the FSA for human-rights abuses of security forces and government supporters.

Although seen as heroes on the ground, FSA fighters, operating in loose units, struggled to cope with the military's superior firepower and organisation. Lacking command and control, the FSA had difficult relations with the SNC, which established a military bureau to coordinate operations and funding. Higher-ranking defectors challenged the authority of the Turkey-based FSA commander, Colonel Riad al-Asaad.

As violence worsened, sectarianism became a more salient, albeit not yet dominant, feature of the uprising. Instances of sectarian violence and provocation multiplied as a result of both regime incitement and communal fears. Alawites, who make up just over 10% of the population overall but dominate the security and intelligence services as well as the elite Republican Guard and Fourth Division, spearheaded the repression. In a calculated effort to prevent defections among Sunni soldiers, ultra-loyalist armed gangs known as the *shabiha* supplemented government forces. There were also reports of the regime arming Alawite villages. An ominous sign of deepening sectarian violence was the massacre in May of 108 people in the town of Houla, nearly half of them children. According to reports, *shabiha* conducted summary executions, forcibly killing entire families. While some Alawites joined the opposition, most continued to support Assad out of fear of retribution and relegation as much as loyalty. Other minorities displayed similar concerns. Although both the SNC and the FSA tried to assuage such fears, minorities as well as many secular Syrians remained wary of the opposition's alleged Islamist leanings.

Battles for territory

By late 2011, significant swathes of territory were under partial rebel control. The FSA held several towns in Idlib province, and in January, they controlled two-thirds of Homs, Syria's third-largest city. The fighting came close to the regime's power bases: in January, many Damascus suburbs were under opposition control, including Saqba and Douma, while government forces were forced to retreat from the town of Zabadani, just 32km from Damascus.

However, in February the government launched a major military offensive across the country in a determined effort to wrest back control. Many rebel gains were reversed as the military retook Zabadani and other cities. In April, government forces went on the offensive in neighbourhoods in Hama. Badly organised and supplied, and lacking artillery and mechanised capabilities, the rebels proved unable to hold territory.

The city of Homs, an early opposition stronghold, played a prominent role in the uprising. Throughout the month-long siege of the neighbourhood of Baba Amr in February 2012, it suffered the heaviest and most sustained fighting between government and opposition forces. The deaths of Western journalists Marie Colvin and Remi Ochlik in a rocket attack galvanised international public and political opinion against the Assad regime. Colvin described the desperate conditions in Baba Amr in her final dispatch, while Paul Conroy, a journalist who managed to get himself smuggled out, gave harrowing testimony from a London hospital, comparing the bombardment of Homs to Rwanda and Srebrenica. Local activists collected and disseminated video footage to highlight the situation in besieged areas.

The regime deployed mortars and artillery, dealing a military setback to the FSA but at the cost of a humanitarian catastrophe. Within weeks, armed rebels made what they termed a tactical retreat to prevent further killing of civilians. On 1 March, government forces took control of the district, which Assad later visited in a show of force. Activists alleged indiscriminate killings and torture of civilians in the following days. Humanitarian access was denied and aid convoys were made to wait. The Syrian Arab Red Crescent was finally allowed into Baba Amr on 7 March: they found it empty, as most of the estimated 10,000 residents had fled. Valerie Amos, UN under-secretary for humanitarian affairs, visited Homs, including Baba Amr, and described it as 'completely devastated'.

Weakened standing

As the regime escalated its crackdown, it launched cosmetic political reforms to create the semblance of responsiveness. On 26 February 2012, a referendum was held on a new constitution that envisioned a pluralistic political system and the ostensible end of the monopoly of the Ba'ath Party. It nevertheless contained provisions that ensured the continued rule of Assad. Boycotted by the opposition and dismissed as a sham by Western and Arab states, the referendum was approved by 89.4% of the voters, on a turnout of 57%. On 7 May, national elections were held to elect a new parliament, with a turnout of 51%. The Ba'ath Party took the majority of seats, and many independents were believed to be regime proxies. In June, a Ba'ath member, Riyad Hijab, was named prime minister.

Other developments further damaged the regime's frail political standing. In March 2012, activists leaked a cache of e-mails said to be from Assad's private e-mail account. They revealed a leadership indulging in luxury and petty behaviour, out of touch with the harsh realities of popular disenchantment, protest and violence across the country. Assad appeared dismissive of political reform.

Regionally, the Assad regime found itself increasingly isolated. Only the Shia-majority states of Iran and, to a much lesser extent, Iraq, still backed Assad, while a divided Lebanon remained naturally wary and anxious about developments in Syria. The Gulf states, on the other hand, were explicit in their opposition to Assad, with the Saudi and Qatari monarchs pushing for the international community to arm the rebels. Most significantly, the

Palestinian group Hamas, a major recipient of diplomatic and financial support from Syria, publicly renounced the Assad regime in February 2012. The move reflected, on the one hand, its growing unease as a Sunni movement at being allied with a regime that was perceived to be repressing its Sunni community, and on the other hand, its own strategic rapprochement with the rising Muslim Brotherhood in Egypt.

Meanwhile Turkey, with which Syria previously had a close relationship, suspended a cooperation agreement and imposed an arms embargo and sanctions. In April, it stopped and searched a German-owned ship that it suspected of carrying arms for the regime. Turkey, along with Lebanon and Jordan, was facing the humanitarian consequences of the uprising, with each country taking in thousands of Syrian refugees.

Absence of international consensus

The Arab League, invigorated by success in Libya and heavily lobbied by Gulf states, attempted to assert itself in the Syrian crisis, with limited success. In November, Syria accepted a League-brokered peace plan to halt the crackdown, but the ceasefire broke down within days. The League suspended Syria's membership and imposed sanctions. After weeks of negotiations, Syria agreed in December to admit a League observer mission. However, the 50-strong team proved too small, too inexperienced, and too dependent on the government to make any real difference. With violence continuing unabated, the mission was criticised as a failure and a farce. After Assad's rejection in January of a League proposal to relinquish power and leave the country, the observers were withdrawn.

As a result, the Arab League referred the issue to the UN. In February, the General Assembly voted overwhelmingly to approve a resolution condemning Assad's crackdown on the uprising. On 1 March, the UN Human Rights Council deplored the 'brutal' actions of the regime, and called for an immediate end to attacks and abuses. However, after much diplomatic wrangling, a watered-down Security Council resolution, calling only for a ceasefire and for dialogue – rather than for Assad to step aside, as the Arab League sought – was vetoed by China and Russia in a move that the US called 'despicable'.

Following this failure, former UN Secretary-General Kofi Annan was appointed joint special envoy of the UN and Arab League for Syria and became the exclusive mediator in the conflict. In March, he proposed a six-point plan to resolve the crisis in Syria, which was adopted unanimously by the Security Council in April. It called for a halt to armed violence, with a withdrawal of military forces from population centres, and an end to the use of heavy weapons. Rebel forces were also to stop fighting. The plan enshrined the right of Syrians to demonstrate peacefully, and demanded the provision of humanitarian assistance to affected areas. Annan also called for the deployment of up to 300 unarmed UN observers to monitor the ceasefire and report breaches. It was hoped that their presence would help inhibit violence and compel compliance.

Pressured by Moscow, and perhaps calculating that he could garner some international credit, Assad accepted the Annan plan. While the SNC too endorsed the plan, opposition activists remained distrustful of Assad's commitments, reporting a military build-up and hundreds of deaths in the days preceding the 12 April deadline. The ceasefire, though superficially observed, was shaky from the start: each side alleged aggression by the other and there were continued clashes in Homs and other rebel strongholds. A bloody government crackdown in Hama in late April cast serious doubt on the success and sustainability of the ceasefire and of the peace plan in general. Continued reports in May of massacres by *shabiha* militia and government shelling of civilian areas drew international outrage, and further dampened prospects that the plan could bring an end to violence. There were renewed calls inside and outside Syria for outside military intervention. Moreover, the effectiveness of the UN observers was debated, with activists accusing the military of hiding tanks and temporarily halting their shelling only while the observers were present.

Two international conferences were held to seek consensus on the best way to resolve the conflict. The inaugural 70-state Friends of Syria meeting was held in Tunis in February 2012, though Russia, China and Iran declined to attend. Calling on Assad to cease violence and allow humanitarian access, nations also committed to implement sanctions against Syria. The meeting marked greater engagement with the opposition, though the final communiqué did not mention intervention or arming the rebels. According to one diplomat, 'The point [was] to make the transition look more inevitable.' A second meeting was held in Istanbul in April. Participating nations endorsed Annan's peace plan and, though they berated Assad, did not explicitly call for him to step down. The SNC was recognised as a legitimate representative of all Syrians and was 'noted' as the main opposition interlocutor with the international community: this stopped short of full recognition, which would see them as a government in waiting. Meanwhile, Gulf states pledged $100m to pay the salaries of armed opposition fighters for three months, though whether, how and to whom this money would be disbursed remained uncertain.

The international community applied sanctions both to punish and pressure the regime. In August 2011, Washington announced sanctions on Syria's energy sector and froze all Syrian government assets in the United States; it continued to push for more and tougher sanctions, including a global arms embargo. The Arab League ended dealings with the Syrian Central Bank, placed travel bans on Syrian officials, and called for the suspension of commercial flights; however, Lebanon and Iraq quietly refrained from applying these measures. The European Union instituted travel bans and asset freezes against major regime figures; in September 2011, it banned crude oil imports from Syria and in February 2012 it blocked trade in gold and precious metals.

Sanctions and unrest had a significant impact on the economy, which contracted by 2% in 2011. European sanctions hit Syria particularly hard as the EU was its biggest trading partner, accounting for 22.5% of Syrian trade. Syria found it difficult to find other buyers for its crude oil, leading to a 30% decline in production. The Syrian pound's value fell sharply.

Quick resolution unlikely

The business community and middle classes of Damascus and Aleppo, once strong pillars of support for the Assad regime, showed signs of unease. Deteriorating economic conditions and increasing insecurity bred dissatisfaction with the regime and hedging behaviour, with some people who nominally were Assad loyalists quietly supporting the resistance.

Worrying trends emerged that had the potential to validate the narrative of the Syrian regime and solidify minority support: a rise in car bombs and the possible involvement of jihadist groups in Syria. Five suicide bombs killed dozens in Damascus, while Aleppo was hit by blasts in March. The government blamed foreign terrorists and there were signs that Arab fighters had been fighting alongside some rebel groups, though in small numbers and in an ad hoc way. US intelligence reported that al-Qaeda and other radical groups had developed a presence in Syria, where the sectarian dimension of the conflict could make for a hospitable environment. Ayman al-Zawahiri, al-Qaeda's leader, explicitly called on his followers to enter Syria to fight the Assad regime.

At mid-2012, the government retained military superiority and it appeared that opposition forces were unable to oust Assad on their own. Defections from the political and security elite remained few, indicating strong loyalty but also a perception that Assad's chances of survival remained high. Fears about Syria's future abounded: of a prolonged civil war, of an Islamist takeover, of sectarian killings, of a proxy war, of regional contagion, of loss of control of weapons of mass destruction. With the West perceived as timid, Russia inflexible and the Arab world divided, the Syrian regime and its opponents were largely left face to face.

Lebanon: looming shadow of Syria

Syria's travails found resonance in Lebanese political and sectarian dynamics. The cabinet, dominated by factions allied with Assad, had to walk a thin line to avoid a sectarian escalation. As a result, Lebanese politics became more polarised and complex. Friction within the coalition government was highlighted by outspoken support for the Syrian opposition by Druze political leader Walid Jumblatt and an attempt by Najib Mikati, the prime minister, to maintain an official policy of 'disassociation'. Lebanon consequently opposed Arab League and UN resolutions condemning and imposing sanctions on Syria, and declined to attend the Friends of Syria meetings.

After decades of Syrian interference in Lebanese affairs, Syria's downward trajectory left many Christians torn between fear of rising Sunni Islamism and deep distrust of the Assad regime. Shi'ites, too, grew anxious about the fate of Assad, whose alliance with Hizbullah, Lebanon's major political and military organisation, contributed to its rise. Indeed, sectarian tensions increased, and often broke out into violence, particularly in areas bordering Syria in the north and northeast, where many Sunnis sympathetic to the Syrian revolution lived alongside pockets of pro-Assad Alawites and Shi'ites affiliated with Hizbullah.

Firefights broke out in the tense northern city of Tripoli between pro- and anti-Assad groups, as well as along the Syrian–Lebanese border and in the capital Beirut. Dozens were killed and wounded, prompting the deployment of the army to restore order. The army, a respected institution weakened by its fragile cross-sectarian make-up and competing loyalties in the officer corps, found itself managing a politically volatile situation and high popular expectations of what it could achieve. Action, inaction and blunders on its part stoked tensions. In May, the arrest of an anti-Assad activist in Tripoli, accused of being an al-Qaeda member by a pro-Assad security agency, triggered a major escalation that spread to Beirut and other areas, during which the military killed a prominent cleric.

The civil war in Syria bled directly into Lebanon, which struggled to cope with more than 20,000 refugees. Supporters and agents of the Syrian regime operated in Beirut, and dissidents were kidnapped and rendered to Syrian authorities. Supporters of the Assad regime accused the Free Syrian Army of smuggling arms and aid through north Lebanon and the eastern Bekka

Valley, and claimed that Lebanese were providing shelter and political cover to rebels and jihadist fighters. Meanwhile, there were protests against Syrian incursions which resulted in civilian deaths and demanded in vain that the army defend the border and protect refugees. Thus, Lebanese society was sharply split by the uprising, and Syria's long shadow continued to loom over domestic politics.

Ever since the Hizbullah-led March 8 alliance had come to power in Lebanon in January 2011 after triggering a collapse of the anti-Syrian March 14 coalition, acrimony between – and often within – the two factions had increased. The latter bloc, led by former Prime Minister Saad Hariri's Sunni-dominated Future Movement, was vociferous in its condemnation of the Syrian regime and its actions. Its rallies and media provided a platform for anti-regime Syrian activists, and its members called for more political and humanitarian support for the Syrian revolution. The issue served as a rallying cry for the party, as did an alleged assassination attempt against an anti-Assad Christian leader, Samir Geagea. Meanwhile, Hizbullah stood by its Syrian ally, with its leader Hassan Nasrallah echoing Assad's narrative by depicting the uprising as a foreign plot and urging Syrians to support their president's timid reforms. He repeatedly appealed to the Syrian opposition to engage in unconditional dialogue with the regime. However, with increasing violence and negative media coverage, an anxious Hizbullah found itself in a politically tenuous position. Many accused the movement of providing material support to the regime and of intimidating Syrian dissidents in Lebanon. More importantly, Hizbullah struggled to justify its backing of Assad, given its declared goal of battling oppression and injustice. The prospect of Assad weakening posed difficult challenges for the organisation, including securing supply lines from Iran into Lebanon so as to ensure that its Lebanese rivals did not contest its political and military superiority.

Against this backdrop, the UN Special Tribunal for Lebanon, charged with investigating the 2005 killing of former Prime Minister Rafik Hariri and other assassinations of anti-Assad political and media figures, finally began work. Although its credibility was questioned by many Lebanese, it issued arrest warrants for four senior Hizbullah members. However, responsibility for making the arrests fell on the Lebanese government which, given Hizbullah's clout, proved unable to act. Nasrallah accused Israel of masterminding the assassination and rejected cooperation with the tribunal. The question of whether the cabinet would authorise payment of Lebanon's share of the tribunal's funding, and if not, what the consequences would be, became contentious. However, Mikati secured a last-minute political deal that allowed indirect funding.

Jordan: waiting for genuine reform

To diffuse growing dissatisfaction in Jordan that escalated in 2011, King Abdullah II pushed forward with political reforms. However, these were perceived as slow and timid, opening the monarchy to further criticism from the traditional Islamist and leftist opposition. Worryingly for the monarchy, tribal groups and former military officers, usually aligned with the government, joined these groups in voicing discontent. The drive for change has led to four different governments in Jordan since the beginning of 2011, all of which have struggled to balance reform with structural obstacles to change.

In September 2011, King Abdullah approved long-awaited constitutional amendments designed to liberalise the political system. These included the establishment of a constitutional court, independent oversight of elections and greater protection of free expression. The changes, however, were not implemented in a timely way and provoked criticism from Islamist and leftist members of parliament. This, coupled with a chaotic electoral redistricting process, led to protests and violence.

In a rare display of parliamentary power, a majority within parliament asked the king to appoint a new prime minister. After serving only eight months, Marouf al-Bakhit, who had been appointed following three weeks of street protests during the Arab uprisings, was sacked by King Abdullah and blamed for the slow and unsteady pace of reform. He was replaced by Awn al-Khasawneh, a former judge at the International Court of Justice, who was charged with rejuvenating the near-moribund reform process. Although the Islamist opposition led by the Muslim Brotherhood declined an offer to join his cabinet, it appeared that a rapprochement between the government and the Islamists was under way. In January 2012, the prime minister met with key leaders of the Brotherhood, following which the opposition cancelled a large planned protest. Conciliatory measures were taken by both sides. The government released key Islamist prisoners, while the Muslim Brotherhood refrained from meeting Hamas leader Khaled Meshal during a visit to Jordan.

Plans for the Brotherhood's political wing, the Islamic Action Front, to join the government failed in April 2012 after Jordan passed a new and controversial election law. The law, which increased the female quota in parliament and for the first time allowed national political party lists with proportionally assigned seats, did not meet the demands of the opposition.

The opposition alleged that a limit of 15 seats in parliament, along with gerrymandered districts, would favour regime loyalists and would not create a multiparty political system. Protests soon broke out across Jordan and opposition parties boycotted elections. Later that month, parliament voted to add an amendment to the electoral law forbidding political parties established on a religious basis. This measure, which passed with 46 votes of 83, would effectively ban the Muslim Brotherhood and was seen by the opposition as payback for not joining Khasawneh's cabinet. It led to continued street protests and political instability.

As unrest continued, Khasawneh tendered his resignation after only six months in the job, citing continuous interference in his work by the royal court and the intelligence services. King Abdullah publicly rebuked him in a letter expressing frustration that electoral reform measures had been implemented too slowly. Fayez Tarawneh, a former prime minister and chief of the Royal Court, was appointed to succeed Khasawneh. The opposition condemned his appointment as maintaining the conservative old order.

Corruption continued to dominate Jordan's political debate. In his appointment letter to Tarawneh, the king, himself perceived as having allowed his relatives and allies to prosper in questionable ways, reaffirmed Jordan's commitment to combating corruption. This was ostensibly a key component of Jordan's strategy to navigate the political turbulence of the Arab world. Omar Maani, former mayor of Amman, was arrested on fraud charges in December 2011. In February 2012, Mohammed Dahabi, former director of the Jordanian Intelligence Service, was charged with money laundering and corruption. Many considered the charges against Dahabi to be politically motivated. Additionally, Bakhit's government was marred by corruption allegations: before becoming prime minister, Bakhit had approved the development of a casino by the Dead Sea without government approval.

Saudi Arabia: regional moves

As Saudi Arabia battled to quiet domestic opposition, it also strove to enhance its standing in its strategic struggle for regional influence against Iran. Its efforts to promote unity within the six-member Gulf Co-operation Council (GCC), and its backing of Syrian rebels rising against Assad, were key to this strategy.

Domestically, scattered constituencies continued to struggle to build momentum for a national reform movement. Inspired by activism in neighbouring Bahrain, Shia activists in the Eastern Province tried to mobilise in cities such as Qatif and Alahsa, demanding greater equality and an end to discrimination. At least five demonstrators were shot by security forces in early 2012. The government denied responsibility for the deaths, claiming the protesters were killed in crossfire between security forces and armed 'masked men'. It blamed the unrest on an 'unnamed foreign power' – a reference to Iran, which it also accused of stirring the uprising in Bahrain.

Saudi authorities imprisoned founders of newly formed liberal organisations, including the Saudi Civil and Political Rights Association and the Islamic Umma Party, an organisation whose demands include greater political rights, transparency and an end to absolute monarchy. A budding women's-rights movement engaged in increasingly defiant acts of protest. In June 2011, a video posted online by activist Manal al-Sharif, in which she openly defied the country's driving ban on women, encouraged women in Riyadh and Jeddah to mimic her actions and led to the arrest of five women. The driving ban is not enshrined in written law but is the result of religious rulings by the country's leading clerics. Hundreds of women also rallied in March 2012 at King Khalid University in Abha to protest against gender discrimination and poor management of services on campus.

Building on earlier measures to pre-empt unrest, including a $130bn package of economic and social benefits, King Abdullah bin Abdulaziz Al Saud passed further reforms. Women were given the right to vote and stand in the next round of municipal elections scheduled for 2015, and to be members of the Majlis ash-Shura, the consultative assembly. The king dismissed the head of the morality police amidst complaints that the organisation was growing too aggressive.

In the year to mid-2012, the successive loss of two crown princes compounded speculation about the future succession. The line of royal succession does not pass from father to son, but has passed between brothers who are direct descendants of the kingdom's founder, King Abdulaziz bin Saud. In October 2011, Prince Sultan bin Abdulaziz Al Saud, who had been crown prince since King Abdullah's accession in 2005, died at the age of 80. In his place, Interior Minister Prince Nayef bin Abdulaziz Al Saud was designated as the heir. But he too died at the age of 78 in June 2012, and King Abdullah then named 76-year-old Prince Salman bin Abdulaziz Al Saud as crown prince. Prince Salman had been governor of Riyadh for nearly 50 years until his promotion to defence minister in 2011. He was known as a moderate and a pragmatist, seen as unlikely to steer far from the policies of cautious economic and social liberalisation begun by the 87-year-old King Abdullah. Prince Salman's younger brother, Prince Ahmed bin Abdulaziz was named interior minister.

The appointment of Prince Salman delayed any decision over a generational shift in power, which was expected to give rise to fierce internal contestation between different branches of the royal family. In 2006 King Abdullah established an allegiance council intended to make decisions over the succession, made up of 34 high-ranking princes who represent each of the lines of the ruling family that were born to the kingdom's founder. The council has the power to approve a choice made by the present king, or to vet its own nominations and bypass the king. However, there was no evidence that its powers had been activated.

Saudi Arabia sought to enhance its regional standing by championing an initiative to shift the GCC (which also includes Bahrain, Kuwait, Oman, Qatar and the United Arab Emirates (UAE)) towards closer union. During the council's annual summit held in Riyadh in December 2011, King Abdullah encouraged states to move towards unity in response to growing threats and turmoil in the Gulf. Analysts interpreted this as a call to enhance collective security cooperation as a means of guarding against internal rebellion and presenting a united front against a potentially nuclear-armed Iran.

In February 2012, Bahrain's state-run news agency reported that King Hamad bin Isa Al Khalifa had met King Abdullah for the purpose of developing the GCC into a unified entity. In May, statements from government officials in Bahrain and Saudi Arabia suggested that a union between the two states might be announced at the 14th GCC advisory summit in Riyadh, scheduled for later that month. At that summit, the GCC announced that a committee had been formed to study the formation of the union and that more time was needed to work on the details. Whether a GCC initiative has any chance of success in the face of regional rivalries, and whether states such as Qatar and the UAE would be willing to cede power to a Saudi-led initiative, however, remained unclear. Critics of the initiative pointed to the absence of a common market and gaps in the cooperative regional security architecture as evidence that it was premature.

Saudi Arabia's support for the Mubarak regime during Egypt's revolution and subsequent coolness towards the new actors emerging on the Egyptian political scene contributed to a downturn in relations between the two countries. Riyadh appeared concerned by the rise of the Muslim Brotherhood and a possible change in the foreign policy of Egypt, which under Mubarak had been a reliable ally. In April, Saudi Arabia recalled its ambassador to Cairo following demonstrations and the storming of its embassy to protest at the detention of an Egyptian human-rights activist in Saudi Arabia over allegations of drug trafficking. The embassy reopened a week later after Egyptian politicians and clerics visited Riyadh to rekindle ties. Activists, however, continued to accuse Riyadh of attempting to influence Egypt's domestic political affairs by financing Islamist groups and supporting the ruling military council. Still, in May, Saudi Arabia's finance minister announced that the country was in the process of finalising a $2.7bn aid package for Egypt, citing 'historic relations of brotherhood' between the two countries. Activists in Tunisia and Libya accused Saudi Arabia of supporting and financing Islamist and anti-revolutionary forces in their countries.

Saudi Arabia pressed for the arming of the opposition against the Assad regime, a close ally of Iran. In February 2012, at the inaugural meeting of the Friends of Syria, Saudi Foreign Minister Prince Saud al-Faisal described the arming of the Free Syrian Army as an 'excellent idea'. In March, officials from Saudi Arabia and Jordan said King Abdullah had asked his Jordanian counterpart to permit the delivery of weapons to rebels in Syria through Jordan, in exchange for economic assistance. However, both the United Nations and the United States opposed the move, the latter on the grounds that weapons might end up in the hands of al-Qaeda and fuel a long-term sectarian civil war. Top officials from Saudi Arabia and other Gulf states were notably absent from an Arab League summit calling on Assad to begin political dialogue through a UN-brokered peace plan, indicating a further shift of Saudi support away from a diplomatic solution.

Bahrain: political and social deadlock

Following the crackdown on anti-government protesters and declaration of a state of national emergency in the first part of 2011, King Hamad established an independent commission of inquiry. Hopes that its report would pave the way for a political solution to the country's crisis were dampened, however, as clashes continued between security forces and anti-government protesters.

The Bahrain Independent Commission of Inquiry was established in July 2011, headed by war-crimes expert Cherif Bassiouni and including other international lawyers. The commission's final report, published in November, provided harrowing details of 'a culture of non-accountability' within the country's security agencies and abuses of protesters in February and March, including beatings, electrocution and rape. The systematic use of torture against detainees had caused five confirmed deaths, it said. The report also detailed the destruction of Shia houses of worship by government authorities, the expulsion of students and employees from their workplaces, and the deaths of 35 individuals during the unrest. The report criticised special security courts established under the state of national emergency, which 'denied most defendants elementary fair trial guarantees'. It found no evidence of Iranian involvement in the unrest, contradicting the regime's narrative that attributed the protests to a Tehran-backed conspiracy to overthrow it.

The government responded by establishing a national commission to oversee implementation of the report's recommendations and by vowing to establish accountability for abuses. But hopes that the report could foster social reconciliation were soon dashed, as opposition groups declined to participate in the commission on the grounds that they were not offered enough seats.

In the weeks following the report's release, the government announced measures such as the revocation of the arrest powers of a security agency implicated in abuses, and the overturning of death sentences for two protesters convicted of killing a policeman. It appointed John Yates, former assistant commissioner of London's Metropolitan Police, and John Timoney, former chief of the Miami Police Department, to oversee police reforms. Other changes included the reinstatement of workers and students dismissed on grounds of political expression, the establishment of training programmes for judiciary and prosecution personnel on human-rights law, and the transfer of political cases to civilian courts. Some 20 medical staff jailed by a military court for between five and 15 years after treating protesters during unrest in March 2011 had their appeal transferred to a civilian court.

Anti-government groups dismissed reform efforts as mere 'window-dressing' and continued to call for greater political rights. Activists alleged that abuses by security forces were continuing, and that dozens of people had been killed since the report made its revelations, mostly as a result of tear-gas inhalation.

The release of numerous videos showing police beating protesters aggravated tensions. Amnesty International reported that a detained student had been tortured. In March 2012, Human Rights Watch reported that the government 'had not adequately addressed critical recommendations made by the independent commission, including establishing accountability for crimes such as torture'. It noted that 21 leading activists convicted solely of offences relating to freedom of expression had not had their cases reviewed. In mid-June, a Bahrain court of appeal acquitted nine medics and cut the jail terms of nine others for their role in anti-government protests. Two 15-year sentences were upheld against doctors who fled the country, and other reduced prison terms ranged from one month to five years. Rights groups condemned the sentences, stating that the majority of the doctors had been tortured in custody.

As a rumoured dialogue between the government and opposition failed to materialise, observers attributed official inaction to a rift within the ruling family between hardline elements and the country's moderate Crown Prince Salman bin Hamad Al Khalifa.

Perceived government intransigence led to continued protests in villages across the country. In early 2012, a march of 100,000 people calling for democracy and equal rights demonstrated the continued power of the opposition to mobilise its supporters. A growing chasm between the demands of the formal and informal opposition was reflected in divergent tactics. Formal opposition groups, including the Islamist bloc Al Wefaq and secular Wa'ad, continued to press for constitutional reforms, greater powers for the elected parliament, and an end to corruption. The February 14 Coalition, a group of anonymous online activists who organised the first protests in 2011, took a harder stance, advocating the overthrow of the regime. Coalition supporters, mainly young people in rural areas, used a wide array of increasingly violent tactics, including burning tyres and the use of Molotov cocktails against the security forces. In April, a small explosion in Al Eker village was reported to have injured seven policemen, marking a further escalation.

Prospects for a political settlement were further dampened by the increasingly hardline stance of groups backing the regime, which is part of the Sunni minority. They opposed any dialogue with the opposition. Cracks, however, also appeared among pro-government elements as youth groups began to compete with more established figures for control of the movement. In parallel, pro-government groups with ties to the Muslim Brotherhood articulated grievances on issues such as corruption.

Kuwait: parliamentary wrangling

Events in Kuwait in the year to mid-2012 were dominated by wrangling in parliament over corruption allegations levelled at Prime Minister Sheikh Nasser Mohammed al-Ahmed Al Sabah. Political pressures ultimately forced his resignation and that of the cabinet in November 2011, triggering early elections.

The prime minister quit after anti-government protesters stormed the parliament building, resulting in injuries to five policemen. Opposition MPs accused Sheikh Nasser of diverting hundreds of millions of dollars of state funds to his private accounts, and of using the country's foreign embassies to do so. MPs also demanded reforms paving the way for direct election of the prime minister, who is currently appointed by the emir, Sheikh Sabah al-Ahmed Al Sabah, and who must be a member of the royal family.

In the February 2012 elections, the loosely grouped opposition gained greater representation, with Islamists and tribal candidates making the largest gains. Candidates affiliated with the Muslim Brotherhood increased their representation from one seat to five, and Salafist candidates also made marked gains. The results reflected an appetite for reform driven by both young people and the socially conservative base.

The country's bedoun (stateless) population continued to rally for citizenship rights. Kuwait is home to between 100,000 and 180,000 stateless persons out of an overall population of 2.7 million. Many claim to be descended from desert nomads who did not acquire citizenship. However, the government claims most bedoun are illegal immigrants who intentionally destroyed their documents as a means of acquiring Kuwaiti nationality. In January 2012, police used water cannons and tear gas to disperse hundreds of protesters who had gathered to call for citizenship rights. Protesters continued to defy the ban on demonstrations imposed by the Ministry of Interior.

The approval by parliament of wage rises for striking workers in the oil industry set off a wave of copy-cat strikes by employees who sought to pressure the government for similar increases. In October 2011, 3,000 striking customs officials refused to give clearance to tankers loaded with oil for export. In March, strikers at Kuwait Airways agreed to suspend their action following talks between the labour union and the government. The government has also been under pressure from workers to increase its already generous civil-service salaries, which cost the country over $4bn annually. The head of the parliamentary budget committee warned about the sustainability of such increases.

Oman: regional mediator

In 2011, Oman contained domestic unrest through a combination of reformist and repressive measures that included the dismissal of 14 cabinet ministers and the arrest of several activists. Political opposition settled down in 2012, allowing the sultanate to capitalise on its positive relations with both Iran and Western states and to act as an intermediary between them.

In November, three French aid workers who had been kidnapped in Yemen by an al-Qaeda offshoot group, al-Qaeda in the Arabian Peninsula (AQAP), were released following the Omani government's intervention in negotiations. Oman's mediation efforts also led to the release from an Iranian prison of two American hikers held for over two years after they had allegedly crossed the border from Iraqi Kurdistan. Oman paid bail of 10bn Iranian rials ($400,000) for each of the hikers, in addition to $500,000 it had paid in 2010 for release of a third member of the group. Oman's cordial relations with Iran were reflected in an increase in energy cooperation.

However, concerns over a thriving smuggling trade between Oman and Iran were raised by German Foreign Minister Guido Westerwelle during a visit to Muscat. The black market has thrived since the imposition of sanctions on Iran as a result of the ability of small speedboats to navigate the Strait of Hormuz and evade detection. Germany called on Oman to take additional steps to stop circumvention of sanctions.

Qatar: extending its reach
The global profile of Qatar continued to grow as the emirate took steps to further lengthen its diplomatic reach. Holding the rotating chairmanship of the Arab League, Qatar spearheaded regional efforts to unseat Syrian President Assad. In January 2012, Prime Minister Sheikh Hamad bin Jasim Al Thani became the first Arab leader to call publicly for military intervention to 'stop the killing'.

Syria then accused Qatar of arming and financing rebels, a claim the Qatari leadership denied. In March, Qatar joined Turkey in inviting Syria's fractious opposition, the Syrian National Council, to a Friends of Syria conference in Istanbul. Rumours of Qatari transfers of weapons to the Syrian opposition grew following allegations by Mustafa Abdul Jalil, head of Libya's NTC, that Qatari forces had armed and trained rebel groups in Libya. This followed Qatari pledges to lead international efforts to train the Libyan military and re-integrate militia units into new security institutions following the removal of Gadhafi. In a symbol of gratitude, Libya's leadership renamed a central plaza in Tripoli 'Qatar Square'. Questions over the extent of Qatari involvement in Libya's domestic politics led to tensions between the two states. There were allegations that Qatar was providing financial backing to Abdel Hakim Belhaj, Islamist head of Tripoli's military council, thereby contravening its public commitment to support the NTC.

Qatar lent its diplomatic weight towards brokering a resolution to the conflict in Darfur, western Sudan. In July 2011, the Sudanese government and a coalition of rebel groups signed a peace agreement in Doha, the Qatari capital, although this did not halt violence in Darfur. Qatar helped to broker the February 2011 Doha Declaration, an agreement between the rival Palestinian groups, Fatah and Hamas, under which the parties agreed to form an interim national unity government under President Mahmoud

Abbas pending elections. It also sought to act as a mediator in reconcilia-tion talks between the Afghan Taliban and the US government, inviting the Taliban to establish a political office in Doha. The Taliban said this would help the group 'come to an understanding with other nations', raising hopes that the office might provide a base for negotiations, but the talks stalled.

United Arab Emirates: activists detained

The UAE faced international criticism for the arrest of 11 political activists in March and April 2012, and for the government's decision to close the local offices of two international organisations.

Those arrested were members of the Reform and Social Guidance Association (Al Islah), a reformist organisation with links to the Muslim Brotherhood. Among them was Sultan bin Kayed al-Qasimi, chairman of Al Islah and a member of the ruling family of Ras al-Khaimah, one of the smaller emirates. Five activists detained in 2011 were also charged on the grounds they had insulted the country's leadership, but were released in November after their sentences were commuted by President Khalifa bin Zayed al-Nahyan. In March, government authorities also closed down the local offices of the National Democratic Institute, an organisation with links to the US Democratic Party, and the Konrad Adenauer Stiftung, a non-governmental organisation with ties to German Chancellor Angela Merkel's Christian Democratic Union.

Amidst increasing tensions between Iran and the Gulf states, the six GCC countries condemned as 'provocative' a visit by Iranian President Mahmoud Ahmadinejad to Abu Musa, one of three islands whose ownership is dis-puted between the UAE and Iran. In a joint statement, the GCC states said the visit contradicted 'good neighbourly policies' and demanded Iran end its occupation of the islands and respond to UAE calls to reach a solution through direct negotiations or an international tribunal.

Yemen: continued instability

The year to mid-2012 saw the end of nearly 34 years in power for President Ali Abdullah Saleh. He had returned to Sana'a, the capital, in September 2011 after being taken to Saudi Arabia for medical treatment in June when he was seriously wounded in a bomb attack on his palace. On 23 November he signed a GCC-brokered plan – he had agreed a similar plan three times previously, beginning in April 2011, only to back away on each occasion – under which he agreed to permanently hand power to his vice-president within three months in exchange for immunity from prosecution. He duly stepped down in February 2012, and was replaced by his vice-president, Abd Rabbuh Mansur al-Hadi.

Under the GCC agreement, elections were held in February in which Hadi was the only candidate listed on the ballot paper. There was to be a division of parliamentary seats between his ruling party and a coalition of established opposition groups, the Joint Meeting Parties. Houthi groups, southern secessionists and newly formed youth coalitions rejected the arrangement on the grounds that it did not provide for their inclusion within the political system. Critics also noted that the agreement failed to mandate reform of the security forces, which remain dominated by members of Saleh's tribe.

As it grappled with an uneasy political transition, Yemen continued to face threats from AQAP insurgents in the south, and secessionist Houthi rebels in the north. While the expansion of AQAP has depended in part on its recruitment of fighters from Somalia, Pakistan and Saudi Arabia, it has also been successful in recruiting local Yemeni fighters. The government suffered a blow when AQAP fighters overran troops and bases in Abyan province, and used tanks and heavy weapons to drive government forces out of several towns. The group later withdrew from the towns of Ra'ada and Al Bayda following a peace agreement with government leaders in those areas, but remained in control of several other towns in Shabwa and Abyan provinces. Officials said AQAP had set up its own police force and judicial system in the towns it controlled. This was the first time that AQAP had secured territorial control anywhere in the Gulf. It used the territory as a launch-pad for a series of kidnappings. In March 2012, a Swiss teacher and Saudi diplomat were kidnapped, and a Yemeni government official was later seized. The group demanded hefty ransom payments and the release of nine prisoners in Saudi Arabia in return for release of the hostages.

The government responded to AQAP's campaign by intensifying its military efforts against the group. US–Yemeni security cooperation was also stepped up. In September 2011, a US drone strike had killed Anwar al-Awlaki, an American-born cleric accused of inspiring and plotting terrorist attacks on US soil. Hadi requested increased US counter-terrorism cooperation and a new influx of US military trainers and advisers. Senior US army officials were quoted as saying that counter-terrorism units would be allowed to target individuals in Yemen plotting attacks on US soil, even in instances where those individuals could not be identified by name. AQAP, which had previously made attempts to bomb international aircraft, clearly still harboured the intent to carry out attacks on US citizens. In May 2012 it emerged that it had supplied a bomb, intended to be carried in the underwear of a passenger on a US airliner, to a man who, in fact, was a foreign agent and subsequently gave information about militants' whereabouts to the US Central Intelligence Agency. An air strike on a vehicle in the capital of Abyan province killed three militants who were linked to the plot. Analysts estimated that, by mid-year, the United States had launched up to 64 drone attacks on Yemeni soil since January 2012. Meanwhile, the long-standing Houthi rebellion continued with the aim of creating an independent state on the border with Saudi Arabia. The group's adherents belong to the Zaydi Shia sect, and are viewed as heretics by hardline Sunni Islamists. There were growing clashes between Houthi rebels and AQAP, with eight people killed in fighting on the outskirts of Sa'da on 21 April.

Conflict compounded the impact of a drought and water shortages on Yemen's impoverished rural communities. In March, the UN World Food Programme reported that levels of food insecurity had doubled since 2009, with 5m of the country's 25m population going hungry on a regular basis. Government mismanagement fuelled the crisis, with residents of towns complaining that economic policies had paid inadequate attention to resolving worsening food and water shortages and had instead poured money into expensive construction projects.

Yemen's changing political landscape also paved the way for social initiatives. In January, online activists declared a 'Day Without Qat' to encourage Yemenis to reduce consumption of the popular plant, which contains an amphetamine-like stimulant. The plant is widely viewed to have detrimental social effects and to handicap working-age Yemenis. Its cultivation also strains Yemen's dwindling water resources. Following widespread support for the initiative, activists declared a second 'Day Without Qat' in April.

Israel and Palestine: Deadlock and Stagnation

Israeli–Palestinian negotiations stalled throughout the year to mid-2012 amid upheaval in the Arab world, regional disinterest and American fatigue. Israeli reluctance to take risks in the face of changing regional dynamics and shifting Palestinian strategies contributed to this lack of progress. If unity agreements on both sides strengthened ruling coalitions, they also contributed to the negotiations' stasis.

Changing regional dynamics affected Israel's perception of its security situation. Egyptian–Israeli ties, shaken by the fall of Mubarak and the end of the strategic certainty that governed bilateral relations, teetered on the brink. Growing activity by militant groups, repeated bombings of a pipeline that transports gas to Israel and Jordan, and concerns that Libyan arms were trickling into Gaza required the deployment of the Egyptian military on the Sinai Peninsula after a decades-long absence. The firing of rockets against Israel from Egyptian soil and the takeover and ransacking by Egyptian demonstrators of the Israeli Embassy in Cairo, after an incident in which Israeli border guards killed Egyptian counterparts, necessitated high-level intervention by Washington. Israel grew concerned about the rise of the Muslim Brotherhood, with which Hamas formally associated in 2012, and its possible impact on the peace treaty and on Palestinian dynamics. Israeli ties to Turkey also suffered as a result of the continuing tensions over the storming by Israeli commandos of a Turkish ship in 2010, with Ankara throwing out the Israeli ambassador and downgrading relations.

Despite external frictions and domestic turbulence, Israeli Prime Minister Benjamin Netanyahu remained steadfastly in power. When challenged within the right-wing Likud Party, he won the contest with 77% of the vote. His main opposition challenger, former Foreign Minister Tzipi Livni, was defeated by Shaul Mofaz for the leadership of Kadima, which was the largest party in the Knesset but was losing popularity. A surprise consequence was the announcement in May 2012 of the formation of a national unity government that included Kadima, Labor and Likud, handing Netanyahu a stunning political victory and a stable majority in parliament.

Palestine's recognition bid

The daring push by the Palestinian Authority (PA) for recognition of Palestine as a sovereign state at the United Nations General Assembly during its September 2011 meeting inflamed tensions and passions. The move, driven by Palestinian frustration at perceived Israeli obstruction of a two-state solution, met strong opposition from the United States and Israel, who argued that such a unilateral move would undercut the spirit of peacemaking. However, it garnered sympathy, if not support, from European, Arab and other states, heightening Israeli concerns about growing diplomatic isolation.

The request for full recognition and Palestinian membership of the UN proved popular among Palestinians and other Arabs. PA President Mahmoud Abbas, whose approval ratings had fallen in recent years, hoped to rekindle international support and regain diplomatic traction. Several factions, including the Popular Front for the Liberation of Palestine and the Democratic Front for the Liberation of Palestine, backed the proposal. Hamas, accusing Abbas of relinquishing rights to pre-1967 territory, opposed the bid, but stated that it would not get in the way of the establishment of a Palestinian state.

The statehood campaign met total and relentless Israeli opposition. Since the Palestinian bid had enough votes at the UN General Assembly, Israel focused its efforts on the Security Council, hoping that veto-yielding Western states would end the process. The United States put pressure on the Palestinian leadership to return to negotiations with Israel and commit to negotiations to achieve Palestinian statehood. The US Congress passed resolutions denouncing the initiative, demanded that the administration use its veto at the UN to block the Palestinian motion and threatened to withdraw US aid. As a result, the United States stated that it would oppose the bid. Some European states tried to broker a compromise that would have the PA accept status as an observer rather than a full-member state.

On 29 September, the PA announced that it secured eight votes, one short of the majority required to pass the proposal in the UN Security Council in the absence of a veto. Meanwhile, the PA also applied for full membership to UNESCO. This was approved on 31 October by 107 votes to 14 with 52 abstentions, triggering a US legal requirement to stop funding for the organisation. Europe was divided on the issue: France and Spain voted for Palestine's membership, Italy and the United Kingdom abstained, and Germany voted against. The Palestinians were unable to carry the momentum gained at UNESCO to the Security Council, where the bid was stalled.

Israeli–Palestinian tensions

Amidst the Palestinian push at the UN, the Quartet (the UN, EU, US and Russia) urged the resumption of direct negotiations between Israel and Palestine, with the United States pushing for meetings between officials of each side. In October 2011, Netanyahu accepted the renewal of negotiations without preconditions as a way of undermining the Palestinian bid. However, the issue of Israeli settlement expansion remained a nonstarter for the Palestinians, with Abbas stating he would not participate in any talks until construction was halted. In January 2012, King Abdullah of Jordan attempted to revive the moribund process by inviting Palestinian and Israeli officials to Jordan to resume the talks, which had been stalled for over a year. Talks failed after Israeli negotiators stated publicly that Israeli borders in any future two-state solution would include existing settlement blocks.

The saga of Israeli Staff Sergeant Gilad Shalit, captured in Gaza in June 2006, ended on 11 October 2011 when Israel and Hamas agreed on the release of 1,027 Palestinian prisoners in exchange for him. The deal was brokered by Egypt, the first major act of Egyptian–Israeli cooperation after the Egyptian uprising. The first phase of the deal occurred on 18 October with 477 prisoners released – 130 to Gaza, 100 to the West Bank and 203 deported from Israel and Palestinian territories. Many of the deported prisoners had previously been sentenced to life imprisonment for perpetrating and supporting attacks against Israel. On the same day, Shalit was transferred from Gaza to Egypt and on to Israel; 550 Palestinian prisoners were released in the second phase of the deal in December 2011. The release of Shalit appeared to have a positive effect on the Egyptian–Israeli relationship, demonstrated by a public Israeli apology for the deaths of Egyptian security officers and an Israeli–Egyptian prisoner swap.

Low-level Israel–Gaza tensions continued. In March 2012, Israel launched several air strikes in Gaza, killing ten Palestinians, including a leader of a popular resistance committee. In reprisal, 90 rockets were fired into Israeli territory, of which the majority were intercepted by the *Iron Dome* anti-rocket system. Border clashes broke out between the Israel Defense Forces (IDF) and Palestinian militant groups. Egypt brokered a ceasefire agreement, which temporarily halted violence. However, violence along the Gaza border rose in April and May. IDF troops discovered improvised explosive devices along patrol routes. Rockets fired from the Sinai toward the Israeli resort town of Eilat led the IDF to preemptively deploy military units near the Egyptian border.

A growing Palestinian interest in civil disobedience and in non-violent action took Israel by surprise. Palestinian prisoners in Israeli jails embraced a new protest tactic: hunger strikes to protest against harsh detention conditions, including solitary confinement. The size of the movement and the media attention it got put Israeli authorities on the defensive. Palestinian society mobilised in support of the 2,000 prisoners who joined the hunger strike. Hamas and Islamic Jihad announced that they would not adhere to ceasefire agreements with Israel if any of the prisoners on hunger strike were to die. The EU and Turkey issued statements demonstrating concern for the well-being of the hunger strikers. On 14 May, in a deal mediated by Egypt and the PA, hundreds of Palestinians prisoners agreed to end their strike after winning concessions from Israel to improve prison conditions and limit detentions without trial.

Israeli fissures

Just as Palestinians were taking tentative steps toward reconciliation, new divisions appeared in Israeli society. A pattern emerged of violence by settlers against Palestinian civilians but also against IDF personnel. Violence against Palestinian targets by settlers included attacks on religious sites, bullying and harassment of civilians, destruction of private property and killing of civilians. In December 2011, settlers attacked an army base, fearing that their outposts would be dismantled. This incident, along with outrage about settler aggressiveness in the West Bank, forced Netanyahu to announce the trial in military courts of radical settlers.

Simultaneously, the behaviour and privileges of ultra-orthodox Jews, exempt from mandatory military service and benefiting from extensive access to social services, were increasingly questioned in Israeli society. Groups of extremist Haredim protested the establishment of a girls' school in their neighbourhood in Jerusalem, leading to clashes and intimidation of pupils. Ultra-orthodox harassment of women in public buses also drew condemnation.

Controversy over the Tal Law (named after former Supreme Court Justice Tzvi Tal), which exempts some religious groups from military service, also increased. Defence Minister Ehud Barak announced that the ministry was preparing an alternative to the law. Reservist IDF soldiers and political activists protested against its possible extension, viewing it as perpetuating unfair burdens on the rest of Israeli society. This movement received political support and acknowledgement from the government. In February 2012, the High Court of Justice ruled that the Tal Law in its current form was unconstitutional and could not be extended. This led to outrage among ultra-Orthodox communities and right-wing political parties. The government later announced that it would draft a new bill intended to share the burden of military service more equally.

Another new front in Israeli politics opened in July 2011 as the largest protests in the nation's history unfolded. A group of protesters built tents on a main street in Tel Aviv to draw attention to growing living costs and shortage of housing. The development of tent camps on main streets as a means of protest quickly spread to other cities. Israeli student groups signed on to the protest movement. The first official rally for the 'J14 movement', named after the date of its establishment, drew an estimated 20,000 participants from varying socioeconomic and religious backgrounds. The rally opposed not only the high cost of living but also the deterioration of basic public services such as health and education.

In reaction, Netanyahu announced emergency student housing programmes and an initiative to add 50,000 apartments to the housing market. As protests and the construction of tent camps continued, the government announced further measures to solve the housing shortage. Netanyahu set up a committee chaired by Professor Manuel Trajtenberg to propose solutions to socio-economic issues. These moves did little to quell the protest movement, and nationwide rallies continued. A series of protests on 3 September drew over 460,000 people. However, the J14 movement slowly began to lose momentum due to fractured leadership, and the government dismantled the main encampment in Tel Aviv in October.

Palestinian unity talks

Palestinian politics remained fractured between Fatah and Hamas. Fatah's traditional reliance on international and Arab support and patronage suffered from the aftershocks of the Arab uprisings and the UN membership bid. At the turn of the year, Abbas, the Fatah leader, faced a complex situation: the popularity Fatah gained from the UN bid came at the cost of falling US support; meanwhile, the loss of his key ally Mubarak and the rise of the Muslim Brotherhood promised a more complex relationship with Egypt; and his technocratic prime minister Salam Fayyad's success in improving the economy and strengthening institutions were not sufficient to assuage his population. This led Fatah finally to acknowledge the need for a unity deal with Hamas. Previous attempts to negotiate such a deal had failed and Fatah remained hesitant about sharing power with Hamas.

Likewise, Hamas faced serious considerations, including the effect of the conflict in Syria on its alliance with the Assad regime. Seeking new sources of support, its leaders visited Egypt and Turkey. In January 2012, Hamas left its base in Syria and resettled in Qatar, which offered to host its political, but not military, leaders.

In November 2011, Hamas and Fatah leaders met in Cairo to announce a new partnership. In response, the Israeli government froze PA funds. In January, Hamas Prime Minister Ismail Haniya gave permission for the Central Elections Commission to operate in Gaza so that Palestinian elections could be scheduled for May (they were, in the event, postponed). In return, Abbas's Gaza residence, seized in 2007, was returned to Fatah. In February, Hamas's Khaled Meshal and Fatah's Abbas met in Doha to put the latter at the head of an interim unity government charged with organising the election, scheduled to be held in late 2012. Even then, distrust between the two sides delayed any real progress and there remained considerable scepticism about whether the Doha agreement could be implemented.

Iran: Nuclear Confrontation Escalates

The nuclear dispute between Iran and the Western world escalated over the past year as both sides upped the pressure. By May 2012, Iran had produced enough low enriched uranium (LEU) for about four nuclear weapons, if further enriched, and had quadrupled the number of centrifuges producing medium-enriched uranium by initiating operations at the deeply buried Fordow facility. Reports by the UN nuclear watchdog about evidence of past and possibly ongoing weapons-development work convinced most observers that the programme had a military purpose. Most governments also agreed with US public assessments that Iran was not yet building a bomb. Because the depth of the Fordow plant puts it out of reach of Israeli bombers, however, Israel's defence minister warned that Iran's nuclear programme would soon enter a 'zone of immunity'. Amidst talk of war at the beginning of 2012, Iran threatened to close the Strait of Hormuz. Tough US and EU sanctions that sharply reduced Iranian oil exports, with a further drop expected later in the year, kept Israeli bombing plans at bay and brought Iran to the negotiating table. Yet three rounds of talks between April and June produced no agreement to limit Iran's nuclear programme or any quid pro quo on sanctions relief.

As Iran's external conflict escalated, internal conflicts abated. A power struggle between religious and secular leaders was settled in favour of Supreme Leader Ayatollah Ali Khamenei, whose allies dominated parliamentary elections in March 2012. Western strategy presupposes that biting sanctions will persuade Khamenei to compromise for fear that the economic pinch will cause political unrest, threatening the regime. Despite 22% inflation, rising unemployment and a 50% drop in the value of the currency, however, there were few signs of popular discontent like that seen in the Arab world. And notwithstanding the troubles afflicting their Syrian ally, Iranian leaders held to a narrative that political winds in the Middle East were blowing in their favour. They similarly discounted the prospect of an Israeli attack. If diplomacy were to fail to limit Iran's nuclear progress, however, that calculus risked being sorely mistaken.

Enrichment progress

In defiance of the UN Security Council's mandate to suspend enrichment operations and of efforts by certain governments to forestall progress through sabotage and assassinations, Iran expanded its programme in several ways. In the 12 months to May 2012, the number of operating centrifuges increased by 50% to almost 9,000. Most of these were installed in the underground facility at Natanz and were being used to enrich uranium to about 3.5%, the level necessary to fuel nuclear power plants. Iran has no current need to produce its own enriched fuel because its sole power plant at Bushehr runs on fuel from Russia. In early 2012, 35 years after construction began, the reactor was finally commissioned and by April was operating at 75% of capacity, although in May it was announced that it would face indefinite delays in achieving full electricity production.

Iran's enrichment programme is touted as a backup to the Russian fuel, but more importantly is being pursued as a security hedge. The 6,200kg of LEU produced by May 2012 is sufficient for about four nuclear weapons, if further enriched to 90% purity. Monthly production was up to 229kg per month, almost 50% higher than the previous year.

Of greater concern, Iran employed 1,370 centrifuges, a fourfold increase over a year, to produce 20%-enriched uranium and was installing more. This is the level that is necessary for fuel for the Tehran Research Reactor (TRR), which is used to produce medical isotopes. However, uranium enriched to this level is very close to being usable for nuclear weapons. Enrichment to 20% accomplishes 90% of the effort needed for weapons-grade uranium. Most of Iran's 20% enrichment work was being conducted in the Fordow facility, built 80–90m deep beneath mountain rock, which started production towards the end of 2011. By May Iran had produced 146kg of the 20% product. This was getting close to the amount (185kg) that is theoretically needed for an implosion weapon. (At least half again as much is needed for a less technically sophisticated gun-type weapon.) However, about a third of Iran's 20% product was converted to oxide form for fuel, which suggested that Iran was not rushing towards weapons production. At its current level of technology, Iran cannot easily reverse this chemical process. Iran began testing the fuel by irradiating it at the TRR.

Almost all of Iran's operating centrifuges are of a first-generation type that has low efficiency. Development work on second-generation models was continuing slowly. Iran reportedly cannot produce the high-strength materials – maraging steel or carbon fibre – that are required for faster-spinning advanced centrifuges. Sanctions and export controls restricted its ability to acquire foreign materials. About 300 centrifuges of two kinds of second-generation model were installed over the past year. President Mahmoud Ahmadinejad announced in February that Iran was introducing a 'fourth' generation model but, as of the May quarterly report by the International Atomic Energy Agency (IAEA), the UN's nuclear watchdog, it had not been installed.

Notwithstanding Iran's technical difficulties and the absence of evidence that it had sought to produce a nuclear weapon, IAEA reports left little doubt about the underlying purpose of Iran's nuclear programme. A revealing report in November 2011 laid out the evidence the agency had collected of what appeared to be a comprehensive plan to develop all the key technologies for an implosion-type nuclear weapon. It was reported, for example, that Iran had conducted tests of bomb components and received bomb designs from the A.Q. Khan black-market network. It was also reported that a former Soviet nuclear-weapons expert spent six years in Iran lecturing on topics such as high-explosives initiation and diagnostics. He is said to have helped Iran construct a large high-explosives test chamber at the Parchin military complex for high-explosives tests that the IAEA termed 'strong indicators of possible weapon development'. The former Soviet expert said he was helping Iran make nano-diamonds using the same explosion techniques employed in nuclear warheads, but the IAEA was not given an opportunity to see any of the fruits of his labour or to interview any of his students.

Although much of the information about weapons development work had been previously mentioned in media reports and was not yet confirmed, it now had the imprimatur of the IAEA, which deemed the information to be 'credible'. The IAEA received intelligence from ten countries and carried out its own investigations. Most of the weapons work detailed in the report took place before 2004. Only four of the report's 65 paragraphs about explosives-development work described activity that continued after 2003, but the IAEA said some of this work might still be ongoing. In a press interview in January, IAEA Director General Yukiya Amano said: 'What we know suggests the development of nuclear weapons.'

For several years Iran had refused to provide satisfactory answers to the IAEA's questions about what the agency called nuclear activities with a 'possible military dimension'. Saying the reports were based on unfounded allegations, Iran also refused access to individuals and places named in the reports, including Parchin. Although the nuclear-related work there was alleged to have taken place almost a decade ago, the IAEA hoped that environmental sampling would confirm the reports. Because recent overhead imagery suggested that the building in question was being sanitised, the IAEA urgently sought a visit. When senior IAEA officials visited Iran in late January, they were given reason to believe that they would be able to visit Parchin during a follow-up meeting three weeks later. But hardliners in Tehran refused to allow such a visit. Iran instead focused discussion on a 'structured approach' for addressing IAEA questions in which it sought, for example, to limit the agency's right to revisit issues if new information arose. Amano said the restrictions would make it impossible for the agency to properly carry out its verification work. Visiting Tehran on 21 May 2012, Amano was sent home with promises of cooperation but no signed agreement. Although he claimed agreement had been reached in principle on a modalities plan, Iran apparently wanted to hold on to any concessions for use in separate talks with the major powers.

Progress in the enrichment programme led to some shortening of intelligence assessments about how long it could take Iran to build a weapon. US Defense Secretary Leon Panetta said in December that if Iran made a decision to build a nuclear weapon it would take about a year, but there was no indication that Iran had made such a decision. The US intelligence community also held to its position that Iran had stopped actively working on nuclear-weapons development in late 2003 and had not restarted it. The latest assessment judged, however, that selective components for nuclear weapons might still be under development. This caveat was in accordance with the IAEA's assessment that Iran's structured work on weapons development stopped in 2003 but that some aspects of it continued. Iran, for its part, continued to insist that its nuclear programme was entirely peaceful. Ahmadinejad raised some questions about this stance when in June 2011 he openly reinforced Iran's ability to make weapons, saying that 'if we want to make a bomb, we are not afraid of anybody'. An article circulated on websites connected to the government in February drew a distinction between possession and use of nuclear weapons. Later, Khamenei repeated his 2005 fatwa against nuclear weapons without drawing this distinction.

Cautious engagement

Although conservative commentators in the West dismissed Khamenei's fatwa, the administration of US President Barack Obama sought to use it for diplomatic effect. Prodded by Turkish Prime Minister Recep Tayyip Erdogan, US Secretary of State Hillary Clinton said the religious prohibition was a 'good starting point' ahead of impending negotiations, which she said Iran should use to demonstrate the sincerity of that conviction. Earlier,

Khamenei himself offered a positive appraisal of comments on 6 March 2012 by Obama, who said diplomacy could still resolve the nuclear stand-off, and decried loose talk of war. Khamenei said those were 'good words' and showed 'an exit from illusion'.

The mutual expressions of respect, qualified though they were, contributed to positive atmospherics in April 2012 when Iran for the first time in 15 months met with its negotiating partners from the E3+3 (France, Germany and the United Kingdom plus China, Russia and the United States – also known as the P5+1, the five permanent members of the UN Security Council plus Germany) led by EU foreign-policy chief Catherine Ashton. The previous meeting in January 2011 ended with Iran refusing to consider any limitations on its nuclear programme until sanctions were lifted and its right to enrichment was accepted. In September, Iranian Supreme National Security Council Secretary Saeed Jalili wrote to Ashton expressing a readiness to hold fresh talks 'for cooperation on common issues'. In reply, Ashton wrote on 21 October that the six were willing to meet if Tehran was prepared to 'engage seriously in meaningful discussions' so that real progress could be made on the nuclear issue. It took Iran several more months to respond, during which there were false claims that a letter had been sent by Tehran but not received and that Obama had written to Khamenei in January calling for direct talks.

Various opportunities for US–Iran engagement were missed in the second half of 2011. In September Ahmadinejad repeatedly offered to suspend 20% enrichment if Iran received fuel for the TRR. Foreign Minister Ali Akbar Salehi repeated the offer, but there were doubts whether either could deliver, given that Ahmadinejad had been overruled two years earlier when he agreed to a similar fuel-swap proposal. Also in September, the head of Iran's Atomic Energy Organisation, Fereydoun Abbasi, expressed a willingness to put the country's nuclear programme under 'full IAEA supervision' for five years if sanctions were lifted. What 'full supervision' meant was never clarified but nor was there any publicly reported effort to pursue the opening. A third Iranian 'goodwill' gesture was the release of two American hikers who had been imprisoned on espionage charges two years earlier after they inadvertently wandered into Iranian territory. The atmospherics of the release were tarnished, however, when Ahmadinejad a week earlier promised release within days, only to have Iran's judiciary overrule him, saying it had exclusive authority to order their release. The hikers were released on $500,000 bail in time for Ahmadinejad's annual speech to the UN General Assembly, but not before his domestic opponents had made their point. (See pp. 236–7 on Oman).

Jalili's acceptance in February of Ashton's invitation was business-like and without preconditions. Because of tensions with Turkey over Syria, Iran was unenthusiastic about the proposed Istanbul venue but eventually conceded. Meanwhile there were other signs in March of reduced tension between the United States and Iran. On 5 March, Iran's Supreme Court ordered the retrial of an Iranian-American former US Marine, who had been sentenced to death on charges of working for the CIA. A week later the United States deported an Iranian arms dealer who had been arrested in 2007 in a sting operation in the Republic of Georgia. The US Treasury Department began an investigation into a former governor of Pennsylvania on charges that he took money from the exile Mujahedin-e Khalq (MEK) to seek its removal from the US State Department's list of terrorist organisations. The State Department had resisted pressure from a number of former US officials to delist the MEK, a group that Tehran despises and accuses of conducting assassinations in Iran.

The Istanbul meeting on 14 April was judged positive on both sides. Iran was pleased by the E3+3's agreement that negotiations would be conducted within the framework of the Nuclear Non-Proliferation Treaty. This supported Iran's claim to the right to enrich uranium, which is not prohibited by the treaty. The major powers were pleased that Iran engaged constructively on issues regarding its nuclear programme, unlike during the previous talks. It also seemed to be a positive sign that Jalili had been publicly designated as the representative of the Supreme Leader, which suggested he had the authority to strike a deal that would not unravel politically, as had happened with a tentative deal he had made while representing Ahmadinejad in 2009. There were danger signs, however. Jalili continued to refuse to meet bilaterally with his US counterpart and Ashton rebuffed his insistent requests for a delay in imposition of EU oil sanctions. She did agree to his request to meet next time in Baghdad, despite the security and logistical hurdles.

Puncturing hopes for a diplomatic breakthrough, the Baghdad meeting on 23–24 May produced no results. The E3+3 aimed for an early set of confidence-building measures to stop the enrichment activity that was of most concern – and was also driving talk of a preventive Israeli air strike. Iran was asked to stop 20% enrichment, to shut down activity at Fordow and to export its stockpile of 20%-enriched uranium. If such steps could be agreed, it was anticipated that later negotiations could address the issue of lower levels of enrichment. In exchange for giving up 20% enrichment, Iran would receive fuel to run the TRR, assistance with safety improvements at that reactor and spare parts for aircraft. Iran, however, expected much more in the form of sanctions relief and expressed bitter disappointment when it was not offered. Paltry though the West's opening offer may have been, Iran's expectations exceeded the realm of the possible. Although Ahmadinejad the previous autumn had proposed to stop 20% enrichment in exchange only for research reactor fuel, Iranian leaders now insisted on the lifting of sanctions set to take effect by 1 July (see below). Claiming it could now fabricate fuel on its own, Iran said it no longer needed foreign fuel for the TRR. Yet it was not clear that the Iranian-produced fuel was safe to use.

In focusing on early confidence-building measures, the E3+3 employed the form, albeit not much of the substance, of a Russian proposal from the previous summer of a step-by-step approach. Moscow's plan called for Iran gradually to address IAEA questions in exchange for a progressive easing of sanctions. Although specifics of the plan were not released, it apparently focused on transparency measures and not on halting Iranian enrichment. The Western capitals worried that such an approach risked giving Iran a green light to acquire a capability to break out of the NPT and rapidly produce nuclear weapons. For the sake of harmony they adopted the trappings of the Russian step-by-step proposal with reciprocal measures but insisted on suspension of 20% enrichment as a first step.

Israel and, reportedly, Britain and France were worried that even if talks proved to be unproductive, Obama would be content to keep negotiations going until the November 2012 American election in order to avoid the image of failed diplomacy and the possibility that this would trigger a military attack. After the round in Istanbul, Israeli Prime Minister Benjamin Netanyahu complained that Iran had been given a 'freebie' to continue its nuclear programme without restriction. Left unsaid was that Iran was continuing enrichment anyway, and that the sanctions it was under hardly made this programme cost free.

Prior to a third round of talks in Moscow on 18–19 June, Iran sought to improve its bargaining position by claiming it was in 'the initial phases of manufacturing atomic submarines'. If so, this would give Iran an ostensible excuse to enrich uranium above 20%, since nuclear submarine reactors run on fuel enriched between 20 and 90%. But it is highly unlikely that Iran, especially when facing severe sanctions, could join the small handful of nations capable of producing nuclear submarines.

The Moscow talks were no better than the round in Baghdad and, in some ways, were worse. Iran re-raised old issues about the legality of Security Council sanctions and pressed both for the lifting of all sanctions and for recognition of what it saw as its right to enrichment. It demanded that these steps be taken before it would accept any limits to its programme. The E3+3 demanded that Iran first accept limits and offered no sanctions relief. No further talks were scheduled at the official level, although lower-level 'technical' discussions were agreed as a means of keeping diplomacy alive. French and US officials warned that if talks did not succeed soon, more sanctions would be in store for Iran.

Sanctions stepped up

Over the past year the economic pressure confronting Iran has evolved from 'smart' sanctions targeted at proliferation-related activity to comprehensive sanctions directed at the oil-export lifeline of the Iranian economy. The targeted sanctions imposed by four Security Council resolutions from 2006–10 restricted Iran's ability to acquire foreign materials needed for certain advances in its nuclear and missile programmes. These raised the cost of doing business for Iran, but not enough to force the leadership to reconsider its stance on nuclear issues. Unilateral measures adopted in the year to mid-2012 by the United States and the European Union changed the stakes, however, and were seen as bringing Iran to the negotiating table. (See essay, pp. 61–74.)

On 21 November 2011, the US Treasury designated the entire Iranian banking sector as a jurisdiction of primary money-laundering concern. Canada and the UK similarly blocked their banks from conducting business with Iran. In protest, a mob stormed the British Embassy in Tehran, heavily vandalising buildings in two compounds and sparking a diplomatic crisis for Iran. The mob was led by Basij militia posing as students, whose actions were condoned by parliamentary speaker Ali Larijani. In response, the UK closed its embassy and expelled Iranian diplomats from Britain. Several countries withdrew ambassadors in protest and the move contributed to an EU decision late in the year to stop all oil imports from Iran.

The US Treasury's action was not enough for the US Congress, which passed legislation that threatened to deny access to the US banking system financial institutions anywhere in the world that conduct transactions with the Central Bank of Iran related to Iran's petroleum industry. The new law, adopted as part of a defence-spending bill, and signed by Obama on New Year's Eve, took full effect on 28 June 2012. A national-interest waiver allowed the president to postpone enforcing these prohibitions for six-month renewable periods for countries that he determined had 'significantly reduced' their Iranian oil imports. What counts as a significant reduction is reviewed on a case-by-case basis. Obama made this determination in March for nine states and Japan. On 11 June, India, Malaysia, South Africa, ri Lanka, Taiwan and Turkey were similarly exempted. China, rgest buyer, and Singapore, which uses some Iranian oil in ...ined products it blends, were added to the exemption list on 29 June.

In January 2012 the EU adopted additional measures of its own. It imposed a phased embargo on Iranian crude-oil imports, taking full effect on 1 July so as to give Greece, Italy and Spain time to find alternative suppliers. The embargo prohibited the import, purchase and transport of crude oil and petroleum products from Iran as well as EU investments in Iranian oil and natural gas industries. The EU ban also prohibited the provision of insurance and reinsurance to the Iranian government and designated Iranian entities. Given the near-monopoly held by EU-based reinsurance companies, particularly for maritime reinsurance, this prohibition could affect 95% of Iran's tanker fleet. Consideration was given to postponing the ban on third-party liability insurance and environmental liability insurance if negotiations with Iran proved to be fruitful. At mid-2012, the full measure remained in place. In anticipation of the measure, the Japanese parliament passed legislation providing for national guarantees on insurance for Iranian crude cargoes. China apparently also undertook to provide for national guarantees. Some other states, such as South Korea, cut Iranian oil imports to zero due to the insurance ban. The intention of the US and EU sanctions was not to take all Iranian oil off the market, which could cause a spike in prices, but to squeeze Iranian hard-currency revenues. When China and India began to pay for Iranian oil in local currencies or through bartering mechanisms for food and consumer goods, it was not necessarily seen as an evasion of sanctions, since it deprived Iran of hard-currency earnings.

In March 2012, the EU extended its sanctions against 30 of the largest Iranian banks, including the central bank, excluding them from making use of the Belgian-based SWIFT (Society for Worldwide Interbank Financial Telecommunication) financial communications system, which is used by nearly every bank around the world. About 14 smaller Iranian financial institutions were not covered by the ban and were subsequently used as intermediaries by the banned banks.

Meanwhile, the US Congress prepared new sanctions legislation that would seek to blacklist every Iranian bank as well as the National Iranian Oil Company, the National Iranian Tanker Company and foreign firms that had joint ventures with Iranian companies on petroleum and uranium projects. Among other measures being considered was an amendment that would penalise any bank that did business with an Iranian financial institution.

The double blow of US sanctions on banks and EU sanctions on oil exports had an immediate negative impact on the Iranian economy, costing the nation an estimated $4.5bn a month in lost oil revenues. Ahmadinejad described the new sanctions as 'the heaviest onslaught on a nation in history'. Iran's currency, the rial, lost about 50% of its value at the beginning of the year, opening up a wide gap between the official and unofficial exchange rates that exacerbated economic distortions and corruption. The inflation rate reached 22% in June, with food inflation exceeding 50%, and the official unemployment rate of 15% masked a huge underemployment problem. The International Energy Agency estimated that oil exports dropped to between 1.2 and 1.8 million barrels a day, down from approximately 2.5 million barrels a day in 2011. Oil exports had accounted for over 80% of hard-currency earnings and over 50% of central-government revenues.

Over the winter, the economic impact of the oil sanctions was partially offset by an oil price rise of $20–25 per barrel, which largely represented a risk premium amidst talk of war. During the series of meetings between Iran and the E3+3, however, the price fell back $15 a barrel. To make up for the cutback in Iranian oil sales, Saudi Arabia increased production. Oil fields in Iraq and Libya also came back on line quicker than some had expected. To further calm oil markets, in May 2012, the United States persuaded the G8 countries to make an unprecedented agreement to release oil from their strategic reserves if sanctions or conflict with Iran led to a surge in prices.

In response to the sanctions, Iranian tankers began to turn off their electronic ship-locating systems before making port calls to foil monitoring by Western intelligence agencies. Rather than closing down oil fields, which could permanently damage production, Iran stored unsaleable oil in a large fleet of supertankers moored offshore. To encourage local production of consumer goods, authorities banned 600 previously imported items. Iran, however, was not about to go bust: it still had about $90bn in hard-currency reserves and gold. While the economic growth rate was well below the government's 8% target, it was still at 2% in 2011, according to the IMF. Some analysts, however, claimed that GDP contracted sharply in 2011–12.

Lame duck president

There were some signs that sanctions had produced disagreement within the regime. In April, former President Akbar Hashemi Rafsanjani, who was retained as chairman of the Expediency Council, an advisory panel to the supreme leader, said the West would not have been able to impose oil sanctions if Iran had forged good relations with Saudi Arabia. Meanwhile a number of economic stakeholders in Iran were said to be lobbying the government to take steps to ease the pressure. Ahmadinejad faced sharp criticism over his handling of the economy, in particular a subsidy-reform programme launched in December 2010 that in the end simply replaced universal price subsidies on food and fuel with cash grants for almost the entire population except the business sector. Ahmadinejad was partially correct when he sought to pin the blame on Western sanctions, but he did not succeed in rallying the population around the flag in nationalist outrage.

In fact, Ahmadinejad faded from significance, losing entirely in a power struggle with Khamenei that had begun in 2010. The same week in September 2011 in which Ahmadinejad was rebuked by Iran's judiciary for exceeding his authority in announcing release of the American hikers, the judiciary launched proceedings against several of Ahmadinejad's associates in a $2.6m embezzlement case. The CEOs of Bank Melli and Bank Saderat both resigned from their positions as a result. In November, Larijani's role in the storming of the British Embassy was interpreted by Ahmadinejad supporters as an effort to undermine his ability to conduct foreign policy. Further signalling Ahmadinejad's political irrelevance, Khamenei in December alluded to the possibility of removing the position of president altogether and moving to a form of government led by a prime minister elected by parliament. In the spring, the Majlis finally succeeded in forcing Ahmadinejad to make an appearance in the parliamentary chamber to answer complaints.

Parliamentary elections on 2 March 2012 sealed Ahmadinejad's lame-duck status. Supporters of Khamenei won over 60% of the vote, while candidates aligned with the president took only 6%, although he might have closet support among some of the independents who won 30% of the seats. Reformist politicians were excluded from the election altogether, including through disqualification by the Guardian Council. In addition to consolidating Khamenei's power, the election was significant in terms of the announced 64% participation rate. As the first nationwide voting since the disputed June 2009 presidential election, the high turn-out and incident-free polling indicated a return to political normality.

This state of normality included a repressive security apparatus. Green Movement leaders Mehdi Karroubi and Mir Hossein Mousavi were kept under extrajudicial house arrest. In October, actress Marzieh Vafamehr was sentenced to 90 cane lashes and a year in jail for appearing in the film 'My Tehran For Sale', which criticised Iran's harsh policies on the arts. In any case, the reformist movement appeared to have nearly disappeared. The year to mid-2012 saw few political protests of any sort and no hint of the kind of populist uprising that toppled Arab governments throughout the region. Yet disquiet lingered beneath the surface, not least over the rising inflation and other economic woes. Western strategy banked on Khamenei being worried enough about this discontent to adjust his strategic calculations over the nuclear issue.

Troubled ally

Iran's leaders maintained that what they called the 'Islamic awakening' in the Arab world benefited Iran by reducing America's role. Yet the ferment in Arab states was no zero-sum game for Tehran, which saw its influence and popularity shrink due to its support for the brutal Bashar al-Assad regime in Syria. Iranian arms transfers to Syria included two shipments interdicted by Turkey. Tehran was also accused of sending trainers to assist Syrian security services and electronic eavesdropping equipment to spy on opposition networks. Iran's support for Assad was not unqualified, as it urged concessions to Syrian dissidents' calls 'for freedom and justice'. This nuance was not enough. The sectarian nature of the growing civil war in Syria, where Sunnis increasingly opposed the Shia offshoot Alawite minority, underscored the problems Iran faced in trying to appeal to the Arab street. Among the casualties was Iran's influence over Hamas, which condemned Assad and agreed to a prisoner swap with Israel.

Differences over the future of Syria also ruptured Iran's relations with Turkey, which called for Assad to leave. Iran and Turkey also were at odds over Ankara's decision in September 2011 to host a radar system as part of NATO's missile shield. Iran saw the radar not as a defensive system but as a means of enabling an Israeli air strike against Iranian nuclear facilities by neutralising an Iranian missile response.

Iran's relations with Arab Gulf neighbours worsened when Ahmadinejad in mid-April paid an unprecedented visit to the island of Abu Musa, which is claimed by the United Arab Emirates but has been under Iranian control since 1971. The visit seemed to be calculated to stoke Iranian nationalism, and indeed it was defended by all parts of the political spectrum. But the visit created a diplomatic tempest, with the Gulf Co-operation Council (GCC) issuing a condemnation. GCC countries were also quick to take up accusations of increased Iranian political outreach and arms shipments to rebel groups in Yemen. American officials who had previously dismissed such reports said there was now credible evidence of at least limited material support from Iran, mirroring in smaller scale the kind of support that the Iran Revolutionary Guard Corps (IRGC) Quds Force was providing to Syria.

Covert war

The role of the Quds Force in Yemen and Syria was but one front in what many analysts described as a subterranean war between Iran and the United States and its allies. One aspect of the conflict was exposed in vivid and (for the US) embarrassing relief in November 2011 when Iran employed GPS spoofing to safely capture a highly classified RQ-170 stealth drone that was being used to monitor nuclear sites. Tehran also claimed to have broken up a US spy ring. Unnamed US officials acknowledged that a handful of informants in Iran had been exposed.

The *New York Times* presented new evidence that the Stuxnet computer virus that had knocked out 20% of Iran's centrifuges in 2010 was launched by the United States with Israeli assistance, in a controversial programme that began under George W. Bush in 2006 and was accelerated by Obama in the first months of his presidency in 2009. During the past year, two other computer malware programmes apparently directed against Iran came to light. Those two codes, dubbed Duqu and Flame, apparently preceded Stuxnet and unlike that worm were designed to spy, not destroy.

The most deadly and controversial aspect of the alleged covert war was a continuing string of assassinations of Iranian nuclear experts, to which Iran sought to respond in kind. On 23 July 2011, scientist Daryoush Rezaei was shot dead outside his Tehran home. On 11 January 2012, a bomb attached to his car killed Mostafa Ahmadi Roshan, who was in charge of procurement for the Natanz uranium-enrichment facility. He was the fifth nuclear-related specialist to be killed since 2007. The United States disavowed complicity in both attacks and strongly condemned such killings. Press reports tied the assassinations to Israel, operating through the MEK. Media reports also alleged that Israel had provided support to the Jundullah militant group, which operates in southeastern Iran. According to one report, Mossad operatives posed as CIA agents to recruit members of Jundullah to carry out terrorist attacks in Iran.

Iran apparently decided to retaliate by attempting to stage its own assassinations. On 11 October, the United States charged a dual US–Iranian citizen, Manssor Arbabsiar, and Gholam Shakuri, a commander in the Quds Force, with plotting to murder the Saudi ambassador to the United States, Adel al-Jubeir, in a Washington restaurant. The evidence was based on phone transcripts and wire transfers. Al-Jubeir had gained notoriety in Iran by being quoted in a 2008 US diplomatic dispatch, later released by the WikiLeaks website, saying the United States should 'cut off the head of the snake' in reference to Iran. Iranian authorities denounced the accusations, and there was scepticism elsewhere about the plot, which supposedly involved a Mexican drug cartel and a former used-car salesman.

However, it did appear that an Iranian retaliatory campaign was under way in which Iran-linked operatives allegedly sought to kill Israeli, Saudi and US diplomats in seven countries. The cases included a plot targeting the American Embassy in Azerbaijan in November; a car bombing in New Delhi on 13 February 2012 that wounded the wife of an Israeli diplomat; an alleged plot to kill Israeli diplomats on 14 February in Bangkok that was thwarted when a car bomb exploded prematurely; a similar magnetic bomb that was found attached to an Israeli diplomatic vehicle the same week in Tbilisi, Georgia; and attempted assassinations in Turkey and Pakistan.

A covert war may also have been behind mysterious accidents at Iranian missile and industrial plants. On 12 November 2011 two massive explosions at the al-Ghadir IRGC missile base 40km southwest of Tehran killed 17 people, including General Hassan Tehrani Moghaddam, the father of Iran's ballistic-missile programme. Al-Ghadir was thought to be a testing centre for *Sajill*-2 solid-fuelled missiles. Although Iran declared it an accident, post-incident imagery suggested foul play to some analysts. An explosion in December at the new Ghadir steelworks in Yazd that reportedly was set to produce maraging steel, a key material for advanced centrifuges, also led some analysts to suspect sabotage, despite Iranian denials. Similarly a reported explosion in November near the uranium-conversion facility at Esfahan sparked media inquiries, but the report was never confirmed apart from evidence that some buildings near a tunnel entrance had been razed.

War worries

Throughout the year to mid-2012, predictions of a preventive Israeli military strike against Iranian nuclear facilities were frequently heard. In late October, Israel's largest-circulation daily newspaper claimed that Netanyahu and Defence Minister Ehud Barak were rounding up cabinet votes in favour of a strike. In March, a respected *Washington Post* columnist said Panetta believed there was a 'strong likelihood' that Israel would strike Iran in April, May or June, before Iran's nuclear programme entered what Barak had begun describing as a 'zone of immunity', when Israeli strikes against it would not be effective. Barak spoke of nuclear work being increasingly spread over several sites, in particular the expansion of work at the underground facility at Fordow. Although new US 'bunker buster' bombs may be able to penetrate the 80–90m of rock above the enrichment halls there, Israeli leaders drew the conclusion from discussions with visiting US officials that Obama would neither take military action against Iran in 2012, nor go along with unilateral action by Israel. Netanyahu and Barak thus reportedly determined that if diplomacy failed to stop the Iranian programme they would have to take matters into their own hands and not inform the United States in advance of a strike. On more than one occasion they spoke publicly of taking military action, though in more measured terms than those employed by some Iranian officials. In May, Iranian military chief of staff Major-General Hassan Firouzabadi said: 'The Iranian nation is standing for its cause and that is the full annihilation of Israel.'

When Netanyahu visited Washington in March, Obama sought to persuade him to give diplomacy a chance. Top White House and Pentagon officials repeatedly warned Israel that a preventive air strike would only delay Iran's programme for three years at most. Among other negative consequences, they argued that an attack would be destabilising to the global economy and would set back the struggle against global jihadism. They insisted that a military strike was unnecessary because Iran was not about to produce weapons, and that oil sanctions were beginning to work in bringing Iran back to the negotiating table. Many former defence and intelligence officials voiced the same conclusions, although to threaten military strikes was a strategy favoured by a significant segment of the American body politic. In November, Mitt Romney, who later became the presumptive Republican presidential candidate, proclaimed: 'If we re-elect Barack Obama, Iran will have a nuclear weapon. And if you elect Mitt Romney, Iran will not have a nuclear weapon.' Senators from both parties let it be known that if Obama decided to attack Iran's nuclear facilities, he would have strong bipartisan support in Congress.

In an interview in the *Atlantic* magazine and in remarks to the American Israel Public Affairs Committee lobbying group, Obama asserted he was not bluffing when he said it was unacceptable for Iran to have a nuclear weapon, but that efforts to produce a weapon would be a red line for the United States. For Israel, by contrast, the stated red line was Iran becoming 'nuclear capable'. What this meant was unclear given that, in most respects, Iran already was nuclear capable.

The prospects for an Israeli strike were deemed to have increased when Netanyahu in May brought the Kadima Party into a coalition that included 94 members of the 120-seat Knesset. Yet a fierce backlash emerged among retired security officials who publicly questioned the utility of a military strike and even the competence of the political leadership to conduct it. Former Shin Bet domestic intelligence chief Yuval Diskin on 20 April deemed Netanyahu and Barak 'messianic' and 'unfit for war'. Ex-Mossad head Meir Dagan also lashed out, repeating his assessment that bombing Iran before all other approaches had been exhausted was the 'stupidest thing I have ever heard'. Even sitting military chief Benny Gantz described Iran as 'very rational' and unlikely to develop a bomb. Such public criticism was unprecedented in Israel and appeared to be stimulated by a real concern that Netanyahu and Barak were bent on a military course. Some analysts predicted that if diplomacy did not succeed in limiting Iran's nuclear programme, an Israeli strike was a 50–50 proposition before November.

No matter who won the US presidential election, the Iranian nuclear issue looked likely to reach a crisis stage in the coming year.

Iraq: Maliki Strengthens Dominance

Two interlinked dynamics dominated events in Iraq in the year to mid-2012: the final withdrawal of US forces in December 2011, eight years and nine months after the US-led invasion, and a far-reaching political crisis caused by the increasingly authoritarian behaviour of Prime Minister Nuri al-Maliki. As the ramifications of both continued to unfold, the long-term viability of the system imposed after the 2003 invasion was coming into question.

On 15 December 2011, in a fortified compound at Baghdad International Airport, US Secretary of Defense Leon Panetta oversaw the formal end of America's military presence in Iraq. As the last troops slipped across the Kuwaiti border, Panetta gave a restrained and rather sombre speech. This was because it was Iraqi public opinion that had finally forced US troops out of the country. The Status of Forces Agreement (SOFA) negotiated by the George W. Bush administration in 2008 had set the end of 2011 as the deadline for the removal of all US military forces. Under its rubric American combat troops left Iraq's towns and cities in June 2009. To meet his election promises, President Barack Obama then accelerated the removal of all combat forces by August 2010. However, by April 2011, it became clear that the US government was keen to renegotiate the SOFA to allow between 10,000 and 20,000 American troops to remain, to be justified by their role in rebuilding the Iraqi police and military.

This followed an unsuccessful attempt in June 2011, by Secretary of Defense Robert Gates and Chairman of the Joint Chiefs of Staff Admiral Mike Mullen to gain the government's permission for the troops to stay, to secure legal protection for them from Iraqi law, and to win approval for this from Iraq's parliament. During his visit to Baghdad, Gates indicated that the United States wanted to keep a minimum of 8,000 soldiers in Iraq after December 2011, and Panetta, having succeeded Gates, followed him to Baghdad in August with a similar plea. However, Iraq's ruling elite could not find the necessary consensus.

Maliki had already made clear his view when he told the *Wall Street Journal*: 'The withdrawal of forces agreement expires on December 31, 2011. The last American soldier will leave Iraq.' In August, Moqtada al-Sadr, the radial Shia cleric whose party had the largest number of seats in parliament, said: 'We should stand together to reject the presence of the infidel occupier and the armies of darkness and we refuse any presence of bases or trainers.' By October, it was evident that senior members of Iraq's ruling coalition, constrained by popular opinion, could not give the US military even the minimum terms it needed to remain. Obama announced the final withdrawal, in effect recognising that American troops had been forced out of the country by popular opinion and divisions within the ruling elite.

The State Department and the Central Intelligence Agency then took charge of US plans to influence Iraqi politics after troop withdrawal. Initial plans for the post-withdrawal embassy envisaged a staff of 15,000–16,000 diplomats and contractors, spread between the largest American embassy in the world in Baghdad and consulates in Basra, Irbil and Kirkuk. The CIA laid plans to keep its largest station, which had 700 staff at its peak. However, even these largely civilian plans for influence were undermined by two unforeseen constraints. Firstly, Iraqi government policy appeared to be aimed at reducing America's diplomatic influence. The Prime Minister's Office took direct responsibility for approving every US diplomatic visa, dramatically slowing down the process of bringing American personnel in and out of the country. Once US troops had departed, Iraqi government officials placed constraints on American diplomatic access to civil servants and politicians. Secondly, US government budgetary constraints forced the postponement of plans to set up consulates in Mosul and Kirkuk. The CIA likewise announced plans to cut its staff in Baghdad by 40%. Overall, the departure of US troops in December 2011 was a much bigger watershed than the American government had anticipated. Iraqi opinion and American budget cuts conspired to reduce US influence and to give Iraqi politics free rein.

Power-sharing agreement fails

However, the indigenous logic that shaped Iraqi politics forced the country into an extended crisis. The roots could be traced back to two sources: the increasing power of Maliki, and the divided outcome of the March 2010 elections, the third since regime change. The prime minister's State of Law coalition won 89 seats, and the largely secular nationalist Iraqiyya coalition led by Iyad Allawi managed to mobilise Sunni voters in Baghdad and across the northwest and won 91 seats. This left the balance of power with an overtly Shia religious coalition, the Iraqi National Alliance, with 70 seats and the Kurdish Alliance with 43 seats.

It took 249 days to build the third government of national unity since the invasion. Negotiations were shaped by two opposing fears: on one hand that Maliki's growing power would lead to dictatorship if he were reappointed and, on the other, that an increase in the influence of the Sunni population in a potential Allawi government could lead to the unravelling of the post-invasion political settlement. The compromise, arrived at in the November 2010 'Irbil Agreement', focused on Maliki signing a 15-point list designed to limit his power. Concessions included the appointment of interior and defence ministers not aligned to the prime minister, the transfer of counter-terrorism forces from Maliki's control to the Ministry of Defence, and strengthening of chains of command over the army and police force. The centrepiece of the agreement was the formation of a National Council for Strategic Policy that Allawi would chair. All major policy decisions would be sent to this council for approval before they were enacted by parliament.

But the Irbil Agreement failed to curb the power of the prime minister and led to a political crisis that, at mid-2012, dominated Iraqi politics. Plans for the National Council for Strategic Policy quickly became mired in party-political disagreements. Then, for the first seven months after the Irbil Agreement, Maliki rejected all candidates for the security ministries proposed by Iraqiyya. In June 2011, in direct contravention of the agreement, he appointed his close adviser Falih al-Fayyad as acting minister of national security. In August, he picked the minister of culture, Saadoun al-Dulaimi, as acting minister of defence while retaining the post of acting minister of interior for himself. By designating weak politicians or people who were personally tied to him as acting ministers, Maliki successfully retained control over the army, police force and intelligence services. He circumvented both the Irbil Agreement and the constitutional demand for cabinet posts to be validated by parliament.

As he set about abrogating the stipulations of the Irbil Agreement, the prime minister also undermined the oversight mechanisms put in place during the US occupation. The Independent High Electoral Commission (IHEC) was set up to oversee and guarantee fair elections. It managed to do this in the elections of 2005 and again in March 2010. However, Maliki blamed the organisation for his failure to obtain a parliamentary majority. His coalition attempted to push a vote of no confidence in the IHEC through parliament. Although this failed in April 2012, IHEC head Faraj al-Haidari and another senior official were arrested on corruption charges. The small amount of money involved, $130, indicated the political motivations behind the charges.

A similar dynamic surrounded the resignation of Judge Raheem Uqaili in September 2011. Uqaili was head of the Integrity Commission, an independent oversight body set up by the United States to tackle corruption. He was the third head of the commission to resign and, like his predecessors, blamed government interference in the commission's work.

Maliki moves against opposition

Fears about Maliki's authoritarian tendencies reached their peak on the evening that the last US troops left the country, 15 December 2011. Iraqi troops and tanks, led by Maliki's son, surrounded the houses of Vice-President Tariq al-Hashemi, Minister of Finance Rafi al-Issawi and Deputy Prime Minister Saleh al-Mutlaq – all senior members of Allawi's Iraqiyya coalition. They were placed under temporary house arrest. Hashemi was then allowed to fly to Irbil, capital of the Kurdish Regional Government (KRG), but three of his bodyguards were arrested. After four days the bodyguards appeared on television and made confessions denouncing the vice president for paying them to carry out assassinations and bombings. When judges issued an arrest warrant for Hashemi, three more confessions from policemen in the northwestern town of Fallujah were added. They claimed that the vice president, the finance minister and senior regional members of their party had set up and run a death squad, Hamas of Iraq, in Fallujah from 2006 onwards. Suspicions that the confessions had been extracted by torture were apparently confirmed on 15 March when one of the bodyguards, Amir Sarbut Zaidan al-Batawi, died in prison. Issawi and Mutlaq were subsequently released from house arrest and returned to their jobs in government. Hashemi, on the other hand, refused to return to Baghdad, arguing he would be unable to gain a fair trial. He travelled to Qatar and Turkey, meeting with Qatar's emir, Sheikh Hamad bin Khalifa al-Thani, Prime Minister Sheikh Hamad bin Jassim bin Jaber al-Thani and Turkey's Prime Minister Recep Tayyip Erdogan. This was an attempt to rally regional opinion in support of his own case – and also to establish an anti-Maliki coalition.

It would be hard to overstate the political importance of Hashemi's arrest and the subsequent trial begun in his absence. The fact that he was neither particularly popular nor effective as a politician may have made him more vulnerable to arrest than other senior members of Iraqiyya. There was a great deal of debate across Iraqi public opinion and amongst Baghdad's diplomatic corps about the veracity of the charges against him. There was little doubt that the confessions of his bodyguards were extracted through the extended use of torture. While it was certainly possible that Hashemi could have been complicit in the use of violence for political ends, the same charge could be levelled against the majority of Iraq's ruling elite. The timing and nature of the charges laid against Hashemi clearly indicated a political motivation. The fact that Issawi was also targeted indicated this was a move against the whole of Iraqiyya's senior leadership. It was part of a wider dynamic that saw Maliki's allies deploy the power of the judiciary and the police in combination with torture to achieve their political ends.

Given the increasing centralisation of power in the prime minister's hands, key Iraqiyya politicians, particularly Speaker of Parliament Osama al-Nujaifi and Hashemi, concluded that regional decentralisation was the only way to limit Maliki's domination. The Iraqi constitution gave provinces the right to form autonomous regions, following a vote of the provincial council and a referendum. Nujaifi and then Hashemi encouraged three provinces north of Baghdad – Anbar, Salahaddin and Diyala – to make this move. The three provinces, which have Sunni majorities, delivered a large percentage of Iraqiyya's votes in the 2010 election.

Maliki's response was to unleash a wave of arrests across the area. Nevertheless, in October 2011 Salahaddin Council voted to move forward with a referendum, followed by Diyala in December, with Anbar council threatening to follow a week later. More worrying still for Maliki, the oil-rich Shia-majority provinces of Basra and Wasit in the south had attempted the same move in 2010 and 2011. Faced with constitutionally legitimate attempts to weaken the central state's dominance, Maliki unleashed further repression and exerted his influence over Iraq's election commission to ensure that the referendums never took place. Blaming the moves in Salahaddin on Ba'athists, he used this as justification for further waves of repression in the provinces seeking greater autonomy. In a speech in Basra in February 2012, he challenged the notion of power sharing that had underpinned Iraqi politics since 2003, arguing that it brought into government, 'incompetent, inexperienced, and sometimes corrupt figures'. He said that this 'will not help in the reconstruction process. If we were forced to accept it for a while, we should not accept it any longer. Efficiency should be the criterion for any public position.'

Maliki's desire to move decisively against the federalist threat may have dictated the timing of Hashemi's arrest. In December, the vice president threw his support behind the federalist movements, saying the people involved 'are unwilling to accept further injustice, corruption and bad management from the central government'. Two days later, his house was surrounded by troops and the arrests were made. Maliki's move was a determined attempt to stop a threat to his campaign to centralise power in his own hands.

Opposition responses

Iraqiyya launched a boycott of parliament and the cabinet that lasted until early February. However, this appeared to have little effect on Maliki, while reducing its own influence on government. Maliki encouraged five members of parliament to break away and form a rival 'White Iraqiyya' group.

The move against Hashemi solidified fears amongst the wider ruling elite that their own safety and the future of Iraqi democracy could come under threat. In April Masoud Barzani, president of the Kurdistan Region, took this message directly to Washington, where he told the administration that 'Iraq is facing a serious crisis ... it's coming towards one-man rule'. Barzani's outspoken criticism opened the possibility of a cross-party alliance to remove Maliki. On 28 April, Barzani hosted a political summit in Irbil attended by Iraqi President Jalal Talabani, Allawi, Sadr and Nujaifi. They sent the prime minister a letter containing eight demands to be met within 15 days. If Maliki failed to comply, they threatened to remove him from office through a vote of no confidence.

Maliki, calculating that his opponents could not muster a parliamentary majority of 163 votes, showed no sign of meeting their demands. He gambled correctly. A series of opposition manoeuvres did not come any where near delivering the votes needed. Maliki showed that he had far greater strategic capacity than any of his rivals for power. He retained the backing of the United States and Iran, both of whom feared the instability that might be unleashed if he were unseated. Sadr, although increasingly vocal in calling for Maliki's removal, was constrained by his Iranian allies and his extended residence in the Iranian holy city of Qom. This left the senior politicians running Iraqiyya as the main opposition to Maliki, but they proved to be relatively inept as politicians and unable to act in concert, let alone to build the coalition needed to oust Maliki. As a result, he seemed as secure in his job as at any time since his appointment in 2006.

Kurdish friction

The leading role Barzani took in orchestrating the campaign against Maliki reflected declining relations between Irbil and Baghdad. Since 2003, the KRG had struggled to increase its political, economic and strategic autonomy from Baghdad.

The main issue was its right to independently negotiate contracts with multinational oil companies to export oil from the territory it controlled. Iraq had not passed a national oil law and the Iraqi constitution was ambiguous on this point. Irbil utilised this legal grey area to sign 43 exploration contracts on more favourable terms than the 18 signed by the government in Baghdad. The KRG's ambitions reached a new height in October 2011 when it signed an exploration deal with ExxonMobil, one of the world's largest oil companies. This gave rise to two issues. Firstly, the Iraqi government had made it clear that oil companies signing separate deals with the KRG would be excluded from the rest of the Iraqi market, and Exxon already had a contract with the Iraqi government to develop the southern field, West Qurna-1. Secondly, two of the six areas covered by the new ExxonMobil agreement were in territory that formally lay within Baghdad's area of geographic control but within which the KRG had deployed troops. The agreement therefore directly destabilised relations between the KRG and Baghdad and risked heightening sectarian tensions. Under pressure from the Iraqi government ExxonMobil agreed to freeze its contracts with the KRG while Baghdad and Irbil attempted to negotiate a solution.

Barzani's dispute with Maliki led him to assert the possibility that the KRG might secede from Iraq – a threat that was not new and which tended to increase when the KRG felt insecure. The KRG received 17% of Iraq's national budget, $11 billion in 2012. Although plans to develop its own oil reserves were well advanced, these would not replace the resources received from Baghdad. Thus threats of secession, although frequently made, did not appear viable.

Social pressures

Political disputes may not have put Maliki's premiership in serious doubt, but did exacerbate the weakness and incoherence of an already malfunctioning state. The failure of the government to deliver improvements in the lives of ordinary Iraqis was a major source of popular alienation with the ruling elite and anger at the government. Until 2011, the US State Department collected data from all of Iraq's 18 provinces, in an attempt to judge whether the lack of state services was driving political unrest and violence. In July 2011, it judged that 16 provinces were 'very unstable' due to poor delivery of electricity, water, sewerage and transport infrastructure. Unemployment was high – estimated by the government at 11%, but by the Iraq Knowledge Network, an NGO, at 26% and by the World Bank at closer to 40%.

The government recognised that poor services and high unemployment were, along with continued violence, the three major problems it faced. It was seeking to create 59,000 new public sector jobs in 2012 alone. However, electricity supply problems underlined the obstacles to its reconstruction plans. It estimated that the national grid was delivering 60% of demand. However, the US State Department estimated in July 2011 that the figure was 51%. The Iraq Knowledge Network survey showed that the average household received just 7.6 hours of electricity a day. This was despite the fact that both the US and the Iraqi authorities had consistently targeted the electricity sector as a key priority. American expenditure on the sector totalled $11bn by 2011, with the Iraqi government planning to invest $4.1bn in electricity infrastructure in the 2012 budget. However, corruption continually hampered investment efforts. This was highlighted by the forced resignation of Electricity Minister Ra'ad Shalal al-Ani, after only six months in the job. He was accused of signing $1.8bn worth of contracts with bogus Canadian and German firms. High-profile corruption cases and poor service delivery alienated the general population from the ruling elite.

The question that dominated Iraq was therefore whether, after the American withdrawal and amidst an extended political crisis and poor infrastructure, the state could continue to impose order on the country. The departure of US troops did not lead to a sustained upsurge in violence, which fell in 2011. There was a renewed campaign of mass-casualty attacks in January 2012 and attacks aimed at Shia pilgrims in March and April. However, the trend was comparable to 2011. Overall, Iraq's security services appeared competent enough to stop politically motivated violence rising to levels seen in the civil war that raged from 2005 to 2008. This was in large part because of their size: in January 2012, the security forces employed 933,103 people, spread between the Ministry of Defence, Ministry of Interior and the prime minister's Counter-Terrorism Force. The fact that these forces were primarily designed to impose order on the population, not to protect the country from external aggression, was reflected in the fact that the Ministry of Interior's numbers were double those of the Ministry of Defence. Iraq's army was described by senior US military commanders as 'the most capable counterinsurgency force in the Middle East and Central Asia'.

By 2011 the army had been due to move out of the country's cities and take a more conventional role in border defence. However, this strategic realignment was postponed at the end of 2011, in recognition that the police force was not yet up to the task. The police force, formed of locally recruited staff, was more prone to fall under the influence of sectarian and political actors, and was considered more unreliable than the army. The departure of US forces also left Iraq unable to defend its own airspace, forcing the government to buy 36 F-16 aircraft from the United States at a reported cost of $3bn – an order that seriously concerned Barzani. However, the first squadron was not due to become fully operational until 2016.

As the attacks in January and March 2012 indicated, the main challenge to the country's security forces was from al-Qaeda in Mesopotamia. During 2011, the organisation managed to regroup and develop its capacity to launch up to about 20 mass-casualty attacks per month across central and northern Iraq. As it evolved into a largely indigenous organisation, it moved away from suicide bombers and relied instead on car bombs. US and Iraqi estimates suggested its membership stood between 1,000 and 3,000. Though it had the ability to hit 'soft targets' – public spaces where large numbers gather – it did not appear to have the capacity to achieve its ultimate goal, that of driving Iraq back into sectarian civil war.

Iraqi politics were finally free of overt foreign control. The country did not, as some feared, see a rapid return to inter-communal violence and civil war. However, Maliki's continued centralisation of power pointed to major weaknesses in the reconstructed political system. By mid-2012, he was so dominant that his critics seemed unable to remove him.

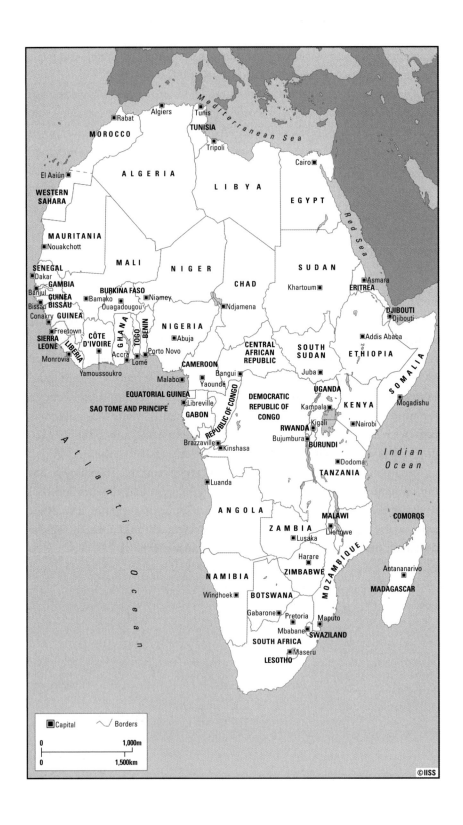

Chapter 7

Africa

The path to stability and democracy in Africa faced challenges across the continent in the year to mid-2012. *Coups d'état* in Mali and Guinea Bissau were particular reminders of the chronic difficulties faced by African nations, as were the tensions that surrounded electoral processes in countries such as Côte d'Ivoire, Kenya, Liberia and Zimbabwe. Islamist violence in Nigeria underlined the vulnerability to extremist influences of areas afflicted by poverty and inequality. Also pointing to the region's fragility were the spillover effects in sub-Saharan Africa of unrest in the Arab world, which had toppled three North African regimes in 2011. Among these effects were destabilising flows of returnees, and protests inspired by the Arab uprisings. Overall, events in the 12-month period suggested that, while the continent as a whole has been making significant economic progress, continuation of this positive trend remained vulnerable to political and ethnic disputes, authoritarian governance and in some places to extremism – as well as to natural disasters such as drought and famine. The brightest development was unexpected progress towards a long-hoped-for political settlement in Somalia, backed by military advances against the al-Shabaab militia group in which several countries participated.

West Africa: Spillover from Northern Troubles

The wave of unrest associated with the Arab uprisings of 2011, which toppled regimes in Tunisia, Egypt and Libya, spread from North Africa to some West

African countries, which witnessed protests and violent incidents from early 2011 onwards. Of particular concern was the influx of returnees and weapons from Libya to countries such as Algeria, Chad, Egypt, Ghana, Mali, Mauritania, Niger and Nigeria. Among the associated local challenges were reduced availability of food, excessive burdens on families and fragile infrastructure, and potential increases in criminality, violence and even conflict – ideal recruiting ground for extremists. In Burkina Faso and Senegal the spillover manifested in protests demanding greater equality, government transparency and defence of democratic values. In Mali change took a more violent form, resulting in a coup and the loss of government control over the north of the country. Guinea Bissau was again the scene of a military coup, and the Economic Community of West African States (ECOWAS) dispatched troops to the country. In Nigeria, nationwide protests and strikes were staged in vehement opposition to the removal of fuel subsidies. The Islamist sect Boko Haram remained a serious security threat as it engaged in more frequent and deadlier attacks.

Elsewhere, there were election-related tensions. A political crisis developed around the results of the presidential elections in Liberia. In Côte d'Ivoire the situation remained fragile, even though there was progress towards political reconciliation following the crisis that shook the country after the 2010 presidential elections.

What was described by the International Organisation for Migration as 'one of the largest migration crises in modern history' saw 706,000 people, mainly from African countries but also from Bangladesh, the Philippines and Vietnam, leave Libya between March and September 2011. In 2012 the movement of returnees continued, albeit more slowly. Chad and Niger received by far the largest numbers, followed by Ghana and Mali. Up to 99% of returnees to West African countries were male, with 80% between the ages of 20 and 40 – a social group particularly at risk of unemployment.

In addition, the flow of weapons contributed to the emergence of new militant groups and the strengthening of existing ones. One example was the establishment in mid-2011 of the Movement for Oneness and Jihad in West Africa (MOJWA), which was responsible for numerous kidnappings in the Sahel. It aimed to establish sharia law across West Africa, but broke away from al-Qaeda in the Islamic Maghreb (AQIM) because it opposed Arab domination of the leadership.

Rebellion and coup in Mali

Mali suffered the most from the effects of the Arab upheavals. After the Libyan conflict ended, well-armed pro-Gadhafi mercenaries returned to

Mali and strengthened the ranks of Tuareg separatists – and in particular, the Movement for the National Liberation of the Azawad (MNLA). Tuareg nomads across the Sahel had been opposing local governments since the 1960s, especially in southern Algeria, northern Mali and northern Niger. In 2009 both Mali and Niger had declared the Tuareg movement defeated. They failed, however, to integrate fighters within their regular armies as required by peace agreements. Many fighters then relocated to Libya. Tuaregs are believed to have received training and weapons from the Gadhafi regime and to have links with AQIM.

The MNLA led a Tuareg uprising in northern Mali in January 2012 in which dozens of rebels and Malian soldiers were killed and over 200,000 people displaced, many fleeing to neighbouring Niger. The Malian military proved ill equipped to fight the northern rebellion and lacked sufficient government support. Mounting public protests culminated in a military coup by junior officers who overthrew the government of President Amadou Toumani Touré on 21 March. They installed a junta, the National Committee for the Reestablishment of Democracy and the Restoration of the State, which pledged to 'return power to a democratically elected president as soon as national unity and territorial integrity were restored' in northern Mali. Both Western and African powers refused to recognise the new government and demanded its removal, and international aid was suspended. The inability of the new leader, Captain Amadou Sanogo, to control his troops led to looting and chaos. (See *Strategic Geography*, pp. X–XI.)

The MNLA quickly exploited the crisis and managed, jointly with MOJWA and their Salafist partners Ansar al-Din, to take control of several cities in the north, including Kidal, Gao and Timbuktu. This was a particular concern for neighbouring Mauritania and Niger, which feared that instability in northern Mali would provide an ideal ground for religious extremism, especially in the form of Ansar al-Din and AQIM. In their view, the Malian government had always failed to adopt effective measures against these groups. Similar criticism had long been made by Algeria, which had deployed troops to the border to support Mali in counter-terrorism operations against AQIM in December 2011.

April proved a critical month. Following international condemnation, the military junta transferred power to a civilian government, though it appeared to keep a large measure of control, including over state media. Parliamentary speaker Dioncounda Traoré was sworn in as interim president on 12 April. Meanwhile, the MNLA declared independence for the state of Azawad in northern Mali, a claim immediately rejected by the African Union (AU) and ECOWAS. Traoré threatened to wage 'total war' against the separatists, and hundreds of northern youths gathered in Bamako, the capital, demanding weapons to fight the Tuareg rebels.

On 28 April Sanogo rejected ECOWAS's plan to deploy 3,000 troops to Mali, intended to help counter the crisis and ensure a peaceful transition expected to last one year. Two days later soldiers loyal to Touré, now hiding in Senegal, attempted a counter-coup which was foiled by the junta after fighting in the capital that led to several casualties.

In May, the MNLA and Ansar al-Din began to enforce a moderate sharia system in Azawad. An agreement between the two to merge, however, proved short lived; the MNLA said Ansar al-Din's plan to introduce strict sharia law across northern Mali was at odds with its secular values. MNLA was uneasy at the prospect of an 'Arabisation' of the Tuareg way of life. In June, a three-day conference of Arab tribes from the greater Azawad region was held in Mauritania to discuss the MNLA's declaration of independence for Azawad state, and the expulsion of al-Qaeda from northern Mali. Representatives from over 120 Azawad Arab tribes bemoaned the fact that their people were victims of a vicious conflict between the Malian state, on the one hand, and Tuaregs and terrorists on the other. The formation of a military force to remove al-Qaeda from Timbuktu, where the advent of Islamists had brought the introduction of Islamic rule in its harshest form, was announced.

As of June 2012, Mali's election plans remained unclear and the deployment of troops by ECOWAS did not appear to be imminent. Most of the north was outside the government's control and Timbuktu remained in the hands of AQIM and Ansar al-Din.

Protests in Senegal and Burkina Faso
Senegal is the only West African country that has not suffered a coup or civil war since independence from France in 1960. However, riots broke out in June 2011, prompted by opposition to President Abdoulaye Wade's proposed constitutional amendments to introduce the post of vice-president and reduce the number of votes needed to be elected president. This wave of discontent gave rise to the M23 movement, which claimed that the changes proposed by Wade would allow him to secure re-election more easily and then resign in favour of his unpopular son Karim, who already held four ministerial portfolios and controlled a large portion of the government budget.

Wade had been in power since 2000, but amendments to the constitution passed in 2008 stipulated that no president should have more than two seven-year terms in office (the 2001 constitution had allowed two five-year terms). Nevertheless, the 86-year-old president sought to stand for a third time. M23 became the driving force behind most protests, expanding to embrace a broad democratisation agenda and bringing together young people, civil-society groups and political factions.

The run-up to the 2012 presidential election was tainted by violent protests against Wade's attempt to hold on to power. Critics claimed that a court ruling allowing the president to run for a third term was given by corrupt judges who had been bribed to rule in favour of the president. The most intense violence took place on 17–18 February in Dakar, the capital, resulting in the deaths of six people. Besides contesting the legitimacy of Wade's candidacy, protesters voiced popular discontent with his presidency, stemming from rising prices and unemployment, corruption, nepotism and outlandish spending projects. Given this context, it came almost as a surprise that the elections took place peacefully. Former prime minister and Wade's protégé Macky Sall defeated Wade and promised that, as president, he would reduce presidential terms from seven to five years and strictly enforce the two-term limit. However, Sall, who had been a supporter of his predecessor, faced the possibility of renewed protests against chronic complaints such as rampant unemployment.

The year to mid-2012 saw Burkina Faso recovering from the wave of protests that disrupted the country in the first half of 2011. Sporadic civilian protests and military looting, often reflecting deep resentment of the political establishment, had begun in the capital Ouagadougou in March 2011 and a mutiny by the Presidential Guard on 15 April 2011 led to several days of unrest, with looting of shops and burning of buildings. Riots quickly spread to at least four other major cities, prompting the Ghanaian government temporarily to suspend trade relations.

Two key sources of discontent among the civilian population were ever-increasing food prices in one of the world's poorest countries, and popular disillusion with the political elite, corrupt bureaucracy, opaque judicial system and often brutal police. There was a series of mutinies within the army throughout 2011 to protest against poor living conditions and failure to pay allowances.

President Blaise Campaore, serving his fourth term, curbed the protests, appointed a new prime minister and army chief of staff, made concessions such as increasing salaries of certain categories of employees, and began a restructuring of the armed forces including the demobilisation of around 600 soldiers. However, the ruling party continued to operate with little transparency and, in February 2012, new protests broke out against poor infrastructure and the rising cost of living. While the security situation improved, it was unclear whether the causes of the unrest had truly been addressed.

Another coup in Guinea Bissau

Since independence from Portugal in 1974, Guinea Bissau has seen four successful coups, of which the latest took place in April 2012. No elected president has yet served a full term.

In July and August 2011, thousands of people mounted protests in Bissau, the capital, against Prime Minister Carlos Gomes Junior, who was believed to be responsible for obstructing the investigation into the murder of President João Bernardo Vieira, the army chief of staff and other figures in 2009. In October, UN Secretary-General Ban Ki-moon requested a mandate extension for the UN Integrated Peace-Building Office in Guinea-Bissau (UNIOGBIS) in light of the country's worsening security crisis. Angola also announced the indefinite extension of its military assistance mission. The latter proved particularly crucial, and the deployment of forces and the provision of material support were key in repelling an attempted coup on 26 December, when a group of renegade soldiers, allegedly led by navy chief Rear Admiral José Americo Bubo na Tchuto, attempted to remove army chief General Antonio Indjai, and forced the prime minister to seek refuge at the Angolan embassy. Admiral na Tchuto is a controversial public figure, suspected of planning a coup against the president in 2008 and identified by the American government as an international drug kingpin.

In a country where political and military power struggles are the norm, the December events hardly came as a surprise. And if the ability to thwart the coup was an encouraging sign, the death of President Malam Bacai Sanha on 9 January due to illness was a warning that more instability was on the horizon. The appointment of Raimundo Pereira, president of the National Assembly, as interim president was immediately rejected by the opposition, which demanded elections. These were scheduled for 18 March.

The first round of elections took place peacefully; they were described as free and fair by international observers, although opposition leaders denounced them as fraudulent and rejected the results. Prime Minister Gomes won the first round, receiving 49% of the vote. But before a run-off vote could take place on 29 April, soldiers staged a coup, detaining Gomes,

Pereira and other senior officials. They seized government buildings and closed the national airspace to prevent foreign delegations from travelling to the country to mediate the crisis. On 16 April the formation of a Transitional National Council was announced by the military junta, led by General Indjai, together with some political leaders.

The coup put pressure on international bodies, especially ECOWAS, to intervene. When the junta failed to comply with a 72-hour ultimatum to accept the deployment of 629 soldiers and police and to embrace a 12-month transition to civilian rule, ECOWAS imposed sanctions, soon followed by the Community of Portuguese Language Countries (CPLP) and the European Union. On 18 May the first 70 paramilitary police arrived from Burkina Faso to relieve a 270-strong Angolan contingent (MISSANG) that had been in Guinea Bissau for around 12 months to provide support and training to the army. By the end of May the rest of the ECOWAS contingent arrived, made up of Nigerians (140 police, 160 soldiers), Burkinabé (70 additional paramilitary police) and Senegalese (189). On 22 May the military junta, having held power for six weeks, announced a return to civilian rule and 28 government ministers were nominated, predominantly from former opposition parties, and excluding all members of the ousted government.

Nigeria: protests and extremist violence

Nigeria, the continent's most populous country and the second richest in sub-Saharan Africa, confronted a daunting set of security challenges including religious extremism, sectarian violence, maritime piracy and organised crime. The two issues that dominated the year to mid-2012 were the growing violence perpetrated by the Islamist group Boko Haram, and protests against removal of fuel subsidies.

Boko Haram, which means 'Western education is forbidden' in Hausa, originated in the northeastern state of Borno. It had terrorised the country with attacks and killings since the early 2000s, with the supposed goal of establishing sharia law and ridding Nigeria of Western influence and education. Violence had increased since 2009 as the group began to venture outside its traditional strongholds in the north and threatened Abuja, the capital and central Nigeria. This prompted the deployment of the army to eliminate or contain the violence.

Attacks in 2011 included Nigeria's first suicide bombing, which targeted the National Police HQ in Abuja on 16 June, killing six people; the bombing of the UN building in Abuja on 26 August, which left at least 24 people dead; and a series of attacks on churches on Christmas Day in central and northern

Nigeria. These demonstrated a growing tactical sophistication, including better planning and mastery of bomb-making. Boko Haram quickly graduated from machetes and drive-by shootings to more complex attacks in a way that suggests exposure to outside Islamist groups. In January 2012 Nigerian Foreign Minister Mohamed Bazoum said intelligence indicated that Boko Haram had trained in AQIM's camps in the Sahel as well as in Somalia with al-Shabaab. Similar claims were made by the foreign minister of Mali, Soumeylou Boubeye Maiga, as well as by the Algerian government and the US Africa Command (AFRICOM).

The government's response to Boko Haram's attacks was widely criticised as ineffective. This weakened the image of President Goodluck Jonathan who, in spite of ambitious promises, proved unable to contain the violence and also failed to address the socio-economic grievances that appeared to be the real drivers behind discontent in the north. Nigeria has long been characterised by a north–south divide with the poorer, less developed Muslim north resenting the richer, Christian south which benefits from the oil infrastructure of the Delta region.

In autumn 2011 increased house-to-house searches by the Joint Task Force (JTF) in Maiduguri, capital of Borno state, prompted Boko Haram to move its base to Damaturu, capital of Yobo state, to which, in turn, additional forces were deployed to strengthen an already substantial military presence. The federal government approved the establishment of permanent operational bases for JTFs in the states of Adamawa, Bauchi, Borno, Gombe, Taraba and Yobe. Troops returning from peacekeeping operations in Kaduna, north-central Nigeria, and elements of the army's 1st Division were put on stand-by to join the JTFs. In addition, there was unconfirmed speculation that some of the 2,400 troops who had been under UN command in Darfur, Sudan, would be assigned to operations in the northeast. The deployment of the army produced mixed results and at times made things worse. Soldiers were unsuited for dealing with civilians and often adopted a heavy-handed approach. Moreover, ethnic tensions between soldiers and the civilian population increased the level of mistrust between the northern population and the central government.

The Christmas Day attacks prompted Jonathan to declare a state of emergency in areas that had become Islamist strongholds, and to increase the military presence at key flashpoints. He rejected an ultimatum issued by Boko Haram on 2 January that demanded all Christians living in the north leave within three days and all Muslims in the south return to northern states. The expiry of the ultimatum was marked by explosions in Maiduguri and Damaturu, which killed over 100 people and caused 90,000 people in Damaturu to flee their homes. On 20 January Boko Haram members wearing police uniforms entered five prisons in the city of Kano, freeing all inmates. They then bombed the buildings, the local branch of the State Security Service and two immigration offices in the group's deadliest attack, resulting in at least 211 deaths.

Attacks against security personnel and churches continued relentlessly through to mid-2012. A first attempt at peace talks between the government and Boko Haram took place in March but brought no results. One of the conditions for a ceasefire made by the group's leader Abubakar Shekau was the release of all Boko Haram members from prison, a proposal unacceptable to the government. Attempted negotiations with moderate members of the sect continued through back channels, but violence did not diminish and the United States was considering the inclusion of Boko Haram on its list of designated terrorist organisations. This proposal, strongly supported by the US Department of Justice, was controversial. While it would give the United States greater power to combat the movement, it would also raise Boko Haram's profile and could even strengthen it. This in turn could drive a more intense military campaign on the part of the government, without addressing the root causes of the problem, which were poverty and inequality.

Amid this tense climate and growing discontent, on 1 January 2012 Jonathan announced the elimination of fuel subsidies, one of the few perks enjoyed by ordinary Nigerians, and the deregulation of the refined-fuel industry in line with recommendations made by the International Monetary Fund. This move was met by week-long strikes across the country led by the main trade unions.

The measure led to an increase in price per litre from 65 naira ($0.40) to 140 naira ($0.89) at petrol stations, and from 100 ($0.64) to 200 naira ($1.28) on the black market. Although Nigeria was Africa's top oil producer, with output of 2 million barrels per day, its four refineries could not meet demand and operated at around 23% of capacity. For this reason, most oil was exported in an unrefined state and the government had to import fuel and pay importers to keep prices low. Jonathan lamented the high costs of this practice – in 2011 1.3 trillion naira (about $8bn) were spent, as opposed to the budgeted 248bn naira – and promised that the money saved through the removal of subsidies would be used to improve infrastructure. Adding to popular frustration was the fact that the president acknowledged that years of mismanagement and corruption had been the key reasons behind the high spending, but he appeared to be taking no steps to address this, and was instead penalising ordinary citizens, 90% of whom live on less than $2 a day.

Strikes brought Nigeria to a standstill as protesters closed Abuja airport, blocked roads and closed down public offices. Oil and gas workers' trade unions threatened to shut down all production. Police used tear gas and beatings, sometimes fatal, to disperse protesters across the country. Six days of strikes, estimated to have cost the economy $600m a day, came to an end on 16 January when Jonathan agreed to an immediate 30% reduction of fuel prices to 97 naira ($0.60) per litre. The protests, the largest for years, indicated the level of popular mistrust of the government, with the fuel-subsidy issue acting as a unifying cause for demands for accountability, perhaps partly inspired by the Arab uprisings.

Election-related tension in Côte d'Ivoire and Liberia

Efforts at reconciliation got under way in Côte d'Ivoire, which had suffered upheaval and conflict after the incumbent Laurent Gbagbo, though beaten in the 2010 presidential elections, refused to step down. His arrest in April 2011, following a ten-day siege of the presidential residence, carried out by UN and French troops, paved the way for Alassane Ouattara to be inaugurated as president. The Constitutional Court, which had previously dismissed the election results, conceded that Ouattara had been the legitimate winner of the presidential elections. Ouattara stressed his commitment to reconciliation and peace following the violence which claimed at least 1,000 lives. The launch of a Commission on Dialogue, Truth and Reconciliation, headed by former Prime Minister Charles Konan Banny, went some way to address this.

In legislative elections held in December 2011, Ouattara's Rally of the Republicans (RDR) secured 127 of 254 seats while the Democratic Party of Côte d'Ivoire (PDCI) won 77. The results strengthened the president's position, but produced tensions between the RDR and PDCI, which alleged electoral fraud. Gbagbo's Ivorian Popular Front (FPI) boycotted the polls. It had also suspended its participation in the Independent Electoral Commission, arguing that RDR had excluded it from decisions. Preventive measures were taken to ensure stability throughout the country and around 25,000 Ivorian and 7,000 UNOCI troops were deployed.

In November 2011 Gbagbo was transferred to the International Criminal Court, where he faced four charges of crimes against humanity, including murder, rape and inhuman acts alleged to have been carried out by his troops between December 2010 and April 2011. This was later extended to war crimes committed since September 2002, when the country's first civil war began. The situation in Côte d'Ivoire remained fragile and Gbagbo's appearance in The Hague was likely to stoke political tensions in a country deeply divided and polarised. While the security situation had improved, violent incidents continued to be reported across the country, including between communities mostly in the west. In a report published in June 2012, Human Rights Watch highlighted the practice used by anti-government rebels to recruit child soldiers in Liberia to conduct raids across the border, targeting mainly villages where the population supported Ouattara. According to the report at least 40 Ivoriens had been killed since July 2011 in four cross-border attacks.

In Liberia, disputes broke out after the first round of the country's second free presidential elections in October 2011. The incumbent President Ellen Johnson Sirleaf's chief opponent was Winston Tubman, a former UN envoy to Somalia and nephew of a previous Liberian leader. Though the vote was declared free, fair and transparent by ECOWAS, the African Union, the Carter Center and other observers, it was nonetheless fraught with controversy. Sirleaf took 43.9% of the first round vote with Tubman winning 32.7%, on a high 71.6% turnout. Tubman's party, the Congress for Democratic Change (CDC), demanded a recount, an investigation into fraud and the establishment of an interim government similar to those set up after disputed elections in Kenya and Zimbabwe in 2008. As chairman of ECOWAS, Nigerian President Goodluck Jonathan invited Tubman and his running mate George Weah to Abuja for crisis talks on 3 November. However, Jonathan failed to convince Tubman to participate in the 8 November run-off elections. The situation deteriorated when four of his supporters were killed by the police in what Tubman called an 'assassination attempt' during a demonstration that spilled out of party headquarters in Monrovia. The next day, Sirleaf won the run-off vote with 90% of a much lower 40% turnout.

Having begun her second term with diminished political authority, the president tried to reduce tensions by setting up a Special Independent Committee to look into the killings. Often described as having done more than any previous Liberian leader to address corruption, she faced criticism for suppressing free speech and cracking down on the opposition by closing four popular opposition radio and television stations. Sirleaf said broadcasters had propagated hate messages and incited people to violence. She faced additional criticism when she appointed her eldest son head of the

National Oil Company and offered senior government positions to friends and relatives.

Meanwhile, the people of both Liberia and Sierra Leone waited to hear the verdict in the five-year-long war-crimes trial of former Liberian President Charles Taylor at the International Criminal Court in The Hague. On 3 May, the 64-year-old was found guilty on 11 counts, including rape and murder, relating to the Sierra Leone civil war. The prosecutors in the trial urged that he be given an 80-year sentence for backing rebels in Sierra Leone, who had killed tens of thousands of people, in exchange for 'blood diamonds' collected by slaves. On 30 May Taylor was sentenced to 50 years in prison, six of which he had already served, to be spent in the United Kingdom.

Somalia: Signs of Renaissance

Somalia made both political and military progress over the year to mid-2012, raising hopes that a country plagued by conflict for over two decades might see a brighter future. After so many years without effective central government, Somalia's leadership took important steps towards creating a new political framework. As a result, there seemed a real prospect of a smooth handover to end the eight-year tenure of the Transitional Federal Government (TFG).

Though there were significant political divisions between Somalia's president, prime minister and parliamentary speaker, the key players sought to put their differences aside and to work towards ending the mandate of transitional institutions and establishing a new government by August 2012. By mid-year, a draft constitution had been completed and parliamentarians had agreed on the shape of the future government.

In parallel to these tentative political steps, there were significant military advances against the al-Qaeda-linked Islamist terrorist group Harakat al-Shabaab al-Mujahideen, or al-Shabaab, which had waged an insurgency since 2006 and controlled a large part of the country. TFG forces gained significant momentum, assisted by African Union peacekeepers and by the intervention late in 2011 of Kenyan and Ethiopian forces. In past years, the TFG had exerted no real authority at all. But more recently it brought Mogadishu, the capital, under its control following the expulsion of al-Shabaab fighters, who until August 2011 still controlled most of the city.

In addition to political and military challenges, the government had to deal with a famine between July 2011 and February 2012 which killed an estimated 80,000 people, displaced 1.5 million others and left 2.3m – a quarter of the population – requiring urgent assistance.

Political framework

Since Somalia's government collapsed in 1991 after clan-based opposition groups ousted President Siad Barre, the international community had been involved in at least a dozen attempts to establish a legitimate central authority. Political reform finally began to gain traction in the wake of the Kampala Accord, signed in June 2011 by President Sharif Sheikh Ahmed of the TFG and Speaker of the Transitional Parliament Sharif Hassan Sheikh Aden.

The accord ended months of infighting and jockeying for power. The rift between the president and the speaker, and their respective supporters, centred on the mandate of the transitional institutions, originally tasked to deliver national elections and a new constitution by August 2011. A parliamentary vote in February 2011 which sought to extend the mandate by three years, escalated tensions. The United Nations came out against the extension; the African Union and the Intergovernmental Authority on Development (IGAD) supported the move, hoping it would give Somalia time to achieve sufficient security and stability for elections to be held.

The Kampala Accord was a compromise between the president, who had supported the extension, and the speaker, who had opposed it. The accord deferred elections for one year to allow for adequate preparation. It enabled the appointment of Prime Minister Abdiweli Mohamed Ali, and set the tone for future governmental reform. A substantial effort was made to halt destructive political practices and both the president and the speaker committed to improve their relationship and 'refrain from media recriminations, threats of impeachment and the dismissal of parliament' – common occurrences over the last few years.

Following the Kampala Accord, all eyes turned to the 'roadmap', signed in September 2011 by Prime Minister Ali as well as by representatives of the breakaway Puntland region, the central Galmudug region, and the pro-government, moderate Sufi militia Ahlu Sunna Wal Jama'a (ASWJ). Representatives of the UN, AU, the Arab League and IGAD also signed the agreement. The roadmap set benchmarks and deadlines to ensure that timetables for parliamentary reform and the drafting of a new constitution stayed on track.

Garowe, capital of Puntland, hosted the First National Constitutional Conference for Somalia in December 2011. The outcome was the 'Garowe principles', followed by the Second National Constitutional Conference for Somalia in February 2012 and the 'Garowe II principles'. Together they established the framework for a bicameral federal legislature, consisting of a lower house of 225 representatives and an upper house of elders. Parliament would be drawn from Somalia's traditional regions and reflect the country's clan structure; 30% of its members were to be women. The 'Garowe II principles' recognised 18 territories as administrative regions, with Puntland and Galmudug as states within the federation. It was agreed that the upper house would have 54 members, and that each of the administrative regions would have three representatives. In addition, they established provisions for a 1,000-member National Constituent Assembly, nominated by all roadmap signatories and civil society, charged with formulating laws, conflict resolution and the implementation of the constitution. The self-declared independent state of Somaliland, which broke away when the Somali government collapsed in 1991, refused to take part in the political process.

The draft constitution was completed on time, but its adoption proved more difficult and the deadline was missed. One of the strongest objections came from Puntland President Abdirahman Mohamed Farole, who said it failed to define the federal system of government and to clearly distribute power and resources between federal and state institutions. The pro-Mogadishu ASWJ also warned against the draft. A consultative meeting on the outstanding issues concluded on 23 May in Addis Ababa. After three days of heated talks, all signatories committed to push the political process forward. Some of the deadlines were missed but participants agreed to put differences aside in order to meet the August transition deadline.

Political progress helped galvanise the international community into giving further support to the TFG to resolve the long-running conflict. In February 2012, Somalia's challenges were the focus of an international conference called by the UK government in London. Delegates from over 50 countries were presented with an ambitious agenda for the country's future political framework, as well as for the funding of the African Union Mission in Somalia (AMISOM), tackling al-Shabaab and combating piracy off the Somali coast. Turkey, which hosted a conference on Somalia in June 2012, also played a major role. It contributed over $350m in humanitarian aid during the famine. In addition, Turkey re-opened its embassy in Mogadishu and built refugee camps, and in March 2012 Turkish Airlines opened the first regular commercial service to Mogadishu in over two decades.

Military gains

Political progress was accompanied by significant military gains against al-Shabaab, putting the Islamist militia on the defensive. TFG forces, assisted by AMISOM troops, were given a considerable boost when Ethiopia and Kenya intervened in Somalia. AMISOM played a key role in pushing al-Shabaab out of Mogadishu in August 2011. Later, Kenyan troops took control of border towns in a move towards the port of Kismayo, al-Shabaab's economic hub. Kenya first deployed its troops to Somalia's Juba Valley in October 2011. *Operation Linda Nchi* (Protect the Country) was aimed at protecting Kenya's North Eastern Province from unrest across its border and preventing al-Shabaab from spreading its influence in Kenya. Kenyan troops experienced setbacks due to the difficult terrain and by mid-2012 Kismayo was still in al-Shabaab's hands.

Meanwhile, Ethiopian forces advanced in the Mudug, Hiraan and Galguduud regions. They moved into Somalia in November 2011 and, together with ASWJ and Somali troops, carried out a number of successful military operations against al-Shabaab. They backed, equipped and trained the ASWJ, which had become prominent in 2008 when it took up arms against al-Shabaab in central Somalia. In 2010, the ASWJ joined Somali government forces in exchange for control of a number of ministries and diplomatic posts.

After capturing the strategic city of Beledweyn in December, the combined forces advanced on and captured Baidoa, al-Shabaab's stronghold, in February and El Bur, another key al-Shabaab base in central Somalia, in March. Ethiopian forces had been scheduled to withdraw by the end of April 2012, handing over liberated areas, including Baidoa, to TFG and AMISOM troops. Encouraged by their success in Beledweyn and Baidoa, President Meles Zenawi said Ethiopian forces were gearing up to liberate Kismayo. Ethiopian troops were reported to have withdrawn from at least five towns in central Somalia in June, but officials said they would remain in the country until the TFG had organised itself to fend off any hostile attacks and until all parties had ratified the constitution. Meanwhile, Kenyan forces announced plans to expand beyond their traditional stronghold of Kuday, south of Kismayo.

Military efforts were further boosted by a decision of the UN Security Council in February 2012 to increase the African Union peacekeeping force to nearly 18,000 troops. The effect would be to place 4,660 Kenyan troops under AU command, fighting alongside troops from Uganda, Burundi and Djibouti. UNSCR 2036, in addition to increasing the number of troops, also approved the AU's request to extend AMISOM's presence to three sectors outside Mogadishu. The mandate of the peacekeeping force itself was also strengthened, since AMISOM was given the authorisation to use 'all necessary measures' to reduce the threat from al-Shabaab.

The United States played a role in supporting the TFG's efforts, including missile attacks on al-Shabaab from unmanned aerial vehicles (UAVs). These had been widely reported from June 2011, and in October US officials confirmed that a base in Ethiopia from which UAVs were launched was operational – though they said the drones would be used for surveillance only. In June 2012, however, Washington confirmed that the United States had been taking 'direct action' against al-Shabaab. The TFG welcomed targeted missile strikes on al-Shabaab provided innocent civilians were not harmed.

Al-Shabaab appeared to have been weakened by the offensive carried out in 2011 and early 2012. Ethiopian and Kenyan forces, with logistical backing from the United States, France and the United Kingdom, squeezed al-Shabaab in a pincer movement from the west and south. Al-Shabaab was itself weakened by Somalia's 2011 famine, which was caused in part by East Africa's worst drought in over six decades. Somalia's instability compounded its effects: the guerrilla group's failure to feed local populations under its control, coupled with its refusal to allow humanitarian organisations access to provide aid, alienated many of its supporters. In addition, al-Shabaab reportedly suffered from the loss of lucrative areas in Mogadishu and other regions. In the UN resolution expanding AMISOM's mandate, the Security Council imposed a ban on the export of Somali charcoal – a business estimated to have generated at least $15m a year in revenues for al-Shabaab through Kismayo.

There were indications that the al-Shabaab leadership was in disarray, particularly after the death in June 2011 of Fazul Abdullah Mohammed, a senior al-Qaeda operative who was also al-Shabaab's military leader. He was killed by Somali troops when shooting broke out after he was stopped at a checkpoint. In February 2012, al-Qaeda leader Ayman al-Zawahiri officially announced that al-Shabaab had merged into al-Qaeda, but the Somali government interpreted this as an indication that al-Shabaab was feeling the pressure. Nevertheless, the re-branded 'al-Qaeda in Somalia' remained an international concern. According to Andrew Mitchell, Britain's international development minister, 'there are more British passport holders engaged in terrorist training in Somalia than in any other country in the world'. Western intelligence agencies estimated that the number of foreign jihadists operating in al-Shabaab was in the low hundreds.

Despite being pushed out of Mogadishu, al-Shabaab showed it was still capable of carrying out spectacular attacks in the capital. In October 2011, the group detonated a truck loaded with fuel drums at the gate of a government ministry, killing more than 100 people. It carried out a suicide attack inside the presidential compound in March 2012, and then another suicide attack on the newly re-opened Somali National Theatre that killed several people, including the president of the Somali Olympic Committee.

AMISOM troops were deployed outside Mogadishu for the first time in April 2012. The 100 soldiers – 50 Burundian and 50 Ugandan soldiers – were the advance team for 2,500 troops that would be deployed in phases and be stationed alongside Ethiopian troops. The aim was to relieve Ethiopian troops in the west and take control, in support of the Somali government, throughout south-central Somalia.

Persistent piracy

Despite the progress being made in the capital, piracy stemming from the Somali coast remained a threat to shipping, and attacks were reported in the Gulf of Aden, Arabian Sea and northern Indian Ocean. The number of Somali-originated incidents increased from 219 in 2010 to 236 in 2011; however, the number of successful hijackings decreased from 49 to 28. Ransoms cost the shipping industry about $160m in 2011.

Progress in combating piracy was attributed partly to a booklet on Best Management Practices for Protection against Somali Based Piracy (BMP4), produced by the shipping industry in August 2011, with the aim of helping ships to avoid, deter or delay attacks. In addition to the naval anti-piracy operations of many countries, many commercial vessels began to carry armed guards as they transited the area.

In March 2012, the EU agreed to expand its *Operation Atalanta*, allowing its military forces to attack targets on land as well as at sea. EU defence ministers agreed warships could target boats and fuel dumps. On 15 May, EU naval forces conducted their first raid near the port of Haradhere, a popular onshore pirate safe haven, and several fast-attack pirate boats were destroyed. In addition, during the London conference on Somalia, headway was made on anti-piracy law enforcement, allowing for transfer and prosecution of arrested pirates. The decision to set up a Regional Anti-Piracy Prosecutions Intelligence Coordination Centre, based in the Seychelles, would help to address the longstanding problem of prosecuting apprehended pirates.

Sudan and South Sudan: After the Split

In the year following the separation of Sudan and South Sudan, relations between the two states were strained. Fighting in three disputed border regions intensified, and disagreements over sharing of oil revenues prompted the South to suspend its exports of oil through production facilities located in the North. In April 2012, the unsettled status of borders and disputes over oil revenues led to direct confrontations between the two countries. Southern troops occupied the area of Heglig for ten days, leading to bombardment of the area by the Sudanese army. The escalation in hostilities prompted the UN Security Council to issue a resolution demanding an immediate end to the violence and the resumption of talks between the two sides.

Other long-standing problems continued to fester in Sudan: the signing of a Darfur peace agreement in July 2011 between the government and an umbrella organisation of rebel groups gave rise to hopes for the end of chronic fighting in the western region of the country. However, major factions refused to become party to the accord, instead announcing an alliance aimed at toppling President Omar al-Bashir. Khartoum also responded to a continuing rebellion in its periphery states by bombing towns and villages, prompting thousands to seek refuge in mountainous areas, and creating a growing humanitarian crisis.

In South Sudan, violence between tribal groups in the largest state of Jonglei and in the border regions caused an exodus of refugees into other areas of the country and into Ethiopia, and threatened to exacerbate the impact of drought.

North–South disputes within Sudan

In 2011, a referendum in favour of independence passed with 98% approval, leading to the independence of South Sudan in July of that year. The referendum was a key element of the Comprehensive Peace Agreement signed between the two states in 2005, which marked the end of a 23-year civil war that cost an estimated two million lives. Since the split, conflicts between Sudan's armed forces and rebel groups over territories along the border between the two states escalated. This was partly the result of the failure of the government in Khartoum to implement a key aspect of the agreement, which required the North to carry out 'popular consultations' in its border states of South Kordofan and Blue Nile following regional elections. Although elections did take place in May 2011, they were widely viewed as rigged and brought to power as governor of South Kordofan Ahmed Haroun, one of three Sudanese leaders indicted by the International Criminal Court for orchestrating crimes against humanity in Darfur.

As governor, Haroun suspended the consultation process, and violence flared. In June, Sudan's armed forces began aerial bombardment of villages in the Nuba Mountains of South Kordofan, similar to bombing campaigns during the 1990s which had resulted in the deaths of 200,000 civilians. While the government maintained that the raids were only on rebel military targets, aid workers accused Sudan of targeting civilians and directly blocking the provision of aid.

The main rebel group in the area, the South People's Liberation Army–North (SPLA-N), was part of a larger movement fighting for the South's independence during the civil war. South Sudan denied that it was supporting the SPLA-N. The group refused to disarm and said it would continue fighting for the independence of South Kordofan, Blue Nile and Unity states. In March, a spokesman for the UN High Commission for Refugees told journalists that refugees were crossing into South Sudan from Blue Nile state, fleeing bombardment and the threat of further violence. It was estimated that as many as 350,000 people had taken refuge in the Nuba Mountains, where malnutrition and starvation claimed thousands of lives. Aid agencies reported that the government of Sudan was continuing to block humanitarian aid to the affected areas. The UNHCR also estimated that tens of thousands of Sudanese refugees fled into neighbouring Ethiopia and South Sudan after fighting broke out. In response, the UN deployed 4,000 Ethiopian peacekeepers to the disputed territory of Abyei, but they were unable to contain the escalation in violence.

Oil confrontation
With border disagreements straining relations between North and South, disagreements over sharing of oil revenues added to tensions. While approximately two-thirds of the formerly united country's oil fields were located in the South, most processing and export facilities were located in the North. Prior to separation, Sudan exported 500,000 barrels of oil per day and split oil revenues nearly equally between authorities in the two areas. After independence, the North charged the landlocked South a 'transit fee' of about $32 per barrel to use its export and processing facilities. Exports continued for months despite the absence of an agreement on fees. But in December 2011, Sudan began to confiscate oil to meet unpaid fees. Calling the diversion of its oil 'blatant theft', the South Sudan government suspended production of oil, which accounted for 95% of its economy. China, which bought 5% of

its crude oil imports from both countries, urged the governments to reach agreement. In May, the World Bank warned that the continued suspension of oil would likely cripple South Sudan's struggling economy and place 'catastrophic pressure' on its currency. In March, a newspaper with close ties to the government reported that Bashir had warned his cabinet to 'expect the worst' in the dispute. This followed reports that military officers had warned him not to go to war due to challenges facing the army.

South Sudanese troops entered the disputed border town of Heglig on 10 April 2012. The area, home to the richest oil fields along the 1,800km border, accounted for nearly half of Sudan's oil output. Sudan labelled the seizure an 'act of aggression' and vowed to retake the town. The South accused the North of indiscriminately bombing the area. The AU adopted a seven-point plan intended to bring the two countries back to the negotiating table, and on 12 April the UN Security Council adopted a resolution based on the plan, which demanded a ceasefire within 48 hours and a 'complete, immediate, and unconditional' end to all fighting. South Sudanese troops withdrew from Heglig on 20 April and retreated to the Panakuac region. Military spokesmen from the South continued to report bombing of the border area despite the retreat. Khartoum said it would continue military operations against South Sudan's troops as long as they remained on its territory.

While the two governments remained deadlocked over oil, some progress was made in talks over border demarcation and movement of people between the two states. In April 2012 they signed framework agreements in Addis Ababa, the Ethiopian capital, to allow nationals of each state the rights to enjoy 'freedom of residence, freedom of movement, freedom to undertake economic activity, and freedom to acquire and dispose of property'. This followed negotiations facilitated by an AU High Level Implementation Panel led by former South African President Thabo Mbeki. It marked the first sign of progress over issues arising from the separation. At mid-2012, the parties were expected to finalise the details at a summit in the South Sudan capital Juba in the near future. The two sides also signed a framework agreement in Addis Ababa in February 2012 which activated a joint verification mission tasked with monitoring the border zone and reporting violations.

Sudan's Darfur hopes frustrated

Hopes for a resolution to the conflict in the western Darfur region grew in July 2011 with the signing of a peace agreement in Doha, Qatar, between the Sudanese government and the Liberty and Justice Movement, an umbrella group of various rebel organisations. This was the latest effort to end a conflict in which an estimated 300,000 people or more were killed and 2.7m driven from their homes since 2003. The new agreement established a Darfur Regional Authority tasked with holding a referendum on whether to keep the territory as a single unified region or divide it into smaller regions governed by the regional authority. It allowed the Sudanese president to appoint a vice-president from the Darfur region.

However, the agreement was weakened by the refusal of several rebel groups to sign it, including the Justice and Equality Movement (JEM) and factions of the Sudan Liberation Army led by Minni Minnawi and Abdel Wahid. Violence continued, with two UN peacekeepers killed in an ambush in October and 52 soldiers kidnapped in February 2012 by the JEM. The group released 49 UN–AU peacekeepers but continued to detain three Sudanese soldiers accompanying them. In December, the Sudanese army announced the killing of JEM leader, Khalil Ibrahim, during a shootout. It accused the rebel groups of continuing military operations, but residents said the Sudanese military was indiscriminately bombing villages and towns suspected of hosting rebels. In March 2012, a court sentenced to death six JEM members on charges including terrorism, illegally carrying arms, and murder. In March, the head of the Darfur regional authority, Al-Tijani al-Sisi, said that a referendum over the status of Darfur would be conducted within the next four months. It was also expected that a continuing severe drought would worsen the conflict, with food shortages set to exacerbate existing tensions.

South Sudan: Jonglei fighting

Fighting between rival Lou Nuer and Murle tribal groups within Jonglei threatened to destabilise the new country. Tit-for-tat attacks between the tribes, which have a long history of fighting over cattle, increasingly focused on population centres, with entire villages burned, women and children abducted and property looted. In August 2011, 58 bodies were found amidst burned huts in Bier county, Jonglei state. In March 2012, the state governor said that at least 233 people had been confirmed dead in the latest bout of cattle raids and revenge attacks. This followed the killing of hundreds of Murle in early January by a force of 6,000 mainly Lou Nuer fighters. The UN said some 350,000 people had been displaced as a result of inter-communal violence in 2011, and that 15,000 Lou Nuer had fled to western Ethiopia to escape the clashes.

UN Special Representative for South Sudan Hilde Johnson identified violence in Jonglei state as the first test of the new government's capacity to ensure security of civilians. President Salva Kiir launched a programme to disarm Jonglei civilians, sending 12,000 soldiers and police to collect an estimated 30,000 weapons, a process which the government estimated could take up to a year. The government accused the North of arming rival tribes, a charge denied by Khartoum. The area remained awash with small arms following the end of the civil war between the two states.

In March 2012, South Sudan's cabinet announced an emergency meeting to discuss further challenges, including an expected food shortage. According to the Agriculture Ministry, crop production fell by 70% in 2011 as a result of below-normal and poorly distributed rainfall. Food shortages were particularly acute in other conflict-affected states. The shortage in South Sudan was linked to the wider drought sweeping across the region. According to the World Food Programme, the number of people facing shortages in South Sudan would rise from 3.3 to 4.7m in 2012 as a result of poor harvests.

A year after its birth, South Sudan's independence had failed to provide a lasting solution to disputes with its Northern neighbour. A looming humanitarian crisis within the border states, coupled with continued deadlock over oil-sharing revenues, threatened to add further pressures to an already volatile political arena.

South and East Africa: Political Wrangling

Zimbabwe: fractious politics

In the year to mid-2012 Zimbabwe's fractious Government of National Unity (GNU) limped on, with ever widening divisions between the Zimbabwe African National Union–Popular Front (ZANU-PF) and its two partners – the two wings of the Movement for Democratic Change (MDC) – in the coalition. There were repeated calls from hardliners in all three parties to end the three-year-old GNU. Each party was aware, however, that a unilateral exit from the coalition would almost certainly result in a loss of regional and international standing for whichever party chose this course. Timelines for the planned constitutional referendum and the next general election dominated political discourse. The death in mysterious circumstances of former army chief Solomon Mujuru did little to calm mounting anxieties.

Contentious drafting process
In late 2010, the Constitutional Select Committee of parliament (COPAC) had been established as a multiparty forum to drive the production of a draft

constitution. Paul Mangwana (ZANU-PF) and Douglas Mwonzora (MDC-Tsvangirai) were appointed co-chairs, and Edward Mkhosi (MDC-Ncube) deputy chair. COPAC spearheaded nationwide public consultations, in which more than a million Zimbabweans participated. However, many meetings were marred by inter-party violence and a number had to be cancelled. With the bulk of consultations concluded, COPAC faced pressure from the government to deliver a draft constitution as soon as possible. Deadlines came and went, and it became increasingly clear that clear that 2012, not 2011 was a more realistic target year for the referendum.

Pressure from the military added to the tensions within COPAC. In February 2012, Mangwana was summoned by army chief General Constantine Chiwenga for an update on the process. This followed the dismissal by the co-chairs of Brigadier Douglas Nyikayaramba as a technical adviser to COPAC.

Contentious issues in the drafting included presidential powers and term limits; separation of powers between the executive and the legislature; whether or not there should be a prime ministerial post as well as a presidency; devolution; legalisation of homosexual rights; and whether or not the Zimbabwean diaspora should be allowed to vote. ZANU-PF, the party of President Robert Mugabe, pressed for strong presidential powers while the MDC argued for reduced powers, devolution and the diaspora vote. Hardline critics such as former ZANU-PF Information Minister Jonathan Moyo dismissed the entire process as irrelevant and pushed for early elections. Meanwhile, Lovemore Madhuku, head of the National Constitutional Assembly which had successfully campaigned for a 'no' vote in a 2000 referendum on a previous draft constitution, insisted that the current process was not people-driven and should be shunned. Although Mugabe and ZANU-PF pressured COPAC to deliver a draft constitution immediately, senior ZANU-PF and military figures rejected a draft presented in a workshop by Mangwana.

The 88-year-old Mugabe insisted that elections must be held in 2012, with or without a referendum, while the MDC and South African mediators said they could only be held after a referendum, and favoured polls in 2013. Under the existing constitution, Mugabe as president could dissolve parliament and call for immediate elections, but it remained to be seen whether he would play this card. Finance Minister Tendai Biti (MDC-T) said the government had no funds for elections. Nor was there complete support even within ZANU-PF for elections in 2012, as many MPs feared losing their seats.

Casting a shadow over these political processes was the behaviour of the Joint Operational Command, which brings together the heads of the army, air force, intelligence and prisons. After Police Chief Augustine Chihuri and Brigadier Nyikayaramba stated publicly in 2011 that the military would not allow anyone other than Mugabe to be in power, in 2012 Mugabe renewed the contracts of all the service chiefs, despite opposition from the MDC.

As they did in 2008, the security forces prepared for the elections as a military operation. Senior military commanders were deployed to Zimbabwe's provinces, with some soldiers billeted at schools. The decade-old alliance between the military, the ZANU-PF Youth League and the War Veterans was augmented by a wider alliance which included many of Zimbabwe's traditional chiefs and church leaders. Targeted intimidation and attacks on the opposition continued both in rural areas and in Harare, Mutare and other towns. In Mbare township in Harare, the Chipangano criminal gang, a ZANU-PF militia, attacked MDC supporters and took control of the lucrative 'flea market' bazaar in the heart of the township. But the military did not confine itself to the opposition; following infighting within ZANU-PF, more than 50 senior military personnel met in Mutare in April 2012, reportedly to establish a roadmap for the military to rebuild ZANU-PF party structures. A number of military men reportedly wanted to stand in the elections – a possibility that alarmed many within ZANU-PF as it recalled 2008, when the military seized control of both the party and the country.

Factionalism

Mugabe's ZANU-PF continued to be riven by factionalism. On 15 August 2011 the charred body of Solomon Mujuru, former head of the Zimbabwe Defence Forces and husband of Vice-President Joice Mujuru, was found in his farmhouse 30 miles outside Harare. The bizarre circumstances of his death, and his political prominence, led to speculation that he had been murdered by political or military rivals. For more than a decade Mujuru had been a political fixer and the power behind the rise of his wife to the vice-presidency – she was thought to be a future candidate for the presidency. The Mujurus were bitter rivals of Defence Minister Emmerson Mnangagwa, who was reported to have his own presidential ambitions. With contradictory findings from police and independent forensic reports, there was mounting speculation that Mujuru had been murdered as a result of his outspokenness, and also to foil his wife's ambitions.

In December 2010 disclosures by the WikiLeaks website had exposed links between the US government and the MDC and its leader, Prime Minister

Morgan Tsvangirai. But the MDC had the last laugh; a further tranche of US diplomatic cables released by WikiLeaks in September–October 2011 showed that senior ZANU-PF officials including Vice-President Mujuru, Jonathan Moyo and others had had meetings with the Americans in which they spoke about the crisis within ZANU-PF and the need for Mugabe to step down. Although ZANU-PF dismissed the revelations in public, the disclosures added to the intense factionalism engulfing the party. A number of factors contributed to disharmony: uncertainties about the health of Mugabe, who frequently visited Singapore for medical check-ups; fears of electoral defeat; the Mnangagwa–Mujuru rivalry; and the emergence of a younger group known as 'Generation 40' under Indigenisation Minister Saviour Kasukuwere.

In March–April 2012, district council elections were the catalyst for a wave of intra-ZANU-PF violence. So serious was the situation that the party politburo convened an extraordinary meeting at which Mugabe was ratified as the party's candidate for elections and it was agreed that party protocols on seniority would be followed regarding succession. This was seen as a rebuke to Mnangagwa, who was some way behind Mujuru and others in party seniority.

South Africa, as the regional facilitator, said it would not allow elections in Zimbabwe without the referendum and the resolution of outstanding issues in the agreement which had created the GNU. This led to increasingly acerbic relations and calls from Harare for replacement of President Jacob Zuma as a mediator – a contrast with the cosy relations between ZANU-PF and Thabo Mbeki, Zuma's predecessor as president and mediator. At mid-2012, Zimbabwe's future hung in the balance.

South Africa: ANC under pressure

Although the ruling African National Congress (ANC) remained the dominant force in South Africa, celebrations in 2012 to mark its centennial could not hide internal anxieties and growing dissatisfaction with the party among both its own faithful and the electorate. Although the economy had recovered to show steady growth since the 2008 recession, unemployment remained a major problem at around 35%. In municipal elections in 2011, the opposition Democratic Alliance (DA) party increased its share of the vote from 17% to 25%.

The ANC, founded in 1912 in Bloemfontein (now Mangaung), is Africa's oldest liberation movement. The protracted struggle against racism and for liberation in South Africa and the region remains highly emotive and the sacrifices which were made continue to provide enormous empathy for the ANC among a majority of South Africans. Among its achievements since taking power in 1994 were: racial reconciliation; a constitution enshrining civil, social and legal rights; free primary and intermediate education; and social welfare grants lifting many of the most vulnerable out of destitution. Since becoming president in 2009, Zuma steered a pragmatic course and resisted populist economic policies.

However, in December 2012 the ANC faced a rigorous test *at party elections* to be held in Mangaung. The party's grassroots would have their say, and no position could be viewed as safe – as former President Thabo Mbeki discovered at the 2007 Polokwane elections, where he was voted out as ANC leader. Urban poverty had increased and perennial strikes in the health and education sectors reflected increasing dissatisfaction among professionals. Corruption remained a major concern, and opposition critics accused the ANC of blurring the boundaries between party and state. As if this were not enough, the battle between Zuma and Julius Malema, the firebrand leader of the ANC Youth League, underscored tensions. The ANC's partnership with the Youth League had been a major element of the party's success, but seemed under intense stress ahead of the Mangaung meeting.

In November 2011 the party suspended Malema, who had played a key role in Zuma's election as party leader. Malema had since achieved notoriety for his militancy and outspokenness and for challenging the ANC hierarchy. He was tolerated for a time, but throughout 2010 and 2011 he continued to criticise Zuma. In addition, his relationship with ZANU-PF undermined the ANC's posture as a neutral mediator on Zimbabwe. Worse still, his call for the ANC to send commando teams into Botswana to remove what he called the 'puppet regime' of Ian Khama proved too much. The ANC found Malema and four other Youth League leaders guilty of bringing the party into disrepute, sowing divisions within the party and propagating racism. Malema was suspended from party membership for five years and removed as Youth League leader. However, the Youth League refused to accept the verdict and insisted that Malema would remain its leader.

There were also fears that the South African Police leadership was being politicised and drawn into the ANC's increasingly bitter internal power struggles. Although statistics indicated that levels of violent crime decreased by 3% in 2011, there were concerns about police competence. In October 2011 Bheki Cele was suspended as chief of police after being implicated in a corruption investigation. In February 2012 Richard Mdludli, head of the Crime Intelligence Unit, was suspended after being charged for murder.

South Africa had mixed success internationally in the year to mid-2012. Its UN Security Council vote for Resolution 1973, authorising intervention in Libya, was heavily criticised by ANC hardliners. The subsequent NATO military venture led to bitter diplomatic fallout. The AU's diplomatic mission to broker peace between Muammar Gadhafi and the rebels had failed and Zuma's espousal of Gadhafi as a 'brother leader' drew criticism from the Libyan people. South Africa's initial reluctance to recognise the National Transitional Council led to a rift with Nigeria and other African states which accepted the new realities in Libya. South Africa's bid for leadership of the African Union stalled: in elections for AU Commission chair in Addis Ababa in January 2012, there was deadlock between incumbent Jean Ping of Gabon and South African challenger Nkosazana Dlamini-Zuma. Ping won a narrow victory after three rounds of voting, but failed to achieve the necessary two-thirds majority to win outright. AU leaders agreed Ping would stay on temporarily.

While the ANC continued to be under pressure to 'fix' the Zimbabwe problem, it was able to record some achievements: South Africa was invited to join the BRIC group of emerging nations, and also hosted a UN climate change conference in Durban at which it was agreed to reach a global deal on carbon emissions by 2015.

Malawi: death of a president

The dominant political event in Malawi was the death on 5 April 2012 of President Bingu wa Mutharika, who died of heart failure at the age of 78 after eight years in office. The accession of Joyce Banda as acting president changed Malawi's political landscape and looked likely to have a regional impact belying the country's small size.

Mutharika had been a key proponent of investing in Africa's agriculture as a continent-wide development strategy. He won international praise for his programme of state subsidies to small-scale farmers, especially women. There were improvements in irrigation, and private–public sector partnerships in agriculture. Malawi initiated an innovative system of food vouchers for peasant farmers and discounts for maize seed.

However, the last years of his rule were overshadowed by increasing authoritarianism. In mid-2011, food and fuel price increases, 36% unemployment and hikes in the cost of living precipitated nationwide protests. These protests, particularly in the cities of Lilongwe, Karaonga and Mzuzu, led to a police and army crackdown in which dozens of civilians were killed and hundreds arrested. The repression led to a falling out between Mutharika and Western donors, who demanded a return to democracy as a precondition for renewed aid. The IMF also insisted on fiscal reform as the price for new loans. Mutharika, emboldened by his growing friendship with Mugabe, denounced Western conditionality and imperialism and insisted that Malawi did not need Western support and would find supportive friends in Asia.

There had been a history of disagreements between Banda and Mutharika, not least over Mutharika's desire to anoint his brother Peter as his successor. Within days of her accession as acting president, Banda set Malawi on a course towards renewed democracy. Hardline Mutharika loyalists, including Foreign Minister Peter Mutharika, were purged, as was former first lady Callista Mutharika, who was removed from her position as co-ordinator of the Safe Motherhood Initiative. A number of human-rights activists were brought into the new 'reconciliation' cabinet. In a landmark decision in May 2012, Banda announced that the ban on homosexuality would be removed from Malawian law.

Banda requested that Sudan's President Bashir not attend the July 2012 AU Summit in Lilongwe, as he was subject to an arrest warrant from the International Criminal Court. Banda's request ran counter to the AU consensus on non-cooperation with the ICC: Malawi was one of the few African countries which supported the ICC stance. On a visit to Liberia, Banda joined President Sirleaf in stating that Africa would have a new generation of leaders, many of whom would be women.

Although most Malawians appeared to welcome the ascent of the more liberal Banda, she needed to tread carefully ahead of the 2014 presidential elections. The military played a key role in ensuring a democratic succession, refusing to countenance the imposition of Peter Mutharika. But it was unclear whether Banda would be able to manage tensions within the government. In addition, the military contained many Mutharika loyalists. Hardline critics accused Banda of being too pro-Western and of wanting to return Malawi to aid dependency. Nevertheless, as Africa's second female head of state and as a liberal, Banda was challenging the old order of leaders in the region. Malawi looked to be one of the most watched countries for the rest of the decade.

Democratic Republic of the Congo: no election surprise

Incumbent Joseph Kabila won the December 2011 presidential elections with 49% of the vote, beating his nearest rival Etienne Tshisekedi, who received 32%. The opposition and EU and Carter Center observers decried what they said were serious irregularities in the poll. Voting was marked by violence, pre-marked voting papers, missing voter lists and other discrepancies. However, while noting the flaws, the AU and other African and developing-world monitors declared the election to be broadly successful.

A week later, Tshisekedi declared himself president and had himself sworn in by party loyalists at his headquarters in Kinshasa. But if he was hoping to repeat the success of Alessane Ouattara in Côte d'Ivoire a year earlier, he was to be disappointed. Tshisekedi's gambit found no takers, and Kabila was recognised as the winner by the Supreme Court. Although there were clashes between supporters of the two candidates, there was much less violence than after the 2006 elections.

The security situation in the eastern Congo continued to be of concern; in late 2011 and into 2012, there were a series of army mutinies. Soldiers who had been integrated into the national army from the former rebel group National Congress for the Defence of the People (CNDP) defected from their army units and engaged in battles with the army in Nord-Kivu province. By April 2012 more than 10,000 civilians had fled their homes after attacks by the new rebel forces, who formed a new military group known as the March 23 Movement, allegedly led by former CNDP Chief of Staff General Bosco Ntaganda. It was unclear to what extent the movement was a threat to the national forces, but eastern Congo remained an area where militia groups held sway. Peace in the eastern Congo seemed set to remain elusive.

Kenya: towards elections

Throughout 2011 and into 2012 political dynamics in Kenya centred on the elections due in early 2013. Kenya's November 2011 military intervention in Somalia also attracted a great deal of attention and highlighted the country's desire to establish itself as a regional power.

The run-up to the general elections was likely to be tense, in light of the violence that followed the previous elections in 2007, after which a new con-stitution was adopted. Setting a date for the vote was highly contentious, with President Mwai Kibaki preferring a 2013 date but Prime Minister Raila Odinga demanding a 2012 vote. Kibaki announced that he would not contest the elections, after serving two terms. In theory, this left Odinga as the front runner, but this was far from assured. With his Orange Democratic Party riven by infighting, a breakaway wing ODM-Kenya emerged, led by Vice-President Kalonzo Musyoka. This split followed rumours that a 'G7' political pact had been agreed between political grandees allied against Odinga, sup-posedly including long-time Odinga rivals Deputy Prime Minister Uhuru Kenyatta, former Education Minister William Ruto and Assistant Minister

Aden Dualle. Opinion polls throughout 2011 showed both the ODM and the ODM-Kenya parties losing popularity as a plethora of potential presidential candidates emerged. Meanwhile, the pre-electoral political coalitions that Kenyan parties have traditionally formed were barred under the newly adopted Kenya Parties Bill.

In January 2012 the ICC served indictments on Kenyatta and Ruto, as well as former Cabinet Secretary Francis Muthaura and radio executive Joshua Arap Sang. All faced charges of crimes against humanity for their alleged roles in inciting the violence which followed the 2007 elections. All denied the charges, and Kenyatta and Ruto insisted they would contest the 2013 elections – Kenyan law does not prohibit those facing charges from running for office. However, it remained to be seen whether their parties and ethnic constituencies would continue to support their presidential aspirations. Kenyatta was a leading figure among the Kikuyu, while Ruto was a senior figure among the Kalenjin. The issue was complex because both men were expected to play major roles in pre-electoral peace building to allay fears of a military rearmament and possible renewed conflict between the tribes ahead of the elections.

In October 2011 the Kenya Defence Forces launched *Operation Linda Nchi* (Protect the Country) against the al-Qaeda-linked al-Shabaab guerrilla group in Somalia (see above, pp. 282–7). The invasion of Somalia's Juba Valley was a response to repeated predations by al-Shabaab and other militant groups along the Kenya–Somalia border. A spate of kidnappings of tourists along Kenya's coast, and fears that militants were mingling with Somali refugees in border camps, forced Kenya to intervene. Although the operation was launched without prior regional or international consultations, there was broad public support for it amongst the Kenyan public. In March 2012, the Kenyan forces were formally incorporated into the 9,000-strong AMISOM force, which was due to expand to nearly 18,000 personnel under its UN mandate. It was unclear, however, how long the Kenyan forces would remain in Somalia and there were concerns about whether there was an exit strategy. What was clear, though, was that Kenya had staked its claim to join Uganda, Rwanda and the DRC as a regional military power.

Uganda: where's Kony?

Although incumbent President Yoweri Museveni had won the 2011 elections with 68% of the vote, his position appeared to be eroded somewhat during the year to mid-2012. Protests against rising inflation, fuel-price increases and unemployment were crushed by the police and military, leaving about

36 people dead and scores arrested. The crackdown targeted journalists and opposition media, with some newspapers temporarily closed. There were continued strikes over pay by teachers, taxi drivers and academics.

The question of presidential term limits was highly contentious. The opposition's call for term limits was opposed by Museveni's ruling National Resistance Movement (NRM). But within the NRM itself, the big question was whether Museveni, president since 1986, would seek to hand-pick a successor. The issue was divisive within the party, with Justice Minister General Kahinda Otafiire calling it 'impossible and incredible' that Museveni could choose his replacement.

Uganda's war against the Lord's Resistance Army (LRA) came vividly to international attention in 2012. The LRA, which had fought the Ugandan military and terrorised civilians in northern Uganda for nearly two decades, was driven out of the north after a military offensive in 2005. Its leader Joseph Kony and remnants of the group dispersed across central Africa and the LRA was considered finished as an effective fighting force. Since then, however, there had been LRA depredations in South Sudan and the DRC. In March 2012 the American NGO Invisible Children released the 'Kony 2012' video, which rapidly garnered more than 100 million views on the Internet. The video showed his past activities and called for his capture, putting pressure on the governments of Uganda and other countries. In October 2011, US President Barack Obama sent about 100 troops to help Uganda deal with the LRA. In May 2012 Ugandan forces announced the capture of Caesar Acellam, a top LRA field commander, but Kony remained at large.

The impact of 'Kony 2012' was extraordinary in that it provided millions in the West with an unusual glimpse of events on a continent which is insufficiently known or understood in the outside world. That glimpse was undoubtedly unrepresentative of trends across Africa, where many countries had experienced marked economic and political progress. Yet the events of the year to mid-2012, including coups, protests and violence, revealed the chronic obstacles that threaten further advances.

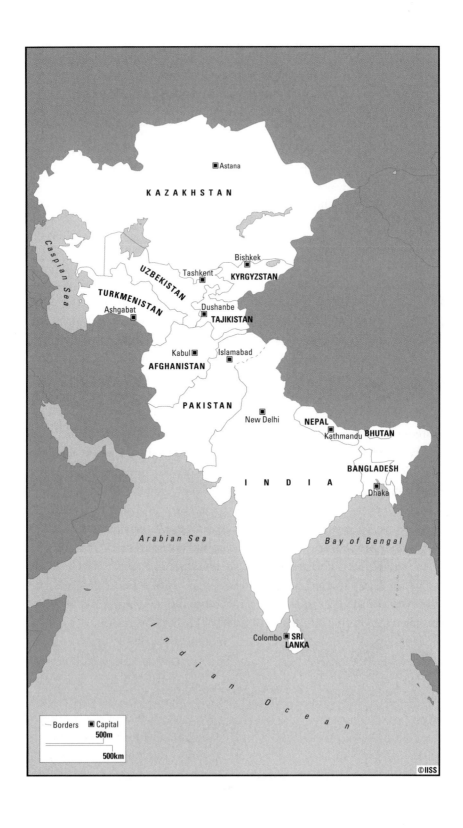

Astana

KAZAKHSTAN

Caspian Sea

Bishkek

Tashkent

UZBEKISTAN

KYRGYZSTAN

TURKMENISTAN

Dushanbe

Ashgabat

TAJIKISTAN

Kabul

Islamabad

AFGHANISTAN

PAKISTAN

New Delhi

NEPAL

Kathmandu

BHUTAN

BANGLADESH

I N D I A

Dhaka

Arabian Sea

Bay of Bengal

Indian Ocean

Colombo **SRI LANKA**

Borders ■ Capital
500m
500km

©IISS

Chapter 8
South Asia and Afghanistan

India: Policy Inertia

India went through another troubled year in 2011–12, although its internal security situation improved and its external strategic options expanded. The primary problem was the economy, which lost much of its momentum while the government struggled to cope with the challenges of operating as a fractious coalition. The result was a widespread perception of policy paralysis.

The Congress Party, which leads the coalition, lost ground in key state elections. But the principal opposition party, the Bharatiya Janata Party (BJP), did little better. The country therefore faced the prospect that general elections due in May 2014 could deliver a fragmented mandate and make it difficult to form a stable government.

The Congress Party lost elections for state legislatures in Punjab and Goa, and was virtually wiped out by a breakaway formation in several by-elections in Andhra Pradesh, the largest state in South India, which had until recently been considered a Congress bastion. Victories in the small states of Uttaranchal and Manipur were little compensation. But the big shock for the party came in a poor showing in elections to the legislative assembly of the largest state, Uttar Pradesh; it won just 28 seats in a house of 403. The campaign had been led by Rahul Gandhi, putative heir to the party leadership, and the setback put paid to any immediate plans of giving him a more prominent role in either the party or the government. Indeed, he was scarcely to be seen in the subsequent weeks, in parliament or elsewhere.

The opposition BJP did only slightly better, in the elections and after-wards. The party was caught in a succession battle when, at its national executive meeting, there were attempts to present the long-serving Gujarat chief minister Narendra Modi, a controversial figure because of his alleged role in anti-Muslim riots in 2002, as a future party leader, and perhaps as its prime ministerial candidate in the 2014 elections. Some senior party leaders showed their unhappiness by staying away from meetings. The party's most important ally, which runs the government in the state of Bihar, was openly critical, and even broke ranks to support the Congress candidate for election as India's president, a largely ceremonial post.

The July 2012 presidential election, which former Finance Minister Pranab Mukherjee, a Congress stalwart, was expected to win, saw coalition alliances becoming fluid. One member party of the ruling coalition refused to endorse Mukherjee, while some of the parties sitting on the fence supported him. The parties of the left were split down the middle. The campaign appeared to be a portent of what might happen if the 2014 general elections failed to deliver a clear mandate to one coalition or the other, and added to the uncertainty about the future.

Improving internal security

The country's internal security situation continued to improve in the year to mid-2012. Whether it was the disputed state of Jammu & Kashmir, the troubled states of the hilly northeastern part of the country, or the Maoist Naxalite insurgency in the forested heartland, the situation was noticeably better, as measured by the number of incidents and casualties, compared to previous years. Several leading Maoists had been killed or captured in recent years, perhaps a result of better intelligence, inter-state coordination and enhanced preparedness and communications. The Kashmir Valley was quiet after the turbulent summer of 2010, though there was some tension after the centuries-old shrine of a Sufi saint was burnt down in an accidental fire. Infiltration from the Pakistani side of the Line of Control that divides Kashmir was at its lowest level for many years. This changed atmosphere encouraged tourism in the summer to climb to record levels – over two million, according to some counts. Notwithstanding the improved conditions, a report commissioned by the central government to explore solutions to the state's issues and to engage with all shades of opinion was greeted in May 2012 with disappointment because it stopped short of suggesting specific political solutions and recommended further committee work. The worry in some circles was that unrest might erupt again if the present period of quiet was not used to work towards long-term solutions.

P. Chidambaram remained active as home minister, setting up a new security architecture he had developed after taking charge following the terrorist attack on Mumbai in 2008. The National Intelligence Grid was set up to link databases for actionable intelligence, to combat terrorism and internal security threats. Also up and running was the National Investigation Agency, to tackle the most important terrorist cases. But a National Centre for Counter-Terrorism (loosely based on a US model) ran into stiff opposition from state governments that felt their police powers were being encroached upon.

Internationally, India found itself in an unusual position: being courted by the United States with zeal. Washington signalled that India figured prominently in its calculations for the 'rebalancing' of its force posture towards Asia. US Secretary of Defense Leon Panetta, visiting New Delhi, offered a new element that India had wanted: joint development of weapon systems. 'We must move beyond a focus on individual arms sales to regular cooperation that increases the quantity and quality of our defence trade', Panetta said. Washington was also moving to reform export controls that had stood in the way of weapons transfers to India. India has joint projects with Russia for developing fifth-generation strike aircraft and the *Brahmos* cruise missile, and with Israel for advanced versions of the ship-borne *Barak* surface-to-air missile system. Panetta's announcement marked the rapid emergence of the United States as India's main supplier of defence equipment. Although a prize order for 126 fighter aircraft went to France's Dassault, leaving US manufacturers bitterly disappointed, India has ordered over $8 billion worth of US military hardware, with more purchases in the pipeline.

India cautiously welcomed the American embrace. New Delhi has traditionally anchored its foreign policy in its search for 'strategic autonomy' – avoiding being seen as belonging in a particular camp. In particular, India was alert to how China viewed the developing relationship with the United States, and was anxious not to project it as a containment strategy aimed at China. Given the history of military conflict over a disputed border, and China's superior defence capabilities, the last thing New Delhi wanted was to provoke Beijing into striking a hostile attitude. Beijing had noticeably hardened its posture in border-settlement talks when the Indo-US nuclear accord was being worked through during the second term of the George W. Bush administration. However, the many benefits to India of closer engagement with the United States were obvious, and diplomats in New

Delhi worked hard to broaden engagement through the strategic dialogue between the two countries.

Meanwhile, a vital diplomatic breakthrough came in June 2012 with Saudi Arabia's decision, prodded by the United States, to hand over to India a key suspect in the planning and supervision of the Mumbai attacks. This signalled a new level of engagement on security matters with the traditionally pro-Pakistan Saudi regime. Relations also improved in the immediate neighbourhood, with Bangladesh and post-reform Myanmar, which Prime Minister Manmohan Singh visited in September 2011 and May 2012 respectively.

Another hopeful sign was Pakistan's announcement that India would obtain 'most–favoured-nation' trading status by the end of 2012. However, negotiations on how to disengage militarily along the Saltoro Ridge, which is occupied by Indian forces and overlooks the Siachen Glacier, went nowhere as the two countries restated established positions. An expected agreement on a more liberal visa regime came unstuck at the last minute. Though some Indian visitors to Pakistan sensed a change in the country's civilian mood, including within the government, and a growing realisation of the futility of continued hostility between the two countries, this had yet to find reflection in a change of posture by the Pakistani army. Opinion polls conducted by Pew Research showed that 59% of Pakistanis still saw their greatest threat coming from India, with the Taliban coming in second at 23%.

A more delicate dance was meanwhile under way with China, both a strategic rival and a vast market. A two-pronged policy vis-à-vis Beijing continued, with India seeking greater engagement and at the same time moving to prevent Chinese dominance in the region and to avoid conflict over the long-running border dispute. Bilateral trade continued to flourish, with China (including Hong Kong) becoming India's largest trade partner. But there was growing concern about the 2:1 imbalance between Indian imports and exports, and about Chinese dominance of key sectors such as power-generation equipment. New Delhi was reconsidering a proposal, rejected two years earlier, to impose customs duty on imports of such equipment, with pressure mounting from domestic suppliers who had surplus capacity. Some Chinese companies seemed to have decided to set up factories in India, to increase localisation and reduce the risk that they would be excluded.

Perhaps reflecting its view that India was not a strategic challenger, China came out with a studied response to the test launch in April 2012 of the *Agni* V long-range, nuclear-capable missile. A Foreign Ministry spokesman in Beijing said India and China were not competitors but partners. State television added that it was a historic moment for India, but that the rocket (which can reach Beijing and Shanghai) was no threat to China. Four Indian naval ships called at Shanghai in June as part of a tour that included port calls in Vietnam and the Philippines, both of which have disputes with China in the South China Sea, and also in South Korea and Japan. The Indian navy opened a new base in the Lakshadweep Islands, off India's southern tip and in the middle of the busy sea lanes from the Persian Gulf to the Malacca Strait.

The message from the naval outreach into East Asia and other developments in West and Central Asia was that India wished to extend its area of influence beyond its immediate, South Asian neighbourhood. A proposed 1,680km-long gas pipeline from Turkmenistan via Afghanistan and Pakistan came a step closer to reality when the countries involved signed a gas-sale agreement in May. The $7.6bn 'peace pipeline', running through a troubled region, was slated to begin delivering gas in 2018. In Kyrgyzstan in June 2012, India unveiled its new 'Connect Central Asia' policy to bolster political and economic engagement with the region. Separately, India was pushing to revive a 12-year-old proposal for an International North–South Corridor for cargo transportation that would run from Russia to India and improve Indian access to the energy-rich Central Asian nations, using the Iranian port of Bandar Abbas. Indian companies were looking to exploit large iron-ore and other mineral resources in Afghanistan, proposing to ship them out via an Indian-financed railway line to the Iranian port of Chahbahar and from there to ports on India's west coast. What these plans made clear was that India was not about to abandon Iran because of Western pressure; the country was far too important in strategic terms – a fact that US officials seemed to understand and agree with privately. Some observers likened these moves, mimicking existing Chinese inroads into Central Asia, to a new Great Game – a jockeying for influence and access to vast natural resources to feed two hungry, rapidly growing economies.

Economic inertia

Many of the worries about Chinese dominance flowed from India's relative economic under-performance: the two economies were of roughly the same size when China embarked on its modernisation programme in the late 1970s, but by 2012 China's economy had become four times the size of India's. Over the year to mid-2012, poor handling of the economy and the failure to push through essential economic reforms became strategic liabilities for India. Economic growth declined to 6.5% in the year to March 2012, down from 8.4% in each of the previous two years. With growth in industrial production averaging no more than 2.8% through the financial year, and flat or falling towards the end of the year, exports lost all momentum. In a country that perennially suffers from shortages of electricity, power stations were shutting down or reducing generation for want of gas and coal, due to insufficient domestic investment and higher import costs. A delayed start to the 2012 monsoon cast a cloud over agricultural prospects as well, even as water shortages began to be seen in both towns and villages, capping a summer of discontent. The financial year 2012–13 thus promised to be another difficult one, especially since consumer-price inflation remained stubbornly high at over 10%. Some observers began to talk of 'stagflation' which, though seeming inappropriate for one of the world's fastest-growing economies, expressed frustrations with economic management.

The yawning trade deficit (a record 4% of GDP, taking into account trade in both goods and services) led to a loss of confidence in the rupee, which fell against the dollar by some 25% over 12 months. The stock market saw a 20% fall during calendar 2011. Business confidence was low, and the legislative, policy and other roadblocks in the way of virtually all projects – even after two decades of economic reform – meant that the production of capital goods plummeted.

It did not help that, at the end of 2011, the government first announced and then partially rolled back the opening up of the retail sector to foreign investment. In March 2012, it also presented to parliament a reformist budget for the railways, but changed its essential elements in a matter of days, accompanied by drama over a change of railway minister. The government attracted international criticism for pushing through retrospective changes in tax law that opened up a series of cases involving international companies including Vodafone, the communications group. Long-delayed action on correcting diesel and other fuel prices was pushed back even further after a hike in petrol prices sparked strong reactions, raising the prospect of a spike in petroleum subsidies that could damage budget plans for the second year in a row. Meanwhile, a third cabinet minister resigned in the wake of corruption charges.

Negative sentiment on India's prospects found voice in the rating agencies, as Standard & Poor's and then Fitch changed the country's outlook from stable to negative. S&P warned that India could become the first BRIC country to lose its investment-grade rating. The government brushed aside such criticism as undeserved, but it reflected the general mood in business circles. In June 2012, Prime Minister Singh, a former reformist finance minister, assumed direct charge of the finance ministry from Mukherjee, giving himself a chance to redeem his government's and his personal reputation. However, many of the issues that needed urgent attention were hostage to opposition from coalition partners or to parliament, where the ruling coalition lacked a majority in the upper house. The Congress Party was itself divided between those who would give priority to rapid growth and others who favoured ambitious social-welfare programmes with the objective of making growth 'inclusive'. Experts noted that, with the central fiscal deficit hovering between 5% and 6% of GDP (with state budgets having a further deficit of about 2.5% of GDP), the government's ability to spend on new welfare commitments that the Congress Party would like to make (expanded nationwide distribution of heavily subsidised grain, and universal health care) was severely constrained.

The longer-term question was about the sustainability of economic growth in an uncertain global environment. Even at 6.5% annual GDP growth, India would remain among the fastest-growing large economies. Some observers reckoned that, in the current environment, the sustainable, non-inflationary growth rate was no more than 7.5%, well short of the 9.5% reached in the middle years of the last decade, but equal to what had been achieved in the four years since the onset of the financial crisis in 2008. However, the government was chary of admitting to such relatively modest targets, and the Planning Commission was expected to set a five-year target of 8–8.5% annual growth, linked somewhat unrealistically to ambitious reform measures. However, independent economists forecast the year to March 2013 to show growth of 6–6.5%, or even lower.

Failure to sustain reasonably rapid growth and employment, at a time of high inflation, held the potential to spark discontent in a predominantly young workforce, dent India's image as a rising economic power, reduce the capacity to spend on defence when a major re-armament programme was under way, and hinder the ability to project the country's power and reach beyond the confines of its immediate neighbourhood. More importantly, it threatened to create scope for China to assert its dominance over the entire region, and to hem India in both economically and strategically.

However, with only one annual budget to be presented to parliament before elections in 2014, the government faced the familiar temptation to hand out pre-election inducements in the hope of winning votes. This was risky given the size of the deficit and of public debt, which at about 70% of GDP, was more than twice the average for developing economies.

Renewing defence

The modernisation of defence forces, long neglected or mismanaged, gathered momentum in the year to mid-2012. Procurement decisions began to accelerate after a leaked letter from the outgoing army chief to the prime minister listed large gaps in the country's defence as a consequence of delays in equipment purchases. Consistent with the pattern of recent years, the navy set the pace. In a speech at the IISS in London, navy chief Admiral Nirmal Kumar Verma stated that 47 ships and submarines were on order, of which 44 were from Indian shipyards. A re-fitted 45,000-tonne aircraft carrier supplied by Russia began sea trials and was expected to become the navy's second operational carrier by the end of 2012. Russia also provided an *Akula*-class nuclear attack submarine on a ten-year lease. With the indigenously built SSBN *Arihant* undergoing sea trials, the navy was poised to complete the nuclear triad with a retaliatory-strike capability that would as the navy chief said, provide India's nuclear insurance 'from the sea'. The navy planned to have at least two fully operational and combat-worthy carriers available at any given time.

Helicopters seemed set to move to the front rank in new purchase decisions, with a planned acquisition for all three services that seemed to total as many as 1,000, including Russian Mi-17s, Boeing's heavy-lift *Chinooks* and *Apache Longbow* attack helicopters, and large numbers of utility and combat helicopters to be built domestically. Acquisitions approved during the year to mid-2012 included a $660 million contract for light howitzers that could be airlifted to mountainous areas such as the border with China. But perhaps the most ambitious modernisation programme related to re-shaping the infantry, with new body armour, weapons, communications and hand-held target-acquisition devices, under the F-INSAS (Futuristic Infantry Soldier as a System) programme. More than 450 infantry and paramilitary battalions were expected to be so equipped by 2020, the date most frequently mentioned for completing the transformation and immediate expansion of the armed forces. Four new infantry divisions were being created, two of them as part of a mountain strike corps in case of conflict with China. New airstrips were operational in remote and mountainous Ladakh and the northeast. Tank squadrons were being modernised and expanded, while the artillery was to benefit from the new howitzer order.

One effect of the modernisation programme was that India looked likely to retain its newfound status as the world's largest arms importer. However, even though defence spending had grown, it remained under 2% of GDP, and was much smaller than China's defence budget. The changes reflected the fact that Pakistan had receded as a threat, with that country withdraw-ing many troops from the Kashmir Line of Control (where a nine-year-old ceasefire still held), and no longer presented a strong conventional threat to India. The long-term strategic threat was seen in New Delhi as coming from a resurgent China, and it was for this reason that the rapidly developing strategic relationship with the United States had become a vital factor.

Pakistan: Internal and External Friction

Tensions between the military, the civilian leadership and the judiciary in Pakistan sharpened in the year to mid-2012, leading to political turmoil and fears of military intervention in domestic politics yet again. At the same time, the country faced a dire economic situation and an energy crisis, with crip-pling power cuts in major cities. While the army and paramilitary fought against jihadist militants, violence continued in the largest city, Karachi. Relations with the United States deteriorated, while those with Afghanistan remained troubled.

Despite this catalogue of problems, Yousuf Raza Gilani in February 2012 became Pakistan's longest-serving prime minister. In June, however, he was replaced after a ruling by Supreme Court Chief Justice Iftikhar Chaudhry dis-qualified him as a member of parliament and consequently as prime minister.

The security situation improved in most parts of the country, with a decrease in the number of extremist and terror attacks nationwide. Another positive sign was that the peace process with India continued, and there were encouraging prospects with regard to trade liberalisation.

Political issues
The killing of al-Qaeda leader Osama bin Laden in Pakistan by US special forces in May 2011 had been a major blow to the Pakistani army. The American raid on a house in Pakistan's military heartland, close to its main army training academy, had gone undetected – and so apparently had bin Laden's presence in the area. The army faced unprecedented public criticism at home, while internationally it was seen as either complicit or incompetent regarding bin Laden's whereabouts for the previous several years.

The raid led directly to the 'Memogate' affair, which in turn led to the resignation of Hussain Haqqani, Pakistan's ambassador to the United States. Although details were murky, Haqqani was reported to have dictated a memorandum to Mansoor Ijaz, an American businessman of Pakistani origin, indicating that the army wanted to bring down the government. The memo was allegedly written, with the aim of obtaining US assistance, at the behest of President Asif Ali Zardari. It was passed by Ijaz indirectly to Admiral Mike Mullen, chairman of the Joint Chiefs of Staff, in October 2011. Ijaz described the series of events, without naming Haqqani, in a column in the *Financial Times*.

The army reacted angrily to Ijaz's disclosure of the memo. It denied that it had intended to overthrow the civilian government and alleged a 'conspiracy' against the army. References to the army and Inter-Services Intelligence (ISI) chiefs as 'bad boys' in communication between Ijaz and Haqqani did not help. A subsequent judicial commission concluded in June that there was no evidence that Zardari had either authorised the preparation of the memo or directed that it be sent to the US administration. It determined that Haqqani had prepared the memo and had led Ijaz to believe that it had the authority of Zardari. It remained unclear whether Washington had ever taken any action in response.

The affair accentuated the deep fissures between the army and the civilian government. Gilani said publicly, in reference to the ISI, that 'there can't be a state within the state. They have to be answerable to this parliament.' Early the following month, when army chief General Ashfaq Parvez Kayani was in China, Gilani criticised the army for making unconstitutional and illegal depositions to the Supreme Court on the Ijaz memo without seeking prior government approval. The military responded that Gilani's accusations had 'serious ramifications with potentially grievous consequences for the country'.

In January 2012, Gilani dismissed Defence Secretary Naeem Khalid Lodhi, a former army officer, for 'gross misconduct and illegal action' for directly submitting the army and ISI chiefs' deposition on the memo to the Supreme Court. The same day, the commander of the Rawalpindi-based 111 Brigade of X Corps was unexpectedly replaced. This sparked intense media speculation, as this unit had spearheaded military coups in the past. Yet both the government and the army attempted to play down any aspect of confrontation. In March, ISI Director-General Lieutenant-General Ahmed Shuja Pasha retired and was succeeded by Lieutenant-General Zaheerul Islam, a former Karachi corps commander. Meanwhile, the National Assembly passed an unprecedented resolution calling on the government to legislate for a comprehensive framework law to regulate the role and functioning of the intelligence and security agencies.

In January, an activist Supreme Court led by Chief Justice Chaudhry reopened the hearing of a 20-year-old petition filed by retired Air Marshal Asghar Khan alleging that the ISI had rigged the 1990 general elections by bankrolling the creation of the Islami Jamhoori Ittehad (IJI), a right-wing political coalition, to prevent the Pakistan People's Party (PPP) – then led by Benazir Bhutto, Zardari's wife – from winning the elections. The following month the Supreme Court ordered seven men from Baluchistan, held for more than a year and a half by intelligence services in connection with terror attacks, to be brought to court. Chaudhry also accused the paramilitary Frontier Corps of involvement in the disappearance of a third of all the missing persons in the country's restive southwest province. He had himself previously been a centre of controversy when he was suspended in 2007 by President Pervez Musharraf, a decision that prompted unrest and hastened Musharraf's own departure. Chaudhry was reinstated in 2009 by Gilani.

In February, the Supreme Court announced that it would press contempt charges against Gilani for failing to reopen a $10 million corruption case against Zardari. The case had been dropped after Musharraf's October 2007 National Reconciliation Ordinance had granted amnesty to politicians accused of various crimes. Gilani had refused since 2009 – when the ordinance had been declared unconstitutional – to write a letter to the Swiss government regarding an investigation into the president's finances in the 1990s on the basis that Zardari had immunity as head of state. Although the government tried its best to delay proceedings, on 26 April the Supreme Court found Gilani guilty of contempt of court, but gave him only a token jail term of barely 30 seconds in the courtroom. On 19 June, however, Chaudhry ruled that, as a convict, Gilani was to be disqualified as a member of parliament and consequently as prime minister. Neither Zardari nor the weakened PPP-led coalition government challenged the decision, and Gilani resigned. A subsequent Supreme Court ruling suggested that his successor as prime minister, Raja Pervez Ashraf, would face a similar predicament over the reopening of corruption charges against Zardari.

This triangular political struggle helped the rise of Imran Khan, a former cricket star, and his Tehreek-e-Insaf (Movement of Justice) Party. Surprisingly large popular rallies took place in support of Khan due largely to an anti-incumbency posture among the middle class. He attracted high-profile defectors from other parties, such as the PPP's former Foreign Minister Shah Mahmood Qureshi. But it was not clear whether he would be able to build on the political momentum he had created in time for the next general elections, due to be held by February 2013.

The economic situation was particularly gloomy. Growth estimates for 2012 were reduced to 3.2% from 3.7%, with a spiralling budget deficit, 10% inflation, diminished aid flows and vastly reduced foreign investment. Manufacturing industries were suffering from energy shortages, which led to riots in the streets. In an election year, the 2012/13 budget proposed a hike in ad hoc relief allowance for government employees and pensioners for the fifth consecutive year, without imposing any new tax. Yet Pakistan's remittances from abroad were at a high of $13bn and it paid back a $1.2bn instalment to the International Monetary Fund.

Security environment

The security situation improved in most parts of Pakistan, although a high tempo of violence was maintained in the tribal areas, Khyber Pakhtunkhwa and Karachi, and to a lesser degree in Baluchistan. This was largely a result of action by the security forces against the leadership of the main terror group, the Tehrik-e-Taliban Pakistan (TTP) or Pakistan Taliban. The total number of extremist and terror attacks declined, as did the number of suicide attacks.

The military and paramilitary presence in Swat helped keep order. Some 150,000 regular soldiers – nearly a third of the army – were deployed in northwest Pakistan, with extended tours of duty that put them under stress. Significant operations were carried out in February 2012 in the Kurram Agency and in May in Miranshah, North Waziristan. The latter took place after an army convoy was ambushed and nine soldiers were killed by the TTP. Some civilians were forced to leave their homes, but the operation was limited to Miranshah and did not spread further.

Pakistan's largest city Karachi was described by the Human Rights Commission of Pakistan as being 'deeply fractured' and in the grip of 'linguistic, ethnic and sectarian polarisation'. Nearly 660 people were killed in violent attacks in Karachi in July and August 2011, stoked by the main political parties with representation in the federal government. Local authorities were helpless when on 15 April about a hundred TTP militants staged the country's largest prison break in Bannu in Khyber Pakhtunkhwa, freeing over 380 inmates. Unrest also continued in Baluchistan with ethnic or sectarian killings. The deadliest attack on 20 September saw 26 Shia pilgrims killed by a group of gunmen.

In October, a disparate alliance of 40 religious parties and extremist groups banded together as the Difa-e-Pakistan (Defence of Pakistan) Council (DPC) in a bid to capitalise politically on rising nationalism and discontent within the country. This brought together extremist groups and former army officers including the Jamaat-ud-Dawa (JuD), the Jamaat-e-Islami Party and the anti-Shia Sipah-e-Sahaba. While the DPC's rhetoric tapped into latent anti-Indian sentiment, its defining trait remained anti-American. According to a Pew opinion poll, about three-quarters of Pakistanis considered the US an enemy.

The DPC provided several opportunities for JuD chief Hafiz Saeed, the alleged planner and coordinator of the 2008 Mumbai terror attacks and founder of the banned Lashkar-e-Taiba (LeT) terror group, to address public rallies in an inflammatory tone. The United States announced a $10m reward for the capture or any information leading to Saeed's capture. Yet he was able to appear in public and to mock this bounty as the government sought proof of the allegations against him.

Mutual mistrust

US–Pakistan relations became severely strained following the US raid against bin Laden. A truck bomb in Afghanistan's Wardak province in September that injured 77 American soldiers was blamed on the Pakistan-based Haqqani terror network, as was an attack on the US Embassy and NATO headquarters in Kabul three days later. On 22 September, Mullen, on the point of retiring as chairman of the Joint Chiefs, accused the Haqqani network of acting 'as a veritable arm of Pakistan's Inter-Services Intelligence agency'. Mullen had been a key interlocutor between the Pakistan military and the US administration. While his statement was not endorsed by the White House, it led to greater scrutiny of Pakistan's ties to the Haqqani group and its safe havens in the North Waziristan region of Pakistan's tribal areas. While the Pakistani military leadership acknowledged that the ISI had contacts with the Haqqani group, it denied support or endorsement of it.

The relationship worsened with a US air attack on 26 November on a Pakistani border post at Salala in the Mohmand Agency that killed 24 Pakistani soldiers. The incident, in which US forces attacked what were perceived as Taliban insurgents along Pakistan's border with Afghanistan, lasted several hours. A Pentagon inquiry concluded that the strike was accidental, citing an 'overarching lack of trust' between the US and Pakistan, with US forces only informing Pakistan of the 'general location of the raid'. Pakistan rejected the US report. Its own account stated that the strike was 'unprovoked' and 'deliberate at some level'. Even after being informed of the mistake, US forces 'continued firing with impunity'.

In response to the attack, Pakistan ordered the evacuation of US military and intelligence personnel from the Shamsi air base in Baluchistan, the operating base for US drone strikes in the tribal areas – which were already criticised in Pakistan as counter-productive, illegal and a violation of national sovereignty. Drone attacks ceased for nearly two months, but resumed in early 2012. Several key al-Qaeda and Afghan Taliban militants were killed.

Pakistan also closed down two supply routes for NATO forces in Afghanistan, via Torkham in Khyber Pakhtunkhwa and Chaman in Baluchistan. These were being used for non-lethal military supplies, including 80% of NATO's equipment and 40% of its fuel requirements. The effect was to triple the Alliance's transport costs, requiring an additional $100m a month. Pakistan also refused to attend the second Bonn International Conference on Afghanistan in early December.

Pakistan's parliamentary Committee on National Security was tasked with formulating guidelines for revised terms of engagement with the United States and NATO. After four months, it recommended an immediate cessation of drone attacks inside Pakistan, cessation of infiltration into Pakistan on any pretext including hot pursuit, and denial of access to Pakistani territory and air space for the transport of arms and ammunition to Afghanistan.

Zardari was invited to attend NATO's Chicago summit in May in the expectation that a deal on the supply routes could be made. But no agreement was reached, as Pakistan sought $5,000 per truck transiting its territory instead of the previous rate of $250. An expected meeting between Zardari and US President Barack Obama did not take place. Drone strikes continued, and while the United States expressed its 'deepest regrets' and 'condolences' for the Salala strike, it refused to issue a formal apology. Relations were further strained when a Pakistani doctor was sentenced to 33 years in prison for helping the United States find bin Laden.

Meanwhile Washington, angered over bin Laden's previous presence in Pakistan, suspended $800m in military aid, which accounted for one-third of annual US security aid to the country. Although the US State Department requested Congress to approve $2.4bn for Pakistan for fiscal 2013 to meet economic requirements, the Senate Appropriations subcommittee on foreign aid voted to approve only $1bn. Amidst these fundamental differences, US–Pakistan military ties were hampered. Only in late March 2012 did General James Mattis, the US regional commander, and General John Allen, NATO commander in Afghanistan, visit Pakistan and meet Kayani.

Afghan positioning

Pakistan's relationship with Afghanistan appeared to be one of strategic ambiguity in preparation for the withdrawal of NATO combat forces by the end of 2014. On the one hand, Pakistan sought a stable and peaceful Afghanistan without any reference to a 'friendly' government in Kabul. It agreed that an Afghan-led and Afghan-owned reconciliation process was vital for reaching an intra-Afghan political settlement. It was also apparently not interested in Taliban control of Afghanistan or the creation of a Taliban mini-state in Afghanistan or any fragmentation of the country.

On the other hand, Pakistan wanted Afghan Pashtuns to be appropriately represented in the Kabul government and especially in the army. It continued to provide safe havens and training grounds to the Afghan Taliban and other insurgents, and did not attempt to put pressure on the Haqqani network, with which it was reported to have close links. Pakistan also made clear that it could not bring the Taliban to the negotiating table. In exasperation at Pakistan's attitude on safe havens, US Secretary of Defense Leon Panetta, visiting Kabul in June 2012, stated that 'we are reaching the limits of our patience here and for that reason it is extremely important that Pakistan take action'.

Pakistan's role with regard to Afghan insurgent groups was obscure. It emerged that Islamabad had facilitated contact between the US government and the Haqqani network. But it prevented the Taliban from talking directly to the Afghan government. The September 2011 murder of former Afghan President Burhanuddin Rabbani, who was responsible for government negotiations with the Taliban, was alleged to have been carried out at the behest of the Pakistani security establishment. In late June, Pakistan protested a cross-border attack allegedly by TTP militants based in Afghanistan that killed 17 soldiers in Upper Dir, Khyber Pakhtunkhwa province.

Indian thaw

On her first official visit to India in July 2011, Pakistani Foreign Minister Hina Rabbani Khar stressed that the peace dialogue between the two countries should be 'uninterrupted and uninterruptible' and expressed keenness to normalise trade relations; annual bilateral trade was a meagre $2.7bn. In line with this goal, on 2 November the Pakistani cabinet unexpectedly agreed to grant India most-favoured-nation (MFN) status without any link to the Kashmir dispute, reciprocating India's 1996 decision. Instead of trade limited to items on a 'positive list', there was instead to be a small 'negative list', allowing commerce in about 90% of goods compared with only 17% earlier. This was to be phased out by the end of 2012 to complete the process of normalisation of trade. The Pakistani army appeared supportive of the move.

There was, however, little progress on other aspects of the peace dialogue. After 140 Pakistani soldiers and civilians were killed in an avalanche in the Gayari sector of the Siachen Glacier on 7 April, Kayani called for the long-running Siachen conflict to be resolved. Yet, at a subsequent meeting, both countries held firmly to their traditional positions, with no sign of compromise. Pakistan sought immediate demilitarisation of the glacier by both sides, while India sought three sequential prerequisites of authentication, delineation and demarcation of respective troop positions on the Saltoro Ridge along the 110km-long Actual Ground Position Line (AGPL). Pakistan opposed this on the grounds that it would 'legitimise' India's position on the glacier. At the same time, there was little progress on the trial in Pakistan of seven alleged co-conspirators in the 2008 Mumbai terror attack or of cooperation on counter-terrorism. There was no serious attempt to start high-level military-to-military contacts or to begin a formal India–Pakistan dialogue on stability in Afghanistan during the withdrawal of NATO combat forces. Yet, in an encouraging sign, Prime Minister Singh accepted Zardari's invitation on 8 April to visit Pakistan at a 'mutually convenient date', a shift from his earlier position that such a visit would only take place after substantive outputs on the peace process had been realised. Overall, the dominant concern in Pakistan remained the lack of effective governance and decision-making on key domestic issues including countering extremism and terrorism, ending urban violence, tackling economic problems and ending power shortages. By June 2012, with a new prime minister in a tenuous position vis-à-vis the Supreme Court, Pakistan seemed to be in a transitional mode as it headed towards general elections.

Afghanistan: State's Weakness Threatens Transition

A planned transition of responsibility for security from NATO-led troops to Afghanistan's security forces continued over the year to mid-2012. But the military campaign against the Taliban insurgency made little progress, as did efforts to end the conflict through negotiation. The country remained mired in political disputes and official corruption.

In November 2010, NATO leaders and President Hamid Karzai agreed that Afghan authorities would take the lead for security throughout the country by the end of 2014. By that time, all NATO combat troops would have left. After 2014, it was intended to form a new US-led force for a training and counter-terrorism mission.

The period was marked by a series of incidents involving US military personnel that inflamed Afghan public opinion. In January 2012, a video showing US marines abusing the bodies of dead Taliban fighters caused an outcry across the country. Even greater outrage was triggered by news a month later that US soldiers at Bagram air base had disposed of copies of the Koran seized from prisoners by burning them. This triggered a week of deadly rioting. In March a US Army sergeant, Robert Bales, was charged with murdering 17 Afghan civilians in the Panjwayi district of Kandahar during a night-time rampage.

There were also several incidents where Afghan personnel turned their weapons on foreign troops. Since 2007 more than 80 NATO soldiers have been killed in this way, and incidents in 2012 resulted in the deaths of American, British and French soldiers.

Transition arrangements
At mid-2012, 75% of the Afghan population was living in districts where Afghan forces were responsible for security, and the transfer of remaining districts was due to take place by mid-2013. At that point Afghans would take the lead in all combat operations, with the NATO-led International Security Assistance Force (ISAF) adopting a supporting and advisory role.

Several of the countries contributing a total of up to 140,000 troops during 2011 announced plans to reduce them as the deadline approached. The United States was steadily drawing down its forces from a peak of about 100,000. France would pull most of its troops out by the end of 2012, and the Netherlands and Canada had already withdrawn combat troops. Australia said most of its soldiers would leave by the end of 2013.

The transition plan depended crucially on the capacity of the Afghan National Security Forces (ANSF). The army had almost reached its target strength of 195,000 and the police strength was 149,000, close to the 157,000 target. However, it was agreed at a NATO Summit in Chicago in May 2012 that the combined total should be reduced to 228,500, with an estimated annual budget of $4.1 billion, so that financing could be more sustainable. With Karzai promising to supply $500m annually, Washington sought promises from allies to cover a further $1.3bn.

The reduction forced NATO's training mission to shift efforts from increasing the size of the ANSF to building support and logistical capabilities while improving leadership and management. NATO and Afghan initiatives, including an improved force rotation and leave schedule, sought with some success to reduce attrition and absentee rates.

By April 2012, 40% of military operations were led by the ANSF and only 10% were executed by ISAF units without ANSF partners. Operations by the Afghan National Army (ANA) in Helmand province, for example, were conducted with little ISAF assistance. ISAF's assessment was that, of 168 battalions, the number characterised as 'effective with advisers' had increased from 101 to 138. However, police training made less progress, with capability development at least two years behind that of the ANA.

To cover the intended US military presence after 2014, the US government proposed a new Status of Forces Agreement. Washington's plan was to retain control of the largest military bases and use them to train Afghan forces. By mid-2012, this had not been agreed.

There were two main contentious issues: control of Afghan detainees, and night-time raids carried out by ISAF on suspected Taliban leaders. Karzai argued that Afghan prisoners should not be in the hands of foreigners, and that the United States should hand over all detention facilities to the Afghan government. In March 2012, it was agreed as a first step that the detention centre at Bagram air base, the largest in Afghanistan, would be handed over to Afghan control but that the United States would have a veto on prisoner releases.

The use of night raids and house searches by NATO special forces was seen by American commanders as an effective tool in fighting the Taliban. Afghans, however, saw them as a gross intrusion into private family life, and as causing unnecessary damage and loss of life. In an effort to resolve this, it was agreed that Afghan troops would take the lead in future operations, and that Afghan soldiers would be the only ones entering homes.

The successful outcome of these negotiations meant an Afghan–US Strategic Partnership Agreement could be signed in Kabul by Obama and Karzai. The agreement was intended to reassure Afghanistan's ruling elite that the United States would remain committed to the country after 2014, and to counter Taliban propaganda that insurgents would be able to march into Kabul after US combat operations ceased.

Slow military progress

Southern and eastern Afghanistan remained ISAF's main areas of operation. It appeared that efforts to clear and hold populated areas, particularly in

Helmand and Kandahar provinces, had led to some improvement in security. ISAF continued offensive operations elsewhere, including in Kunduz and Balkh provinces.

ISAF claimed to have 'broken and reversed Taliban momentum', an assertion supported by a 9% reduction in insurgent attacks on ISAF in 2011 compared to 2010, the first such reduction for some years. There was also a modest fall in US, NATO and ANSF casualties compared with the previous year. However, UN figures showed 2011 was the worst year for civilian deaths, with more than 3,000 fatalities, despite NATO efforts to limit artillery, missile and air-strikes. The UN blamed the insurgents for the majority of deaths, especially their use of improvised explosive devices (IEDs).

Although UN statistics showed an increase in complex and 'spectacular' attacks, they also suggested that insurgent groups were less successful in areas where there was a high density of NATO and Afghan forces. NATO spokesmen claimed that this demonstrated not only the tactical success of clearance operations, but also the impact of attacks on insurgent leaders. This, they said, had resulted in a significant reduction in the Taliban's motivation and competence. An unusually harsh winter also reduced insurgent activity.

However, there was a significant increase in attacks in eastern Afghanistan. US Defense Secretary Leon Panetta told Congress that 'the topography, the cultural geography and the continuing presence of safe havens in Pakistan gave the insurgents advantages in eastern Afghanistan that they have lost elsewhere in the country'. Insurgents also launched a series of attacks on high-profile targets in Kabul, including the Intercontinental Hotel in June 2011, the British Council in August and the US Embassy and ISAF headquarters in April 2012. There were similar attacks outside Kabul, including in Uruzgan province, Kandahar city and Jalalabad. Though these were defeated by the ANSF with assistance from ISAF, they sought to reinforce claims of an inevitable insurgent victory after 2014. Afghan forces and NATO responded by increasing 'layered defences' around Kabul, which the Afghan authorities claimed had thwarted hundreds of attempted attacks on the city.

Insurgent efforts to assassinate Afghan security and government officials had some notable successes, especially in Kandahar where several senior officials were killed. In addition, two influential figures close to Karzai were assassinated in July 2011: Jan Muhammad Khan (his special adviser) and Ahmed Wali Karzai (his half-brother and an important Pashtun power-broker).

Dealing with the Taliban

Slow progress in the military campaign gave impetus to Afghan and American efforts to engage Taliban groups in talks on a negotiated settlement. However, little progress was made.

The first reliable reports of face-to-face meetings between the Taliban and US officials were made public in May 2011. These indicated that mid-level employees of the US State Department and the CIA had met with Tayyab Agha, the former secretary of Taliban leader Mullah Omar. The first meeting had taken place in Qatar in January 2011, followed by subsequent meetings in Germany and again in Doha. By June then-Secretary of Defense Robert Gates confirmed that talks were taking place but added a note of caution, stating that they could only be successful if the Taliban were placed under such military pressure that negotiations could be seen as a positive alternative to fighting. Even if this happened, he added, it could be months before any progress was made. Secretary of State Hillary Clinton labelled this strategy 'fight, build and talk'. The depth of the US commitment to negotiations as a central plank of their post-2015 strategy was shown when Clinton confirmed that America had opened discussions not only with the Taliban but also with the Pakistan-based Haqqani network, one of the most effective insurgent groups operating in Afghanistan.

The United States also explored ways to increase incentives for both organisations to take part in negotiations. This included an agreement from the UN Security Council to lift sanctions on certain former Taliban personnel. The sanctions, imposed in 1999, banned 144 people from travelling abroad or opening bank accounts. In July 2011, the US, UK and Afghan governments successfully proposed that 14 names would be removed from the list, as an indication to the Taliban that the international community both backed the negotiations and was willing to assist former fighters who chose to lay down their arms. A second initiative was proposed by the Taliban to test the US commitment to negotiations. It proposed that Washington release five 'high-level' detainees from the US military prison at Guantanamo Bay, Cuba. Amongst the five was reported to be Mohammed Fazl, a senior Taliban commander who had allegedly been responsible for ordering the murder of thousands of Afghan Shi'ites between 1998 and 2001. These plans, unsurprisingly, caused concern both in the American Congress and amongst Afghanistan's ruling elite. Arguments against such a deal stopped the Guantánamo prisoners being transferred to Afghanistan. Instead, the United States embarked on a 'strategic release' programme in Afghanistan, quietly setting free a number of detainees from Parwan prison at Bagram in a covert operation that did not trigger the ire of Congress in Washington or allies in Kabul.

The Afghan government's approach to negotiations with the Taliban was mercurial. In June 2011, as negotiations began, Massoum Stanekzai, a minister with responsibility for reconciliation, described talks between the government and the insurgency as 'systematic', adding: 'Peace is a process not a deal. Overall I think we can be cautiously optimistic.' However, Stanekzai narrowly escaped death on 20 September 2011 when an emissary apparently sent from the Taliban to negotiate turned out to be a suicide bomber. Former President Burhanuddin Rabbani, head of the Afghan High Peace Council, was killed. The assassination of the government's lead negotiator mobilised those within the ruling elite who had long been opposed to the process, and forced Karzai to suspend the process. He said: 'Their messengers are coming and killing. So with whom should we make peace? I cannot find Mullah Mohammad Omar, where is he? I cannot find the Taliban council. Where is it?'

However, on his release from hospital in November, Stanekzai pushed for the resumption of negotiations with additional conditions. By December, the government had issued an 11-point memo that laid down terms for restarting talks. These included accepting the opening of a Taliban liaison office in Qatar, the right of the government to agree to other countries' involvement in talks and the demand that Pakistan back the talks. Karzai visited Islamabad in February 2012 to encourage Pakistani agreement. While there he also gained the approval of Maulana Samiul Haq, so-called 'father of the Taliban', in whose seminary a number of Taliban leaders had studied. Haq called the talks a 'noble cause'. A further breakthrough occurred in May 2012 when Salahuddin Rabbani was appointed to take over from his father as head of the Afghan High Peace Council, in an attempt to entice the ex-Northern Alliance groups into the peace process.

With the Afghan and US governments increasingly committed to negotiations with the insurgents, the attitude of Pakistan and the Taliban remained uncertain. Pakistan, although publicly supportive, was reportedly worried that successful negotiations would allow the Taliban to gain independence from its paymasters in Islamabad. The government pointedly refused to give explicit backing to the talks in Qatar. Reports suggested that when it became public that Tayyeb Agha was leading the negotiations with the US, authorities surrounded his family home in Pakistan. This led to Karzai, in a theatrical gesture, promising senior members of the Taliban and their families protection from the Pakistani government in Afghanistan if they engaged in serious negotiations.

The Taliban had always demanded the complete withdrawal of US forces from Afghanistan as a prerequisite for talks. However, Mullah Omar issued an Eid message in August 2011 confirming that talks had indeed been started with the Americans and raised the possibility of the organisation entering into some form of power sharing in Kabul. This was seen as a strong message to those fighting in his name that negotiations were under way and could possibly result in a settlement. The Taliban agreed in January 2012 to open an office in Qatar as the main conduit for talks.

However, confirmation of the talks brought both confusion and opposition from fighters and mid-level Taliban commanders. NATO air strikes had killed veteran Taliban field commanders, who were replaced by younger and more hard-line leaders. A series of interviews carried out by a US government Special Operations Task Force with 4,000 suspected Taliban detainees held in Afghanistan's prisons indicated that the rank and file were bullish about their ability to retake power once US forces had left. This implied that NATO's tactics had been effective in removing a number of commanders but had done little to break the Taliban's will or convince them of the need to negotiate with either the Americans or the government in Kabul. This view was confirmed in a February CNN interview with Zabiullah Mujahid, a Taliban spokesman. Mujahid confirmed negotiations with the US in Qatar but said the Taliban would never open talks with the 'puppet' Karzai government. The Taliban then suspended talks with the United States in the wake of the murder of 17 Afghan civilians in Panjwayi in March, for which an American soldier was charged. In May Arsala Rahmani, a member of the High Peace Council, was murdered. Rahmani had been a deputy minister of education in the Taliban government, and was then imprisoned but released in 2005. The Karzai government used him as an informal conduit to the Taliban as he was one of the 14 people removed from the UN sanctions list. His assassination cast further doubt on the Taliban's commitment to peace talks.

Unstable politics, endemic corruption

Beyond the insurgency, democratic politics in Afghanistan added to the instability of the country. Long-running arguments surrounded the aftermath of the September 2010 parliamentary elections and plans for the 2014 presidential elections. The uncertainty surrounding both highlighted the continued weakness of institutional authority and the lack of agreed procedures for regulating elections. If left unsolved, these problems would become increasingly troublesome over the next three years as the country was due to have provincial council elections in 2013, presidential elections in 2014 and parliamentary elections in 2015.

The outcome of the 2010 parliamentary elections indicated the potential of the coming ballots to destabilise Afghanistan in the midst of NATO troop withdrawal. Afghanistan's Independent Electoral Commission rejected 1.3m of 5.6m ballots cast and disqualified 21 of 249 successful candidates. However, Karzai, worried that the ruling would threaten his base amongst the country's Pashtuns, set up a special court to re-examine the results. The impasse this caused created a bitter rift between the legislature and the president and forced Karzai to rule by decree because parliament refused to pass any law or authorise the president's choice of cabinet members.

In June 2011, the special court, unrecognised by either the Independent Electoral Commission or the international community, ruled that 62 members of parliament needed to be replaced. Parliamentarians refused to recognise the legitimacy of the ruling and by August Karzai was forced to back down. This allowed the electoral commission to announce a compromise ruling that excluded only nine members of parliament, rather than the 21 they had initially named. Those excluded were chosen from across the country, with two coming from Herat province and one each from Paktika, Badakhshan, Baghlan, Samangan, Helmand, Faryab and Zabul.

The chaotic aftermath of the 2010 elections gave rise to fears that the presidential elections scheduled for 2014 might destabilise the country to such an extent that the timetable for troop withdrawals could be put in danger. However, the electoral commission refused to countenance a delay and published a list of reforms it wanted by the polling date. These included an improved system for voter registration and for post-election assessment of possible fraud. However, for the changes to become law they would have to pass through parliament, a number of whose members were still disputing the commission's ruling on the 2010 elections.

Karzai, constitutionally barred from running for a third term, repeatedly stated that he had no ambitions to stay in power. However, the diplomatic community in Kabul was worried that, citing security concerns, he might seek to extend his term for another two years – a move that would not only be unconstitutional but would cause renewed conflict amongst the ruling elite.

Corruption posed the greatest threat to the coherence of the country's nascent state institutions. Far from diminishing, the problem continued to grow. The UN Office on Drugs and Crime found in July 2011 that ordinary Afghans were paying twice as much in bribes each year as they had two years previously. Khan Afzal Hadawal, deputy governor of the Bank of Afghanistan, estimated that $8bn was smuggled out of the country in 2011, in addition to $4.5bn which was overtly flown out of Kabul airport. It was estimated that $1bn of the $8bn donated to Afghan reconstruction over the previous eight years had been lost to corruption. It was clear that Afghanistan's ruling elite, from the president downwards, had little or no commitment to reducing official corruption. In November 2011, central bank governor Abdul Qadir Fitrat fled the country claiming his life had been threatened because of his investigations into high-level corruption. In December, Drago Kos, head of the international commission monitoring corruption in Afghanistan, threatened to resign, citing the indifference of Karzai to pervasive corruption.

The problem was shown in sharp focus in the collapse of Kabul Bank and the government's failure to prosecute anyone over this. Before 2010, the bank was seen as one of Afghanistan's post-2001 success stories. Sherkhan Farnood and Khalilullah Ferozi, respectively chairman and chief executive, ingratiated themselves with Karzai by bankrolling his re-election campaign in 2009. In return the government gave the bank responsibility for paying the wages of civil servants, soldiers and the police, with the result that 430,000 government employees had accounts with it. Meanwhile the bank was making large unsecured loans to numerous senior members of the political establishment without any formal paperwork. Things came to a head when it gave Mahmoud Karzai, brother of the president, and Abdul Haseen Fahim, brother of vice president General Muhammad Qasim Fahim, multi-million dollar loans to buy a stake in the bank. When this was revealed, it caused a run on the bank's deposits, bringing it to the verge of collapse. The government took over the bank and found that $910m was unaccounted for.

Given the political influence of the bank's major debtors, criminal proceedings against the chairman and chief executive stalled. Attempts to recover the missing money raised only $150m. Faced with a prime example of Afghanistan's culture of impunity, the International Monetary Fund refused to lend the country more money until the government developed a robust plan for prosecuting Kabul Bank's senior staff and funding its bailout through increased taxation. The IMF's refusal to lend money stopped the flow of Western aid, raising the possibility of bankruptcy. It took 18 months for the government to convince the IMF that it had sustainable plans to deal with Kabul Bank and could thus be in receipt of further international funds. However, there remained profound doubts that the ruling elite could develop a commitment to good governance.

At mid-2012, the Afghan state remained weak, riddled with corruption and vulnerable to interference by Pakistan. There was no clear evidence that this state of affairs would not continue as the 2014 transition approached.

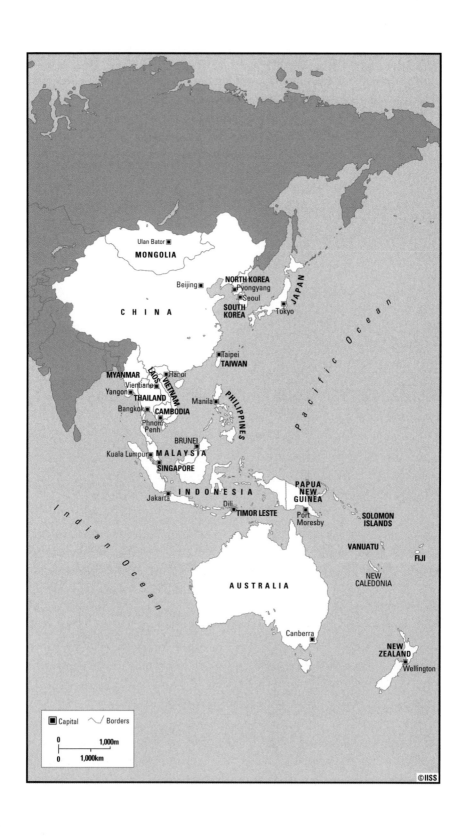

MONGOLIA

Ulan Bator ■

Beijing ■

CHINA

NORTH KOREA
Pyongyang ■
■ Seoul
SOUTH
KOREA

JAPAN

Tokyo ■

Taipei ■
TAIWAN

MYANMAR
LAOS
Vientiane ■ VIETNAM ■ Hanoi
Yangon ■
THAILAND
Bangkok ■ ■ CAMBODIA
Phnom
Penh ■

Manila ■

PHILIPPINES

BRUNEI ■

Kuala Lumpur ■ MALAYSIA
■ SINGAPORE

INDONESIA

Jakarta ■
Dili ■
TIMOR LESTE

PAPUA
NEW
GUINEA
Port ■
Moresby

SOLOMON
ISLANDS

VANUATU

FIJI ■

NEW
CALEDONIA

AUSTRALIA

Canberra ■

NEW
ZEALAND
■ Wellington

Pacific Ocean

Indian Ocean

■ Capital   ⁀ Borders

0   1,000m

0   1,000km

©IISS

Chapter 9

Asia-Pacific

China: Domestic Crisis, Foreign Progress

As Chinese power continued to grow over the past year according to several measures, nations in the Asia-Pacific and beyond increasingly worried whether China would rise peacefully, but also looked to Beijing to contribute more actively to global governance. China's internal problems, however, remained daunting. Chinese citizens stepped up demands that their leaders more staunchly defend their country's interests around the world as well as address grievances at home. Chinese leaders sought to cope with these rising internal and external expectations as they set in motion a major leadership transition that will unfold at the 18th Party Congress in autumn 2012.

The scandal that erupted in March was the biggest political crisis to face the Chinese leadership in decades. Political intrigue centred on Politburo member Bo Xilai, Chongqing's Communist Party secretary and scion of one of the country's revolutionary founding fathers. The affair was sparked when Bo's police chief, Wang Lijun, sought political asylum at the US consulate in Chengdu on 6 February. Four days previously, the government of Chongqing had announced that Wang had been transferred to a non-police role, reinforcing rumours that he had fallen out with Bo. As more details emerged, it became clear that Wang held vital evidence that implicated Bo's wife, Gu Kailai, and associates in the murder of British businessman Neil Heywood on 14 November 2011, and that Bo and the Chongqing government may have attempted to quash the investigation. Heywood had been a long-time associate of Gu, and the two allegedly had a falling out over a financial dispute that involved the illegal transfer out of the country of large sums of money. Sources claimed that Heywood threatened to expose Gu's activity, which may have served as motive for the murder. The Bo family reportedly had amassed a fortune totalling over a hundred million dollars, in part through extortion and other forms of corruption. With revelation of the government cover-up, Bo's hopes for a spot on the Politburo Standing Committee were torpedoed. He was sacked as Chongqing's party boss and suspended from the Politburo and the Central Committee for suspected 'serious violations of discipline'. His wife was placed under judicial investigation on 'suspicion of intentional homicide'.

Bo's populist style, flagrant public campaigning for advancement, and espousal of Maoist-era policies and campaigns posed threats to the Communist Party and its leaders' commitment to decision-making based on consensus. Although the case was intensely political, the Chinese leaders concluded that it would be treated solely as a criminal case and urged the party to close ranks to ensure a stable leadership transition. As Bo disappeared from public view, rumours circulated on Chinese social-media websites of a coup plot by Bo and his supporters to bring down the top leadership in Beijing. Censors worked to limit speculation and Chinese media reported in April that over 210,000 microblogging posts and 42 websites had been removed in a 'rumour clean-up'.

Chinese Premier Wen Jiabao used the crisis to renew calls for economic and political 'structural reform'. He argued that, unless such reforms, especially leadership reform, were pursued, 'the gains we have made in this area will be lost, new problems that have cropped up in China's society will not be fundamentally resolved and such a historic tragedy as the Cultural Revolution may happen again'. However, as Wen was on his way out of the top leadership, such calls for reform may once more have fallen on deaf ears. Rather than propose a reformist agenda, an authoritative commentary in the party's mouthpiece in the wake of the Bo Xilai episode reminded cadres to 'stick to the overall work principle of seeking progress while maintaining stability'.

China's external relations, meanwhile, remained troubled, despite efforts to defuse tensions with many of its neighbours. Friction over maritime issues simmered with Japan, the Philippines, Vietnam and South Korea. Heightened uncertainty about China's strategic intentions among its neighbours led to appeals for greater US engagement in the region. Washington's resulting 'pivot' to Asia made Beijing uneasy and increased anxiety that the United States was determined to contain China's re-emergence as a major power. Economic, political and military initiatives to bolster American presence and influence in the Asia-Pacific region, combined with outbursts of assertive Chinese behaviour and advances across a range of military capabilities, intensified strategic competition between Washington and Beijing. Frequent US–China communication and consultation helped alleviate concerns and damp down suspicions, but the risk of drift toward strategic rivalry persisted.

US–China relations remain steady

Preserving a stable bilateral relationship, managing differences and advancing cooperation were objectives shared by Chinese leader Hu Jintao and US President Barack Obama over the past year. The US and Chinese governments continued joint efforts to implement the consensus reached by their presidents in January 2011 that the countries would 'work together to build a cooperative partnership based on mutual respect and mutual benefit'.

In late June, with subsequent rounds in October and in March 2012, the two governments convened the Asia-Pacific Consultations, a new mechanism aimed at reducing mistrust and misperception and identifying potential new areas of bilateral cooperation to manage growing US–Chinese friction in the region. But when Obama received the Dalai Lama at the White House in mid-July, Beijing accused the United States of 'seriously interfering' in China's internal affairs and charged that the meeting 'damaged' bilateral relations and 'violated solemn commitments' that the Obama administration had 'made repeatedly'. As retribution, the Chinese quietly postponed a relatively insignificant planned visit to China by Robert Einhorn, the State Department's special adviser for non-proliferation and arms control. At the same time, however, Beijing signalled that, despite its dissatisfaction with the president's affront to Chinese sovereignty over Tibet, Sino-American ties would remain on a positive track.

In mid-August, US Vice President Joe Biden travelled to China for a six-day visit. The main objective of the trip was to meet Hu Jintao's successor, Vice President Xi Jinping, and lay the groundwork for a subsequent visit by Xi to the United States the following year. Biden and Xi spent approximately ten hours together in formal and informal settings. They ate noodles together in a small restaurant in Beijing, and travelled to Chengdu, capital of Sichuan province. Both sides hailed the visit as a success that further strengthened US–Chinese ties.

But there was yet another setback to the US–China relationship in September, when the Obama administration announced approval of a new

$5.85 billion arms-sale package for Taiwan that included a major retrofit pro-gramme to upgrade Taiwan's 145 F-16A/B fighters. Ties between the US and Chinese militaries had been on a positive trajectory in summer 2011, with a successful visit by Admiral Mike Mullen to China in July, the first by a US chairman of the Joint Chiefs of Staff in four years. Mullen and his counterpart General Chen Bingde agreed to continue regular communication through a new telephone link; to exchange visits by commanders from one of the People's Liberation Army's military regions and the US Pacific Command; and to conduct joint humanitarian rescue and disaster-relief drills, joint anti-piracy exercises in the Gulf of Aden, hospital-ship exchanges and joint medical drills in 2011–12.

None of these exchanges were realised. In keeping with previous Chinese reactions to US arms sales to Taiwan, Beijing suspended visits between the PLA and the US military. In a departure from past practice, however, the PLA agreed to proceed in December with the Defense Consultative Talks, the annual high-level dialogue between the two militaries. The meeting was held in accordance with the understanding reached between Obama and Hu in January 2011 that a healthy, stable and reliable military-to-military rela-tionship is an essential part of a positive, cooperative and comprehensive US–China relationship. The head of the Chinese delegation, Deputy Chief of the PLA General Staff Ma Xiaotian, reiterated demands that the United States remove the obstacles to the development of bilateral military ties: US arms sales to Taiwan, US legislation that restricts exchanges between the two militaries, and the conduct of high-frequency close-in reconnaissance activi-ties by US warships and planes against China.

Military-to-military relations were, gradually, fully restored, though the fact that both militaries were devoting ever-greater energies to fighting a potential war against the other made dialogue and cooperation difficult. An agenda for US–China defence exchanges in 2012 was agreed upon in April and was kicked off by a visit by China's Defence Minister Liang Guanglie to the United States in May.

Xi Jinping's visit to the United States proceeded on schedule in February 2012, providing an opportunity for China's incoming leader to gain a better understanding of the Sino-US relationship and the United States. No break-throughs were achieved, but none were expected, since Xi could not upstage the incumbent leader Hu Jintao. Nevertheless, China's leader-in-waiting impressed Americans as self-assured and competent. His conversations with Obama, Biden, Secretary of State Hillary Clinton and Secretary of Defense Leon Panetta suggested that, like his predecessors, Xi attached great importance to the preservation of stable and cooperative Sino-US relations. Moreover, Xi's demonstration of his ability to manage the vitally important US–China relationship likely strengthened his position back home.

On 3–4 May, the fourth round of the Strategic and Economic Dialogue (S&ED) was held in Beijing. Once again, Clinton and Treasury Secretary Tim Geithner joined their Chinese co-chairs, Vice Premier Wang Qishan and State Councillor Dai Bingguo. The S&ED is the premier bilateral dialogue mechanism and is emblematic of the institutionalisation of the US–China relationship. Both countries view the S&ED as part of a joint effort to increase mutual understanding, dispel misperceptions, build deeper mutual trust and expand cooperation. According to the joint statement released after the meeting, the fourth S&ED 'reviewed progress over the four rounds of the S&ED in deepening strategic trust and advancing President Barack Obama and President Hu Jintao's shared vision for building a US–China cooperative partnership based on mutual respect and mutual benefit'. Clinton told the media that the discussions were productive and were 'a testament to how far we've come in building a strong and resilient relationship'.

The issue of human rights in China temporarily leapt to the forefront of the bilateral relationship when Chinese dissident Chen Guangcheng made a dramatic escape from house arrest and sought refuge in the American embassy in Beijing on the eve of the opening of the fourth round of the S&ED. After some confusion about whether Chen wanted to remain in China or seek political asylum in the United States, and several days of intense negotiations, a deal was reached that would enable Chen to go to the United States to study law and take his family members with him. It was a reminder, however, of the fragility of the bilateral relationship and the fundamental differences between the two countries' political systems and values.

US–China economic friction intensified over the past year. Bilateral trade volume in 2011 reached a record $446.6bn and was forecast to surpass $500bn in 2012. However, according to US Census Bureau figures, the bilateral trade deficit reached a record $295bn in 2011, up from $273bn in 2010. Throughout the past year, the United States continued to prod China to speed up the renminbi's appreciation and called for China to cease its unfair trade practices and 'play by the rules' of the international economic system. Beijing generally defended Chinese policies and occasionally criticised US protectionist trade policies and fiscal irresponsibility.

Trade tensions escalated as both sides filed trade disputes with the World Trade Organisation (WTO) and levelled anti-dumping and anti-subsidy tariffs against each other. In December 2011, for example, Washington announced it would bring Beijing's anti-dumping measures against US poultry exports to the WTO; a week later China placed anti-dumping and anti-subsidy tariffs on cars and SUVs imported from the United States. In May 2012, the United States applied anti-dumping tariffs on over 31% of solar panels imported from China and then imposed countervailing duties on Chinese wind-tower imports, decisions which some trade experts warned could heighten trade tensions. In his June 2012 statement at the WTO's Trade Policy Review (TPR) of China, Deputy US Trade Representative Michael Punke noted that since China's 2010 TPR, Washington had initiated five trade cases against China. China has issued complaints of its own against the United States at the WTO. On 8 June, the WTO ruled in favour of China in a case involving US anti-dumping duties on imports of Chinese saw blades and frozen shrimp.

Some relief from the economic discord came in April, as China began to enact a series of financial-policy adjustments. Officials announced a wider trading band for the renminbi against the dollar and lifted some restrictions on capital flows in and out of the country; allowed retail investors to purchase and sell some investments through Hong Kong; and permitted the sale of renminbi-denominated bonds in London. Additionally, China's current-account surplus continued to shrink dramatically, reaching 3% of GDP in 2011 (down from a peak of 10.1% in 2007). The Obama administration welcomed these shifts, along with the 13% rise in the value of the renminbi in the prior two years and more than 40% appreciation since 2005, saying that the 'cumulative effect' was 'significant and very promising'. Less progress was made, however, in other areas of the economic relationship, such as expanding access for US companies to the Chinese market and intellectual-property-rights protection for foreign entities in China. At the S&ED in May, however, China agreed to allow foreign investors to take larger stakes in Chinese securities joint ventures; to review policies that provide 'attractive financing' (which foreign corporations consider unfair) for its exports; and to remove regulatory conditions and subsidies that unfairly benefit state-owned enterprises. The United States, for its part, agreed to support China's bid to include the renminbi in the IMF's basket of reserve currencies.

Cooperation between Washington and Beijing was complicated by a series of Obama foreign-policy initiatives that were dubbed the US 'pivot' to Asia. At the Asia-Pacific Economic Cooperation (APEC) Forum in Honolulu, Hawaii, in November, Obama made a big push for the Trans-Pacific Partnership (TPP), a potential multilateral free-trade agreement that would set new high standards for free and open trade and investment. The TPP was widely viewed in China as an effort to prevent Beijing from dominating trade arrangements in the Asia-Pacific through its relatively low-standard free-trade agreements with its neighbours. It was also seen as an attempt to exclude China from a new round of regional trade integration.

On the heels of the APEC meeting, Obama travelled to Australia and launched the military component of the US pivot with great fanfare. He announced plans to begin rotational deployments of US Marines to Darwin, expanding the US military presence in Asia beyond South Korea and Japan. Subsequently, the United States and the Philippines agreed to consider ways to expand American access to Philippine ports and airfields to re-fuel and service US warships and planes. Singapore agreed to allow the US Navy to deploy up to four littoral combat ships to the city-state on a rotational basis and launched nascent military cooperation with Vietnam. The reorientation of America's long-term national-defence planning to focus on emerging challenges posed by China was further suggested in January 2012 when Obama rolled out a new strategic-defence guidance that highlighted the need to counter anti-access/area-denial threats from China and Iran. The Pentagon stepped up efforts to develop a new operational concept known as Air–Sea Battle to preserve US and allied air-sea-space superiority in the Asia-Pacific region. (See *Strategic Geography*, pp. IV–V).

Politically, the United States bolstered relations with its traditional allies; promoted ties with new partners in the Asia-Pacific region, including Indonesia and India; and made a breakthrough in relations with Myanmar, a country with close, long-standing ties to Beijing. Attending the East Asia Summit for the first time in Bali in November, Obama reiterated the US commitment to ensuring freedom of navigation in the South China Sea and stressed the need to settle sovereignty disputes in accordance with international law, an obvious signal to China. US officials underscored that the rebalancing of US strategy towards Asia was not aimed at containing or strategically encircling China. Rather, US policy initiatives were presented as a long-overdue reweighting of American attention to protect and advance US interests, exploit opportunities and reassure US allies and friends of American staying power and commitments in the region, especially as the United States prepared to make radical cuts in its defence budget. But assertions by the US president and members of his cabinet that the United States welcomed China's rise and hoped to expand cooperation with China failed to assuage Chinese worries. Concern also mounted around the region that intensifying US–China rivalry could have negative consequences.

The US presidential election campaign also fuelled Chinese worries about the future stability of US–China relations. Republican candidate Mitt Romney charged China with manipulating its currency, stealing American intellectual property, hacking into American computers and killing American jobs. If elected, he pledged to implement a series of measures to cope with the challenges posed by China, including levying targeted tariffs on Chinese firms that use unfair trade practices or misappropriate American technology, designating China a currency manipulator and imposing countervailing duties, and ending US government procurement of Chinese goods until Beijing joins the WTO's Government Procurement Agreement.

In addition, Congress and various interest groups lambasted Beijing for refusing to accept global rules and norms on a range of issues. US concerns mounted about China's expanding capabilities in cyber, space, nuclear and conventional weapons. In July 2011, General Chen Bingde, member of the Central Military Commission and chief of general staff of the PLA, publicly confirmed China's development of the DF-21D, an anti-ship ballistic missile intended to put US aircraft carriers at risk. In August 2011, China's first aircraft carrier, the re-fitted *Varyag*, set sail on its maiden voyage and, according to the deputy commander of the PLA Navy, was to be commissioned by the end of 2012. At the National People's Congress in March 2012, China announced an 11.2% increase in military spending.

China on the world stage

Challenges to regional and global security from mid-2011 to mid-2012 put China in the spotlight and tested whether Beijing would contribute positively to the resolution of international problems as its economic clout expanded. On Iran, Syria and North Korea, whose actions aroused international concern and the attention of the UN Security Council, China's record was mixed.

After the International Atomic Energy Agency (IAEA) reported in November 2011 that there was 'credible' evidence that Iran had pursued – and was perhaps still pursuing – all the key technologies needed for a nuclear weapon, the European Union and the United States worked assiduously to ratchet up pressure on Iran's leaders in an effort to persuade them to abandon any illicit part of their nuclear programme. India, Japan and South Korea took steps to reduce Iranian oil imports, and the EU began to ramp up an oil embargo on Tehran which was to take full effect on 1 July 2012. China objected to the imposition of sanctions outside the UN and refused to cut its oil imports from Iran, despite strong pressure from the United States.

In January, Washington imposed sanctions on a Chinese company, Zhuhai Zhenrong, for selling refined oil to Iran, though the move was largely symbolic since the company did not do business with the United States. Either due to price disputes or subtle Chinese efforts to pressure Iran – or both – Chinese imports of Iranian crude oil declined in the first quarter of 2012. Beijing continued to support Tehran's right to peaceful use of nuclear energy at the same time that it stepped up cooperation with the other members of the P5+1 to resolve the dispute with Iran over its nuclear programme.

As violence against anti-regime protesters in Syria increased in late 2011 and early 2012, the UN Security Council voted on 4 February on a resolution which backed an Arab peace plan to facilitate a political transition and restore peace. China, along with Russia, vetoed the resolution, a move condemned by many countries. US Ambassador Susan Rice said she was disgusted by the vetoes that 'prop up desperate dictators'. French Ambassador Gérard Araud said 'history will judge harshly' those who protected the Assad regime. China defended its action, insisting that pressuring the Syrian government would not help resolve the problems in that country. Another factor in Beijing's decision to use its veto was the lesson drawn from its prior abstention on UNSCR 1973 in March 2011 which authorised member states to take all necessary measures to protect civilians in Libya. From China's perspective, that resolution had been abused by NATO to use force to oust Libyan leader Muammar Gadhafi. In the Syrian case, China and Russia were determined to block an attempt to use UN-sanctioned armed intervention to carry out regime change.

Faced with charges from the international community that the veto spurred even greater bloodshed in Syria, Beijing adopted an unusually active diplomatic stance to promote a political solution. China sent a special envoy to Damascus in February and again in March, and threw its weight behind a six-point peace plan put forward by international envoy Kofi Annan. Signalling greater cooperation with the international community, China, along with Russia, backed a Security Council resolution in mid-April authorising the deployment of UN military observers to monitor a ceasefire between the Syrian government and opposition fighters. China's Foreign Ministry said the country was willing to contribute members to the UN observer team in Syria.

The bloodshed in Syria continued unabated with the massacre of over 100 civilians on 25 May in Houla. The UN's top human-rights body, composed of 47 nations, supported a US- and Arab-led resolution condemning the 'outrageous use of force against the civilian population' by 'pro-regime elements' and Syrian government troops. Only Russia, China and Cuba voted against the resolution.

In autumn 2011, China encouraged a US–North Korean deal that held out promise to pave the way for the resumption of the Six-Party Talks aimed at denuclearisation of North Korea. Progress was halted when North Korean leader Kim Jong-il died suddenly on 17 December. When US–North Korea negotiations resumed in February, an agreement was struck in which Pyongyang would suspend its nuclear programmes and missile launches and would invite IAEA inspectors back into the country in return for 240,000 tonnes of food assistance from the United States. The deal collapsed a few weeks later, when North Korea announced plans to launch a satellite in violation of UN Security Council resolutions, despite private urging by Beijing to forgo any provocative moves.

North Korea's attempted satellite launch on 13 April failed, but nevertheless prompted condemnation from the international community. China worked with the United States and other Security Council members on the wording of a UNSC Presidential Statement that resulted in the tightening of sanctions on North Korea and expressed the determination of the council to take action in the event that North Korea launched missiles or conducted nuclear tests in the future.

China tries to ease tensions with neighbours

After a period of rising tensions between China and the Philippines and Vietnam in May and June 2011 over competing claims in the South China Sea, Beijing returned to a posture of restraint and reassurance toward its Southeast Asian neighbours. To assuage growing worries among many ASEAN members that an economically more powerful China was beginning to throw its weight around, in July 2011 Beijing negotiated a largely symbolic but nonetheless important agreement establishing guidelines for implementing the 2002 Declaration on the Conduct of Parties (DOC) in the South China Sea.

In November, Wen and the leaders of the ten ASEAN member nations met in Bali at a summit commemorating the 20th anniversary of China–ASEAN dialogue relations. Just prior to the meeting, the Chinese Foreign Ministry published a special report detailing the impressive progress made in China–ASEAN relations since the dialogue began. At the end of the meeting the leaders issued a joint statement reaffirming their commitment to effectively implement the DOC and 'work towards the eventual adoption, on the basis of consensus, of a code of conduct in the South China Sea'. At a meeting on the implementation of the DOC held in Beijing in January 2012, senior representatives from China and ASEAN member states agreed to hold a series of workshops during the year on maritime disaster prevention and mitigation, marine ecological environment and surveillance technology, search and rescue, and marine ecology and biological diversity.

Over the year to mid-2012 Beijing took additional steps to improve its tarnished image and reduce neighbouring countries' incentives to enhance cooperation with the United States to counterbalance Chinese power. During a visit to China by Philippine Foreign Secretary Albert del Rosario in July, the two sides agreed not to let disagreements on maritime disputes affect the broader cooperative relationship. This understanding was reaffirmed in a joint statement released in September when Hu hosted Philippine President Benigno Aquino. Chinese State Councillor Dai Bingguo visited Vietnam in September in an effort to lower frictions and improve relations. The following month, during a visit to China by Vietnamese party leader Nguyen Phu Trong, the two governments signed an accord setting basic principles to guide the settlement of maritime issues. China and Vietnam subsequently established a working group to demarcate and develop the southern portion of the Gulf of Tonkin near the disputed Paracel Islands. Xi Jinping further strengthened Sino-Vietnamese bilateral ties during his visit to Hanoi in December.

Nevertheless, low-level disputes between China and other South China Sea claimants cropped up sporadically during the year. The Philippines' construction of a garrison building on Patag Island in the Spratlys prompted Chinese warnings to expect 'consequences' if steps to militarise the Spratlys continued. In March, China detained 21 Vietnamese for illegal fishing around disputed islands after over a year of refraining from such detentions in favour of levying fines and confiscating catches. There was another flare-up in April, when the Philippine navy attempted to detain Chinese fishermen it charged were poaching on Scarborough Shoal and Chinese vessels moved in to protect the fishermen.

China's trade with and investment in Southeast Asia continued to grow at a double-digit annual pace. At the China–ASEAN meeting in November 2011, Wen announced a $476 million China–ASEAN maritime cooperation fund and pledged another $10bn in loans for ASEAN in addition to $15bn in loans pledged two years earlier.

The March 2011 earthquake and tsunami in Japan created an opening for improved Sino-Japanese relations, which had become icy after a 2010 incident in which a Chinese fishing boat collided with Japan Coast Guard vessels in the East China Sea. Subsequently, bilateral high-level visits and defence relations resumed, but underlying problems were not addressed and the relationship remained contentious. At the IISS Shangri-La Dialogue in June, Chinese and Japanese defence ministers agreed to resume defence ties and to establish a maritime crisis management system. Yoshihiko Noda, Japan's new prime minister, later conveyed uneasiness regarding China's lack of military transparency, but emphasised that he wanted to strengthen relations. Noda and Hu met in Beijing in December and agreed to proceed with the maritime project but did not make progress on joint development of resources in the East China Sea.

Although relations appeared to be improving, Japan voiced increasingly explicit concerns about China's military posture, particularly after China announced that it would conduct sea trials of its first aircraft carrier in August 2011. These worries were reflected in Japan's 2011 Defence White Paper, which cited China's 'overbearing' behaviour in the South China Sea and East Asia. Chinese patrol ships and fishing boats continued to enter Japan's exclusive economic zone and contiguous zone, sometimes without prior notification. Despite this, there were no major incidents at sea like the clash in 2010, and both sides exercised caution. For example, an incident in November 2011 in which a fishing-boat captain was detained for entering Japanese waters was quickly resolved with the release of the captain after he paid a fine.

In 2012, Sino-Japanese ties were strained again by territorial disputes. In February, China prevented Japan Coast Guard ships from conducting surveys near the Chunxiao gas field, which lies in disputed territory. Then, in March, Japan assigned names to islands in the Senkaku/Diaoyu archipelago, leading to an outcry from both China and Taiwan. Beijing also strongly denounced a plan by Tokyo's governor to use public funds to purchase four islands in the Senkakus for sale by a private owner.

Despite the political tensions, the Sino-Japanese economic relationship flourished. Bilateral trade reached a record $344.9bn in 2011, an increase of 14.3% from 2010 levels. Japanese export growth to China was not as high as initially expected due to the earthquake, but still managed to reach record highs.

China and South Korea worked to improve their bilateral relationship, which soured after China's refusal to condemn North Korea's sinking of the *Cheonan* corvette in March 2010. The first China–South Korea 'strategic defence dialogue' in July 2011 resulted in an agreement to increase bilateral military exchanges as well as cooperation on peacekeeping and anti-piracy efforts. At a bilateral summit in January 2012, Presidents Lee Myung-bak and Hu Jintao agreed to negotiate a bilateral free-trade agreement. They set a goal of increasing bilateral trade to $300bn by 2016. Sino-Korean trade rose 19% in 2011 to $246bn, according to Chinese customs data.

Despite these steps, tensions spiked over maritime jurisdiction after a Chinese fisherman stabbed a South Korean Coast Guard officer in December 2011. In March, a Chinese official asserted that Suyan (Socotra) Rock, which is 4.6 meters below sea level at low tide, lay in Chinese waters and was rightfully Chinese. South Korea insisted that the rock, which it calls Ieodo, was in its 200nm exclusive economic zone. The two countries agreed to resolve the dispute through negotiations. They also differed over the repatriation of North Korean defectors.

At the fifth annual trilateral summit of Chinese, Japanese and South Korean leaders, an agreement was reached to begin negotiations on a regional free-trade area. The three nations together account for 90% of the East Asian economy and trade among them grew to $690bn in 2011.

China and North Korea worked to strengthen and deepen their relationship as they commemorated the 50th anniversary of their bilateral Friendship Treaty. In the second half of 2011, several high-level exchanges were conducted. North Korean Premier Choe Yong-rim visited China in September. Chinese delegation visits to North Korea were led by Guo Shengkun, an alternate member of the Chinese Communist Party Central Committee, and Li Jinai, director of the General Political Department of the PLA. After Kim Jong-il's death, all the members of China's Politburo Standing Committee, including Hu, visited the North Korean Embassy in Beijing to express China's condolences. A joint message from all the major arms of the Chinese government and party expressed strong support for North Korea, noting that the two countries were 'linked by mountains and waters and stand together sharing weal and woe'. It concluded that the 'Chinese people will stand together with the DPRK people forever'. In 2012 high-level exchanges between China and North Korea slowed, however. Invitations from Beijing to North Korea's leader Kim Jong-un were left unanswered, perhaps due to Kim's observation of a mourning period or to Sino-North Korean tensions after Pyongyang's satellite launch proceeded in defiance of Chinese warnings.

Cross-strait relations advance

Cross-strait relations continued on a positive trajectory based on a shared understanding that Beijing and Taipei would address easy issues before difficult ones and tackle economic matters before more sensitive political and security matters. After the signing of 15 agreements between the two sides in the first three years of Taiwanese President Ma Ying-jeou's four-year term, progress slowed. This was due in part to anticipation of Taiwan's January 2012 elections, but also because the low-hanging fruit had been harvested, while more thorny matters that required more intensive negotiations were yet to be put on the agenda.

Nevertheless, a few gains were achieved between mid-2011 and mid-2012. In November, an accord on nuclear-safety cooperation was signed at the seventh meeting of Taiwan's Straits Exchange Foundation (SEF) and China's Association for Relations Across the Taiwan Straits (ARATS), the quasi-official negotiating bodies for cross-strait affairs. The two delegations also committed to concluding an investment-protection accord, viewed by both sides view as a high priority and which was expected to be signed before the end of June. Due attention was also paid to further promoting trade liberalisation through the Economic Cooperation Framework Agreement (ECFA) that went into effect in September 2010 followed by the implementation of the 'early harvest' programme for tariff reductions or exemptions in January 2011. The Cross-Strait Economic Cooperation Committee (CSECC), launched in January 2011 to facilitate talks on the implementation, interpretation and coordination of the 'early harvest' list and other ECFA-related matters, convened in Hangzhou in November 2011. The two sides endorsed an agreement on cross-strait industrial cooperation and also agreed to establish reciprocal offices for their trade associations in early 2012. Over the next two years, the mainland and Taiwan expected to conclude tariff reduction or exemption talks for more than 5,000 further items that were not included on the ECFA 'early harvest list,', and to sign two additional cross-strait agreements on investment and customs cooperation.

The cross-strait economic and trade relationship continued to flourish. Some 41 cities on the Chinese mainland and nine cities in Taiwan had implemented cross-strait direct flights, with 558 passenger flights and 56 cargo flights every week. Chinese mainland authorities allowed five Taiwanese commercial banks to set up branches on the mainland and approved three Taiwanese companies to be listed on the mainland's stock market. The mainland also allowed six Taiwanese financial organisations to invest in its capital market.

As Taiwan's presidential campaign heated up in late 2011 and the polls showed a close race among the three candidates – the incumbent President Ma Ying-jeou, Democratic Progressive Party (DPP) Chairwoman Tsai Ing-wen, and People First Party candidate James Soong – Beijing's fears of a DPP win and a return to pro-independence policies such as were pursued by Taiwan's first DPP president Chen Shui-bian (2000–08) increased. Nevertheless, China refrained from making demonstrations of military force or using harsh rhetoric to intimidate Taiwan's voters, having learned from the 1996 and 2000 elections that such actions were often counterproductive. Instead, the mainland attempted to win the support of Taiwan's farmers and fishermen for Ma's cross-strait policies by purchasing fruit and milkfish. In addition, Beijing facilitated the return of Taiwan compatriots living on the mainland to vote, and mainland Chinese officials warned that if Tsai were elected and refused to accept the '1992 Consensus' on 'one China', cross-strait dialogue and cooperation would be suspended.

The presidential and legislative elections held in Taiwan on 14 January 2012 returned Ma to power with a Kuomintang majority in the legislature for another four years. Ma's victory, with a solid six-percentage-point lead over Tsai, his main rival, portended continued stability in cross-strait relations and good prospects for managing US–China differences over Taiwan. Beijing was relieved by the outcome, which proved the correctness of Hu's policy of seeking 'peaceful development' across the strait and averted a debate on the mainland's Taiwan policy on the eve of the 18th Party Congress. The mainland's Taiwan Affairs Office welcomed the election results and said that it was 'willing to join hands with all walks of life in Taiwan on the basis of continuing to oppose "Taiwan independence" and uphold the "1992 Consensus"'.

With a smaller margin of victory in 2012 than in 2008 – 6% compared to 17% – Ma and his administration were expected to have a diminished ability to dominate the policy agenda. The revitalised opposition and deep popular support for maintaining the cross-strait status quo (86.2% in an April 2012 poll) would limit what Ma could accomplish in his second term. The direction of cross-strait relations looked to remain unchanged, but the pace of reconciliation was likely to slow. Although Beijing did not hide its desire to sign a peace accord with Taiwan during Ma's second term, the upsurge of criticism in Taiwan of such an accord when Ma floated it during the campaign as part of his 'golden decade' national vision suggested that, while scholars from both sides of the strait might informally exchange views on political issues, formal negotiations on a peace accord were unlikely to get under way anytime soon.

In his 20 May inaugural address, Ma did not mention the possibility of a peace accord as he had four years earlier. Instead, he put forward a new concept of 'one Republic of China, two areas'. Since Beijing believes that the ROC ceased to exist when the People's Republic of China was established in 1949, the mainland's Taiwan Affairs Office responded by noting that the two sides of the strait continue to belong to one China and their relationship 'is not one of nation-to-nation'.

China–Europe relations improve

China's role in the EU sovereign-debt crisis dominated China–EU relations over the course of the year and was at times a source of contention, due to Beijing's unwillingness to make a commitment to provide financial support. Despite continued assurances from officials regarding China's confidence in the eurozone and its intention to buy more sovereign debt throughout 2011, the lack of clear pledges spread distrust of China in Europe. At the November 2011 G20 Summit in France, which the EU hoped to use to obtain clear financial support from China, Chinese Vice Minister of Finance Zhu Guangyao said Beijing had 'no concrete plans' to invest in the European Financial Stability Facility (EFSF) and maintained it was 'too early' to discuss further investments. It was not until February 2012, when Wen said China was considering 'involving itself more' by offering support via the EFSF and the European Stability Mechanism (ESM), that some of Europe's uncertainty eased. Wen also declared China was 'open and positive' about additional funding through the IMF.

Even with the crisis, China–EU economic relations remained largely stable, and frequent high-level bilateral visits and dialogues helped to sustain the relationship. Bilateral trade reached over $560bn in 2011, an 18% increase over 2010. The EU continued to be China's biggest trading partner and export market, as well as China's main source of technology transfer. The EU also remained China's biggest source of imports, having surpassed Japan in May 2011. Meanwhile, China became the EU's second-largest trading partner, behind the United States, and the EU's largest source of imports. While Chinese exports to the EU declined rapidly through autumn 2011, total exports to the EU over the course of the year grew by approximately 3%, reaching €292.1bn (about $386bn). EU exports to China grew by 20.3% in 2011, reaching a record-breaking €136.2bn (about $180bn). The EU's trade deficit with China of €155.9bn (about $206bn) in 2011 was down by 9% from 2010.

The most notable high-level dialogue was the 14th China–EU Summit, held 14–15 February 2012. However, even though a joint press statement listed 31 points of agreement and mutual understanding, there was no mention of the eurozone crisis, nor any specific actions by Beijing to help bolster its European partners, even though Wen had pledged China's continued support at the meeting.

China's restrictions on rare-earth exports caused another a stir. On 13 March 2012, the EU joined the United States and Japan in taking joint complaints against China to the WTO. EU Trade Commissioner Karel De Gucht stated that China's rare-earth measures 'hurt [the EU's] producers and consumers in the EU and across the world, including manufacturers of pioneering hi-tech and "green" business applications'. Beijing defended its rare-earth policy, arguing that the restrictions were fair, in line with WTO regulations, and necessary to protect the environment.

China–Norway ties also remained tense as Beijing continued to punish Oslo for awarding the Nobel Peace Prize to Chinese dissident Liu Xiaobo in October 2010. China continued to refuse to resume talks on a bilateral free-trade agreement. When China sought permanent observer status at the Arctic Council in early 2012, Norwegian media called in a tit-for-tat action for Oslo to block Beijing's bid, which would have restricted Chinese influence in multilateral dialogues on Arctic security, energy development, and trade and shipping routes. The government nevertheless announced its support of China's bid in February 2012. Despite the positive step, the following month Norwegian Prime Minister Jens Stoltenberg described bilateral relations as still 'very static'.

Domestic challenges mount
As China prepared for its once-a-decade leadership transition in autumn 2012, pressure was on to keep a lid on both sources and expressions of discontent. To this end, maintaining economic growth and social stability remained key priorities, but the economic slowdown and ongoing ethnic tensions between the Han Chinese and the Tibetan and Uighur minorities posed major challenges.

Maintaining social stability was especially problematic. In 2011, an estimated 180,000 'mass incidents' and civil disturbances took place across the country, most of which were aggravated by economic discontent. Western sources indicated Chinese unemployment averaged 6.5% in 2011, a slight increase from 2010; however, the Chinese Ministry of Human Resources and Social Security reported that, by the end of the year, unemployment held at 4.1%, below the government's 5% target. Household income was estimated at $8,400 in purchasing-power parity terms, still far below the world's average of $11,800. Corruption, economic inequality and illegal land seizures were common complaints among protesters. According to Yu Jianrong from the Chinese Academy of Social Sciences (CASS), land disputes are behind 65% of all mass incidents.

Protests in the village of Wukan, Guangdong province, grabbed the international spotlight when residents clashed with local authorities over illegal land seizures in September 2011. By December 2011, the villagers had succeeded in ousting party officials and police, who responded by sealing off the village. Senior provincial officials eventually compromised with the villagers, declaring their demands 'reasonable' and pledging to investigate the alleged corruption. New village elections were held in Wukan in early 2012. Wang Yang, Communist Party secretary of Guangdong province, one of China's more reform-minded leaders who could be elevated to the Standing Committee of the Politburo at the upcoming 18th Party Congress, earned plaudits for his handling of the situation.

In addition to the economic factors behind civil unrest, public demands for greater protection of human rights and civil freedoms, combined with an increase in racial tensions, plagued Chinese society and challenged the party's goal of achieving social harmony. Friction between the Tibetan and Uighur communities and the Han Chinese majority intensified over the course of the year, fuelled by what Tibetans and Uighurs considered oppressive restrictions on language, culture and religious practices by Beijing. Between March 2011 and June 2012, there were 38 documented cases of Tibetan self-immolation, the most serious Tibetan protests since 2008. Beijing continued to blame the Dalai Lama for inciting social unrest within the Tibetan community, calling him a 'splittist'. In July 2011, violent clashes involving Uighurs in Xinjiang resulted in 32 deaths and dozens injured. 'Separatist groups' with ties to terrorist networks have often been blamed for the province's ethnic tensions.

Officials responded to both sets of incidents by increasing the already high paramilitary presence, expanding re-education programmes and periodically carrying out harsh crackdowns. Beijing refused to acknowledge the socioeconomic factors at play in Tibet and Xinjiang, and showed no signs of willingness to adjust its approach to dealing with the spike in unrest among both minority populations.

Amid ongoing concerns about maintaining economic growth and social stability, the fifth and final session of the 11th National People's Congress (NPC) was held in Beijing on 5–14 March 2012. Ahead of the meeting, Wen delivered his annual government work report to the congress, highlighting the government's plan to rebalance the economy by increasing domestic consumption and shifting away from China's current reliance on exports. Although the 12th Five-Year Plan unveiled in 2011 focused on economic restructuring, little progress had been made and Beijing was still facing the problem of a high domestic savings rate paired with low domestic demand. The work report also set a 7.5% target for economic growth over the course of 2012. This was consistent with the 7% GDP growth-rate target announced in the 12th Five-Year Plan for 2011–15.

GDP growth slowed to 9.5% in 2011 compared to 10.3% in 2010, and was expected to slow further in 2012 due to the eurozone crisis. The debt incurred from the domestic stimulus plan, the housing bubble and inflation was also expected to constrain economic growth. In addition to the GDP growth target, Wen announced a target of 4% inflation for the year. China's inflation rate is estimated to have hit as high as 5.4% in 2011. In early June foreign analysts believed inflation to have cooled throughout the spring, falling as low as 3.2% in May, well within the government's 2012 target. Wen also highlighted continued health-care system reforms focused on cost reductions, and announced a continuation of housing-market controls to stabilise prices.

The 2012 budget released during the NPC reflected Beijing's concern to sustain economic development and stability. Key items included a 16.4% increase in education and health-care spending, a 21.9% increase in social-security and employment spending, and a 7.7% increase for 'public safety', terminology used to refer to China's internal security forces. China's 2012 defence budget increased by 11.2% to 670bn renminbi ($106.4bn). NPC spokesman Li Zhaoxing stated this was 'reasonable and appropriate', and was aimed at safeguarding 'national sovereignty and territorial integrity' rather than threatening other countries. Li also noted that defence spending had dropped as a percentage of China's GDP from 1.33% in 2008 to 1.28% in 2011.

One piece of legislation that was passed at the congress was an amendment to the Criminal Procedure Law that was controversial both in China and abroad. The revision made confessions, witness testimony and depositions extracted through illegal means inadmissible in court. Despite these and other positive changes, the amendment also stipulated procedures allowing for police detentions. The amendment permitted police to confine suspects under 'residential surveillance' for up to six months, did not require the investigating agency to disclose the suspect's whereabouts or provide reasons why a person was detained, and allowed police to waive a 24-hour notification to relatives if they determined it would 'impede the investigation'.

Korean Peninsula: Succession and Suspicion

The death of Kim Jong-il in December 2011 produced a much-anticipated dynastic succession in North Korea that went without a hitch in terms of mustering domestic support. However, the young new leader, Kim Jong-un, failed his first foreign-policy test: on 29 February, Pyongyang agreed to a moratorium relating to its nuclear and missile programmes, but weeks later it broke the deal by launching a space rocket that exploded two minutes after take-off. This turn of events, combining diplomatic disaster with technological loss of face, killed any chances in the foreseeable future of improvement of relations with the United States or of addressing North Korea's nuclear challenge through the moribund Six-Party Talks.

Kim Jong-un's inept diplomacy, and the vitriolic propaganda campaign he unleashed against South Korean President Lee Myung-bak, flew in the face of a softening of attitudes in South Korea. If the North were to seek rapprochement, it would probably find a receptive partner in whoever is elected president when Lee's term ends in 2013. But Seoul's horizons are ever more global, not merely inter-Korean. A free-trade agreement with the United States finally took effect in 2012, another was signed with the United Kingdom and a third was under negotiation with China, which is South Korea's largest trading partner. Lee's hosting of the second nuclear security summit was further evidence of South Korea's global reach.

Dynastic Succession

On 17 December 2011, Kim Jong-il, the 69-year-old supreme leader of the Democratic People's Republic of Korea (DPRK), died of a heart attack while travelling on a train, though the news was held for two days before being broadcast to a stunned nation. The mantle of leadership immediately passed to his designated successor, third son Kim Jong-un, thought to be 28 or 29, who was named 'supreme commander of the armed forces'.

Amid a show of mass wailing at Kim Jong-il's funeral, seven senior party and military officials were particularly prominent. They were apparently chosen to be the new leader's mentors or quasi-regents. Most notable among them was Kim Jong-il's brother-in-law, Jang Song-taek, now the second most (if not the most) powerful man in the nation. For the event, Jang wore an army uniform for the first time in public, seeming to underscore the central role of the military. There was no doubting that the 'military first' policy propagated by Kim Jong-il was continuing under his son. Yet the Korean Workers' Party also continued the revival it had undergone in the former leader's last few years. His official obituary, for example, listed the Central Committee of the party as first among the signatory institutions.

At a rare Party Delegates' Conference on 11 April 2012 and a meeting of the rubber-stamp Supreme People's Assembly two days later, Kim Jong-un was formally appointed as the first secretary of the party and the first chairman of the National Defence Commission (the highest organ in the state), thereby completing the process of succession. He was now *de jure* head of the army, party and state. Meanwhile, the leadership of the party and military was reshuffled to promote close allies of the Kim family including Choe Ryong-hae, who became one of five members of the Politburo Presidium of the Korean Workers' Party and a member of the General Political Bureau of the Korean People's Army, among other new titles.

The succession appeared to be proceeding without internal trouble. By the end of June 2012 no evidence of discontent or rivalry had marred the unified support pledged to Kim Jong-un by all elements of the regime. No purges or demonstrations had been reported. The regime would have been watching anxiously the fate of leaders in the Arab world and the turn of events in Myanmar which, in line with its democratisation and rapprochement with the United States, agreed to break military ties with Pyongyang. While the death of Kim Jong-il might yet prove to be the beginning of the demise of the DPRK, there was as yet no sign of it.

Nuclear freeze: too good to be true

Though Kim Jong-un's initial efforts at maintaining domestic unity were successful, he began his tenure on the foreign-policy front with a massive miscalculation compounded by a humiliating technical failure. Following a series of bilateral discussions that began in summer 2011, North Korea and the United States on 29 February ('Leap Day') announced a set of reciprocal measures. Pyongyang agreed to a moratorium on nuclear tests and long-range missile launches, as well as on uranium-enrichment activities at its Yongbyon complex, with monitoring of the latter by the IAEA. The freeze was to last 'while productive dialogues continue'. In exchange, Washington agreed to provide 240,000 tonnes of nutritional assistance, delivered over the course of 12 months. Distribution of the food aid was to be monitored by Korean-speaking Americans and it was to be in the form of high-protein supplements, rather than grain, so that it could be less easily misused to supplement army rations. As a diplomatic nicety, the US State Department insisted that it was not a 'food for freeze' deal, in that two sets of discussions took place on separate tracks. It was North Korea that sought the linkage.

The agreement appeared to augur well for the new leader's foreign-policy vision. True, the nuclear moratorium was incomplete in that North Korea did not undertake to stop work at other enrichment facilities outside Yongbyon. At least two such undeclared facilities must exist: a plant to produce uranium hexafluoride, and a pilot plant that would have been used as a model for constructing the 2,000-machine centrifuge facility that was displayed to visiting American academics in November 2010. There was also suspicion, but little evidence, of highly enriched uranium (HEU) production at a secret site.

From the US perspective, the agreement seemed too good to be true: about $200m of food aid, which Washington might normally have provided on humanitarian grounds in any case, in exchange for a freeze of activities in both the nuclear and missile areas that had provoked so much international concern. And so it proved. Just 16 days later, North Korea announced that it would conduct a space launch to put an 'earth observation satellite' into orbit during mid-April celebrations marking the centenary of the birth of 'Great Leader' Kim Il-sung, father of Kim Jong-il. The satellite was to be carried by a rocket dubbed *Unha-3*, launched from a new site on the West (China) Sea. According to North Korea, the satellite launch did not fall into the category of the 'long-range missile launches' which were to be suspended under the Leap Day agreement. The DPRK insisted on its sovereign right to launch a peaceful satellite. Yet the United States had made clear during the negotiation that a space launch would invalidate the deal. UN Security Council Resolution 1718, passed in 2006, specifically banned North Korea from conducting 'any launch using ballistic missile technology' and Resolution 1874, passed in 2009, prohibited 'all activities related to [North Korea's] ballistic missile programme'. Satellite-launch rockets and ballistic missiles are intricately linked, sharing the same bodies, engines and other development processes. Demanding that North Korea call off the satellite launch, Washington indicated it would derail the food-aid pledge on the grounds that a country that did not honour its freeze agreement could not be trusted to honour the monitoring arrangements for food aid. For North Korea, however, there was no turning back.

Pyongyang sought to salvage the deal by quickly inviting IAEA inspectors to visit Yongbyon. But regardless of how useful it would be for inspectors to ascertain whether the enrichment facility was working and how well, IAEA Director-General Yukiya Amano knew the agency could not proceed in the absence of an understanding with the United States.

The prospective rocket launch was seen as highly provocative by North Korea's neighbours. Pyongyang sought to demonstrate peaceful intent by launching the rocket southward, to the west of the Korean peninsula and the Philippines, rather than over Japan as in two previous tests. A new launch tower on the west coast was used for this purpose, though the tower was notably larger than the *Unha*-3, meaning it could accommodate longer-range missiles. Pyongyang also informed the International Civil Aviation Organisation and the International Maritime Organisation. Yet mindful of the potential for a course deviation, both Japan and South Korea threatened to shoot down the rocket if it threatened their territory.

By going ahead with a test on 13 April, North Korea lost the food aid and any prospect for better relations with the administration of US President Barack Obama. Pyongyang also angered its Chinese ally, which had counselled restraint. Worst of all, the rocket misfired, breaking apart about two minutes after lift-off. The humiliation could not have been worse. Any inclination by authorities to cover up the mishap, as had been attempted with two previous space launches, was obviated by the presence of scores of journalists who had been invited to observe the launch and who began receiving phone calls from their home offices informing them of the failure. Four hours after the explosion, it was reported by DPRK news media.

Pundits puzzled over why North Korea carried out the launch despite the obvious incongruity with the February deal. The answer seemed to be that Kim Jong-il had given the go-ahead for a launch before he died. In any weighing of policy priorities, the 'military first' policy ensures that generals have the upper hand. The greater mystery was why North Korea agreed to a deal to suspend long-range missile launches, knowing that one would soon take place. If Kim Jong-un believed he could have both the deal and the launch because Obama would forgive the deceit, he was badly advised. With the break-up of the rocket, he got neither.

Responding only a day later and employing somewhat stronger language than that adopted after the previous rocket launch in 2009, the Security Council 'strongly condemned' the action and warned the North of further consequences if it carried out another missile launch or nuclear test. A sanctions committee of the Security Council added three DPRK state companies to the list of those blacklisted under previous resolutions. China made clear it would not permit a new resolution imposing further sanctions on Pyongyang and vetoed most of the approximately 40 entities that the United States, Japan, South Korea and the European Union sought to add to the list. Yet China's agreement to go along with even a small expansion of the sanctions list was a sure sign of Beijing's displeasure with its client.

The outstanding question was whether Chinese pressure would dissuade North Korea from taking the further step of conducting a third nuclear test. In early April, satellite photos showed growing piles of dirt next to a previously used nuclear-test tunnel, and the South Korean media speculated that North Korea was preparing to test a bomb using HEU. The escalatory pattern of spring 2009 looked set to be repeated: a space launch followed by a Security Council condemnation, followed by a nuclear test. A need to overcome the humiliation of the failed space launch seemingly added to the reasons for a nuclear test. By mid-2012, however, no test had taken place, and there were unconfirmed reports that Pyongyang privately promised China and the US it would not test. To underscore its nuclear status, however, the preamble to the constitution was amended in April to proclaim that Kim Jong-il had turned the nation into a 'nuclear-armed state'.

Sputtering diplomacy

Following the break-down of the Leap Day agreement, US policy towards North Korea reverted to a policy of 'strategic patience', under which Washington would not seek diplomatic engagement in the absence of a demonstrable change in DPRK behaviour. The collapse of the deal also dashed any prospects for resumption of the Six-Party Talks, the negotiating forum involving China, Japan, Russia, the United States and North and South Korea that in 2005 and 2007 had produced stuttering progress toward the goal of DPRK denuclearisation before repeatedly running aground.

Six-Party Talks have not been held since December 2008, mostly because of North Korea's missile and nuclear tests in spring 2009 and its dismissive attitude towards diplomacy. In 2011, however, Pyongyang changed its tune: what some observers called a 'smiling diplomacy' was judged more in tune with its quest for food aid. North Korea signalled that if Six-Party Talks resumed, issues such as temporarily suspending nuclear tests and ballistic-missile launches and allowing IAEA inspection of the enrichment facility at Yongbyon could be 'discussed and settled'. Japan, South Korea and the United States insisted, however, on a reversal of the sequence. Before it could resume Six-Party Talks, North Korea would first have to demonstrate its commitment to the denuclearisation goal, including by verifiably stopping the enrichment operations that had been revealed since the talks were last held. Washington also made clear that before it would agree to any bilateral talks, Pyongyang must first engage with the South.

Surprising many observers, in July North Korea did just that, holding a substantive discussion with the South's nuclear negotiator on the side-lines of the ASEAN Regional Forum in Bali. The meeting, and a short ministerial bilateral that followed, paved the way for the resumption of bilateral talks with the United States. The nuclear negotiators met again in Beijing on 21 September, presaging additional US–DPRK meetings the next month in Bangkok, and then Geneva, for what Washington called 'exploratory discussions'. In those talks, North Korea sought a peace treaty with the United States, to replace the armistice that codified the end of hostilities in the 1950–53 Korean War. Without South Korea as an equal party to the treaty and an end to North Korea's nuclear-weapons programme, however, a peace treaty was a non-starter.

North Korea was more likely to find success in its other objective of acquiring American food aid. It pressed for 330,000 tonnes of grain, which was the undelivered amount from an earlier deal in 2008 to provide 500,000 tonnes. This time the United States offered 240,000 tonnes, based on an assessment of the amount needed to satisfy nutritional requirements for the most vulnerable segments of the population. The day before Kim Jong-il died, negotiators reportedly came close to an agreement.

When talks resumed after the funeral, the two sides concluded the agreement on the nuclear suspension. Rather than a joint document, Washington and Pyongyang made coordinated statements that differed in some ways. The US statement, for example, said IAEA inspectors would 'confirm the disablement' of the 5MW reactor and associated facilities at Yongbyon. The reactor, which had produced most of the plutonium for North Korea's weapons programme, had not been in operation since it was partially disabled in summer 2007 under the terms of a previous agreement.

It was not clear why North Korea had not resumed plutonium production. But one reason was almost certainly the fact that it was pursuing an alternative path to nuclear weapons through uranium enrichment. Gas-centrifuge enrichment facilities are easy to hide, and HEU is deemed a more attractive export commodity, attractive to terrorist groups because of the relative ease of constructing gun-type HEU weapons (in contrast to the implosion type required for plutonium). In addition, North Korea could claim that its enrichment programme was peaceful in purpose, to produce fuel for the experimental power reactor under construction at Yongbyon. Satellite imagery in April 2012 showed the reactor containment building to be nearly completed, although the reactor was still at least one to two years away from being operational.

As an ancillary to the suspension agreement, the United States and North Korea also agreed to resume joint operations to recover the remains of US service members from the Korean War, about 8,000 of whom remain unaccounted for. In 2005 the US suspended the efforts to recover human remains that had been under way for ten years. Resumption was deemed an important confidence-building measure. The collapse of the Leap Day agreement, however, put the recovery effort on ice.

Centenary celebration

For years North Korea had been proclaiming that 2012, the 100th anniversary of the birth of Kim Il-sung, would signal the arrival of a status as a 'strong and prosperous nation'. The prosperous part of that goal is belied by the nation's enduring poverty. There were some signs of economic progress: a massive unfinished hotel that had long disrupted the Pyongyang skyline finally received a set of outer windows, for example. And a joint venture with an Egyptian mobile-phone company signed up its one-millionth subscriber in February 2012. Yet the (South Korean) Bank of Korea, which publishes the most reliable economic statistics on North Korea (which produces no regular statistics itself), reported that real GDP in the North fell by 0.5 % in 2010, the fourth contraction in five years. Foreign residents of Pyongyang reported further deterioration in electricity and water supply. In autumn 2011 UN agencies reported severe water shortages in areas outside Pyongyang, and the situation worsened the following spring, when North Korea experienced what it said was the nation's most severe drought in half a century.

With prosperity nowhere in sight, the regime had all the more reason to emphasise the power of its military, capped by nuclear and missile capabilities. When 2012 dawned, the slogan evolved slightly, heralding a 'strong and thriving country'. The subtle change reflected awareness that claims of economic strength were obviously unrealistic. The new-year editorial that lays out annually the regime's main message even acknowledged that the 'food problem is a burning issue in building a thriving country'. The 'food problem' – North Korea's chronic inability to produce enough to feed the population – has been acknowledged for years. But as usual, the editorial sought the solution in exhortations to increase yields by working harder rather than acknowledging that systemic reforms were necessary either to incentivise more private-sector production, or to earn more foreign exchange to purchase foreign foodstuffs.

At a military parade on 15 April, Kim Jong-un made his first public speech, in which he stressed the need to strengthen the military, calling this his 'first, second and third' priorities. Emphasising the nation's newfound power, he credited his father and grandfather with developing nuclear weapons. But more remarkable than the content of the 20-minute speech was the similarity of voice, appearance and body language to that of his charismatic grandfather, Kim Il-sung. It was as if the traits had skipped a generation; the recently deceased Kim Jong-il almost never spoke in public and had neither the girth nor gregariousness displayed by his father and now by his son.

New missile paraded

At the IISS Shangri-La Dialogue in June 2011, then-US Secretary of Defense Robert Gates expressed concern that North Korea was developing a road-mobile intercontinental ballistic missile (ICBM) that could pose a direct threat to the United States. Many non-governmental experts were sceptical that North Korea could make the leap to ICBMs, given the failure to date of all three of its long-range missile tests, and that it could produce the large vehicles that would be necessary to make ICBMs road-mobile. The failed test of the *Unha*-3 on 13 April contributed to doubts about North Korea's ability to develop and field ICBMs.

At the end of a military parade on 15 April, North Korea showcased six new missiles that appeared to support Gates's contention. Close examination of the missiles, dubbed the KN-08 by Western analysts, showed that they were mock-ups, apparently of a new system under development. Until it is tested, and therefore observable, however, North Korea cannot be said to have an ICBM capability.

More intriguing than the mock-ups were the 16-wheel vehicles that transported them. The transporter-erector-launchers were based on a chassis imported from a subsidiary of the China Aerospace Science and Industry Corp. China said the export did not violate UN sanctions because the chassis was not a complete vehicle and was sold to a DPRK civilian agency ostensibly for forestry work. The false end-user justification gave North Korea the off-road mobility it had been seeking for longer-range missiles. The vehicles were noticeably longer than the KN-08 mock-ups that they carried, which suggests that they were procured for longer-range systems.

North–South relations

On 30 August 2011, Lee Myung-bak replaced hardline unification minister Hyun In-taek with Yu Woo-ik, who had been ambassador to China. Lee's presidency had thus far been marked by a tougher, less open approach to the North than that of his predecessors. But the ministerial change signalled a shift in tactics – and an acknowledgement that Lee's policies had achieved little success in advancing reconciliation or reducing the North Korean threat, and that he would soon be entering his last year in office. Yu began to oversee a somewhat more flexible approach: for example, he approved a joint North–South archaeological project north of the demilitarised zone (DMZ). Seoul gradually relaxed its demand that, as a condition for food aid, the North must first apologise for the deadly attacks in 2010 on the *Cheonan*, a South Korean naval corvette sunk by a North Korean torpedo, and on Yeonpyeong Island. Concerned about his legacy and with an eye to parliamentary elections in spring 2012, Lee even began to drop hints of seeking a North–South summit.

North Korea, however, showed little interest in assisting Lee in improving his legacy. Working-level North–South talks had been held in secret in May 2011 in Beijing to try to work out language that the South could construe as an apology. On 1 June, Pyongyang noisily revealed the talks, claiming the South had 'begged' for them and had sought to bribe DPRK officials. For several months in the second half of 2011, inter-Korean relations became surprisingly business-like, as Pyongyang was at the same time engaged in outreach to Washington. In the aftermath of Kim Jong-il's death, however, the North's attitude again turned hostile. Seoul expressed sympathy to the people of North Korea and cancelled an annual illumination of large Christmas-tree-shaped towers near the DMZ, which Pyongyang had found offensive. But the DPRK state media took offence that the South Korean government did not send a condolence delegation, had put troops on alert and strictly limited the number of South Korean citizens allowed to visit the North to pay respects. Thus began a DPRK campaign of vitriol against the South Korean president.

In spring 2012, anti-Lee propaganda went into overdrive, employing the most vitriolic language and vile caricatures in memory. Pyongyang chose to take offence at Lee's hosting of 53 global leaders for a nuclear-security summit in March, even though, being devoted to countering nuclear terrorism, the agenda had nothing to do with North Korea. On 23 April, following an announcement of a new cruise missile (see below), North Korean state media announced that 'special actions' would soon be initiated aimed at destroying the South Korean president and his government as well as named newspapers and television networks within 'three to four minutes through unique, unprecedented means'. Rallies were staged throughout North Korea to fan death threats. The North began jamming the global-positioning systems of aircraft using Seoul's airports and of vessels in nearby waters.

China–DPRK relations

Throughout 2011, Chinese high-level political and economic exchanges with the North had continued at an impressive pace. China pressed North Korea to improve relations with both the United States and South Korea, and to follow the Chinese model of economic reform. Although the latter exhortation did not stick, the diplomatic message did resonate, as North Korea assiduously sought a resumption of Six-Party Talks. Then, in expressing condolences on the death of Kim Jong-il, China explicitly endorsed Kim Jong-un's leadership succession. The Chinese leadership expressed a willingness to host the young man at an early date.

Thus, when the North's announcement of its plans for a rocket launch derailed China's diplomatic efforts, the anger in Beijing was palpable. Attending the nuclear-security summit, President Hu Jintao gave unprecedented public advice to Pyongyang to focus instead on improving its people's livelihood. China allowed a resolution at the UN Human Rights Council condemning violations in North Korea to pass by consensus – and following the rocket launch, it allowed a more forceful Security Council response. China then permitted several detained North Korean refugees to travel to South Korea, rather than repatriating them to the North as had been Beijing's practice.

In early May, uniformed North Koreans seized three Chinese fishing boats and held the 29 crew captive for two weeks, demanding ransom. Beijing's decision to release news about the fishermen's mistreatment – they were reportedly beaten, stripped and nearly starved – reflected China's disgust with its supposed ally. The incident was also interesting in that it appeared to show a breakdown of central government control in North Korea.

These moves reflected not just China's pique at the North but also its growing economic ties with the South. Two-way trade in 2011 totalled $220bn, dwarfing the $5bn trade between China and North Korea. Small though the latter figure was by comparison, it represented an increasing DPRK dependence on China, which accounted for nearly 60% of North Korea's overall trade.

Dependency on China does not sit well with Pyongyang. In an effort at counter-balancing, Kim Jong-il in August 2011 made his first visit to Russia since 2002, travelling by train to Ulan-Ude in southeast Russia for a meeting with then-President Dmitry Medvedev. The Russians promoted their two-decade-old vision of a gas pipeline through North Korea to the South, and the two leaders agreed to joint working groups on the idea. But no tangible progress was made. Meanwhile, a Russian delegation visiting Pyongyang reached a settlement on North Korea's outstanding debt to the former Soviet Union, which had long been hampering economic cooperation. However, like China, Russia does far more business with the South.

South Korean muscle-flexing

North Korea's rocket launch fanned populist sentiments in South Korea in favour of matching Pyongyang's nuclear challenge in kind. Reflecting an increasingly popular view in conservative circles, National Assemblyman Chung Mong-joon, a potential presidential candidate, argued for the re-introduction of US tactical nuclear weapons, which were removed from South Korean soil in 1991 by President George H.W. Bush. Neither Washington nor Seoul wants this, but the South did seek US approval for the fielding of missiles that could reach every corner of North Korea, even though this would exceed previously agreed range limits. In line with Missile Technology Control Regime (MTCR) requirements, Seoul had agreed to limit its ballistic missiles to a 300km range with a 500kg warhead. The defence ministry announced on 19 April that it had deployed a new cruise missile, the *Hyunmu*-3C, believed to have a range of 1,500km carrying a 450kg payload. Cruise missiles are not covered by the MTCR, but Seoul had reportedly agreed with Washington on a 500km range for those systems. Lee said bilateral discussions would soon produce a new agreement. Meanwhile, South Korea was seeking permission from the United States to reprocess plutonium through a 'pyroprocessing' technique that it argued was less susceptible to being misused for production of weapons-grade plutonium, an argument not wholly convincing to Washington.

Another significant military development was the start of construction on a naval base on Jeju Island in January 2011. When completed in 2014 at a cost of $970m, it will house 20 warships including submarines and *Aegis*-equipped destroyers. The base, which is intended to protect sea lines of communication, has faced stiff resistance from leftists and local fishermen. American naval ships will be able to dock at the base, which has led to belief that its purpose is to counter China, not North Korea. *Aegis* systems stationed in Jeju will not have the requisite range to protect most of South Korea from DPRK missiles. The island is close to Socotra Rock (which the Koreans call Ieodo, and the Chinese call Suyan Rock), a submerged reef claimed by both South Korea and China. Oil and mineral deposits may lie beneath the surrounding waters.

While the naval-base construction provided a focal point for anti-US protests, another source of debate about relations with the United States was finally put to rest with the ratification in November 2011 of the Korea–US Free Trade Agreement. First signed in 2007, the agreement aims mutually to remove all duties and tariffs by 2017 and is projected to increase bilateral trade by 15%. Two months after the deal, South Korean exports to the US had risen by 11%. Labour unions in both countries opposed the deal over fear of job losses. It was passed by the US Congress just in time for a state visit by Lee. This paved the way for ratification by the National Assembly of South Korea, where the lopsided vote of 151–7 belied the intensity of the opposition to it in previous years.

Seoul then began negotiations with Beijing on a free-trade agreement with China. However, relations were soured by China's practice of repatriating North Korean refugees, which led to protests outside the Chinese embassy in Seoul. Four South Korean human-rights activists who tried to assist refugees were detained in Dalian, and the killing of a South Korean coast guard officer by a Chinese fisherman, who was resisting arrest for illegal fishing, also strained relations. But these developments were later offset by China's anger at North Korea's missile launch.

In May, South Korea and Japan reached the final stages on two military pacts, which also aim to develop trilateral military cooperation with the US. Firstly, a General Security of Military Information Agreement (GSOMIA) would stipulate the sharing of military intelligence, primarily regarding North Korea, and search and rescue information. Seoul would particularly benefit from shared intelligence from Japan's six *Aegis*-equipped destroyers and airborne early warning and control systems. The GSOMIA also represents a step towards integrating South Korea into the US–Japan ballistic-missile-defence (BMD) framework. Secondly, an Acquisition and Cross-Servicing Agreement (ACSA) would cover the provision of food, fuel and medical supplies in joint military activities. President Lee and Japanese Prime Minister Yoshihiko Noda agreed on 13 May to conclude the agreements at the end of the month, but the event was postponed due to the sensitivity among the Korean public over historical issues. Seoul has signed ACSA agreements with ten countries, and GSOMIA agreements with 24, and even opened talks on similar pacts with China.

Electoral manoeuvres

Seoul's October mayoral by-election revealed discontent with the political elite, and foreshadowed National Assembly elections the following spring. It was won by Park Won-soon, an independent candidate with a history of political activism, after IT entrepreneur Ahn Cheol-soo, another independent and the favourite to win, abruptly resigned from the race. The popularity of independents suggested that the electorate was disappointed with the current crop of political leaders, and speculation that Ahn was planning to run for president was later confirmed.

In the face of negative poll numbers, the ruling Grand National Party (GNP) in late January announced that it would remove from its party platform a clause calling for political reform and human-rights improvements in North Korea. Many people felt that the finger-wagging attitude toward North Korea had brought nothing but heightened confrontation. In a further attempt to distance itself from its past, the GNP then changed its name to Saenuri (New Frontier) Party just two months before the 11 April parliamentary election. Presidential candidate Park Geun-hye was brought back to run the party and successfully distanced herself from the unpopular President Lee, partly due to her past as a relative outsider in the party. The party essentially reinvented itself as centrist in response to voters' demands for better welfare policies, among other issues.

These changes had the desired effect. Against all expectations, Saenuri retained its majority in the 300-seat National Assembly by just two seats. However, it lost 15 seats, and the opposition Democratic United Party (DUP) gained 46 on a low turnout of 54.3%. The DUP failed to produce an expected victory because of both policies and scandals. The party's attacks on the US Free-Trade Agreement and the Jeju naval base, both of which were initiated under former president and DUP leader Roh Moo-hyun, created doubts about its fitness to rule. Extensive surveillance of citizens by the Prime Minister's Office was revealed days before the election, with the bulk of the documents apparently dating from Roh's administration. Party leader Han Myun-sook stepped down following the defeat, and the party was left with no obvious candidate for the presidential elections in December 2012. Ahn Cheol-soo, though an independent, looked the most likely candidate for the left-of-centre DUP. Park Geun-hye, daughter of late President Park Chung-hee, was considered the leading candidate for the conservatives, especially after leading Saenuri to parliamentary victory. But she faced competition from Chung Mong-joon, among others.

Dark clouds ahead

In an article in the US journal *Foreign Affairs* in summer 2011, Park emphasised themes of engagement, trust-building and inter-Korean cooperation, using a new phrase, 'trustpolitik'. Whatever the precise nature of this approach, the next president of South Korea will be expected to make some move toward reconciliation. Whether North Korea will be a willing partner is unclear: Pyongyang's state media has already taken to lambasting Park. In any case, Washington is unlikely itself to want to gamble any more political capital to seek a deal with Pyongyang, whoever wins the US presidential election. The danger is that North Korea, if feeling ignored and aggrieved, will again try to attract attention in the worst way.

Japan: Elusive Search for Stability

After one of the most traumatic periods in post-war Japanese history, the country spent the year to mid-2012 searching for domestic and international stability. The previous year had seen the triple disaster in March 2011 of the Great Tohoku Earthquake, tsunami and meltdown at the Fukushima No. 1 nuclear plant – known in Japan as the '3.11 disasters'. The government's response to the disasters provoked domestic discontent. Meanwhile, relations with China and Russia were adversely affected by wrangling over territorial issues.

By late 2011, Japan appeared to have achieved a new equilibrium, with a change of political leadership, re-assertion of US–Japan alliance ties, and the restoration of cordial ties with China. In early 2012, however, familiar problems of domestic political gridlock and tensions with China and North Korea, and even some renewed doubts about US alliance commitments, had returned.

Noda's fishy business

Following months of speculation, Prime Minister Naoto Kan of the Democratic Party of Japan (DPJ) resigned on 2 September 2011 after just over 15 months in office. He was succeeded by his finance minister, Yoshihiko Noda, who became the third DPJ prime minister in three years and the country's sixth since 2006 – in effect, a new leader each year.

Kan's premiership largely foundered on his unsure response to the 3.11 disasters, and his related attempts to raise the consumption tax to help pay for reconstruction and restore the public finances. His administration was criticised for a lack of transparency and coordination in its response to the Fukushima accident, although his declaration in July that Japan would seek eventually to end the use of nuclear power did resonate with the public. Although by May 2012 all of the country's commercial reactors had been shut down for interim safety reviews, debate raged over whether they should be restarted, and on 19 June Noda gave the go-ahead for two to do so, something that would take six weeks. (See *Strategic Geography*, pp. VIII–IX.)

Despite shutting down all reactors, the government's public-approval ratings dropped below 20%, a threshold that had traditionally been seen as marking irrecoverable decline. Meanwhile, elements of the DPJ, including Kan's predecessor Yukio Hatoyama and powerful rival Ichiro Ozawa, worked to undermine his authority within the party. They criticised his indecisive leadership, strict fiscal stance and proposed higher consumption taxes; the latter two policies ran contrary to the DPJ's 2009 election pledges. The main opposition Liberal Democratic Party (LDP) harassed Kan in the National Diet and submitted a no-confidence motion in June. He was only able to defeat this by promising to resign as soon as his administration passed three key pieces of legislation to respond to 3.11.

By August the government was able to pass a second supplementary budget, legislation on bond issues to finance disaster recovery, and a renewable-energy law. Kan then kept his promise to resign, triggering a party-leadership election. The front-runners were originally former Foreign Minister Seiji Maehara and Trade Minister Banri Kaieda (the latter backed by Ozawa), but Noda eventually emerged as the clear winner. He was deemed acceptable by the various internal DPJ groupings because of his previous low profile; he characterised himself as a dojo loach (an undistinguished freshwater fish found at the bottom of muddy waters working hard for its living), and suggested he would devote himself to the basics of improving Japan's politics and economy.

Noda made a competent start, appointing key members of different DPJ groupings, including some of Ozawa's supporters, to key party and cabinet positions, so as to establish party consensus. Kan had sought to marginalise Ozawa, suspending his party membership while he awaited trial on charges of infringing electoral-financing laws.

However, Noda soon ran into political trouble: his government failed to find ways to reduce spending and remained intent on tackling the budget deficit through a higher consumption tax. This proved highly unpopular with the public, which was already paying the cost of earthquake reconstruction, and feared a further squeeze on living standards. In addition, Noda indicated that Japan would negotiate to join the Trans-Pacific Partnership (TPP), a regional free-trade agreement that the United States also plans to join. But the trade-liberalisation measures that would be required are vociferously opposed by agricultural and medical organisations concerned at the opening up of Japan's rice and health-care markets to greater competition. By April, Noda admitted that the TPP might have to take second place to the consumption-tax rise. Meanwhile, plans to re-start a number of nuclear reactors to meet a looming shortfall in energy production encountered stiff local opposition, amid fears that adequate safeguards were not yet in place.

Noda's cabinet eventually agreed to present a bill to the Diet in early summer 2012 on increasing the consumption tax from 5% to 10% by 2014. Having publicly staked his political future on the outcome, the prime minister's prospects were uncertain. The DPJ was divided over the issue; opponents resigned from internal party posts and a dozen members left the party altogether. Ozawa, who had by then regained his party membership following his acquittal in late April, was seeking to use the issue to force Noda to resign. On the tax issue, the DPJ's majority in the lower house of the Diet looked precarious. Moreover, the party was likely to require cooperation from the LDP in the upper house, where it lacked a majority. But even though the LDP's policy was also to raise the consumption tax, it pledged to oppose it in order to force a general election. Noda may thus fail in his bid to raise the consumption tax, leading to his resignation. One possibility was that he could obtain the support of the LDP in exchange for calling a general election in autumn 2012, a year early.

Shift back towards US

The DPJ had pledged, after forming a government under Hatoyama in 2009, a greater degree of strategic autonomy from the United States. This was marked by attempts to re-affirm the centrality of East Asia for Japanese diplomacy, while seeking to refashion the US alliance to focus more on regional contingencies and less on global contingencies such as Afghanistan and Iraq. The DPJ, moreover, had been intent on revisiting the 2006 agreement with the United States for the relocation of the US Marine Corps (USMC) air station at Futenma to Nago in Okinawa Prefecture.

Hatoyama, meeting domestic and US opposition to this plan, was forced to revert to accepting the original agreement, and resigned as a result. The Kan and Noda administrations then gradually swung back to a stance similar to that of the LDP, positioning the US–Japan alliance as central to Japan's foreign-policy strategy. These efforts were reinforced by the legacy of goodwill produced by the US contribution to 3.11 disaster relief through the mobilisation of its forces in *Operation Tomodachi*.

This emphasis on the bilateral alliance under Kan and Noda was demonstrated by their effective abandonment of support for the East Asian

Community (EAC) as the preferred future mechanism for macro-regional cooperation. Instead they emphasised the East Asia Summit (EAS). The United States was not envisaged as a member of the EAC, whereas it has been a full participant in the EAS since 2011. Japan thus sought to bring US presence to bear to check China's influence on the design of regional cooperation frameworks. Similarly, in economic policy the DPJ shifted priority to the TPP, which is set to become a de facto US-led cooperation framework. The DPJ thus signified that it supported models for regional cooperation in which the United States and Asia-Pacific standards would dominate, to which it hopes China will ultimately have to subscribe and, by so doing, accept limits on its capability to construct a counter-region centred on East Asia. How far Japan can push this vision will be dependent on its domestic political commitment to the TPP, as well as the United States' own domestic political constraints and protectionist pressures.

In the security dimension, the DPJ adhered even more strongly to the bilateral relationship. In June 2011 Japan and the United States convened the Security Consultative Committee (SCC), known as the '2+2' as it brought together the foreign and defence ministers of both states. With an eye on the tensions with China the previous year, the SCC updated for the first time since 2007 the 'common strategic objectives' of the alliance, pledging to continue to press China on military transparency; increase military complementarities between the Japan Self Defense Force (JSDF) and the US military; and enhance cooperation to deal with the regional challenges of ballistic missiles, anti-access/area-denial, cyber security and maritime security, including expanded bilateral intelligence, information and reconnaissance (ISR) activity. The committee emphasised that US–Japan cooperation would expand to include enhanced trilateral ties with Australia and South Korea, and with the ASEAN states and India. The SCC again met in April 2012 prior to Noda's summit with President Obama in Washington, and reiterated the need for 'dynamic defence' cooperation in ISR, matching Japan's new defence doctrine announced in 2010.

Japan's tilt back towards the United States was also reflected in an agreement that jointly developed technologies for the SM-3 Block IIA interceptor for *Aegis*-based ballistic-missile defence could be transferred to third countries; and the decision by the Japan Ministry of Defense in December to select Lockheed Martin's F-35A to replace the Air Self Defense Force's (ASDF) ageing F-4Js. Tokyo also broadly supported Washington's declaration of a 'rebalancing' or 'pivot' towards Asia in the Pentagon's January 2012 strategic guidance document. Nevertheless, Japanese policymakers, despite shifts on both sides of the Pacific back towards greater cooperation, still entertained concerns about the current and future strength of the alliance. The US return to Asia may have been welcomed by Japan, but doubts remained over the substance of the strategy, given that the United States was reducing defence expenditure and had not yet made clear exactly what level of capabilities and force presence it would maintain in the region in the longer term. In particular, Japanese defence analysts were anxious that the United States might not have sufficient future dispositions to overcome China's anti-access/area-denial capabilities, thus leaving Japan's sea lines of communication and territorial security at risk. Moreover, Japanese analysts questioned the strength of Washington's commitment to Japan's defence in specific contingencies. Many expressed doubts that the United States would actually come to Japan's assistance and risk conflict with China in the event of a fait accompli in which the latter seized the disputed Senkaku/Diaoyu Islands in the East China Sea.

Japanese policymakers, moreover, were quietly disappointed by the US reaction to North Korea's missile test in April 2012. Although Washington strongly condemned the test as a breach of UN resolutions 1718 and 1874 and February's US–North Korea agreement, and then suspended food aid, it appeared reassured that the failure of the missile launch meant that North Korea was still some way from being able to threaten the US mainland. Tokyo thus saw Washington as more concerned over the greater issue of North Korean nuclear proliferation and preventing a third North Korean nuclear test. This reinforced the perception that the United States might be less willing to pressure North Korea over its missile programme lest it trigger a subsequent nuclear test (as happened on previous occasions), thereby demoting Japanese security on the list of US priorities.

Finally, security ties continued to be dogged by the problem of the Okinawa bases. The Noda administration attempted to bring the Futenma relocation forward, presenting an environmental-impact survey for the Nago site to Okinawa Prefecture in December to open the way for construction of the facility. But the political mood in the prefecture had been turning increasingly against the relocation, not least because of a scandal surrounding the remarks and subsequent dismissal in November of a defence official who likened the relocation to the 'rape' of the prefecture. In the meantime, criticism of the Futenma plan grew in the United States as well; a sceptical Congress cut the budget for the relocation to Guam and senior senators suggested considering moving the air station to merge with USAF Kadena in Okinawa instead.

In an attempt to break the logjam, and avert the threat to the relocation plans from the increasing domestic opposition on both sides, Washington and Tokyo agreed in April to, in effect, 'delink' the Futenma relocation from the rest of the base realignments due to occur under the 2006 Defence Policy Review Initiative. The US would initiate the relocation of 4,700 USMC personnel (rather than the original 8,000) from Okinawa to Guam without predicating these moves on a resolution of the Futenma issue. But while delinking was helpful in the short term, it carried the longer-term risk of reducing the incentives for both sides to tackle the issue, which might lead to the USMC facility remaining in its current location, engendering further future local opposition to US bases in Okinawa. Japan thus avoided, for the time being, possible US requests for it to specify financial support for the maintenance of the runway at Futenma which might have been taken to indicate Japanese acquiescence in the non-relocation of the facility. Moreover, Tokyo appeared to have successfully beaten off US requests to increase its funding for the relocation of USMC personnel from Okinawa to Guam, even though the number of Marines now moving had actually been reduced. Futenma thus looked set to rumble on as a problem for bilateral ties.

China and Korea: unease and competition

After a disastrous downturn in 2010–11, with deep tensions over the disputed Senkaku/Diaoyu Islands leading to the suspension of diplomatic exchanges and an alleged Chinese embargo on rare-earth-mineral exports, Sino-Japanese relations improved in the year to mid-2012. Economic interdependency continued to grow, but political and security ties remained uneasy.

The Japan–China–South Korea Trilateral Cooperation Dialogue (TCD) forum held in Japan in May 2011 provided an opportunity for the restoration of ties. Prime Minister Kan, Chinese Premier Wen Jiabao and South Korean President Lee Myung-bak visited the disaster-hit Tohoku region and pledged enhanced cooperation in nuclear safety and crisis management. Japan and China conspicuously avoided any discussion at the TCD of territorial issues. Noda, as the new prime minister, was then able to meet Chinese President Hu Jintao at the G20 and APEC summits in October and November, and visited Beijing in December for meetings with Hu and Wen. Japan thus managed to stabilise bilateral relations and damp down controversial issues such as conflicting territorial claims and the colonial past. (Noda had in the past been an open supporter of prime ministerial visits to Yasukuni Shrine, disputing the legality of the conviction of the class-A war criminals enshrined there, but declared that neither he nor his cabinet would pay visits to avoid provoking China and South Korea). In the economic sphere, Noda and Wen agreed in December that Japan would purchase Chinese government bonds and that the two countries would increase the use of each others' currencies in bilateral trade.

At the same time, though, Japan's policymakers expressed frustration over China's lack of reciprocation on attempts to engage on the thornier bilateral issues and move ahead with a truly 'mutually beneficial strategic relationship' (as it had been designated since 2006). Japan's leaders called repeatedly, but to no avail, for the resumption of bilateral talks, suspended since 2010, on the joint exploitation of natural-gas fields in the East China Sea. Defence planners expressed their discontent at what they saw as a lack of transparency in China's military build-up, and were especially concerned by the enhanced maritime power and activities of the People's Liberation Army Navy (PLAN) around Japan's territorial waters. In June the PLAN sent its largest squadron to date – 11 warships, including a *Sovremenny*-class destroyer – close to Okinawa Prefecture, and in July a PLAN flotilla comprising one *Luzhou*-class destroyer and a frigate followed the same route. The PLAN's sea trials of its first aircraft carrier in the past year also generated concern in Japan over Beijing's military intentions and power-projection ambitions. Moreover, an active debate took place in Japan about the possibility that China might now look to impose its territorial will on Japan by force and, armed with new anti-access/area-denial capabilities, seek to take the Senkaku/Diaoyu Islands. Such speculation was given greater currency by Tokyo Governor Shintaro Ishihara's announcement in April that he was engaged in negotiations with the private owners to purchase four of the Senkaku/Diaoyu Islands for the metropolitan government. Ishihara's intention was to draw attention to the issue and jolt the central government into reinforcing its hold on the islands, but the effect was to goad China into condemning the move.

In the meantime, the government moved more quietly to strengthen its claims to island territories. In May 2011, it completed formally naming ten uninhabited islands in Japanese territorial waters, and named another 39 in March 2012, including the Senkaku/Diaoyu islets. It registered a further 23 as state property. All this strengthened Japan's potential legal claims for exclusive economic zones (EEZ). Moreover, in April the Japanese government reported that the UN Commission on the Limits of the Continental Shelf had recognised 310,000 square kilometres of seabed around the tiny atoll of Okinotorishima as part of Japan's continental shelf. This was an area equivalent to 82% of Japan's total land territory and gave it access to potentially vast seabed resources. However, China and South Korea disputed Japan's claim to designate Okinotorishima as a rock and thus its claim to the surrounding EEZ, and it appeared that the commission's decision (which has not yet been published) was based not on the status of Okinotorishima but on other Japanese islands. Nevertheless, the April decision looked likely to further stoke territorial tensions.

Japan's general suspicion of China was compounded by the response to the North Korean missile test-launch in April. Tokyo had experienced no direct North Korean provocations since the failed 2009 missile test, but had watched with concern North–South clashes over the sinking of the *Cheonan* corvette and the Yeonpyeong incident in 2010, as well as the potential for domestic instability with the transition to the Kim Jong-un regime in the North. Japan's policymakers thus received the news that North Korea was preparing another 'satellite' launch in 2012 as a new direct provocation and dangerous ramping up of the North's threat to Japan and the rest of the international community. Despite North Korea's protestations that it was seeking to launch a civilian satellite, and that the announced trajectory and range of the launch was far south, towards the Philippines and away from Japan's main islands (in contrast to the 2009 test, which passed over Japan), the Japanese government designated the launch as in effect a missile test and mobilised its full panoply of missile-defence assets to defend against the possibility of a misdirected trajectory or debris falling on its territory. The ASDF deployed seven PAC-3 batteries on the mainland and in Okinawa Prefecture, along with 500 Ground Self Defense Force troops, and the Maritime Self Defense Force deployed three *Aegis* destroyers in the Sea of Japan and East China Sea. The government's stance, allied with extraordinary mass-media reporting, create a considerable sense of anticipation and anxiety in Japan.

In the event, the failure of the missile test proved anti-climactic. Despite its lengthy preparations and deployment of capabilities, Tokyo's response was found to be wanting. Japan remained reliant on US space-based early-warning sensors for notification of the launch, and the government was berated by the LDP and media for undue delays in relaying information to the public. Perhaps the greatest benefit to the defence establishment was the chance to rehearse the deployment of forces on the southernmost islands to defend against a putative Chinese invasion.

Despite the failure of the test, Tokyo remained intent on punishing Pyongyang for what it viewed as a transgression of UN resolutions, but was frustrated by the fact that, unlike in 2009, it did not hold a rotating seat on the Security Council, and by its reliance on Washington to lead the effort to persuade China to take action. Japanese policymakers were disappointed by Washington's unwillingness to push for anything other than a condemnatory statement from the UNSC chair, and were reminded that it was principally Chinese reluctance to pressure North Korea that put Japanese security at risk.

Away from the Korean Peninsula, Japan–China rivalry continued over the issue of resource diplomacy. The Fukushima accident and the necessity to reduce reliance on nuclear power meant that Japan had to significantly increase imports of fossil fuels. Its energy difficulties were compounded by the fact that it had agreed with the United States to reduce the percentage of its oil imports from Iran from 22% to 17% as part of international sanctions.

Japan managed to secure pledges from Russia and Australia to increase Liquefied Natural Gas (LNG) supplies. Nonetheless, it embarked on vigorous diplomacy to try to plug the gaps in its requirements. Yukio Edano, economy and trade minister, visited Saudi Arabia, the United Arab Emirates (UAE) and Kuwait in October 2011, seeking stable supplies in return for pledges to restart negotiations on an Economic Partnership Agreement (EPA) with the Gulf Co-operation Council and provide support for infrastructure. The Prime Minister's Office reportedly established a Resource Diplomacy Strategy Committee to ensure access to energy and rare-earth resources. Such proactive energy diplomacy, not witnessed since the oil shocks of the 1970s, was evident in an agreement on an EPA with Saudi Arabia to facilitate energy supplies, and plans for an EPA with Mongolia to enhance access to its rich coal reserves.

Defence policy: real dynamism?

The DPJ had been expected to be soft on defence issues, but this was one area of policy where the government in fact consistently fostered quite radical change. In line with the 2010 National Defense Programme Guidelines (NDPG), the DPJ continued to allow the JSDF to shift towards a 'dynamic defence' doctrine, characterised by technologically advanced forces, power-projection capabilities and rapid reaction to provocation and regional contingencies. The MSDF continued to plan to acquire advanced destroyers, submarines, DDH-22 light helicopter carriers and new P-1 patrol aircraft; while the ASDF began procurement of the C-2 transport and selected the F-35A. The choice of the F-35A over the Eurofighter *Typhoon* and Boeing F/A-18 was controversial, because unlike the Eurofighter it is not strictly an air-superiority fighter; nor is it yet operationally capable or combat tested, with a probable delivery date not before the end of the decade; and the Japanese defence industry will receive few opportunities to maintain competency in fighter production as it is an off-the-shelf import. Nevertheless, a fleet of 42 F-35As will eventually provide the ASDF with a formidable fifth-generation multi-role aircraft with stealth characteristics, which should match up well against, if perhaps not totally surpass, Chinese capabilities. The importance Japan attaches to the stealth capabilities of the F-35A, and its greater associated strengths in an air-defence penetration rather than air superiority role, suggests an interest in developing an offensive counter-air doctrine for the ASDF. This type of capability might be used to strike against North Korean missile bases or even the Chinese mainland in a contingency, marking a radical departure in Japan's defence-oriented posture.

Meanwhile, the GSDF and ASDF responded to China's military rise by strengthening the defences of Miyako, Yonaguni, Ishigaki and Iriomotejima, the southernmost islands in Okinawa Prefecture close to Taiwan. The GSDF deployed a new coastal surveillance unit and formed a first response unit for information gathering and defending the islands. In addition, the GSDF was to form a new anti-aircraft artillery group for rapid air deployment to the southern islands. The ASDF deployed mobile radar equipment on these four southernmost Japanese islands this year. The GSDF, ASDF and MSDF conducted joint exercises, supported by the United States, in Honshu based on a scenario in which there was a need to retake one of the southern islands. These exercises involved ASDF F-2 and F-15 fighters and MSDF P-3C patrol aircraft providing cover for ASDF C-130 transports to drop GSDF parachute forces.

Further afield, Tokyo showed a determination to maintain a military presence that counters Beijing's growing global influence. The continued deployment of MSDF destroyers and P-3Cs in anti-piracy operations in the Gulf of Aden, including the construction in Djibouti in mid-2011 of the first overseas military base for the JSDF in the post-war period, enabled Japan to keep a watch on China's maritime activities. From January 2012 the GSDF dispatched around 300 personnel for reconstruction missions in South Sudan. Tokyo was also reported in April to be considering revising the legal constraints on dispatching the JSDF to allow the use of weapons for not just self-defence but also to defend UN peacekeepers from other states.

Most radically, in December the DPJ decided to breach Japan's long-running ban on the export of military technology. In the past, Japan had made only partial exemptions for key projects with the United States and for technologies that could be used for humanitarian assistance. It will now exempt joint international development projects as well. This move opened up the possibility of collaboration with states other than the United States, and UK Prime Minister David Cameron agreed a joint statement on the development of military technologies during a visit to Tokyo in April.

Outlook: political realignments and regional tensions

As of mid-2012, Japan's domestic and international scene appeared to have returned to a state of uncertainty after stabilising, to a degree, at the end of 2011. Noda looked unlikely to last in his post beyond September: he might either be forced out of office over a failure to raise the consumption tax, or be obliged to call elections. But a general election looked unlikely to lead to a clear outcome. Neither the DPJ nor the LDP was expected to gain a majority due to low public support. New local parties centred on regional governments, leading a 'Tea Party'-style grassroots revolt against national politics, such as Osaka Mayor Toru Hashimoto's Ishin no Kai (Osaka Restoration Association), could lock the national parties out of a large number of National Diet seats. The next government looked likely to be based on some grand coalition between the DPJ and LDP, or a major reconfiguration and merger of political parties. Japan's domestic political volatility looked likely to continue.

Nor did the prospects for stable international ties appear particularly bright. Japan–China relations remained difficult. The possibility of another North Korean nuclear test held the potential to further stimulate Japanese military growth, as did the fact that ties with Washington appeared not to be rock solid. Regardless of the outcome of the presidential election, the United States did not appear to be an entirely safe haven for Japan: in April 2012, the first full bilateral summit since 2009 revealed continuing gaps between US and Japanese perceptions on key issues.

Australia: All the Way with the USA

If Australia's strategic debate in recent times has centred around the question of which side Canberra would 'choose' in the event of growing competition between China and the United States, this year brought indications that it has already made that choice. The deepening of the US–Australia alliance relationship was a dominant motif throughout the year to mid-2012. In September 2011, marking the 60th anniversary of the ANZUS alliance, annual Australia–United States Ministerial Consultations (AUSMIN) delivered a joint communiqué significant in at least two key respects.

Firstly, using language reminiscent of the ANZUS Treaty itself, for the first time cyber-security issues were explicitly designated as directly relevant to the alliance relationship: 'in the event of a cyber attack that threatens the territorial integrity, political independence or security of either of our nations, Australia and the US would consult together and determine appropriate options to address that threat'. Secondly, the communiqué placed heavy emphasis on the Indo-Pacific – as opposed to the traditional Asia-Pacific conceptualisation – suggesting to some commentators a paradigmatic shift in the way that Canberra and Washington were thinking about the region in which Australia resides and with which America is increasingly eager to engage.

The centrepiece of the deepening of the US–Australia alliance occurred in November 2011, when US President Barack Obama visited Australia for the first time. Despite twice postponing what turned out to be a very short visit, at only 28 hours, Obama was well received in a country where this particular US president remained hugely popular. The visit was also one of strategic significance. Speaking before the Australian parliament, Obama reassured one of America's closest allies that cuts in US defence spending would not come at the expense of America's Asian presence. Reinforcing that message, Obama and Australian Prime Minister Julia Gillard announced in Darwin that up to 2,500 US Marines would be deployed to Australia's north on a rotational basis and that the US Navy would also gain increased access to a port (HMAS *Stirling*) in Perth, Western Australia. The first deployment of approximately 200 personnel arrived in Darwin in April 2012 and it is anticipated that the number will be increased to 2,500 within five to six years. The marines will spend up to three months of their deployment based in Darwin and the remainder engaging with US security partners in the Asia-Pacific region.

One of the most notable aspects of this enhancement in the US–Australia strategic relationship was the lack of opposition to it within Australia. To be sure, some prominent figures voiced their dissent. The veteran pro-US foreign-policy commentator Owen Harries responded by observing that 'the crucial question is this: is America's current economic and political trouble a sign of serious structural decline? To make bets, to make commitments when this is unknown is ridiculous.' Former senior defence official Hugh White and former Chief of the Australian Army Peter Leahy – both now prominent university professors – each expressed concern that the Darwin deployment would complicate Australia's relations with China. Yet political opposition was next to non-existent (in contrast to President George W. Bush's controversial 2003 visit 'Down Under' when he was heckled in the Australian parliament) while the Australian public was effusive. Indeed, according to polling conducted by the Sydney-based Lowy Institute for International Policy, 82% of Australians regarded the US alliance as important to their country's security, while 55% were in favour of permitting the US to base troops on Australian soil.

Fractious politics

This level of consensus was not apparent in other areas of Australia's domestic politics, which became increasingly fractious. Tensions within the ruling Labor Party came to a head in February 2012, when Foreign Minister Kevin Rudd resigned unexpectedly while on an official visit to the US. Upon his return, Rudd challenged Gillard for the party leadership. Although opinion-poll figures indicated overwhelming public support for Rudd to be reappointed as prime minister, his challenge was soundly defeated by a margin of 71 legislators to 31.

In a popular appointment, Rudd was replaced as foreign minister by the former premier of the state of New South Wales, Bob Carr. His strong foreign-policy credentials – particularly his long-standing connections with senior US policymakers – were widely considered an asset to a struggling prime minister not renowned for her expertise in this area. Consistent with this, Carr's first major overseas visit was to the United States. While his appointment helped to minimise the vacuum that would otherwise have been left by the highly proactive Rudd, the latter's return to the backbenches did little to ease leadership speculation. In particular, a number of high-profile scandals continued to hang over the government, including accusations of improper credit-card usage by one member of parliament and allegations of sexual harassment against the speaker of the House of Representatives. Given the slim majority on which the government rested – it depended on the support of independent MPs – there remained much uncertainty over whether it would see out its term.

Foreign-policy initiatives

Gillard took steps to establish her own foreign-policy credentials. In September 2011, for instance, she commissioned a White Paper on *Australia in the Asian Century*. This would consider present and future economic, political and strategic trends in Asia, the opportunities and challenges these pose for Australia, and the role of regional and global cooperation in approaching them. The ultimate stated purpose was to provide 'a national blueprint for Australia at a time of transformational economic growth and change in Asia'. The process, which involved quite extensive public consultation, was being led by former Secretary of the Treasury Ken Henry, and the White Paper was scheduled for release in mid-2012.

In November 2011, Gillard then unexpectedly announced a proposal – a personal initiative on her part – to reverse a long-standing ban on Australian exports of uranium to India. This ban had been in place since the 1970s and derived largely from Labor Party policy that Australia would not sell uranium to countries that were not party to the Nuclear Non-Proliferation Treaty (NPT). The government of John Howard had come close to reversing the ban and reportedly would have done so had he been re-elected as prime minister in 2007. Gillard succeeded in gaining support for its removal.

Three factors appear to have contributed to this decision. Firstly, the timing of Gillard's initial announcement on the eve of the Obama visit was significant, made as it was against the backdrop of deepening strategic ties between the US and India. Secondly, the ban was increasingly seen as inhibiting economic and political progress in the Australia–India relationship, undermining the Asian Century strategy that Gillard had initiated. Thirdly, continuation of the ban in the face of India's economic rise had caused some commentators to question her government's competence.

While Gillard's foreign-policy credentials were given a significant boost by Labor Party support to remove the ban, later developments again called into question the competence of her government in the areas of defence and national security. Much criticism centred around Minister for Defence Stephen Smith, especially over his treatment of allegations of sexual misconduct involving cadets at the Australian Defence Force Academy (ADFA). ADFA Commandant Bruce Kafer was suspended over his handling of the incident. However, Smith delayed for several months the release of the report that exonerated Kafer and ultimately led to his reinstatement. The defence minister was widely criticised for this delay, by among others four of Australia's most highly respected retired generals. There was further criticism of the government's failure to implement the force structure outlined in a 2009 Defence White Paper, particularly after A$5.5bn worth of cuts were made to the 2012/13 defence budget, leaving Australia spending 1.56% of GDP on defence, the lowest level since the late 1930s. In the days immediately prior to this budget announcement Gillard announced that a new Defence White Paper scheduled for 2014 would be published a year earlier.

Looking towards the future, the rise of Indonesia gained increased prominence in Australia. Much attention was focused on deepening security ties between Canberra and Jakarta, which had initially gained traction in the wake of the 2002 Bali bombings (which killed 88 Australians) and took a further step forward with the holding of inaugural 2+2 talks between the Australian and Indonesian foreign and defence ministers in March 2012. Polling conducted in November and December 2011 by the Lowy Institute for International Policy registered a marked improvement in popular Indonesian attitudes towards Australia. In July 2011 a controversial Australian ban on live-cattle exports to Indonesia was lifted. On a less positive note, however, Indonesian Foreign Minister Marty Natalegawa cautioned that the deployment of US Marines to Australia could provoke 'a vicious circle of tension and mistrust'. Polling also suggested that the Australian public – particularly older Australians – remained distrustful of Indonesia.

New Zealand: Economic and Budget Pressures

The biggest news story of the period for New Zealand occurred in November 2011, when the country hosted the Rugby World Cup and broke a 24-year drought to win the tournament. The victory provided a ray of sunshine in an otherwise troubled period for New Zealand. Still reeling from the devastating Christchurch earthquake of February 2011, which killed 185 people, the region was hit by a series of severe aftershocks in early 2012. While there were no fatalities or reports of significant damage, scientists suggested that aftershocks of this nature could continue in Christchurch for years. The country as a whole continued to suffer the economic aftershock of the earthquake, compounded by the effects of the global recession.

Notwithstanding these challenges, Prime Minister John Key won a second term in November 2011. The former investment banker's National Party won 48% of the vote, increasing its share and winning 59 of the 121 seats in parliament, meaning that with the support of its partners – ACT New Zealand and United Future, each of which won one seat – it was able to secure a majority. Key subsequently announced a confidence and supply arrangement with the Maori Party, which won three seats. The main opposition Labour Party won 34 seats and the Greens a record 14 seats. Key's main objective was to eliminate a NZ$18.4bn (US$13.75bn) budget deficit, principally by reducing government stakes in a number of assets including energy companies and the airline Air New Zealand.

Developments in the areas of foreign affairs and defence included a budget-cutting proposal to reduce the size of the Ministry of Foreign Affairs, which was heavily criticised by officials – only four of New Zealand's serving ambassadors opted not to sign a letter opposing it – and by agricultural exporters. The plan was returned to the drawing board. Meanwhile, a restructuring of the New Zealand Defence Force (NZDF) was under way, implementing an October 2011 defence capability plan which followed a 2010 Defence White Paper. The changes were intended to create an integrated NZDF centred around a Joint Amphibious Task Force capable of independent action in the South Pacific and of participating in a larger coalition operation overseas. Towards this end, New Zealand will spend about NZ$3bn on enhancing its armed forces over the coming decade, with a view to being able to deploy an 800-strong force over a three-year period in a mid-intensity environment. Finally, reflecting improved US–New Zealand security ties that are likely to deepen even further during Key's second term, the first joint exercise in 26 years to take place on New Zealand soil between US troops and the NZDF occurred in April 2012.

Southwest Pacific: Heightened Outside Interest

The 40th-anniversary meeting of the Southwest Pacific's paramount multilateral organisation – the Pacific Islands Forum (PIF) – was held in Auckland, New Zealand, in September 2011. While the leaders of Australia and New Zealand have traditionally been the highest profile attendees at this gathering, the 2011 meeting was also attended by UN Secretary-General Ban Ki-moon, along with the president of the European Commission and the foreign ministers of France and Indonesia. A number of countries lobbying for permanent seats on the UN Security Council also sent representatives, with a view to securing votes from small Pacific island states. Of particular note was the size and diversity of the US delegation, which was headed by a deputy secretary of state and included a total of 50 representatives from the White House, the Departments of State, Defense and Commerce, USAID, the Coast Guard and the Peace Corps. China sent an eight-strong delegation headed by Vice Foreign Minister Cui Tiankai.

One notable absentee was Fiji, banned from attending since its December 2006 military coup. However, New Zealand Prime Minister Key appeared to soften an earlier stance that Fiji's military leader Commodore Frank Bainimarama needed to return the country to democracy immediately. He said PIF re-admission might be possible if Fiji 'demonstrated that they are on a pathway to democracy and the holding of those elections in 2014 as promised'. Optimism was maintained in early 2012 with Bainimarama's announcement that regulations introduced in 2009 censoring the media and prohibiting meetings of more than three people were to be relaxed. Sceptics noted that a concurrent amendment of the country's 40-year-old Public Order Act extended these controls and, indeed, enshrined them in law by legalising arrest without warrant and detention for periods of up to 14 days. In March 2012, however, Bainimarama announced a wide-ranging process of consultation on a new constitution and continued to promise that elections would be held by September 2014.

Papua New Guinea was plunged into a constitutional crisis which originated in April 2011 when Prime Minister Michael Somare underwent the first of three operations for a serious heart condition in Singapore. His family announced in June that he would not be resuming his office for health reasons. However, when parliamentarians replaced Somare's nominated acting prime minister with the recently demoted Treasurer and Finance Minister Peter O'Neill, Somare refused to accept the decision and indicated that he would complete his term, which was due to end in June 2012. The supreme court ruled in Somare's favour by three votes to two in December 2011, leaving the country with two prime ministers, two cabinets, two governors-general and two police commissioners. The crisis appeared to have been resolved on 20 December 2011, when Michael Ogio – who was appointed governor-general (the representative of Queen Elizabeth II, the country's constitutional monarch) during Somare's prime ministership and was widely viewed as the legitimate holder of the office – reversed an earlier decision and declared O'Neill to be prime minister. A failed military coup led by a small number of Somare supporters occurred in January 2012. In February 2012 suggestions that a general election might be delayed due to problems with voter registration led to threats from Australian Foreign Minister Bob Carr that this would provoke sanctions. The hope was that the June 2012 election could bring an end to political instability. However, in May 2012 the Supreme Court ruled again that the O'Neill government was illegal, to which the Papua New Guinea parliament responded by declaring a state of emergency in the capital city of Port Moresby, and in the Southern Highlands and Hela provinces.

Southeast Asia: Political Change

Important domestic political developments were under way in several Southeast Asian states during the year to mid-2012. In Myanmar, pro-democracy leader Aung San Suu Kyi entered into a tentative partnership with President Thein Sein, which led to members of her party being elected to parliament, to the easing of Western sanctions, and to her own first forays outside the country since 1988. In Thailand, the government led by Yingluck Shinawatra faced strong domestic opposition, aimed particularly at its apparent plans to engineer the return to Thailand of the premier's brother, former Prime Minister Thaksin Shinawatra. In Malaysia, there was growing political contestation following the January 2012 acquittal from criminal charges of opposition leader Anwar Ibrahim and ahead of a general election, while in Indonesia political attention was increasingly focused on the legislative and presidential elections scheduled for 2014. Simultaneously, Southeast Asia was the focus of greater strategic attention than at any time since the 1980s, as China escalated its pressure on other claimants to features in the South China Sea while the United States adopted a new geopolitical posture which the Obama administration referred to as a 'rebalance to the Asia-Pacific'.

Myanmar: reforms take wing

Myanmar's politics were characterised by dramatic changes. During the second half of 2011, there were growing signs that the government formed under President Thein Sein in March was serious about implementing political and economic reforms. The motivations for the reform programme were unclear. However, expanding the government's international legitimacy seemed to be a key consideration. The regime apparently wanted to widen Myanmar's economic and politico-strategic options after two decades of increasing dependence on China, which had become necessary as political repression and human-rights abuses provoked punitive economic sanctions from Western states. A further trigger may have been the government's wish to smooth the way for Myanmar to take its turn as chair of the Association of Southeast Asian Nations (ASEAN) in 2014, having been forced to relinquish a previous opportunity in 2006 under pressure from fellow ASEAN states.

Aung San Suu Kyi, the 1991 Nobel Peace Prize winner, had been released in November 2010 after spending 15 of the previous 21 years under house arrest. Following meetings with Labour Minister Aung Kyi, in August 2011 the leader of the National League for Democracy (NLD) flew to the administrative capital Naypyidaw to meet Thein Sein for the first time. Following the meeting, Aung San Suu Kyi said she believed that the president 'genuinely wishes for democratic reforms' and expressed cautious optimism regarding Myanmar's political future. The meeting apparently resulted in tentative agreement from Thein Sein that the government would not harass the NLD, though it remained an illegal organisation, and that Aung San Suu Kyi would be allowed to travel freely. The NLD leader impressed on the president that there could be no progress until his government released political prisoners, and before the end of August the parliament passed legislation allowing exactly this. For her part, Aung San Suu Kyi promised to consider important concessions that would help the government reduce the country's international economic isolation.

Over the following months, a working relationship developed between the president and the NLD leader, which was reportedly characterised by a degree of genuine warmth, based in part on Thein Sein's manifest respect for Aung San Suu Kyi as the daughter of Myanmar's nationalist hero and founder of the country's army, General Aung San. This proved so central to Myanmar's continuing political evolution that some observers questioned the viability of the reform process in the absence of either of these two key actors. In late 2011, reforms gathered pace to a degree that would have seemed impossible earlier in the year. In September, against a background of rising popular outcry (echoed by Aung San Suu Kyi) about the potential environmental and human impact of a huge hydroelectric dam on the Irrawaddy River at Myitsone, being built and financed by Chinese interests, Thein Sein announced its termination – contradicting government assertions only weeks earlier that the government fully supported the project.

In October, the government released approximately 300 political prisoners, out of an estimated total of approximately 2,000, as part of a wider amnesty. During the same month, the parliament passed legislation, approved by the International Labour Organisation, allowing labour unions, acknowledging the right to strike, and providing legal protection for union members and strikers. Crucially, in early November the government sponsored legislative amendments aimed at encouraging the NLD to accept the prevailing political system and to re-register as a political party.

These and other reforms such as the relaxation of media censorship brought positive reactions regionally and internationally. At their November 2011 summit in Bali, ASEAN leaders agreed that Myanmar should take its turn as the association's chair in 2014. In December, US Secretary of State Hillary Clinton visited Myanmar, met both Thein Sein and Aung San Suu

Kyi, and announced that the United States would no longer block international financial assistance from the World Bank and International Monetary Fund or aid under the United Nations Development Programme. The United States and Myanmar agreed to discuss upgrading their diplomatic relations and exchanging ambassadors. Clinton also invited Myanmar to join the Lower Mekong Initiative, a US-sponsored regional association focused on water issues. The British and French foreign ministers followed Clinton's visit with their own trips to Myanmar in January.

Shortly before Clinton's visit, Aung San Suu Kyi revealed that she would stand as a parliamentary candidate in forthcoming by-elections for 48 vacant parliamentary seats. In mid-December, the government approved the NLD's re-registration. By January 2012, Aung San Suu Kyi had sufficient confidence in the reform process to say that 'Burma is on the verge of a breakthrough to democracy'. Shortly afterwards, the government released more political prisoners, including prominent opposition activists such as student leader Min Ko Naing (who had been detained for most of the time since 1988), former Prime Minister Khin Nyunt (in jail since 2004), Shan leader Khun Tun Oo, and militant monk Shin Gambira who had helped lead the abortive 'Saffron Revolution' in 2007. As a direct result of the amnesty, which US President Barack Obama described as 'a substantial step forward for democratic reform', Washington announced within hours that it was restoring full diplomatic relations.

Despite widespread optimism regarding the prospects for political change in Myanmar, the relationship between ethnic-minority groups (many of which had mounted long-running insurgencies against the political centre) and the government remained unstable and sometimes violent (see *Strategic Geography*, p. XV). For its part, the opposition NLD did not seem to have formulated a clear policy regarding the minorities beyond calling for 'unity' and for greater international aid and investment in ethnic-minority areas. The main armed conflict was between government forces and the Kachin Independence Army (KIA), the military wing of the Kachin Independence Organisation (KIO), following the breakdown of a 17-year-old ceasefire in June 2011. Though peace talks began in Ruili, China in January 2012, Kachin sources claimed that approximately 20,000 combat troops from Myanmar's army were deployed in the continuing offensive against the KIO. In March, Thein Sein, saying he had ordered the army to cease offensive operations, appealed to the KIO to join further talks and outlined a three-part peace process. In May 2012, UN Secretary-General Ban Ki-moon called for an end to fighting in Kachin state after receiving a letter from the KIA which accused Myanmar's army of ethnic cleansing. During negotiations in June 2012 the government proposed that both sides pull back their forces to reduce the potential for conflict. However, the KIO stood firm on its demand that the army should withdraw from what it saw as its territory, and clashes continued on an almost daily basis.

By mid-2012, Myanmar's government claimed that it had reached peace agreements with ten ethnic-minority insurgent groups (notably including the Karen National Union in January 2012), and that the KIO was the only such group not to have agreed to a ceasefire. However, fighting between government forces and the Shan State Army (SSA) continued intermittently, and in early July the SSA told Thein Sein that it would end its ceasefire if Myanmar's army did not 'suspend hostilities'. A struggle between local military commanders and the SSA for control of lucrative narcotic-trafficking routes appeared to underlie this intermittent conflict.

The ethnic-minority conflicts had little impact on campaigning for the 1 April 2012 by-elections. As NLD leader, Aung San Suu Kyi campaigned not just in the constituency that she was contesting in Yangon, but despite evident physical exhaustion travelled widely throughout Myanmar, receiving tumultuous and adulatory welcomes wherever she went. The result of the elections was a landslide victory for the NLD, which won 43 of the 44 seats it contested (the exception being in a constituency where its candidate was disqualified) – a result that surpassed even the opposition party's own expectations. Even constituencies substantially populated by government officials and military personnel in Naypyidaw fell to the NLD. Though the resulting NLD presence in parliament would be relatively small at 6% of total seats, its victory in the by-elections was of huge symbolic importance. The humiliation of the regime-backed Union Solidarity and Development Party, effectively a proxy for the army, indicated that a similar voting pattern in the general election scheduled for 2015 would almost certainly lead to a huge parliamentary majority for the NLD, despite the fact that 25% of legislative seats are reserved for military appointees. In May, NLD members of parliament, including Aung San Suu Kyi, took their parliamentary oaths despite an earlier controversy when the party said party members could not do this, because the oath included a pledge to 'protect' the constitution, to which the party objected on principle.

International reaction to the by-elections was highly positive. Clinton said the United States would ease restrictions on investment to allow NGOs to operate in Myanmar if their projects were aimed at meeting 'basic human needs' or promoting democracy, and would soon name an ambassador to

Myanmar. However, she also noted that 'sanctions and prohibitions will stay in place on individuals and institutions that remain on the wrong side of these historic reform efforts'. Foreign economic interest in resource-rich Myanmar escalated rapidly. Two weeks after the by-elections, British Prime Minister David Cameron made the first visit in decades by a Western leader to Myanmar and jointly with Aung San Suu Kyi called for the suspension of international sanctions against the country in recognition of the changes that were happening there. Once home, though, Cameron told the British parliament that while Myanmar's regime was taking steps towards democracy, 'we should be extremely cautious'. Japan agreed to waive billions of dollars' worth of Myanmar's debt and to recommence financial aid, which had been suspended since 1988. Shortly afterwards, European Union foreign ministers announced that the EU would suspend economic sanctions for a year, and Norway removed all restrictions on aid, finance and visas. Ban Ki-moon addressed Myanmar's parliament and called for the continued lifting of sanctions. South Korean President Lee Myung-bak, visiting in May, offered a wide-ranging aid package and expanded cooperation in energy and other resource development. Soon afterwards, the Thai government announced that it had approved more than $1bn in projects to support construction of a deep-sea port and industrial zone in southern Myanmar. Indian Prime Minister Manmohan Singh visited and spoke of establishing a bilateral 'roadmap' for boosting bilateral economic ties.

Aung San Suu Kyi's first visits outside Myanmar since 1988 were another milestone. She went to Thailand in May 2012, primarily to speak at a World Economic Forum meeting. This provoked Thein Sein to cancel his own engagement to address the same forum; one of the president's advisers accused the opposition leader of a 'lack of transparency' and indirectly raised concerns over the durability of the working relationship between Myanmar's two key figures. While in Thailand, Aung San Suu Kyi also addressed migrant workers from Myanmar and visited a camp for Karen refugees near the border. In June, she undertook a longer trip to Europe, receiving her Nobel Peace Prize 21 years late at a ceremony in Oslo, and also visiting France, Ireland, Switzerland and the UK.

Meanwhile, the reform process continued. In May, the government announced a further relaxation of media controls. While Aung San Suu Kyi was in Europe, Thein Sein presaged a second phase of reforms, which he said would include reductions in the state's role in some economic sectors. Speaking at the IISS Shangri-La Dialogue in Singapore on 2 June, Minister of Defence Hla Min confirmed that Myanmar had no plans to continue with a nuclear research programme that had earlier provoked international concern (though in response to a question regarding whether the country would submit to inspections by the International Atomic Energy Agency, he said that there was 'nothing to investigate'). Asked whether the quota of parliamentary seats reserved for the armed forces could be reduced, Hla Min said that 'when appropriate, there will be a gradual decline from 25%'. This was the first time that any government spokesman had admitted this possibility.

At mid-2012, any prognosis for Myanmar's future political development needed to include significant caveats. The reform process remained incomplete. The military continued to hold effective veto power, and the extent of its support for Thein Sein remained unclear. The continuing process seemed fragile in that it evidently depended on two key personalities, Thein Sein and Aung San Suu Kyi, neither of whom appeared to be in robust health. The country still lacked an independent judiciary to safeguard human and civil rights and, according to Aung San Suu Kyi, 330 political prisoners remained in jail.

Ethnic-minority troubles also persisted, and not only in Kachin and Shan areas, where human-rights abuses continued. Against the background of long-running persecution of the Rohingya people (most of whom were Muslims, and stateless) in western Myanmar's Rakhine state, a significant new conflict erupted in early June 2012 after nine Muslim Rohingya people were killed in revenge for the rape and murder of an Arakanese woman. Riot police were soon exchanging gunfire with Muslims, the army deployed troops, and it was reported that 14 villages had been razed. By late June, 78 people had died, almost 32,000 people had been displaced by the violence, and Bangladesh reported that it had returned almost 1,000 people who had crossed into its territory as a result of the fighting. The conflict highlighted Myanmar's ethnic and religious heterogeneity and the type of complex internal security challenges that any future administration would face.

Thailand: Yingluck's first year
While political developments in Myanmar provided good reasons for cautious optimism regarding that country's trajectory, those in Thailand gave cause for concern over its future political stability. Following the Pheu Thai Party's clear-cut victory in the July 2011 general election, the first session of the new House of Representatives (in which Pheu Thai and four smaller allies held almost 300 of the total of 500 seats) voted on 5 August overwhelmingly to approve party leader Yingluck Shinawatra's nomination as prime minis-

ter. Four days later, Yingluck – the sister of former Prime Minister Thaksin Shinawatra, who had been deposed by a military coup in 2006 – announced her cabinet. In a clear effort to start her time as national leader as uncontroversially as possible, leaders of the United Front for Democracy Against Dictatorship or 'Red Shirt' movement were not given ministerial roles. The group, which supported Thaksin, had mounted violent demonstrations against the previous government of Abhisit Vejjajiva, culminating in what amounted to urban warfare in central Bangkok in May 2010. Nevertheless, few Thais doubted that Yingluck was effectively a proxy for Thaksin, who remained in exile in Dubai because he faced jail if he returned to Thailand, as the result of a successful criminal prosecution in absentia for corruption. Many believed that Yingluck was effectively a temporary place-holder pending Thaksin's eventual return, and that Thaksin was a puppet-master who controlled the new government on a day-to-day basis.

Yingluck's administration immediately faced a major challenge in the form of a disastrous flood resulting from the heaviest rainfall experienced in Thailand for half a century. Responding to this natural calamity was necessarily a priority for the new government for the remainder of 2011. The new prime minister oversaw the establishment of centralised flood monitoring and relief operations and began tours of flood-affected provinces a week after taking office, as well as promising government investment in long-term flood-prevention projects. However, the flood – which lasted until January 2012 – affected 65 of the country's 77 provinces, inundated parts of Bangkok, resulted in 815 deaths and caused an estimated $45bn in economic damage, particularly to the manufacturing sector. With seven major industrial estates flooded and out of operation, manufacturing supply chains were disrupted, affecting automobile production elsewhere in Southeast Asia and causing a global shortage of hard disk drives. Efforts to mitigate the disaster provoked controversy and criticism from the opposition, particularly in relation to the flood's impact on Bangkok, where the government's Flood Relief Operations Centre and the opposition-controlled Bangkok Metropolitan Administration were often at loggerheads. Much criticism was directed at Yingluck and her government for underestimating the scale of the flood, and for conveying inconsistent messages and inadequate warnings. The construction of flood barriers sometimes led to disputes: residents of Bangkok suburbs were unhappy that their homes were flooded in order to protect the city centre. In some instances, local people sabotaged barriers. Former Prime Minister Abhisit, now opposition leader, and military commanders lobbied in October for the government to declare a state of emergency in order to protect the flood barriers but Yingluck refused to do so, possibly out of fear that such a move could provide a pretext for renewed military interference in politics.

With the flood's recession in January, Yingluck (reportedly under Thaksin's direction) reshuffled her cabinet, apparently in an effort both to reinforce its solidarity and to respond to criticism of the government's performance. Some of the choices for new ministers were controversial, particularly because they included Red Shirt leaders such as Nattawat Saikua, who became a deputy minister. A key appointment was that of retired Air Chief Marshal Sukumpol Suwanatat, a classmate of Thaksin from their time as military cadets, who was moved from the transport portfolio to become defence minister. Sukumpol was a leading 'watermelon' military officer ('green outside, red inside') and Thaksin reportedly assigned him the task of amending the Defence Ministry Administration Act to allow greater political influence over military promotions so that pro-Thaksin officers could be promoted to more prominent military positions.

Despite the major distraction of the flood, Yingluck's administration did start moving to enact important policy initiatives during its early months. A key objective for Pheu Thai was to rebalance Thailand's society and economy to boost domestic consumption, according to Kittirat Na-Ranong, the new deputy prime minister in charge of economic policy. In Kittirat's view, the fact that exports accounted for 72% of GDP highlighted the need to 'reduce our dependence on others' and to 'guard against the perils of globalisation', particularly in light of the economic turmoil in the United States and Europe.

A crucial element of Pheu Thai's economic strategy was to raise the incomes of Thailand's poor. During the election campaign the party had promised to legislate for a nationwide 40% increase in the daily minimum wage to 300 baht ($9.50) if the party took power. However, pressure from small and medium enterprises (which had earlier forced Abhisit to scale back to a 25% increase his own similar promise) resulted in delayed and only partial implementation. Nevertheless, on 1 April 2012 the minimum wage for Bangkok and six surrounding provinces increased to 300 baht and elsewhere by lesser amounts, to the benefit of an estimated seven million workers in total. The government still aimed for a 300 baht minimum wage nationwide by 2015. It also increased the monthly starting salary for graduate civil servants to 15,000 baht ($475).

A second important promise was the 'rice-mortgage' scheme, intended to raise rural income by buying padi (unmilled rice) from Thailand's eight million rice farmers at 15,000 baht a tonne, double the price prevailing before the election. While the scheme, which came into effect in October 2011, undoubtedly helped the farmers, who responded eagerly by selling their grain to the government, it had important ramifications for Thailand's role as the world's largest rice exporter. Rather than exporting the rice at a loss, the government stockpiled huge amounts, which exporters would otherwise have sold on the international market, and it was unclear how much rice was held in warehouses and when and at what price it would eventually be sold. By July 2012 Thailand's rice exports had declined 44%. Critics argued that the policy was misguided: big farmers were gaining most from the increased prices, and government funds would have been better directed towards helping small rice growers to increase their productivity.

During the first half of 2012, political debate in Thailand focused on the question of whether Thaksin might return to Thailand and assume a legitimate and direct role in the country's politics, perhaps as prime minister. An important report commissioned by the parliamentary committee on national reconciliation from the politically independent but state-funded King Prajadhipok's Institute (KPI) in April made detailed recommendations for a gradual process of reconciliation between the two main sides in Thailand's long-running political conflict. Among its recommendations were an amnesty for people who had participated in protests and the dropping of corruption charges previously brought by the defunct Assets Scrutiny Committee (which had been appointed by the architects of the 2006 coup) against members of Thaksin's administration including the former prime minister himself. In early April, government MPs and senators ensured a vote in favour of forwarding the KPI proposals to the cabinet for consideration with a view to using them as the basis for a reconciliation bill. During the Songkran (Thai new year) celebrations in April, Thaksin visited neighbouring Laos and Cambodia, where he addressed large-scale rallies of his Red Shirt supporters. Saying that he hoped to return to Thailand during the 'auspicious' current year, Thaksin claimed that he had no wish to become prime minister again, though he expected to be an 'adviser' to his sister in that role.

Also during April, the government ensured the indefinite extension of the current parliamentary sitting in order to allow the rewriting of the 2007 constitution, which had been promulgated by the military-appointed government following the coup that deposed Thaksin; the planned revision had been part of Pheu Thai's election manifesto. Critics claimed that this 'charter amendment' process was aimed, above all, at providing another route for Thaksin to return to Thailand, as it was anticipated that the new constitution would include an amnesty clause.

In mid-April, Abhisit warned of a 'political tsunami' if the government tried to 'whitewash' Thaksin to allow his return, while the government's Yellow Shirt opponents in the People's Alliance for Democracy (PAD)began organising demonstrations against the government's reconciliation and constitutional amendment bills. During May, the Constitutional Court accepted petitions from the opposition Democrat Party and others that questioned the legality of the government's promotion of constitutional change, charging that this involved an attempt to undermine Thailand's political system based on the constitutional monarchy. With the opposition warning that the country would descend into a new political crisis if the government did not follow a Constitutional Court ruling to delay the constitutional-amendment bill's third reading, in mid-June the government ended the parliamentary session, effectively postponing further debate on both bills. Yingluck said that the government would proceed with the constitutional amendment at 'the right time', but Red Shirt legislators including Nattawat Saikua fiercely criticised what they saw as the government's timidity.

While the government emphasised to the court that it had no intention of interfering with the constitutional monarchy, by mid-2012 the future of the government itself was under threat as the court began a review of the proposed constitutional amendment: if it was found to threaten the monarchy, the Pheu Thai Party could be disbanded. Though it would have been feasible for Yingluck to set up a new party as the basis for her government, large-scale and possibly violent demonstrations seemed likely. A widespread view among government supporters was that this intervention against the executive's legislative power amounted to an attempted judicial coup. However, in the event, the court dismissed the complaints against the government, effectively defusing the looming crisis. Nevertheless, its ruling complicated efforts to change the constitution by insisting that the government would need approval from a referendum before the constitution could be rewritten, which could only be done section by section. A Pheu Thai spokesman said that the government was likely to proceed down that route.

Thailand's political scene remained in ferment despite the Constitutional Court's ruling. The government remained under pressure from two directions: its own Red Shirt supporters, who had pressed for the enactment of both the national-reconciliation and constitutional-amendment bills; and from the parliamentary opposition and the Yellow Shirt activists of PAD. An impending problem remained Thaksin's potential return and the possibly violent political instability that would almost certainly provoke. Moreover, the passage of time inevitably brought the royal succession closer, and it was widely appreciated that this could itself provoke instability. However, one significant factor on the government's side remained Thailand's continuing strong overall economic performance, with the IMF forecasting GDP growth for 2012 at 5% and for 2013 at 7% despite the impact of the 2011 floods.

Violence in Thailand's far south continued, with insurgents carrying out frequent attacks using roadside bombs and grenade launchers as well as firearms, increasingly against 'soft' targets such as village defence volunteers, local government officials and schoolteachers rather than the army and police. More evidence emerged of links between insurgents and drug gangs after three bombs in Sungai Kolok in Narathiwat province killed four people, including three Malaysian tourists, in September 2011, in what the army claimed was a revenge attack for a recent police drug raid. In late March 2012, in one of the insurgency's most lethal coordinated attacks, car bombs in Yala City, Hat Yai and the Mae Lan district of Pattani province killed 14 people and injured 340. Meanwhile, according to an Amnesty International report in May 2012, the security forces continued to ill-treat and torture detainees. In June, Deputy Prime Minister Yutthasak Sasiprapa, a retired general and former defence minister, said controversially that the violence in the south was under control and that the armed forces had quelled unrest there, a claim that NGOs and also King Prajadhipok's Institute contested. Yingluck's government routinely extended the state of emergency in the three provinces of Narathiwat, Pattani and Yala every three months, but showed no signs of getting to grips with the violence – which had killed more than 5,000 people since 2004 – any more effectively than its predecessor. The violence showed no sign of expanding into other parts of Thailand.

Maritime Southeast Asia: elections in prospect

In Malaysia and Indonesia there was a growing sense of political uncertainty ahead of national elections expected during 2012 in the former country, and scheduled for 2014 in the latter. In Malaysia, the Barisan Nasional (National Front) coalition government led by Prime Minister Najib Tun Razak and with his United Malays National Organisation (UMNO) as its main component continued to face significant political opposition. The most recent general election in 2008 had resulted in significant gains for opposition parties, which were grouped into a loose coalition led by former Deputy Prime Minister Anwar Ibrahim, and it was widely expected that the government would lose support again – and possibly even lose power – in the next national election, which needed to be held by June 2013. Although polls indicated that Najib's moves to reform the economy and to scrap repressive legislation including the Internal Security Act (a move announced in September 2011) had significantly improved his personal popularity, according to a poll in April 2012 the government itself remained unpopular with 42% of the population.

The main opposition to Najib's government came from non-Malays (particularly Chinese) opposed to the racism of the government's policies favouring ethnic Malays and other indigenous people, from Muslims (most of them Malays) who wanted an Islamic state, and from people of all ethnic groups who wished to overturn the cronyism and corruption that many alleged were endemic in government. The last category made their views known in the Bersih ('clean') 2.0 and Bersih 3.0 mass demonstrations against corruption in Kuala Lumpur and other Malaysian cities in July 2011 and April 2012.

The Pakatan Rakyat opposition coalition led by Anwar Ibrahim argued that good governance and social justice would be key to the country's future social cohesion and economic growth, and that Najib's reforms were essentially cosmetic. It promised not only to move decisively to control corruption, but also to increase health spending substantially and to cancel the university-fee debts of a whole generation of students. The opposition received a major fillip in January 2012 when Anwar was acquitted of criminal charges (for sexually assaulting an assistant in what is widely rumoured to have been a 'sting' operation by the authorities) at the end of a trial that had begun in 2010.

By mid-2012, the general election was widely believed to be imminent and there was much speculation regarding the most likely date. After police used tear gas and water cannon to break up the Bersih 3.0 demonstration in Kuala Lumpur in April and opposition leaders were subject to physical harassment and death threats, there was widespread concern in Malaysia that the election could be violent, particularly if, as seemed possible, the ruling coalition again lost support. Some polls suggested that the Barisan Nasional could even lose power. Given that the coalition had been in power since the independence of peninsular Malaysia in 1957, this would be a momentous development with potentially dramatic consequences.

By many measures, Indonesia appeared increasingly successful under the leadership of President Susilo Bambang Yudhoyono, who was re-elected for his second term in 2009. However, the country's anti-corruption efforts met with only partial success: graft remained widespread in Indonesia's public sector and during 2011–12 corruption was the pre-eminent issue in Indonesian politics as it became clear that it had tainted leading politicians from the president's Democratic Party, notably in connection with

Indonesia's staging of the Southeast Asian Games in 2011. By January 2012, the corruption allegations had caused schisms in the Democratic Party, with Party Chairman Anas Urbaningrum and Deputy Secretary-General Angelina Sondakh implicated as well as former Treasurer Muhammad Nazaruddin, who in April was sentenced to a jail term. The popularity of the party, which had won 20% of the votes in the 2009 legislative election on an anti-corruption platform, declined precipitously and its prospects in the 2014 elections were severely undermined.

Indonesia's economy continued to grow strongly: after relatively slow economic expansion of 4.5% in 2009, in 2010 GDP growth returned to the 6% level of 2007–08. There was 6.5% growth in 2011. New foreign investment in 2012 was expected to amount to more than $19bn. The country's membership in the G20 recognised its overall economic success, and it was sometimes seen as an honorary member of the BRICS category of large, fast-growing states. There was a tangible sense of greater prosperity in the capital Jakarta, where the roads were clogged with new vehicles. Yet the government faced multiple economic challenges, notably including the fact that 80% of the country's massive and still-expanding oil and gas revenues were diverted to pay for oil subsidies, which the administration had not succeeded in slashing to the extent it wished. In March 2012, the government's efforts to secure parliamentary approval for a cut in subsidies which threatened to raise fuel prices by one-third provoked violent demonstrations across the country. After the Prosperous Justice Party (PKS) – the country's most important Islamic party and the fourth-largest parliamentary party – opposed the government's plan to cut subsidies, it was threatened with expulsion from the governing coalition, to which it had belonged since 2004. Following a parliamentary vote (in which the PKS joined the opposition) against the subsidy cuts but instead for a compromise plan, the government was forced to back down. But this by no means resolved the issue, which would still need to be tackled in the future.

Indonesia faced an upcoming leadership transition in 2014, when Yudhoyono must step down on completing his second term. It was almost certain that his presidential successor would lead a coalition government in which one or more of the major secular parties (the Democratic Party, Golkar and the Indonesian Democratc Party–Struggle (PDI-P)) would be partnered with a range of smaller parties including some, such as the PKS, which are to a greater or lesser extent Islamist in their political orientation. Among a wide range of potential candidates for 2014, the most popular according to opinion polls were Megawati Sukarnoputri (leader of the PDI-P, daughter of President Sukarno, and herself a former president whose record was mediocre at best); Prabowo Subianto (a controversial former general and son-in-law of former President Suharto); and Aburizal Bakrie (leader of the Golkar Party and one of Indonesia's most successful non-Chinese businessmen). In June, Golkar announced that Bakrie would be the party's official candidate.

Indonesia's major remaining internal security problem is in West Papua, where most local people still apparently repudiate Indonesian rule. In late 2011, large-scale labour disturbances supplemented the long-running if low-intensity insurgency and pro-independence demonstrations as an element in the Papuan unrest, with a strike at the multinational Freeport company's massive Grasberg mine (the largest single source of tax revenue in Indonesia), combined with deteriorating local security, causing the company to cease operations for three months. There was also an upsurge in violent incidents perpetrated by the Organisasi Papua Merdeka (OPM, Free Papua Movement), including two attacks by insurgents on an airport in the country's mountainous heartland, as well as a rash of shootings and stabbings in the provincial capital, Jayapura. Against this background of violence, Papuan leaders asked for discussions with the Indonesian government, which the sultan of Yogyakarta offered to moderate. However, Yudhoyono made clear in June 2012 that while he was willing to talk to Papuan nationalists, he was unwilling to discuss the popular demand for a referendum on Papua's independence, saying that 'Papua and West Papua are legitimate Indonesian regions'.

South China Sea: zone of contention
Competition over territorial claims in the South China Sea continued to generate tension there, particularly as a result of the assertive activities of Chinese government agencies in relation to features claimed by Southeast Asian countries. During 2011, it seemed that Beijing was adopting a more moderate approach towards its claims, in the interests of repairing its relations with Southeast Asian capitals, which had shown signs of strengthening their strategic relationships with the United States. At the ASEAN Regional Forum meeting in Bali in July 2011, China agreed to accept the Guidelines for the Implementation of the Declaration on the Conduct of Parties in the South China Sea, in which all state parties to the dispute – Brunei, China, Malaysia, the Philippines and Vietnam – agreed to 'exercise self-restraint in the conduct of activities that would complicate or escalate disputes'. This agreement seemed to indicate a degree of reconciliation between Beijing

and Hanoi: in May–June 2011, Chinese paramilitary vessels had harassed Vietnamese survey ships, and there had been large anti-Chinese demonstrations in Hanoi and Ho Chi Minh City. It soon became evident that China was using economic incentives to undermine Vietnam's objections, and in October 2011 General Nguyen Phu Trong, Vietnam Communist Party secretary-general, visited Beijing and signed a Five-Year Economic Trade Cooperation Development Plan as well as a bilateral agreement on the settlement of maritime disputes. Chinese Vice-President Xi Jinping visited Hanoi in December 2011, and the two countries subsequently established a working group to demarcate part of the Gulf of Tonkin.

Chinese efforts to win over the Philippines were less successful. President Benigno Aquino visited Beijing in August–September 2011, and returned to Manila with Chinese promises of $13bn in investments. However, relations deteriorated rapidly after a stand-off between a Philippine navy frigate and two Chinese paramilitary surveillance vessels close to Scarborough Shoal, a feature claimed by both China and the Philippines. By mid-June, both sides had withdrawn their vessels because of the beginning of the typhoon season. In July, though, a Chinese frigate ran aground on Hasa Hasa Shoal, within the Philippines' Exclusive Economic Zone, again stoking tensions. Soon afterwards, the annual ASEAN Ministerial Meeting (AMM) took place in Phnom Penh. Philippine Foreign Secretary Albert del Rosario ensured that the meeting discussed the Scarborough Shoal issue, and then asked (with support from several other member states and the ASEAN secretariat) for the matter to be mentioned in the AMM's concluding joint statement. Remarkably, as chair of the meeting, Cambodian Foreign Minister Hor Namhong refused to issue the joint statement if the Philippines insisted that it should mention Scarborough Shoal. It was unprecedented for the AMM not to issue a final statement, and this turn of events constituted a major setback for ASEAN's credibility. It was widely reported that Cambodia had come under pressure not to include any mention of Scarborough Shoal from China, which has developed substantial economic and political influence in Cambodia since the late 1990s and which wished to continue dealing with ASEAN claimants in the South China Sea bilaterally rather than as a bloc.

US 'rebalance': the Southeast Asian dimension
During 2012, a major theme in US policy towards Asia was the strengthening of its military deployments and partnerships in the region. The Pentagon's Defense Strategic Guidance document in January talked of 'pivoting' US national security efforts towards Asia; however, within several months, US

officials – such as Secretary of Defense Leon Panetta when he spoke at the IISS Shangri-La Dialogue in Singapore in June – were avoiding this terminology, which did not quite suggest the strong long-term sense of commitment that Washington wished to convey. Instead, they spoke of the United States' 'rebalance to the Asia-Pacific'. According to Panetta, 'as part of this rebalancing effort we are … strengthening our presence in Southeast Asia and in the Indian Ocean region'. In addition to rotating US Marines and supporting aviation units through Northern Australia, the United States would deepen its strategic cooperation with Thailand; pursue 'mutually beneficial capability enhancements' with the Philippines, while working to improve its 'maritime presence'; forward-deploy Littoral Combat Ships to Singapore; and enhance security partnerships with India, Indonesia, Malaysia, New Zealand and Vietnam. (See *Strategic Geography*, pp. IV–V.)

Panetta also talked about the United States' strong support for Asia's 'deepening regional security architecture', including his own involvement in the ASEAN Defence Ministers Meeting Plus, which involved the ten ASEAN defence ministers and those of eight key dialogue partners. On the South China Sea, he emphasised US support for efforts 'to develop a binding code of conduct that would create a rules-based framework for regulating the conduct of parties' there. More specifically, the 'clear and consistent' US position on Scarborough Shoal was that it wished to see restraint and diplomatic resolution. It had made this clear to both the Philippines and China.

The US was less clear, however, regarding how it would respond to an escalating crisis in the South China Sea between China and the Philippines. While the United States and the Philippines were bound by a bilateral Mutual Defense Treaty dating from 1952, it was unclear if the treaty applied in the event of conflict over features that Manila claimed in the South China Sea (particularly as the treaty pre-dated these claims). If the United States asserted that the treaty would apply, this might embolden the Philippines and thereby risk entangling America in a minor conflict of no strategic importance to itself; making clear that the treaty did not apply, however, would risk encouraging Chinese adventurism. Nevertheless, the United States seemed determined to enhance the capabilities of the Philippine armed forces. In talks involving the foreign and defence secretaries of both the United States and the Philippines, tentative agreement was reached in April 2012 on the supply of second-hand F-16 combat aircraft and an additional frigate-sized ship from the United States, in exchange for US use of Philippine air bases.

In the longer-term, one intriguing possibility was that Washington might also develop security relations with a reforming Myanmar. Panetta hinted at this, saying that discussions about 'how we can improve our defence relationship with their country' would be 'part-and-parcel' of encouraging Myanmar's reforms. Given the extent to which Myanmar was thought to have fallen into China's geopolitical orbit prior to the reform process that Thein Sein began in 2011, such a development could represent a hugely significant strategic windfall for the United States.

Chapter 10

Prospectives

Old certainties and recent conventional wisdoms about international affairs are now under persistent challenge. The questions being asked are fundamental. Will the eurozone and the European Union survive in their current shape? What will be the balance of power in the Middle East given a resurgent Muslim Brotherhood in Egypt and deepening internal conflict in Syria? Can a new generation of Chinese leaders cope with the internal contradictions of the Chinese polity and a possible slowdown in growth? While rising powers in Asia and South America seem to be getting closer to the top of the global power hierarchy, do they know what to do when they get there? On what issues is American power still crucial? These, and a legion of other questions with multiple possible answers, are so constantly being asked that global affairs seem inherently unstable.

In this age of flux, the uncertainty generated is all the greater because of the diffusion of power and the many different forms power takes. There is 'military', 'diplomatic', 'economic', 'financial', 'market', 'people', 'reputational' and 'idea' power. If there is a balance of power today, it is only the balance between these different *types* of power. The German state fights the power of the market, the Egyptian army the power of the people; states in economic decline find their international reputations weakened, those with financial power can gain more diplomatic clout. Ideas, whether of nationalism, economics, religion or politics, are distributed at an intense pace over the Internet and across borders, requiring business and governments to react quickly, so much so that speed itself has become an attribute of power. To the neologisms of 'hard power', 'soft power' and 'smart power' could be added 'fast power': the ability to shape events at speed effectively. Militaries prize rapid-deployment forces, financial houses computer-generated trades, diplomatic establishments the quick 'win' of the special envoy. 'Fast power' of course can cause mistakes, which is yet another reason why the sense of instability is heightened, as governments, businesses and others are forced to react at speed to events that shift at such pace.

The processes of careful deliberation will continue to bump uncomfortably against the realities of fast-paced developments in the European Union. In the year ahead, the debate on how the euro is saved will become hard to distinguish from the debate over how Europe should be shaped. Chancellor Angela Merkel in Germany has announced a race against the markets to establish the fiscal union and 'a common domestic policy' in Europe, in order to save the euro. Non-eurozone countries have an interest in encouraging a process that can stabilise the currency long term, but the same countries, and the United Kingdom in particular, will want to ensure the independence of their fiscal and monetary decision-taking while maintaining access to the single market. It will take some effort of mutual diplomatic restraint to ensure that the relations between the eurozone and non-eurozone countries do not turn into a game of Russian roulette. The UK (or others) cannot use the crisis to renegotiate the parts of its membership of the EU it does not like, while Germany (or others) cannot try to use the crisis to squeeze non-eurozone countries into a political union they cannot accept.

The logic of the situation suggests that an inner core of eurozone countries and multiple outer cores of non-eurozone countries with different relations to the European centre be established. This would preserve the euro and keep a wider community of European nations together. But a Europe of concentric circles, once favoured by personalities such as former French Premier Édouard Balladur, is perhaps too logical an outcome for such a politically charged crisis. High-speed muddling through will be the order of the day for the next year in Europe as arrangements continue to be patched together to maintain the single currency. There will come a point when intramural negotiations will need to take a more formal shape, less to articulate policy and more to determine structure. Delaying that moment of quasi-constitutional reckoning may be in the interests of many, while drawing it closer may be the instinct of others. Fashioning an outcome that has a look of permanence about it will be as important as it will be difficult.

Neighbourhood policy and especially an imaginative diplomatic and geo-economic approach towards the Middle East will be a key EU foreign-policy priority at this time. Yet sustaining an effective negotiation with Iran, handling the changes in North Africa and facilitating positive change in Syria will fall more to the stretched capacities of Europe's bigger powers than to the still uncoordinated staff of the European External Action Service managed by Europe's high representative, Catherine Ashton. Development aid and economic assistance will remain key instruments of policy, but European impact on the changing geo-strategic shape of the Middle East will be limited.

The future balance of power in the Levant is the most delicate. Egypt will be consumed by its need to find the right modus vivendi between the Muslim Brotherhood and the army, and to settle a constitutionally guaranteed sharing of powers between the various branches and agencies of influence that commands some public respect. In these circumstances, it is hard to see Egypt playing its usually hefty regional diplomatic role. That vacuum will be filled by others, including the Gulf states which, with their suspicions of Iran, are defining most issues in sectarian terms and responding accordingly. The freelance diplomacy and occasional military assistance undertaken in Syria by various Gulf Co-operation Council states is symptomatic of this reality. The future of the Assad regime may well be dark, but the delay in his quitting the scene, which could be quite long, may further infect the region. Jordan and Lebanon have reason to worry about the stability of their own domestic order as the Syrian state further degenerates. The relative quiet in the occupied territories is not certain to endure and if there were a resumption of violence there and Palestinians were seen to be suffering, the now more animated 'Arab street' elsewhere could demand more of their governments (or themselves) than ritualised condemnation. Israel has special reason, in current circumstances, to be wary of an outbreak of violence in Palestine, not least because of the fragility of its other flanks. Egypt's control over the Sinai is weak. The situation in southern Lebanon is tense as Hizbullah weighs its own options at a time when Syria is internally stressed and Iran under external pressure. The Shia movement is asking itself existential questions, and these could invite unhappy answers. An accidental conflict between Israel and Hizbullah in Lebanon is an ever-present risk. Finally, the fact that chemical-weapon storage depots and associated delivery systems are to be found between Damascus and the Golan Heights makes Syria's border with Israel also troubling. The risk that chemical weapons could fall into the wrong hands and cross borders to others is an important strategic reason why outside powers are right to emphasise a political solution. Danger signs in the Levant are multiplying and the impact of any of them being realised is high. The region is living 'day-by-day'; diplomatic engagement from the outside needs to be as intense.

In comparison, the risk scenarios in the Asia-Pacific appear less frenetic and more tightly bound by the economic incentives that most countries have to maintain peace. That restraint on strategic impertinence does not apply to North Korea, and the ability of a third-generation Kim to keep his internal power-base intact without engaging in regular external provocation is unknown. Better understood is that South Korea will feel obliged to respond to any militarily significant challenge. Public opinion will not easily accept that North Korean aggression can only invite magnanimity or diplomatic protest. The need to maintain a deterrent capacity rests on being ready to respond and show the risks of the use of force, and that maxim will weigh on South Korean policymakers. While the tensions across the Taiwan Strait remain much diminished, those throughout the South China Sea have risen. With nine different Chinese agencies responsible for policing and protecting China's expansively drawn interests in the South China Sea, the chance of accidents and conflict between China and the other claimant states is ever-present. Business is affected because of the offshore energy available, but only the larger companies will feel able to persist with exploration agreements in such a charged atmosphere. A code of conduct for the South China Sea (and ways of enforcing it) remains a diplomatic imperative.

Movement towards it will partly depend on how confident the new Chinese leadership is as it emerges from a less than smooth transition. The Bo Xilai scandal will have left its marks, but if the result is a very tightly disciplined and smaller politburo of seven rather than nine leaders, and a less factionalised ruling order, then the prospect for accelerating domestic reform and keeping regional disputes contained may be stronger. The US pivot to Asia will have irritated China, though it was partly brought on by the strategic demand created by Asian states that are simultaneously excited about China's economic promise and intimidated by its rising power. China's assertiveness in previous years served to legitimise the United States as a resident Asian power for others. In time, the United States will want to develop confidence-building measures with China analogous to those it negotiated in the past with the Soviet Union. An agreement to avoid incidents at sea and to ensure that conflict is limited would be a natural strategic goal for Washington. The Chinese are likely to see such arrangements as offering a 'seatbelt to a speeding driver', in effect allowing the United States to become less risk averse. Rules of the road, as between China and its neighbours, or between China and the United States, will be hard to come by, yet they will be a central feature of Asian defence diplomacy in the years ahead.

As the Asian economic growth story continues to be written, even with breaks in the narrative in India, and some uncertainty about China, the importance of domestic politics is on the rise. (See *Strategic Geography*, pp. II–III.) Indian business pines for a stronger government, investors in Indonesia wonder about who will succeed President Susilo Bambang Yudhoyono in 2014, the ruling National Front coalition in Malaysia will face a real challenge once elections are called, while the concessions made by the governing People's Action Party in Singapore to popular concerns especially over foreign workers make business leaders there fret. Thai politics, meanwhile, remain possessed by the prospect of a return to the country by Thaksin Shinawatra, whose sister is managing to maintain power in Bangkok. As ASEAN leaders watch with interest how a version of coalition politics emerges in Myanmar, they will be alert to the growing complexity of their own domestic political challenges. Public opinion will increasingly impose on them the duty to marry national stability and economic openness at the altar of fairer and more open political competition. Southeast Asian politics are entering a period of generational change, and of real excitement. Potential political transitions will carry significance and have regional as well as national implications.

The fascination of the Asian economic success story and interest in the Pacific century have extended powerfully into Latin America. Many economies have done well from the Chinese appetite for resources, but their growth is also a function of better national economic policies. The Latin American 'Pacific Four' of Chile, Colombia, Mexico and Peru are strengthening their trade relations with each other and are looking outwards. In June 2012 they formed a 'Pacific Alliance' to improve economic integration and organise their policies more effectively towards Asia. Joint trade between the four may soon reach $9 billion, comparing favourably to the $5.5bn of trade in 2010 between the Mercosur countries of Argentina, Brazil, Paraguay and Uruguay. For the four countries, soon possibly joined by Panama, moving out of the Brazilian orbit may be an important psychological motivation, but the prize is to be at the forefront of the new South–South trade routes.

The financial, economic and political traffic between leading Asian, Latin American, Middle Eastern and African states is an important geo-economic trend. The roads on which that traffic is carried remain unpaved, bumpy and subject to accidents. Tensions, for example between Brazil and China over trade dumping and currency manipulation, have been high. The decision to agree a $30bn currency swap allowing payments to be settled in their own currencies is to be seen largely in terms of China's ambition to move settlements away from the US dollar. In general, as trade increases between the Southern countries, so will political interaction and potential tensions. The BRIC countries may have their summits, but the mortar has not bonded, and as the United States becomes a less hyper-dominant setter of the global agenda, it also is less of a useful object of resentment or blame. As China, India, Brazil and others claim greater extra-regional influence, their interests could well diverge as often as they coalesce. Their small neighbours may also want to protect themselves from potential regional dominance and, in Africa, Asia, Latin America and the Middle East, many smaller powers are developing their diplomatic independence and flair. Outside powers cannot count on dealing principally with 'regional champions': Brazil in Latin America, or Egypt in the Levant, or Nigeria in Africa, as the diversity of regional international relations increases. International diplomacy is much more complex. With the rising powers uncertain about how to develop a genuinely global agenda and the United States preferring to let regional powers take the lead where possible, strategic nationalism continues to rise. In almost every region of the world, countries are now putting their faith as much in 'self-reliance' as in the effectiveness of their regional organisations. National hedging against the failure of regional institutions is as prevalent in the security realm as in the financial.

It is into this more plural order that an American president will step in January 2013. The rest of the world will be less interested in the result of the November 2012 elections than any other poll of the last 60 years. The fascination and promise of President Barack Obama, always unfairly exaggerated, has substantially ebbed internationally as it has dimmed nationally. His re-election would not be treated as having immediate dramatic consequences. Mitt Romney, the presumptive Republican candidate, is neither greatly feared nor especially admired internationally. There would be interest in his approach to the Iran file and to relations with Russia and China, but the expectation remains that American foreign-policy adventurism ended with the George W. Bush administration and that a more cautious management approach will in different shades colour future US administrations.

For all governments, in fact, foreign policy has become a mixture of political risk management and trade promotion. Shaping favourably the domestic politics of other countries is still an ambition of the greater powers, but its labour-intensive nature leaves most jobs incomplete. The greatest proliferation risk is that of 'ungoverned spaces'. Yemen and parts of Africa – Mali is the latest example – remain hugely unstable. Past ventures have given pause to those advised to intervene in Syria, as there is justified concern that an external military intervention would accelerate disintegration that could not be contained within the state. In the year ahead, the challenges of dealing with the proliferation of non-governed state territory will increase. Changes in the way countries deal with the criminal networks that deal in drugs could make this problem more manageable. As the IISS argued in a 2012 *Adelphi* book, *Drugs, Insecurity and Failed States: The Problems of Prohibition*, law-enforcement efforts need to move away from low-level interdictions and arrests towards a more strategic, intelligence-led approach that focuses on the top-tier criminals who derive most from the trade. More international commitment to attack the proceeds of organised criminal groups would be an important priority. While Colombia has scored relative successes against drugs, some production has shifted to Peru. Transit states in West Africa, Central America and Mexico are still struggling to deal with the effects of the drug trade. The debate begun at the 2012 Organisation of American States summit in Cartagena, on new approaches to dealing with transnational drug-related crime and violence, needs to be continued. The privatisation of violence is a feature of the international drugs economy; the renationalisation of the monopoly over organised military force is an overwhelming task, but one on which more international cooperation is required. In this context, everything from agreements on small-arms control to cooperation combating transnational crime is needed.

Yet this is now a counsel of perfection, as foreign-policy energy is sapped by the need to rebuild economically at home. Western defence budgets are shrinking to produce smaller but purportedly 'more agile' militaries that still need time to lick wounds accumulated during too many recent wars. Western foreign-affairs ministries are re-tooling to perform trade tasks, sometimes grandly styled 'economic statecraft'. In the 'Southern' countries, the rising powers have to concentrate too on more vibrant domestic politics and on confidence-building in the neighbourhood. As world politics becomes more global, leadership priorities have become more parochial. There may be a global power shift going on, but the transition will be a long one, and those gaining a greater share of global power have no obvious plan for how they will use it. In that transition, and during that shift, private forces will have more of a say and more of an impact. Public policy responsibilities cannot now fall only on the narrowing shoulders of government. Companies acting abroad need to go beyond corporate social responsibility and develop virtual foreign policies if they are to protect their interests and the environments in which they succeed. The media and NGOs who are active internationally are now expected to assume greater responsibility for the impact of their actions. In the age of privatised power, with so many international agencies of power, we are witnessing the privatisation of foreign policy. In that context, strategic thinking may be a conceit, but its absence is even more dangerous. That leaves only one policy prescription: 'Keep calm, and carry on'.

Index